Springer Proceedings in Mathematics & Statistics

Volume 140

More information about this series at http://www.springer.com/series/10533

Springer Proceedings in Mathematics & Statistics

This book series features volumes composed of select contributions from workshops and conferences in all areas of current research in mathematics and statistics, including operation research and optimization. In addition to an overall evaluation of the interest, scientific quality, and timeliness of each proposal at the hands of the publisher, individual contributions are all refereed to the high quality standards of leading journals in the field. Thus, this series provides the research community with well-edited, authoritative reports on developments in the most exciting areas of mathematical and statistical research today.

L. Andries van der Ark • Daniel M. Bolt
Wen-Chung Wang • Jeffrey A. Douglas
Sy-Miin Chow
Editors

Quantitative Psychology Research

The 79th Annual Meeting of the Psychometric Society, Madison, Wisconsin, 2014

Springer

Editors
L. Andries van der Ark
University of Amsterdam
Amsterdam, The Netherlands

Daniel M. Bolt
University of Wisconsin
Madison, WI, USA

Wen-Chung Wang
The Hong Kong Institute of Education
Hong Kong, Hong Kong SAR

Jeffrey A. Douglas
University of Illinois
Champaign, IL, USA

Sy-Miin Chow
The Penn State University
University Park, PA, USA

ISSN 2194-1009 ISSN 2194-1017 (electronic)
Springer Proceedings in Mathematics & Statistics
ISBN 978-3-319-19976-4 ISBN 978-3-319-19977-1 (eBook)
DOI 10.1007/978-3-319-19977-1

Library of Congress Control Number: 2015945591

Springer Cham Heidelberg New York Dordrecht London

Printed on acid-free paper

Springer International Publishing AG Switzerland is part of Springer Science+Business Media (www.springer.com)

Preface

This volume is a collection of presentations given at the 79th annual International Meeting of the Psychometric Society (IMPS) held at the University of Wisconsin-Madison, in Madison, Wisconsin during July 21–25, 2014. The meeting attracted 380 participants from 26 countries, with 242 papers being presented, along with 56 poster presentations, 5 pre-conference workshops, 5 keynote presentations, 4 invited speaker presentations, 4 state-of-the-art lectures, and 8 invited symposia. We thank the University of Wisconsin-Extension staff, as well as the faculty and students from the Department of Educational Psychology at the University of Wisconsin, Madison for hosting this very successful conference.

This volume continues a tradition started after the 77th meeting in Lincoln, Nebraska, of publishing a proceedings volume from the conference so as to allow presenters to quickly disseminate their ideas to the broader research community, while still undergoing a thorough review process. The 78th meeting in Arnhem was also followed by a proceedings. With the third proceedings, we now have a series that is expected to be continued next year with submissions from the 80th IMPS meeting in Beijing, China.

We asked the authors to use their presentations at the meeting as the basis of their chapters, possibly extended with new ideas or additional information. The result is a selection of 26 state-of-the-art chapters addressing a diverse set of topics, including item response theory, factor analysis, structural equation modelling, time series analysis, mediation analysis, propensity score methods, cognitive diagnostic models, and multi-level models, among others.

The proceedings of the 77th and 78th meeting were initiated by Roger E. Millsap, the editor of Psychometrika. Just before finalizing the proceedings of the 78th meeting, on May 9, 2014, Roger suddenly passed away. This volume is the first proceedings not initiated by Roger. We dedicate it to him.

Amsterdam, The Netherlands — L. Andries van der Ark
Madison, WI, USA — Daniel M. Bolt
Hong Kong, Hong Kong SAR — Wen-Chung Wang
Urbana-Champaign, IL, USA — Jeffrey A. Douglas
University Park, PA, USA — Sy-Miin Chow

Contents

Chapter 1
Extending the Use of Multidimensional IRT Calibration as Projection: Many-to-One Linking and Linear Computation of Projected Scores

David Thissen, Yang Liu, Brooke Magnus, and Hally Quinn

Abstract Two methods to make inferences about scores that would have been obtained on one test using responses obtained with a different test are *scale aligning* and *projection*. If both tests measure the same construct, scale aligning may be accomplished using the results of simultaneous calibration of the items from both tests with a unidimensional IRT model. If the tests measure distinct but related constructs, an alternative is the use of regression to predict scores on one test from scores on the other; when the score distribution is predicted, this is projection. Calibrated projection combines those two methods, using a multidimensional IRT (MIRT) model to simultaneously calibrate the items comprising two tests onto scales representing distinct constructs, and estimating the parameters describing the relation between the two scales. Then projection is done within the MIRT model. This presentation describes two extensions of calibrated projection: (1) the use of linear models to compute the projected scores and their error variances, and (2) projection from more than one test to a single test. The procedures are illustrated using data obtained with scales measuring closely related quality of life constructs.

Keywords linking • projection • calibration • scale aligning

1.1 Introduction

It is often desirable to obtain scores that are in some sense comparable from disparate tests that measure the same or closely related constructs. For example, the empirical examples in this presentation are motivated by the possibility that PROMIS® pediatric and adult scales may be used in the same cross-sectional or

D. Thissen (✉) • Y. Liu • B. Magnus • H. Quinn
Department of Psychology, The University of North Carolina at Chapel Hill, Chapel Hill, NC 27599, USA
e-mail: dthissen@email.unc.edu; liuy0811@live.unc.edu; brooke.magnus@unc.edu; hallyq@live.unc.edu

L.A. van der Ark et al. (eds.), *Quantitative Psychology Research*, Springer Proceedings in Mathematics & Statistics 140, DOI 10.1007/978-3-319-19977-1_1

longitudinal research, with the (different) pediatric and adult scales each used within their age-range. Test score linking facilitates data analysis in such situations.

Holland (2007) provided a modern framework for test score linking; he wrote that "linking refers to the general class of transformations between the scores from one test and those of another, ... linking methods can be divided into three basic categories called predicting, scale aligning, and equating." For linking scores from disparate scales, such as the PROMIS® pediatric and adult scales, only predicting scores from one with the other, or aligning the two scales, are viable candidates.

A commonly used method of scale aligning has been calibration, which uses item response theory (IRT) models and methods to place the items from each of two scales on the same metric. After that is done, standard computation of IRT scale scores from any subset of the items (which could include all of the items on only one scale) yields comparable scores. However, calibration has heretofore been limited to situations in which a unidimensional IRT model is suitable for all items from both scales jointly—that is, both scales measure the same construct.

For two scales that measure different constructs, even if the two constructs are highly related, predicting scores on one scale from those on the other yields more correct results. Such predictions are based on regression models, but often the regression model is elaborated to produce a distribution across the score range as a prediction; that is called projection.

Usually projection has been based on standard regression models, which consider the values of the predictor variable(s) fixed. *Calibrated projection* (Thissen et al. 2011) is a relatively new statistical procedure that uses IRT to link two measures, without considering the scores on the predictor scale to be fixed, and without the demand of conventional calibration that the two are measures of the same construct. In calibrated projection, a multidimensional IRT (MIRT) model is fitted to the item responses from the two measures: θ_1 represents the underlying construct measured by the first scale, with estimated slopes a_1 for each of the first scale's items and fixed values of 0.0 for the items of the second scale. θ_2 represents the underlying construct measured by the second scale, with estimated slopes a_2 for each of the second scale's items and fixed values of 0.0 for the items of the first scale. The correlation between θ_1 and θ_2 is estimated.

After calibration, the MIRT model may be used to provide IRT scale score estimates on the scale of the second measure, using only the item responses from the first measure. Figure 1.1 illustrates calibrated projection: The x-axis variable is θ_1, the underlying construct measured by the first scale (for Fig. 1.1, that is the PROMIS pediatric Anxiety scale), and the y-axis variable is θ_2, the underlying construct measured by the second scale (in Fig. 1.1, PROMIS adult Anxiety). The two latent variables are highly correlated, as indicated by the density ellipses around the regression line. Given the item responses on the pediatric Anxiety scale, IRT methods may be used to compute the implied distribution on θ_1; two of those are shown along the x-axis in Fig. 1.1, for summed scores of 13 and 44. The estimated relation between θ_1 and θ_2 is then used to project those distributions onto the y-axis, to yield the implied distributions on θ_2, the adult construct.

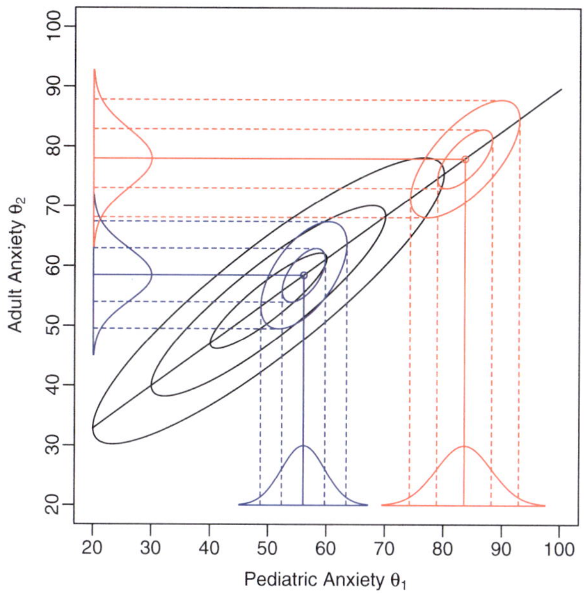

Fig. 1.1 The x-axis variable is θ_1, the underlying construct measured by the first scale, in this case the PROMIS pediatric Anxiety scale; the y-axis variable is θ_2, the underlying construct measured by the second scale, in this case the PROMIS adult Anxiety scale. Both scales report scores in T-score units. The correlation between the two latent variables is indicated by the large density ellipses. The implied distributions on θ_1 for summed scores of 13 (*blue*) and 44 (*red*) on the pediatric Anxiety scale are shown along the x-axis, along with the corresponding implied bivariate distributions, and those on θ_2, the adult Anxiety construct, along the y-axis

The means of the implied distributions on the θ dimensions are the IRT-based scale scores, and the standard deviations of those distributions are reported as the standard errors of those scores. The projection links the scales in the sense that each score on the pediatric scale yields a score on the adult metric.

In subsequent sections, we will illustrate calibrated projection from the PROMIS pediatric Anxiety (Irwin et al. 2010) scale to the corresponding adult scale (Pilkonis et al. 2011) and vice versa, using new data and pre-existing item parameters for the two PROMIS scales as the mechanism to link the results back to the original scales. Then we will describe a linear approximation to the IRT computations, and illustrate the extension of calibrated projection to use more than one scale as the basis for projection.

1.2 Calibrated Projection, Illustrated with PROMIS Anxiety

The original development of calibrated projection (Thissen et al. 2011) made use of the same data that were used to set the scale for the PROMIS Asthma Impact

Scale (PAIS), so there was no need to link a new set of data back to any existing scale. In contrast, the illustrations here are drawn from the linkage of the PROMIS pediatric and adult scales that measure similar constructs; both the pediatric and adult scales are now based on published item banks with reference metrics derived from their (separate) original calibrations. New data were collected for this project, from a sample of 874 persons in the age range 14–20 who responded to short forms of both the pediatric and adult PROMIS scales.

The item banks of all of the PROMIS scales comprise items with five response alternatives. The items have been calibrated using the graded IRT model (Samejima 1969, 1997), which describes the probability of each item response as a function of a set of item parameters (*a*s and *c*s), and $\boldsymbol{\theta}$, the latent variable(s) measured by the scale, as follows: The conditional probability of response $u = 0, 1, \ldots, m-1$ is

$$T_u(\boldsymbol{\theta}) = T_u^*(\boldsymbol{\theta}) - T_{u+1}^*(\boldsymbol{\theta}) \tag{1.1}$$

in which $T_u^*(\boldsymbol{\theta})$ is a curve tracing the probability of a response in category u or higher: $T_0^*(\boldsymbol{\theta}) = 1$, $T_m^*(\boldsymbol{\theta}) = 0$, and for $u = 1, 2, \ldots, m-1$

$$T_u^*(\boldsymbol{\theta}) = \frac{1}{1 + \exp(-(\mathbf{a}'\boldsymbol{\theta} + c_u))}. \tag{1.2}$$

The original unidimensional parameters for the short-form items for the PROMIS pediatric and adult Anxiety scales are in Table 1.1, recast in a two-dimensional format in which θ_1 is the underlying construct measured by the pediatric Anxiety scale and θ_2 is the underlying construct measured by the adult Anxiety scale.

To begin the process of linking the two Anxiety scales with each other, and back to their original (published) scales, the item parameters in Table 1.1 were used as fixed values, and the population parameters (mean vector and covariance matrix) for the latent variables θ_1 and θ_2 were estimated by maximum likelihood. Estimation of the MIRT parameters and subsequent computation of the scale scores was done using the IRTPRO software (Cai et al. 2011).

For the Anxiety scales, the estimated covariance matrix from the fixed (original calibration) parameters and the current data *C*, with $\theta_1 \equiv \theta_{\text{ped}}$ and $\theta_2 \equiv \theta_{\text{ad}}$, is

$$\hat{\boldsymbol{\Sigma}}_C = \begin{bmatrix} 1.650(0.11) & \\ 1.174(0.07) & 1.047(0.06) \end{bmatrix}. \tag{1.3}$$

The estimated correlation of the two latent variables is $\hat{\rho}_C = \frac{1.174}{\sqrt{1.650 \times 1.047}} = 0.893$. It is convenient to define the ratio of the variance of the adult latent variable to that of the pediatric latent variable, $\hat{k}_{\text{ad}}^2 = \frac{1.047}{1.650} = 0.635$.

To compute projected scores on a scale set in a hypothetical calibration population that is the same as the reference population for the pediatric scale, we need an estimate of the covariance matrix of the two latent variables in that population. That estimate has three components: The variance of the pediatric latent variable,

$\hat{\sigma}_{\text{ref(ped),ped}}$, is 1.0 (that set the original scale); the variance of the adult latent variable, $\hat{\sigma}_{\text{ref(ped),ad}}$, is $\hat{k}^2_{\text{ad}}$, obtained from the ratio of the two variances in the current data; and the covariance is $\hat{\rho}_C\hat{k}_{\text{ad}}$, using the correlation from the current data. So the covariance matrix used to project from the pediatric scale to the adult scale is:

$$\hat{\boldsymbol{\Sigma}}_{\text{ref(ped)}} = \begin{bmatrix} 1.0 & \\ \hat{\rho}_C\hat{k}_{\text{ad}} & \hat{k}^2_{\text{ad}} \end{bmatrix} = \begin{bmatrix} 1.000 & \\ 0.711 & 0.635 \end{bmatrix} . \tag{1.4}$$

We also need to compute the predicted value of the adult scale mean in that population. We use linear regression to compute that estimate, based on $\hat{\boldsymbol{\Sigma}}_C$ and the estimated mean vector for the current data, which in this example is

$$\hat{\boldsymbol{\mu}}_C = \begin{bmatrix} 0.631(0.05) \\ 0.868(0.04) \end{bmatrix} . \tag{1.5}$$

The regression estimate of the adult scale value for the pediatric scale mean of 0.0 uses an estimate of the slope

$$\beta_1 = \hat{\rho}_C \frac{\hat{\sigma}_{C,\text{ad}}}{\hat{\sigma}_{C,\text{ped}}} = 0.893 \frac{\sqrt{1.047}}{\sqrt{1.650}} = 0.711 , \tag{1.6}$$

and the intercept

Table 1.1 Item parameters for the PROMIS pediatric and adult Anxiety scales, based on their original calibrations

Item	Label	a_1	a_2	c_1	c_2	c_3	c_4
1	Pediatric-Anxiety1-8	1.51	0	1.29	−0.27	−2.80	−4.31
2	Pediatric-Anxiety2-2	1.89	0	0.48	−1.12	−3.24	−4.76
3	Pediatric-Anxiety2-9	1.81	0	1.42	−0.45	−2.87	−4.79
4	Pediatric-Anxiety2-1	1.71	0	0.74	−0.88	−3.00	−4.54
5	Pediatric-Anxiety2-6	1.50	0	0.60	−0.76	−2.78	−3.97
6	Pediatric-Anxiety1-7	1.48	0	1.01	−0.43	−2.84	−4.25
7	Pediatric-Anxiety1-3	1.84	0	0.44	−0.89	−2.83	−4.08
8	Pediatric-Anxiety2-4	1.83	0	−0.46	−1.67	−3.34	−4.69
9	Adult-EDANX01	0	3.60	−1.23	−3.92	−7.06	−9.72
10	Adult-EDANX40	0	3.88	−1.89	−4.91	−8.20	−11.26
11	Adult-EDANX41	0	3.66	−1.33	−3.78	−6.52	−9.59
12	Adult-EDANX53	0	3.66	0.85	−2.18	−5.72	−9.14
13	Adult-EDANX46	0	3.40	0.74	−2.15	−5.59	−9.28
14	Adult-EDANX07	0	3.55	−1.92	−3.71	−6.62	−8.47
15	Adult-EDANX05	0	3.36	0.64	−2.01	−5.28	−8.21
16	Adult-EDANX54	0	3.35	1.71	−1.04	−4.19	−7.69

$$\beta_0 = \hat{\mu}_{C,\text{ad}} - \beta_1 \times \hat{\mu}_{C,\text{ped}} = 0.868 - 0.711 \times 0.631 = 0.419. \tag{1.7}$$

Assuming the same relationships between the pediatric and adult scales observed in the current data C would have held if the calibration sample for the pediatric scale had also been the reference sample for the adult scale, the mean for the adult scale would have been

$$\hat{\mu}_{\text{ad}} = 0.419 + 0.711 \times 0.0 = 0.419 \ . \tag{1.8}$$

Assembling all this, calibrated projection of pediatric item responses onto the adult scale uses the item parameters for the pediatric items in Table 1.1, the population mean vector

$$\hat{\boldsymbol{\mu}}_{\text{ref(ped)}} = \begin{bmatrix} 0.0 \\ \hat{\mu}_{\text{ad}} \end{bmatrix} = \begin{bmatrix} 0.0 \\ 0.419 \end{bmatrix} , \tag{1.9}$$

and covariance matrix $\hat{\boldsymbol{\Sigma}}_{\text{ref(ped)}}$ from Eq. (1.4).

To project item responses onto the pediatric scale, the computations in this section are reflected appropriately, reversing the roles of the pediatric and adult latent variables.

1.3 A Linear Approximation to Calibrated Projection

In calibrated projection, the projected score on the θ_2 dimension, given the score on the θ_1 dimension, is computed using two-dimensional numerical integration of the conditional posterior distribution, two of which are illustrated in Fig. 1.1. However, it is numerically the case that the predictions so-computed are, within rounding error, a linear function of the predictor scores, specifically

$$\widehat{\text{EAP}}[\theta_2] = \beta_0 + \beta_1 \text{EAP}[\theta_1] \ . \tag{1.10}$$

in which the values of β_0 and β_1 are computed as described in the previous section. So for the Anxiety examples, we can compute

$$\begin{aligned} \widehat{\text{EAP}}[\theta_2] &= \beta_0 + \beta_1 \text{EAP}[\theta_1] \\ &= 0.419 + 0.711 \text{EAP}[\theta_1]. \end{aligned} \tag{1.11}$$

This linear relationship is exact, due to the linearity of conditional expectations. However, no exact relationship has thus far been found for the values of $\text{SD}[\theta_2]$. An approximation that appears empirically useful combines two sources of variance: the error variance of the predicting value, $\text{SD}^2[\theta_1]$, and the residual variance around the regression line, $V_{\text{Res},2}$. The residual variance is

$$V_{\text{Res},2} = (1 - \hat{\rho}_C^2)\hat{\sigma}_{C,2}^2 \tag{1.12}$$

so for the projection from the pediatric scale to the adult scale it is

$$V_{\text{Res},2} = (1 - 0.893^2)1.047 = 0.212 \ . \tag{1.13}$$

Using these values, approximate conditional standard errors of the projected values can be computed for the projection from the pediatric scale to the adult scale as

$$\widehat{\text{SD}}[\theta_2] = \sqrt{\beta_1^2 \text{SD}^2[\theta_1] + V_{\text{Res},2}} = \sqrt{0.711^2 \text{SD}^2[\theta_1] + 0.212} \ . \tag{1.14}$$

1.3.1 Comparing the Results from the Linear Approximation with Calibrated Projection for PROMIS Anxiety

It is not convenient to show the results of projection for scores based on response patterns, because there are so many. However, tabulation of the responses for summed scores covers the entire range and can be useful to provide illustration and checks on the results. The first five columns of Table 1.2 illustrate calibrated projection for the summed scores for the pediatric Anxiety scale, with projection to the adult Anxiety scale. All results are shown using the T-score scale common to all PROMIS measures.

The pediatric EAP[θ_1] and SD[θ_1] values in Table 1.2 are those published as the scoring table for the Anxiety measure. The adult EAP[θ_2] and SD[θ_2] are those computed using two-dimensional quadrature, the item parameters in Table 1.1, and the population mean vector and covariance matrix from Eqs. (1.4) and (1.9). The rightmost four columns of Table 1.2 show the results obtained with the linear approximation described in the preceding section. Columns 6 and 7 show the values of adult $\widehat{\text{EAP}}[\theta_2]$ computed using equation 1.11, and the difference between the calibrated projection EAPs and the linear approximation. Columns 8 and 9 show the values of adult $\widehat{\text{SD}}[\theta_2]$, and the ratio of the approximation to the calibrated projection values. In this case the values from the linear approximation are about 1.2 times larger than those from calibrated projection; but most would still round to the same integral values on the T-score scale.

1.3.2 Summary of Comparisons for Seven PROMIS Scales

In the course of a project to link some of the pediatric PROMIS scales to their adult counterparts, we have computed the results for calibrated projection and the linear approximation described in the preceding section for seven scales. Because all were done twice, once from the pediatric items to the adult scales and a second time from

Table 1.2 The first five columns show the calibrated projection IRT scores (EAPs) and standard errors (SDs) for summed scores on the pediatric measure (only even summed scores are shown to save space)

Pediatric summed score	Calibrated projection				Linear approximation			
	Pediatric		Adult					
	EAP[θ_1]	SD[θ_1]	EAP[θ_2]	SD[θ_2]	$\widehat{\text{EAP}}[\theta_2]$	EAP[θ_2]− $\widehat{\text{EAP}}[\theta_2]$	$\widehat{\text{SD}}[\theta_2]$	$\widehat{\text{SD}}[\theta_2]$/ SD[$\theta_2$]
0	32.3	5.8	41.7	5.5	41.6	0.0	6.2	1.1
2	39.2	4.7	46.5	4.9	46.5	0.0	5.7	1.2
4	43.3	4.2	49.5	4.7	49.5	0.0	5.5	1.2
6	46.7	3.9	51.8	4.6	51.8	0.0	5.4	1.2
8	49.6	3.8	53.9	4.5	53.9	0.0	5.3	1.2
10	52.3	3.7	55.8	4.5	55.8	0.0	5.3	1.2
12	54.8	3.7	57.6	4.5	57.6	0.0	5.3	1.2
14	57.3	3.7	59.3	4.5	59.4	0.0	5.3	1.2
16	59.7	3.7	61.1	4.5	61.1	0.0	5.3	1.2
18	62.1	3.7	62.8	4.5	62.8	0.0	5.3	1.2
20	64.5	3.7	64.5	4.5	64.5	0.0	5.3	1.2
22	67.0	3.7	66.3	4.5	66.3	0.0	5.3	1.2
24	69.6	3.7	68.1	4.5	68.1	0.0	5.3	1.2
26	72.3	3.7	70.0	4.5	70.0	0.0	5.3	1.2
28	75.2	3.8	72.0	4.5	72.1	−0.1	5.3	1.2
30	78.6	4.1	74.5	4.6	74.5	−0.1	5.4	1.2
32	83.5	4.7	78.0	4.9	78.0	−0.1	5.7	1.2

The last four columns show the results obtained with the linear approximation

the adult item responses to the pediatric scales, there are a total of 14 examples. The latent variables measured by all of the pairs of scales are highly correlated; correlations ranged from 0.86 to 0.95. For all 14 linkings, the linearly approximated EAPs for each summed score were essentially identical to those obtained with numerical integration in calibrated projection, as was illustrated for the Anxiety pediatric to adult projection in Table 1.2.

The degree to which $\widehat{\text{SD}}[\theta_2]$ approximates SD[θ_2] as computed by numerical integration in calibrated projection remains an empirical question. While it is not feasible to check that for all response pattern scores, it is easy to evaluate the approximation for the posterior standard deviations associated with each summed score on the scale that is used for projection. An example is shown in Table 1.2, in which the ratio of $\widehat{\text{SD}}[\theta_2]$ to SD[θ_2] varies only between 1.1 and 1.2. Table 1.3 shows the minimum and maximum values of that ratio for all 14 of the PROMIS pediatric–adult projections. Across 13 of the 14 cases, the ratio is between 1.0 and 1.3. For many applications, reported standard errors that are zero to 30 % larger than the "exact" values would probably present no problems. The exception is the projection of the Upper Extremity scale from the pediatric to the adult measure, for which $\widehat{\text{SD}}[\theta_2]$ is 1.3–1.6 times larger than SD[θ_2].

Table 1.3 The minimum and maximum values of the ratio $\widehat{SD}[\theta_2]/SD[\theta_2]$ for all 14 of the PROMIS pediatric-adult projections

	Pediatric to adult		Adult to pediatric	
Pediatric domain	Minimum	Maximum	Minimum	Maximum
Anxiety	1.1	1.2	1.0	1.0
Depressive symptoms	1.1	1.2	1.1	1.1
Anger	1.2	1.3	1.1	1.2
Fatigue	1.3	1.4	1.1	1.1
Pain interference	1.2	1.3	1.0	1.0
Physical functioning—mobility	1.1	1.2	1.0	1.1
Physical functioning—upper extremity	1.3	1.6	1.0	1.3

Table 1.4 Proportions of values of EAP[θ_2] for each scale combination that are within ± 1 SD and ± 2 SD of the values obtained using the linear approximation to calibrated projection

	Pediatric to adult		Adult to pediatric	
Pediatric domain	± 1 SD	± 2 SD	± 1 SD	± 2 SD
Anxiety	0.69	0.93	0.72	0.92
Depressive symptoms	0.70	0.93	0.71	0.93
Anger	0.72	0.95	0.74	0.94
Fatigue	0.71	0.94	0.75	0.94
Pain interference	0.75	0.92	0.77	0.95
Physical functioning—mobility	0.71	0.93	0.69	0.91
Physical functioning—upper extremity	0.54	0.95	0.53	0.95

The point of reporting values of $\widehat{SD}[\theta_2]$ (or SD[θ_2]) as standard errors for the IRT scale scores is to provide a confidence interval the covers the true value $100(1-\alpha)\,\%$ of the time. With the data collected for linking the pediatric and adult scales, we have the values of EAP[θ_2] for each projection, so we can compute the proportion of those values that are included in any specified confidence range. Table 1.4 shows those proportions for confidence intervals computed as $\widehat{EAP}[\theta_2] \pm \widehat{SD}[\theta_2]$ and $\widehat{EAP}[\theta_2] \pm 2\widehat{SD}[\theta_2]$, which should be about 0.68 and 0.95, respectively, if the standard errors are nearly correct and the errors are approximately normal. Across 13 of the 14 cases, the ± 1 SD proportions are between 0.69 and 0.77, while the ± 2 SD proportions are between 0.91 and 0.95. While the ± 1 SD proportions tend to be a little too large, the ± 2 SD proportions are slightly too small. So no improvement could be made on one (e.g., making the SD smaller to reduce the ± 1 SD proportions) without making the other worse (the example would make the ± 2 SD proportions too small).

The exceptional values in Table 1.4 are the ± 1 SD proportions for the Upper Extremity scales, which are 0.53–0.54 instead of 0.68. This anomaly is due to a distributional peculiarity for those scales: In these data, 21 % of the respondents have a perfect (maximum) score on both scales. That produces a single point mass in the distributions with 21 % of the data. The fact that these large blocks of 21 % have residuals between 1 and 2 SDs from zero reduces the observed proportion within ± 1 SD from the nominal 0.68 to 0.53–54. Setting that anomaly aside, the coverage proportions suggest that the approximation works well across the linkings that have used it thus far. For future use, it is easy to check its accuracy, by constructing a table like Table 1.2, and comparing the calibrated projection computations for summed scores with the approximation.

1.4 Projection from Two Scales to One, Illustrated with PROMIS Physical Functioning

1.4.1 Calibrated Projection from Two Scales

In this section we extend calibrated projection to use a MIRT model for item responses to three scales. Two measures form the basis of the projection, with θ_1 representing the underlying construct measured by the first scale, with estimated slopes a_1 for each of the first scale's items and fixed values of 0.0 for the other items, and θ_2 representing the underlying construct measured by the second scale, with estimated slopes a_2 for each of the second scale's items and fixed values of 0.0 for the other items. θ_3 represents the underlying construct measured by the third scale, the target scale of the projection, with estimated slopes a_3 for each of the third scale's items and fixed values of 0.0 for the other items. The correlations among all three θs are estimated.

The context for this extension of calibrated projection, and the linear approximation, involves the linking between the PROMIS pediatric Physical Function (PF) scales (Mobility and Upper Extremity/Dexterity; DeWitt et al. 2011) and the adult PF scale (Fries et al. 2014). The results for the Physical Function scales in Tables 1.3 and 1.4 were produced by linking the two pediatric scales separately to the omnibus adult scale; in this section, we will link the two pediatric scales jointly with the adult scale. To do so, we will use the published calibration item parameters for the three unidimensional scales in Table 1.5, where they are expressed as components of a three-dimensional MIRT model, in which θ_1 is pediatric PF-Mobility, θ_2 is pediatric PF-Upper Extremity/Dexterity, and θ_3 is adult PF.

For the PF scales, the estimated covariance matrix from fixed parameters and the current data C, with $\theta_1 \equiv \theta_{\text{ped-Mobility}}$, $\theta_2 \equiv \theta_{\text{ped-UpperExtremity}}$, and $\theta_3 \equiv \theta_{\text{ad-PF}}$, is

$$\hat{\boldsymbol{\Sigma}}_C = \begin{bmatrix} \hat{\boldsymbol{\Sigma}}_{\theta_1,\theta_2} & \hat{\boldsymbol{\Sigma}}_{\theta_{1-2},\theta_3} \\ \hat{\boldsymbol{\Sigma}}'_{\theta_{1-2},\theta_3} & \hat{\sigma}^2_{\theta_3} \end{bmatrix} = \begin{bmatrix} 1.548(0.02) & & \\ 2.189(0.03) & 3.393(0.08) & \\ 1.286(0.07) & 1.841(0.09) & 1.200(0.10) \end{bmatrix}. \qquad (1.15)$$

The estimated correlation matrix among the three latent variables is

Table 1.5 Item parameters for the PROMIS pediatric and adult Physical Function (PF) scales, based on their original calibrations

Item	Label	a_1	a_2	a_3	c_1	c_2	c_3	c_4
1	Pediatric-PF-Mobility1-3	3.11	0.00	0.00	5.95	5.42	3.55	1.40
2	Pediatric-PF-Mobility3-9	2.62	0.00	0.00	8.32	6.72	5.29	2.65
3	Pediatric-PF-Mobility4-4	1.96	0.00	0.00	5.69	4.72	3.20	0.97
4	Pediatric-PF-Mobility4-8	3.27	0.00	0.00	10.18	8.67	6.36	4.31
5	Pediatric-PF-Mobility4-3	3.00	0.00	0.00	8.28	7.65	5.78	4.29
6	Pediatric-PF-Mobility2-7	1.82	0.00	0.00	5.78	4.53	3.46	1.73
7	Pediatric-PF-Mobility2-4	1.97	0.00	0.00	5.51	4.73	3.87	2.53
8	Pediatric-PF-Mobility1-1	2.36	0.00	0.00	5.55	4.66	3.15	1.17
9	Pediatric-PF-UpperExtremity2-3	0.00	2.33	0.00	7.63	5.85	3.78	–
10	Pediatric-PF-UpperExtremity4-1	0.00	1.67	0.00	6.45	4.97	3.79	1.26
11	Pediatric-PF-UpperExtremity3-11	0.00	2.53	0.00	7.32	6.97	6.02	3.82
12	Pediatric-PF-UpperExtremity4-10	0.00	1.89	0.00	6.90	5.58	4.54	2.31
13	Pediatric-PF-UpperExtremity3-4	0.00	2.67	0.00	8.99	6.60	4.74	–
14	Pediatric-PF-UpperExtremity3-9	0.00	2.25	0.00	6.59	5.62	4.30	1.56
15	Pediatric-PF-UpperExtremity2-2	0.00	2.54	0.00	10.00	8.20	7.36	4.68
16	Pediatric-PF-UpperExtremity3-7	0.00	2.46	0.00	7.11	6.77	5.37	3.67
17	Adult-PFA1	0.00	0.00	3.31	3.71	1.66	−0.43	−1.99
18	Adult-PFC36	0.00	0.00	4.46	6.38	4.50	2.63	1.03
19	Adult-PFC37	0.00	0.00	4.46	10.30	7.27	4.68	2.54
20	Adult-PFA5	0.00	0.00	4.14	9.81	6.71	4.31	2.19
21	Adult-PFA3	0.00	0.00	2.95	6.64	3.72	1.65	−0.09
22	Adult-PFA11	0.00	0.00	4.83	9.56	7.39	5.36	2.17
23	Adult-PFA16	0.00	0.00	3.37	10.58	8.63	6.44	4.18
24	Adult-PFB26	0.00	0.00	3.32	10.52	9.56	7.77	5.84
25	Adult-PFA55	0.00	0.00	3.58	11.99	9.49	7.41	5.30
26	Adult-PFC45	0.00	0.00	3.11	9.67	8.65	6.87	4.54

Note: For two of the Pediatric Upper Extremity items, two response categories were collapsed in calibration so there are only three intercepts for those items

$$\hat{\mathbf{R}}_C = \begin{bmatrix} 1.000 & & \\ 0.955 & 1.000 & \\ 0.944 & 0.912 & 1.000 \end{bmatrix}, \tag{1.16}$$

and the estimated mean vector for the current data is

$$\hat{\boldsymbol{\mu}}_C = \begin{bmatrix} \hat{\boldsymbol{\mu}}_{\theta_1,\theta_2} \\ \hat{\mu}_{\theta_3} \end{bmatrix} = \begin{bmatrix} -0.634(0.06) \\ -0.269(0.10) \\ -0.332(0.05) \end{bmatrix}. \tag{1.17}$$

To compute estimates of the mean and covariance matrix among the latent variables for a hypothetical joint reference distribution for the pediatric and adult scales, and for use in the linear approximation to calibrated projection, we need the regression coefficients for θ_3 on θ_1 and θ_2, which are

$$\hat{\boldsymbol{\beta}} = \begin{bmatrix} \widehat{\beta_1} \\ \widehat{\beta_2} \end{bmatrix} = \hat{\boldsymbol{\Sigma}}^{-1}_{\theta_1,\theta_2} \hat{\boldsymbol{\Sigma}}_{\theta_{1-2},\theta_3} = \begin{bmatrix} 0.724 \\ 0.076 \end{bmatrix} ; \tag{1.18}$$

the intercept is

$$\hat{\beta}_0 = \hat{\mu}_{\theta_3} - \hat{\boldsymbol{\beta}}' \hat{\boldsymbol{\mu}}_{\theta_1,\theta_2} = 0.147 . \tag{1.19}$$

To obtain the mean vector for the hypothetical joint reference distribution for the pediatric and adult scales, we proceed as we did in Sect. 1.2, and compute the predicted value of the adult mean from the regression equation,

$$\hat{\mu}_{\mathrm{ad}} = \beta_0 + \beta_1 \times 0.0 + \beta_2 \times 0.0 = 0.147 + 0.724 \times 0.0 + 0.076 \times 0.0 = 0.147 , \tag{1.20}$$

so the mean vector used to project from the pediatric scale to the adult scale is:

$$\hat{\boldsymbol{\mu}}_{\mathrm{ref(ped)}} = \begin{bmatrix} 0.000 \\ 0.000 \\ 0.147 \end{bmatrix} . \tag{1.21}$$

Assembly of an estimate of the covariance matrix for the hypothetical pediatric-adult reference population is more challenging than it was in the two-dimensional case described in Sect. 1.2. However, we proceed with a similar series of steps: (a) We set the variances of the two pediatric measures, θ_1 and θ_2, to the reference value of 1.0. (b) We use the estimate of the correlation between θ_1 and θ_2 obtained from the current data. (c) We compute a proportionally adjusted estimate of the variance for the adult θ_3. (d) Finally, we combine the estimates of the correlations of θ_1 and θ_2 with θ_3 from the current data with the estimate of the variance of θ_3 to obtain the covariances.

The new challenge appears in step (c): In Sect. 1.2 we used the ratio of the adult variance to the pediatric variance as the adjustment factor $\hat{k}^2$; however, here there are two pediatric variances. In principle, it might be possible to use a ratio constructed from any combination of the two pediatric variances. In this illustration we use the weighted combination that is the regression prediction of adult θ_3 from pediatric θ_1 and θ_2. We compute the variance of the predictions of adult θ_3 in the current data as

$$\hat{\upsilon}_C^2 = \beta_1^2 \hat{\sigma}^2_{C;\theta_1} + \beta_2^2 \hat{\sigma}^2_{C;\theta_2} + 2\beta_1\beta_2\hat{\sigma}_{C;\theta_1,\theta_2} = 1.070 , \tag{1.22}$$

in which the variances and covariance are obtained from the upper left-hand block of the matrix in Eq. (1.15). We compute the (hypothetical) variance of predictions in the reference pediatric sample as

$$\hat{\upsilon}_Z^2 = \beta_1^2 + \beta_2^2 + 2\beta_1\beta_2\hat{\rho}_{C;\theta_1,\theta_2} = 0.634 . \tag{1.23}$$

Then the predicted variance of adult θ_3 is computed as

$$\hat{k}_2^2\hat{\sigma}_{\theta_3}^2 = \frac{\hat{\upsilon}_Z^2}{\hat{\upsilon}_C^2}\hat{\sigma}_{\theta_3}^2 = \frac{0.634}{1.070}1.200 = 0.711 \ . \tag{1.24}$$

Combining that estimate of the adult variance with the correlations in Eq. (1.16) completes the covariance matrix used to project from the pediatric scale to the adult scale:

$$\hat{\boldsymbol{\Sigma}}_{\text{ref(ped)}} = \begin{bmatrix} 1 & & \\ \hat{\rho}_{\theta_1,\theta_2} & 1 & \\ \hat{\rho}_{\theta_1,\theta_3}\hat{k}_2,\hat{\sigma}_{\theta_3} & \hat{\rho}_{\theta_2,\theta_3}\hat{k}_2\hat{\sigma}_{\theta_3} & \hat{k}_2^2\hat{\sigma}_{\theta_3}^2 \end{bmatrix} = \begin{bmatrix} 1.000 & & \\ 0.955 & 1.000 & \\ 0.796 & 0.769 & 0.711 \end{bmatrix} . \tag{1.25}$$

Calibrated projection, using the item parameters in Table 1.5 and the population mean vector and covariance matrix in Eqs. (1.21) and (1.25) yields the results in the first seven columns of Table 1.6 for the summed scores of pediatric PF Mobility and Upper Extremity/Dexterity combined.

1.4.2 *Linear Approximation, from Two Scales to One*

To compute the linear prediction of the θ_3 score, we use the regression equation with coefficients from Eqs. (1.18) and (1.19),

$$\begin{aligned} \widehat{\text{EAP}}[\theta_3] &= \beta_0 + \beta_1\text{EAP}[\theta_1] + \beta_2\text{EAP}[\theta_2] \\ &= 0.147 + 0.724\text{EAP}[\theta_1] + 0.076\text{EAP}[\theta_2] \end{aligned} \tag{1.26}$$

and the EAP estimates for θ_1 and θ_2 as the predictor values.

Using reasoning analogous to that expressed in Eqs. (1.12)–(1.14), we compute the residual variance from the regression equation as

$$V_{\text{Res}} = \hat{\sigma}_{\theta_3}^2 - \hat{\upsilon}_C^2 = 1.200 - 1.070 = 0.130 \ , \tag{1.27}$$

and the estimated posterior standard deviations as

$$\begin{aligned} \widehat{\text{SD}}[\theta_3] &= \sqrt{\beta_1^2\text{SD}^2[\theta_1]+\beta_2^2\text{SD}^2[\theta_2]+2(\beta_1\beta_2\text{Cov}[\theta_1,\theta_2])+V_{\text{Res}}} \\ &= \sqrt{0.724^2\text{SD}^2[\theta_1]+0.076^2\text{SD}^2[\theta_2]+2(0.724\times 0.076\text{Cov}[\theta_1,\theta_2])+0.130} \end{aligned} \tag{1.28}$$

in which $\text{Cov}[\theta_1, \theta_2]$ is the error covariance associated with $\text{EAP}[\theta_1]$ and $\text{EAP}[\theta_2]$, with the results shown in the rightmost four columns of Table 1.6.

Table 1.6 The first seven columns show the calibrated projection IRT scores (EAPs) and standard errors (SDs) for summed scores on the pediatric measures combined (only even summed scores are shown to save space)

	Calibrated projection						Linear approximation			
	Pediatric				Adult					
SS	EAP[θ_1]	SD[θ_1]	EAP[θ_2]	SD[θ_2]	EAP[θ_3]	SD[θ_3]	$\widehat{\text{EAP}}[\theta_3]$	d	$\widehat{\text{SD}}[\theta_3]$	r
0	8.7	3.8	7.9	3.5	18.3	4.0	18.4	−0.1	4.7	1.2
2	12.1	3.4	11.6	3.1	21.1	3.8	21.1	−0.1	4.5	1.2
4	14.2	3.2	13.8	2.9	22.7	3.7	22.8	−0.1	4.4	1.2
6	15.8	3.0	15.6	2.8	24.1	3.6	24.1	0.0	4.3	1.2
8	17.3	2.9	17.1	2.7	25.2	3.5	25.3	0.0	4.2	1.2
10	18.5	2.8	18.4	2.6	26.3	3.5	26.3	0.0	4.2	1.2
12	19.7	2.7	19.6	2.5	27.2	3.4	27.2	0.0	4.2	1.2
14	20.7	2.7	20.7	2.5	28.0	3.4	28.1	0.0	4.1	1.2
16	21.8	2.6	21.7	2.5	28.9	3.4	28.9	0.0	4.1	1.2
18	22.7	2.6	22.7	2.5	29.6	3.4	29.7	0.0	4.1	1.2
20	23.7	2.6	23.7	2.5	30.4	3.4	30.4	0.0	4.1	1.2
22	24.6	2.5	24.6	2.5	31.1	3.3	31.1	0.0	4.1	1.2
24	25.5	2.5	25.6	2.5	31.8	3.3	31.9	0.0	4.1	1.2
26	26.4	2.5	26.5	2.5	32.6	3.3	32.6	0.0	4.1	1.2
28	27.3	2.5	27.4	2.5	33.3	3.3	33.3	0.0	4.1	1.2
30	28.2	2.4	28.3	2.6	34.0	3.3	34.0	0.0	4.0	1.2
32	29.1	2.4	29.2	2.6	34.7	3.3	34.7	0.0	4.0	1.2
34	30.0	2.4	30.2	2.6	35.5	3.3	35.5	0.0	4.0	1.2
36	30.9	2.4	31.1	2.6	36.2	3.3	36.2	0.0	4.0	1.2
38	31.9	2.4	32.1	2.7	37.0	3.3	37.0	0.0	4.0	1.2
40	32.9	2.4	33.1	2.7	37.8	3.3	37.8	0.0	4.0	1.2
42	33.9	2.4	34.1	2.8	38.6	3.3	38.6	0.0	4.1	1.2
44	35.0	2.5	35.2	2.8	39.5	3.3	39.5	0.0	4.1	1.2
46	36.1	2.5	36.3	2.9	40.4	3.4	40.4	0.0	4.1	1.2
48	37.4	2.6	37.6	3.0	41.4	3.4	41.4	0.0	4.1	1.2
50	38.7	2.6	38.9	3.1	42.5	3.4	42.5	0.0	4.1	1.2
52	40.2	2.8	40.4	3.2	43.7	3.5	43.7	0.0	4.2	1.2
54	42.0	2.9	42.1	3.3	45.1	3.6	45.1	0.0	4.3	1.2
56	44.1	3.2	44.2	3.6	46.8	3.7	46.8	0.0	4.4	1.2
58	46.8	3.7	46.9	4.1	49.0	4.0	49.0	0.0	4.6	1.2
60	50.6	4.2	50.5	4.5	51.9	4.3	51.9	0.0	4.9	1.1
62	59.8	6.5	59.7	6.6	59.3	5.9	59.3	0.0	6.3	1.1

The final four columns show the results obtained with the linear approximation. SS is the summed score on the pediatric scales, $d = \text{EAP}[\theta_3] - \widehat{\text{EAP}}[\theta_3]$, and $r = \widehat{\text{SD}}[\theta_3]/\text{SD}[\theta_3]$

As was the case with the one-to-one calibrated projections and their approximations, the values of the linear approximation $\widehat{\text{EAP}}[\theta_3]$ in Table 1.6 are essentially within rounding error of the numerically integrated values EAP[θ_3]. The ratios of the approximate standard errors $\widehat{\text{SD}}[\theta_3]$ to SD[θ_3] are between 1.1 and 1.2, as they were in the one-to-one projections. When the linear approximation values $\widehat{\text{EAP}}[\theta_3]$ and $\widehat{\text{SD}}[\theta_3]$ are combined to produce confidence-interval estimates for the values of response-pattern EAP[θ_3] for each respondent in the current data, the proportions covered by the ± 1 SD and ± 2 SD intervals are 0.70 and 0.92, respectively, the former slightly exceeding the target value of 0.68 while the latter is slightly less than the target 0.95, exactly as observed in the one-to-one projections.

In the case of two-to-one projection, the linear approximation does not yield the level of computational simplicity that it did for one-to-one projection, because two-dimensional MIRT scoring is required for θ_1 and θ_2, to obtain the error covariance term in equation 1.28. Given that one is required to compute two-dimensional MIRT scores for the predictor scores, it is probably more straightforward to simply use calibrated projection to compute the three-dimensional MIRT scores that include the estimate for θ_3 as well. Nevertheless, the linear approximation remains a potentially useful pedagogical tool.

1.5 Conclusion

While calibrated projection serves effectively to remove the restriction that IRT calibration could hitherto be used only to link scales that measure the same construct, it is also admittedly mysterious to compute scores on one scale using only item responses from another. The linear approximation presented here is easier to implement, because the projected scores are computed as linear combinations of scores on the basis scales. This also makes apparent the use of regression or prediction in the procedure. The standard errors are computed as the square root of a weighted combination of the error variances of the predicting scores, plus a component due to the imprecision of the regression, all of which is very easy to understand.

While the accuracy of the approximation of the standard error estimates described here remains an empirical question, it is easy to check for summed scores for any particular projection by comparing them to values obtained by numerical integration in calibrated projection. Taken as a whole, the combination of calibrated projection and the linear approximation proposed here extends the scope of linking procedures based on IRT.

References

Cai, L., Thissen, D., & du Toit, S. (2011). *IRTPRO Version 2: Flexible, multidimensional, multiple categorical IRT modeling [Computer software manual]*. Chicago, IL: Scientific Software International.

DeWitt, E. M., Stucky, B. D., Thissen, D., Irwin, D. E., Langer, M., Varni, J. W., et al. (2011). Construction of the eight item PROMIS Pediatric Physical Function Scales: Built using item response theory. *Journal of Clinical Epidemiology, 64*, 794–804.

Fries, J. F., Witter, J., Rose, M., Cella, D., Khanna, D., & Morgan DeWitt, E. (2014). Item Response Theory (IRT), Computerized Adaptive Testing (CAT), and PROMIS: Assessment of physical function (PF). *Journal of Rheumatology, 41*, 153–158.

Holland, P. W. (2007). Framework and history for score linking. In N. J. Dorans, M. Pommerich, & P. W. Holland (Eds.), *Linking and aligning scores and scales* (pp. 5–30). New York, NY: Springer.

Irwin, D., Stucky, B. D., Langer, M. M., Thissen, D., DeWitt, E. M., Lai, J. S., et al. (2010). An item response analysis of the Pediatric PROMIS Anxiety and Depressive Symptoms Scales. *Quality of Life Research, 19*, 595–607.

Pilkonis, P. A., Choi, S. W., Reise, S. P., Stover, A. M., Riley, W. T., & Cella, D. (2011). Item banks for measuring emotional distress from the Patient-Reported Outcomes Measurement Information System (PROMIS™): Depression, anxiety, and anger. *Assessment, 18*, 263–283.

Samejima, F. (1969). Estimation of latent ability using a response pattern of graded scores. *Psychometric Monograph* (No. 18).

Samejima, F. (1997). Graded response model. In W. van der Linden & R. K. Hambleton (Eds.), *Handbook of modern item response theory* (pp. 85–100). New York: Springer.

Thissen, D., Varni, J. W., Stucky, B. D., Liu, Y., Irwin, D. E., & DeWalt, D. A. (2011). Using the PedsQL™ 3.0 Asthma Module to obtain scores comparable with those of the PROMIS Pediatric Asthma Impact Scale (PAIS). *Quality of Life Research, 20*, 1497–1505.

Chapter 2
The Reliability of Diagnosing Broad and Narrow Skills in Middle School Mathematics with the Multicomponent Latent Trait Model

Susan Embretson, Kristin Morrison, and Hea Won Jun

Abstract The multicomponent latent trait model for diagnosis (MLTM-D; Embretson and Yang, Psychometrika 78:14–36, 2013) is a conjunctive item response model that is hierarchically organized to include broad and narrow skills. A two-stage adaptive testing procedure was applied to diagnose skill mastery in middle school mathematics and then analyzed with MLTM-D. Strong support for the reliability of diagnosing both broad and narrow skills was obtained from both stages of testing using decision confidence indices.

Keywords Diagnostic models • Item response theory • Multidimensional models • Decision confidence reliability

Diagnostic assessment has become increasingly prominent in the last few years (Leighton and Gierl 2007; Rupp et al. 2010). Several explanatory item response theory (IRT) models (i.e., Hensen et al. 2009; von Davier 2008) have been developed using latent classes to assess patterns of skill or attribute possession by examinees. Since the number of classes increases exponentially with the number of skills that are assessed, the models are typically applied to tests with less than ten skills.

However, using high-stakes broad achievement or proficiency tests that may include 20 or 30 skills, to diagnose more specific skills or skill clusters has several potential advantages. First, the content aspect of validity, as explicated in the *Standards for Educational and Psychological Testing* (2014), is supported, since the tests typically represent skills deemed important by expert panels. Second, proficiencies in the skills represented on the tests have practical importance.

The research in this report was partially supported by a Goal 5 (Measurement) grant from the *Institute of Educational Science* Grant R305A100234 to Georgia Institute of Technology, Susan Embretson, Principal Investigator.

S. Embretson (✉) • K. Morrison • H.W. Jun
Georgia Institute of Technology, 654 Cherry Street, Atlanta, GA 30332, USA
e-mail: susan.embretson@psych.gatech.edu

L.A. van der Ark et al. (eds.), *Quantitative Psychology Research*, Springer Proceedings in Mathematics & Statistics 140, DOI 10.1007/978-3-319-19977-1_2

Decisions about examinees, as well as their instructional support systems, are based on the overall test scores. Third, remedial instructional materials may be coordinated with these tests for examinees who are not deemed to achieve mastery. For example, the *Blending Assessment with Instruction Project* (BAIP; 2010) provides online tutorials that are coordinated with achievement tests administered for Grade 3 to Grade 8. Fourth, the diagnostic assessment would be efficient if the broad tests have sufficiently reliable information about skills. However, this last advantage is questionable because commonly used subscale scores often do not have sufficient reliability (Sinharay 2010) particularly when the subscales are highly intercorrelated.

The purpose of this study is to examine the reliability of diagnosis from heterogeneous tests for mastery of skill clusters and specific skills (Fig. 2.1). An example of a two-stage adaptive diagnostic system is presented that was applied to mathematics achievement in middle school. The methods employed differ from using subscale scores in several important ways. First, the study employs a diagnostic IRT model. In the current study, a diagnostic model that is appropriate for a heterogeneous test, the multicomponent latent trait model for diagnosis (MLTM-D; Embretson and Yang 2013), is applied. Second, the broad achievement test is not necessarily viewed as sufficient for diagnosis. Instead, the broad test is Stage 1 in a multistage adaptive testing (MST) design for diagnosis. Stage 2 testing can be adapted to those skill clusters that are not sufficiently reliable in Stage 1. An interesting issue is the extent to which diagnosis may be sufficiently reliable from the Stage 1 heterogeneous test. Third, since the goal is to provide diagnosis, not accurate score locations on a continuum, different indices for reliability may be appropriate. Since diagnosis depends on cutlines, decision accuracy and consistency indices may be applied (Lewis and Sheehan 1990).

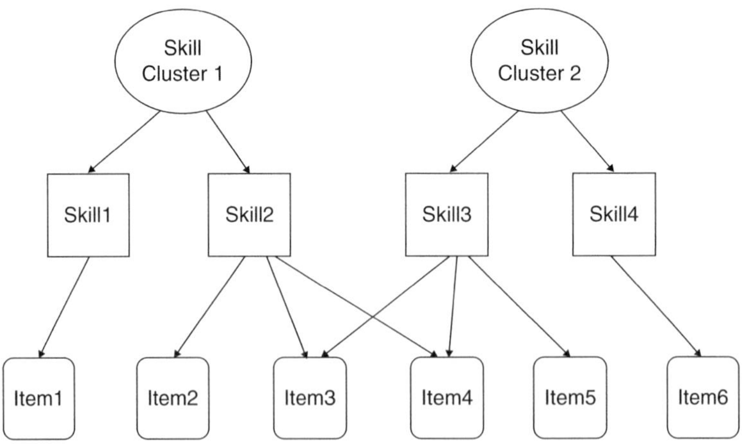

Fig. 2.1 Hierarchical blueprint structure

Prior to presenting results from the two-stage diagnostic testing of mastery of skills in middle school mathematics, an overview of the diagnostic model and procedures, as well as a consideration of appropriate reliability indices, is presented.

2.1 Background

2.1.1 Diagnostic Modeling of Heterogeneous Tests

The diagnostic model. The MLTM-D is a confirmatory model that is appropriate for hierarchically organized test domains with complex items. That is, separately defined areas of competency are represented on the test and more narrowly defined skills are clustered into these broader areas (see Fig. 2.1). Some items may involve skills from only one cluster while other items may involve skills from two or more clusters. To implement MLTM-D, two sets of scores are required: C_{ixk} is the involvement of component k in item i (i.e., the skill cluster), and $Q_{ixm(k)}$ is the score for item i on skill/attribute m with component k. The probability that the response of person j to the total item iT, X_{ijT}, is correct depends on the probability of solving the relevant skill clusters, as follows:

$$P\left(X_{ijT}=1\right)=\prod_{k}P\left(X_{ijk}=1\right)^{cik} \quad (2.1)$$

and

$$P(X_{ijk}=1)=1/(1+\exp(-1.7(\theta_{jk}-\sum_{m}\eta_{km}q_{ikm}+\eta_0))), \quad (2.2)$$

where X_{ijk} is the response of examinee j to component k on item i, θ_{jk} is the trait level of examinee j on component k, q_{ikm} is the score for stimulus feature m in component k for item i, η_{km} is the weight of feature m on component k, and c_{ik} is the involvement of component k in item i. The within component model for MLTM-D is similar to a linear logistic test model (LLTM; Fischer 1973). It should be noted that X_{ijk} is not directly observable, but that the associated parameters can be estimated from response patterns in the data.

Setting mastery boundaries in MLTM-D. For skill clusters, mastery levels can be set by locating skills on the components of MLTM-D. These probabilities are often set for the test as a whole by expert panels, but they also may be applied to skills and skill clusters in MLTM-D. Define $\overline{P}_m$ as the mean predicted probability of solving items on component k for θ_k. Then the cutline τ_k for component k may be found so that $\overline{P}_m \geq y$, where y is a specified probability for mastery.

For specific skills, as for component mastery, a probability for mastery, y, also must be specified. Specific attributes or skills are located on the common scales for component traits and items by their parameter estimates. Assuming that skill m is specified by a binary variable q_{km} for each relevant component, the estimated η_{km} indicates skill position on the theta scale where P_{km} equals .50. However, mastery of skill m must be located at a specified probability, y, within each relevant component. That is, the location of skill m in component k, γ_{mk}, is determined by the probability of solving skill m, P_{km}, such that $P_{km} = y$ if $\theta_k = \gamma_k$. Skill mastery for examinee j on skill m in component k is scored as 1 if $\theta_{jk} \geq \gamma_{m(k)}$, otherwise skill mastery is scored as 0. Number of skills mastered for component k is the sum of the mastered skills. It should be noted that interpretability of skill mastery depends on the strength of prediction of item difficulty by the skills involved.

2.1.2 *Assessing Reliability and Decision Accuracy*

Empirical reliability. Reliability of component estimates in MLTM-D may be obtained by traditional methods, which depend on the how the traits are estimated (see du Toit 2003). For *expected a posteriori* estimates (EAP), assuming the Rasch model specified within components in MLTM-D, empirical reliability for component k is given as:

$$\rho_t = \sigma^2_{\theta k} / \left(\sigma^2_{\theta k} + \overline{\sigma^2_{\varepsilon k}} \right), \tag{2.3}$$

where $\sigma^2_{\theta k}$ and $\overline{\sigma^2_{\varepsilon k}}$ are the variance of θ_k and the mean error variance, respectively, for component k.

Decision accuracy. If MLTM-D component estimates are used for mastery decisions, cutlines are applied as described above, decision accuracy estimates may be more appropriate for describing score properties. Decision accuracy has often been defined in terms of IRT estimates (Lewis and Sheehan 1990; Rudner 2005; Wainer et al. 2005). While these researchers were primarily interested in providing indices for decision accuracy for the test as a whole (not components or skill clusters), the underlying basis of the indices is interesting to consider. Rudner (2005), for example, placed the mastery cutline for the test, τ_w, on the estimated plausible distribution of theta, θ^*_j, for each person, assuming $\theta^*_j \sim N\left(\theta_j, \sigma^2_\varepsilon\right)$. For $\theta_j \geq \tau_w$, the proportion of $\theta^*_j \geq \tau_w$ would indicate accuracy. Conversely, for $\theta_j < \tau_w$, the proportion of $\theta^*_j < \tau_w$ would indicate accuracy. Thus, decision accuracy depends on both distance from the cutline and the standard error of measurement.

Given this formulation of procedures, decision confidence, ζ_j, also can be expressed for each person as follows:

$$\zeta_j = max\left(P^M_j,\ P^{NM}_j\right), \tag{2.4}$$

where P^M_j is probability of mastery (theta equal to or above cutline) and P^{NM}_j is the probability of non-mastery or $1 - P^M_j$. In turn, P^M_j is obtained as follows:

$$P_j^M = \mathrm{P}\left(\theta_j^* \geq \tau_w\right) \int_\tau^\infty \frac{1}{\sqrt{2\pi}} e^{-ty^2/2} dt$$

and

$$\mathrm{t} = \left(\theta_j^* - \theta_j\right) / \sigma_{\widehat{\theta}j}^2. \tag{2.5}$$

Equation 2.4 also may be applied to subscales or component estimates.

Skill diagnosis and decision accuracy. The reliability of skill diagnosis depends on the distribution of plausible trait levels within each component. As explicated above, the expected number of skills mastered for each component depends on the mastery location, γ_{mk}, and the estimated trait level, θ_j. An expectation that is based on the reliability of θ_j would base the expectation on the distribution of plausible thetas. For a decision confidence of .85, for example, a lower boundary for theta, θ_{jLB}^*, can be defined as $\mathrm{P}(\theta_j^* \geq \theta_{jLB}^*) = .85$ based on the plausible distribution of theta for examinee j, $\theta_j^* \sim N\left(\theta_j, \sigma_\varepsilon^2\right)$. The number of mastered skills in component k would be the sum of skills for which $\theta_{jLB}^* \geq \gamma_{mk}$.

2.2 Two-Stage Assessment of Mathematics Achievement

This study was conducted in cooperation with a state testing program that was administered at the end of the school year to assess proficiency in mathematics. Thus, Stage 1 of testing is the year-end test used for state accountability. Stage 2 testing consists of adaptive test forms to diagnose varying patterns of skill clusters.

2.2.1 *Method*

Examinees. The examinees were middle school students who were administered both stages of testing. While Stage 1 is required of all students, Stage 2 testing was conducted on a voluntary basis with participating classrooms. For Grade 6 and Grade 7, respectively, 713 and 311 students participated.

Tests. The year-end test was hierarchically organized to include both broad and narrow skills. At the highest level was four areas of mathematics: Number, Algebra, Geometry, and Data. Within each area were indicators, which specified the more specific skills. Items were scored by a panel of educators for the involvement of multiple skills. Approximately 20 % of items involved more than one area of mathematics. The number of operational items on the year-end tests was 73 and 71, respectively, for Grade 6 and Grade 7. For Grade 6, the majority of items represented Number and Geometry, due to the blueprint specifications. Both Algebra and Data were represented by only a few items. For Grade 7, only Data was represented by a small number of items.

The Stage 2 tests consisted of items that were developed to measure the same areas and indicators as the Stage 1 tests, but to be administered at the beginning of the school year to students now in Grade 7 and Grade 8. The items had been previously calibrated within the year-end tests. Sixteen forms of both the *Background Skills Test* were constructed. Two levels of difficulty were available for each area, hence 4^2 forms were needed. Although the background test for Grade 8 had the same number of items for each area, for a total of 32 items, the background test for Grade 7 had fewer available items for both Algebra and Data, similar to the Stage 1 test. Hence the tests included only 24 items.

Procedure. All tests were computer administered. Stage 1 testing was conducted at the end of the school year while Stage 2 conducted at the beginning of the next school year.

Estimation of mastery. Marginal maximum likelihood estimated MLTM-D item parameters were used in both Stage 1 and Stage 2 estimation of trait levels (Embretson et al. 2014). Item parameter estimates were based on minimum sample sizes of 5000 randomly selected examinees from the year-end mathematics achievement tests. A previous study on this population had found good overall fit of MLTM-D as compared to other IRT models (Embretson 2015) and good fit of the items.

The Stage 1 item parameters were used to estimate component trait levels (i.e., the four areas of mathematics) for all students in each grade level (32,000 students) using EAP with normal priors (0,1). These estimates were then used to select the most informative test for the participating students in Stage 2. Stage 2 trait estimates on each component were obtained using EAP, with the Stage 1 estimates as serving as individual priors for each examinee. Mastery of the skill clusters, the four areas of mathematics, and the more narrow skills, the indicators within the areas, were obtained using the procedures described in the Sect. 1. The probability standard, y, to determine mastery was the probability that had been set by the state board of education for the whole test. This standard was applied to determine mastery for both the components and the skills within components.

2.3 Results

Descriptive statistics and empirical reliability. Table 2.1 presents descriptivestatistics (means, standard deviations, mean standard errors, and empirical reliabilities) for the Stage 1 and Stage 2 MLTM-D estimates for the four areas. The participating students means and standard deviations may be compared to the population data, estimated as N(0,1). For Grade 7, the mean trait level estimate for each area is negative, indicating that the participating students were somewhat lower than the population. For three components, the standard deviations are somewhat lower than the population. The standard error of measurement for Algebra and Data, both of which had fewer items than the other two areas, was relatively large. Similarly, the empirical reliability for these two tests was smaller than .70, which is often deemed to the minimal level for research purposes. The highest empirical reliability was for Number, which was nearly .80. Thus, the reliability results did

Table 2.1 Descriptive statistics and empirical reliabilities of estimates for two grade levels

		Stage 1				Stage 2			
Grade	Standard	Mean	SD	Mean SE	Empirical reliability	Mean	SD	Mean SE	Empirical reliability
7N = 713	Number	−.249	.905	.453	.799	−.373	.900	.394	.839
	Algebra	−.148	.895	.705	.617	−.205	1.01	.608	.735
	Geometry	−.338	.953	.480	.797	−.643	.892	.421	.818
	Data	−.318	1.150	.807	.670	−.680	1.168	.731	.719
8N = 311	Number	−.051	1.006	.569	.758	.071	1.061	.498	.819
	Algebra	.274	1.017	.534	.784	.194	1.000	.486	.808
	Geometry	−.003	.967	.493	.793	−.119	.920	.440	.814
	Data	.167	.782	.626	.609	.133	.949	.541	.755

Table 2.2 Descriptive statistics for decision confidence by testing stage and grade level

		Stage 1			Stage 2		
	Standard	Mean	SD	Percent $\zeta_j \geq .85$	Mean	SD	Percent $\zeta_j \geq .85$
Grade 7	Number	.885	.139	.699	.892	.133	.743
	Algebra	.906	.128	.727	.925	.123	.821
N = 713	Geometry	.884	.144	.684	.887	.138	.687
	Data	.908	.131	.742	.905	.121	.725
Grade 8	Number	.882	.142	.716	.902	.136	.742
	Algebra	.948	.121	.880	.958	.099	.894
N = 311	Geometry	.918	.133	.803	.913	.144	.790
	Data	.878	.131	.671	.891	.144	.739

not strongly support estimates for the four areas from Stage 1 of testing alone. The Stage 2 results, however, were stronger. Empirical reliabilities are greater than .70 for both Algebra and Data, while Number and Geometry were greater than .80.

For Grade 8, the means for Number and Geometry were close to the population means, while Algebra and Data were somewhat higher. Similarly, the standard deviations are close to the population values, except for Data, which was lower. The standard errors are also higher for Data. The empirical reliabilities are in the high .70s for Number, Algebra and Geometry, but Data is substantially lower at .609. It should be noted that in Grade 8, Data is represented by substantially fewer items than the other areas. As for Grade 7, the reliability results did not strongly support scale estimates for the four areas. The Stage 2 results, however, yielded reliabilities greater than .80 for all areas except Data, which had a reliability of .755.

Decision accuracy. Table 2.2 presents descriptive statistics on decision accuracy. It can be seen that the mean decision confidence for both Grade 7 and Grade 8 for all areas is quite strong, as it is in the high .80s and low .90s for all areas in Stage 1. The mean decision confidence, ζ_j, was only slightly higher after Stage 2. Table 2.2 also presents the percentages of examinees with ζ_j greater than .85. For Grade 7, the percentage ranged from .684 to .742 in Stage 1, and from .725 to .821 in Stage 2.

Thus, the percentage with ζ_j greater than .85 increased somewhat with the second stage of testing. Similarly, for Grade 8, the percentage ranged from .671 to .880 in Stage 1, and from .739 to .884 in Stage 2. Again, moderate increases from the second stage of testing were observed.

Skill mastery. Table 2.3 presents the mean number of skills mastered for each area by testing stage and grade level. Skill mastery was obtained using both estimated trait levels, θ_j, and the boundary trait levels, θ^*_{jLB}, as described above. Since the number of skills specified in the blueprint differs between areas, the means vary. Most importantly is the *root mean square error* (RMSE) shown in Table 2.3 which estimates the difference between the estimated and boundary thetas. This may be taken as an indicator of reliability. Generally RMSE is somewhat greater when skill mastery is estimated in Stage 1 of testing versus Stage 2. For Grade 7, the results reflect the smaller number of skills tested for Algebra and Data, and the small number of items on both Stage 1 and Stage 2 tests. RMSE is low after Stage 1 for both Algebra and Data, and little change is observed after Stage 2 of testing. For Number and Geometry, RMSE decreases more substantially from Stage 1 to Stage 2 of testing. For Grade 8, RMSE for number of skills ranges from 1.145 to 1.229 for Number, Algebra and Geometry, but is 1.646 for Data after Stage 1 testing. RMSE decreases for all areas after Stage 2 testing.

2.4 Discussion

This study examined the reliability of heterogeneous tests for diagnosing mastery of skill clusters and specific skills. It was found that the results depended most strongly on the method used to assess reliability. Use of multistage testing increased reliability somewhat, but the results depended on the method used to assess reliability.

The most important finding was that scale score reliability for skill clusters, even when assessed in a diagnostic model, was not substantial from a single stage of testing. While the empirical reliabilities were sufficient for research purposes, with estimates in the .70s, using these score to inform individuals is somewhat questionable. While the second stage of testing did increase reliabilities, the reliabilities were in the low .70s or low .80s. Whether or not this level of reliability is adequate depends on score use.

In contrast, when decision accuracy was used to estimate reliability, the results were much stronger. The average decision confidence was approximately .90 after a single stage of testing. The mean decision confidence increased only slightly after the second stage of testing. An alternative perspective to examine the percentage of examines for whom a specified level of decision confidence was reached. When this level was set at .85, the percentage of individuals with sufficient levels of reliability ranged from 67.1 to 88.0 % across areas and grade levels after the first stage of testing. These percentages ranged from 72.5 to 89.4 % after the second stage of

Table 2.3 Descriptive statistics on skill mastery at estimated and boundary trait levels by testing stage and grade level

		Estimated theta		Boundary theta		
		Mean	Std. deviation	Mean	Std. deviation	RMSE
Grade 7	Stage 1					
	Number	4.833	2.812	3.706	2.779	1.513
	Algebra	1.688	.466	1.495	.519	.436
	Geometry	6.063	2.319	4.918	2.732	1.729
	Data	1.701	.537	1.446	.711	.510
	Stage 2					
	Number	4.673	2.699	3.680	2.641	1.360
	Algebra	1.757	.432	1.545	.520	.458
	Geometry	5.751	2.418	4.754	2.603	1.470
	Data	1.645	.572	1.354	.671	.539
Grade 8	Stage 1					
	Number	5.112	1.497	4.287	1.884	1.229
	Algebra	6.251	1.566	5.548	2.016	1.212
	Geometry	4.845	1.459	4.083	1.723	1.145
	Data	4.841	1.515	3.441	1.824	1.646
	Stage 2					
	Number	5.216	1.401	4.564	1.808	1.030
	Algebra	6.193	1.611	5.554	2.005	1.091
	Geometry	4.719	1.518	4.003	1.690	1.082
	Data	4.512	1.719	3.593	1.974	1.221

testing. Thus, for diagnosing mastery of skill clusters, a single stage of testing appears to be adequate for the majority of examinees. These results suggest that the second stage of testing may be needed only for a small percentage of examinees to adequately assess skill cluster mastery.

The stronger reliability found for decision confidence indices, rather than scale scores, could be true for many tests if used for diagnosis. Decision confidence indices depend not only on the reliability of the individual trait level estimates, but also on the placement of the mastery cutlines relative to the trait level estimates. Thus, for some tests, with cutlines near the mean of the trait level distribution, stronger results for reliability from decision confidence indices is unlikely.

The results on the mastery of specific skills were comparable, in that the second stage of testing made a small improvement. Skills were examined in the context of decision accuracy, with a specified level of .85. The second stage of testing reduced the uncertainty about the number of skills above mastery by a small amount. Future research could examine for which examinees this assessment is important. That is, if instructional materials are available on the separate skills, greater accuracy for assessing mastery of each one could optimize instructional efficiency.

References

Du Toit, M. (2003). *IRT from SSI*. Lincolnwood, IL: Scientific Software International, Inc.
Embretson, S. E. (2015). The multicomponent latent trait model for diagnosis: Applications to heterogeneous test domains. Invited paper for *Applied Psychological Measurement* (pp. 6–30).
Embretson, S. E., & Yang, X. (2013). A multicomponent latent trait model for diagnosis. *Psychometrika, 78*, 14–36.
Embretson, S. E., Morrison, K., & Jun, H. (2014). *Implementation of a multistage adaptive testing system for diagnosing mathematical deficits in middle school*. Report IES1001A-2014 for Institute of Educational Sciences Grant R305A100234. Atlanta, GA: Cognitive Measurement Laboratory, Georgia Institute of Technology.
Fischer, G. H. (1973). The linear logistic test model as an instrument in educational research. *Acta Psychologica, 37*, 359–374.
Hensen, R. A., Templin, J. L., & Willse, J. T. (2009). Defining a family of cognitive diagnosis models using log-linear models with latent variables. *Psychometrika, 74*, 191–210.
Leighton, J. P., & Gierl, M. J. (2007). *Cognitive diagnostic assessment for education*. New York: Cambridge University Press.
Lewis, C., & Sheehan, K. (1990). Using Bayesian decision theory to design a computerized mastery test. *Applied Psychological Measurement, 14*, 367–386.
Rudner, L. M. (2005). Expected classification accuracy. *Practical Assessment Research & Evaluation, 10*, 1–4.
Rupp, A. A., Templin, J., & Hensen, R. A. (2010). *Diagnostic measurement: Theory, methods, and applications*. New York: Guilford Press.
Sinharay, S. (2010). How often do subscores have added value? Results from operational and simulated data. *Journal of Educational Measurement, 47*, 150–174.
von Davier, M. (2008). A general diagnostic model applied to language testing data. *British Journal of Mathematical and Statistical Psychology, 61*, 287–307.
Wainer, H., Wang, X. A., Skorupski, W. P., & Bradlow, E. T. (2005). A Bayesian method for evaluating passing scores: The PPoP curve. *Journal of Educational Measurement, 42*, 271–281.

Chapter 3
New IRT Models for Examinee-Selected Items

Wen-Chung Wang and Chen-Wei Liu

Abstract Examinee-selected-item (ESI) design, in which examinees are required to respond to a fixed number of items in a given set of items (e.g., responding to two items in five given items; leading to ten selection patterns), has the advantages of enhancing students' learning motivation and reducing their testing anxiety. The ESI design yields incomplete data (i.e., only those selected items are answered and the others have missing data). It has been argued that missing data in the ESI design are missing not at random, making standard item response theory (IRT) models inappropriate. Recently, Wang et al. (Journal of Educational Measurement 49(4):419–445, 2012) propose an IRT model for examinee-selected items by adding an additional latent trait to standard IRT models to account for the selection effect. This latent trait could correlate with the intended-to-be-measured latent trait, and the correlation quantifies how stronger the selection effect and how serious the violation of the assumption of missing at random are. In this study, we developed a framework to incorporate this model as a special case and generate several new models. We conducted an experiment to collect real data, in which 501 fifth graders took two mandatory items and four pairs of mathematic (dichotomous) items. In each pair of items, students were first asked to indicate which item they preferred to answer and then answered both items. This is referred to as the "Choose one, Answer all" approach. These new IRT models were fit to the real data and the results were discussed.

Keywords Item response theory • Examinee-selected items • Selection effect • Missing data

In most achievement testing, examinees are required to complete all items. In some cases, examinees are allowed to respond to a fixed number of items in a given set of items. These items referred to as examinee-selected (ES) items and this design is referred to as the examinee-selected-item (ESI) design. The ESI design

W.-C. Wang (✉) • C.-W. Liu
The Hong Kong Institute of Education, 10 Lo Ping Road, Tai Po, New Territories, Hong Kong, China
e-mail: wcwang@ied.edu.hk; cwliu@ied.edu.hk

L.A. van der Ark et al. (eds.), *Quantitative Psychology Research*, Springer Proceedings in Mathematics & Statistics 140, DOI 10.1007/978-3-319-19977-1_3

may reduce test anxiety, raise motivation for learning, and stimulate self-access and self-adaptive learning (Wainer and Thissen 1994). The 1989 Advanced Placement Examination in Chemistry is an example of the ESI design, which consists of both mandatory (all examinees are required to answer) and ES items, in multiple-choice or constructed-response format. Another example is the 2010 Geography, History, and Mathematics subjects of the National Matriculation Entrance Tests in China, consisting of both mandatory and ES items.

The ESI design brings challenges to psychometrics. Allowing choices will inevitably cause problems in comparing scores obtained from different selection patterns because different items often (if not always) have different difficulties. Although IRT enables score comparison when different examinees respond to different items (e.g., computerized adaptive testing or large-scale assessment such as the Program for International Student Assessment; PISA), either the item difficulty has to be known in advance or the assumption of missing at random (MAR; Rubin 1976) has to be valid for those unselected items. Otherwise, scores are no longer comparable when different examinees respond to different items.

Previous studies have attempted to fit IRT models to ES items. Wainer et al. (1991) developed equating strategies for ES items and observed the items selected by different groups of examinees have different parameters. Fitzpatrick and Yen (1995) observed that the selection behaviors vary across genders and grades and the use of mandatory items is crucial for equating. Wainer et al. (1994) examined the score comparability in the ESI design and found the missing data to unselected items are missing not at random (MNAR) because the missing responses are related to examinees' ability levels. Standard IRT models, which assume MAR, are no longer appropriate for ES items.

Later on, Wang et al. (1995) conducted an experiment with the Choose-One-Answer-All (COAA) design, in which examinees are required to indicate which item in a given pair of multiple-choice items do they prefer to respond and then answer both items. Such a design creates a complete dataset with responses to all items, so the parameters of all items can be calibrated using conventional IRT models. They then treated the unselected items as missing data and evaluated the assumption of MAR in ES items. The results clearly point to MNAR, making standard IRT models inapplicable when the ESI design is implemented. Bridgeman et al. (1997) conducted the same experiment on constructed-response items and drew the same conclusion that the missing data to unselected items are MNAR. Bradlow and Thomas (1998) conduct simulation studies to demonstrate that the difficulties of easy items are systematically underestimated, whereas those for difficult items are systematically overestimated, which is an indication of MNAR. These experimental or simulation studies lead to a conclusion that the item parameter equating is problematic and conventional IRT models are inappropriate for ES items.

It is of great interest to understand how examinees make a choice in the ESI design. Wang (1999) gathered empirical data from Hawaii and found that examinees' perception of item difficulty is associated with their selection behavior in ES items. Examinees tend to select seemingly easy and familiar items. Wainer and Thissen (1994) showed that examinees do not always select items cleverly and less proficient examinees tend to do a worse job in selection than more proficient examinees. Allen et al. (2005) used logistic regression to assess the relationship between the target ability and selection behavior and found that the higher the ability level, the more clever the choice is.

Despite these clear research findings, there are some attempts to fitting conventional IRT models to empirical ES items. Lukhele et al. (1994) fitted the graded response model (GRM; Samejima 1969) to mandatory items and the nominal response model (Bock 1972) to ES items in the chemistry subject of the College Board's Advanced Placement exams. Nonresponses to unselected items were assumed to be MAR in their study, without any empirical validation. If such an assumption was violated (it is very likely according to the above experiments), their conclusions would be misleading. Thus, their findings were jeopardized. Wang et al. (1995) fitted latent mixture models to ES items, which actually require knowledge of the distributions of the latent variable that dominates the missingness. In reality, such knowledge is applicable only when missing data are observed (e.g., in the OCAA design). To sum up, it is very likely that nonresponses to unselected items are MNAR. If so, conventional IRT models are no longer valid.

Recently, Wang et al. (2012) proposed the examinee-selected item model (ESIM) to account for the selection effect in ES items. In the ESIM, the selection effect is summarized by a latent variable (can be referred to as test wisdom), which is added to standard IRT models, such as the rating scale model (Andrich 1978) or the partial credit model (Masters 1982) when ES items are polytomous. In the ESIM, it is the target latent trait θ that the test intends to measure that determines the response functions of mandatory items, whereas it is θ and the test-wisdom latent variable γ jointly determine the response functions of ES items. θ and γ are assumed to follow a bivariate normal distribution. Their correlation depicts the magnitude of the selection effect. A positive correlation indicates that more capable examinees gain more benefit from making a clever choice than less capable examinees; a negate correlation indicates that less capable examinees gain more benefit from making a clever choice than more capable examinees (this is not very likely to occur in practice); a zero correlation indicates no selection effect and thus nonresponses to unselected items can be treated as MAR and standard IRT models become feasible. In their empirical example of the 2009 History test of the National Matriculation Entrance Examinations in China, which consisted of 28 mandatory items (25 multiple-choice items and 3 open-ended items) and 6 ES items from which 2 items were to be answered, a moderate and positive correlation ($r = .49$) was found, which is why the γ variable is referred to as test wisdom (Wang et al. 2012).

The ESIM belongs to bi-factor IRT models (Li et al. 2006; Rijmen 2010), in which mandatory items are assumed to measure a single dimension of θ, whereas ES items are assumed to measure two dimensions of θ and γ. While the ESIM appears promising for ES items, it is of great importance to embed it into a general framework so that its feasibility can be further increased and customized and general models can be invented. In this study, we developed such a general framework to incorporate the ESIM as a special case and conducted a brief simulation study to evaluate parameter recovery. We adopted the COAA design to collect real data on a mathematics test. These new models as well as conventional ones were fit to the real data and their results were compared.

3.1 The Experiment

We developed an algebra test for fifth graders according to the mathematical subject guidelines. A math teacher was consulted and ten fifth graders piloted the test for item revision. The final version of the test consisted of ten constructed-response dichotomous items. Among the ten items, the first two were mandatory and the other eight items were formed into four pairs. The COAA design was adopted. A total of 501 fifth-graders from Shenzhen and Guangzhou, China participated in this experiment. They were instructed to preview each pair of items, indicate their preference should they be requested to choose one item to answer, indicate their reasons for making such a choice, and then answer both items. The testing time was 40 min, which was long enough to let all students finish the test. Before formal testing, the students were given a trial to familiarize the COAA design. No personally identifiable information was collected. Because 17 students did not indicate their preferences and were thus excluded, the remaining sample had 484 students.

3.2 Conventional Raw-Score Analysis

In the COAA design, the original dataset can be arranged in two ways: a complete dataset with responses to all the ten items, and an incomplete dataset with responses to the two mandatory items and four selected items. We calibrated the parameters of the ten items in a complete dataset with the Rasch model (Rasch 1960). Table 3.1 shows the difficulty estimates and the percentage of preference, for each item. Among the four pairs of items, there was a "clever" choice (the easier item was preferred more often) in the second and fourth pairs, and an "unclever" choice (the more difficult item was preferred more often) in the third pair. Taken as a whole, a small clever choice was found in the test.

The percentages of preference in Table 3.1 were calculated across all students, which did not tell whether more capable students tended to make a clever choice more often than less capable students. We thus computed the number of times a student selected the easier item in a pair across the four pairs, resulting a score of "clever choice" from 0 to 4. We then plotted the scores of clever choice against the raw total scores (from 0 to 10), shown in Fig. 3.1. It seemed that the mean clever choice score increased slightly as the raw total score increased. The Mann–Kendall test (Kendall 1975; Mann 1945) was conducted to assess the monotonic trend of the increment. It was found that there was a significant upward trend

Table 3.1 Item parameter estimates obtained from the complete dataset and percentage of preference for each item

	Item no.	Difficulty	Preference
Mandatory	1	0.51	
Mandatory	2	0.38	
Pair 1	3	2.49	49 %
	4	−0.58	51 %
Pair 2	5	0.50	26 %
	6	−0.60	74 %
Pair 3	7	−1.18	46 %
	8	−0.96	53 %
Pair 4	9	−0.27	36 %
	10	−1.69	64 %

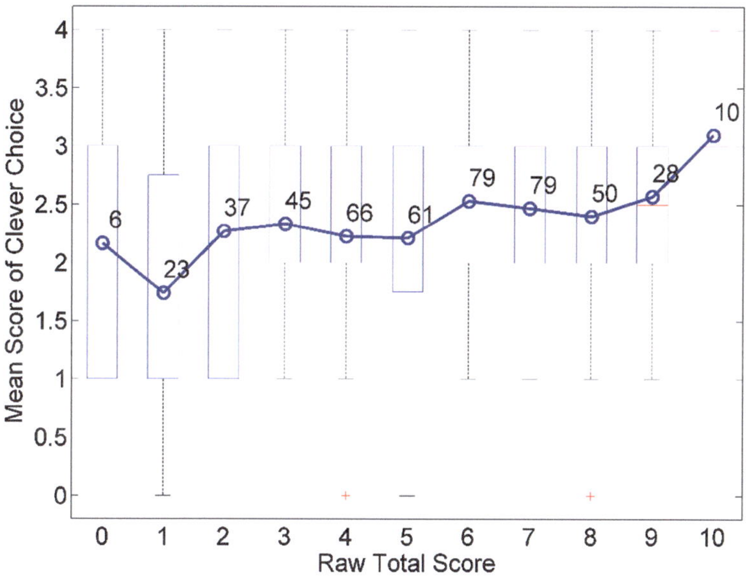

Fig. 3.1 Relationship between the score of clever choice and the raw total scores. *Note*. The numbers in the figure are the numbers of students in that raw total score

($\tau = 0.67$, $\sigma^2 = 165$; $p = .005$), suggesting more capable students tended to make clever choices more often than less capable students.

To further examine the selection effect in each pair, we plotted the percentages of clever choice against the raw total scores for each pair, shown in Fig. 3.2. The Mann–Kendall test was again conducted to assess the monotonic trend of the increment for each pair. The results showed there was a significant upward trend for the first ($\tau = 0.53$, $\sigma^2 = 165$; $p = .029$) and second pairs ($\tau = 0.56$, $\sigma^2 = 165$; $p = .020$), but not for the third ($\tau = 0.36$, $\sigma^2 = 164$; $p = .138$) and fourth pairs ($\tau = 0.20$, $\sigma^2 = 165$; $p = .436$). The familywise error rate of the four tests was of no concern, so the *p*-value was not corrected for multiple tests. Overall, a small clever choice effect was found.

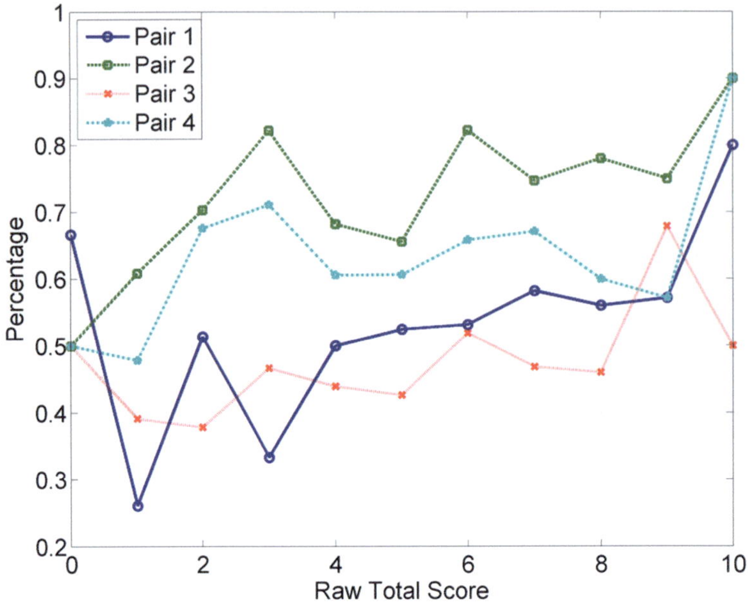

Fig. 3.2 Relationship between the percentage of clever choice and the raw total score for the four pairs of items

Table 3.2 Proportions of correctness in the four pairs of items and the choice preferences

Item no.	Difficulty	Preferred item 3	4	5	6	7	8	9	10
3	2.49	0.10	0.12						
4	−0.58	0.58	0.65						
5	0.50			0.39	0.41				
6	−0.60			0.53	0.65				
7	−1.18					0.76	0.69		
8	−0.96					0.73	0.65		
9	−0.27							0.52	0.57
10	−1.69							0.74	0.83

Note. The difficulty parameters were estimated from the complete dataset

With the COAA design, it was possible to observe responses to both items in a pair and examine whether students tended to select the easier item in a pair. The results are shown in Table 3.2. Take pair 1 (including items 3 and 4) as an example. The IRT difficulties of items 3 and 4 were 1.46 and −0.35, respectively. Item 4 was much easier than item 3. For students preferring item 3, the proportions of correctness in items 3 and 4 were 0.10 and 0.58, respectively. For students preferring item 4, the proportions were 0.12 and 0.65, respectively. It appeared that students

Table 3.3 Reasons of preference in examinee-selected items

Pair	Easy to solve	Easy to understand	Familiarity	Small numbers	Formula available	Short item	Others
1	0.51	0.26	0.15	0.06	0.07	0.01	0.02
2	0.53	0.30	0.14	0.14	0.05	0.06	0.04
3	0.45	0.26	0.15	0.09	0.07	0.01	0.03
4	0.58	0.11	0.14	0.09	0.12	0.05	0.03
Mean	0.52	0.23	0.14	0.10	0.08	0.03	0.03

preferring the easier item (item 4) had a higher percentage of correctness on both items than that for students preferring the more difficult item (item 3). The same finding was observed for the other three pairs.

From the above analyses, it can be concluded that there was a small selection effect. If the selection effect is large but ignored by applying standard IRT models that assume MAR to ES items, the ability levels for students making a clever choice (preferring the easier item) will be overestimated, whereas those for making an unclever choice (preferring the more difficult item) will be underestimated. In addition, item parameter estimates will be biased. Given that the selection effect in this experiment appeared rather small in this particular dataset, fitting standard IRT models might do little harm.

With respect to the reasons of preference, seven options were provided for students to choose: (1) easy to solve, (2) familiar with the item, (3) small numbers in the item, (4) easy to understand, (5) short item length, (6) formula available to solve the item, and (7) others (please specify). The results are shown in Table 3.3. Apparently, easy to solve was the most popular reason, followed by easy to understand and familiar with the item. It seems that students selected items based on their perceived easiness and familiarity.

3.3 New IRT Models

The preliminary raw-score analysis was based on the complete data, which was made possible from the COAA design. In reality, the COAA is not implemented and only the incomplete data are available. Below, we show how to fit new IRT models to the incomplete dataset to recover the selection effect and yield parameter estimates that were close to those obtained from the complete dataset.

Let $\Pr_{nik}$ be the probability of being in category k of item i for person n and the item responses follow a multivariate Bernoulli distribution. The target latent trait θ is linked to $\Pr_{nik}$ as:

$$f^{\text{link}}(\Pr_{nik}) = \alpha_i\theta_n - \delta_{ik} \tag{3.1}$$

where θ_n is the latent trait of person n and is often assumed to follow a standard normal distribution; α_i is the slope (discrimination) parameter of item i; δ_{ik} is the intercept parameter for category k of item i. When the cumulative logit link function is used, Eq. (3.1) becomes the logistic version of the GRM (Samejima 1969). For dichotomous items, the logistic version of the GRM becomes the two-parameter logistic model (Birnbaum 1968). When the slope parameters are further constrained to be unity, the Rasch model (Rasch 1960) is formed:

$$f^{\text{link}}\left(\text{Pr}_{ni}\right) = \theta_n - \delta_i \tag{3.2}$$

where Pr_{ni} is the probability of success on item i for person n; δ_i is the difficulty of item i; the others are defined previously. In this study, we focused on one-parameter IRT models.

The selection effect in ES items may result from personal preference or intuition, response habit, or others. Whatever they are, they are irrelevant to the target latent trait θ and thus should be partitioned out from θ. Throughout this study, it is assumed the underlying factors of making a choice in ES items can be summarized by a latent variable γ. For commutation simplicity, we may call γ "test wisdom," as done in Wang et al. (2012). When Eq. (3.1) or (3.2) is fit to ES items (treating the missing data of unselected items as MAR), the selection effect in ES items is not accounted for, so the resulting θ estimates will be contaminated by those irrelevant factors and thus become unfair.

The following IRT models are proposed to account for the selection effects in ES items, from simple to complex. First of all, it is assumed that those selecting the same sets of ES items have the same level of γ. For example, there were four pairs of ES items in the test, resulting in a total of 16 selection patterns. Let the selection patterns be indexed as s ($s = 1, \ldots, S$). The corresponding IRT model is as follows:

$$f\left(\text{Pr}_{ni}\right) = \theta_n - \delta_i + \gamma_s, \tag{3.3}$$

where γ_s describes the selection effect for those persons with selection pattern s; the others are defined previously. For model identification, the mean of γ_s is set at zero, together with common constraints in standard IRT models (e.g., the mean of θ_n is constrained at zero). A positive γ increases the probability of success (i.e., a clever choice); a negative γ decreases the probability of success (an unclever choice); a zero γ has no impact on the probability of success. If γ_s is equal to zero for all s, then Eq. (3.3) becomes Eq. (3.2).

Second, it is assumed in Eq. (3.3) that all persons come from the same distribution (often, θ $N(\mu, \sigma^2)$). It is possible that those having different selection patterns have different means on the latent trait θ. If so, Eq. (3.3) can be extended as:

$$f\left(\text{Pr}_{ni}\right) = \theta_{ns} - \delta_i + \gamma_s, \tag{3.4}$$

where θ_{ns} is the latent trait of person n with selection pattern s and is assumed to be normally distributed with mean μ_s and common variance σ^2; the others are defined previously. For model identification, at least one mandatory item is needed. Besides, the grand mean of μ_s should be at zero.

Third, in Eqs. (3.3) and (3.4) the selection effect is a fixed effect, indicating that those persons having the same selection pattern s share the same selection effect of γ_s. This constraint can be released and the selection effect can be a random effect. There are several ways of formulating random effects. Take Eq. (3.3) as a starting point. It can be extended as:

$$f(\Pr_{ni}) = \theta_n - \delta_i + \gamma_n, \tag{3.5}$$

where θ_n and γ_n are assumed to follow a bivariate normal distribution; the others are defined previously. Equation (3.5) is a dichotomous version of the ESIM (Wang et al. 2012). To be more general, Eq. (3.5) can be further extended as:

$$f(\Pr_{ni}) = \theta_{ns} - \delta_i + \gamma_{ns}, \tag{3.6}$$

where θ_{ns} and γ_{ns} are assumed to follow a bivariate normal distribution, for each selection pattern s (s = 1, ..., S); the others are defined previously. To identify this general model, both the grand means of θ_{ns} and γ_{ns} across selection patterns are constrained at zero. Furthermore, at least one mandatory item is required. Equations (3.3–3.6) are referred to as the general examinee-selected-item models (GESIMs).

The association between θ and γ can help explain the selection effect. A positive association indicates that more capable persons tend to benefit from ES items more than less capable persons, whereas a negative association indicates that less capable persons tend to benefit more.

3.4 Parameter Estimation

Traditional parameter estimation procedures such as the marginal maximum likelihood with expectation-maximization algorithms (MML-EM) (Bock and Aitkin 1981) and the Bayesian methods via Markov chain Monte Carlo (MCMC) algorithms (Patz and Junker 1999) are feasible for the parameter estimation of the GESIMs. In general, MML-EM is more efficient than MCMC in low dimensional models. In the present study, we consider only two latent variables, θ and γ; so the MML-EM procedure implemented in M*plus* (Muthén and Muthén 1998–2012) was used to estimate the parameters.

3.5 IRT Results

We fit the Rasch (Eq. 3.2) to the complete dataset (denoted as Rasch-c) to obtain parameter estimates. These estimates were treated as a gold standard, to which those obtained from fitting other models to the incomplete data were compared. We then fit the Rasch (denoted as Rasch-i), Eqs. (3.3–3.6) (denoted as GESIM3–GESIM6, respectively) to the incomplete data. The appendix lists the M*plus* codes for the GESIM6.

The Akaike information criterion (AIC) was used to compare models (Akaike 1974). To make the AIC applicable for model comparison between the Rasch-i and the other GESIMs, the Rasch-i was formulated as a simplified version of the GESIM5, in which θ_n and γ_n were constrained independent. The AIC values were 5978 for the Rasch-i, 5979 for the GESIM5, 5986 for the GESIM3, 6000 for the GESIM4, and 6054 for the GESIM6. It seems that the Rasch-i and GESIM5 were the two best fitting models, suggesting the selection effect was not evident. In the GESIM5, the θ and γ variances were 0.64 and 0.09, respectively, and the correlation was .24 ($p = .03$), indicating a small selection effect.

The item parameter estimates of the Rasch-c, Rasch-i, and GESIM5 are listed in Table 3.4. It appeared that those item parameter estimates obtained from the three models were very similar. Figure 3.3 shows the relationship in the θ estimates (expected a posteriori estimates) obtained from the Rasch-c, Rasch-i, and GESIM5, respectively. It seemed that the estimates obtained from the Rasch-i and GESIM5 were shrunken toward zero, as compared to those from the Rasch-c. The shrinkage was mainly because the test length in the Rasch-c was ten items, whereas that in the Rasch-i and GESIM5 was six items, so the estimates in the Rasch-i and GESIM5 were subject to the shrinkage toward the prior mean (zero) more seriously than those in the Rasch-c. The θ estimates from the Rasch-i and GESIM5 were almost identical. In short, there was little difference in fitting the Rasch-i and the GESIM5 to this particular dataset because the selection effect was rather small. However, it should be noted that the GESIMs may have a better fit than the Rasch-i in other datasets. For example, in Wang et al. (2012), the polytomous GESIM5 had a better fit than the polytomous Rasch-i. Furthermore, the advantage of the GESIMs over the Rasch-i is that the former can yield an estimate for the selection effect (no matter how small it is), whereas the latter assumes the selection effect is ignorable.

Table 3.4 Item difficulty estimates for the ten items in the Rasch-c, Rasch-i, and GESIM5

Item no.	Rasch-c	Rasch-i	GESIM5
1	0.51	0.49	0.47
2	0.38	0.37	0.35
3	2.49	2.52	2.53
4	−0.58	−0.68	−0.68
5	0.50	0.48	0.48
6	−0.60	−0.74	−0.74
7	−1.18	−1.36	−1.36
8	−0.96	−0.78	−0.78
9	−0.27	−0.11	−0.11
10	−1.69	−1.96	−1.97

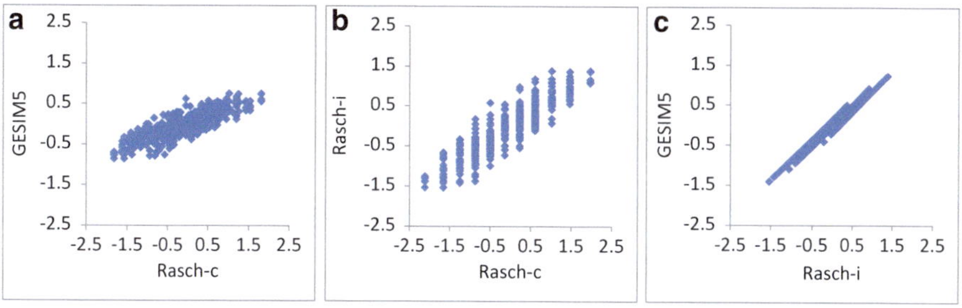

Fig. 3.3 Relationships in the person parameter estimates between the Rasch-c and the Rasch-i (**a**), between the Rasch-c and the GESIM5 (**b**), and between the Rasch-i and the GESIM5 (**c**)

3.6 A Simulation Study of the GESIM6

3.6.1 Design and Analysis

We conducted a brief simulation to evaluate the parameter recovery of the GESIM6. There were ten mandatory dichotomous items and six ES dichotomous items from which two items were to be selected. There were a total of 15 selection patterns (groups) and each pattern had a sample size of 500 or 1000. The means of the θ and γ variables for the 15 groups were both set at -1, -1, -1, -0.5, -0.5, -0.5, -0.5, 0, 0.5, 0.5, 0.5, 0.5, 1, 1, and 1, respectively. The variances of the θ and γ variables for the 15 groups were all set at 1. The correlations between θ and γ for the 15 groups were randomly generated from a uniform distribution between 0.3 and 0.9. The difficulty parameters were between -2 and 2 for the ten mandatory items, and between -1 and 1 for the six ES items, with an equal increment between two adjacent items. There were 100 replications under each of the two sample-size conditions. After the data were simulated from the GESIM6, the data-generating model was fit to the data using M*plus*. The bias and root mean square error (RMSE) in parameter estimates across replications were computed to evaluate the parameter recovery.

3.6.1.1 Results

The bias and RMSE in the estimates for the means and variances of θ and γ, and their correlations under the two sample-size conditions are shown in Fig. 3.4. It was evident that σ_{γ}^{2} was recovered less satisfactorily than the other parameters. The relatively poor estimation for σ_{γ}^{2} was mainly there were only two selected ES items, which were too short to yield a reliable estimate for σ_{γ}^{2}. For the item parameter estimates, the bias ranged from -0.004 to 0.008 and the RMSE from 0.021 to 0.088 when $N = 500$; the bias ranged from -0.007 to 0.009 and the RMSE from 0.015 to 0.066 when $N = 1000$, suggesting a very good recovery. In summary, the parameter recovery of the GESIM6, although not perfect, was satisfactory.

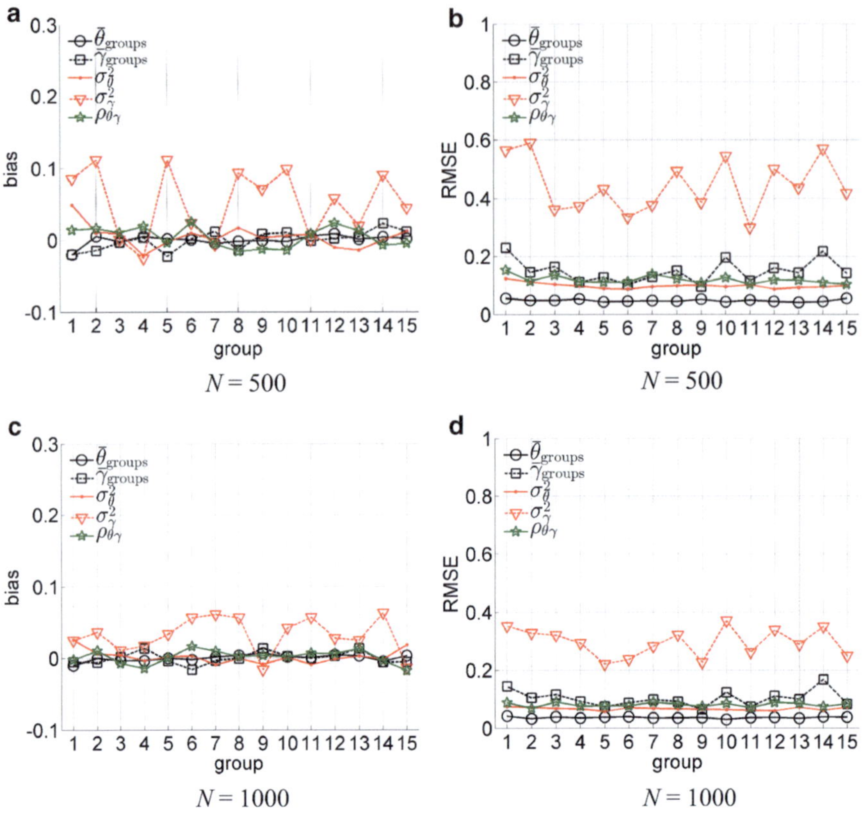

Fig. 3.4 Bias and RMSE for the estimates of means, variances, and correlations of θ and γ in the GESIM6

3.7 Concluding Remarks

The ESI design has advantages and is still common used in some high-stakes examinations. It could alleviate testing anxiety and boost motivation for learning. However, it creates psychometric problems due to selection effect. It has been demonstrated that missing data in unselected items are often MNAR, which invalidates standard IRT models that hold the MAR assumption. To tackle this problem, Wang et al. (2012) proposed the ESIM to account for selection effect in ES items, in which various sources of selection effect are summarized by a latent variable (referred to as test wisdom). In this study, we develop a framework that incorporates the ESIM as a special case. In the new GESIMs, the selection effect for each selection pattern can be a fixed effect or a random effect. The association between the target latent trait θ and the latent variable γ describes the magnitude of the selection effect. The stronger the association, the larger the selection effect will be, and thus the less justifiable of fitting standard IRT models. The parameters of the GESIMs can be estimated with M*plus*, so no efforts are needed to develop parameter estimation procedures or computer software. The brief simulation study confirms the feasibility of the most general GESIM6, although it requires a large sample size and a large number of ES items to yield reliable estimates for person distributional parameters.

We adopt the COAA design to collect data from fifth graders on two mandatory items and four pair of items and ask them to indicate the reasons why they chose an item from a pair. Most students make a choice based on their perceived item easiness and familiarity. Conventional raw-score analysis indicates a small selection effect, in which those who scored higher on the test tend to make a clever choice more often than those who scored lower. To account for the selection effect more accurately, we fit the new GESIMs together with the Rasch model to the incomplete data. Using the AIC for model comparison, we found that the Rasch-i and the GESIM5 (where the selection effect was treated as a random effect as it was in the ESIM) have similar fit. The correlation between θ and γ was .24 in the GESIM5, indicating a small selection effect. The correlation of .24 was smaller than that of .49 found by Wang et al. (2012), which might be because only four pairs of ES dichotomous items are adopted in this experiment whereas the six ES items are polytomous in Wang et al.'s study. Unfortunately, we were not able to increase the test length or to adopt polytomous items due to limited testing time and scoring resource. Had the test length been increased and/or polytomous ES items been adopted, the selection effect would have been more apparent and the GESIMs would have outperformed conventional IRT models more significantly. Future studies are called for to validate this inference.

Future studies may also aim at the following issues. It is of great interest to understand whether different groups of students have different degrees of "test wisdom." As documented by Fitzpatrick and Yen (1995) and Wainer and Thissen (1994), the selection behaviors in ES items are different across genders, grades, or ethnic groups. To address this issue statistically, we can add these covariates into the GESIMs to predict the γ variable, which can be easily done with M*plus*. In the experiment, the items were dichotomous. In many practical situations, ES items are often polytomous (e.g., essay items). It is of great importance to adopt the OCAA design on polytomous items and evaluate how the GESIMs would perform. In some large-scale surveys, such as the Program for International Student Assessment (PISA) and the National Assessment of Educational Progress (NAEP), two-staged sampling is often adopted, in which a set of schools are first sampled, and a set of students are then sampled from each selected school. It is likely that students from the same school are more homogeneous on the variable of interest (e.g., mathematical proficiency) than those from different schools. In recent years, multilevel IRT models (Fox 2005; Fox and Glas 2001; Wang and Qiu 2013) have been developed to account for such a multilevel data structure. It is of great interest to embed the GESIMs within a multilevel framework.

Acknowledgment This study was supported by the General Research Fund, Hong Kong (No. 844112).

Appendix: M*plus* Codes for the GESIM6 in the Empirical Example

```
TITLE: GESIM! y1-y2: Mandatory items; y3-y10: ES items; group: index
DATA: FILE IS imcomdata.txt;
VARIABLE: NAMES ARE y1-y10 group; CATEGORICAL ARE y1-y10;
                  USEVARIABLES = y1-y10 group; MISSING ARE ALL (-9);
               CLASSES = c(16); KNOWNCLASS = c(group = 11-26);
               CLUSTER IS group;
ANALYSIS: TYPE = MIXTURE COMPLEX; ESTIMATOR IS MLR;
               LINK = LOGIT; ALGORITHM=INTEGRATION;
               COVERAGE = .00;
MODEL: %OVERALL%
               f1 BY y1-y10@1; f2 BY y3-y10@1; f1 with f2;
               %c#1%
               f1 with f2; f1*; f2*; [f1*] (c1f1); [f2*] (c1f2);
               %c#2%
               f1 with f2; f1*; f2*; [f1*] (c2f1); [f2*] (c2f2);
               ! Add the rest code in the same manner from group 3 to 15
               %c#16%
               f1 with f2; f1*; f2*; [f1*] (c16f1); [f2*] (c16f2)
MODEL CONSTRAINT:
c16f1 = -(c1f1 + c2f1 + c3f1 + c4f1 + c5f1 + c6f1 +
c7f1 + c8f1 + c9f1 + c10f1 + c11f1 + c12f1 + c13f1 + c14f1 + c15f1);
c16f2 = -(c1f2 + c2f2 + c3f2 + c4f2 + c5f2 + c6f2 +
c7f2 + c8f2 + c9f2 + c10f2 + c11f2 + c12f2 + c13f2 + c14f2 + c15f2);
OUTPUT: TECH1; SAVEDATA: FILE IS fscore.txt; SAVE = FSCORES;
```

References

Akaike, H. (1974). A new look at the statistical model identification. *IEEE Transactions on Automatic Control, 19*(6), 716–723.

Allen, N. L., Holland, P. W., & Thayer, D. T. (2005). Measuring the benefits of examinee-selected questions. *Journal of Educational Measurement, 42*(1), 27–51.

Andrich, D. (1978). A rating formulation for ordered response categories. *Psychometrika, 43*(4), 561–573.

Birnbaum, A. (1968). Some latent trait models and their use in inferring an examinee's ability. In F. M. Lord & M. R. Novick (Eds.), *Statistical theories of mental test scores* (pp. 395–479). Reading, MA: Addison-Wesley.

Bock, R. D. (1972). Estimating item parameters and latent ability when responses are scored in two or more nominal categories. *Psychometrika, 37*(1), 29–51.

Bock, R. D., & Aitkin, M. (1981). Marginal maximum likelihood estimation of item parameters: Application of an EM algorithm. *Psychometrika, 46*(4), 443–459.

Bradlow, E. T., & Thomas, N. (1998). Item response theory models applied to data allowing examinee choice. *Journal of Educational and Behavioral Statistics, 23*(3), 236–243.

Bridgeman, B., Morgan, R., & Wang, M.-m. (1997). Choice among essay topics: Impact on performance and validity. *Journal of Educational Measurement, 34*(3), 273–286.

Fitzpatrick, A. R., & Yen, W. M. (1995). The psychometric characteristics of choice items. *Journal of Educational Measurement, 32*(3), 243–259.

Fox, J. P. (2005). Multilevel IRT using dichotomous and polytomous response data. *British Journal of Mathematical and Statistical Psychology, 58*(1), 145–172.

Fox, J.-P., & Glas, C. A. (2001). Bayesian estimation of a multilevel IRT model using Gibbs sampling. *Psychometrika, 66*(2), 271–288.

Kendall, M. G. (1975). *Rank correlation methods* (4th ed.). London: Charles Griffin.

Li, Y., Bolt, D. M., & Fu, J. (2006). A comparison of alternative models for testlets. *Applied Psychological Measurement, 30*(1), 3–21.

Lukhele, R., Thissen, D., & Wainer, H. (1994). On the relative value of multiple-choice, constructed response, and examinee-selected items on two achievement tests. *Journal of Educational Measurement, 31*(3), 234–250.

Mann, H. B. (1945). Nonparametric tests against trend. *Econometrica: Journal of the Econometric Society, 13*, 245–259.

Masters, G. (1982). A Rasch model for partial credit scoring. *Psychometrika, 47*(2), 149–174.

Muthén, L. K., & Muthén, B. O. (1998–2012). *Mplus user's guide* (7th ed.). Los Angeles, CA: Muthén & Muthén.

Patz, R. J., & Junker, B. W. (1999). A straightforward approach to Markov chain Monte Carlo methods for item response models. *Journal of Educational and Behavioral Statistics, 24*(2), 146–178.

Rasch, G. (1960). *Probabilistic models for some intelligence and attainment tests* (Expanded edition, 1980. Chicago: The University of Chicago Press, ed.). Copenhagen: Institute of Educational Research.

Rijmen, F. (2010). Formal relations and an empirical comparison among the bi-factor, the testlet, and a second-order multidimensional IRT model. *Journal of Educational Measurement, 47*(3), 361–372.

Rubin, D. B. (1976). Inference and missing data. *Biometrika, 63*(3), 581–592.

Samejima, F. (1969). Estimation of latent ability using a response pattern of graded scores. *Psychometrica Monograph, 17*, 1–100.

Wainer, H., & Thissen, D. (1994). On examinee choice in educational testing. *Review of Educational Research, 64*(1), 159–195.

Wainer, H., Wang, X.-B., & Thissen, D. (1994). How well can we compare scores on test forms that are constructed by examinees' choice? *Journal of Educational Measurement, 31*(3), 183–199.

Wainer, H., Wang, X.-B., & Thissen, D. (1991). *How well can we equate test forms constructed by examinees?* (Program Statistics Report 91-55). Princeton, NJ: Educational Testing Service.

Wang, W.-C., Jin, K.-Y., Qiu, X.-L., & Wang, L. (2012). Item response models for examinee-selected items. *Journal of Educational Measurement, 49*(4), 419–445.

Wang, W.-C., & Qiu, X.-L. (2013). A multidimensional and multilevel extension of a random-effect approach to subjective judgment in rating scales. *Multivariate Behavioral Research, 48*(3), 398–427.

Wang, X. B. (1999). *Understanding psychological processes that underlie test takers' choices of constructed response items*. Newtown, PA: Law School Admission Council.

Wang, X.-b., Wainer, H., & Thissen, D. (1995). On the viability of some untestable assumptions in equating exams that allow examinee choice. *Applied Measurement in Education, 8*(3), 211–225.

Chapter 4
Gauss–Hermite Quadrature in Marginal Maximum Likelihood Estimation of Item Parameters

Seock-Ho Kim, Yu Bao, Erin Horan, Meereem Kim, and Allan S. Cohen

Abstract Although many theoretical papers on the estimation method of marginal maximum likelihood of item parameters for various models under item response theory mentioned Gauss–Hermite quadrature formulas, almost all computer programs that implemented marginal maximum likelihood estimation employed other numerical integration methods (e.g., Newton–Cotes formulas). There are many tables that contain quadrature points and quadrature weights for the Gauss–Hermite quadrature formulas; but these tabled values cannot be directly used when quadrature points and quadrature weights are specified by the user of computer programs because the standard normal distribution is frequently employed in the marginalization of the likelihood. The two purposes of this paper are to present extensive tables of Gauss–Hermite quadrature for the standard normal distribution and to present examples that demonstrate the effects of using various numbers of quadrature points and quadrature weights as well as different quadrature formulas on item parameter estimates. Item parameter estimates obtained from more than 20 quadrature points and quadrature weights with either Gauss–Hermite quadrature or the Newton–Cote method were virtually identical.

Keywords Gauss–Hermite quadrature • Item response theory • Marginal maximum likelihood estimation • Parameter estimation

4.1 Introduction

In Bock and Lieberman (1970, pp. 182–183) the use of Gauss–Hermite quadrature can be found:

S.-H. Kim (✉) • Y. Bao • E. Horan • M. Kim • A.S. Cohen
Department of Educational Psychology, The University of Georgia,
323 Aderhold Hall, Athens, GA 30602-7143, USA
e-mail: shkim@uga.edu; yubao02@uga.edu; ehoran@uga.edu; mrkim15@uga.edu; acohen@uga.edu

L.A. van der Ark et al. (eds.), *Quantitative Psychology Research*, Springer Proceedings in Mathematics & Statistics 140, DOI 10.1007/978-3-319-19977-1_4

Although the definite integral in (4) cannot be expressed in closed form, it is easy to evaluate to any practical degree of accuracy by numerical methods. The preferred method for this purpose is Gauss-Hermite quadrature, which approximates the above integral by the sum

$$(5) \qquad \frac{1}{\surd(\pi)} \sum_{l=1}^{m} A_l \left\{ \prod_{j=1}^{n} \Xi[\gamma_j, \alpha_j, k_{ij}, \surd(2)X_l] \right\}. \tag{4.1}$$

Stroud and Secrest (1966) have prepared extensive tables of the coefficients A_l corresponding to the quadrature points X_l. In the computations for this paper, we have employed 40 points of quadrature corresponding to 20 positive and 20 negative values of X_l taken from the table for 64 point quadrature in Stroud and Secrest.

It can be noted that Stroud and Secrest (1966) used quadrature points (i.e., nodes) x_i instead of X_l and quadrature coefficients (i.e., weights) A_i instead of A_l in their tables. Note that the exact definitions of the terms in Eq. (4.1) can be found in Bock and Lieberman (1970, pp. 180–182) and are not repeated here in detail. Bock and Lieberman (1970) rather cleverly avoided the use of x_i or x_l because these frequently designate item responses in many psychometric literature. It is not all clear why the subset of quadrature points was used in Bock and Lieberman (1970) in their implementation. Nevertheless, based on the required degree of precision, the quadrature points $|x_i|$ and weights A_i for the number of quadrature points $N = 2(1)64(4)96(8)136$ (i.e., $N \equiv m$ in Eq. (4.1), and parentheses contain the width of increments; Stroud and Secrest 1966, pp. 217–252) can be used in estimation. A less extensive table can be found in the tenth printing of Abramowitz and Stegun (1972, p. 924). Abramowitz and Stegun (1972) used abscissas $\pm x_i$, weight factors w_i, and $n = 2(1)20$ (i.e., $n \equiv m$ in Eq. (4.1)) for the number of zeros of Hermite polynomials that were compiled from Salzer et al. (1952) in which $|x_i^{(n)}|$, $\alpha_i^{(n)}$, and $n = 1(1)20$ were used for the zeros, weight factors, and the degrees, respectively. In addition, Shao et al. (1964) contain a table of zeros and Gaussian weights of the Hermite polynomials for $n = 2^{3(1)6}$ (i.e., $n \equiv k$ in Shao et al. 1964).

Another use of Gauss–Hermite quadrature can be found in the seminal paper by Bock and Aitkin (1981, p. 445):

This probability can be approximated to any practical degree of accuracy by Gauss-Hermite quadrature, i.e., by the sum

$$\sum_{k}^{q} P(\mathbf{x} = \mathbf{x}_i | X_k) A(X_k), \tag{4.2}$$

where X_k is a tabled quadrature point (node) and $A(X_k)$ is the corresponding weight (see Stroud and Secrest 1966).

It should be noted that the quadrature points and quadrature weights from Stroud and Secrest (1966) cannot be directly used in Eq. (4.2) but these ought to be properly modified as $X_k \equiv \sqrt{2}x_i$ and $A(X_k) \equiv A_i/\sqrt{\pi}$, assuming that subscripts are accordingly adjusted. Note that the exact definitions of the terms in Eq. (4.2) can be found in Bock and Aitkin (1981, pp. 444–445). Also note that X_l and A_l from Bock and Lieberman (1970) are, respectively, not the same as X_k and $A(X_k)$ from Bock and Aitkin (1981) in addition to the trivial difference in subscripts.

Although many theoretical papers that presented marginal maximum likelihood estimation mentioned Gauss–Hermite quadrature (e.g., Drasgow 1989, p. 80; Mislevy 1984, p. 367; Mislevy 1986, p. 180; Muraki 1984, p. 13; Rigdon and Tsutakawa 1983, p. 570; Tsutakawa 1984, p. 275; Zwinderman and van den Wollenberg 1990; p. 76), all practical computer programs might not use the method as a default (e.g., Cai 2013; Cai et al. 2010; Mislevy and Bock 1984, 1985, 1986, 1990; Muraki and Bock 1993, 2002; Thissen 1986; Thissen et al. 2002). The paper by Thissen (1982, pp. 178–179) about marginal maximum likelihood estimation of the Rasch model didn't use Gauss–Hermite quadrature, however, and can be seen as an exception.

Note that values from nearly all available tables for Gauss–Hermite quadrature cannot be directly used as X_k and $A(X_k)$. Hence, this paper presents tables. There are two purposes of this paper. One purpose is to present tables of Gauss–Hermite quadrature for the standard normal distribution. The other purpose is to present examples that used various numbers of points of Gauss–Hermite quadrature and Mislevy's histogram (i.e., a Newton–Cotes method; see De Ayala 2009, p. 71).

4.2 Gauss–Hermite Quadrature

There are many different notations for Gauss–Hermite quadrature (e.g., Davis and Rabinowitz 1975, pp. 173–175; Hildebrand 1974, pp. 395–397; Krylov 1962, pp. 129–130). In this section we will simply use the notation from Stroud and Secrest (1966) with n in place of their N, because the book was referred in Bock and Lieberman (1970) and Bock and Aitkin (1981). The formula of Gauss–Hermite quadrature (Stroud and Secrest 1966, p. 22) is

$$\int_{-\infty}^{\infty} e^{-x^2} f(x)dx \approx \sum_{i=1}^{n} A_i f(x_i). \tag{4.3}$$

Eventually, we will report the values of $\sqrt{2}x_i$ and $A_i/\sqrt{\pi}$ as X_k and $A(X_k)$ for the standard normal distribution that is frequently used as the prior distribution of ability parameters. It will be instructive, nevertheless, to discuss some important characteristics of Gauss–Hermite quadrature as in Eq. (4.3).

Abramowitz and Stegun (1972, p. 890) contained

$$\int_{-\infty}^{\infty} e^{-x^2} f(x)dx = \sum_{i=1}^{n} A_i f(x_i) + R_n, \tag{4.4}$$

where

$$R_n = \frac{n!\sqrt{\pi}}{2^n(2n)!} f^{2n}(\xi) \tag{4.5}$$

for some $-\infty < \xi < \infty$ (see also Salzer et al. 1952). The order and the theoretical approximation errors can be obtained using such a formula.

In order to approximate the integral we need for a given n values of x_i and A_i. The values or abscissas of x_i are the ith zero or root of Hermite polynomials $H_n(x)$. The corresponding weights are

$$\frac{2^{n-1}n!\sqrt{\pi}}{n^2[H_{n-1}(x_i)]^2}. \tag{4.6}$$

There are numerous representations or formulae of Hermite polynomials (see, e.g., Hochstrasser 1972, pp. 771–802). According to Rodrigues's formula,

$$H_n(x) = (-1)^n e^{x^2} \frac{d^n}{dx^n}(e^{-x^2}) \tag{4.7}$$

and $H_0(x) = 1$ by definition. Other Hermite polynomials include (see Gradshteyn and Ryzhik 1994, p. 1057):

$$\begin{aligned}
H_1(x) &= 2x \\
H_2(x) &= 4x^2 - 2 \\
H_3(x) &= 8x^3 - 12x \\
H_4(x) &= 16x^4 - 48x^2 + 12 \\
H_5(x) &= 32x^5 - 160x^3 + 120x \\
H_6(x) &= 64x^6 - 480x^4 + 720x^2 - 120 \\
H_7(x) &= 128x^7 - 1344x^5 + 3360x^3 - 1680x \\
H_8(x) &= 256x^8 - 3584x^6 + 13440x^4 - 13440x^2 + 1680 \\
H_9(x) &= 512x^9 - 9216x^7 + 48384x^5 - 80640x^3 + 30240x \\
H_{10}(x) &= 1024x^{10} - 23040x^8 + 161280x^6 - 403200x^4 + 302400x^2 - 30240 \\
H_{11}(x) &= 2048x^{11} - 56320x^9 + 506880x^7 - 1774080x^5 + 2217600x^3 - 665280x \\
H_{12}(x) &= 4096x^{12} - 135168x^{10} + 1520640x^8 - 7096320x^6 + 13305600x^4 \\
&\quad -7983360x^2 + 665280 \\
&\vdots
\end{aligned}$$

There will be n real roots of x_i for $H_n(x) = 0$. The roots are referred to Gauss–Hermite quadrature nodes. For small n, analytical solutions exist and roots or abscissas x_i are:

$$\begin{aligned}
H_1(x) &: x_i = 0 \\
H_2(x) &: x_i = \pm\frac{1}{\sqrt{2}}
\end{aligned}$$

$$H_3(x) : x_i = \pm\frac{\sqrt{3}}{\sqrt{2}}, \quad 0$$

$$H_4(x) : x_i = \pm\sqrt{\frac{3+\sqrt{6}}{2}}, \quad \pm\sqrt{\frac{3-\sqrt{6}}{2}}$$

$$H_5(x) : x_i = \pm\sqrt{\frac{5+\sqrt{10}}{2}}, \quad \pm\sqrt{\frac{5-\sqrt{10}}{2}}, \quad 0$$

$$\vdots$$

The abscissas that have the same absolute value but different signs will share the same weight. The weights are referred to Gauss–Hermite quadrature weights. The corresponding weights A_i to the above roots are:

$$H_1(x) : A_i = \sqrt{\pi}$$

$$H_2(x) : A_i = \frac{\sqrt{\pi}}{2}$$

$$H_3(x) : A_i = \frac{\sqrt{\pi}}{6}, \quad \frac{2\sqrt{\pi}}{3}$$

$$H_4(x) : A_i = \frac{\sqrt{\pi}}{12+4\sqrt{6}}, \quad \frac{\sqrt{\pi}}{12-4\sqrt{6}}$$

$$H_5(x) : A_i = \frac{3\sqrt{\pi}}{140+40\sqrt{10}}, \quad \frac{3\sqrt{\pi}}{140-40\sqrt{10}}, \quad \frac{8\sqrt{\pi}}{15}$$

$$\vdots$$

Although it is possible to find analytical roots of cubic, quartic, and quintic functions (i.e., real roots from $H_6(x)$ to $H_{11}(x)$), numerical solutions are in general employed to find x_i and A_i. As mentioned earlier, the values are tabulated and reported to various values of n.

Because the standard normal distribution is used, we need to evaluate

$$\frac{1}{\sqrt{2\pi}}\int_{-\infty}^{\infty} e^{-y^2/2} g(y)dy \approx \sum_{i=1}^{n} A_i^{'} g(y_i). \tag{4.8}$$

With $x = y/\sqrt{2}$, $dx = dy/\sqrt{2}$, $f(x) = g(y)/\sqrt{\pi}$, and the same interval of integration $(-\infty, \infty)$, the integral becomes $\int e^{-x^2} f(x)dx$. The values of $y_i = \sqrt{2}x_i$ and $A_i^{'} = A_i/\sqrt{\pi}$ can be obtained based on the Hermite-Gauss formula (see Kennedy and Gentle 1980, p. 84). Hence, we need n real roots of x_i for $H_n(x) = 0$, and multiplying values by $\sqrt{2}$ to yield $\sqrt{2}x_i$.

For small n, analytical solutions exist and roots or abscissas $\sqrt{2}x_i \equiv X_k$ are:

$$H_1(x) : X_k = 0$$

$$H_2(x) : X_k = \pm 1$$

$$H_3(x) : X_k = \pm\sqrt{3},\quad 0$$

$$H_4(x) : X_k = \pm\sqrt{3+\sqrt{6}},\quad \pm\sqrt{3-\sqrt{6}}$$

$$H_5(x) : X_k = \pm\sqrt{5+\sqrt{10}},\quad \pm\sqrt{5-\sqrt{10}},\quad 0$$

$$\vdots$$

The abscissas that have the same absolute value but different signs will share the same weight. The corresponding weights $A_i/\sqrt{\pi} \equiv A(X_k)$ are:

$$H_1(x) : A(X_k) = 1$$

$$H_2(x) : A(X_k) = \frac{1}{2}$$

$$H_3(x) : A(X_k) = \frac{1}{6},\ \frac{2}{3}$$

$$H_4(x) : A(X_k) = \frac{1}{12+4\sqrt{6}},\ \frac{1}{12-4\sqrt{6}}$$

$$H_5(x) : A(X_k) = \frac{3}{140+40\sqrt{10}},\ \frac{3}{140-40\sqrt{10}},\ \frac{8}{15}$$

$$\vdots$$

Appendix 1 contains zeros x_i and Gaussian weights A_i of the Hermite polynomials for $n = 10, 20$. For the standard normal distribution, Appendix 2 contains zeros $x_i\sqrt{2} \equiv X_k$ and weights $A_i/\sqrt{\pi} \equiv A(X_k)$ for $n = 10, 20$. The file, gausshermite2-20.txt, that contains zeros x_i and Gaussian weights A_i of the Hermite polynomials for $n = 2(1)20$, and the file, gausshermitenormal2-20.txt, that contains $x_i\sqrt{2} \equiv X_k$ and weights $A_i/\sqrt{\pi} \equiv A(X_k)$ for $n = 2(1)20$ for the standard normal distribution in both the portable document format—pdf and in the text format are available from the authors. The more extensive files, gausshermite.txt and gausshermitenormal.txt, in pdf as well as in the text format for $n = 2(1)200$ are also available from the authors. Stroud and Secrest (1966, pp. 34–36) contain Fortran subroutines and a function for the Gauss–Hermite quadrature formula.

Note that there are other ways to obtain the tabled values for Gauss–Hermite quadrature. Let's consider some other currently available ways for general Gauss quadrature formulas. According to Stroud and Secrest (1966, p. 1), Gauss quadrature formulas have the form

$$\int_a^b w(x)f(x)dx \approx \sum_{i=1}^{n} A_i f(x_i), \tag{4.9}$$

where $w(x)$ is a weight function which is greater than zero on the interval $[a, b]$. The x_i are called the points or nodes of the formula and the A_i are called coefficients or weights. Such formulas are called Gaussian quadrature formulas. The Gaussian quadrature formulas are obtained as applications of the theorem on Gaussian nodes (Cheney and Kincaid 1985, pp. 193–194). Gauss (1876) with his Latinized name of Carolo Friderico Gauss studied them first (i.e., dated 1814 Sept. 16) for the special case $w(x) = 1$.

Algorithms for six well-known kinds of orthogonal polynomials (i.e., Legendre polynomials, Chebyshev polynomials of the first kind, Chebyshev polynomials of the second kind, Jacobi polynomials, Laguerre polynomials, and Hermite polynomials; see Thisted 1988, pp. 282–288) are presented by Golub and Welsch (1969) and implemented in a Fortran subroutine called gaussq.f in the Netlib software repository (Smyth 1998). The same algorithms are implemented in the package "statmod" (Smyth 2014) in the statistical computing software R (R Core Team 2010). The statmod package was used in the R implementation of marginal maximum likelihood estimation (Johnson 2007, p. 10). Note that there are several R packages, for example, "gaussquad" (Novomestky 2013) and "fastGHQuad" (Blocker 2014), that can produce Gauss–Hermite quadrature notes and weights. Press et al. (1996, p. 1062) contain a Fortran 90 subroutine for obtaining the abscissas and weights of the Gauss–Hermite quadrature formula. Use of the statmod package in R seems to be the easiest way to obtain Gauss–Hermite quadrature points and weights. Also using R, these values can be easily transformed to the points and weights for the standard normal distribution.

4.3 Effect of the Number of Quadrature Points

Using numbers of quadrature points of 10, 20, 30, and 40, Seong (1990) compared the item and ability parameter estimates obtained by the Stroud and Secrest (1966) values with those obtained by the composite midpoint rule of open type (Burden and Faires 1985, pp. 158–169; Jeffrey 2000, pp. 315–318; cf. Hildebrand 1974, p. 96). The composite midpoint rule is also referred to the Mislevy's histogram solution (see Mislevy and Stocking 1989, p. 66). De Ayala et al. (1995, p. 387) referred to the latter as the Mislevy vertical line graph method. Because a set of uniformly spaced points are used, the method is of the Newton–Cotes type (De Ayala 2009, p. 71; Linz and Wang 2003, p. 133). In this paper the quadrature that used uniformly spaced points is called the Newton–Cote method.

To compare results from employing different numbers of quadrature points and weights in Gauss–Hermite quadrature, the Law School Admission Test—Section 6 (LSAT6; Bock and Lieberman 1970) with five-items by 1000 examinees were

Table 4.1 Item parameter estimates from Gauss–Hermite quadrature using different numbers of quadrature points

Parameter	Number of quadrature points					
Item	2	4	6	8	10	12+[a]
a_j						
1	0.82719	0.82369	0.82431	0.82456	0.82456	0.82456
2	0.71212	0.73029	0.72395	0.72360	0.72361	0.72361
3	0.78430	0.88188	0.88911	0.88908	0.88900	0.88899
4	0.67176	0.69395	0.69006	0.68977	0.68976	0.68977
5	0.68373	0.66168	0.65728	0.65715	0.65716	0.65716
b_j						
1	−3.34630	−3.36523	−3.36341	−3.36261	−3.36260	−3.36261
2	−1.39913	−1.35888	−1.36815	−1.36869	−1.36868	−1.36868
3	−0.31188	−0.28252	−0.28016	−0.28012	−0.28014	−0.28014
4	−1.91504	−1.85394	−1.86243	−1.86311	−1.86312	−1.86311
5	−3.02401	−3.10635	−3.12414	−3.12478	−3.12473	−3.12472

[a] 12(2)20(10)80

calibrated using marginal maximum likelihood estimation. The data set was not grouped in response patterns and consists of a four-column identification code and the five item responses for each of 1000 examinees. The two-parameter logistic model was used with the scaling constant $D = 1$. The numbers of quadrature points used were 2(2)20(10)80.

The computer program in Fortran used 20 expectation and maximization cycles and 2 Newton cycles (cf. de Toit 2003, pp. 126–127). The initial values were those used in the second phase of BILOG-MG (see Lord 1980, pp. 33–34). Item parameter estimates from employing more than 10 quadrature points (i.e., 12–80) were the same up to five decimal places. Table 4.1 contains the LSAT6 item parameter estimates.

The item discrimination parameter estimates are plotted along with the number of quadrature points in Fig. 4.1. The item difficulty parameter estimates are plotted along with the number of quadrature points in Fig. 4.2.

4.4 Comparison of Computer Programs

There are many computer programs that can yield item parameter estimates under marginal maximum likelihood estimation. Two main approaches employed in the programs to perform marginalization are the Newton–Cote method and Gauss–Hermite quadrature. It can be noted that in almost all programs the default method is the Newton–Cotes method. The computer programs compared in conjunction with the quadrature methods include BILOG-MG, PARSCALE, MULTILOG, IRTPRO, and flexMIRT.

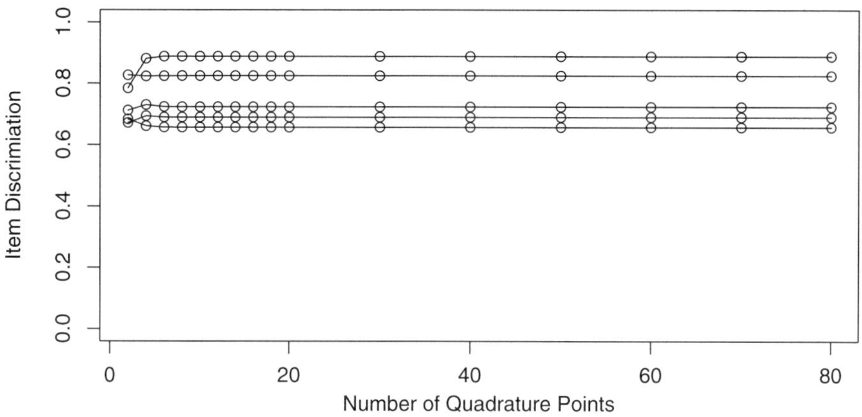

Fig. 4.1 LSAT6 item discrimination estimates plot

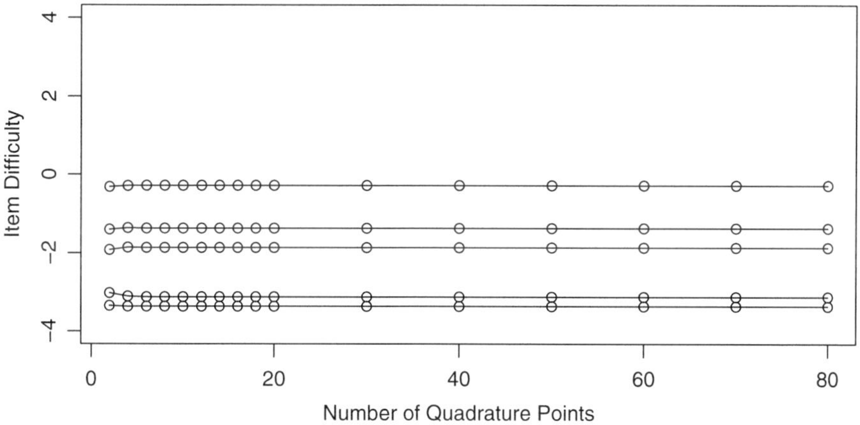

Fig. 4.2 LSAT6 item difficulty estimates plot

Note that it is also possible to obtain item parameter estimates for the two-parameter model under marginal maximum likelihood estimation using Gauss–Hermite quadrature from the computer program TESTFACT (Wilson et al. 1991; Wood et al. 2002) when it is used to perform one-dimensional factor analysis (de Toit 2003, p. 492). TESTFACT is one of the programs that uses Gauss–Hermite quadrature, but the program is developed for performing factor analysis of dichotomously scored items. In such an analysis, 50 seems to be the maximum number of quadrature points. Note that item discrimination in TESTFACT is expressed on the normal metric. It can also be noted that the computer program OPLM (Verhelst et al. 1994) can yield item parameter estimates for the Rasch model via marginal maximum likelihood estimation.

Table 4.2 LSAT6 item parameter estimates from item response theory computer programs

Parameter	BILOG-MG		PARSCALE		MULTILOG		IRTPRO		flexMIRT	
Item	NC	GH	NC	GH	NC	GH	NC	GH	NC	GH
a_j										
1	0.813	0.784	0.809	0.808	0.82	NA	0.83	0.83	0.83	NA
2	0.714	0.687	0.732	0.732	0.72	NA	0.72	0.72	0.72	NA
3	0.877	0.845	0.901	0.901	0.88	NA	0.89	0.89	0.89	NA
4	0.680	0.655	0.693	0.693	0.69	NA	0.69	0.69	0.69	NA
5	0.648	0.625	0.658	0.657	0.66	NA	0.66	0.66	0.66	NA
b_j										
1	−3.409	−3.538	−3.397	−3.399	−3.36	NA	−3.36	−3.36	−3.36	NA
2	−1.388	−1.441	−1.364	−1.364	−1.37	NA	−1.37	−1.37	−1.37	NA
3	−0.284	−0.295	−0.280	−0.280	−0.28	NA	−0.28	−0.28	−0.28	NA
4	−1.890	−1.962	−1.864	−1.864	−1.87	NA	−1.86	−1.87	−1.87	NA
5	−3.167	−3.288	−3.128	−3.129	−3.12	NA	−3.11	−3.13	−3.12	NA

The default setting of BILOG-MG for obtaining item parameter estimates of the LSAT6 data for the two-parameter logistic model under marginal maximum likelihood estimation uses 15 equally spaced quadrature points from −4 to 4. Item parameter estimates from the default Newton–Cotes method (NC) in BILOG-MG are reported in Table 4.2. In fact, the NC columns contain the results from the default settings of the respective programs. The item parameter estimates from BILOG-MG using Gauss–Hermite quadrature (GH) with 10 quadrature points are also reported in Table 4.2. A user must supply the quadrature points and weights for Gauss–Hermite quadrature based on the standard normal distribution to obtain the GH results reported in Table 4.2.

The default setting of PARSCALE (Muraki and Bock 2002) for obtaining item parameter estimates of the LSAT6 data for the two-parameter logistic model under marginal maximum likelihood estimation uses 30 equally spaced quadrature points from −4 to 4. Item parameter estimates from the default NC in PARSCALE are reported in Table 4.2. The item parameter from PARSCALE using GH with 10 quadrature points are also reported in Table 4.2. The GH results are obtained from the program generated Gauss–Hermite quadrature points and weights by using the prior distribution keyword (de Toit 2003, p. 277; Muraki and Bock 1993, p. 64).

The default setting of MULTILOG (Thissen et al. 2002) for obtaining item parameter estimates of the LSAT6 data for the two-parameter logistic model under marginal maximum likelihood estimation uses 19 equally spaced quadrature points from −4.5 to 4.5. Item parameter estimates from the default NC in MULTILOG are reported in Table 4.2. It may be possible to use Gauss–Hermite quadrature in MULGILOG by employing the keywords QP and DE (Thissen 1986, p. 28). Because weights based on the standard normal distribution produced seemingly inconsistent results and the current version of the program manual didn't include such a DE keyword from the earlier versions, the GH results cannot be properly obtained.

The default setting of IRTPRO (Cai et al. 2010) for obtaining item parameter estimates of the LSAT6 data for the two-parameter logistic model under marginal maximum likelihood estimation uses 49 equally spaced quadrature points from −6 to 6. Item parameter estimates from the default NC in IRTPRO are reported in Table 4.2. The item parameter from IRTPRO using GH with 10 quadrature points is also reported in Table 4.2. The GH results are obtained from selection of the quadrature option GH in IRTPRO.

The default setting of flexMIRT (Cai 2013; Houts and Cai 2013) for obtaining item parameter estimates of the LSAT6 data for the two-parameter logistic model under marginal maximum likelihood estimation uses 49 equally spaced quadrature points from −6 to 6. Item parameter estimates from the default Newton–Cotes type (NC) in flexMIRT are reported in Table 4.2. The flexMIRT manual (see Houts and Cai 2013, p. 143) does not provide a way to obtain item parameter estimates using GH.

Overall, all programs yielded very similar results and some of them produced seemingly identical results up to the decimal points reported in the main outputs of the respective programs. Note that nearly the same results of item parameter estimates can be obtained by changing the settings of each computer program. Demonstrating how to obtain the same results from these programs, however, was not the purpose of the current investigation.

In addition the LSAT6 data, in order to evaluate the similarity of results from various computer programs employing different quadrature methods, a relatively large data set containing student responses to a college English placement test was analyzed with the same eight different cases reported in Table 4.2. The data file actually analyzed for the current study contained dichotomously scored item responses from 3657 examinees for the 115 item test. There were originally 117 items but two of them were removed due to the near zero value (original item 34) and the negative value (original item 35) of the biserial correlation. There were five options for each item and so the data set can be analyzed under the three-parameter model in general. Because priors may necessarily be imposed on the guessing parameters (i.e., the lower asymptotes) of the three-parameter model and the computer programs use different forms of such priors, the two-parameter logistic model was used to assess the effect of the quadrature methods.

The 115 items from the English test were analyzed with the above five IRT computer programs, but eight different cases existed because only three could employ Gauss–Hermite quadrature. Actually the estimation method used (i.e., marginal maximum likelihood estimation) may not be the default estimation option for some programs (e.g., BILOG-MG). The numbers of the default quadrature points for the respective programs were not changed for this larger English test data. The number of quadrature points used for Gauss–Hermite quadrature was 20 following a suggestion in BILOG-MG (e.g., $2 \times \sqrt{\text{test length}}$; see also De Ayala et al. 1995, p. 388). Due to the fact that a relatively large data set was used, all programs yielded practically the same item parameter estimates.

The calibration results of the English test data indicated that all computer programs regardless of using either NC or GH yielded fully comparable item parameter estimates under the two-parameter logistic model. Except for three pairs (BILOG-MG-NC and BILOG-MG-GH; BILOG-MG-NC and PARSCALE-GH; BILOG-MG-GH and PARCALE-GH) all eight sets of item discrimination estimates yielded pairwise Pearson correlations of unity. The three exceptional pairs yielded $r = 0.999$. All eight sets of item difficulty estimates yielded pairwise Pearson correlations of unity. All programs yielded almost identical, albeit not exactly the same, results for the item parameter estimates of the English test.

4.5 Discussion

When the ability distribution to be integrated out in the marginalization is assumed to be normal, the Gauss–Hermite quadrature points and weights under the standard normal distribution may be a theoretically correct choice to use. Most of the current computer programs do not use the Gauss–Hermite quadrature as a default. It can be noted that in some application settings, the latent distribution of ability is to be concurrently characterized with item parameters (i.e., estimation of either hyper-parameters of the ability distribution or discrete histogram-type characterization of the ability distribution). In such a situation (Bock and Aitkin 1981; Mislevy 1984; Sanathanan and Blumenthal 1978), Gauss–Hermite quadrature may not be appropriate, and other methods (e.g., adaptive Sympson's rule; Sanathanan and Blumenthal 1978, p. 797) should be utilized.

In the estimation of ability parameters, the expected a posteriori (EAP) estimation may not require Gauss–Hermite quadrature (Bock and Mislevy 1982). For example, the investigation of the EAP estimates by De Ayala et al. (1995) didn't use Gauss–Hermite quadrature. Also Bock and Mislevy (1982) indicated that the prior distribution in some testing situation (e.g., adaptive testing) need not have a form of the standard normal distribution. Hence, Gauss–Hermite quadrature might not be used in some situations. Hence, the Newton–Cotes method may provide a more coherent framework for estimation of all parameters.

The values from the available tables of the nodes and weights for Gauss–Hermite quadrature cannot be directly used when a user wants to specify them. So we presented extensive tables of Gauss–Hermite quadrature for the standard normal distribution. We also presented examples that demonstrate the effects of using various numbers of quadrature points and quadrature weights as well as different quadrature formulas on item parameter estimates. In sum, item parameter estimates obtained from more than 20 quadrature points and quadrature weights with either Gauss–Hermite quadrature or Newton–Cote method were virtually identical. More thorough investigations similar to Seong (1990) are needed for other item response theory models and other estimation procedures.

Appendix 1

```
N =  10
XI
-3.436159118837738E+00 -2.532731674232789E+00 -1.756683649299880E+00 -1.036610829789513E+00 -3.429013272237046E-01
 3.429013272237046E-01  1.036610829789513E+00  1.756683649299880E+00  2.532731674232789E+00  3.436159118837738E+00
AI
 7.640432855232643E-06  1.343645746781229E-03  3.387439445548111E-02  2.401386110823148E-01  6.108626337353258E-01
 6.108626337353258E-01  2.401386110823148E-01  3.387439445548111E-02  1.343645746781229E-03  7.640432855232643E-06

N =  20
XI
-5.387480890011237E+00 -4.603682449550741E+00 -3.944764040115622E+00 -3.347854567383215E+00 -2.788806058428129E+00
-2.254974002089274E+00 -1.738537712116586E+00 -1.234076215395323E+00 -7.374737285453945E-01 -2.453407083009013E-01
 2.453407083009013E-01  7.374737285453945E-01  1.234076215395323E+00  1.738537712116586E+00  2.254974002089274E+00
 2.788806058428129E+00  3.347854567383215E+00  3.944764040115622E+00  4.603682449550741E+00  5.387480890011237E+00
AI
 2.229393645534086E-13  4.399340992273155E-10  1.086069370769280E-07  7.802556478532085E-06  2.283386360163550E-04
 3.243773342237865E-03  2.481052088746362E-02  1.090172060200233E-01  2.866755053628341E-01  4.622436696006098E-01
 4.622436696006098E-01  2.866755053628341E-01  1.090172060200233E-01  2.481052088746362E-02  3.243773342237865E-03
 2.283386360163550E-04  7.802556478532085E-06  1.086069370769280E-07  4.399340992273155E-10  2.229393645534086E-13
```

Appendix 2

```
N =  10
XK
-4.859462828332313E+00 -3.581823483551926E+00 -2.484325841638953E+00 -1.465989094391158E+00 -4.849357075154976E-01
 4.849357075154976E-01  1.465989094391158E+00  2.484325841638953E+00  3.581823483551926E+00  4.859462828332313E+00
A(XK)
 4.310652630718300E-06  7.580709343122154E-04  1.911158050077032E-02  1.354837029802678E-01  3.446423349320191E-01
 3.446423349320191E-01  1.354837029802678E-01  1.911158050077032E-02  7.580709343122154E-04  4.310652630718300E-06

N =  20
XK
-7.619048541679765E+00 -6.510590157013650E+00 -5.578738805893197E+00 -4.734581334046053E+00 -3.943967350657314E+00
-3.189014816553388E+00 -2.458663611172368E+00 -1.745247320814127E+00 -1.042945348802751E+00 -3.469641570813560E-01
 3.469641570813560E-01  1.042945348802751E+00  1.745247320814127E+00  2.458663611172368E+00  3.189014816553388E+00
 3.943967350657314E+00  4.734581334046053E+00  5.578738805893197E+00  6.510590157013650E+00  7.619048541679765E+00
A(XK)
 1.257800672437891E-13  2.482062362315165E-10  6.127490259982936E-08  4.402121090230865E-06  1.288262799619300E-04
 1.830103131080495E-03  1.399783744710101E-02  6.150637206397688E-02  1.617393339840000E-01  2.607930634495547E-01
 2.607930634495547E-01  1.617393339840000E-01  6.150637206397688E-02  1.399783744710101E-02  1.830103131080495E-03
 1.288262799619300E-04  4.402121090230865E-06  6.127490259982936E-08  2.482062362315165E-10  1.257800672437891E-13
```

References

Abramowitz, M., & Stegun, I. A. (Eds.). (1972). *Handbook of mathematical functions with formulas, graphs, and mathematical tables.* New York, NY: Wiley.

Blocker, A. W. (2014). fastGHQuad: Fast Rcpp implementation of Gauss-Hermite quadrature. R package version 0.2.

Bock, R. D., & Aitkin, M. (1981). Marginal maximum likelihood estimation of item parameters: Application of an EM algorithm. *Psychometrika, 46*, 443–459; *47*, 369 (Errata).

Bock, R. D., & Lieberman, M. (1970). Fitting a response model for *n* dichotomously scored items. *Psychometrika, 35*, 179–197.

Bock, R. D., & Mislevy, R. J. (1982). Adaptive EAP estimation of ability in a microcomputer environment. *Applied Psychological Measurement, 6*, 431–444.

Burden, R. L., & Faires, J. D. (1985). *Numerical analysis* (3rd ed.). Boston, MA: Prindle, Weber & Schmidt.

Cai, L. (2013). *flexMIRT: Flexible multilevel multidimensional item analysis and test scoring (Version 2) [Computer software].* Chapel Hill, NC: Vector Psychometric Group.
Cai, L., Thissen, D., & du Toit, S. (2010). *IRTPRO: Item response theory for patient-reported outcomes [Computer software].* Skokie, IL: Scientific Software International.
Cheney, W., & Kincaid, D. (1985). *Numerical mathematics and computing* (2nd ed.). Pacific Grove, CA: Brooks/Cole.
Davis, P. J., & Rabinowitz, P. (1975). *Methods of numerical integration.* New York, NY: Academic.
De Ayala, R. J. (2009). *The theory and practice of item response theory.* New York, NY: The Guilford Press.
De Ayala, R. J., Schafer, W. D., & Sava-Bolesta, M. (1995). An investigation of the standard errors of expected a posteriori ability estimates. *British Journal of Mathematical and Statistical Psychology, 47*, 385–405.
de Toit, M. (Ed.). (2003). *IRT from SSI.* Lincolnwood, IL: Scientific Software International.
Drasgow, F. (1989). An evaluation of marginal maximum likelihood estimation for the two-parameter logistic model. *Applied Psychological Measurement, 13*, 77–90.
Gauss, C. F. (1876). Methodus nova integralium valores per approximationem inveniendi [The new method of integral values by finding approximation]. In *Carl Friedrich Gauss Werke* (Vol. 3, pp. 163–196). Göttingen, Germany: Königlichen Gesellschaft der Wissenschaften.
Golub, G. H., & Welsch, J. H. (1969). Calculation of Gauss quadrature rules. *Mathematics of Computation, 23*, 221–230.
Gradshteyn, I. S., & Ryzhik, I. M. (1994). *Table of integrals, series, and products* (5th ed.) (A. Jeffrey, Trans.). San Diego, CA: Academic.
Hildebrand, F. B. (1974). *Introduction to numerical analysis* (2nd ed.). New York, NY: McGraw-Hill.
Hochstrasser, W. (1972). Orthogonal polynomials. In M. Abramowitz & I. A. Stegun (Eds.), *Handbook of mathematical functions with formulas, graphs, and mathematical tables* (pp. 771–802). New York, NY: Wiley.
Houts, C. R., & Cai, L. (2013). *flexMIRT user's manual version 2.0.* Chapel Hill, NC: Vector Psychometric Group.
Jeffrey, A. (2000). *Handbook of mathematical formulas and integrals* (2nd ed.). San Diego, CA: Academic.
Johnson, M. S. (2007). Marginal maximum likelihood estimation of item response models in R. *Journal of Statistical Software, 20*(10), 1–24.
Kennedy, W. J., Jr., & Gentle, J. E. (1980). *Statistical computing.* New York, NY: Marcel Dekker,
Krylov, V. I. (1962). *Approximate calculation of integrals* (A. H. Stroud, Trans.). New York, NY: Macmillan.
Linz, P., & Wang, R. L. C. (2003). *Exploring numerical methods: An introduction to scientific computing using MATLAB.* Boston, MA: Jones and Bartlett.
Lord, F. M. (1980). *Applications of item response theory to practical testing problems.* Hillsdale, NJ: Lawrence Erlbaum Associates.
Mislevy, R. J. (1984). Estimating latent distributions. *Psychometrika, 49*, 359–381.
Mislevy, R. J. (1986). Bayes modal estimation in item response models. *Psychometrika, 51*, 177–195.
Mislevy, R. J., & Bock, R. D. (1984). *BILOG II: Item analysis and test scoring with binary logistic models—User's guide.* Mooresville, IN: Scientific Software.
Mislevy, R. J., & Bock, R. D. (1985). Implementation of the EM algorithm in the estimation of item parameters: The BILOG computer program. In D. J. Weiss (Ed.), *Proceedings of the 1982 Item Response Theory and Computerized Adaptive Testing Conference* (pp. 189–202). Minneapolis, MN: University of Minnesota, Department of Psychology, Computerized Adaptive Testing Laboratory.
Mislevy, R. J., & Bock, R. D. (1986). *PC-BILOG: Item analysis and test scoring with binary logistic models [Computer software].* Mooresville, IN: Scientific Software.
Mislevy, R. J., & Bock, R. D. (1990). *BILOG 3: Item analysis and test scoring with binary logistic models [Computer software].* Mooresville, IN: Scientific Software.

Mislevy, R. J., & Stocking, M. L. (1989). A consumer's guide to LOGIST and BILOG. *Applied Psychological Measurement, 13*, 57–75.

Muraki, E. (1984). *Marginal maximum likelihood estimation for three-parameter polychotomous item response models: Application of an EM algorithm*. Paper presented at the Annual Meeting of the American Educational Research Association, New Orleans, LA.

Muraki, E., & Bock, R. D. (1993). *PARSCALE: IRT based test scoring and item analysis for graded open-ended exercises and performance tasks [Computer software]*. Chicago, IL: Scientific Software International.

Muraki, E., & Bock, R. D. (2002). *PARSCALE: Maximum likelihood item analysis and test scoring—polytomous model [Computer software]*. Chicago, IL: Scientific Software International.

Novomestky, F. (2013). gaussquad: Collection of functions for Gaussian quadrature. R package version 1.0-2.

Press, W. H., Teukolsky, S. A., Vetterling, W. T., & Flannery, B. P. (1996). *Numerical recipes in Fortran 90: The art of parallel scientific computing* (2nd ed.). New York, NY: Cambridge University Press.

R Core Team. (2010). *R: A language and environment for statistical computing*. Vienna, Austria: R Foundation for Statistical Computing. Retrieved from http://www.R-project.org.

Rigdon, S. E., & Tsutakawa, R. K. (1983). Parameter estimation in latent trait models. *Psycometrika, 48*, 567–574.

Salzer, H. E., Zucker, R., & Capuano, R. (1952). Table of the zeros and weight factors of the first twenty Hermite polynomials. *Journal of Research of the National Bureau of Standards, 48*, 111–116.

Sanathanan, L., & Blumenthal, S. (1978). The logistic model and estimation of latent structure. *Journal of the American Statistical Association, 73*, 794–799.

Seong, T.-J. (1990). *Validity of using two numerical analysis techniques to estimate item and ability parameters via MMLE: Gauss-Hermite quadrature formula and Mislevy's histogram solution*. Paper presented at the Annual Meeting of the National Council on Measurement in Education, Boston, MA.

Shao, T. S., Chen, T. C., & Frank, R. M. (1964). Tables of zeros and Gaussian weights of certain associated Laguerre Polynomials and the related generalized Hermite polynomials. *Mathematics of Computation, 26*, 598–616.

Smyth, G. K. (1998). Numerical integration. In P. Armitage & T. Colton (Eds.), *Encyclopedia of biostatistics* (pp. 3088–3095). Chichester: Wiley.

Smyth, G. K. (2014). statmod: Statistical modeling. R package version 1.4.20.

Stroud, A. H., & Secrest, D. (1966). *Gaussian quadrature formulas*. Englewood Cliffs, NJ: Prentice-Hall.

Thissen, D. (1982). Marginal maximum likelihood estimation for the one-parameter logistic model. *Psychometrika, 47*, 175–186.

Thissen, D. (1986). *MULTILOG version 5 user's guide*. Mooresville, IN: Scientific Software.

Thissen, D., Chen, W.-H., & Bock, R. D. (2002). *MULTILOG [Computer software]*. Lincolnwood, IL: Scientific Software International.

Thisted, R. A. (1988). *Elements of statistical computing: Numerical computation*. New York, NY: Chapman and Hall.

Tsutakawa, R. K. (1984). Estimation of two-parameter logistic item response curves. *Journal of Educational Statistics, 9*, 263–276.

Verhelst, N. D., Glas, C. A. W., & Verstralen, H. H. F. M. (1994). *One parameter logistic model (OPLM) [Computer software]*. Amhem: Cito.

Wilson, D. T., Wood, R., & Gibbons, R. (1991). *TESTFACT: Test scoring, item statistics, and item factor analysis (386/486 Version) [Computer software]*. Chicago, IL: Scientific Software International.

Wood, R., Wilson, D., Gibbons, R., Schilling, S., Muraki, E., & Bock, R. D. (2002). *TESTFACT: Test scoring, item statistics, and item factor analysis (Version 4.0) [Computer software]*. Lincolnwood, IL: Scientific Software International.

Zwinderman, A. H., & van den Wollenberg, A. L. (1990). Robustness of marginal maximum likelihood estimation in the Rasch model. *Applied Psychological Measurement, 14*, 73–81.

Chapter 5
GPU-Accelerated Computing with Gibbs Sampler for the 2PNO IRT Model

Yanyan Sheng, William S. Welling, and Michelle M. Zhu

Abstract Item response theory (IRT) is a popular approach used for addressing large-scale statistical problems in psychometrics as well as in other fields. The fully Bayesian approach for estimating IRT models is usually memory and computational expensive due to the large number of iterations. This limits the use of the procedure in many applications. In an effort to overcome such restrictions, previous studies proposed to tackle the problem using massive core-based graphic processing units (GPU), and demonstrated the advantage of this approach over the message passing interface (MPI) by showing that a single GPU card could achieve a speedup of up to 50×. Given that GPU is practical, cost-effective, and convenient, this study aims to seek further improvements using a single GPU card.

Keywords Item response theory • Bayesian estimation • MCMC • Two-parameter IRT model • High performance computing • CUDA • Optimization

5.1 Introduction

Item response theory (IRT) is a popular approach used for describing probabilistic relationships between correct responses on a set of test items and continuous latent traits (see Bock and Aitkin 1981; Mislevy 1985; Patz and Junker 1999; Tutakawa and Lin 1986). In addition to educational and psychological measurement, IRT models have been used in other areas of applied mathematics and statistical research, such as US Supreme Court decision-making processes (Bafumi et al. 2005), alcohol disorder analysis (Beseler et al. 2010; Feske et al. 2007; Gilder et al. 2011; Martin

Y. Sheng (✉)
Quantitative Methods, Department of Counseling, Quantitative Methods, & Special Education, Southern Illinois University, Carbondale, IL 62901, USA
e-mail: ysheng@siu.edu

W.S. Welling • M.M. Zhu
Department of Computer Science, Southern Illinois University, Carbondale, IL 62901, USA
e-mail: wwelling@library.tamu.edu; mzhu@siu.edu

L.A. van der Ark et al. (eds.), *Quantitative Psychology Research*, Springer Proceedings in Mathematics & Statistics 140, DOI 10.1007/978-3-319-19977-1_5

et al. 2006), nicotine dependency (Courvoisier and Etter 2008; Panter and Reeve 2002; Rose and Dierker 2010), multiple-recapture population estimation (Fienberg et al. 1999), and psychiatric epidemiology (Orlando et al. 2000; Reiser 1989; Tsutsumi et al. 2009), to name a few.

5.1.1 Gibbs Sampling for IRT Models

IRT has the advantage of allowing inferences regarding the effects of items and persons on the responses through distinct sets of model parameters. As a result, a primary concern associated with IRT research has been on parameter estimation. Specifically of concern are the statistical complexities that can often arise when item and person parameters are simultaneously estimated (see Baker and Kim 2004; Birnbaum 1969; Bock and Aitkin 1981; Molenaar 1995). Recent attention has focused on fully Bayesian estimation methods where Markov chain Monte Carlo (MCMC, Smith and Roberts 1993; Tierney 1994) simulation techniques are used. Albert (1992) applied Gibbs sampling (Geman and Geman 1984), one of the most efficient MCMC algorithms, to the two-parameter normal ogive (2PNO; Lord and Novick 1968) model, which takes the form

$$P(y_{ij} = 1) = \Phi(\alpha_j\theta_i - \beta_j) = \int_{-\infty}^{\alpha_j\theta_i-\beta_j} \frac{1}{\sqrt{2\pi}} e^{\frac{-t^2}{2}} dt \tag{5.1}$$

for modeling the probability that person i obtains a correct response on item j, where $i = 1, \ldots, n$ and $j = 1, \ldots, k$, α_j and β_j denote item parameters and θ_i denotes the continuous person trait parameter.

Despite its many advantages, the fully Bayesian approach for estimating IRT models is both memory and computationally expensive, which further limits its actual applications. Typically, item response data are based on n subjects' responses to k items at one occasion, and a Markov chain requires 5000–10,000 iterations to reach convergence for such IRT models. Each implementation of the algorithm could take five or more minutes to complete by a single desktop when n and k are relatively small (e.g., $n = 1000$, $k = 10$) (Sheng and Headrick 2007). This fact makes it impractical for users to utilize the algorithm for various applications of IRT, such as item calibration and scoring in large-scale standardized testing situations, and item analysis in test development and scale construction. Other examples include using IRT (1) to diagnose patients for certain mental disabilities in psychiatry where the urgency of starting treatment for a disability is essential, (2) to calibrate item parameters for a CAT system where a large item pool with sufficient numbers of good quality items is required, and (3) in the massive open online courses (MOOCs) where sample sizes and test frequencies are often quite large.

In addition to these applications, the computation expense limits researchers in conducting Monte Carlo studies where a large number of replications is desirable. In the IRT literature, simulation studies commonly utilize 25 replications only (Harwell et al. 1996), which makes it difficult to empirically evaluate the property of the population distribution of the model parameters. Even with such a small number of replications, the entire execution may take weeks or even months to finish. The delayed research findings in turn limit the advance of IRT research in developing more complicated models.

In general, the serial implementation of the Gibbs sampler is limited in both practical applications and theoretical developments. Consequently, achieving a considerable speedup with well-designed parallel algorithms on an inexpensive and convenient execution platform would make it more practical for researchers or practitioners to implement IRT models using MCMC. In an effort to achieve this, previous studies investigated high performance computing (HPC) using the message passing interface (MPI) (Pastias et al. 2012; Sheng and Rahimi 2012) or the massive core-based graphic processing units (GPU) (Sheng et al. 2014). Given the theoretical and empirical advantages of the latter over the former, this paper focuses on GPU.

5.1.2 Massive Core GPU Computing

With the current trend of having increasing processor core counts, it is necessary to investigate software that can concurrently use all of the hardware resources. As a result, HPC employs supercomputers, computer clusters, and graphics processors to tackle problems with computing and memory intensive computations. HPC utilizes the concept of parallel computing to run programs in parallel and achieve a much smaller execution time with high efficiency and low overhead.

With a great many processing elements, CUDA (Compute unified device architecture) enabled GPU is of growing research interest for data decomposition-based parallel applications. As of 2012, the peak floating-point throughput of many-thread GPU is ten times that of a multicore CPU. Such a gap between CPU and GPU is due to two factors: First, the design of CPU is optimized for sequential algorithms with a complicated control logic and a large cache. Latency (time required to complete a task) can be reduced by such designs but the throughput (number of tasks executed in a fixed time) will be sacrificed. Second, the memory bandwidth of delivering data from the memory to the processor is about six times faster for GPU than CPU, for which the bandwidth usually serves as the bottleneck in many applications (Kirk and Hwu 2013). Hence, even a single GPU card is capable of delivering much improved performances.

The data size and the data-parallelism nature of the MCMC procedure with a high throughput requirement make GPU an ideal platform for fast and efficient execution. A typical GPU program utilizes thousands of threads simultaneously and can achieve an extremely high system throughput. On the contrary, a high-end multicore microprocessor CPU typically has only four to eight cores and multiple megabytes of on-chip cache for strong sequential code performance.

Indeed, Sheng et al. (2014) demonstrated the advantage of the CUDA-enabled GPU over MPI by showing that a single GPU card could achieve a speedup of up to 50× for implementing MCMC with an IRT model, and that as the data size increases, the benefit of using GPU would be even higher. However, in their study, the performance of the GPU program was improved via optimizing global memory access and enabling massive thread-level parallelism. With the recently released CUDA 5.0, it is believed that more advanced optimization techniques, such as dynamic parallelism (DiMarco and Taufer 2013), data streaming, shared memory, and parallel reduction (Harris 2007), are expected to make the GPU-accelerated high performance Gibbs sampling algorithm more efficient and practically more attractive. This study is hence to seek further improvements using a single GPU card.

The remainder of the paper is organized as follows. Section 5.2 illustrates the approach we adopted in the present study to optimize the CUDA GPU algorithm. In Sect. 5.3, the effect of two important optimization approaches is investigated by comparing their performances with those from the parallel algorithm without implementing them. General guidelines are provided in this section suggesting the appropriate method under specific test situations. Finally, a few concluding remarks are made in Sect. 5.4.

5.2 Methodology

This study was performed using a Tesla K20c GPU on an Intel Core 2 Quad CPU with 8 GB of RAM.

5.2.1 Serial Algorithm

For the 2PNO IRT model defined in Eq. (5.1), the Gibbs sampler involves updating three sets of parameters in each iteration, namely, an augmented continuous variable Z_{ij} (which is positive if $y_{ij} = 1$ and negative if $y_{ij} = 0$), the person parameter θ_i, and the item parameters $\boldsymbol{\xi}_j$, where $\boldsymbol{\xi}_j = (\alpha_j, \beta_j)'$ from their respective full conditional distributions, namely,

$$Z_{ij}|\cdot \sim \begin{cases} N_{(0,\infty)}(\alpha_j\theta_i - \beta_j, 1), & \text{if} \quad y_{ij} = 1 \\ N_{(-\infty,0)}(\alpha_j\theta_i - \beta_j, 1), & \text{if} \quad y_{ij} = 0 \end{cases}, \tag{5.2}$$

$$\theta_i|\cdot \sim N\left(\frac{\sum_j (Z_{ij} + \beta_j)\alpha_j}{\sum_j \alpha_j^2}, \frac{1}{\sum_j \alpha_j^2}\right), \tag{5.3}$$

$$\boldsymbol{\xi}_j|\cdot \sim N((\mathbf{x}'\mathbf{x})^{-1}\mathbf{x}'\mathbf{Z}_j, (\mathbf{x}'\mathbf{x})^{-1})I(\alpha_j > 0), \tag{5.4}$$

where $\mathbf{x} = [\boldsymbol{\theta}, -1]$, and the prior distributions are assumed to be $\theta_i \sim N(0,1)$, $\alpha_j \sim U(0, \infty)$, and $p(\beta_j) \propto 1$ (see, e.g., Albert 1992; Sheng and Headrick 2007).

Hence, with starting values $\boldsymbol{\theta}^{(0)}$ and $\boldsymbol{\xi}^{(0)}$, observations $(\mathbf{Z}^{(\ell)}, \boldsymbol{\theta}^{(\ell)}, \boldsymbol{\xi}^{(\ell)})$ can be simulated from the Gibbs sampler by iteratively drawing from their respective full conditional distributions as specified in Eqs. (5.2)–(5.4). Specifically, to go from $(\mathbf{Z}^{(\ell-1)}, \boldsymbol{\theta}^{(\ell-1)}, \boldsymbol{\xi}^{(\ell)-1})$ to $(\mathbf{Z}^{(\ell)}, \boldsymbol{\theta}^{(\ell)}, \boldsymbol{\xi}^{(\ell)})$, there are three transition steps:

1. Draw $\mathbf{Z}^{(\ell)} \sim p(\mathbf{Z}|\boldsymbol{\theta}^{(\ell-1)}, \boldsymbol{\xi}^{(\ell-1)})$;
2. Draw $\boldsymbol{\theta}^{(\ell)} \sim p(\theta|\mathbf{Z}^{(\ell)}, \boldsymbol{\xi}^{(\ell-1)})$;
3. Draw $\boldsymbol{\xi}^{(\ell)} \sim p(\boldsymbol{\xi}|\mathbf{Z}^{(\ell)}, \boldsymbol{\theta}^{(\ell)})$.

This iterative procedure produces a sequence of $(\boldsymbol{\theta}^{(\ell)}, \boldsymbol{\xi}^{(\ell)})$, $\ell = 0, \ldots, L$. To reduce the effect of the starting values, early iterations in the Markov chain are set as burn-ins to be discarded. Samples from the remaining iterations are then used to summarize the posterior density of item parameters $\boldsymbol{\xi}$ and ability parameters $\boldsymbol{\theta}$.

5.2.2 GPU Implementation and Optimization

CUDA is a heterogeneous programming model specially designed for general purpose GPU computing. It operates in CPU (host) and GPU (device). Code developed on the host not only manages memory on both the host and device, but also launches kernels that are functions executed on the device. These kernels are executed by an array of threads (sequences of executions) in parallel. Specifically, a kernel launches a grid of thread blocks so that threads of the same block can communicate. This way, CUDA virtualizes the physical hardware, where a thread is a virtualized scalar processor and thread blocks are virtualized multiprocessors. A typical sequence of operations for a CUDA program involves the following steps: (1) declare and allocate host and device memory; (2) allocate and initialize host data; (3) transfer data from the host to the device; (4) execute kernels; and (5) transfer results from the device to the host.

To implement the Gibbs sampler for the 2PNO IRT model, the CUDA-enabled GPU parallel algorithm begins with copying the data matrix $\mathbf{y}$ to the device, which then assumes the tasks of updating model parameters θ_i, α_j, β_j, and calculating results. Using the triple chevron notation that contains the kernel launch parameters, we defined a kernel per update to specify the number of blocks and the number of threads per block for decompositions of the data matrix and model parameters. Hence, each kernel has a random state indexed in a grid or a list. Specifically, the data matrix $\mathbf{y}$, which is of size $n \times k$, was decomposed over a two-dimensional grid of $r \times c$ blocks with a defined number of threads (see Fig. 5.1). This way, each block on the device receives a sub-matrix $\mathbf{y}_{B_{ij}}$ of size $g_r \times g_c$, where $g_r = n/r$ and $g_c = k/c$.

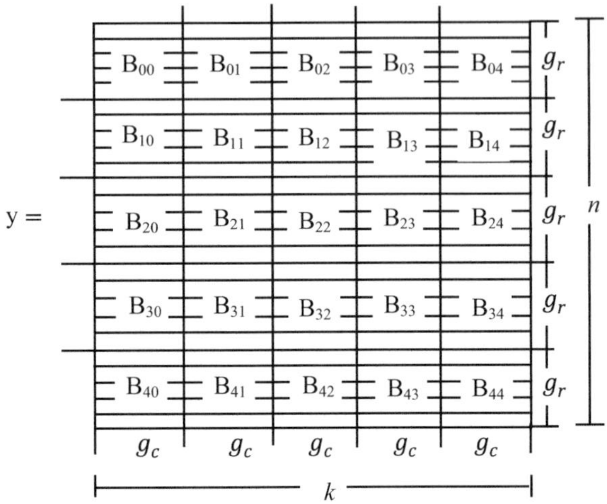

Fig. 5.1 Decomposition of the data matrix **y** over a grid of $(r = 5) \times (c = 5)$ blocks

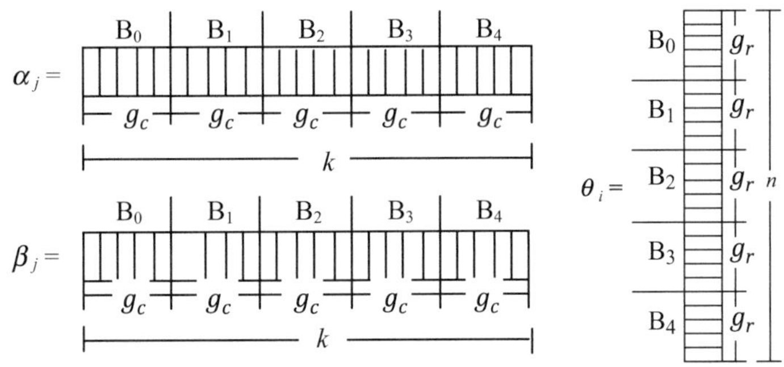

Fig. 5.2 Decomposition of item parameters (*left panel*) and person parameters (*right panel*) over a list of $r = 5$ or $c = 5$ blocks

In addition, each item (person) parameter was decomposed over a list of r (c) blocks as depicted in Fig. 5.2.

The algorithm was implemented in ANSI C with utilization of the cuRAND library (NVIDIA 2010) for random number generations and normal cumulative densities. We employed the curand_normal2_double device API method for its efficiency in generating two pseudorandom numbers at once, and the efficiency of memory access.

The program adopts statically allocating memory at compile time because of its simplicity and efficiency in memory for addressing two-dimensional arrays and optimal memory alignment. For more detailed implementation and optimization, Figs. 5.3 and 5.4 display a basic control diagram between the CPU host and the GPU device for updating various variables in the algorithm. Specifically, after the initial matrices (e.g., dev_Z), vectors (e.g., dev_AVZ, dev_GVZ), and input values (dev_Y) are stored in the device memory with random states allocated (rngStatesAG),

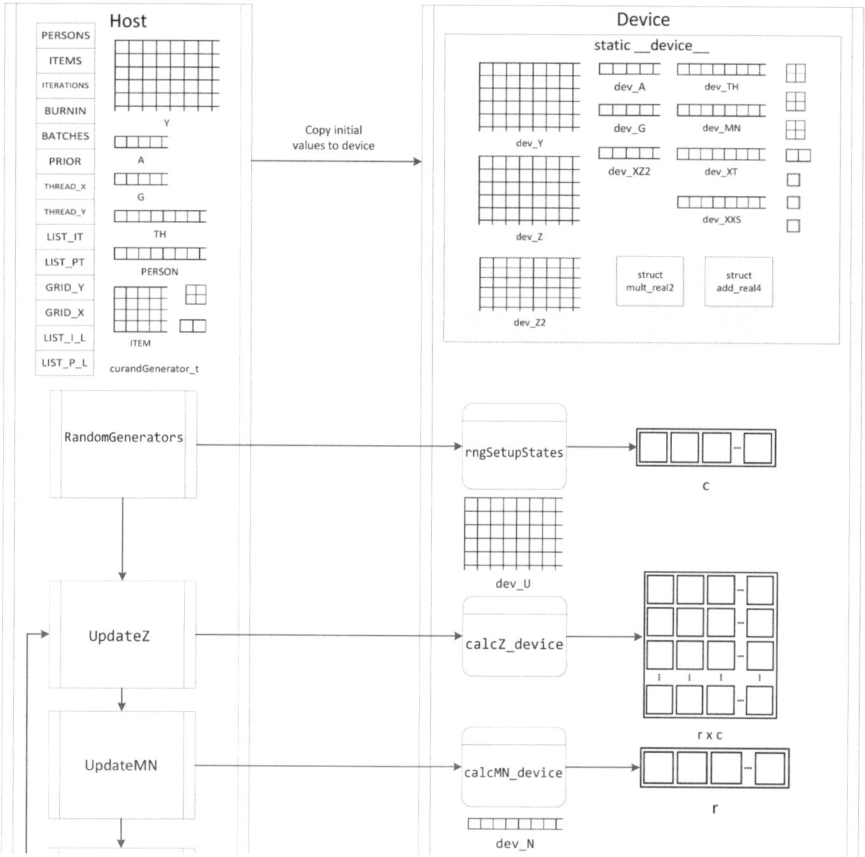

Fig. 5.3 Control diagram (part 1) between the device and the host for the optimized CUDA program

the Gibbs sampler begins. The first update is in the kernel of updating **Z** (calcZ), which decomposes the data matrix **y** on a two-dimensional grid and calculates the augmented data **Z** (see Fig. 5.1). This kernel requires the device to generate a matrix of uniform random numbers (dev_U). Calculating the mean for θ (calcMN) is a separate kernel that is decomposed on a one-dimensional list of r blocks (see Fig. 5.2). Updates of θ (calcTH) are decomposed similarly but require the device to randomly generate a vector of numbers from a standard normal distribution (dev_N). Updates of α and β (calcAG) are decomposed on a one-dimensional list of c blocks (see Fig. 5.2). This update requires passing a pointer to a vector of random states on the device (rngStatesAG). Calculating the posterior estimates for item or person parameters, performed at the end of each iteration after the burn-in stage utilizing running averages (trackStatistics, copyStatistics, sumStatistics), is also parallelized using a one-dimensional list of c or r blocks. This approach has considerable improvement in memory efficiency as posterior samples of item and

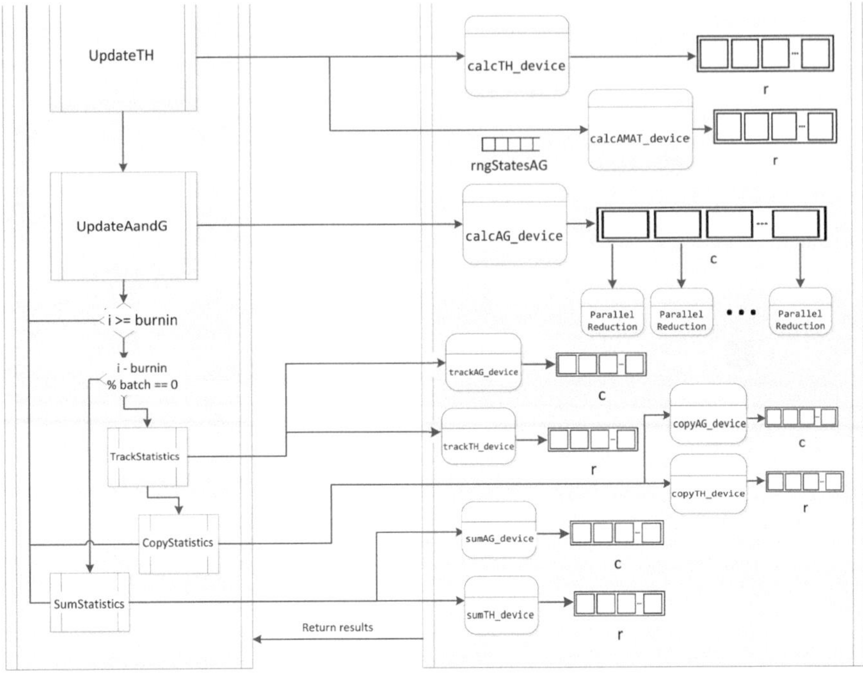

Fig. 5.4 Control diagram (part 2) between the device and the host for the optimized CUDA program

person parameters do not have to be gathered for computing the posterior estimates and standard errors after the completion of a Markov chain. The program stops when the device sends all the results back to the host.

It is noted that the update of θ has been optimized using a template library, Thrust (Hoberock and Bell 2010). With the use of two custom defined C structure operators (one for vector addition and the other for inverse vector multiplication), a transform reduce method from the Thrust library was successfully implemented to improve the performance when operating $\mathbf{x}'\mathbf{x}$, a $2 \times n$ by $n \times 2$ matrix multiplication, in Eq. (5.4).

The Thrust library was invoked from the host side, while streams were used to transfer data between host and device primarily, asynchronously overlapping the computation of the transform reduce. Specifically, two streams were utilized so that stream one was used to asynchronously copy $\mathbf{x}$ in Eq. (5.4) from device to host, which was further passed to the transform reduce calculation within a thrust:device_vector to be invoked in parallel on the device; stream two was used to asynchronously copy $\mathbf{x}'\mathbf{x}$ back to the device for the results to be sent back to the host when the Thrust transform reduce was complete. It is noted that the latter may not be a significant improvement as $\mathbf{x}'\mathbf{x}$ is simply a 2×2 matrix.

In addition, parallel reduction was implemented using the Kepler architecture (Luitjens 2014), where massive thread parallelism, dynamic parallelism (DiMarco and Taufer 2013), and shared memory were utilized for calculating $\mathbf{x}'\mathbf{Z}_j$ in Eq. (5.4) for each kernel.

5.2.3 Performance Analyses

The main advanced optimization techniques successfully implemented in the parallel algorithm are transform reduce via the use of the Thrust library and parallel reduction. In order to investigate the effect of each technique on the performance of the GPU computing with the implementation of Gibbs sampling for the 2PNO IRT model, experiments were carried out in which tests with n persons ($n = 500$, 1000, 2000, 5000, 10,000, 20,000, 50,000) and k items ($k = 20, 50, 100, 200$) were considered. In each experiment, Gibbs sampling was implemented to run a single Markov chain with a total of 10,000 iterations using CUDA (with a single GPU card) that has:

1. no parallel reduction or transform reduce (GPU1),
2. parallel reduction (GPU2),
3. transform reduce (GPU3),
4. both parallel reduction and transform reduce (GPU4).

The performances of these GPU programs were evaluated with respect to the total execution time. The three programs with parallel reduction and/or transform reduce (namely, GPU2, GPU3, and GPU4) were further compared using the relative speedup over that without these optimizations (GPU1), which is defined as:

$$S_r = T_1 \,/\, T_i, \tag{5.5}$$

where T_1 is the execution time for GPU1 and T_i is that for each of the GPU2, GPU3, and GPU4 programs.

5.3 Results

For the fully crossed $7 \times 4 \times 4 = 112$ design, each implementation was replicated 3 times. The execution time was averaged across these replications and the results are summarized in Figs. 5.5 and 5.6. A close examination of the figures suggests:

- GPU2 performs similarly to GPU1 for $k < 100$, with a slight advantage to GPU2 when sample sizes go over 5000. However, when $k \geq 100$, GPU2 is not as efficient as GPU1 for $n \leq 5000$.
- GPU3 consistently performs better than GPU1, with a relative speedup ranging from 1.5× to 3.4×. Its speedup over GPU1 increases up to two times with increased sample sizes, which is consistent across the four test length conditions (see Fig. 5.6).
- With a relative speedup over GPU1 ranging from 0.3× to 18×, GPU4 is mostly desirable for large sample size and small test length conditions (e.g., $n > 2000$ and $k = 20$). It requires increasingly lesser amounts of time than GPU1 when

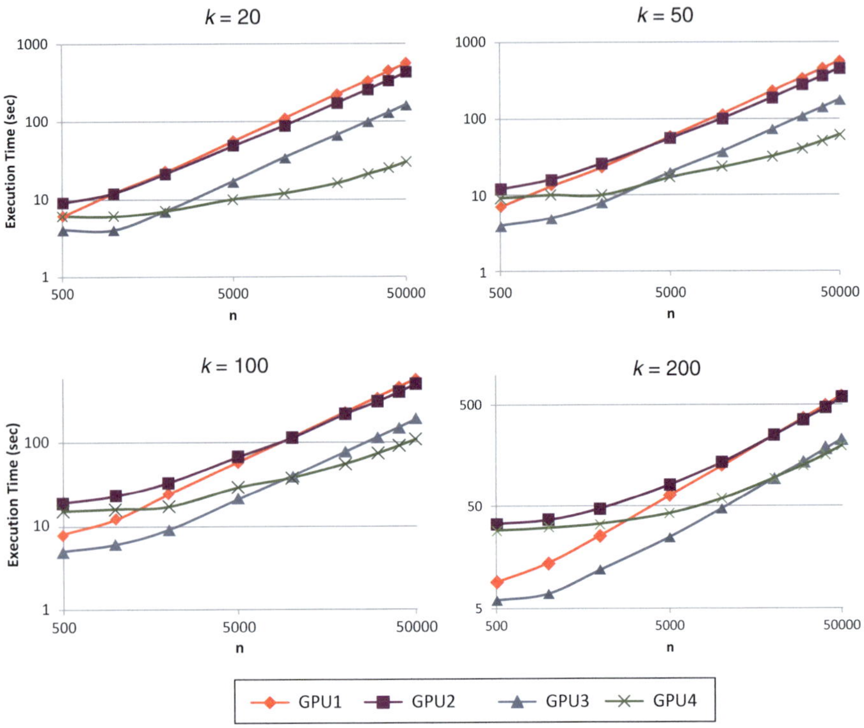

Fig. 5.5 Execution time for implementing the CUDA parallel program of Gibbs sampling for tests and samples with different sizes

sample size increases. However, the amount of speedup reduces considerably with increased test lengths.

In general, transform reduce alone improves the computation efficiency by having a relative speedup of up to 3.4× over the GPU program without either transform reduce or parallel reduction. Moreover, parallel reduction works well only when paired with transform reduce.

It is noted that sample size and test length effects are different with the two optimization techniques. With increased sample sizes, transform reduce improves the speed steadily whereas parallel reduction improves it exponentially. On the other hand, increased test length has little effect on transform reduce, but it substantially reduces the speedup of parallel reduction. This can be explained by the fact that parallel reduction was used for calculating $\mathbf{x}'\mathbf{Z}_j$, which becomes more efficient when a larger n is used. However, when test length increases, the increased amount of overhead resulted from performing dynamic parallelism and utilizing shared memory overweighs the gain in computation when sample size is not sufficiently large.

For the two GPU programs that performed best, GPU3 and GPU4, a set of guidelines can be established with respect to the conditions to use them. Specifically,

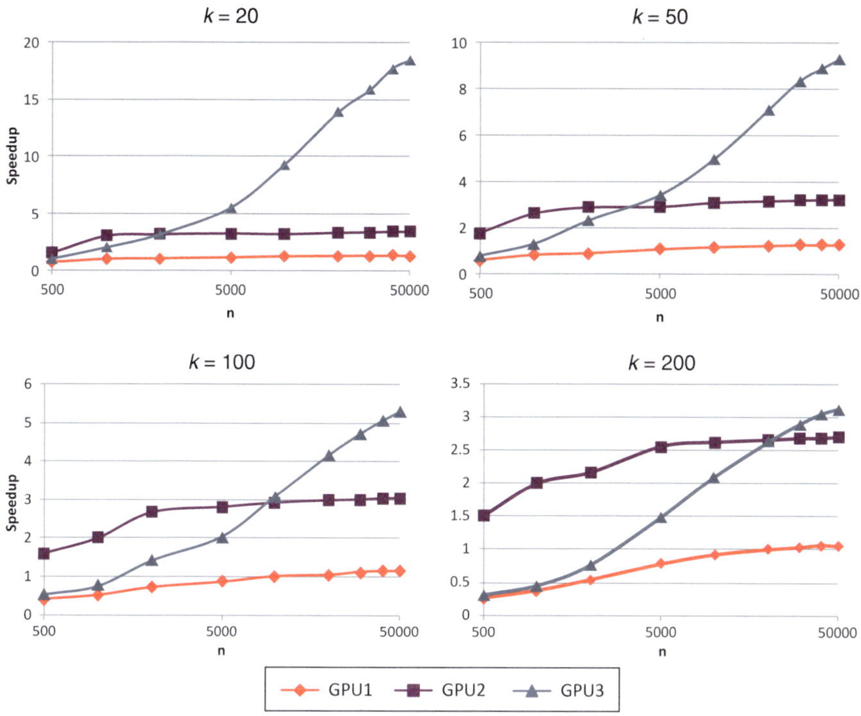

Fig. 5.6 Speedup of GPU2, GPU3, and GPU4 relative to GPU1 for tests and samples with different sizes

for short tests, i.e., $k \leq 50$, transform reduce alone (GPU3) works the best with $n \leq 2000$, whereas the program with parallel reduction and transform reduce (GPU4) is most helpful for $n > 2000$ (see Fig. 5.5a, b). When $k > 50$, the threshold increases. For tests with 200 items, transform reduce (GPU3) alone outperforms the other approaches for sample sizes as large as $n = 20{,}000$ (see Fig. 5.5d).

To further evaluate the performance of the four GPU programs, their execution times were compared with that of the sequential algorithm using the speedup, which is defined as:

$$S = T_S \, / \, T_P, \tag{5.6}$$

where T_S is the execution time for the fastest sequential algorithm and T_P is that for the parallel algorithm. For the purpose of comparing the speedup with those based on the parallel program developed by Sheng et al. (2014), we used the same data size conditions (i.e., $n = 500, 1000, 2000, 5000, 10{,}000$). Figure 5.7 clearly indicates that the optimized GPU program can reach a speedup of up to 80× over the sequential implementation. For example, for data with binary responses of 5000 persons to 200 items, the program takes only 25 s to complete a single Markov chain

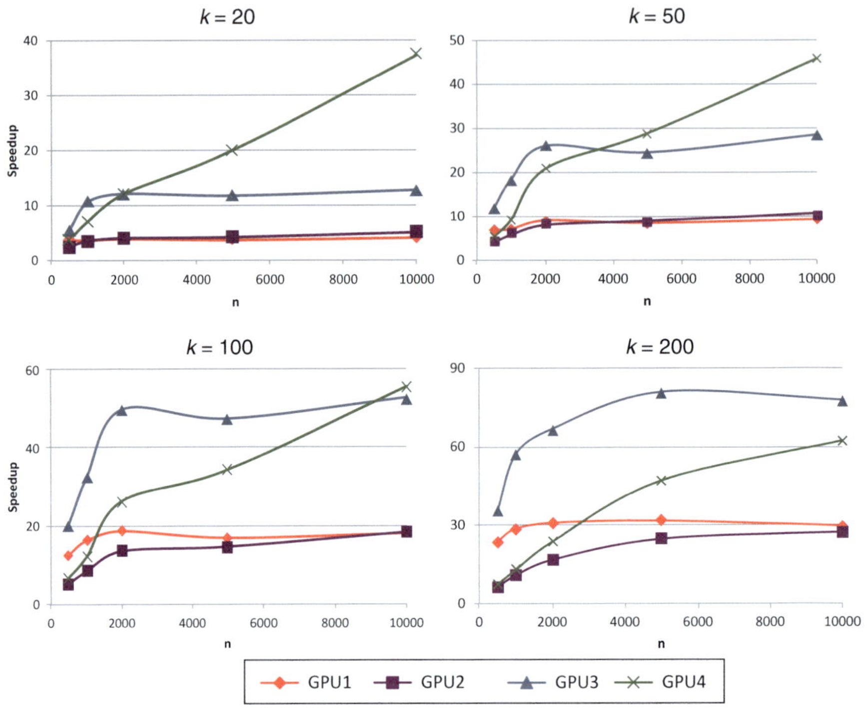

Fig. 5.7 Speedup of implementing the CUDA parallel program over sequential algorithm for tests and samples with different sizes

with 10,000 iterations (see Fig. 5.7d). This is a significant improvement over the original speedup of 50×, making the GPU accelerated computing more attractive.

5.4 Discussion

This study optimized a CUDA GPU-accelerated high performance Gibbs sampling algorithm for the 2PNO IRT model with the purpose of achieving higher speedup and efficiency. With the use of additional advanced optimization techniques by utilizing CUDA 5.0, a more efficient program can be developed with CUDA GPU. The algorithm was implemented using the ANSI C programming language and the CUDA interface. Two advanced optimization techniques, transform reduce and parallel reduction, were evaluated and compared. Results indicated that transform reduce consistently improves the computation efficiency of the Markov chain, whereas parallel reduction works exceptionally well with large sample sizes and short test lengths when paired with transform reduce. In addition, given that the performance of parallel reduction depends on different sample size and test length conditions, a set of guidelines are provided for situations in which to use it.

Although this paper only focuses on a simple IRT model, its methodology and results shed light on developing a GPU-based Gibbs sampler for more complicated IRT models. In the IRT literature, the model can be more complex by assuming multiple latent traits, or assuming priors for hyperparameters. Tests for such models typically involve more than 20 items and/or a larger sample size, where the GPU accelerated parallel computing is theoretically appealing.

Finally, this study achieved further speedup and improved efficiency of the Gibbs sampler for the 2PNO IRT model through a massive-core GPU computing via the use of advanced optimization techniques. It will also be interesting to consider a different decomposition scheme with MPI such as the 2D decomposition suggested by Georganas (2013), or use a hybrid CUDA, MPI and/or OpenMP parallel programming as recommended by Karunadasa and Ranasinghe (2009), Oancea and Andrei (2013) and Yang et al. (2011).

References

Albert, J. H. (1992). Bayesian estimation of normal ogive item response curves using Gibbs sampling. *Journal of Educational Statistics, 17*(3), 251–269.

Bafumi, J., Gelman, A., Park, D. K., & Kaplan, N. (2005). Practical issues in implementing and understanding Bayesian ideal point estimation. *Political Analysis, 13*(2), 171–187.

Baker, F. B., & Kim, S. H. (2004). *Item response theory: Parameter estimation techniques*. (2nd ed.). New York: Dekker.

Beseler, C. L., Taylor, L. A., & Leeman, R. F. (2010). An item-response theory analysis of DSM-IV alcohol-use disorder criteria and "binge" drinking in undergraduates. *Journal of Studies on Alcohol and Drugs*, 71(3), 418–423.

Birnbaum, A. (1969). Statistical theory for logistic mental test models with a prior distribution of ability. *Journal of Mathematical Psychology, 6*(2), 258–276.

Bock, R. D., & Aitkin, M. (1981). Marginal maximum likelihood estimation of item parameters: Application of an EM algorithm. *Psychometrika, 46*(4), 443–459.

Courvoisier, D., & Etter, J. F. (2008). Using item response theory to study the convergent and discriminant validity of three questionnaires measuring cigarette dependence. *Psychology of Addictive Behaviors, 22*(3), 391–401.

DiMarco, J., & Taufer. M. (2013). Performance impact of dynamic parallelism on different clustering algorithms. In *SPIE Defense, Security, and Sensing*, International Society for Optics and Photonics.

Feske, U., Kirisci, L., Tarter, R. E., & Plkonis, P. A. (2007). An application of item response theory to the DSM-III-R criteria for borderline personality disorder. *Journal of Personality Disorders, 21*(4), 418–433.

Fienberg, S. E., Johnson, M. S., & Junker, B. W. (1999). Classical multilevel and Bayesian approaches to population size estimation using multiple lists. *Journal of the Royal Statistical Society, Series A, 162*(3), 383–392.

Geman, S., & Geman, D. (1984). Stochastic relaxation, Gibbs distributions, and the Bayesian restoration of images. *IEEE Transactions on Pattern Analysis and Machine Intelligence, 6*(6), 721–741.

Georganas, E. (2013). *High performance parallel Gibbs sampling for IRT models*. Poster session presented at ParLab Winter Retreat, Berkeley, USA.

Gilder, D. A., Gizer, I. R., & Ehlers, C. L. (2011). Item response theory analysis of binge drinking and its relationship to lifetime alcohol use disorder symptom severity in an American Indian community sample. *Alcoholism: Clinical and Experimental Research, 35*(5), 984–995.

Harris, M. (2007). *Optimizing parallel reduction in CUDA*. Presentation packaged with CUDA Toolkit, NVIDIA Corporation.

Harwell, M., Stone, C. A., Hsu, H., & Kirisci, L. (1996). Monte Carlo studies in item response theory. *Applied Psychological Measurement*, 20(2), 101–126.

Hoberock, J., & Bell, N. (2010). *Thrust: A parallel template library*. http://thrust.github.io/.

Karunadasa, N. P., & Ranasinghe, D. N. (2009). Accelerating high performance applications with CUDA and MPI. In *2009 International Conference on Industrial and Information Systems (ICIIS)* (pp. 331–336).

Kirk, D. B., & Hwu, W. W. (2013). *Programming massively parallel processors: A hands-on approach* (2nd ed.). Burlington, MA: Addison-Wesley.

Lord, F. M., & Novick, M. R. (1968). *Statistical theories of mental test scores*. Boston: Addison-Wesley.

Luitjens, J. (2014). *Faster parallel reduction on Kepler*. Retrieved from http://devblogs.nvidia.com/parallelforall/faster-parallel-reductions-kepler/.

Martin, C. S., Chung, T., Kirisci, L., & Langenbucher, J. W. (2006). Item response theory analysis of diagnostic criteria for alcohol and cannabis use disorders in adolescents: Implications for DSM-V. *Journal of Abnormal Psychology, 115*(4), 807–814.

Mislevy, R. J. (1985). Estimation of latent group effects. *Journal of the American Statistical Association, 80*(392), 993–997.

Molenaar, I. W. (1995). Estimation of item parameters. In G. H. Fischer & I. W. Molenaar (Eds.), *Rasch models: Foundations, recent developments, and applications* (pp. 39–51). New York: Springer.

NVIDIA. (2010). *CUDA CURAND library*. Santa Clara, CA: NVIDIA Corporation.

Oancea, B., & Andrei, T. (2013). Developing a high performance software library with MPI and CUDA for matrix computations. *Computational Methods in Social Sciences, 1*(2), 1–10.

Orlando, M., Sherbourne, C. D., & Thissen, D. (2000). Summed-score linking using item response theory: Application to depression measurement. *Psychological Assessment, 12*(3), 354–359.

Panter, A. T., & Reeve, B. B. (2002). Assessing tobacco beliefs among youth using item response theory models. *Drug and Alcohol Dependence, 68*(1), 21–39.

Pastias, K., Rahimi, M., Sheng, Y., & Rahimi, S. (2012). Parallel computing with a Bayesian item response model. *American Journal of Computational Mathematics, 2*(2), 65–71.

Patz, R. J., & Junker, B. (1999). A straightforward approach to Markov chain Monte Carlo methods for item response model. *Journal of Educational and Behavioral Statistics, 24*(2), 146–178.

Reiser, M. (1989). An application of the item-response model to psychiatric epidemiology. *Sociological Methods and Research, 18*(1), 66–103.

Rose, J. S., & Dierker, L. C. (2010). An item response theory analysis of nicotine dependence symptoms in recent onset adolescent smokers. *Drug and Alcohol Dependence, 110*(12), 70–79.

Sheng, Y., & Headrick, T. C. (2007). An algorithm for implementing Gibbs sampling for 2PNO IRT models. *Journal of Modern Applied Statistical Methods, 6*(1), 341–349.

Sheng, Y., & Rahimi, M. (2012). High performance Gibbs sampling for IRT models using row-wise decomposition. *ISRN Computational Mathematics, 2012*(264040), 1–9.

Sheng, Y., Welling, W. S., & Meng, M. M. (2014). A GPU-based Gibbs sampler for a unidimensional IRT model. *ISRN Computational Mathematics*, 2014 (368149), 1–11.

Smith, A. F. M., & Roberts, G. O. (1993). Bayesian computation via the Gibbs sampler and related Markov chain Monte Carlo methods (with discussion). *Journal of the Royal Statistical Society, Series B, 55*(1), 3–23.

Tierney, L. (1994). Markov chains for exploring posterior distributions. *The Annals of Statistics, 22*(4), 1701–1728.

Tsutsumi, A., Iwata, N., Watanabe, N., de Jonge, J., Pikhart, H., Fernndez-Lpez, J. A., et al. (2009). Application of item response theory to achieve cross-cultural comparability of occupational stress measurement. *International Journal of Methods in Psychiatric Research, 18*(1), 58–67.

Tutakawa, R. K., & Lin, H. Y. (1986). Bayesian estimation of item response curves. *Psychometrika, 51*(2), 251–267.

Yang, C.-T., Huang, C.-L., & Lin, C.-F. (2011). Hybrid CUDA, OpenMP, and MPI parallel programming on multicore GPU clusters. *Computer Physics Communications, 182*, 266–269.

Chapter 6
Collusion Detection Using Joint Response Time Models

Anne Thissen-Roe and Michael S. Finger

Abstract One method for detecting test collusion, or large-scale answer sharing, is the divergence framework (Belov, Journal of Educational Measurement 50: 141–163, 2013). It uses Kullback–Leibler divergence and a psychometric model to identify groups of test-takers with unusual person-fit distributions. A second phase examines individuals within anomalous groups. Another line of research considers collusion detection methods that depend on the identification of aberrant response times. These methods can be integrated for greater power, using joint statistical models for item response and response time. Here, we explore the value added when collusion detection is conducted under the divergence framework, using two joint models of responses and response times: the lognormal model within a hierarchical framework (van der Linden, Journal of Educational and Behavioral Statistics 31:181–204, 2006; van der Linden, Psychometrika 72:287–308, 2007), and a model extended from the diffusion family of models for choice reaction time (Ratcliff, Psychological Review 85:59–108, 1978; Ratcliff et al., Psychological Review 106:261–300, 1999).

Keyword Response time

6.1 Introduction

In a large-scale examination program, test security is of great concern. Statistical methods can be used to monitor applicant data for suspicious individual records or test centers, or to detect compromised content.

One such method for detecting test collusion, or large-scale answer sharing, is the divergence framework (Belov 2013). It depends on assessing the fit of a psychometric model to the answer choices of groups of test-takers, using Kullback–Leibler divergence to identify those groups with unusual person-fit distributions. A follow-up investigation is conducted on the person-fit of individuals within

A. Thissen-Roe (✉) • M.S. Finger
Comira, 777 Mariners Island Boulevard Suite 200, San Mateo, CA 94404, USA
e-mail: athissenroe@comiratesting.com; mfinger@comiratesting.com

L.A. van der Ark et al. (eds.), *Quantitative Psychology Research*, Springer Proceedings in Mathematics & Statistics 140, DOI 10.1007/978-3-319-19977-1_6

anomalous groups, compared to the distribution of non-members. Meaningful, measurable groups whose boundaries can envelop an instance of collusion include schools, test sites, administration windows, and even social networks. For a relatively innocuous example, if an item administered in two consecutive years became a widely used classroom example in the intervening months, that item might become considerably "easier" for applicants in the second year. Such item compromise is more problematic, but still potentially detectable, when the item-specific training is available only to a subpopulation of applicants in the second year, such as those attending a particular school.

Another, older line of research focuses on the identification of aberrant response times. Intuitively speaking, a test-taker will answer a question very quickly if he or she has memorized the response, and very slowly if he or she is looking it up. A single instance of memorization or reference consultation may not be distinguishable from the wide normal range of response times, but a pattern of anomalous short or long response times, or some of each, can be identified statistically.

Both of these methods, while promising, suffer from limited statistical power to detect colluding individuals within the number of responses made to a single test. However, they can be combined formally for greater power. For example, Belov's protocol can be followed using person-fit statistics derived from a joint statistical model for response correctness and response time.

The present simulation study evaluates the value added when collusion detection is conducted under the divergence framework, using hierarchical joint modeling of responses and response times, to that achieved by the divergence framework using the item response model alone. A variety of conditions have been simulated in order to provide guidance on whether and when joint models of response time are valuable, as well as limiting conditions for when either model is viable. Simulation variables included test length, item response and response time hyperparameters, number of examinees in the target and reference groups, frequency of collusion within the target group, and aberrant response count per colluding individual.

6.2 Collusion Detection

6.2.1 Divergence Framework

Belov (2013) proposed a two-stage process for large-scale collusion detection, in order to ameliorate common issues of low statistical power in direct or pairwise approaches, as well as to encompass computerized adaptive testing (CAT) situations. His process extended prior detection approaches based on model fit; however, he recommended first identifying groups that may be involved in collusion, and then screening individuals within those groups. A highly parallelizable combinatoric search algorithm permitted simultaneous, if computationally intensive, identification of compromised content as a subset of all banked items.

Stage One: Group Identification. The purpose of Stage One is to identify meaningful groups of test-takers in which collusion is likely. First, a model fit statistic is calculated for each individual. Second, for each pair of groups, Kullback–Leibler divergence is calculated between the distributions of individual fit within each group. Third, for each group, the divergence values obtained with every other group are summed. Finally, groups are selected for follow-up investigation if the sum exceeds a critical value.

Stage Two: Individual Identification. The purpose of Stage Two is to identify colluding individuals within the suspect groups identified in Stage One. First, the aggregate distribution of the individual fit statistics is calculated across all groups not identified in Stage One. Second, a critical value is set based on the non-suspect distribution. Third, individuals are identified if their model fit statistics are beyond the critical value.

In theory, any fit statistic for any model can work, but in practice, some work better than others. A better model, that is, more informative or more explanatory, yields better collusion detection. Therefore, model comparison studies on representative datasets are profitable prior to implementing the procedure; general studies of the performance of different models, and their limits of applicability, may also be useful beyond a specific testing program.

Fit statistics vary in utility, as well. Belov recommended a second use of Kullback–Leibler divergence. In this case, divergence is calculated between two discretized posterior distributions of ability, one obtained from potentially compromised items and one obtained from secure items. It is of interest to determine whether a less tailored model fit statistic can be used, in order to provide for simple automation and rapid large-scale screening of incoming datasets from complex testing programs.

6.2.2 Joint Models of Item Responses and Response Times

The divergence method of collusion detection is model-dependent, and therefore benefits from a more informative model. One method of increasing the information obtained from each item is to include response time as well as response correctness. This is conceptually in keeping with prior work on aberrant response detection based on exceptionally short or long response times.

Item responses and response times may be modeled jointly, as paired observations reflecting two latent traits. There are several joint model families; the present work considers two. These are the lognormal model within a hierarchical framework (van der Linden 2006, 2007), and a model extended from the diffusion family of models for choice reaction time (Ratcliff 1978; Ratcliff et al. 1999).

6.2.2.1 The Hierarchical Framework

A hierarchical framework put forth by van der Linden (2006, 2007) permits a population-level association between latent speed and latent ability, as suggested by Carroll (1993). Within the framework, response time is modeled as a function of latent speed, and response correctness as a function of latent ability. The framework calls for an individual to choose a balance of speed and accuracy before beginning the test, and to maintain that balance; the choice is reflected in the individual's latent speed and latent ability parameters.

Any item response model can be used to relate latent ability to response correctness; van der Linden (2007) uses the three-parameter logistic model. A parallel model relates the logarithm of observed response time ($\ln t_j$) to latent speed (τ):

$$P\left(\ln t_j \middle| \tau\right) = \frac{\alpha_j}{t_j\sqrt{2\pi}} \exp\left\{-\frac{1}{2}\left[\alpha_j\left(lnt_j - \left(\beta_j - \tau\right)\right)\right]^2\right\}$$

where α_j is a speed discrimination parameter, and β_j is a time intensity parameter, for item j. An advantage of the framework is its simplicity; the response time model can be fit using standard confirmatory factor analysis software (Finger and Chuah 2009).

6.2.2.2 Diffusion Models

Over the last four decades, researchers in sensory perception and elementary cognition developed a series of choice reaction time models based on underlying random walk processes (see, e.g., Laming 1968; Link and Heath 1975; Stone 1960). In these models, information toward one of two decision thresholds accumulates in many small increments, some of which might fall in opposite directions. The consistency of increment direction, step size, and the distance of the thresholds jointly determines the distribution of reaction times pertaining to each possible decision outcome.

Random walk models are discrete models, with steps in quantized time. Ratcliff (1978) proposed a continuous model for the limit as the time increment goes to zero. This model described a diffusion process analogous to the movement of molecules in a gas, but in a single dimension. A family of diffusion models have been derived in more recent years (see, e.g., Ratcliff and Rouder 1998; Ratcliff et al. 1999; Ratcliff and Tuerlinckx 2002; Ratcliff and Smith 2004; Ratcliff and McKoon 2008). They typically incorporate notions of caution, bias, and information quality. Caution takes the form of boundary separation; that is, the total distance between the two decision thresholds. Bias occurs when the starting position is not at the midpoint between thresholds. Information quality is represented by the drift rate, which is the average velocity toward one or the other threshold over many steps. Increment direction consistency becomes a continuous distribution, with specified variance, of the drift rate; this is usually termed a scaling constant, as it is semantically meaningful, but not mathematically necessary to fit data. The response time distribution is right-shifted by a variously specified element of non-decision time.

The diffusion model is a simple choice reaction time model; it was not developed for "slow" items, in which typical response times are above 1500 ms, or for "complex" items in which the information accumulated may be subdivided into different areas or tasks, or for polytomous items (Ratcliff and McKoon 2008). However, psychometricians already commonly approximate multiple-choice item responses as a single comparison between the correct response and an aggregate of all distractors; for example, the two-parameter and three-parameter logistic models are often used with items having more than two response options. In the absence of a clearly better process model, attempts have been made to adapt the diffusion models to psychometric items.

Tuerlinckx and De Boeck (2005) presented an amalgamation of the diffusion model with the two-parameter logistic model, although their model allowed for only a single latent trait, ability (θ).

Thissen-Roe and Finger (2014) proposed a closely related joint model, the diffusion two-parameter logistic model (D2PL), which includes a latent speed parameter τ. In that model, response time distributions are dependent on latent speed, item demands, and the latent attractiveness (or obviousness) of the response option to the individual, as given in the two-parameter logistic item response model (2PL). An example is shown in Fig. 6.1.

The D2PL has five item parameters (item response parameters a and c, and additional response time parameters w, m and β). The defective probability density function at time t is the partial derivative with respect to t of the defective cumulative density function. This is:

$$g\left(t,\delta,\upsilon\right) = \frac{\pi}{\delta^2} e^{\frac{\upsilon\delta}{2}} \sum_{k=1}^{\infty} k \sin\left(\frac{k\pi}{2}\right) e^{\frac{-1}{2}\left(\upsilon^2+\left(\frac{k\pi}{\delta}\right)^2\right)\left(\frac{t-e^{m\theta+\beta}}{w}\right)}$$

for correct responses and:

$$g\left(t,\delta,\upsilon\right) = \frac{\pi}{\delta^2} e^{\frac{-\upsilon\delta}{2}} \sum_{k=1}^{\infty} k \sin\left(\frac{k\pi}{2}\right) e^{\frac{-1}{2}\left(\upsilon^2+\left(\frac{k\pi}{\delta}\right)^2\right)\left(\frac{t-e^{m\theta+\beta}}{w}\right)}$$

for incorrect responses, where:

$$\upsilon = \frac{a\theta + c}{\delta}$$

and:

$$\delta = e^{-\tau}$$

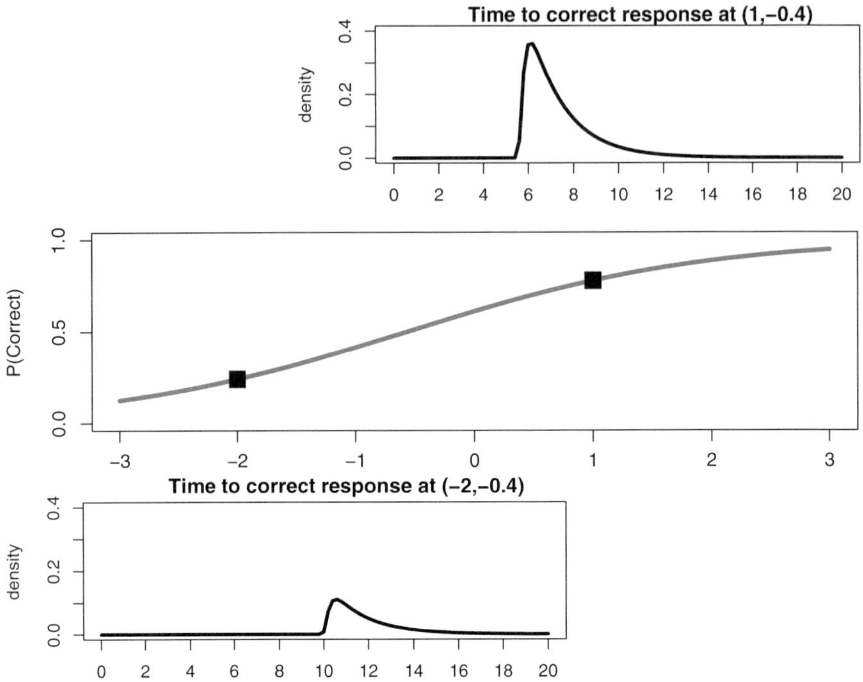

Fig. 6.1 An example of the diffusion two-parameter logistic (D2PL) model. Response time distributions for the correct response are shown for ($\theta = 1$, $\tau = -0.4$) and ($\theta = -2$, $\tau = -0.4$). The correct response is both less likely and slower when ability is lower, even given the same latent speed parameter

The summation is infinite; it may be terminated when its envelope function reaches a threshold for trivial increase of the total. The envelope function is the non-oscillating component:

$$f_{env} = ke^{\frac{-1}{2}\left(v^2+\left(\frac{k\pi}{\delta}\right)^2\right)\left(\frac{t-e^{m\theta+\beta}}{w}\right)}$$

The sum will be slow to terminate in some cases of improbable response times, requiring some hundreds of terms, even if only the nonzero odd terms are actually calculated.

The integral of $g(t,\delta,v)$ over all t equals the probability of each response given θ. That is to say, for any θ, the total probability of a given response at any time is equal to the probability of that response as predicted by the 2PL. In practice, obtaining a reasonable numeric approximation requires interpolation of the density functions at sub-second intervals.

6.3 Study 1: Hierarchical Model

6.3.1 Method

A simulation study was conducted to explore collusion detection in the following practical testing situation: An examination is constructed and calibrated on a large sample of individuals with no prior knowledge of any item. Following calibration, the test is used operationally. During the course of operational use, some test preparation centers provide preknowledge of some items to some of the examinees they serve. The administering group knows which examinees used which test preparation centers, but not which centers provided information about the items.

For the purpose of this study, it was assumed that an educated guess could be made about which items were compromised. For example, in an examination program where half the items are anchor items shared with another form or a previous testing cycle, suspicion might be largely limited to those anchor items.

The primary purpose of the study was to evaluate the contribution of the hierarchical response time model over and above its component item model, in this case the three-parameter logistic model (3PL). It also explored the effect of several situational factors on the successful identification of colluding individuals and centers: the number of centers involved in collusion (five levels), the scale of item compromise (two levels), the incidence of cheating (three levels), and the population correlation of latent ability and latent speed (two levels).

Item parameters for the hierarchical three-parameter logistic model (H3PL; van der Linden 2006) were generated at random according to a consistent set of hyperparameters for ten replicates of each combination of the latter three factors. In total, 120 sets of parameters were used. For each of 50 items on the test, two complete sets of item parameters were generated, representing two processes of item response: one reasoning process occurring under the intended conditions of general candidate knowledge, and one highly effective rapid recognition process occurring in the case of item preknowledge. Parameters for the 3PL model were generated with discrimination $a \sim \text{logN}(0,0.5)$, difficulty $b \sim \text{N}(0,1)$, and lower asymptote $c \sim \text{Beta}(1,5)$. Parameters for the lognormal response time model were discrimination $\alpha \sim \text{logN}(0,0.5)$ and difficulty $\beta \sim \text{N}(3,1)$.

"Cheating" was modeled as a fast recognition process with a high lower asymptote, operationalized by adding a constant 0.8 to $0.2c$, where c is the lower asymptote parameter in the reasoning condition. The a and b parameters are kept unchanged from their reasoning condition counterparts. Response times had the same discrimination distribution, but beta $\sim$ N(2,1). This choice of parameters is equivalent to an 80 % rate of substitution of the correct answer for that which would be obtained otherwise, coupled with a distribution of response times e times faster, consistent with practical observation.

Depending on the condition, 10 or 50 % of items were labeled suspect; of those, one half, at random, were "exposed" and received some responses from the cheating process.

Latent ability (θ) and speed (τ) parameters for each simulee were generated at random from a bivariate normal distribution with a population correlation of either 0.0 or 0.4.

For each set of item parameters, a calibration sample of 10,000 simulees was generated and used to obtain the item parameter estimates then used for analysis. An additional 2000 simulees, distributed across 20 centers with 100 simulees each, constituted the reference (non-collusion) sample. A target (collusion) sample of a further 2000 simulees was subdivided to obtain conditions of 1, 2, 5, and 10 as well as 20 equally sized centers involved in collusion. Within the target sample, 5, 10, or 20 % of simulees were designated as "cheaters," uniformly throughout latent trait space. These simulees used the cheating process for the items on which it was available.

Item parameters for the full joint model, including the population correlation, were estimated simultaneously from the calibration sample data, using a modified EM algorithm in two dimensions. Based on the obtained item parameters, latent ability and latent speed were estimated for all reference and target sample simulees. Two fit statistics were calculated for each simulee: the divergence of the joint posterior of latent ability and speed based on suspect items from the joint posterior based on non-suspect items, within an individual, and the loglikelihood of the entire pattern given the model. Latent ability was also estimated, and both fit statistics calculated, based on the 3PL without reference to response time.

Identification of groups and individuals was carried out independently for each model (H3PL and 3PL) and fit statistic (divergence and loglikelihood), in order to compare the efficacy of each configuration. The critical value for identification of suspect groups was set to one standard deviation above the mean, an intentionally liberal criterion suitable for a first hurdle. The critical value for identification of likely colluding individuals was set to 1.96 standard deviations above the mean of individuals in non-suspect groups, for a casewise Type I error rate of 0.025.

6.3.2 Results

In Stage One, in which suspect centers are labeled, there was a pronounced joint effect of model type, fit statistic, and number of target centers. As shown in Fig. 6.2, the H3PL model and divergence fit statistic yielded higher detection of target centers than any other combination, when there were 1, 2, 5, or 10 target centers. The remainder of the methods were barely above chance detection, as demonstrated by the obtained rate of false positives. At 20 target centers (and, as always, 20 reference centers), the method ceased to be effective for any model and statistic. This is not surprising; divergence between two centers is calculated bilaterally, and the relative positions on the fit statistic are not considered. Two equally sized clusters of centers at different locations on the fit statistic continuum leave the method without a cue to determine which cluster is "reference" and which is "target;" detection is at chance.

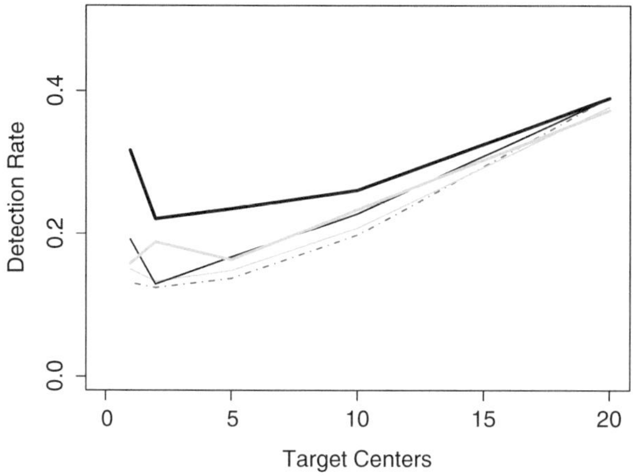

Fig. 6.2 Target center detection rate as a function of the number of target centers in the sample (*horizontal axis*), the model used (*black lines* for H3PL; *light grey* for 3PL), and the fit statistic (*thick lines* for divergence; *thin lines* for loglikelihood). The false positive rate is shown as a *dark grey dotted line*; only the divergence method combined with H3PL (*thick black line*) substantially exceeds it, and only when the number of target centers is smaller than the number of reference centers

The divergence fit statistic yielded better results when cheating behavior was more prevalent within target centers. Both fit statistics yielded better results when 50 % of the items were suspected compromised, versus 10 %; it is intuitive that model misfit occurring on 12 or 13 items out of 50 would be more detectable than misfit occurring on 2 or 3 items. Unexpectedly, the joint models did not perform better when θ and τ were positively correlated than when they were uncorrelated.

In Stage Two, in which individuals are identified, there was a joint effect of model type, fit statistic, and the scale of item compromise. When the two-pass methodology was used with H3PL and the divergence fit statistic, where there were 1–10 target centers, and 25 items (50 %) were suspected with half of those actually compromised, the correct identification rate was 15–22 %. With only five items (10 %) suspected, the correct identification rate was 6–8 %. (The false positive rate was 0.7 %.) The effect was only partly induced by the higher success rate of Stage One in the case of the more severely compromised test. With target centers correctly identified, individuals were detected 53 % of the time in the 50 % compromise case, and 27 % of the time in the 10 % compromise case.

The combination of non-response time 3PL with the divergence statistic fared more poorly: 5–7 % correct in the two-pass, severely compromised case; 1–2 % in the mildly compromised case. When the correct centers were identified, the rates rose to 26 and 12 %. The loglikelihood statistic was even worse, regardless of model. Even with response time in the model, the true centers identified and large-scale compromise, it only detected 9 % of simulated cheaters.

There were no meaningful effects of latent trait correlation or cheating prevalence within colluding samples on individual detection.

6.4 Study 2: Diffusion Model

6.4.1 Method

A second simulation study was conducted under the same practical paradigm, but using the diffusion two-parameter logistic model (D2PL), with the 2PL for comparison. An additional variable of interest was included; test length was either 10, 15, or 20 items, to simulate an analysis of a highly homogenous subtest rather than an entire certification exam.

Item parameters for the D2PL were generated at random according to a parallel set of hyperparameters. The 2PL response model was generated with discrimination $a \sim \text{logN}(0,0.5)$ and intercept $c \sim \text{N}(0,1)$. The response time model used parameters $w \sim \text{logN}(3.2,0.7)$, $m \sim \text{N}(-1.7,0.3)$ and $\beta \sim \text{N}(3.7,0.4)$. Cheating was modeled as an entirely distinct rapid recognition process with a generally higher rate of success; however, reasoning was permitted to be more reliable than recognition for some items and some examinees. Parameters used were $a \sim \text{logN}(-1,0.5)$, $c \sim \text{N}(3,1)$, $w \sim \text{logN}(2.2,0.7)$, $m \sim \text{N}(-0.57,0.1)$, and $\beta \sim \text{N}(2.7,0.4)$.

In the interests of efficiency, and to accommodate the greater computational demands of the D2PL, the same item parameters and calibration sample were used for all three levels of cheating incidence, within a condition defined by test length, scale of compromise, and correlation of ability and speed. However, separate reference and target samples were simulated for the three levels. A total of 120 sets of item parameters were used: ten replicates of each condition.

The remainder of the procedures, including calibration, calculation of fit statistics, and identification of suspect groups and individuals, were carried out as in Study 1.

6.4.2 Results

As in Study 1, in Stage One, the joint model (D2PL) and divergence fit statistic outperformed all other combinations at correctly identifying centers, so long as target centers were in the minority (1, 2, 5 or 10 centers). This result is shown in Fig. 6.3.

Again, the divergence fit statistic yielded better results when cheating behavior was more prevalent within target centers. There were no meaningful effects of scale of compromise, latent trait correlation, or test length.

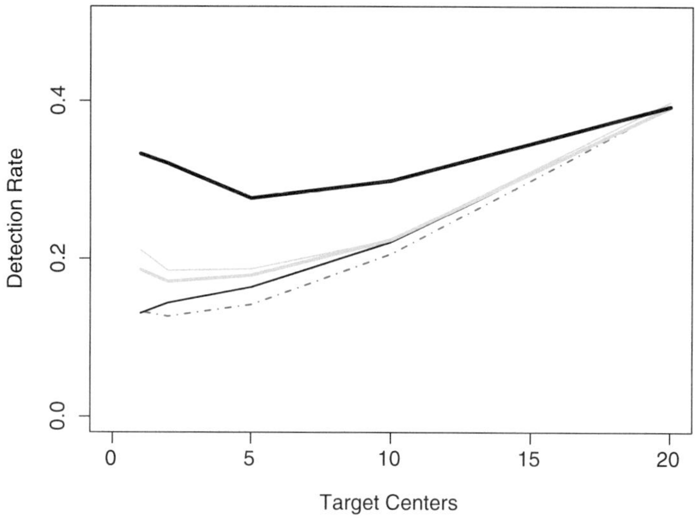

Fig. 6.3 Target center detection rate as a function of the number of target centers in the sample (*horizontal axis*), the model used (*black lines* for D2PL; *light grey* for 2PL), and the fit statistic (*thick lines* for divergence; *thin lines* for loglikelihood). Only the divergence method combined with D2PL (*thick black line*) substantially exceeds the rate of false positives (*dotted line*)

In Stage Two, in which individuals are identified, the joint model and divergence fit statistic again outperformed the other combinations. The two-pass method resulted in 7–10 % correct detection, versus 3–4 % for runner-up 3PL with the divergence fit statistic. With centers correctly identified, the D2PL identified individuals with 22 % accuracy, and the 3PL was 16 % accurate. With the loglikelihood statistic, even with centers correctly identified, the 2PL's accuracy was only 8 %, and the D2PL was actually worse, at 6 %.

There were no meaningful effects of latent trait correlation or test length within colluding samples on individual detection. The effects of cheating prevalence and scale of compromise were inconsistently observed, but in the expected direction where present.

6.5 Discussion

In both studies, there was a clear contribution of joint response time models above and beyond their item response components. The scale of the improvement is influenced by the particular sets of item response and response time model hyperparameters chosen to represent reasoning and recognition (collusion) behaviors. The hyperparameters were not based on any particular dataset and should not, for example, be used to compare the H3PL to the D2PL.

It is also worth noting that the selected hyperparameters led to moderate effect sizes and limited detection, with less than 40 % correct identification of centers and even lower identification rates for individuals. Correct identification could be increased by choosing more liberal critical values, particularly in Stage One. However, increases in detection must be balanced with the need to keep false positive rates low in practical situations, where the consequences of being labeled a "cheater" may be severe. Under the simulated conditions, the observed false positive rates were consistently well below 1 % for individuals.

In the case where homogenous subtests are used for detection, as simulated in Study 2, independent screens based on multiple subtests could generate a longer list of suspects with an indication of priority; further investigation is needed to fully determine true and false positive rates in that case.

Caution should be used in applying these methods of collusion detection, due to the high stakes for test takers and testing programs; independent verification of findings is advisable.

In conclusion, a pair of simulation studies found the inclusion of response time as well as response correctness to benefit model-based collusion detection. Belov's (2013) divergence method is effective when used with joint response time models and its own divergence-based fit statistic, and when colluding groups are the minority; however, the method does not perform as well with a non-tailored fit statistic. Accuracy is higher when the scale of compromise is greater and when cheating is more prevalent (20 % versus 5 %) in groups where compromise exists.

References

Belov, D. I. (2013). Detection of test collusion via Kullback–Leibler divergence. *Journal of Educational Measurement, 50*(2), 141–163.

Carroll, J. R. (1993). *Human cognitive abilities: A survey of factor-analytic studies*. Cambridge, UK: Cambridge University Press.

Finger, M., & Chuah, S. C. (2009). *Response-time model estimation via confirmatory factor analysis*. Paper presented at the Annual Meeting of the National Council on Measurement in Education, San Diego, CA.

Laming, D. R. J. (1968). *Information theory of choice reaction time*. New York: Wiley.

Link, S. W., & Heath, R. A. (1975). A sequential theory of psychological discrimination. *Psychometrika, 40*, 77–105.

Ratcliff, R. (1978). A theory of memory retrieval. *Psychological Review, 85*, 59–108.

Ratcliff, R., & McKoon, G. (2008). The diffusion decision model: Theory and data for two-choice decision tasks. *Neural Computation, 20*, 873–922.

Ratcliff, R., & Rouder, J. F. (1998). Modeling response times for two-choice decisions. *Psychological Science, 9*, 347–356.

Ratcliff, R., & Smith, P. L. (2004). A comparison of sequential sampling models for two-choice reaction time. *Psychological Review, 111*, 333–367.

Ratcliff, R., & Tuerlinckx, F. (2002). Estimating the parameters of the diffusion model: Approaches to dealing with contaminant reaction times and parameter variability. *Psychonomic Bulletin and Review, 9*, 438–481.

Ratcliff, R., Van Zandt, T., & McKoon, G. (1999). Connectionist and diffusion models of reaction time. *Psychological Review, 106*, 261–300.

Stone, M. (1960). Models for choice reaction time. *Psychometrika, 25*, 251–260.

Thissen-Roe, A., & Finger, M. S. (2014). *Speed, speededness, and the price of high information.* Paper presented at the Meeting of the Society for Industrial-Organizational Psychology, Honolulu, HI.

Tuerlinckx, F., & De Boeck, P. (2005). Two interpretations of the discrimination parameter. *Psychometrika, 70*, 629–650.

van der Linden, W. J. (2006). A lognormal model for response times on test items. *Journal of Educational and Behavioral Statistics, 31*, 181–204.

van der Linden, W. J. (2007). A hierarchical framework for modeling speed and accuracy on test items. *Psychometrika, 72*, 287–308.

Chapter 7
The Performance of the Modified Multidimensional Priority Index for Item Selection in Variable-Length MCAT

Ya-Hui Su

Abstract In addition to statistical optimization, an important issue in computerized adaptive testing (CAT) is to fulfill a large number of statistical and non-statistical constraints for the construction of assessments. The priority index (PI) approaches can be used for item selection to monitor many constraints simultaneously. Many previous studies on item selection methods were conducted in fixed-length multidimensional CAT (MCAT); however, studies in variable-length MCAT were paid little attention. To achieve the same level of precision for examinees, the purpose of the study was to investigate the modified multidimensional priority index (MMPI-v) and multidimensional priority index (MPI) in variable-length MCAT through simulations. It was found that the MMPI-v method outperformed the MPI in terms of constraint management, and the MMPI-v used fewer items than the MPI method did to meet the required measurement precision.

Keywords Computer adaptive testing • Priority index • Multidimensional • Item selection • IRT • Variable length

7.1 Background and Purpose

An important issue in computerized adaptive testing (CAT) is to fulfill a large number of statistical and non-statistical constraints for the construction of assessments, such as item exposure control, content balancing, key balancing, and so on. The priority index (PI; Cheng and Chang 2009; Cheng et al. 2009) and multidimensional priority index (MPI; Yao 2011, 2012, 2013) can be used to handle many constraints simultaneously for CAT and multidimensional CAT (MCAT), respectively. The MPI item selection method was developed for the CAT Armed Services Vocational Aptitude Battery (CAT ASVAB), which is a between-item MCAT test. To extend

Y.-H. Su (✉)
Department of Psychology, National Chung Cheng University, No. 168, Sec. 1, University Road, Min-Hsiung Township, Chiayi County 621, Taiwan
e-mail: psyyhs@ccu.edu.tw

L.A. van der Ark et al. (eds.), *Quantitative Psychology Research*, Springer Proceedings in Mathematics & Statistics 140, DOI 10.1007/978-3-319-19977-1_7

the MPI item selection method to a within-item multidimensional framework, the modified multidimensional priority index (MMPI; Su and Huang 2014) was proposed for item selection in fixed-length MCATs.

The stopping rule is used to stop a cyclical item selection process in CATs (Reckase 2009; Wainer 2000). When a stopping rule of fixed-length is considered in CATs, measurement precisions are different for different ability levels and it results in a high misclassification rate, which might be costly. To achieve the same level of precision for examinees, a stopping rule of fixed-precision can be used in CATs. Some examinees may need to take more items and some may need to take fewer items when fixed-precision is considered. The administered tests for certain examinees may be undesirably lengthy or short because the required precision cannot be met or few items have improved the precision significantly. Under the unidimensional framework, some studies have been done on using different stopping rules in CAT (Dodd et al. 1993), such as the minimum standard error (SE) stopping rule, the minimum information stopping rule (Dodd et al. 1989), and the predicted standard error reduction (PSER) stopping rule (Choi et al. 2011). Under the multidimensional framework, many previous studies on item selection methods were conducted in fixed-length MCATs (Mulder and van der Linden 2009; Su and Huang 2014; Wang et al. 2011a, b; Yao 2011, 2012). However, studies on item selection methods were paid little attention in variable-length MCATs (Yao 2013).

The MPI item selection method can be used in MCAT for item selection under the fixed-length (Yao 2011, 2012) and variable-length (Yao 2013) conditions. The MMPI item selection method can be used for item selection in fixed-length MCATs (Su and Huang 2014), but it hasn't been investigated under the variable-length condition. Both the MPI and MMPI item selection methods can be implemented easily and computed efficiently so they are important and useful for operational CAT. However, no thorough simulation study has compared the performance of these two methods in variable-length MCATs. Therefore, the purposes of the study were to investigate the performance of the MPI and MMPI item selection methods on monitoring constraints in MCATs when a stopping rule of fixed-precision was considered.

7.1.1 The Multidimensional Priority Index Method

For each item i, Yao (2011) defined the MPI as

$$\mathrm{MPI}_i = \prod_{d=1}^{D} {f_{id}}^{c_{id}}, \tag{7.1}$$

where the c_{id} is the loading information for item i on dimension d. The term $c_{id} = 1$ if item i is from dimension d, and $c_{id} = 0$ otherwise. For each item selection step, the item with the largest MPI will be selected for administration. The estimated dimension precision, item exposure rate, and content constraints with upper and lower bounds are included to define f_{id} in variable-length MCATs (Yao 2013) as

$$f_{id} = [\max\{[1 - (\frac{p_d}{\widehat{p}_d})^a + \varepsilon_1], 0\}][\max\{(\frac{r_i - n_i/N}{r_i}), 0\}]$$
$$[1_{x_d \le l_d}(\frac{l_d - x_d}{l_d} + \varepsilon_2/x_d) + 1_{x_d > l_d}\max\{1 - (\frac{x_d}{u_d})^b, 0\}], \quad (7.2)$$

where p_d and $\widehat{p}_d$ are the required standard error of measurement (SEM) and the SEM estimates based on the administered items for the dimension d ability estimates, respectively. The first term in Eq. (7.2) is used to achieve the same level of precision for examinees. The larger the SEM, the smaller the precision. The second term in Eq. (7.2) is used to ensure that no item is selected more than a pre-specified item exposure rate r_i. N is the total number of examinees. For each item selection step, n_i is the number of examinees who have seen item i. The third term in Eq. (7.2) is used to handle content specifications. The lower and upper bounds of each dimension d are l_d and u_d, respectively. For each item selection step, x_d is the number of selected items from dimension d. When the constraint is met, no further items will be selected for a specific constraint. The smaller the values of a and b, the larger the weights given to the precision. ε_1 is used to ensure that precision is obtained slightly above the required measurement precision. ε_2 is used to meet the lower bound for the dimension d.

The MPI item selection method was developed to handle the constraints for the CAT ASVAB test (Yao 2011, 2012, 2013), which is the between-item multidimensional test. The items from the same battery are assumed to measure only one distinct latent trait, and the overall assessment is assumed to measure four different latent traits. In practice, some other tests might have a within-item multidimensional structure such that individual items are intended to assess multiple latent traits.

7.1.2 The Modified Multidimensional Priority Index Method

Su and Huang (2014) extended the MPI item selection method to the between-item multidimensional framework with a stopping rule of fixed-length. For each item i, the MMPI is defined as

$$\text{MMPI}_i = Inf_i \times \prod_{k=1}^{j} w_k f_k^{c_{ik}} \times \sqrt{\sum_{k=j+1}^{K} \left[w_k c_{ik} f_k\right)\right]^2}, \quad (7.3)$$

where the c_{ik} is the loading information for item i on constraint k. The term $c_{ik} = 1$ if item i is from constraint k and $c_{ik} = 0$ otherwise. Each constraint k is associated with a weight w_k, which depends on its importance. For each item selection step, the item with the largest MMPI will be selected for administration. The first term in Eq. (7.3) is the item information, which is the determinant of the Fisher information matrix. The second term in Eq. (7.3) includes the between-dimension constraints, such as item exposure control and key balancing in a unidimensional or between-item multidimensional pool. When the item selection is considered in unidimensional CATs, only the first two terms in Eq. (7.3) are included to calculate the MMPI. The third term in Eq. (7.3) includes the within-dimension constraints, such as content balancing in a within-item multidimensional pool.

When considering the flexible content balancing, l_k and u_k are lower and upper bounds of content area k, respectively. μ_k is the number of items to be selected from content area k. L is test length. Then,

$$l_k \leq \mu_k \leq u_k, \tag{7.4}$$

and

$$\sum_{k=1}^{K} \mu_k = L. \tag{7.5}$$

A two-phase item selection is to fulfill the lower bounds in the first phase and the upper bounds in the second phase. To incorporate both upper bounds and lower bounds, f_k for a one-phase item selection strategy can be replaced with $f_{1k}f_{2k}$, which f_{1k} and f_{2k} are defined as

$$f_{1k} = \frac{1}{u_k}\left(u_k - x_k\right), \tag{7.6}$$

and

$$f_{2k} = \frac{(L - l_k) - (t - x_k)}{L - l_k}, \tag{7.7}$$

respectively. f_{1k} measures the closeness to the upper bound whereas f_{2k} measures the closeness to the lower bound. t is the number of items that have already been administered and $t = \sum_{k=1}^{K} x_k$. When f_{2k} is equal to 0, it means that the sum of items from other contents has reached its maximum; $f_{1k}f_{2k}$ is defined as 1 to ensure that items from content k can be still included for item selection. When considering item exposure control, f_k can be defined as

$$f_k = \frac{1}{r_{\max}}\left(r_{\max} - \frac{n_i}{N}\right), \tag{7.8}$$

where the N is the number of examinees who have taken the CAT, n is the number of examinees who have seen item i, and r_{max} is a pre-specified item exposure rate. n_i/N is the provisional exposure rate after N examinees have taken the CATs.

7.2 Method

7.2.1 *Data Generation*

In this study, the multidimensional three-parameter logistic (M3PL; Reckase 1985) model was used for data generation. The probability of getting a correct response for examinee n with d-dimensional latent traits $\boldsymbol{\theta}'_n = (\theta_1, \theta_2, \ldots, \theta_d)$ is defined as

$$p_{ni1} = c_i + (1\text{-}c_i)\frac{\exp\left[\mathbf{a}'_i(\boldsymbol{\theta}_n - b_i\mathbf{1})\right]}{1 + \exp\left[\mathbf{a}'_i(\boldsymbol{\theta}_n - b_i\mathbf{1})\right]}, \tag{7.9}$$

where $\mathbf{a}_i$ is a $d \times 1$ vector of the discrimination parameter; b_i and c_i are the difficulty and the guessing parameters of item i, respectively; and $\mathbf{1}$ is a $d \times 1$ vector of 1s.

The item parameters and pool structure in this study were adapted from Su and Huang's paper (2014). One thousand M3PL items were generated to form a within-item two-dimensional pool, in which 40 % items measured the first dimension, 30 % items measured the second dimension, and the rest 30 % items measured both dimensions. The discrimination parameters were drawn from a uniform distribution on the interval of real numbers (0.5, 1.5) for each dimension, difficulty parameters were drawn from a standard normal distribution, and guessing parameters were drawn from a uniform distribution on (0, 0.4). The numbers of content areas simulated for two dimensions was 3 and 2. All 5000 simulated examinees are drawn from a multivariate standard normal distribution with correlation 0.8.

7.2.2 *Simulation Design*

Eight constraints were considered in the study, including content balancing, required measurement precision, item exposure control, and item information. The corresponding weights, upper bounds, and lower bounds of the constraints list in Table 7.1. Three levels of the required measurement precision, 0.25, 0.30, and 0.35, were used as the stopping rules of fixed-precision in MCAT. The maximum item exposure rates of items were set at 0.20. The determinant of Fisher information matrix was used as item information in MCAT. The maximum a posteriori (MAP) estimation with a multivariate standard normal distribution (correlation is set at 0.8) prior was used to estimate $\widehat{\boldsymbol{\theta}}$.

The MMPI item selection method was developed in fixed-length MCAT (Su and Huang 2014). In this study, the MMPI was modified in a fixed-precision condition, which was named as MMPI-v. This study compared the performance of the MMPI-v and MPI item selection methods in variable-length MCAT. Since the item information was already included by the MMPI-v item selection method in Eq. (7.3), the MPI method in Eq. (7.1) was modified by multiplying item information for item selection. For each item selection step, both methods were

Table 7.1 Constraints and weights for item selection

Constraints	Weight	Lower bound	Upper bound
Dimension 1—Content 1	1	5	9
Dimension 1—Content 2	1	7	13
Dimension 1—Content 3	1	6	11
Dimension 2—Content 1	1	6	14
Dimension 2—Content 2	1	7	16
Required measurement precision	1		0.25/0.30/0.35
Item exposure rate	1		0.20
Item information	1		

multiplied by determinant of Fisher information matrix for item selection. Then, an item with maximum value for the MPI or MMPI-v was selected for administration. Each MCAT item selection method was stopped if the required measurement precision had been achieved.

7.2.3 Evaluation Criteria

The results of the simulations were analyzed and discussed based on the following criteria: constraint management, measurement precision, and test length. The measurement precision was evaluated by the SEM estimates based on the administered items for the dimension d ability estimates. The test length was the averaged test lengths over all examinees while different stopping rules and different MCAT item selection methods were used. The constraint management was to check whether the test sequentially assembling for each examinee met all the specified test-construction constraints. The number of violated constraints for each examinee was recorded, and the averaged number of violated constraints for examinees was calculated by

$$\overline{V} = \frac{\sum_{n=1}^{N} V_n}{N}, \tag{7.10}$$

where V_n represents the number of constraint violations in the nth examinees' test.

7.3 Results

For each dimension, examinees were classified into six levels: $\{\theta < -2\}$, $\{-2 \leqq \theta < -1\}$, $\{-1 \leqq \theta < 0\}$, $\{0 \leqq \theta < 1\}$, $\{1 \leqq \theta < 2\}$, and $\{2 \leqq \theta\}$. Due to the space limitations, the measurement precision and test length of the item selection methods when the required measurement precision was 0.35 and 0.25 were summarized in Table 7.2. The MMPI-v and MPI item selection methods performed well in obtaining the measurement precision to meet the required measurement precision at both levels. When the required measurement precision was 0.35, the MMPI-v item selection method needed 16–20 items whereas the MPI item selection method needed 20–30 items. When the required measurement precision was 0.25, the MMPI-v item selection method needed 25–35 items whereas the MPI item selection method needed 37–45 items. Although both item selection methods could achieve similar measurement precision, the MMPI-v item selection method used fewer items than the MPI method did, which was about 5 and 11 items when the required precision was 0.35 and 0.25, respectively. It was found that more items were needed when the required measurement precision was small. It was also found that more items were needed for examinees with extreme ability.

Since the violation was considered at each examinee level, only the first seven constraints in Table 7.1 were included to evaluate the efficiency of the constraint management. When the required measurement precision was 0.35, the averaged number of violated constraints for the MMPI-v and MPI item selection methods were 0.00 and 0.08 items, respectively. When the required measurement precision was 0.25, the averaged number of violated constraints for the MMPI-v and MPI item selection methods were 0.00 and 2.01 items, respectively. The MMPI-v item selection method performed better than the MPI method in terms of constraint management no matter when the required measurement precision was set high or low.

Table 7.2 Measurement precision and test length for the item selection methods

	MMPI-v				MPI			
	SEM		Test length		SEM		Test length	
Level	Dim1	Dim2	Dim1	Dim2	Dim1	Dim2	Dim1	Dim2
Required measurement precision = 0.35								
1	0.35	0.35	23	25	0.35	0.35	28	30
2	0.35	0.35	20	22	0.35	0.34	23	27
3	0.35	0.34	17	18	0.35	0.34	20	23
4	0.34	0.34	16	17	0.34	0.35	24	20
5	0.35	0.35	19	20	0.34	0.35	27	25
6	0.35	0.35	24	23	0.35	0.35	30	29
Required measurement precision = 0.25								
1	0.25	0.25	35	34	0.25	0.25	43	44
2	0.24	0.25	29	30	0.24	0.25	44	42
3	0.25	0.24	25	26	0.24	0.24	42	38
4	0.25	0.24	28	27	0.25	0.25	39	37
5	0.25	0.25	30	29	0.25	0.25	42	40
6	0.25	0.25	33	32	0.25	0.25	45	42

7.4 Discussion

The MMPI item selection method can be implemented with various constraints efficiently under the fixed-length condition (Su and Huang 2014); however, the measurement precision cannot guarantee be to equal for all examinees. It might misclassify the examinees with extreme abilities. Many previous studies on MCAT item selection methods were conducted under the fixed-length condition; however, studies under the fixed-precision condition were paid little attention. To achieve the same level of precision for examinees, this study investigated the performance of the MMPI-v and the MPI in variable-length MCAT through simulations. It was found that the MMPI-v item selection method used fewer items than the MPI method did to meet the required measurement precision. It was also found that the MMPI-v item selection method outperformed the MPI method in terms of constraint management. The MMPI-v item selection method is recommended for item selection under the variable-length condition.

The MMPI-v item selection method can be implemented easily and computed efficiently. The research findings from this study will advance our knowledge for item selection in variable-length MCAT. However, this study has some limitations that can be addressed in future work. First, the determinant of Fisher information matrix was used as the constraint related to item information in the study. There are different item selection procedures related to item information, such as minimum angle (Reckase 2009), minimize the error variance of the linear combination (van der Linden 1999), Kullback–Leibler (KL) information (Veldkamp and van der Linden 2002), and so on. Yao (2013) found that the KL information used the least numbers of items among five different item selection procedures under the variable-length condition. It might be worth to replace the maximum volume of the information with the KL information for the MMPI-v item selection method and investigate its efficiency under the variable-length condition. Second, the algorithms of the MMPI-v item selection method were derived for M3PL model, which is for multidimensional dichotomous items. It might be useful to be extended for multidimensional polytomous items because the polytomous items provide more information than dichotomous items do. Third, to integrate the MMPI-v item selection method with the other item exposure control or test overlap control procedures needs to be investigated as well.

References

Cheng, Y., & Chang, H.-H. (2009). The maximum priority index method for severely constrained item selection in computerized adaptive testing. *British Journal of Mathematical and Statistical Psychology, 62*, 369–383.

Cheng, Y., Chang, H.-H., Douglas, J., & Guo, F. (2009). Constraint-weighted *a*-stratification for computerized adaptive testing with nonstatistical constraints: Balancing measurement efficiency and exposure control. *Educational and Psychological Measurement, 69*, 35–49.

Choi, S. W., Grady, M., & Dodd, B. G. (2011). A new stopping rule for computerized adaptive testing. *Educational and Psychological Measurement, 71*, 37–73.

Dodd, B. G., Koch, W. R., & De Ayala, R. J. (1989). Operational characteristics of adaptive testing procedures using the graded response model. *Applied Psychological Measurement, 13*, 129–143.

Dodd, B. G., Koch, W. R., & De Ayala, R. J. (1993). Computerized adaptive testing using the partial credit model: Effects of item pool characteristics and different stopping rules. *Educational and Psychological Measurement, 53*, 61–77.

Mulder, J., & van der Linden, W. J. (2009). Multidimensional adaptive testing with optimal design criteria for item selection. *Psychometrika, 74*, 273–296.

Reckase, M. D. (1985). The difficulty of test items that measure more than one dimension. *Applied Psychological Measurement, 9*, 401–412.

Reckase, M. D. (2009). *Multidimensional item response theory*. New York, NY: Springer.

Su, Y.-H., & Huang, Y.-L. (2014). Using a modified multidimensional priority index for item selection under within-item multidimensional computerized adaptive testing. In R. E. Millsap, D. M. Bolt, L. A. van der Ark, & W.-C. Wang (Eds.), *Quantitative psychology research: The 78th annual meeting of the psychometric society* (pp. 227–242). Switzerland: Springer.

van der Linden, W. J. (1999). Multidimensional adaptive testing with a minimum error-variance criterion. *Journal of Educational and Behavioral Statistics, 24*, 398–412.

Veldkamp, B. P., & van der Linden, W. J. (2002). Multidimensional adaptive testing with constraints on test content. *Psychometrika, 67*, 575–588.

Wainer, H. (Ed.). (2000). *Computerized adaptive testing: A primer* (2nd ed.). Mahwah, NJ: Erlbaum.

Wang, C., Chang, H.-H., & Boughton, K. (2011a). Kullback–Leibler information and its applications in multi-dimensional adaptive testing. *Psychometrika, 76*, 13–39.

Wang, C., Chang, H.-H., & Huebner, A. (2011b). Restrictive stochastic item selection methods in cognitive diagnostic computerized adaptive testing. *Journal of Educational Measurement, 48*, 255–273.

Yao, L. (2011, October). *Multidimensional CAT item selection procedures with item exposure control and content constraints*. Paper presented at the (2011) International Association of Computer Adaptive Testing (IACAT) Conference, Pacific Grove, CA.

Yao, L. (2012). Multidimensional CAT item selection methods for domain scores and composite scores: Theory and applications. *Psychometrika, 77*, 495–523.

Yao, L. (2013). Comparing the performance of five multidimensional CAT selection procedures with different stopping rules. *Applied Psychological Measurement, 37*, 3–23.

Chapter 8
A Nonparametric Estimator of a Monotone Item Characteristic Curve

Mario Luzardo and Pilar Rodríguez

Abstract This paper presents a nonparametric approach to estimating item characteristic curves (ICCs) when they should be monotonic. First, it addresses the uni-dimensional case; before generalizing it to the multidimensional case.

This is a two-stage process. The first stage uses a nonparametric estimator of the ICC by means of nonparametric kernel regression; the second uses the above result to estimate the density function of the inverse ICC.

By integrating this density function, we obtain an isotonic estimator of the inverse ICC: symmetrized with respect to the bisector of the unit square, to obtain the ICC estimator. We also present the multidimensional case, in which we proceed on a coordinate-by-coordinate basis.

Keywords Nonparametric • Isotone • Item response theory

8.1 Introduction

The most popular approach to item response theory (IRT) is to use parametric models: such as one-, two- or three-parameter logistic or normal ogive models; the Rasch model is currently the most popular. The literature on these models is extensive: most notably Lord (1980), Hambleton et al. (1991), Fischer and Molenaar (1995), Van der Linden and Hambleton (1997), Boomsma et al. (2001), and Baker and Kim (2004). The models determine the shape of the item characteristic curve (ICC), depending on a fixed, very small number of parameters; but none take non-monotonic items or systematic departures of shape into consideration, and they are not flexible (Douglas 1997; Douglas and Cohen 2001; Ramsay 1991).

M. Luzardo (✉)
School of Psychology, University of the Republic, Montevideo, Uruguay
e-mail: mluzardov@gmail.com

P. Rodríguez
University Center East Regional, University of the Republic, Maldonado, Uruguay
e-mail: prodriguez@cure.edu.uy

L.A. van der Ark et al. (eds.), *Quantitative Psychology Research*, Springer Proceedings in Mathematics & Statistics 140, DOI 10.1007/978-3-319-19977-1_8

In parametric models, methods for estimating ICC include joint maximum likelihood, marginal maximum likelihood, and conditional maximum likelihood estimation; but if the assumptions of uni-dimensionality and local independence are violated, estimations of item parameters and the ability are poor. Departures from the three-parameter model have been noted while the parameter estimates of these models have very large sampling co-variations (Lord 1980).

Several alternative methods, based on quasi-parametric or nonparametric approaches, have been developed to deal with these issues. There has been considerable research on those models which are not based solely on a parametric approach: such as the partial spline model, which is partly parametric and partly nonparametric (Wahba 1990) or models based on a linear combination of basis functions. One of these methods—nonparametric item response theory (NIRT)—was shown to be more flexible than that offered by parametric models. The first nonparametric models were proposed by Mokken (1971), Niemoller and van Schuur (1983), Mokken and Lewis (1982), Sijtsma (1988), and Giampaglia (1990). More recently, Mokken (1997), Sijtsma (1998, 2001), Molenaar and Sijtsma (2000), Junker (2001), and Junker and Sijtsma (2001) presented new results.

Two models stand out: the monotonic homogeneity and double monotonicity models. The mathematical treatment for the former can be found in Holland and Rosenbaum (1986), Holland (1990), Stout (1987, 1990), Junker (1993), and Ellis and Junker (1997). Mokken (1971) showed that if the monotone homogeneity model is assumed, and the prerequisites of uni-dimensionality, local independence and monotonicity are fulfilled, covariance between all item pairs is nonnegative. In addition, Rosenbaum (1984) and Holland and Rosenbaum (1986) proved the conditional association in monotonic latent trait models. Meijer et al. (1990) provided a thoughtful comparison between parametric and nonparametric models; as did De Koning et al. (2002). Readers interested in a basic introduction to NIRT should refer to Sijtsma and Molenaar (2002).

Douglas et al. (1998) provided methods with which to investigate local independence. Methods of studying non-decreasing ICCs from a practical standpoint were presented in Ramsay (1991), Molenaar and Sijtsma (2000), and Douglas and Cohen (2001). Mokken (1971) employed the H coefficient developed by Loevinger (1947) for scale evaluation. He proposed that a scale is weak if $0.3 \leq H < 0.4$, moderate if $0.4 \leq H < 0.5$, and strong if $H \geq 0.5$. Grayson (1988) showed that the total score (conditioned to θ) has a monotone likelihood: such that $\frac{P(X_+=t|\theta)}{P(X_+=s|\theta)}$, $0 \leq s < t \leq n$ is non-decreasing as a function of θ, then $X_+|\theta$ is an optimal statistic for the binary classification.

In order to estimate ability, we must use indirect methods. A first alternative is to utilize the total score, which has monotone likelihood and is positively correlated with the trait. Schriever (1985) suggested using multiple correspondence analyses; the first component of the correlations matrix determining ability. Lewis (1983) favored a Bayesian method, which also makes it possible to obtain confidence intervals for the trait.

Ramsay (1991) presents an alternative method, which aims to estimate the ICC through nonparametric kernel regression, and can be considered a functional data analysis technique. This approach is implemented in TestGraf software (Ramsay

2000). Douglas (1997) proved the joint consistency for the uni-dimensional case while Luzardo and Forteza (2014) proved conditions for joint consistency in the multidimensional one.

As regards monotonic estimates of regression functions, we have found a wide range of methods, such as those proposed by Cheng and Linn (1981), Wright (1981), Friedman and Tibshirani (1984), Delecroix and Thomas-Agnan (2000), or Gijbels (2005) and Mammen (1991). Brunk (1955) proposes a method—later modified by Mukerjee (1988)—for obtaining estimators with similar properties to those of nonparametric regression. Ramsay (1988, 1998) and Kelly and Rice (1990) propose using splines. Ramsay (1988), for example, estimates the functions by taking linear combinations of monotone regression splines. Later, Ramsay (1998) uses a semiparametric approach which requires that the ICC satisfies a second-order differential equation, $D^2P = wDP$ where $w \in L^2$. The solution of this equation is of the form $P(\theta) = C_0 + C_1 \int_0^\theta exp(\int_0^\theta w(x)dx)dx$ where C_0 and C_1 are constants. As a consequence, the estimator is not consistent in general. Finally, Hall and Huang (2001) use the kernel-type estimator with modified weights while Dette et al. (2006) deploy a two-step estimator.

Lee (2007) studies the performance of three nonparametric methods of estimating ICCs, and compares the Ramsay model with isotonic regression and smoothed isotonic regression. The isotonic regression and smoothed isotonic regression methods estimate ICCs under the constraint of monotonicity. This paper will build on the estimator model proposed by Dette et al. (2006) for our estimation of monotonic ICCs in the uni-dimensional and multidimensional cases.

8.2 Multidimensional Ramsay Model

Our model is based on nonparametric kernel regression. Ramsay (1991) introduced this approach in the uni-dimensional case; and Douglas (1997) proved the joint consistency of traits and ICCs.

Let us begin by examining how the Ramsay model (1991) extends to the multidimensional case. A detailed discussion of this—together with the demonstration of joint consistency when the trait is multidimensional—can be read in Luzardo and Forteza (2014). Unfortunately, Bellman's curse of dimensionality limits this development to low dimensions.

Ramsay (1991) considers dichotomous or polytomous items, and estimates traits and ICC by using nonparametric regression methods. Our focus is on the dichotomous model with multidimensional traits; but extension to polytomous items is easy.

Consider n dichotomous items responded to by N examinees. This situation determines the existence of random variables $X_{i,k}$ $i = 1, \ldots, n$, $k = 1, \ldots N$, which indicate the responses of the *kth* subject to the *ith* item $X_{i,k}$, whose value is 1 if examinee i responds to item k correctly, and 0 otherwise.

Variables $X_{i,k}$ depend on d latent traits (Θ_l), y $\mathbf{X} = (X_1, .., X_n)$ represents the random vector of responses to n items; more specifically, $\mathbf{X_k}$ indicates the *kth* person's response vector.

We can notice ability as a random vector in R^d

$$\Theta = (\Theta_1, \ldots, \Theta_d).$$

Assume that $P_i(\theta_k) = P(X_{ik} = 1|\Theta = \theta_k)$ is the probability that an examinee with trait θ_k will respond to item i correctly (Ω, A, P) is a probability space; and—with no loss of generality—that trait Θ has uniform marginal distribution functions on [0, 1].

This hypothesis is not restrictive. It is clear that any conclusion we may draw in this context will work for any marginal distribution, as the ICCs remain unchanged under monotonic transformations. This loss of identifiability is noted by Ramsay (1991, p. 614): "In the context of item analysis, a test cannot yield anything more than rank order information about examinees."

To see this, let us consider a uni-dimensional latent trait τ and its population distribution function H. We know that $H(\tau)$ has uniform distribution on [0,1]. We can therefore estimate $\theta = H(\tau)$ rather than τ because

$$P(\tau) = P(H^{-1}(H(\tau))) = P(H^{-1}(\theta)) = P^*(\theta) \tag{8.1}$$

where

$$P^* = P \circ H^{-1} \tag{8.2}$$

is the ICC related to ability θ. If $\tau = (\tau_1, \ldots, \tau_d)$ is multidimensional with known marginal distribution functions H_l $l = 1, \ldots, d$, the changes are trivial.

As random variables $X_{i,k}$ are Bernoulli variables, then

$$P_i(\theta_k) = P(X_{ik} = 1|\Theta = \theta_k) = E(X_{ik} = 1|\Theta = \theta_k). \tag{8.3}$$

Therefore, the nonparametric regression estimator can be applied; but first it is necessary to estimate the ability vector.

Consider a sequence of vector functions $\mathbf{g_n}$, Borel-measurable on R^n with values on $[0, 1]^d$. These functions must have certain properties for consistent estimators to be obtained. A detailed demonstration of joint consistency in the multidimensional case can be followed in Luzardo and Forteza (2014).

We assume $g_{n,l}$ is the *lth* component of $\mathbf{g_n}$, and for $x \in R^n$

$$\mathbf{g_n}(x) = (g_{n,1}(x), \ldots., g_{n,d}(x)).$$

We further assume that functions $g_{n,l}(X)$ are independent of $\Theta_1, \ldots, \Theta_{l-1}$, $\Theta_{l+1}, .., \Theta_d$ for every $1 \leq l \leq d$, and we define the sequence of functions $\{G_{g_n}\} : R^d \longrightarrow R^d$ in such a way that for every $x = (x_1, \ldots, x_d)$ we have

$$G_{g_n}(x) = (P(g_{n,1}(X) \leq x_1), \ldots, P(g_{n,d}(X) \leq x_d)) = (F_{n,1}(x_1), \ldots, F_{n,d}(x_d)) \tag{8.4}$$

where

$$F_{n,l}(x) = P(g_{n,l}(X) \leq x) \tag{8.5}$$

We also have empirical distributions

$$\hat{F}_{N,l}(x) = \frac{\#\{g_{n,1}(X) \leq x\}}{N} = \frac{\sum_{i=1}^{N} \chi_{\{g_{n,1}(X) \leq x\}}}{N} \tag{8.6}$$

with $l = 1, .., d$; and let us define the functions:

$$\hat{G}_N(x_1, \ldots, x_d) = (\hat{F}_{N,1}(x_1), \ldots, \hat{F}_{N,d}(x_d)) \tag{8.7}$$

Based on the above, we are in a position to estimate the *lth* component of the ability. We use function $g_{n,l}$ to order the subjects, and then take the empirical distribution function; the ability estimator being:

$$\hat{\Theta}_n = \hat{G}_N(g_n(X)) \tag{8.8}$$

We must be careful when obtaining the estimated ability to be used in the ICC estimator. As the number of items is less than the number of subjects, many ties will occur which will have to be broken. For this purpose, a random variable W_n is to be added to each $g_{n,l}$ to obtain a sequence with no ties. Another factor is that the estimation of the trait should be independent of the response to the item: so when the ICC is estimated for item i, this item is removed when calculating the ability estimate, and we obtain $\widehat{\theta_{n,i}}$

Then, the ICC estimator is

$$\hat{P}_i(\theta) = \frac{\sum_{k=1}^{N} K(\frac{\widehat{\theta_{n,i}} - \theta}{h}) X_{ik}}{\sum_{k=1}^{N} K(\frac{\widehat{\theta_{n,k}} - \theta}{h})} \tag{8.9}$$

where K is a kernel and h is the bandwidth. If we know the marginal distribution functions of ability H_l, we can convert the empirical estimators to the appropriate scale using:

$$\hat{\tau} = (\widehat{\tau_1}, \ldots, \widehat{\tau_d}) = (H_1^{-1}(\widehat{\theta_1}), \ldots, H_d^{-1}(\widehat{\theta_d})) \tag{8.10}$$

Bandwidth h must be chosen carefully to control the relationship between skewness and variance of the estimator. If h decreases, so does skewness: as only observations close to θ are actually taken into account, but variance increases. If h increases, variance decreases, as more observations will be included in the calculation but skewness increases. Härdle (1990) presents several methods for choosing the optimal value of h.

8.3 Isotonic Model

In IRT, it is very important to develop models for monotonic items. Ramsay (1998) proposes a procedure; but his method is semi-parametric, because the ICC requires that a second-order differential equation be satisfied, which renders the procedure inconsistent. Recently, Lee et al. (2007) proposed the use of an isotonic regression method promoted by Barlow et al. (1972) as well as Robertson et al. (1988), a least-squares method for data fitting under order restrictions. Our approach is based on the method developed by Dette et al. (2006).

We will now demonstrate an isotonic nonparametric estimator for the ICC. As stated above, this is a normal assumption in IRT. Dette et al. (2006) propose estimating monotonic functions from non-monotonic estimators. These authors consider functions strictly monotonic on [0, 1] with positive derivatives.

Suppose that the distribution of ability τ is $F(\tau)$; and $P(\tau)$ is the ICC: which is increasing, differentiable and monotonic. Denote $\theta = F(\tau)$ and $P^*(\theta) = P(F^{-1}(\theta)) = P(\tau)$. Clearly, $P^*(\theta)$ is increasing on [0, 1], so we can assume with no loss of generality that the trait has uniform distribution in the unit interval.

In this context, we presume that $U_1, \ldots, U_T$ is a sample of random variables with uniform distribution on [0, 1], K_d is a kernel, and h_d is the bandwidth. Then,

$$\frac{1}{TH_d}\sum_{i=1}^{T} K_d(\frac{P^*(U_i) - u}{h_d}) \tag{8.11}$$

is the density estimator for $P^*(U)$.

The density of $P^*(U)$ is $(P^{*-1})'(u)\chi_{[P^*(0),P^*(1)]}(u)$, then upon integration,

$$\frac{1}{Th_d}\int_{-\infty}^{\theta}\sum_{i=1}^{T} K_d(\frac{P^*(U_i) - u}{h_d})du \tag{8.12}$$

is a consistent estimator of P^{*-1} en θ.

It is only natural to replace $P^*(U_i)$ with an estimator of the ICC valued at a set of points equally spaced out on [0, 1], which in our case, we will do by means of the Ramsay model. We will take a grid $0, \frac{1}{T}, ..., \frac{i}{T}, .., 1$ and use the nonparametric regression estimator at each point

$$\widehat{P^*}(\frac{i}{T}) = \frac{\sum_{j=1}^{N} K_r(\frac{\frac{i}{T}-\hat{\theta}_j}{h_r})X_j}{\sum_{j=1}^{N} K_r(\frac{\frac{i}{T}-\hat{\theta}_j}{h_r})} \tag{8.13}$$

where K_r and h_r are the kernel and window of the regression estimator. Then, the inverse monotonic ICC on θ will be

$$\widehat{P^{*-1}}(\theta) = \frac{1}{Th_d}\int_{-\infty}^{\theta}\sum_{i=1}^{T} K_d\left(\frac{\widehat{P^*}(\frac{i}{T}) - u}{h_d}\right)du \tag{8.14}$$

Finally, the estimator of $\widehat{P^*}$ is obtained by reflection of $\widehat{P^{*-1}}$ in relation to $y = x$. To illustrate the multidimensional case, we assume an increasing ICC for each trait; and that the ICC estimator has been obtained via nonparametric regression in two dimensions.

$$\hat{P}_i(\theta_1, \theta_2) = \frac{\sum_{k=1}^{N} K_r(\frac{\widehat{\theta_{1i}}-\theta_1}{h_1}, \frac{\widehat{\theta_{2i}}-\theta_2}{h_2})X_{ik}}{\sum_{k=1}^{N} K_r(\frac{\widehat{\theta_{1k}}-\theta}{h_1}, \frac{\widehat{\theta_{2k}}-\theta}{h_2})} \tag{8.15}$$

where K_r is a dimension-two kernel with compact support $C \subset [0, 1]^2$. We also assume that the kernel, bandwidth and functions used to estimate the traits all fulfill the required hypotheses (Luzardo and Forteza 2014) for this estimator to be consistent.

We then take a grid $0, \frac{1}{T}, .., \frac{i}{T}, .., 1$ for θ_1; and a grid $0, \frac{1}{T}, .., \frac{j}{T}, .., 1$ for θ_2. For each fixed $\theta_2 \in (0, 1)$ we consider the estimator

$$\widehat{H^{-1}}(\theta_1|\theta_2) = \frac{1}{Th_d}\int_{-\infty}^{\theta_1}\sum_{i=1}^{T} K_d\left(\frac{\hat{P}(\frac{i}{T}, \theta_2) - u}{h_d}\right)du \tag{8.16}$$

Function $\widehat{H^{-1}}(\theta_1|\theta_2)$ is strictly increasing on θ_1 for each fixed θ_2. We can calculate the inverse (as a function of θ_1) to obtain $\hat{H}(\theta_1|\theta_2)$. For each fixed $\theta_1 \in (0, 1)$, we calculate

$$\widehat{P^{*-1}}(\theta_1, \theta_2) = \frac{1}{Th_d}\sum_{j=1}^{T}\int_{-\infty}^{\theta_2} K_d\left(\frac{H(\theta_1|\frac{j}{T}) - u}{h_d}\right)du \tag{8.17}$$

Finally, $\widehat{P^*}(\theta_1, \theta_2)$ is calculated through the inverse (as a function of θ_2). The algorithm would be:

Step 1 Using the standard procedure for each $1 \leq i \leq T$ and $1 \leq j \leq T$, calculate

$$\hat{P}(\frac{i}{T}, \frac{j}{T})$$

Step 2 For each $\frac{j}{T}$ with $1 \leq j \leq T$, calculate $H^{-1}(\theta_1|\frac{j}{T})$ through

$$\widehat{H^{-1}}(\theta_1|\frac{j}{T}) = \frac{1}{Th_d}\int_{-\infty}^{\theta_1}\sum_{i=1}^{T} K_d\left(\frac{\hat{P}(\frac{i}{T}, \frac{j}{T}) - u}{h_d}\right)du \tag{8.18}$$

Step 3 Through inversion in relation to θ_1, we obtain $\hat{H}(\theta_1|\frac{j}{T})$ with $1 \leq j \leq T$

Step 4 Calculate

$$\widehat{P^{*-1}}(\theta_1, \theta_2) = \frac{1}{Th_d} \sum_{j=1}^{T} \int_{-\infty}^{\theta_2} K_d(\frac{H(\theta_1|\frac{j}{T}) - u}{h_d})du \tag{8.19}$$

Step 5 Through inversion in relation to θ_2, we obtain $\widehat{P^*}(\theta_1, \theta_2)$.

8.4 Discussion

We believe that the proposed method is an attractive alternative for estimating ICCs where they are increasing, such as in educational contexts.

The method is very flexible, easy to program, and non-iterative: a major advantage over parametric methods in the case of both uni-dimensional and multidimensional models. It is precisely in the multidimensional case where its full power becomes apparent in comparison to parametric methods, on account of the large number of iterations in the case of the latter. Moreover, smooth functions are obtained from the original method, which does not apply with other nonparametric procedures.

As a constraint, we should mention that when working in the $[0, 1]$ interval, we do not obtain the original distribution of the trait and the estimation of ICCs in the original ability scale. However, this difficulty is in any case apparent, as the scales are equivalent in the case of monotonic transformations. If we know the distribution of the trait in the uni-dimensional case, or the marginals in the multidimensional one, the original scales will be obtained. A further significant feature is that the dimension of the latent trait has to be reduced, as the number of observations required for an accurate estimation grows potentially with the number of dimensions.

References

Baker, F. B., & Kim, S.-H. (2004). *Item response theory: Parameter estimation techniques* (2nd ed.). New York: Marcel Dekker.

Barlow, R. E., Bartholomew, D. J., Bremner, J. M., & Brunk, H. D. (1972). *Statistical inference under order restrictions: the theory and application of isotonic regression*. New York: Wiley.

Boomsma, A., Van Duijn, J., & Snijders, A. B. (Eds.). (2001). *Essays on item response theory*. New York: Springer.

Brunk, H. D. (1955). Maximum likelihood estimates of monotone parameters. *Annals of Mathematical Statistics, 26*, 607–616.

Cheng, K. F., & Linn, P. E. (1981). Nonparametric estimation of a regression function. *Zeitschrift fur Wahrscheinlichkeitstheorie und Verwandte Gebiete, 57*, 223–233.

De Koning, E., Sijstma, K., & Hamers, J. H. M. (2002). Comparison of four IRT models when analyzing two tests for inductive reasoning. *Applied Psychological Measurement, 26*(3), 302–320.

Delecroix, M., & Thomas-Agnan, C. (2000). Spline and kernel regression under shape restrictions. In M. G. Schimek (Ed.), *Smoothing and regression: Approaches, computation and application*. New York: Wiley.

Dette, H., Neumeyer, N., & Pilz, K. (2006). A simple nonparametric estimator of a strictly monotone regression function. *Bernoulli, 12*(3), 469–490.

Douglas, J. (1997). Joint consistency of nonparametric item characteristic curve and ability estimation. *Psychometrika, 62*, 7–28.

Douglas, J., & Cohen, A (2001). Nonparametric item response function estimation for assessing parametric model fit. *Applied Psychological Measurement, 25*, 234–243.

Douglas, J., Kim, H. R., Habing, B., & Gao, F. (1998). Investigating local dependence with conditional covariance functions. *Journal of Educational and Behavioral Statistics, 23*, 129–151.

Ellis, J. L., & Junker, B. W. (1997). Tail-measurability in monotone latent variable models. *Psychometrika, 62*, 495–523.

Fischer, G. H., & Molenaar, I. (Eds.). (1995). *Rasch models: Foundations, recent developments and applications*. New York: Springer.

Friedman, J., & Tibshirani, R. (1984). The monotone smoothing of scatterplots. *Technometrics, 26*, 243–250.

Giampaglia, G. (1990). *Lo scaling unidimensionale nella ricerca sociale*. Napoli: Liguori Editore.

Gijbels, I. (2005). Monotone regression. In N. Balakrishnan, S. Kotz, C. B. Read, & B. Vadakovic (Eds.), *The encyclopedia of statistical sciences* (2nd ed.). Hoboken/New York: Wiley.

Grayson, D. A. (1988). Two-group classification in latent trait theory: Scores with monotone likehood ratio. *Psychometrika, 53*, 383–392.

Hall, P., & Huang, L. S. (2001). Nonparametric kernel regression subject to monotonicity constraints. *The Annals of Statistics, 29*, 624–647.

Hambleton, R., Swaminathan, H., & Rogers, H. (1991). *Fundamentals of item response theory*. Thousand Oaks: Sage Publications.

Härdle, W. (1990) Applied nonparametric regression. Cambridge: Cambridge University Press.

Holland, P. W. (1990). On the sampling theory foundations of item response theory models. *Psychometrika, 55*, 577–601.

Holland, P. W., & Rosenbaum, P. R. (1986). Conditional association and unidimensionality in monotone latent variable models. *The Annals of Statistics, 14*, 1523–1543.

Junker, B. W. (1993). Conditional association, essential independence and monotone unidimensional item response models. *The Annals of Statistics, 21*, 1359–1378.

Junker, B. W. (2001). On the interplay between nonparametric and parametric IRT, with some thoughts about the future. In A. Boomsma, M. A. J. Van Duijn, & T. A. B. Snijders (Eds.), *Essays on item response theory* (pp. 247–276). New York: Springer.

Junker, B. W. & Sijtsma, K. (2001). Nonparametric item response theory in action: An overview of the special issue. *Applied Psychological Measurement, 25*, 211–220.

Kelly, C., & Rice, J. (1990). Monotone smoothing with application to dose response curves and the assessment of synergism. *Biometrics, 46*, 1071–1085.

Lee, Y. S. (2007). A comparison of methods for nonparametric estimation of item characteristic curves for binary items. *Applied Psychological Measurement, 31*(2), 121–134.

Lee, Y. S., Douglas, J., & Chewning, B. (2007). Techniques for developing health quality of life scales for point of service use. *Social Indicators Research: An International and Interdisciplinary Journal for Quality-of-Life Measurement, 83*(2), 331–350.

Lewis, C. (1983). Bayesian inference for latent abilities. In S. B. Anderson & J. S. Helmick (Eds.), *On educational testing* (pp. 224–251). San Francisco: Jossey-Bass.

Loevinger, J. (1947). A systematic approach to the construction and evaluation of tests of ability. *Psychological Monographs, 61*(4), 1–49.

Lord, F. M. (1980). *Applications of item response theory to practical testing problems*. Hillsdale: LEA.

Luzardo, M., & Forteza, D. (2014). *Modelo no paramétrico multidimensional para la estimación de los rasgos y de las curvas características del ítem mediante regresión no paramétrica con núcleos*. Montevideo: CSIC.

Mammen, E. (1991). Estimating a smooth monotone regression function. *The Annals of Statistics, 19*, 724–740.

Meijer, R. R., Sijtsma, K., & Smid, N. G. (1990). Theoretical and empirical comparison of the Mokken and the Rasch approach to IRT. *Applied Psychological Measurement, 14*, 283–298.

Mokken, R. J. (1971). *A theory and procedure of scale analysis*. New York/Berlin: De Gruyter.

Mokken, R.J. (1997). Nonparametric models for dichotomous responses. In *Handbook of Modern Item Response Theory*, ed. W. J. van der Linden and R. K. Hambleton, 351–368. New York: Springer.

Mokken, R. J., & Lewis, C. (1982). A nonparametric approach to the analysis of dichotomous item responses. *Applied Psychological Measurement, 6*, 417–430.

Molenaar, I. W., & Sijtsma, K. (2000). *User's manual MSP5 for Windows*. Groningen: iecProGAMMA.

Mukerjee, H. (1988). Monotone nonparametric regression. *The Annals of Statistics, 16*, 741–750.

Niemoller, K., & van Schuur, W. (1983). Stochastic models for unidimensional scaling: Mokken and Rasch. In D. McKay & N. Schofield (Eds.), *Data analysis and the social sciences*. London: Frances Printer Ltd.

Ramsay, J. O. (1988). Monotone regression splines in action. *Statistical Science, 3*(4), 425–461.

Ramsay, J. O. (1991). Kernel smoothing approaches to nonparametric item characteristic curve estimation. *Psychometrika, 56*, 611–630.

Ramsay, J. O. (1998). Estimating smooth monotone functions. *Journal of the Royal Statistical Society. Series B. Statistical Methodology, 60*, 365–375.

Ramsay, J. O. (2000). *TestGraf: A computer program for nonparametric analysis of testing data*. Unpublished manuscript, McGill University.

Robertson, T., Wright, F. T. & Dykstra, R. L. (1988). *Order restricted statistical inference*. New York: Wiley.

Rosenbaum, P. (1984). Testing the conditional independence and monotonicity assumptions of item response theory. *Psychometrika, 49*, 425–435.

Schriever, B. F. (1985). *Order dependence*. Unpublished Ph.D. thesis, Free University, Amsterdam.

Sijtsma, K. (1988). *Contributions to Mokken's nonparametric item response theory*. Amsterdam: Free University Press.

Sijtsma, K. (1998). Methodology review: Nonparametric IRT approaches to the analysis of dichotomous item scores. *Applied Psychological Measurement, 22*, 3–32.

Sijtsma, K. (2001). Developments in measurement of persons and items by means of item response models. *Behaviormetrika, 28*, 65–94.

Sijtsma, K., & Molenaar, I. W. (2002). *Introduction to nonparametric item response theory*. Thousand Oaks: Sage Publications.

Stout, W. F. (1987). A nonparametric approach for assessing latent trait unidimensionality. *Psychometrika, 52*, 589–617.

Stout, W. F. (1990). A new item response theory modeling approach with applications to unidimensionality assessment and ability estimation. *Psychometrika, 55*, 293–325.

Van der Linden, W., & Hambleton, R. (1997). *Handbook of modern item response theory*. New York: Springer.

Wahba, G. (1990). *Spline Models for observational data*. Philadelphia: Society for Industrial and Applied Mathematics.

Wright, E. T. (1981). The asymptotic behavior of monotone regression estimates. *The Annals of Statistics, 9*, 443–448.

Chapter 9
Goodness-of-Fit Methods for Nonparametric IRT Models

Klaas Sijtsma, J. Hendrik Straat, and L. Andries van der Ark

Abstract This chapter has three sections. The first section introduces the unidimensional monotone latent variable model for data collected by means of a test or a questionnaire. The second section discusses the use of goodness-of-fit methods for statistical models, in particular, item response models such as the unidimensional monotone latent variable model. The third section discusses the use of the conditional association property for testing the goodness-of-fit of the unidimensional monotone latent variable model. It is established that conditional association is well suited for assessing the local independence assumption and a procedure is proposed for identifying locally independent sets of items. The procedure is used in a real-data analysis.

Keywords Conditional association • Goodness-of-fit methods • Local independence • Robustness of conclusions when models fail • Unidimensional monotone latent variable model

---

Paper presented at the International Meeting of the Psychometric Society 2014, Madison, Wisconsin, July 21st until July 25th, 2014.

K. Sijtsma (✉)
Department of Methodology and Statistics, TSB, Tilburg University,
Warandelaan 2, 5037 AB, PO Box 90153, 5000 LE Tilburg, The Netherlands
e-mail: k.sijtsma@tilburguniversity.edu

J.H. Straat
Cito Arnhem, Amsterdamseweg 13, 6814 CM Arnhem, The Netherlands
e-mail: hendrik.straat@cito.nl

L.A. van der Ark
University of Amsterdam, Room D7.15, Nieuwe Achtergracht 127,
1018 WS Amsterdam, The Netherlands
e-mail: L.A.vanderArk@uva.nl

L.A. van der Ark et al. (eds.), *Quantitative Psychology Research*, Springer Proceedings in Mathematics & Statistics 140, DOI 10.1007/978-3-319-19977-1_9

9.1 Introduction to the Unidimensional Monotone Latent Variable Model

We discuss the unidimensional monotone latent variable model (UMLVM), which is a nonparametric item response theory (IRT) model also known as the monotone homogeneity model (Sijtsma and Molenaar 2002). Next, we discuss the issues of assessing the goodness-of-fit (GoF) of IRT models and the UMLVM in particular to the data and problems that GoF investigation of IRT models typically encounters. Finally, we propose a new GoF procedure for the UMLVM that selects one item set or several item subsets consistent with the UMLVM's local independence assumption from an initial item set that may or may not be consistent with local independence.

Let θ denote the latent variable, and let X_j denote the random variable for the score on item j ($j = 1, \ldots, J$; J is the number of items in the test). The three assumptions on which the UMLVM is based are the following.

- Unidimensionality (UD): latent variable θ is unidimensional;
- Local independence (LI): the item scores are independent conditional on θ; that is,

$$P(X_1 = x_1, \ldots, X_J = x_J \middle| \theta) = \prod_{j=1}^{J} P(X_j = x_j \middle| \theta).$$

  LI implies Weak LI, for covariances between items defined as

$$\sigma(X_j, X_k \middle| \theta) = 0,$$

  and which proves to be useful in this chapter. It may be noted that Weak LI is a weaker property than LI: LI $\Rightarrow$ Weak LI, but Weak LI $\neq>$ LI;
- Monotonicity (M): The J IRFs are monotone nondecreasing in θ; that is, expectation $E(X_j \middle| \theta)$ is nondecreasing in θ.

The essential difference with parametric IRT models, such as the 1, 2, and 3-parameter logistic models, the (generalized) partial credit model and the graded response model, is that in nonparametric IRT models, such as the UMLVM, the IRFs are not parametrically defined by means of, for example, logistic functions, but are only subjected to order restrictions. For example, let us consider the logistic IRF of the 1-parameter logistic model (Van der Linden and Hambleton 1997a), in which δ_j denotes the item's location or difficulty parameter and 0/1 scoring for example denotes incorrect/correct scoring, so that

$$P(X_j = 1 \middle| \theta) = E(X_j \middle| \theta) = \frac{\exp(\theta - \delta_j)}{1 + \exp(\theta - \delta_j)}.$$

The latent variable θ and the latent item parameter δ_j can be estimated by means of maximum likelihood procedures. However, nonparametric IRT models such as the UMLVM only impose assumption M on the IRFs but do not parametrically define the IRFs, and in the absence of parametric IRFs such as the logistic, nonparametric IRT models do not enable estimating the latent variable θ and the latent item parameter δ_j (but see Mokken and Lewis 1982, for an alternative approach). However, the nonparametric UMLVM is a useful model because it does imply an ordinal scale for person measurement that is suited in most practical testing applications. Next, we discuss the properties of the ordinal scale.

For dichotomous items, the UMLVM implies stochastic ordering of latent variable θ by total score $X_+ = \sum_{j=1}^{J} X_j$ (SOL; Grayson 1988; Hemker et al. 1997). Let C and K be values of X_+, such that $0 \leq C < K \leq J$. Then for any t, SOL is defined as

$$P(\theta > t \big| X_+ = C) \leq P(\theta > t \big| X_+ = K).$$

SOL refers to the ordering of the conditional, cumulative distributions of θ. For the means of these distributions, SOL implies that an increasing total score X_+ produces an increasing mean latent variable θ. Hence, SOL means that X_+ orders persons on θ, and this allows making decisions about relative attribute levels.

For polytomous items, mathematically the UMLVM does not imply SOL but using an extensive simulation study, Van der Ark (2005) demonstrated that SOL holds by approximation and that person reversals with respect to θ due to the use of X_+ usually concern adjacent X_+ values. Thus, rare ordering errors do not seem to cause serious and far-reaching decision errors. In addition, SOL implies weak SOL, defined as

$$P(\theta > t \big| X_+ < x_+) \leq P(\theta > t \big| X_+ \geq x_+),$$

and Van der Ark and Bergsma (2010) proved that the UMLVM implies Weak SOL: SOL $\Rightarrow$ Weak SOL, but Weak SOL $\neq>$ SOL. The dichotomization $X_+ < x_+$ and $X_+ \geq x_+$, typical of using cut scores, orders persons on θ, and allows the use of total score X_+ for assignment of individuals to the categories failure and success in educational testing, rejection and selection in job assessment, and ineligible and eligible for therapy or treatment in clinical settings.

The conclusion is that the UMLVM implies an ordinal scale on θ by means of total score X_+. An interesting note often ignored is that all the parametric models that are mathematical special cases of the UMLVM imply the use of X_+ as an ordinal estimator of θ, thus justifying the use of the much more accessible total score in all applications where this might prove convenient. That is, the 1, 2, and 3-parameter logistic models and their normal-ogive counterparts imply SOL, and the (generalized) partial credit model and the graded response model imply Weak SOL. In the 1-parameter logistic model and its polytomous-item generalization, the partial credit model, total score X_+ is a sufficient statistic for the maximum likelihood estimation of latent variable θ. In other parametric IRT models, this relationship is absent and it is often assumed incorrectly that X_+ has no place in the application of such models. However, it has as an ordinal estimator of the θ scale, and when reasons to resort to the θ scale are absent one can use the ordinal X_+ scale instead.

9.2 Goodness-of-Fit Research for the UMLVM

A good fit of an IRT model to the data is essential for establishing the model's measurement properties for the particular application envisaged. Without a well-fitting model, the measurement specialist and the researcher cannot know whether the measurement properties, in case of the UMLVM an ordinal scale, hold for the test of interest, and the measurement practitioner cannot know whether conclusions about people based on the scale are valid. An important question is when to use the UMLVM as opposed to parametric IRT models. The answer is: When parametric IRT models fail to fit the data well. This may seem to be a modest position, but model-fit failure is the rule rather than the exception and is frequently ignored implicitly assuming that the misfitting parametric IRT model can be used in practice anyway; thus, the UMLVM may be useful in many applications to obtain an IRT model that fits better than a parametric IRT model. We first discuss GoF in general and then address the question of why researchers tend to neglect GoF investigation.

Like any model, IRT models are idealizations of reality and, consequently, they cannot describe the data structure perfectly well. Thus, a GoF investigation will always suggest at least some degree of model misfit. We distinguish three possible outcomes of a GoF investigation. First, one may find that an IRT model provides a reasonable approximation to the data and accept the model as a description of the data. Second, one may conclude that the IRT model shows serious misfit and decide that, for example, the item set should be divided into different subsets each measuring a different attribute or misfitting items should be removed from the item set hoping the IRT model to fit to the remaining item subset. The second outcome may be a reasonable approximation but in principle the result is always some degree of misfit. The third outcome is that the misfit is hopeless and nothing can be done to save the test; that is, as long as one sticks to the IRT model selected to model the data. In each case, in particular when misfit appears hopeless (i.e., option 3) but also when items are rejected because their IRFs are not logistic or have slopes deviating from the majority of the IRF slopes (i.e., option 2) may one resort to an alternative IRT model based on weaker assumptions, such as the UMLVM.

In test construction, GoF investigation appears to be somewhat neglected despite the availability of GoF methods for several IRT models (e.g., Glas and Verhelst 1995; Sijtsma and Molenaar 2002; Van der Linden and Hambleton 1997b). One can only speculate about the reasons for the more general neglect. One reason may be that GoF investigation is complex. First, GoF methods never address the whole model simultaneously but only one model assumption or a pair of model assumptions. For example, several GoF methods exist that assess the combination of UD and LI or only LI, and other methods assess M possibly including a particular parametric shape, but methods that simultaneously assess all assumptions of a model, say, the 1-parameter logistic model or the graded response model, to our knowledge do not exist. Second, GoF methods may be global, assessing the GoF of all items with respect to one or two assumptions simultaneously, or they may be local, assessing whether pairs of items are locally independent or whether the IRF of one particular item is monotone. Third, splitting the item set in subsets or removing an item from the item set produces a smaller data set and affects the GoF results in the next analysis round, possibly causing initially fitting items to show misfit. Combining these different aspects of a GoF investigation is difficult and may easily discourage researchers; De Koning et al. (2002) and Sijtsma et al. (2011) suggest how to consistently perform a complex GoF investigation.

Another reason for GoF neglect is that several GoF methods check a particular observable consequence of a model, following the logic that negative results imply that the IRT model cannot have generated the data. While the logic is correct, it remains unknown which assumption or assumptions were violated in particular. For example, the UMLVM and all its special cases including many parametric IRT models imply positive inter-item correlations but the presence of negative correlations among several positive correlations usually does not inform the researcher which assumption or which assumptions have been violated, only that the model did not generate the data. Hence, the diagnostic value of negative inter-item correlations appears limited.

A comprehensive GoF investigation based on the combination of different methods assessing different assumptions, for all items simultaneously and for individual items and pairs of items, and possibly also considering GoF methods providing little diagnostic information, may produce additional problems. First, a comprehensive GoF procedure typically involves many decisions as the procedure moves along thus introducing results that increasingly capitalize on chance, calling for cross validating the end result. Second, a GoF investigation typically produces a plethora of results that need to be combined so as to enable the researcher to draw a conclusion about the fit of his IRT model to the data. Little research has been done with respect to the question of how to combine the detailed results into one conclusion about GoF.

In the third section of this chapter, we discuss a new GoF method that, when the data are inconsistent with the UMLVM, has two apparent problems that we try to solve: The method does not inform the researcher unequivocally which assumption—UD, LI, or M—is violated and moreover produces an avalanche of detailed results. We investigate which assumption is violated when the method indicates model misfit and we suggest a solution to the problem of multiple detailed results. Many GoF methods assess the UMLVM; for UD assessment see Mokken (1971) and Straat et al. (2013); for LI assessment see Zhang and Stout (1999) and Douglas et al. (1998); and for M assessment see Rossi et al. (2002) and Tijmstra et al. (2013). Sijtsma and Molenaar (2002) and Sijtsma and Meijer (2007) provide overviews.

9.3 Conditional Association

We studied conditional association (CA; Holland and Rosenbaum 1986), which is an observable consequence of the UMLVM, as a potential method for assessing whether the data are consistent with the model's assumption of LI. Let the vector of J item-score variables be denoted by $\mathbf{X}$, and let $\mathbf{X}$ be divided into two mutually exclusive and exhaustive item subsets $\mathbf{Y}$ and $\mathbf{Z}$, so that $\mathbf{X} = (\mathbf{Y}, \mathbf{Z})$. Also, let f_1 and f_2 be nondecreasing functions and let h be any function. Holland and Rosenbaum proved that the UMLVM implies CA,

$$\sigma[f_1(\mathbf{Y}), f_2(\mathbf{Y}) \big| h(\mathbf{Z}) = \mathbf{z}] \geq 0.$$

CA implies that in particular subgroups defined by $h(\mathbf{Z}) = \mathbf{z}$, the covariance between nondecreasing functions $f_1(\mathbf{Y})$ and $f_2(\mathbf{Y})$ is non-negative. Examples (Sijtsma 2003) of CA are:

- $\sigma(X_j, X_k) \geq 0$; all inter-item covariances/correlations are non-negative;
- $\sigma(X_j, X_k \big| X_l = x_l) \geq 0$; within item-score subgroups, all inter-item covariances are non-negative; and
- $\sigma(X_j, X_k \big| R_{(jk)} = r) \geq 0$, rest score $R_{(jk)} = \sum_{i \neq j,k} X_i$, R has realizations r; within rest-score subgroups, all inter-item covariances are non-negative.

These covariances are used separately in several GoF methods for the UMLVM, but here we will investigate whether they can be used for investigating LI.

CA provides the means for testing the GoF of the UMLVM to the data as follows:

- If the covariances are negative, then the UMLVM did not generate the data; and
- If the covariances are positive, then one has found support for the UMLVM (but not proof, which is impossible in sample data).

A drawback for this sort of GoF research is the many covariances generated, among them perhaps negative covariances due to serious model violations but others due to only minor violations and sampling fluctuation, thus rendering it difficult to draw straightforward conclusions about GoF. For example, assume one has 20 items and 5 ordered item scores per item; then, drawing conclusions about GoF would involve a complete and possibly confused inspection that assesses and combines the results from

- 190 covariances $\sigma(X_j, X_k)$;
- 5700 covariances $\sigma(X_j, X_k \big| X_l = x_l)$; and
- 13,680 covariances $\sigma(X_j, X_k \big| R_{(jk)} = r)$.

9.3.1 How to Use CA Failure to Identify UMLVM Misfit?

How are the three cases of CA related to violations of UD, LI, and M? Suppose, we need a multidimensional $\boldsymbol{\theta}$ to explain the associations between the items; then, conditioning on one latent variable θ violates LI and also weak LI, and may also cause non-monotone IRFs reflected by negative (conditional) inter-item covariances. We distinguish two violations of weak LI: positive local dependence (PLD), $\sigma(X_j, X_k \middle| \theta) > 0$, and negative local dependence (NLD), $\sigma(X_j, X_k \middle| \theta) < 0$ (Rosenbaum 1988). What one needs to know is whether, for example, $\sigma(X_j, X_k \middle| X_l = x_l) < 0$ is due to items j and k being PLD or NLD, or whether the negative covariance is due to non-monotonicity of the items' IRFs. We used mathematical results provided by Holland and Rosenbaum (1986) and Rosenbaum (1988) and a computational study to find an answer to questions like these when the three cases of CA provide negative values in sample data (Straat et al. 2014).

The mathematical results showed that even when the UMLVM fails to hold, particular observable covariances are positive; hence, such covariances are useless to assess UMLVM fit. For the other observable covariances, a computational study was used to mimic PLD or NLD for particular item pairs or IRF non-monotonicity for particular items, and to estimate the proportion by which a particular conditional covariance for the corresponding items was negative. Reversely, we argued that the higher the proportion, the higher the power of a particular covariance to identify item pairs that were PLD or NLD, or items that had non-monotone IRFs.

The results of the computational study were the following. Conditional covariances had insufficient power to detect IRF non-monotonicity; hence, they are not suitable for this purpose. The next three types of covariances are suitable for identifying PLD and NLD; that is, they are suited to identify violations of LI. Let a and b be two items from item subset $\mathbf{Y}$, and let c be an item from $\mathbf{Z}$; j indexes any item from the union of both subsets, $\mathbf{X}$. PLD(a, b) means that items a and b are PLD, and NLD(a, b) that both items are NLD. Further, s denotes sample covariance. The next three results appear consistently across different choices of item parameters:

PLD: 1. If PLD(a, c) is investigated, then $s(X_a, X_j \middle| X_c = x_c) < 0$ indentifies PLD;

2. If PLD(a, j) is investigated, then $s(X_a, X_b \middle| R = r) < 0$ identifies PLD;

Note: item b may replace item a; formally, nothing changes.

NLD: 3. If NLD(a, b) is investigated, then $s(X_a, X_b \middle| R = r) < 0$ identifies NLD.

These results show that only a limited number of observable conditional covariances have enough power to be useful in GoF research. The other covariances often have positive values if LI is violated, that is, when the UMLVM fails to fit the data.

9.3.2 Usefulness of CA Failure for Identifying Locally Dependent Items

Straat et al. (2014) proposed a methodology that uses the three specific conditional covariances above for identifying locally dependent items from a larger set, and which therefore are candidates for removal from the test represented by vector **X**. For each of the three covariance results discussed in the previous section, the authors defined unique indices denoted $W^{(1)}$, $W^{(2)}$, and $W^{(3)}$, respectively, that quantify the degree to which the item is suspected to belong to locally dependent pairs. For a set of J items, each of the $J(J-1)$ indices $W^{(1)}$ is a weighted count of negative covariances defined in Result 1 in the previous section [i.e., $s(X_a, X_b \mid X_c = x_c) < 0$, $j = 1, \ldots, J; j \neq a, b$]; each of the J indices $W^{(2)}$ is a weighted count of negative covariances defined in Result 2 in the previous section [i.e., $s(X_a, X_j \mid R = r) < 0$, $j = 1, \ldots, J; j \neq a; r = 1, \ldots, R$]; and each of the $J(J-1)$ indices $W^{(3)}$ is a weighed count of negative covariances defined in Result 3 in the previous section [i.e., $s(X_a, X_b \mid R = r) < 0; r = 1, \ldots, R$]. Each index is the sum of probabilities that a sample conditional covariance s is negative under the null hypothesis that the population covariance σ is non-negative. After a Fisher Z-transformation, sample covariances are assumed to be normally distributed, and the sum of the areas under the normal curve that correspond to the negative scale region on the abscissa defines the value of a W index. A larger negative sum, that is, a larger positive W value, suggests a stronger case for local dependence and thus removing the item from **X**.

Tukey's fences were used to determine whether a W index has a negative value high enough to remove the item from **X**. The authors adjusted a procedure Ligtvoet et al. (2010) used in another context for item selection to their purpose, which was to identify and then remove locally dependent items from **X**. Straat et al. (2014) called the adjusted procedure the CA procedure. In a simulation study, the authors found that CA procedure had a specificity—the proportion of correctly identified LI items or item pairs that were kept in **X**—equal to 89.5 %. The CA procedure's sensitivity was defined for single items and pairs of items and assessed for different versions of local dependence, and varied from approximately 42–90 %.

9.3.3 Real-Data Example: The Adjective Checklist

We analyzed data from the Adjective Checklist (Gough and Heilbrun 1980), which are available in the R package "`mokken`" (Van der Ark 2007, 2012). The data consisted of the scores of 433 students on 218 items from a Dutch version of the Adjective Checklist. Each item is an adjective having five ordered answer categories (0 = completely disagree, 1 = disagree, 2 = neither agree nor disagree, 3 = agree, 4 = completely agree). The respondents were instructed to consider whether an adjective described their personality, and mark the answer category that fitted best

Table 9.1 Item means, item-scalability coefficients, and total-scalability coefficient (standard errors between parenthesis) for two ACL scales

Achievement				Nurturance			
Item	Mean	H_j	(s.e.)	Item	Mean	H_j	(s.e.)
Active	2.471	0.408	(0.030)	Kind	2.771	0.266	(0.036)
Alert	2.395	0.337	(0.036)	Aloof*	2.312	0.190	(0.031)
Ambitious	2.448	0.410	(0.030)	Helpful	2.624	0.264	(0.034)
Thorough	2.259	0.322	(0.036)	Intolerant*	2.998	0.247	(0.034)
Energetic	2.460	0.423	(0.032)	Sympathetic	2.778	0.265	(0.036)
Unambitious*	2.734	0.367	(0.033)	Snobbish*	3.044	0.196	(0.032)
Quitting*	2.811	0.321	(0.036)	Affectionate	2.972	0.207	(0.037)
Determined	2.499	0.384	(0.036)	Hostile*	3.307	0.337	(0.027)
Industrious	2.067	0.372	(0.034)	Friendly	2.806	0.317	(0.032)
Persevering	2.298	0.433	(0.032)	Distrustful*	2.700	0.221	(0.031)
Total scale		0.378	(0.026)	Total scale		0.247	(0.024)

Note: An asterisk indicates adjectives that are negative with respect to the attribute. Tabulated results are based on recoded item scores

to this description. The 218 items constitute 22 scales. For illustration purposes we selected two 10-item scales: Achievement, having item-scalability H_j-values (Sijtsma and Molenaar 2002, chap. 4) greater than 0.3 for all items, and Nurturance, having rather low item-scalability coefficients (Table 9.1). We used the R package "`mokken` (Van der Ark 2007, 2012) to compute the scalability coefficients of the items, and we used the R package "`CAprocedure`" (available from the third author upon request) for the CA procedure. The R-code is provided in the Appendix.

The UMLVM implies that item-pair scalability coefficients (Sijtsma and Molenaar 2002, chap. 4) and item-scalability coefficients are non-negative. For both scales, we found that all item-pair scalability coefficients (not tabulated) and all item-scalability coefficients indeed were positive, lending support to the fit of the UMLVM.

For Achievement, the CA procedure flagged only item pair (Ambitious, Unambitious) for possible PLD (Index $W^{(1)}$). The 10 items produced 90 indices $W^{(1)}$. Based on these 90 indices, Tukey's upper fence was equal to 11.433. For item pair (Ambitious, Unambitious), index $W^{(1)}$ equaled 12.194. For all other item pairs, the $W^{(1)}$ values did not exceed Tukey's upper fence. None of 10 indices $W^{(2)}$ and none of the 45 indices $W^{(3)}$ exceeded the corresponding Tukey's upper fences. The result can be explained by noticing that the reversed scores of Unambitious were used to compute the results, and reversal of the scores renders the items similarly worded, so that a flag for PLD seems reasonable. Because Unambitious had the lower item-scalability value, this item is a candidate for removal.

For Nurturance, the CA procedure flagged item-pair (Hostile*, Distrustful*) for PLD ($W^{(1)} = 18.189$, Tukey's upper fence $= 15.777$), and the items Aloof* ($W^{(2)} = 71.047$, Tukey's upper fence $= 70.741$) and Snobbish* ($W^{(2)} = 74.924$,

Tukey's upper fence = 70.741) for being in a PLD item pair. Aloof* had the lowest item-scalability coefficient and was removed first, followed by Distrustful*, and Snobbish*. After these three items were removed, Intolerant* ($W^{(2)} = 33.027$, Tukey's upper fence = 30.650) was flagged for being in a PLD item pair, and was also removed, leaving six items in the scale. Except for Hostile*, all negatively worded items were removed. An explanation for the large number of flagged items is that the negatively worded items formed a separate dimension.

9.4 Discussion

Conditional association offers possibilities for LI assessment in goodness-of-fit studies of the UMLVM. Given the variable results for CA procedure's sensitivity, it seems worthwhile to study how the procedure can be improved so as to increase its sensitivity. A comparison with alternative procedures assessing LI is useful and should be conducted. In a broader context, we noticed that GoF methods for any statistical model hardly ever address the complete model but target particular assumptions or sets of intimately related assumptions. For nonparametric IRT models the picture is no different but fortunately a large array of GoF methods assessing nonparametric IRT assumptions is available. The assessment of LI seems to be the least well developed. This chapter discussed a contribution to LI assessment. From the researcher's viewpoint a sound methodology that combines the best GoF methods so as to obtain a comprehensive picture of a model's fit to the data with respect to UD, LI and M is another topic we intend to pursue.

A.1 Appendix

R code we used for the real-data example.

```
R> library("CAprocedure")
R> library("mokken")
R> data(acl)
R> # Achievement
R> Ach <- acl[, 11 : 20]
R> coefH(Ach)
R> apply(Ach, 2, mean)
R> CAP(Ach, TRUE)
R> # Nurturance
R> Nur <- acl[, 61 : 70] #
R> coefH(Nur)
R> apply(Nur, 2, mean)
R> CAP(Nur, TRUE)
```

References

De Koning, E., Sijtsma, K., & Hamers, J. H. M. (2002). Comparing four IRT models when analyzing two tests for inductive reasoning. *Applied Psychological Measurement, 26*, 302–320.

Douglas, J., Kim, H., Habing, B., & Gao, F. (1998). Investigating local dependence with conditional covariance functions. *Journal of Educational and Behavioral Statistics, 23*, 129–151.

Glas, C. A. W., & Verhelst, N. D. (1995). Testing the Rasch model. In G. H. Fischer & I. W. Molenaar (Eds.), *Rasch models. Their foundations, recent developments and applications* (pp. 69–96). New York, NY: Springer.

Gough, H. G., & Heilbrun, A. B. (1980). *The Adjective Check List, manual 1980 edition*. Palo Alto, CA: Consulting Psychologists Press.

Grayson, D. A. (1988). Two-group classification in latent trait theory: Scores with monotone likelihood ratio. *Psychometrika, 53*, 383–392.

Hemker, B. T., Sijtsma, K., Molenaar, I. W., & Junker, B. W. (1997). Stochastic ordering using the latent trait and the sum score in polytomous IRT models. *Psychometrika, 62*, 331–347.

Holland, P. W., & Rosenbaum, P. R. (1986). Conditional association and unidimensionality in monotone latent variable models. *The Annals of Statistics, 14*, 1523–1543.

Ligtvoet, R., Van der Ark, L. A., Te Marvelde, J. M., & Sijtsma, K. (2010). Investigating an invariant item ordering for polytomously scored items. *Educational and Psychological Measurement, 70*, 578–595.

Mokken, R. J. (1971). *A theory and procedure of scale analysis*. The Hague, The Netherlands/Berlin, Germany: Mouton/De Gruyter.

Mokken, R. J., & Lewis, C. (1982). A nonparametric approach to the analysis of dichotomous item responses. *Applied Psychological Measurement, 6*, 417–430.

Rosenbaum, P. R. (1988). Item bundles. *Psychometrika, 53*, 349–359.

Rossi, N., Wang, X., & Ramsay, J. O. (2002). Nonparametric item response function estimates with the EM algorithm. *Journal of Educational and Behavioral Statistics, 27*, 291–317.

Sijtsma, K. (2003). Developments in practical nonparametric IRT scale analysis. In H. Yanai, A. Okada, K. Shigemasu, Y. Kano, & J. J. Meulman (Eds.), *New developments in psychometrics* (pp. 183–190). Tokyo, Japan: Springer.

Sijtsma, K., & Meijer, R. R. (2007). Nonparametric item response theory and related topics. In C. R. Rao & S. Sinharay (Eds.), *Handbook of statistics*. Vol. 26, Psychometrics (pp. 719–746). Amsterdam, The Netherlands: Elsevier.

Sijtsma, K., Meijer, R. R., & Van der Ark, L. A. (2011). Mokken scale analysis as time goes by: An update for scaling practitioners. *Personality and Individual Differences, 50*, 31–37.

Sijtsma, K., & Molenaar, I. W. (2002). *Introduction to nonparametric item response theory*. Thousand Oaks, CA: Sage.

Straat, J. H., Van der Ark, L. A., & Sijtsma, K. (2013). Comparing optimization algorithms for item selection in Mokken scale analysis. *Journal of Classification, 30*, 72–99.

Straat, J. H., Van der Ark, L. A., & Sijtsma, K. (2014). *Using conditional association to identify locally independent item sets* (Manuscript submitted for publication).

Tijmstra, J., Hessen, D. J., Van der Heijden, P. G. M., & Sijtsma, K. (2013). Testing manifest monotonicity using order-constrained statistical inference. *Psychometrika, 78*, 83–97.

Van der Ark, L. A. (2005). Stochastic ordering of the latent trait by the sum score under various polytomous IRT models. *Psychometrika, 70*, 283–304.

Van der Ark, L. A. (2007). Mokken scale analysis in R. *Journal of Statistical Software, 20*(11), 1–10.

Van der Ark, L. A. (2012). New developments in Mokken scale analysis in R. *Journal of Statistical Software, 48*(5), 1–27.

Van der Ark, L. A., & Bergsma, W. P. (2010). A note on stochastic ordering of the latent trait using the sum of polytomous item scores. *Psychometrika, 75*, 272–279.

Van der Linden, W. J., & Hambleton, R. K. (1997a). Item response theory: Brief history, common models, and extensions. In W. J. van der Linden & R. K. Hambleton (Eds.), *Handbook of modern item response theory* (pp. 1–28). New York, NY: Springer.
Van der Linden, W. J., & Hambleton, R. K. (Eds.). (1997b). *Handbook of modern item response theory*. New York, NY: Springer.
Zhang, J., & Stout, W. F. (1999). The theoretical DETECT index of dimensionality and its application to approximate simple structure. *Psychometrika, 64*, 213–249.

Chapter 10
A Comparison of Differential Item Functioning (DIF) Detection for Dichotomously Scored Items Using IRTPRO, BILOG-MG, and IRTLRDIF

Mei Ling Ong, Seock-Ho Kim, Allan Cohen, and Stephen Cramer

Abstract This study was designed to provide an empirical comparison of three IRT calibration programs, IRTPRO, BILOG-MG, and IRTLRDIF, all of which can be used for detecting differential item functioning (DIF). The three programs were compared for each of three dichotomous IRT models, the one-parameter logistic, the two-parameter logistic, and the three-parameter logistic models. Results from each of these programs were examined using data from a test designed to predict high school graduation test results in a large Southeastern US state. Results suggested that all three programs detected DIF differently.

Keywords Differential item functioning • IRTPRO • BILOG-MG • IRTL-RDIF • IRT • 1PL • 2PL • 3PL

M.L. Ong (✉)
Department of Education Psychology, University of Georgia,
126H Aderhold Hall, University of Georgia, Athens, GA 30602, USA
e-mail: tmlong@uga.edu

S.-H. Kim
Department of Education Psychology, University of Georgia,
325U Aderhold Hall, University of Georgia, Athens, GA 30602, USA
e-mail: shkim@uga.edu

A. Cohen
Department of Education Psychology, University of Georgia,
125M Aderhold Hall, University of Georgia, Athens, GA 30602, USA
e-mail: acohen@uga.edu

S. Cramer
Department of Education Psychology, University of Georgia,
320A Aderhold Hall, University of Georgia, Athens, GA 30602, USA
e-mail: cramer@uga.edu

L.A. van der Ark et al. (eds.), *Quantitative Psychology Research*, Springer Proceedings in Mathematics & Statistics 140, DOI 10.1007/978-3-319-19977-1_10

10.1 Introduction

Item response theory (IRT) is a general statistical theory describing the relationship between examinee ability and item performance. In order to make certain all items on a test fit to an IRT model are as free as possible from construct irrelevant variance, a differential item functioning (DIF) analysis is often used. An item is said to function differentially when examinees from different groups, conditioning on the latent variable measured by the test, have different probabilities of success (Holland and Thayer 1988). DIF testing is an important step in reducing the likelihood that the items on the test measure variability that is irrelevant to the construct being measured. In this way, DIF can help improve the validity of a test (Thissen et al. 1993).

A number of studies have employed BILOG-MG (Zimowski et al. 2003) for use in detection of DIF (e.g., Kline 2004). Likewise, the computer program IRTLRDIF (Thissen 2001) has also been used for DIF detection (Woods 2009). A new computer program Item Response Theory for Patient-Reported Outcomes (IRTPRO) developed by Cai et al. (2011) has recently been used for DIF detection (e.g., Basokcu and Ogretmen 2014; Woods et al. 2013). Relatively little research has been reported comparing whether DIF detection using IRTPRO is consistent with results from other IRT calibration programs such as BILOG-MG.

The objectives for this study were (1) comparison of DIF detection of two commonly used IRT calibration programs, BILOG-MG and IRTLRDIF, with results from IRTPRO on an empirical data set for the one-parameter logistic (1PL), two-parameter logistic (2PL), and three-parameter logistic (3PL) models and (2) the examination of IRTPRO to determine its effectiveness in detecting DIF.

Previous research on DIF methodology has considered all minorities, such as African Americans, Asians, Hispanics, and Native Americans, to be a single homogeneous group (McNulty and Bellair 2003). Little research has shown that African Americans and Hispanics are similar in this regard (Logan et al. 2012). Therefore, the detection of DIF in this study is performed separately by ethnicity.

A third aspect of this study, therefore, was designed to examine whether DIF occurred between different minority taking a statewide test of social studies. DIF is expected to arise between one or more of these three groups and the majority white sample, however, it is also expected that different patterns of DIF will obtain between the different majority groups and the majority white sample.

10.2 Three Computer Programs for DIF Detection

10.2.1 IRTPRO

IRTPRO is a recently published computer program for use in calibration and test scoring (Cai et al. 2011; Paek and Han 2013). IRT models included in IRTPRO include unidimensional and multidimensional IRT models scored both dichotomously and polytomously. Confirmatory factor analysis and exploratory factor analysis is also possible with IRTPRO. IRTPRO is capable of calibrating large-scale production applications with unrestricted numbers of items or respondents. The response functions of IRTPRO include 1PL, 2PL, 3PL, graded response, partial credit, generalized partial credit, and nominal response models. IRTPRO also applies the Wald test, as proposed by Lord (1980), for DIF detection. It implements the methods of marginal maximum likelihood (MML) and maximum likelihood estimation (MLE) for item parameter estimation. It is also possible to use apply prior distributions for item parameters, in which case IRTPRO calculates Bayesian estimates (Cai et al. 2011).

10.2.2 BILOG-MG

BILOG-MG is an extension of the BILOG 3 program and is specifically designed for dichotomously scored items (Zimowski et al. 2003). It is capable of large-scale production applications with unlimited numbers of items or respondents and can perform item analysis and the scoring of an unlimited number of subtests or subscales. In addition, BILOG-MG can be used for DIF detection as well as for equating of test scores. Item response models analyzed by BILOG-MG include 1PL, 2PL, and 3PL. BILOG-MG applies a likelihood ratio chi-square and implements MML estimation for the item and ability parameter estimation.

10.2.3 IRTLRDIF

IRTLRDIF was developed to implement a version of the likelihood ratio test for DIF for large-scale testing applications (Thissen 2001). Several studies have used IRTLRDIF in previous research (e.g., Steinberg 1994; Wainer et al. 1991; Wang et al. 1995). Item response models analyzed in IRTLRDIF include 2PL, 3PL, and Samejima's polytomous models (Samejima 1997). IRTLRDIF implements the likelihood ratio test and uses MML for item and ability parameter estimation.

10.3 Method

The Georgia High School Graduation Predictor Test (GPT). Data for this study were taken from the Fall 2010 administration of the Georgia High School Graduation Predictor Test (GPT) developed by the Georgia Center for Assessment (GCA) (2007–2012). The GPT consists of four-choice multiple-choice questions and is designed to provide a broad range measure of high school achievement in Social Studies and Science. The Social Studies data were used for this study.

The GPT Social Studies test originally consisted of 80 dichotomously scored items. As analysis of the GPT indicated that Item 26 had a biserial correlation of −0.052, it was dropped from the analysis. The GPT is a standardized test constructed to follow the blueprint for the Georgia High School Graduation Tests (HSGT). Because both the GPT and HSGT were constructed to measure the same content, the GPT is able to predict 11th grade students' future performance on the HSGT (Georgia Department of Education 2010).

Data. The data consist of 2654 respondents who answered all the items on the GPT. Self-reported information indicated that the sample consisted of 872 African Americans, 114 Hispanics, 132 Multi-Racial, and 1536 white examinees. All examinees were enrolled in the 11th grade and attended 18 different high schools from 17 different counties in Georgia. Three comparison groups were used in this study: (1) Whites vs. African Americans; (2) Whites vs. Hispanics; and (3) White vs. Multi-Racial. Whites were treated as the reference group, and African Americans, Hispanics, and Multi-Racial students were treated as separate focal groups in the DIF analysis.

Calibration. Unidimensional IRT models were used for items scored dichotomously, that is, as either correct or incorrect. If an examinee j responds to item i denoted by a random variable U_{ij}, the two scores are coded as $U_{ij} = 1$ (correct) and $U_{ij} = 0$ (incorrect) (Van der Linden and Hambleton 1997). The three IRT models implemented in the programs used in this study were the 1PL model,

$$P_i(\theta) = \frac{1}{1 + e^{-(\theta - \beta_i)}}, \tag{10.1}$$

the two-parameter logistic (2PL) model,

$$P_i(\theta) = \frac{1}{1 + e^{-\alpha_i(\theta - \beta_i)}}, \tag{10.2}$$

and the three-parameter logistic (3PL) model,

$$P_i(\theta) = c_i + (1 - c_i)\frac{1}{1 + e^{-\alpha_i(\theta - \beta_i)}}, \tag{10.3}$$

are employed in this study. In these models, examinee ability is $\theta \in (-\infty, \infty)$. The properties of item i that have an effect on the probability of success, $P_i(\theta)$, are difficulty, $b_i \in (-\infty, \infty)$, discrimination, $a_i \in (0, \infty)$, and the lower asymptote or pseudo guessing parameter, $c_i \in (0, 1)$ (Baker and Kim 2004).

DIF Detection. Thissen (2001) notes that IRTLRDIF does not include the 1PL model. Thus, BILOG-MG and IRTPRO were used to detect DIF with the 1PL model and IRTLRDIF, BILOG-MG, and IRTPRO with the 2PL and 3PL models.

In order to cross-validate the results from the DIF detection methods, this study considered items to contain DIF if BILOG-MG and IRTPRO identified them to have DIF under 1PL. For the 2PL and 3PL models, when the three programs identically detected DIF, those items were identified as functioning differentially.

To investigate DIF under the 1PL, for example, BILOG-MG employs Lord's (1980) technique which tests whether item difficulties differ. The equation is

$$z_i = \frac{\Delta b}{SE_{(G_F - G_R)}}, \tag{10.4}$$

where $\Delta b = \widehat{b}_{F_i} - \widehat{b}_{R_i}$. $\widehat{b}_{F_i}$ and $\widehat{b}_{R_i}$ are the item difficulty parameters for the focal group and the reference group. $SE_{(GF-GR)} = \sqrt{\mathrm{var}(GF) + \mathrm{var}(GR)}$ is the standard errors of the differences between the focal group and the reference group, and z_i is the approximated standard normal deviate. If z_i is less than -1.96 or greater than 1.96 for a two-tailed test, DIF is assumed to exist.

IRTPRO employs the Wald test (Lord 1977), the equation for which is

$$\chi^2 = \left(\widehat{\xi}_{F_i} - \widehat{\xi}_{R_i}\right)' \Sigma^{-1} \left(\widehat{\xi}_{F_i} - \widehat{\xi}_{R_i}\right), \tag{10.5}$$

where $df = p$, p is the number of parameters in the IRT model. $\Sigma^{-1}$is the inverse of the sample variance and covariance matrix of the differences between the item parameter.

For IRTLRDIF, the likelihood ratio test statistic, G^2, was used. The equation for the G^2 is (Thissen 2001)

$$G^2(df) = -2\log L_c - (-2\log L_A), \tag{10.6}$$

where $df = p$, p is the number of parameters. L_c is the compact model, and L_A is the augmented model. $G^2(df)$ is distributed as $\chi^2(df)$ with degrees of freedom, df, equal to the difference between the number of parameters in the augmented and the compact models (Thissen 2001). The critical value of chi-square statistics used in this study and z are given in the footnotes at the bottom of Tables 10.2, 10.3, and 10.4.

10.4 Results

Table 10.1 presents the summary statistics for each minority group and the white comparison group. DIF results are given in Table 10.2. Note that IRTLRDIF was not included in Table 10.2 as it does not handle the 1PL.

For White vs. African American comparisons, 42 DIF items were detected using BILOG-MG, and 36 items using IRTPRO. Both programs yielded the same 36 items, so those items were considered DIF items with the 1PL. Sixteen items advantaged African American examinees, and 20 items advantaged White examinees. In addition, BILOG-MG detected an additional six items as functioning differentially,

Table 10.1 Raw score summary statistics for the GPT

Statistics	Races			
	Whites	African Americans	Hispanics	Multi-racial
Number of items	79	79	79	79
Mean	43.24	36.63	40.46	42.67
Standard deviation	12.59	11.46	10.73	11.752
Coefficient alpha	0.902	0.877	0.859	0.884
Participants ($N = 2654$)	1536	872	114	132

and BILOG-MG detected more than 50 % DIF items in White vs. African American comparisons (i.e., 42 items), because this may have a different cultural background (Hambleton 2006) and community region. For White vs. Hispanic comparisons, six DIF items were detected using BILOG-MG, and five items using IRTPRO. Five of the items were detected as functioning differentially by both programs. Three items favored White examinees, and two favored Hispanic examinees. BILOG-MG detected 12 DIF items and IRTPRO detected five DIF items for White examinees and Multi-Racial examinees. The same five DIF items detected by IRTPRO were also detected by BILOG-MG. Two items favored White examinees, and three items favored Multi-Racial examinees. BILOG-MG and IRTPRO yielded the different result in detecting DIF, and BILOG-MG detected more DIF items than IRTPRO.

Table 10.3 shows the DIF outcomes for the 2PL. DIF was identified only when the three computer programs detected the same items. For White vs. African American comparisons, 29 items were detected as functioning differentially using IRTLRDIF, 19 items using BILOG-MG, and 28 items using IRTPRO. The three programs detected the same 16 items as functioning differentially. Nine items favored White examinees and seven items favored African American examinees.

For White vs. Hispanics comparisons, ten items were detected as functioning differentially using IRTLRDIF, four items using BILOG-MG, and eight items using IRTPRO. Four items were detected as DIF by the three programs. Three items favored White examinees and one item advantaged Hispanic examinees. Ten items were detected using IRTLRDIF, eight items using BILOG-MG, and eight items using IRTPRO. The same five items detected as DIF by all three programs were found for the White vs. the Multi-Racial comparisons. One item favored White examinees and four items favored Multi-Racial examinees.

Both IRTLRDIF and IRTPRO presented almost the same results for the 2PL model. For instance, both yielded the same 26 DIF items for the White vs. African American comparisons, the same eight items for the White vs. Hispanic comparisons, and the same seven items for the White vs. Multi-Racial comparisons. IRTLRDIF and BILOG-MG detected the same 17 DIF items for the White vs. African American comparisons, the same four items for the White vs. Hispanic comparisons, and the same five items for the White vs. Multi-Racial comparisons. BILOG-MG and IRTPRO detected the same 16 items for the White vs. African American examinees, the same four items for the White vs. Hispanic examinees, and

Table 10.2 The summary of BILOG-MG and IRTPRO for three comparison groups with 1PL

Item	Whites vs. Blacks		Whites vs. Hispanics		Whites vs. Multi-Racial	
	BILOG-MG (z)	IRTPRO (χ^2)	BILOG-MG (z)	IRTPRO (χ^2)	BILOG-MG (z)	IRTPRO (χ^2)
1	−5.216*	24.1*	1.057	0.8	−0.077	0.0
2	2.926*	10.7*	2.919*	8.7*	0.137	0.1
7	−3.008*	8.8*	−1.435	2.2	−0.191	0.0
8	−5.442*	27.1*	−1.339	1.9	−2.724*	6.4*
11	−7.861*	51.3*	−1.931	3.6	−2.266*	4.2*
13	6.350*	45.4*	3.412*	12*	1.093	1.6
14	4.554*	24.4*	−0.148	0.1	0.938	1.1
15	4.106*	21.0*	1.723	2.9	0.140	0.1
17	2.820*	10.7*	1.698	3.0	−1.236	1.6
19	1.445	3.9	3.069*	8.9*	0.275	0.2
20	3.445*	15.0*	0.763	0.5	−0.742	0.5
22	−4.257*	16.3*	0.988	0.8	0.000	0.0
23	2.968*	12.1*	0.618	0.3	0.601	0.6
25	2.661*	10.0*	1.010	1.0	−0.385	0.1
26	−4.238*	16.6*	−1.556	2.5	−0.221	0.0
27	−3.442*	11.2*	0.556	0.3	0.377	0.3
28	−3.602*	12.4*	−0.623	0.5	−0.138	0.0
29	−5.848*	29.5*	−1.627	2.7	−1.738	2.5
30	2.256*	7.4*	1.737	2.8	1.241	2.0
31	2.000*	6.2*	−0.256	0.1	1.532	3.0
34	−3.518*	11.5*	−0.469	0.3	−0.706	0.4
44	−8.263*	62.8*	−1.724	3.2	−2.756*	6.6*
49	2.132*	6.8*	0.749	0.5	0.449	0.3
51	−2.314*	5.7*	−3.383*	12.2*	1.707	3.1
52	−4.123*	15.3*	−0.997	1.1	−0.189	0.0
56	4.770*	26.9*	−0.278	0.1	2.510*	6.9*
57	4.016*	19.1*	1.340	1.8	1.377	2.3
59	−2.706*	6.8*	0.107	0.0	1.528	2.5
60	2.179*	7.1*	0.036	0.0	0.532	0.5
61	3.504*	15.7*	1.026	0.1	2.244*	5.9*
62	2.632*	9.2*	0.678	0.5	1.810	3.9
66	2.859*	10.8*	0.234	0.0	0.893	1.1
69	−2.752*	7.4*	1.163	1.1	−0.325	0.1
71	2.886*	10.7*	−0.756	0.7	1.244	2.0
72	3.446*	14.7*	−0.228	0.1	0.500	0.4
74	−4.706*	19.3*	−3.412*	10.5*	−0.316	0.1
78	3.746*	17.4*	0.341	0.1	0.374	0.3

*Two computer programs are consistently identified DIF Items with $p < 0.05$. The critical values are $\chi^2_{(1)} = 3.84$ for IRTPRO and $z = \pm 1.96$ for BILOG-MG

Table 10.3 The summary of IRTLRDIF, BILOG-MG, and IRTPRO for three comparison groups with 2PL

	Whites vs. African Americans			Whites vs. Hispanics			Whites vs. Multi-Racial		
Item	IRTLRDIF (χ^2)	BILOG-MG (z)	IRTPRO (χ^2)	IRTLRDIF (χ^2)	BILOG-MG (z)	IRTPRO (χ^2)	IRTLRDIF (χ^2)	BILOG-MG (z)	IRTPRO (χ^2)
1	6.1*	−2.368*	6.1*	7.5	1.313	6.7	0.7	0.121	1.3
2	12.1*	2.919*	11.0*	9.6*	2.711*	8.6*	0.0	0.198	0.0
3	0.7	1.258	0.5	2.6	1.739	2.4	8.2*	−2.455*	7.5*
4	2.1	0.464	2.1	2.2	0.995	2.3	11.6*	−1.976*	12.3*
8	11.2*	−3.135*	11.0*	2.4	−0.975	3.0	7.5*	−2.277*	7.4*
11	10.3*	−3.083*	10.5*	1.6	−1.148	1.8	3.3	−1.718	3.3
13	32.0*	5.888*	29.7*	11.1*	3.382*	10.6*	1.0	1.216	0.9
14	14.3*	4.198*	13.4*	0.5	−0.300	0.4	1.6	1.049	1.7
15	9.1*	2.768*	8.2*	3.1	1.650	2.9	0.5	0.335	0.4
19	1.0	1.545	0.9	9.1*	2.992*	8.8*	1.3	0.362	1.0
36	10.3*	−2.047*	9.7*	0.5	−0.223	0.4	1.5	−0.925	1.4
38	9.4*	−2.068*	8.5*	3.1	0.058	2.2	5.6	−2.092	5.5
44	36.6*	−5.495*	35.8*	2.4	−1.367	2.1	7.4*	−2.368*	7.7*
45	17.0*	−2.485*	14.7*	3.0	0.175	2.5	2.0	−0.917	1.8
51	12.7	−1.649	12.8	13.9*	−3.547*	13.5*	7.0	1.733	7.4
56	22.0*	4.687*	21.0*	0.8	−0.304	0.7	6.4*	2.580*	6.0*
57	13.6*	3.638*	13.0*	2.2	1.254	2.1	2.1	1.436	2.0
68	6.1*	2.155*	6.1*	4.7	0.972	4.0	0.6	0.533	0.4
72	6.9*	3.040*	6.7*	2.3	−0.358	1.7	0.5	0.588	0.7
78	8.1*	3.430*	7.8*	1.0	0.162	1.1	1.6	0.447	1.6

*Three computer programs are consistently identified DIF Items with $p < 0.05$. The critical values are $\chi^2_{(2)} = 5.99$ for both IRTLRDIF and IRTPRO and $z = \pm 1.96$ for BILOG-MG

the same four items for the White vs. Multi-Racial examinees. The three programs displayed different DIF outcomes. IRTLRDIF and IRTPRO exhibited the highest consistency for DIF detection for the 2PL model.

Table 10.4 presents the DIF outcomes for the 3PL model. For White vs. African American comparisons, 20 items were detected using IRTLRDIF, 14 using BILOG-MG, and 16 using IRTPRO. Nine of these items were the same for the three programs. Six items advantaged White examinees, and three items favored African American examinees. For the White vs. Hispanic comparisons, five DIF items were detected using IRTLRDIF, six items using BILOG-MG, and 14 items using IRTPRO. Three DIF items were detected by all three programs. Two items favored White examinees, and one item favored Hispanic examinees. For the White vs. Multi-Racial comparisons, four items were detected using IRTLRDIF, seven items using BILOG-MG, and ten items using IRTPRO. The three programs detected only one DIF in common. This item advantaged the Multi-Racial group.

Both IRTLRDIF and IRTPRO presented the same 13 DIF items for the White vs. African American comparisons for the 3PL, the same four items for the White vs. Hispanic comparisons, and the same two items for the White vs. Multi-Racial comparisons. IRTLRDIF and BILOG-MG detected the same 12 DIF items for the White vs. African American comparisons, the same three items for the White vs. Hispanic comparisons, and the same two items for the White vs. Multi-Racial comparisons. BILOG-MG and IRTPRO detected the same nine items for the White vs. African American examinees, the same three items for the White vs. Hispanic examinees, and the same two items for the White vs. Multi-Racial examinees. The three programs displayed different DIF outcomes, and IRTPRO detected more DIF items than other computer programs for Whites vs. Hispanics (14) and for Whites vs. Multi-Racial (10) for the 3PL. Results indicated that IRTLRDIF and IRTPRO detected the same items for the 2PL. Summary results of DIF items for the three comparison groups with the three models, 1PL, 2PL, and 3PL, are presented in Table 10.5.

10.5 Summary and Discussion

Most DIF detection procedures have been developed for two-group comparisons such as between a reference group and a focal group. Previous research has tended to consider all minorities as a single homogeneous group (McNulty and Bellair 2003). For instance, several studies mentioned that racial differences in assessment have primarily been developed in reference to comparisons between Whites and minority groups, which include African Americans, Asians, Hispanics, and Native Americans. There is no evidence, for example, that African American and Hispanic examinees are indeed homogeneous in this regard (Logan et al. 2012). Thus, this study shows that DIF detection differs by ethnicity. Previous studies (Coffman and Belue 2009) investigated the scores only for either Whites and African Americans or Whites and Hispanics. This study extends the line of prior research by using three

Table 10.4 The summary of IRTLRDIF, BILOG-MG, and IRTPRO for three comparison groups with 3PL

	Whites vs. African Americans			Whites vs. Hispanics			Whites vs. Multi-Racial		
Item	IRTLRDIF (χ^2)	BILOG-MG (z)	IRTPRO (χ^2)	IRTLRDIF (χ^2)	BILOG-MG (z)	IRTPRO (χ^2)	IRTLRDIF (χ^2)	BILOG-MG (z)	IRTPRO (χ^2)
3	3.8	−0.100	2.0	2.3	1.013	5.7	9.9*	−2.144*	7.9*
13	34.4*	4.256*	35.0*	10.1*	2.150*	12.8*	1.0	0.585	2.8
14	17.1*	2.596*	14.3*	0.5	−0.764	1.2	1.3	0.962	5.1
15	9.8*	2.287*	10.6*	3.4	1.503	6.8	2.2	0.439	6.5
19	1.7	0.673	2.0	8.5*	2.026*	10.9*	4.9	−0.245	0.3
32	23.5*	−4.104*	13.0*	2.4	1.055	6.2	3.9	−1.619	8.3
44	34.2*	−4.245*	28.8*	2.8	−1.758	2.8	7.7	−2.134	8.2
45	12.4*	−2.366*	9.5*	3.4	−0.296	0.4	2.8	−0.978	2.1
51	15.2	−0.585	15.6	14.5*	−3.438*	15.8*	7.6	1.953	10.9
56	32.5*	3.093*	11.4*	1.0	−0.086	1.9	10.3	2.049	4.7
57	17.9*	2.856*	12.3*	1.7	0.607	1.1	2.5	1.108	3.4
78	9.2*	2.463*	12.0*	1.0	−0.630	1.3	0.8	−0.438	0.4

*Three computer programs are consistently identified DIF Items with $p < 0.05$. The critical values are $\chi^2_{(3)} = 7.81$ for both IRTLRDIF and IRTPRO and $z = \pm 1.96$ for BILOG-MG

Table 10.5 The summary of DIF items for three comparison groups using IRTLRDIF, BILOG-MG, and IRTPRO

	Whites vs. African Americans			Whites vs. Hispanics			Whites vs. Multi-Racial		
Programs	1PL	2PL	3PL	1PL	2PL	3PL	1PL	2PL	3PL
IRTLRDIF	NA	29	20	NA	10	5	NA	10	4
BILOG-MG	42	19	14	6	4	6	12	8	7
IRTPRO	36	28	16	5	8	14	5	8	10
IB	NA	17	12	NA	4	3	NA	5	2
IP	NA	26	13	NA	8	4	NA	7	2
BP	36	16	9	5	4	3	5	4	2
IBP	NA	16	9	NA	4	3	NA	5	1

Note: IB = IRTLRDIF and BILOG-MG; IP = IRTLRDIF and IRTPRO; BP = BILOG-MG and IRTPRO; IBP = IRTLRDIF, BILOG-MG, and IRTPRO; NA = Not Available; IRTLRDIF cannot deal with 1PL

comparison groups (1) Whites vs. African Americans; (2) Whites vs. Hispanics; and (3) White vs. a Multi-Racial group, to determine which items function differentially for a specific ethnicity.

In general, DIF results did not differ across the three computer programs. DIF results did differ across computer programs depending on the IRT model in this study. For instance, for the 3PL, IRTLRDIF detected five DIF items, BILOG-MG detected six DIF items, and IRTPRO detected more DIF items, 14, than other computer programs for Whites vs. Hispanics. Consistency was greater rate between IRTLRDIF and IRTPRO for the 2PL and 3PL. IRTPRO DIF results differed in this study. As an example, IRTPRO detected more DIF items for Whites vs. Hispanics (14) and Whites vs. Multi-Racial (10) groups with 3PL.

Future studies should employ both simulated and empirical data in detecting DIF in order to obtain an accurate result to determine whether IRTPRO is equally as effective as BILOG-MG or IRTLRDIF. It is also possible that school-level variables might cause some items to function differentially. Future studies might consider a multilevel DIF analysis to better understand school level variables that may influence the DIF results observed in this study.

References

Baker, F. B., & Kim, S.-H. (2004). *Item response theory—Parameter estimation techniques* (2nd ed.). Boca Raton: Taylor & Francis.

Basokcu, T. O., & Ogretmen, T. (2014). Comparison of parametric item response techniques in determining differential item functioning in polytomous scale. *American Journal of Theoretical and Applied Statistics, 3*, 31–38.

Cai, L., Thissen, D., & du Toit, S. (2011). *IRTPRO 2.1 [Computer software]*. Lincolnwood: Scientific Software International.

Coffman, D. L., & Belue, R. (2009). Disparities in sense of community—True race differences or differential item functioning? *Journal of Community Psychology, 37*, 547–558.

Georgia Center for Assessment. (2007–2012). *The Georgia high school graduation predictor test*. Athens, GA: Author.

Georgia Department of Education. (2010). *Test content descriptions based on the Georgia performance standards social studies*. http://archives.gadoe.org/DMGetDocument.aspx/GHSGT%20Social%20Studies%20Content%20Descriptions%20GPS%20Version%20Update%20Oct%202010.pdf?p=6CC6799F8C1371F6A344D9C15C23A9D859A861593B934AB75F446073BD12714C&Type=D. Accessed 15 Nov 2014.

Hambleton, R. K. (2006). Good practices for identifying differential item functioning. *Medical Care, 44*, S182–S188.

Holland, P. W., & Thayer, D. T. (1988). Differential item functioning and the Mantel-Haenszel procedure. In H. Wainer & H. I. Braun (Eds.), *Test validity* (pp. 129–145). Hillsdale: Lawrence Erlbaum Associates.

Kline, T. J. B. (2004). Gender and language differences on the test of workplace essential skills—Using overall mean scores and item-level differential item functioning analyses. *Educational and Psychological Measurement, 64*, 549–559.

Logan, J. R., Minca, E., & Adar, S. (2012). The geography of inequality—Why separate means unequal in American public schools. *Sociology of Education, 85*, 287–301.

Lord, F. M. (1977). A broad-range tailored test of verbal ability. *Applied Psychological Measurement, 1*, 95–100.

Lord, F. M. (1980). *Applications of item response theory to practical testing problems*. Hillsdale: Lawrence Erlbaum Associates.

McNulty, T. L., & Bellair, P. E. (2003). Explaining racial and ethnic differences in serious adolescent violent behavior. *Criminology, 41*, 709–748.

Paek, I., & Han, K. T. (2013). IRTPRO 2.1 for windows (item response theory for patient-reported outcomes). *Applied Psychological Measurement, 37*, 242–252.

Samejima, F. (1997). Graded response model. In W. J. van der Linden & R. K. Hambleton (Eds.), *Handbook of modern item response theory* (pp. 85–100). New York: Springer.

Steinberg, L. (1994). Context and serial-order effects in personality measurement—Limits on the generality of measuring changes the measure. *Journal of Personality and Social Psychology, 66*, 341–349.

Thissen, D. (2001). *IRTLRDIF v2.0b—Software for the computation of the statistics involved in item response theory likelihood-ratio tests for differential item functioning [Computer software documentation]*. Chapel Hill: L. L. Thurstone Psychometric Laboratory, University of North Carolina.

Thissen, D., Steinverg, L., & Wainer, H. (1993). Detection of differential item functioning using the parameters of item response model. In P. W. Holland & H. Wainer (Eds.), *Differential item functioning* (pp. 67–114). Hillsdale: Lawrence Erlbaum Associates.

Van der Linden, W. J., & Hambleton, R. K. (1997). Item response theory—Brief history, common models, and extensions. In W. J. van der Linden & R. K. Hambleton (Eds.), *Handbook of modern item response theory* (pp. 1–28). New York: Springer.

Wainer, H., Sireci, S. G., & Thissen, D. (1991). Differential testlet functioning—Definitions and detection. *Journal of Educational Measurement, 28*, 197–219.

Wang, X.-B., Wainer, H., & Thissen, D. (1995). On the viability of some untestable assumptions in equating exams that allow examinee choice. *Applied Measurement in Education, 8*, 211–225.

Woods, C. M. (2009). Empirical selection of anchors for tests of differential item functioning. *Applied Psychological Measurement, 33*, 42–57.

Woods, C. M., Cai, L., & Wang, M. (2013). The Langer-improved Wald test for DIF testing with multiple groups—Evaluation and comparison to two-group IRT. *Educational and Psychological Measurement, 73*, 532–547.

Zimowski, M. F., Muraki, E., Mislevy, R. J., & Bock, R. D. (2003). *BILOG-MG [Computer software]*. Lincolnwood: Scientific Software International.

Chapter 11
An Empirical Study of the Impact of the Choice of Persistence Models in Value Added Modeling upon Teacher Effect Estimates

Yong Luo, Hong Jiao, and Robert Lissitz

11.1 Introduction

It seems that the application of value added modeling (VAM) in educational settings has been gaining momentum in the past decade or so due to the interest in using test scores to evaluate teachers or schools, and currently myriads of VAM models are available for VAM researchers and practitioners. Despite the large number of VAM models, McCaffrey et al. (2004) summarized the relations among them and concluded that many can be viewed as special cases of persistence models. In persistence models, student scores are calculated based on the sum of teacher effects across years. Since different students may change teachers every year and have different membership in multiple group units, such models are also referred to as "multiple membership" models (Browne et al. 2001; Rasbash and Browne 2001). Persistence models differ from each other in the value of the persistence parameter, which, ranging from 0 to 1, denotes how teacher effects at the current year persist into the subsequent years, may it be vanished, undiminished, or diminished. The Variable Persistence (VP) model (Lockwood et al. 2007; McCaffrey et al. 2004) had been considered more flexible due to its free estimation of the persistence parameter, while other persistence models constrain its value to be either 0 or 1.

Before the development of the Generalized Persistence (GP) model (Mariano et al. 2010), the issue of construct shift had seldom been investigated in VAM. Construct shift might be a common phenomenon in K-12 testing due to curriculum

Y. Luo (✉)
National Center for Assessment in Higher Education, King Khalid bin Abdul Aziz, West Palm Neighborhood, P.O. Box 68566, Riyadh 11534, Saudi Arabia
e-mail: jackyluoyong@163.com; jakyluoyong@gmail.com

H. Jiao • R. Lissitz
University of Maryland, 1230 Benjamin Building, College Park, MD 20742, USA
e-mail: hjiao@umd.edu; rlissitz@umd.edu

L.A. van der Ark et al. (eds.), *Quantitative Psychology Research*, Springer Proceedings in Mathematics & Statistics 140, DOI 10.1007/978-3-319-19977-1_11

change across grades (Schmidt et al. 2005). Previous VAMs often assume that the current year teacher effect correlates perfectly with the persisting effect in the future years. Such an assumption is overly restrictive and unrealistic since construct shift occurs in reality and the correlation should not be perfect. The GP model relaxes this constraint and allows the correlation to be freely estimated.

While conceptually intuitive, the GP model did not produce considerably different teacher effect estimates than the VP model in an empirical data analysis in the original paper. Specifically, while the GP model had the best model fit among all persistence models, estimates of the current year teacher effects between the GP model and the VP model were extremely highly correlated. Therefore, Mariano et al. (2010) concluded that for that particular data set they used, choosing the GP model over the VP model might not make a difference in terms of teacher effect estimation. Aware of the fact that their conclusions were based on a single data set that has a development scale, they suggested that other data, especially those that are not vertically scaled, should be used to investigate the generalizability of their findings.

To the best of our knowledge, no similar empirical studies that apply the GP model to other data are found in literature and it remains unclear whether their findings are generalizable to other data. Using longitudinal data of math testing scores from an Eastern state from 2008 to 2010 that include four cohorts, the current study fits four different persistence models to those four data sets and compares the findings to those found in the study by Mariano et al. (2010). Specifically, it intends to answer the following research questions:

1. How strong are the correlations between the current year teacher effect and persisting future year teacher effect estimated from the GP model?
2. How well do different persistence models fit those data sets?
3. How similar are the teacher effect estimates produced by different persistence models?

11.2 Different Persistence Models

McCaffrey et al. (2004) summarized the relations among different VAMs and the persistence models. Specifically, they showed that with certain restrictions imposed, the covariate adjustment models (Diggle et al. 1996; Meyer 1997; Rowan et al. 2002), the gain score models (Rowan et al. 2002; Shkolnik et al. 2002), the cross-classified models (Raudenbush and Bryk 2002), and the layered model (Sanders et al. 1997) can all be viewed as special cases of the persistence model.

Assuming a single cohort of students and a single subject, the mathematical equation of the GP model is expressed as follows:

$$Y_{it} = \mu_t + \Sigma_{t^* \leq t} a_{tt^*} \boldsymbol{l}_{t^*} + \varepsilon_{it}. \tag{11.1}$$

In this equation, y_{it} is the test score of student i in year t, μ_t is the year-specific mean for year t, and $\varepsilon_{it}$is the residual error. $\boldsymbol{l}_{t^*}$ is a vector of teacher effects including the current year effect and its subsequent persisting effects till the year t, which, together with the summation from the year t^* to the year t, makes the middle term on the right side of the above equation the accumulation of the current year effect and its persisting effects in the following years till the year t. a_{tt^*} is the persistence parameter which is equal to 1 when $t = t^*$, and between the range of 0 to 1 when $t^* \leq t$. Here it is assumed that each student has only one teacher each year for the sake of simplicity.

The residual error terms $\boldsymbol{\varepsilon}_i' = (\boldsymbol{\varepsilon}_{i1}, \ldots, \boldsymbol{\varepsilon}_{it})$ are assumed to be normally distributed random variables, independent across students. They have a mean of 0 and an unstructured covariance matrix Σ:

$$\boldsymbol{\varepsilon}_i \sim MVN\left(0, \sum\right).$$

For each year t^*, the current year and future year effects of a teacher teaching the current year t^* have a K_{t^*}-dimensional ($K_{t*} = \text{t}-t^*$) multivariate normal distribution with mean vector 0 and unstructured covariance matrix $\boldsymbol{\Gamma}_{\text{t}^*}$:

$$\boldsymbol{l}_{t^*} \sim MVN\left(0, \boldsymbol{\Gamma}_{\text{t}*}\right)$$

It is assumed that the vectors of teachers' effects are independent across both teachers at the same grade and teachers at different grades. Moreover, they are independent of the residual errors.

The primary innovation of the GP model is its relaxation of the assumption that the current year effects and their persisting effects in future years are perfectly correlated. All the previous persistence models, including the "complete persistence" (CP) model (Harris and Sass 2006; Raudenbush and Bryk, 2002; Sanders et al. 1997) and the VP model, assume a perfect correlation between the current year effects and their persisting effects in future years.

The "zero persistence" (ZP) model is a special case of the GP model in the sense that $a_{tt^*} = 0,\ t^* < t$. In other words, teacher effects do not persist into future years. The ZP model, CP model, and VP model have the same mathematical equation as the GP model. The CP model is another special case of the GP model since it constrains $a_{tt^*} = 1,\ t^* < t$, which means teacher effects persist undiminished into future years. In the VP model,$0 < a_{tt^*} < 1,\ t^* < t$, which means that the persisting teacher effects at year t is just the product of $a_{tt^*}$and the current year effect at year t^*. Therefore, the VP model is also a special case of the GP model.

The fact that the GP model is a generalized case of the ZP model, the CP model, and the VP model can also be shown through the different assumptions about the covariance matrix $\boldsymbol{\Gamma}_{t^*}$, which can be decomposed as

$$\boldsymbol{\Gamma}_{t*} = \boldsymbol{S}_{t*}^{1/2}\mathbf{C}_{t*}\boldsymbol{S}_{t*}^{1/2}.$$

In this equation, $\boldsymbol{S}_{t*}^{1/2}$is a nonnegative diagonal matrix of the variances of grade t^* teacher effects in each outcome year $t^* \leq t$ and C_{t*} is the nonnegative definite correlation matrix of those effects.

The GP model places no constraints on either the $\mathbf{S}_{t*}$ and $\mathbf{C}_{t*}$, which means that the variance of the teacher effects are allowed to vary and the correlation set to be arbitrary.

For the ZP model, the CP model, and the VP model, $\mathbf{C}_{t*}$ is constrained to be $\mathbf{J}$, a matrix of all 1s indicating the perfect correlation. These three models are different from each other in the sense that the ZP model constrains $\mathbf{S}_{t*}$to include only one parameter—the variance of the current year teacher effect due to no teacher effect persistence—and zeros elsewhere, the CP model constrains the diagonal parameter of $\mathbf{S}_{t*}$ to be the same, and in the VP model the diagonal parameters of $\mathbf{S}_{t*}$ are just the product of the square of the persistence parameter and the teacher effect in the preceding year.

Following Lockwood et al. (2007), Mariano et al. (2010) also adopted the Bayesian framework (Carlin and Louis 2000; Gelman et al. 1995; Gilks et al. 1996) for the estimation of teacher effects in the GP model and implemented it using WinBUGS (Spiegelhalter et al. 2002). Karl et al. (2012a, b) tackled the estimation issue of multiple membership linear mixed models such as the GP model using the frequentist approach. Specifically, they developed a method to compute maximum likelihood estimates with an EM algorithm. This method takes advantage of matrix sparsity and only inverts a matrix with dimensions depending on the number of random effects rather than on the total number of observations. Compared to the Bayesian estimation framework, this estimation method produces standard errors that will not be influenced by the choice of priors.

11.3 Method

11.3.1 Data

The data contain 3 years of math scores (2008, 2009, and 2010) on a state achievement test from grade 3 to grade 8. The data are not vertically scaled, which corresponds to Mariano et al.'s suggestion of evaluating the performance of the GP model with test data that does not have a developmental scale. In the dataset there are four cohorts: Cohort 1 (grade 3 through grade 5), Cohort 2 (grade 4 through grade 6), Cohort 3 (grade 5 through grade 7), and Cohort 4 (grade 6 through grade 8). Table 11.1 summarizes the sample size of each cohort.

Missing data are common in the sample: only 70 % of the students have fully observed test scores across 3 years. If the missing data issue is ignored, the sample size becomes 8522 for Cohort 1, 8610 for Cohort 2, 8656 for Cohort 3, and 8617 for

Table 11.1 Cohort sample size

	Year		
Cohort	2008	2009	2010
Cohort 1	7246	7336	7273
Cohort 2	7251	7337	7107
Cohort 3	7321	7095	7052
Cohort 4	7374	7282	7201

Table 11.2 Descriptive statistics of math scores in four cohorts

Cohort	Year	Mean	SD	Min	Max
Cohort 1	2008	421	38	310	585
	2009	431	40	297	650
	2010	433	36	309	650
Cohort 2	2008	430	41	317	584
	2009	432	38	329	650
	2010	427	35	335	650
Cohort 3	2008	430	38	327	589
	2009	423	36	240	650
	2010	422	36	321	568
Cohort 4	2008	428	36	314	566
	2009	424	35	309	650
	2010	429	35	320	572

Cohort 4. If the observations with missing data are deleted, the sample size becomes 6074 for Cohort 1, 5850 for Cohort 2, 5842 for Cohort 3, and 6089 for Cohort 4. Fortunately, the GP model is flexible enough to accommodate the missing data issue. Table 11.2 lists the descriptive statistics of each cohort's mean score at each of the 3 years.

11.3.2 Software

While both the Bayesian approach and the maximum likelihood (ML) approach can be used to estimate persistence models, the former one requires the specification of an informative prior distribution for the covariance parameters, the choice of which may affect parameter estimates. Therefore, the ML approach is chosen as the estimation algorithm. Specifically, the R package GPvam (Karl et al. 2012a, b), which employs the maximum likelihood estimation method for the multiple membership mixed models used in VAM, is used in the current study.

11.4 Results

11.4.1 Model Fit of Different Persistence Models

The Akaike Information Criterion (AIC) is used to compare model fit in this study. Table 11.3 lists the AIC values for all the persistence models fit in each of the four cohorts, and the minimum value within each cohort indicating a best fitting model is bolded. The pattern is similar to Mariano et al.'s findings that the GP model provides the best model fit and the ZP model has the worst model fit compared to the other persistence models.

11.4.2 Correlation Among Teacher Effect of Different Years

Table 11.4 presents the correlation values among the current year teacher effects estimates and their persisting effects in subsequent years estimated from the GP model for the four cohorts. The correlations listed in these four tables are all above 0.84, which are much higher than those values found in Mariano et al.'s study (2010). The correlation values among the persisting effects in the subsequent years are all above 0.99, which is also slightly higher than those found in Mariano et al.'s study (2010), which are above 0.9. It was suggested by Mariano et al. that the correlation between the current year effect and the future year effect can be an indicator of the magnitude of construct shift, and the higher correlation values found in the data may indicate that they exhibit a smaller magnitude of construct shift than those used in the original paper.

11.4.3 Correlation of Teacher Effects Produced by Different Persistence Models

Table 11.5 presents the correlation among the current year teacher effect estimation of four different persistence models for the four cohorts. Consistent with Mariano et al.'s findings, the correlation between the VP and the GP models is extremely

Table 11.3 AIC for different models in different cohorts

	Model			
Cohort	ZP	VP	CP	GP
Cohort 1	202556.3	199101.6	199649.4	**198905.5**
Cohort 2	201260.1	197560	198140.3	**197275.5**
Cohort 3	195955.7	193154.8	193716.1	**192795.5**
Cohort 4	196928.4	194391.5	194731.8	**194292.5**

Table 11.4 Correlation in different cohorts

			Year 1			Year 2	
Cohort	Year	Teacher effect	Current	Year 2	Year 3	Current	Year 3
Cohort 1	Year 1	Current	1				
		Year 2	0.988	1			
		Year 3	0.990	0.999	1		
	Year 2	Current				1	
		Year 3				0.896	1
Cohort 2	Year 1	Current	1				
		Year 2	0.995	1			
		Year 3	0.986	0.998	1		
	Year 2	Current				1	
		Year 3				0.846	1
Cohort 3	Year 1	Current	1				
		Year 2	0.984	1			
		Year 3	0.981	0.999	1		
	Year 2	Current				1	
		Year 3				0.977	1
Cohort 4	Year 1	Current	1				
		Year 2	0.998	1			
		Year 3	0.996	0.999	1		
	Year 2	Current				1	
		Year 3				0.957	1

high regardless of the year, and the correlation between the CP and the VP model seems to be less in year 2 and year 3. An interesting observation is that in year 1, the teacher effect estimates of the CP and the VP model seem to be also extremely highly correlated. When it comes to the choice of persistence models, the choice of the GP model over the VP does not make a big difference in terms of teacher effect estimates.

11.5 Discussion

The four data sets used in the current study are not vertically scaled, which aligns well with Mariano et al.'s recommendation of using data sets without common development scales to investigate the generalizability of their findings. This recommendation was driven by their suspicion that the extremely high correlation of teacher effect estimates produced by the GP model and the VP model might be due to the small magnitude of construct shift indicated by the vertical scaling design in their dataset, since one of the assumptions of vertical scaling design is that no major construct shift occurs across grades. Similarly, datasets without vertical

Table 11.5 Correlation among current year teacher effects estimates of different models in different cohorts

			Year 1				Year 2				Year 3			
Cohort	Year	Model	CP	VP	ZP	GP	CP	VP	ZP	GP	CP	VP	ZP	GP
Cohort 1	Year 1	CP	1											
		VP	0.997	1										
		ZP	0.893	0.902	1									
		GP	0.996	0.999	0.912	1								
	Year 2	CP					1							
		VP					0.945	1						
		ZP					0.518	0.739	1					
		GP					0.886	0.976	0.799	1				
	Year 3	CP									1			
		VP									0.844	1		
		ZP									0.322	0.749	1	
		GP									0.776	0.974	0.812	1
Cohort 2	Year 1	CP	1											
		VP	0.996	1										
		ZP	0.801	0.824	1									
		GP	0.994	0.999	0.834	1								
	Year 2	CP					1							
		VP					0.868	1						
		ZP					0.225	0.645	1					
		GP					0.749	0.951	0.762	1				
	Year 3	CP									1			
		VP									0.888	1		
		ZP									0.560	0.852	1	
		GP									0.883	0.986	0.855	1
Cohort 3	Year 1	CP	1											
		VP	0.991	1										
		ZP	0.848	0.890	1									
		GP	0.989	0.999	0.895	1								
	Year 2	CP					1							
		VP					0.911	1						
		ZP					0.650	0.887	1					
		GP					0.909	0.988	0.880	1				
	Year 3	CP									1			
		VP									0.913	1		
		ZP									0.668	0.889	1	
		GP									0.917	0.993	0.879	1

(continued)

Table 11.5 (continued)

			Year 1				Year 2				Year 3			
Cohort	Year	Model	CP	VP	ZP	GP	CP	VP	ZP	GP	CP	VP	ZP	GP
Cohort 4	Year 1	CP	1											
		VP	0.995	1										
		ZP	0.798	0.824	1									
		GP	0.994	0.999	0.830	1								
	Year 2	CP					1							
		VP					0.937	1						
		ZP					0.609	0.822	1					
		GP					0.925	0.992	0.827	1				
	Year 3	CP									1			
		VP									0.855	1		
		ZP									0.443	0.815	1	
		GP									0.832	0.989	0.831	1

scaling design may exhibit large magnitude of construct shift which causes the teacher estimates from the GP model and the VP model to be considerably different.

Consistent with Mariano et al.'s finding, the GP model has the best model fit among the four persistence models, suggesting the existence of variable teacher effects over time in those data sets. While the issue of construct shift versus variable teacher effects seems somewhat complicated, it can be stated that, even if construct shift exists, it does not seem to cause the GP model and the VP model to produce noticeably different teacher effect estimates, and in the four cohorts the correlations between the estimates from those two models are all higher than 0.95. As suggested by Mariano et al., the correlation between the current year effect and the persisting future year effect may be an indicator of the magnitude of construct shift, and the high correlation values presented in Table 11.5 seem to indicate a small magnitude of construct shift in all four data sets.

Another possible explanation for such high correlations is that despite the existence of construct shift of considerable magnitude, teacher effects may be too robust to cause teacher effect estimates from those two models to be different enough. Since all the current data come from standardized tests that have similar test blueprints across grades, it is more likely that despite the lack of vertical scaling design, the magnitude of construct shift, assuming that it exists, is relatively small; therefore, it is more likely that the high correlations found in the current data example be due to the combination of small magnitude of construct shift and the robustness of teacher effects across construct change. To disentangle those two effects, future studies with empirical data sets of considerably different test blue prints across grades should be used to investigate whether the high similarity between the estimates from the GP model and the VP model still exists.

It may seem natural to choose the GP model as the analysis model in practice since it is the most generalized persistence model. However, it produces teacher effect estimates highly similar to those of the VP model despite the GP model's theoretical advantage as a result of its explicit modeling of the construct shift. One advantage of the VP model over the GP model is the computing time: it takes an I7 processor computer about two hours to estimate the GP model and about fifteen minutes to estimate the VP model, which, as a simpler model, should estimate teacher effects with greater precision. Such a time difference should be negligible for empirical data analysis since no replications are required as in large-scale simulation studies. Moreover, with the advance of modern computing power and the development of more efficient estimation algorithms, it is anticipated that the time factor will become less of a concern.

References

Browne, W. J., Goldstein, H., & Rasbash, J. (2001). Multiple membership multiple classification (MMMC) models. *Statistical Modelling: An International Journal, 1*, 103–124.

Carlin, B., & Louis, T. (2000). *Bayes and empirical Bayes methods for data analysis* (2nd ed.). Boca Raton, FL: Chapman and Hall/CRC Press.

Diggle, P. J., Liang, K.-Y., & Zeger, S. L. (1996). *Analysis of longitudinal data*. New York: Oxford University Press.

Gelman, A., Carlin, J., Stern, H., & Rubin, D. (1995). *Bayesian data analysis*. London: Chapman & Hall.

Gilks, W. R., Richardson, S., & Spiegelhalter, D. J. (1996). *Markov chain Monte Carlo in practice*. London: Chapman & Hall.

Harris, D., & Sass, T. (2006). *Value-added models and the measurement of teacher quality*. Unpublished manuscript.

Karl, A., Yang, Y., & Lohr, S. (2012a). Efficient maximum likelihood estimation for multiple membership mixed models used in value-added modeling. *Computational Statistics and Data Analysis, 59*, 13–27.

Karl, A. T., Yang, Y., & Lohr, S. (2012b). *GPvam: Maximum likelihood estimation of multiple membership mixed models used in value-added modeling*. R Package Version 2.0-0. http://cran.r-project.org/web/packages/GPvam/index.html

Lockwood, J., McCaffrey, D., Mariano, L., & Setodji, C. (2007). Bayesian methods for scalable multivariate value-added assessment. *Journal of Educational and Behavioral Statistics, 32*, 125–150.

Mariano, L., McCaffrey, D., & Lockwood, J. (2010). A model for teacher effects from longitudinal data without assuming vertical scaling. *Journal of Educational and Behavioral Statistics, 35*, 253–279.

McCaffrey, D., Lockwood, J., Koretz, D., Louis, T., & Hamilton, L. (2004). Models for value-added modeling of teacher effects. *Journal of Educational and Behavioral Statistics, 29*, 67–101.

Meyer, R. (1997). Value-added indicators of school performance: A primer. *Economics of Education Review, 16*, 183–301.

Rasbash, J., & Browne, W. (2001). Modelling non-hierarchical structures. In A. Leyland & H. Goldstein (Eds.), *Multilevel modelling of health statistics* (pp. 93–103). West Sussex, England: Wiley.

Raudenbusch, S. W., & Bryk, A. S. (2002). *Hierarchical linear models: Applications and data analysis methods, second edition*. Newbury Park, CA: Sage.

Rowan, B., Correnti, R., & Miller, R. J. (2002). What large-scale, survey research tells us about teacher effects on student achievement: Insights from the prospects study of elementary schools. *Teachers College Record, 104*, 1525–1567.

Sanders, W., Saxton, A., & Horn, B. (1997). The Tennessee value-added assessment system: A quantitative outcomes-based approach to educational assessment. In J. Millman (Ed.), *Grading teachers, grading schools: Is student achievement a valid evaluational measure?* (pp. 137–162). Thousand Oaks, CA: Corwin.

Schmidt, W. H., Houang, R. T., & McKnight, C. C. (2005). Value-added research: Right idea but wrong solution? In R. Lissitz (Ed.), *Value added models in education: Theory and applications* (pp. 145–165). Maple Grove, MN: JAM Press.

Shkolnik, J., Hikawa, H., Suttorp, M., Lockwood, J., Stecher, B., & Bohrnstedt, G. (2002). Appendix D: The relationship between teacher characteristics and student achievement in reduced-size classes: A study of 6 California districts. In G. W. Bohrnstedt & B. M. Stecher (Eds.), *What we have learned about class size reduction in California Technical Appendix*. Palo Alto, CA: American Institutes for Research.

Spiegelhalter, D., Thomas, A., Best, N., Gilks, W., & Lunn, D. (2002). *BUGS: Bayesian inference using Gibbs sampling*. Cambridge, England: MRC Biostatistics Unit. www.mrc-bsu.cam.ac.uk/bugs/.

Chapter 12
The Impact of Model Misspecification with Multidimensional Test Data

Sakine Gocer Sahin, Cindy M. Walker, and Selahattin Gelbal

Abstract In this study data were simulated for 5000 examinees on a thirty-item two-dimensional test, using a compensatory MIRT model. Various combinations of simple and complex structure items were examined. Specifically, the numbers of simple structure items on the tests were gradually decreased from 24 to 6, in multiples of six, while simultaneously increasing the number of complex items by the same number of items. In one scenario, the simple structure items were simulated to measure both dimensions equally; in a second scenario, the simple structured items were simulated to measure only the first dimension. The current investigation also varied the correlation between dimensions and the ability distributions on the first and second dimensions. RMSE was used to determine the impact of model misspecification and the results of a unidimensional simulated and scaled test were used for comparison purposes. Results indicated that the underlying structure of multidimensional tests did have an impact on estimation error. However, in some instances fitting a unidimensional model to multidimensional data resulted in estimation error that was not very dissimilar from what was obtained when fitting a unidimensional model to unidimensional data.

Keywords Multidimensionality • Unidimensionality • Item response theory

In unidimensional item response theory (IRT), it is assumed that only one trait or ability underlies an individual's performance on a test. This is the most critical and basic assumption of measurement theory, the assumption that all of the items on an assessment instrument measure only one common thing. (Hambleton et al. 1978) stated that this assumption of unidimensionality is the strictest assumptions

S. Gocer Sahin (✉) • S. Gelbal
Hacettepe University, Hacettepe Universitesi Egitim Fakultesi
Egitim Bilimleri Bolumu, Ankara 06800, Turkey
e-mail: sgocersahin@gmail.com; sgelbal@gmail.com

C.M. Walker
University of Wisconsin-Milwaukee, END 599,
PO Box 413, Milwaukee, WI 53201, USA
e-mail: cmwalker@uwm.edu

L.A. van der Ark et al. (eds.), *Quantitative Psychology Research*, Springer Proceedings in Mathematics & Statistics 140, DOI 10.1007/978-3-319-19977-1_12

underlying the model of latent traits (Hattie 1985). Therefore, this assumption is oftentimes not met on many educational and psychological tests. This is because there are other factors which may affect test performance. For example, other cognitive traits, affective traits such as personality and attitude, and testing conditions may all affect test performance. In order for the assumption of unidimensionality to be met there must only be one dominant factor, or component, which affects the performance of individuals on the test (Hambleton et al. 1991).

Using unidimensional IRT models to scale response data does have some advantages. It is a simpler model, it is readily available in standard psychometric software packages, and has been used in a large number of applications. However, the interaction between an individual and an item is not always as simple as this, in that it cannot be explained by only one dimension. Traub (1992) described the unidimensionality assumption of IRT as a "fragile, sensitive" assumption. Although unidimensional IRT models are frequently used in practice and can be effective for ability estimation under certain circumstances, more complex IRT models were developed to model the complex interaction between an individual and an item (Harrison 1986).

One of the ways to increase the efficiency of IRT models to account for the complex interaction between individuals and items is to define multiple traits of individuals (Reckase 2009). According to Ackerman (1992), multidimensional IRT models were developed because it is technically inappropriate to scale individuals at a single ability level when the unidimensionality assumption was not met. However, in practice it is still most common to use a unidimensional model.

A multidimensional structure can be categorized as simple, approximately simple, or complex (Walker et al. 2006). This can be explained from a factor analytic perspective in a two-dimensional space with each factor being used to represent a dimension. If an item loads on only one factor, with a zero factor loading on the second factor, then it is a simple structured item. If an item loads primarily on one factor but has a small factor loading on the second factor, then it is an approximately simple structured item. If an item loads on both factors in at least a moderate way, then it is a complex item. For example, on a mathematics test designed to assess algebraic reasoning and geometric reasoning, items that were only measuring either algebra or geometry skills would be simple structured items, while items measuring both algebra and geometry would be complex items. When multiple abilities are needed to assess a psychological behavior it is likely that most items in the measure are not simple structured. In this case, if there is one dominant dimension and one or more non-dominant dimensions being measured by test items, the test is said to be *essentially unidimensional* (Stout 1987). In the event that both complex and simple structured items are on a test, the structure of the test is called a mixed structure (Zhang 2005, 2012).

The criticisms of an item structure or a particular model are generally based on the strict and unique traits of that item structure or model. For example, the concept of essential unidimensionality emerged in response to the criticism of the unidimensionality assumption. Likewise, the concept of approximately simple structured items emerged in response to the criticism of the credibility of having only simple structured items on a test. This is also the reason for the conceptualization of tests of mixed structures because it is unrealistic to think that all test items measure only one primary dimension. As previously stated, when simple and complex items exist together, the test is said to be of mixed structure. On the other hand, when approximately simple and complex items exist together on a test, the test is said to be of semi-mixed structure (Zhang 2012).

Although it might be theoretically better to scale response data using multi-dimensional IRT models, these models are not often applied in practice because they are difficult to interpret and it is often difficult and complex to define the underlying dimensions (Luecht and Miller 1992). One might also argue that these models are not used because there is a proliferation of available user-friendly software that can be used to scale response data using unidimensional IRT models, such as MULTILOG and BILOG. Although there are also programs available to fit multidimensional IRT models, such as TESTFACT and NOHARM, ability estimates cannot be obtained from these programs, even though it is possible to obtain item parameters from them (Zhang 2008). Due to these reasons, the use of unidimensional models still dominates the testing industry.

Studies on scaling multidimensional data using unidimensional models are conducted because it is well known that violating the unidimensionality assumption can cause many problems. Yet, these models continue to be widely used in practice because they are easy to apply and interpret. While using a unidimensional model to scale response data from a test with complex items has been previously studied, using a unidimensional model to scale response data from a test that has a semi-mixed structure has not been studied previously. Considering that a semi-mixed test structure is more likely to be encountered in practice, this study reflects a more realistic testing situation. Unidimensionality is not only a trait that refers to items, rather it is the product of an interaction between a measures item structure and underlying person ability distribution. In previous studies, only item traits or only ability distributions were manipulated while the underlying ability distribution was assumed to be multivariate normal. In this study, both item structure and underlying ability distributions are addressed together. Thus, it is the aim of this study to evaluate what happens when the unidimensionality assumption is violated in a more extensive and realistic manner.

12.1 Method

There are some studies in the literature that have considered the impact of modeling a multidimensional test as unidimensional. Zhang (2005, 2012) focused on different estimation algorithms, with both mixed- and simple-structure tests that were modeled using both unidimensional and multidimensional approaches. The results of these simulation studies indicated that when subtests had fewer items a multidimensional approach provided more accurate estimates of item parameters. However, the unidimensional approach worked better as the number of items on the subtest increased. Zhang (2008) estimated approximately simple items as unidimensional. In his study, the number of dimensions, test length, proportions of items sensitive to the secondary dimensions and levels of correlation were all considered as independent variables. In his study, the RMSE decreased as the correlation between dimensions, test length increased and number of items measuring secondary dimensions, and number of secondary dimensions decreased. It is well known that when the correlation between dimensions increases a multidimensional test becomes more unidimensional like (Ansley and Forsyth 1985; Ackerman 1989). In this study we used semi-mixed tests like one of above studies because we hypothesized that the location of complex items can impact ability estimation. The standard error of measurement increases when items are either too difficult or too easy for an examinee. This is because there are studies in the literature that have explored the impact of skewed ability distributions when modeling multidimensional tests as unidimensional (Kirisci et al. 2001). Unlike previous studies, in this research we examined estimating multidimensional tests as unidimensional under neither skewed nor standard normal underlying ability distributions. Rather, normal distributions were considered with different means, to determine the impact of mismatching item difficulty to examinee ability. We also considered different combinations of simple or complex items, the location of simple items on the tests and different correlations because we hypothesized that these would have an impact on estimation.

Specifically, in this study, parameters of semi-mixed two-dimensional tests were estimated using a unidimensional IRT model under two conditions. These conditions include: (1) different underlying ability distributions (either equal or unequal ability distributions between θ_1 and θ_2), and (2) different correlations between dimensions (0.00, 0.45, and 0.90). For all conditions, the number of items was fixed at 30 and the sample size was fixed at $n = 5000$. In total, 72 $(3 \times 4 \times 3 \times 2)$ conditions were studied: three different conditions for underlying ability distributions; four different conditions for the ratio of simple- to complex items; three different conditions for the correlation between dimensions; and two different conditions for the primary dimension being measured by simple structure items (i.e., the first or the second). Data were simulated based on two-parameter multidimensional item response model (Reckase 1997) as expressed in Eq. (12.1).

$$P\left(u_{ij} = 1 \middle| \theta_j\right) = \frac{1}{1 + \exp\left[-1.7\left(a_i\theta_j + d_i\right)\right]} \tag{12.1}$$

where P is the conditional probability that examinee j's response u to item i is correct, θ_j is the ability vector, a_i is the discrimination parameter vector, and d_i is related to the difficulty level. Item parameter and ability estimation were conducted using BILOG. For each condition, 100 replications were conducted.

Although test length was fixed, the structure of test items varied according to the location of simple and complex items on the test. Two scenarios were simulated based on the location and number of mixed items on the test. In the first scenario, all of the simple structured items were simulated to load on only the first dimension. In the second scenario, half of the simple structured items were simulated to load on

Table 12.1 Study pattern concerning the case in which inter-dimensional correlation is 0.00

θ_1	θ_2	Correlations between dimensions	First scenario		Second scenario	
			1. dimension	2. dimension	1. dimension	2. dimension
N(0,1)	N(0,1)	0.00	24S + 6C	6C	12S + 6C	12S + 6C
			18S + 12C	12C	9S + 12C	9S + 12C
			12S + 18C	18C	6S + 18C	6S + 18C
			6S + 24C	24C	3S + 24C	3S + 24C
N(−.5,1)	N(0,1)	0.00	24S + 6C	6C	12S + 6C	12S + 6C
			18S + 12C	12C	9S + 12C	9S + 12C
			12S + 18C	18C	6S + 18C	6S + 18C
			6S + 24C	24C	3S + 24C	3S + 24C
N(0,1)	N(−1,1)	0.00	24S + 6C	6C	12S + 6C	12S + 6C
			18S + 12C	12C	9S + 12C	9S + 12C
			12S + 18C	18C	6S + 18C	6S + 18C
			6S + 24C	24C	3S + 24C	3S + 24C

S Approximately simple item, *C* Complex item expected

the first factor and the other half of the simple structure items were simulated to load on the second factor. The conditions studied are depicted in detail in Table 12.1.

As Table 12.1 illustrates, the current study focused primarily on the pattern of items that were simulated to measure each of the dimensions. These patterns of items were simulated according to two different scenarios and three different underlying ability distributions for the first and second dimension. For example, for one condition 24 simple structured and six complex structured items were simulated. In the first scenario, all simple structured items were simulated to only measure the first dimension. In this scenario, only the six complex items measured the second dimension. When considering the second scenario for this same condition, 6 items were simulated with complex structure, while 12 of the 24 simple structured items were simulated to measure the first dimension and the other 12 were simulated to measure the second dimension. Therefore, in the second scenario both dimensions are being measured equally well by the simulated test. This differs from the first scenario where the test is primarily measuring the first dimension. This condition was studied under three different ability distributions. In the first case θ_1 and θ_2 were generated from a standard normal distribution. In the second case, the mean of the distribution of $\theta_1 \sim N(-0.5, 1)$ was 0.5 lower than θ_2 which was simulated from a standard normal distribution. In the third case, θ_1 was simulated from a standard normal distribution, while $\theta_2 \sim N(-1,0)$ was generated from a distribution with a mean 1 unit lower than θ_1. Table 12.1 was replicated under the two different correlation between dimensions considered in this study which were 0.45 and 0.90.

Discrimination parameters for approximately simple structured items were generated from an $N \sim (1,0.1)$ distribution for the dominant factor and from a Log-$N \sim (-3,0.1)$ distribution(s) for the secondary factors in order to ensure that the discrimination parameters obtained were positive and realistic for the dominant dimension and small and positive for the secondary factor. For similar reasons, the discrimination parameters for both dimensions were generated from an N ~ (1,0.1) for complex items. Difficulty parameters were generated from an N ~ (0,0.1) distribution. Approximately simple structured items were simulated to have an angular distance of less than 20° from the primary dimension being measured by the item. Complex structured items were simulated so that their angular distance from the first dimension was between 20° and 70°.

The RMSE (Root Mean Square Error) statistic, shown in Eq. (12.2), was used to evaluate parameter estimation error, as well as ability estimation error, when multidimensional response data is scaled using a unidimensional IRT model.

$$RMSE = \sqrt{\frac{\Sigma_{n=1}^{N}\left(\overline{\tau}_{nj} - \tau_n\right)^2}{N}} \tag{12.2}$$

In Eq. (12.2), $\overline{\tau}_{nj}$ represents the estimated parameter for parameter for examinee *n* in the *j*th item, τ_{nj} represents the actual parameter for examinee *n* in the *j*th item, and N represents the number of replications. RMSE values were calculated separately for item difficulty, item discrimination, and ability parameters. Furthermore, RMSE was also examined for the average of the two discrimination parameters, for MDISC, and for the average of the two ability parameters. A test, which was simulated to be unidimensional, was also estimated using a unidimensional IRT model to provide a baseline from which the results could be compared. To simulate a unidimensional test, the parameters from a multidimensional test, MDISC (maximum discrimination index), and D were utilized. MDISC is the overall discriminating power of an item which shares the same interpretation as the discrimination parameter in the unidimensional models (Reckase and McKinley 1968).

$$\mathrm{MDISC} = \sqrt{\Sigma_{\mathrm{n}=1}^{\mathrm{k}}\alpha_{\mathrm{ik}}} \tag{12.3}$$

where K refers to the number of ability dimensions. The difficulty level of an item is defined as:

$$D = \frac{-d_i}{MDISC} \tag{12.4}$$

In this equation d_{i} is intercept term. The value of D has the same interpretation as the *b* parameter for the unidimensional IRT. The ability distribution for the unidimensional test was generated from the same underlying distribution that was used to generate the multidimensional tests. The RMSE values obtained from this unidimensional test were used as the baseline criterion to evaluate the magnitude of the errors that were obtained from the multidimensional data.

The reliability of the generated data was evaluated using Cronbach's alpha. Cronbach alpha coefficient is an unbiased estimate of reliability when tests are at least essentially tau-equivalent (Lord and Novick 1968). From an operational aspect, a test that is essentially tau-equivalent has items that are equally discriminating.

In this case, all of the items would have equal factor loadings under the single factor model underlying the test (McDonald 1999). This requirement is quite strict. However, it is well known that Cronbach's alpha is a lower bound estimate of reliability when this requirement is not met (Raykov 1997; Zinbarg et al. 2005). For the simulated data the alpha coefficient ranged between 0.86 and 0.94 for the first scenario, and between 0.80 and 0.94 for the second scenario. Even though Cronbach alpha is not typically used in multidimensional IRT it is used for unidimensional tests. And also more importantly considering the fact that the reliability obtained is a lower bound, this range of values can be considered satisfactory. Therefore, estimates of reliability that may be better suited for multidimensional data were not calculated.

12.2 Findings

The RMSE values obtained from the simulated unidimensional test are presented in Table 12.2. These values will be used as the criterion by which to evaluate the RMSE values obtained when simulated multidimensional test data is scaled using a unidimensional IRT model.

The RMSE values depicted in Table 12.2 correspond to every multidimensional test that was simulated for the various combinations of simple and complex items that were studied. As mentioned before, the unidimensional test was formed from the multidimensional test parameters. Although there were two *a* parameters for a two-dimensional test a single *a* discrimination parameter was generated by using Eq. (12.3) to obtain the a parameter for the unidimensional test. Once again, despite the fact that there were two theta parameters for the two-dimensional test, only one theta was needed for the unidimensional test. Specifically, ability was generated from the same distribution that was used to obtain the multidimensional theta distribution, $N \sim (0,1)$. Since the number of simple and complex items was different in each condition, the tests for these conditions were also different. As the table illustrates, the RMSE value for the discrimination parameter increased as

Table 12.2 RMSE values obtained when fitting a unidimensional IRT model to simulated unidimensional response data

		RMSE for a	RMSE for b	RMSE for Theta
First scenario	24S + 6C = 30	0.038	0.024	0.322
	18S + 12C = 30	0.040	0.023	0.322
	12S + 18C = 30	0.043	0.023	0.322
	6S + 24C = 30	0.045	0.023	0.324
Second scenario	12S + 12SS + 6C = 30	0.038	0.024	0.322
	9S + 9S + 12C = 30	0.040	0.023	0.322
	6S + 6S + 18C = 30	0.043	0.023	0.322
	3S + 3S + 24C = 30	0.045	0.023	0.324

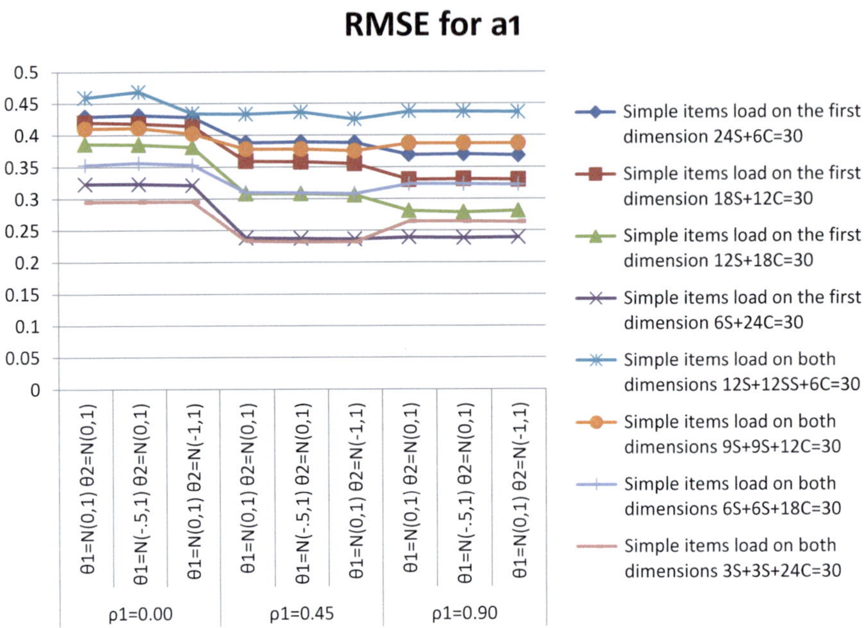

Fig. 12.1 RMSE values for a1 parameter

the number of complex items increased, when the corresponding MDISC values from the multidimensional items to simulate the unidimensional data were used. Little differences were observed in the RMSE values for the difficulty parameters or ability estimates across all test types.

Figure 12.1 illustrates the RMSE values for a_1. It should be noted that all of the results are presented graphically. However, these results are presented in tabular form in Appendix, for the interested reader. As illustrated in Fig. 12.1, for multidimensional semi-mixed tests, a decrease in the RMSE values for the discrimination parameter on the first dimension (a_1) was found as the number of complex items increased for the first scenario, in which simple items loaded only on the first dimension. In addition, in the first scenario, the RMSE values for the a_1 parameters decreased as the correlation between dimensions increased. Finally, Fig. 12.1 illustrates that having different primary and secondary dimension ability distributions did not have much impact on the RMSE values for the a_1 parameter. Also, the errors obtained from all conditions converged in value as the number of complex items increased.

In the second scenario, in which half of the simple structured items load on the first dimension and the other half load on the second dimension, the RMSE values obtained for the a_1 parameters resemble a hyperbolic curve. Specifically, the RMSE was highest for this parameter when the correlation between dimensions was 0.00, lowest when the correlation was 0.45, and somewhere in between when the correlation was 0.90. In this scenario, the RMSE values decreased as the number

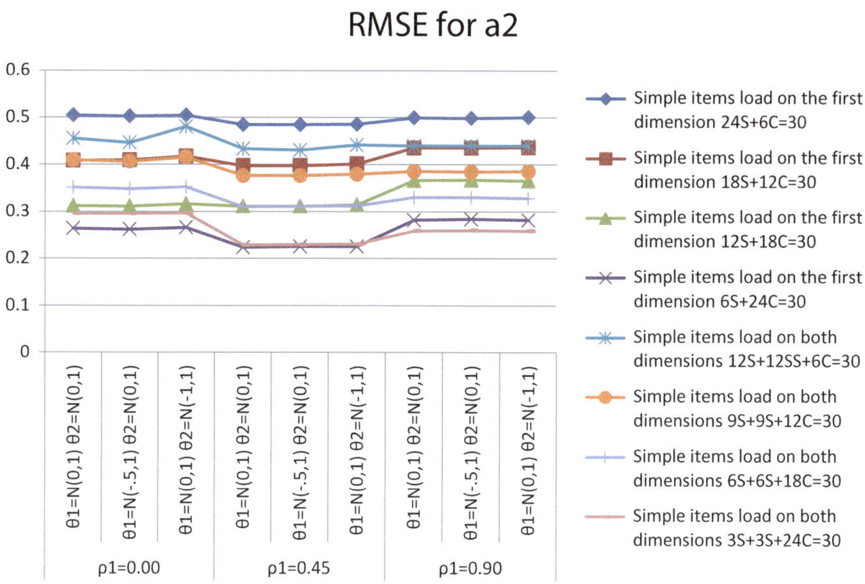

Fig. 12.2 RMSE values for a2 parameter

of complex items increased. As the number of complex items increased, having different ability distributions did not have much impact on the RMSE values for a_1. In general, the pattern of results for a_1 looks fairly random and there was not a clear pattern when comparing the results of the first and second scenarios. However, the results were very similar when the correlation between dimensions was 0.90.

Figure 12.2 depicts the RMSE values for a_2. These results were comparable to the RMSE values that were obtained for the a_1 parameters; however, these results were slightly less stable. Accordingly, for the first scenario, the lowest RMSE value was obtained when the correlation between dimensions was 0.45, and the highest RMSE value was obtained when the correlation between dimensions was 0.90. Once again the RMSE decreased as the number of complex items increased, and once again underlying differences in the mean of ability distributions did not seem to impact the RMSE associated with the a_2 parameter.

For the second scenario, once again the lowest error was obtained when the correlation between dimensions was 0.45, and the highest error was obtained when the correlation between dimensions was 0.00. For this scenario, a lower mean for the ability distribution on the second dimension seemed to impact the error associated with the a_2 parameters slightly more when the correlation between dimensions was 0.00. This impact decreased as the correlation between dimensions increased. However, having a lower mean ability distribution on the first dimension did not have an impact on the errors associated with a_2. The RMSE values associated with a_2 also decreased as the number of complex items increased. Furthermore, the effect of having different underlying mean ability distributions decreased as the number of complex items increased. In general, as the number of complex items decreased, the

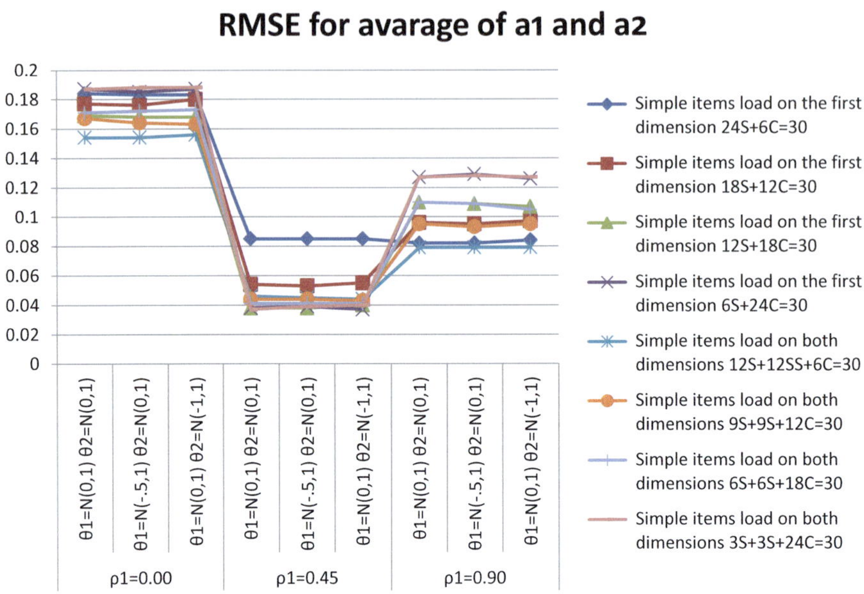

Fig. 12.3 RMSE values for average of a1 and a2 parameters

errors obtained from the second scenario were lower than those obtained from the first scenario. However, no other discernible patterns were observed for the other conditions explored in this study.

Figure 12.3 depicts the results that were obtained when considering the average of a_1 and a_2. As the figure illustrates, for the first scenario, the lowest error was generally obtained when the correlation between dimensions was 0.45, and the highest error was generally obtained when the correlation between dimensions was 0.00. For the first scenario, differing mean ability distributions was not found to impact the average RMSE obtained for the average of the discrimination parameters. No apparent pattern was observed as the number of complex items increased.

For the second scenario, in which simple items were simulated to load on both dimensions, the errors were generally lower than those obtained in the first scenario. When compared with the criterion RMSE values in Table 12.2, the error values for the second scenario are close to the criterion, and some are even better, under certain conditions. Once again, the lowest errors were obtained when the correlation between dimensions was 0.45, and the highest errors were obtained when the correlation between dimensions was 0.00. Moreover, when the correlation between dimensions was 0.45, as the number of complex items increased the errors decreased. However, when the correlation between dimensions was either 0.00 or 0.90, as the number of complex items increased so did the RMSE. As was the case with the first scenario, having different underlying ability distributions on the two dimensions did not seem to impact the error associated with the average discrimination parameter.

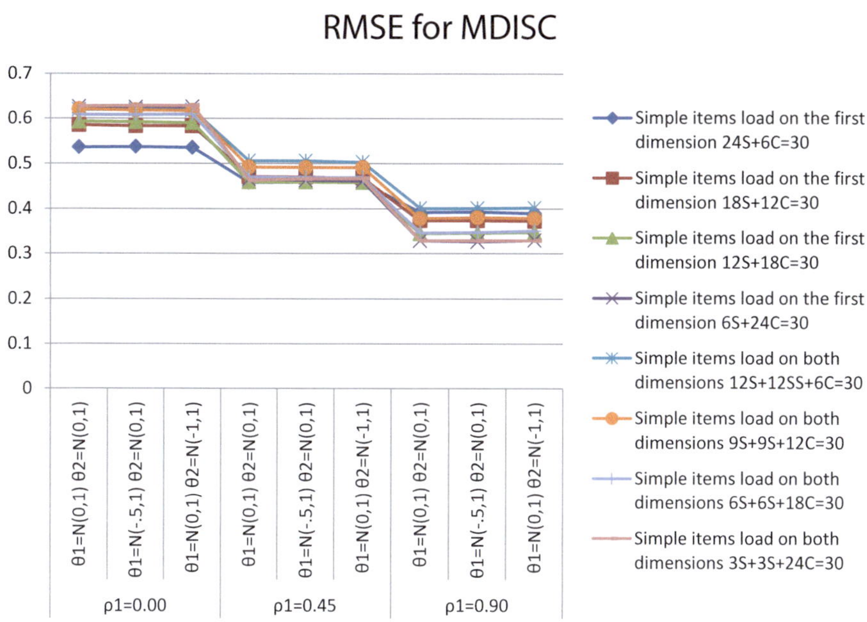

Fig. 12.4 RMSE values for MDISC parameter

Figure 12.4 depicts the RMSE associated with MDISC. MDISC corresponds to the discrimination parameter from a unidimensional IRT model and is calculated based on all of the discrimination parameters in the multidimensional model. Figure 12.4 illustrates an unsurprising pattern for both scenarios as the correlation between dimensions increases. Specifically, as the correlation between dimensions increased, the RMSE values decreased. In addition, when the correlation between dimensions was zero, the RMSE increased as the number of complex items increased. However, when the correlation between dimensions was 0.90, the RMSE values decreased as the number of items increased. When the correlation between dimensions was 0.45 there was no discernible pattern to the RMSE values as the number of complex items increased. As was the case with the average discrimination parameter, having unequal means on the underlying ability distributions did not seem to impact the error associated with MDISC.

Figure 12.4 also illustrates that, in general, the errors obtained in the second scenario were higher than those obtained in the first scenario; however, the errors obtained from both scenarios converged in value as the correlation between dimensions increased. Also in the second scenario the errors seemed to decrease as the number of complex items increased, when the correlations between dimensions were 0.45 and 0.90. As is the case with the first scenario, it can be said that having a mean difference between the underlying distributions did not impact the error associated with MDISC.

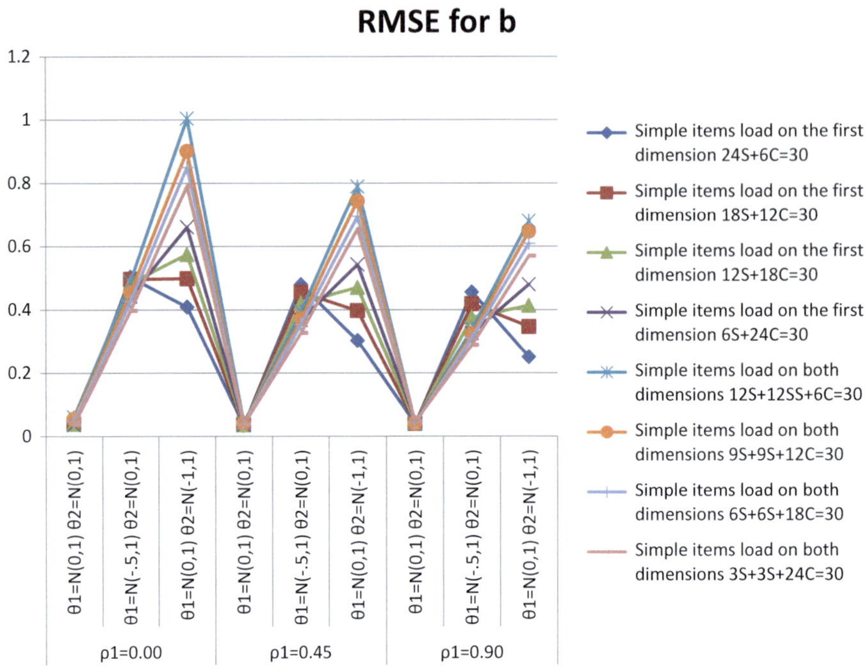

Fig. 12.5 RMSE values for b parameter

The RMSE values obtained for the difficulty parameters are illustrated in Fig. 12.5. As the figure illustrates, this parameter is more unstable and the errors are more substantial than what was observed for the discrimination parameters. In the first scenario, the lowest errors were obtained when the correlation between dimensions is 0.45 and the underlying distributions are both normal; the highest were obtained when the correlation between dimensions is 0.00 and the underlying distribution for one of the dimensions is non-standard normal. Unlike what was observed for the discrimination parameters, having unequal means between ability distributions had a significant impact on the errors associated with the difficulty parameter. When the underlying ability distribution of the first dimension had a lower mean than the second dimension, the errors decreased as the number of complex items increased. However, when the underlying ability distribution of the second dimension had a lower mean than first dimension, the errors increased as the number of complex items increased. When the underlying ability distributions had equal means, a regular pattern was not observed, relative to increasing the number of complex items. When the mean of the primary and secondary distributions were not equal, the error decreased as the correlation between dimensions increased.

For the second scenario, the errors obtained when the underlying ability distribution of the first dimension had a lower mean than the ability distribution of the second dimension was lower than those obtained in the analogous case for the first scenario. For all of the remaining conditions the errors obtained for the

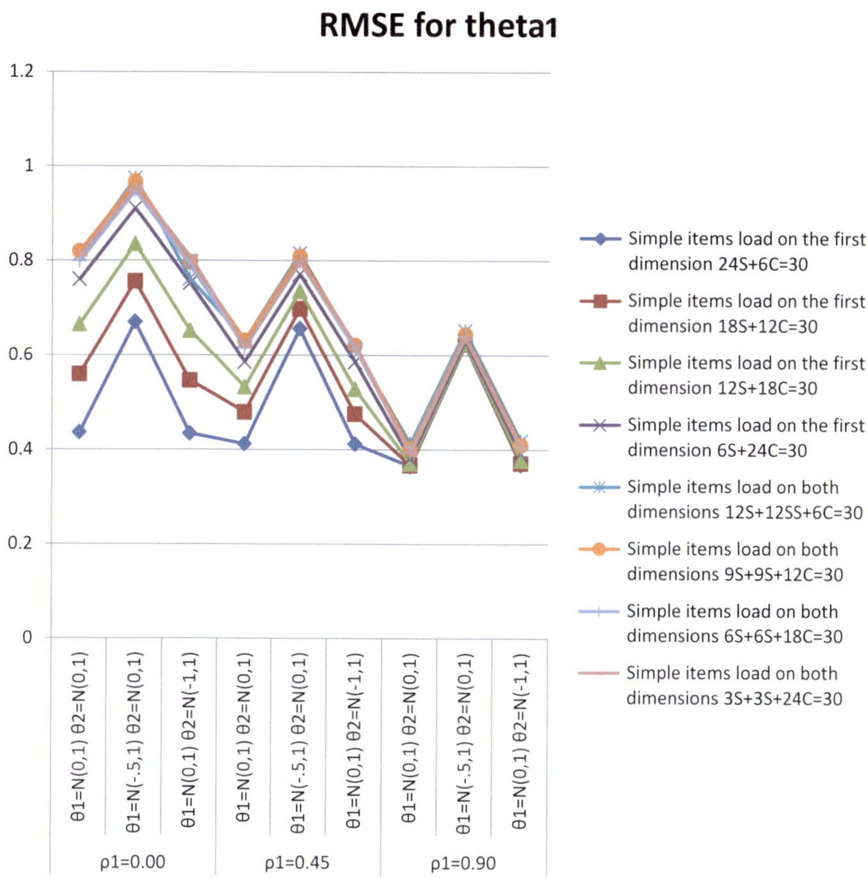

Fig. 12.6 RMSE values for theta1 parameter

second scenario were higher than those obtained in the analogous cases for the first scenario. As is the case with the first scenario, the lowest errors were obtained when the correlation between dimensions was 0.45 and the underlying ability distributions were equal; the highest errors were obtained when the correlation between dimensions was 0.00 and the means of the ability distributions were not equal. For most of the conditions for the second scenario, the errors decreased as the number of complex items increased.

When the RMSE values for the θ_1 ability parameter are examined in Fig. 12.6, it can be observed that, in the first scenario, the errors decreased as the correlation between dimensions increased. Thus, the error obtained for the condition in which the correlation between dimensions was 0.90, and the errors associated with the simulated unidimensional data, used as a baseline criterion, are very similar.

In addition, for the first scenario, the errors increased as the number of complex items increased and having unequal means for the underlying ability distributions on the first dimension impacted the error associated with θ_1.

Figure 12.6 illustrates that the RMSE values obtained from the second scenario were higher than those obtained from the first scenario. A decrease in RMSE values was observed, as the correlation between dimensions increased. No discernible pattern was observed, in terms of the number of complex items. Having a lower mean for the underlying ability distribution on the first dimension compared to the second dimension had a greater impact on the RMSE associated with θ_1 than having a lower mean on the underlying ability distribution on the second dimension in relation to the first. In general, the errors obtained from both scenarios were found to converge, as the correlation between dimensions increased.

When the RMSE values associated with the θ_2 parameter are examined in Fig. 12.7, it can be observed that the average RMSE values decreased as the correlation between dimensions increased, for both scenarios. The RMSE values associated with the condition in which the correlation between dimensions was 0.90 are similar to the criterion RMSE values, obtained from fitting a unidimensional IRT model to unidimensional response data. In general, the errors associated with the second scenario were found to be lower than those associated with the first scenario. While the errors decreased as the number of complex items increased for the first scenario, no discernible pattern was observed as the number of complex items

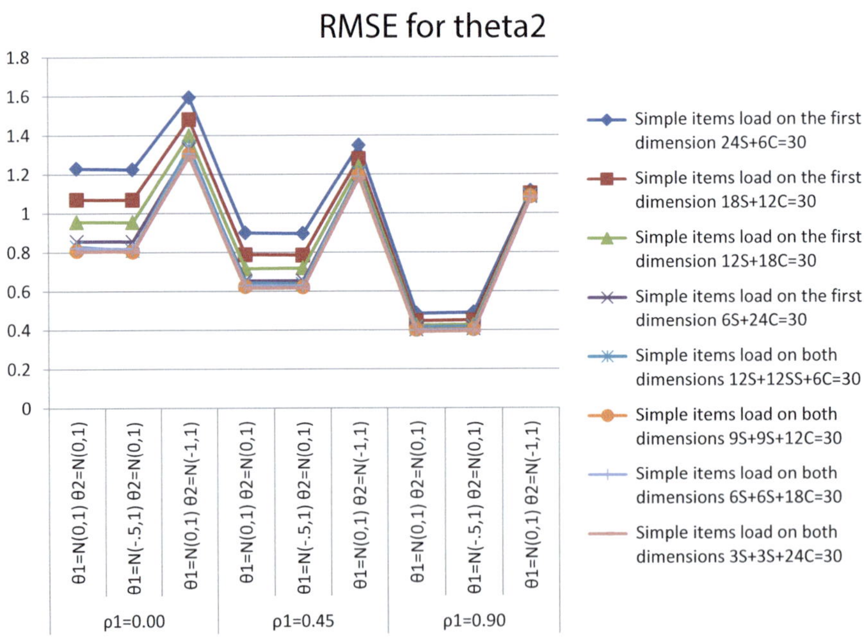

Fig. 12.7 RMSE values for theta2 parameter

increased for the second scenario. When compared to the results obtained for θ_1, for the first scenario, the errors obtained for θ_2 are higher than those obtained for θ_1. In addition, the errors were higher when the mean of the underlying distribution for the second dimension was lower. However, having a lower mean for the underlying distribution on the first dimension did not seem to have much impact on the average RMSE values associated with θ_2. These values are very close to the values obtained when the underlying ability distribution was standard normal.

As illustrated in Fig. 12.8, the average RMSE values obtained for the average of θ_1 and θ_2 are lower than those obtained for either θ_1 or θ_2. Moreover, these errors tended to decrease as the correlation between dimensions increased. In general, the error values obtained for the second scenario were lower than those obtained for the first scenario, and the errors for both scenarios converge as the correlation between dimensions increases. Once again, the errors obtained when the correlation between dimensions was 0.90 and the underlying ability distributions were equal are almost the same as the criterion, when a unidimensional IRT model was used to scale unidimensional response data. For both scenarios, the errors tended to decrease as the number of complex items increased. While the lowest errors were obtained when both underlying ability distributions were from a standard normal distribution, the highest errors were obtained when the mean of the underlying ability distribution of θ_2 was lower than θ_1.

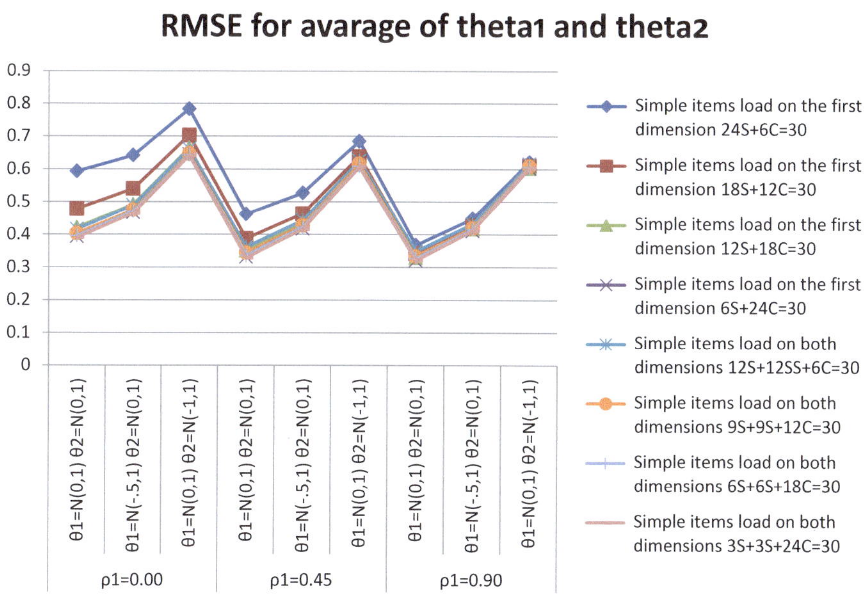

Fig. 12.8 RMSE values for average of theta1 and theta2 parameters

12.3 Discussion

In this study, we calculated the errors for the semi-mixed test structured multidimensional tests, which contain both essentially simple and complex items, after using unidimensional IRT models to estimate the parameters. Two scenarios were simulated that differed according to the location of simple structured items on the test and the number of complex items on the test. In addition to these two scenarios, the impact of having a mean difference between the underlying ability distributions for the primary and second dimensions, as well as the impact of increasing the correlation between dimensions was studied. The errors obtained were evaluated for individual item and ability parameters.

12.3.1 Parameter a

When studies similar to this one, which are currently in the literature, are examined, it can be said that the findings associated with the item parameters obtained in this study are interesting. Previous studies have determined that the error associated with the discrimination parameters decreases as the correlation between dimensions increases (Ansley and Forsyth 1985; Ackerman 1989; Zhang 2008). However, in this study this was not the case, likely due to the different test structures that were simulated. In this study, the test structures in which simple items were simulated to load on only the first dimension are similar to a test that is approximately simple structure. In approximately simple structured tests, the RMSE for the a_1 parameter will decrease as the correlation between dimensions increases. However, the second simulated test structure, in which an equivalent number of simple structured items were simulated to measure each of the two dimensions, resulted in the least error when the correlation between dimensions was 0.45, for all discrimination parameters with the exception of MDISC. MDISC, which corresponds to the discrimination parameter in unidimensional models, behaved as expected, and decreased, as the correlation between dimensions increased. Having a correlation between dimensions of 0.45 also resulted in the least error. Recall that the discrimination parameters and thus the angular distance of items was manipulated in order to control the structure of the mixed test. When simple structure items were simulated to measure only the first dimension, the angle for simple structured items was forced to fall within a range of 0–20° and the angle for complex items was forced to fall within a range of 21–70°. In fact, the average angular distance across all 30 items in the first scenario ranged between 12 and 37°; while the average angular distance across all 30 items in the second scenario ranged between 45 and 55°. The fact that the least error was obtained for the discrimination parameters when the correlation between dimensions was 0.45 is likely due to the fact that the average angular distance of the items is comparable to the correlation between dimensions. Furthermore, as reported in a similar study done by Kahraman (2013), the error associated with the discrimination parameters increases as the correlation between dimensions increases, when modeling multidimensional response data with a unidimensional IRT model and ignoring the second dimension. Kahraman proposed that the projection IRT model be used to estimate the discrimination parameter when modeling multidimensional data as unidimensional. She stated that the discrimination parameter can be estimated with less error by using this model. In future research, the estimation of the discrimination parameters can also be examined by using the projection IRT model.

Despite the fact that MDISC corresponds to the discrimination parameter in unidimensional IRT models, the lowest errors were obtained when considering the average of a_1 and a_2, as was observed in the study conducted by Ansley and Forsyth (1985).

In parallel with studies in the literature that found that the skewness of the underlying ability distributions does not impact the error associated with the discrimination parameters (Kirisci et al. 2001), the results of this study also suggest that having a different underlying ability distributions on the different dimensions does not seem to impact the error associated with the discrimination parameters. In a study conducted by Walker et al. (2006), it was found that the power of DIMTEST, one of the methods of assessing test dimensionality, decreases when the secondary dimensions are excessively skewed and/or have little to no variability. In their study, they found that DIMTEST provide the most accurate result when the average of the secondary dimension is between the range of (−1,+1). In this study, the averages of the underlying skewed distributions were −0.5 and −1.00. However, this did not have much of an effect on the estimation of the discrimination parameters.

For the first scenario, simple structured items were simulated to measure only the first dimension. In this case, when the first dimension is measured better, the measurement of the second dimension is insufficient. Yet, the fact that simple structured items are distributed equally on both dimensions, in the second scenario, implies that the first and second dimensions are measured equally. The fact that the errors associated with the a_2 parameter were lower in the second scenario than the first scenario, and the errors for a_1 and a_2 parameters were similar in the second scenario is likely due to this fact. This also helps to explain why the error decreased as the number of complex items increased. In general, the discrimination parameter values for both dimensions are similar for complex items because both dimensions are measured effectively.

12.3.2 Parameter b

In parallel with previous studies in the literature (Reckase et al. 1988; Ackerman 1989; Zhang 2008), this study also demonstrated that the difficulty parameter is more prone to estimation error under normal conditions. Item difficulty is a parameter related to the ability of examinees. Items that have difficulty parameters that are below the ability of examinees are easy items for those examinees, while items that have difficulty parameters that are above the ability of examinees are difficult items for those examinees. Accordingly, the difficulty of an item is related to the person ability, or theta. Therefore, having different underlying distributions really impacts the ability to estimate the difficulty parameter when fitting a unidimensional IRT model to multidimensional data. As was observed for the discrimination parameters, the lowest error associated with the difficulty parameter was obtained when the underlying ability distributions were normal and the correlation between dimensions was 0.45. However, what is interesting is that the error decreases as the correlation between dimensions increases, and the underlying ability distributions became more distinct.

12.3.3 *Theta Parameter*

The results obtained when estimating ability with a unidimensional IRT model to scale multidimensional data were expected. Errors associated with the unidimensional estimate of ability decreased as the correlation between dimensions increased. In a study conducted by Ansley and Forsyth (1985), in which multidimensional data based upon the non-compensatory IRT model was modeled as unidimensional, the errors associated with θ_1 were smaller than those associated with θ_2 because the average of the true a_1 parameters was greater than the average of the true a_2 parameters, similar to the first scenario in this study. Similarly, in this study, the errors associated with θ_1 were lower than the errors associated with θ_2. In a similar study done by Ackerman (1989), the average of the true a_1 and a_2 parameters were similar to each other, which is similar to the second scenario in this study. The findings obtained in this study corroborate the findings obtained by Ansley and Forsyth (1985), and Ackerman (1989). In the first scenario, the errors associated with θ_1 were lower than those associated with θ_1 in the second scenario. That is because, in the first scenario, the average of the discrimination parameters for the first dimension was higher than the average of the discrimination parameters for the second dimension. However, in the second scenario, since the averages of the discrimination parameters for both dimensions were close to each other, a lower error was obtained for θ_2 in this scenario. In conclusion, if the discrimination for an item is high for a particular dimension, the error associated with the ability parameter for that dimension will be low. Furthermore, in parallel with the finding in the study of Ansley and Forsyth (1985), the error values associated with the average of θ_1 and θ_2 are always lower than the errors associated with only θ_1 or θ_2.

Appendix

			$\rho 1 = 0.00$			$\rho 1 = 0.45$			$\rho 1 = 0.90$		
	RMSE_a1	Results of unidimensional data = criteria	$\theta 1 = N(0,1)$ $\theta 2 = N(0,1)$	$\theta 1 = N(-.5,1)$ $\theta 2 = N(0,1)$	$\theta 1 = N(0,1)$ $\theta 2 = N(-1,1)$	$\theta 1 = N(0,1)$ $\theta 2 = N(0,1)$	$\theta 1 = N(-.5,1)$ $\theta 2 = N(0,1)$	$\theta 1 = N(0,1)$ $\theta 2 = N(-1,1)$	$\theta 1 = N(0,1)$ $\theta 2 = N(0,1)$	$\theta 1 = N(-.5,1)$ $\theta 2 = N(0,1)$	$\theta 1 = N(0,1)$ $\theta 2 = N(-1,1)$
Simple items load on the first dimension	24S + 6C	0.038	0.429	0.431	0.428	0.388	0.389	0.388	0.369	0.370	0.368
	18S + 12C	0.040	0.420	0.418	0.414	0.359	0.358	0.355	0.330	0.331	0.330
	12S + 18C	0.043	0.386	0.385	0.381	0.308	0.308	0.306	0.281	0.279	0.281
	6S + 24C	0.045	0.323	0.323	0.321	0.238	0.237	0.236	0.239	0.238	0.239
Simple items load on both dimensions	12S + 12SS + 6C	0.038	0.459	0.468	0.434	0.433	0.436	0.425	0.437	0.437	0.436
	9S + 9S + 12C	0.040	0.410	0.411	0.402	0.378	0.378	0.375	0.387	0.387	0.387
	6S + 6S + 18C	0.043	0.353	0.356	0.353	0.310	0.309	0.308	0.323	0.323	0.322
	3S + 3S + 24C	0.045	0.295	0.295	0.295	0.233	0.232	0.232	0.264	0.264	0.263

	RMSE for a2	Results of unidimensional data = criteria	ρ1 = 0.00			ρ1 = 0.45			ρ1 = 0.90		
			θ1 = N (0,1) θ2 = N (0,1)	θ1 = N (−.5,1) θ2 = N (0,1)	θ1 = N (0,1) θ2 = N (−1,1)	θ1 = N (0,1) θ2 = N (0,1)	θ1 = N (−.5,1) θ2 = N (0,1)	θ1 = N (0,1) θ2 = N (−1,1)	θ1 = N (0,1) θ2 = N (0,1)	θ1 = N (−.5,1) θ2 = N (0,1)	θ1 = N (0,1) θ2 = N (−1,1)
Simple items load on the first dimension	24S + 6C	0.038	0.504	0.502	0.504	0.484	0.484	0.485	0.499	0.498	0.500
	18S + 12C	0.040	0.408	0.409	0.417	0.397	0.397	0.401	0.435	0.435	0.436
	12S + 18C	0.043	0.312	0.311	0.316	0.311	0.311	0.314	0.366	0.367	0.365
	6S + 24C	0.045	0.263	0.261	0.265	0.223	0.225	0.225	0.281	0.283	0.281
Simple items load on both dimensions	12S + 12SS + 6C	0.038	0.455	0.446	0.480	0.433	0.430	0.441	0.439	0.439	0.439
	9S + 9S + 12C	0.040	0.409	0.406	0.415	0.376	0.376	0.379	0.385	0.384	0.385
	6S + 6S + 18C	0.043	0.351	0.348	0.352	0.310	0.311	0.312	0.330	0.330	0.328
	3S + 3S + 24C	0.045	0.295	0.295	0.296	0.228	0.229	0.230	0.258	0.259	0.258

	RMSE for average of a1 + a2	Results of unidimensional data = criteria	$\rho1 = 0.00$ $\theta1 = N(0,1)$ $\theta2 = N(0,1)$	$\rho1 = 0.00$ $\theta1 = N(-.5,1)$ $\theta2 = N(0,1)$	$\rho1 = 0.00$ $\theta1 = N(0,1)$ $\theta2 = N(-1,1)$	$\rho1 = 0.45$ $\theta1 = N(0,1)$ $\theta2 = N(0,1)$	$\rho1 = 0.45$ $\theta1 = N(-.5,1)$ $\theta2 = N(0,1)$	$\rho1 = 0.45$ $\theta1 = N(0,1)$ $\theta2 = N(-1,1)$	$\rho1 = 0.90$ $\theta1 = N(0,1)$ $\theta2 = N(0,1)$	$\rho1 = 0.90$ $\theta1 = N(-.5,1)$ $\theta2 = N(0,1)$	$\rho1 = 0.90$ $\theta1 = N(0,1)$ $\theta2 = N(-1,1)$
Simple items load on the first dimension	24S + 6C	0.038	0.184	0.183	0.183	0.085	0.085	0.085	0.082	0.082	0.084
	18S + 12C	0.040	0.177	0.176	0.180	0.054	0.053	0.055	0.096	0.095	0.097
	12S + 18C	0.043	0.169	0.168	0.168	0.038	0.038	0.040	0.110	0.109	0.107
	6S + 24C	0.045	0.187	0.185	0.187	0.038	0.039	0.037	0.127	0.129	0.126
Simple items load on both dimensions	12S + 12SS + 6C	0.038	0.154	0.154	0.156	0.046	0.045	0.044	0.079	0.079	0.079
	9S + 9S + 12C	0.040	0.167	0.164	0.163	0.044	0.044	0.043	0.095	0.093	0.095
	6S + 6S + 18C	0.043	0.171	0.172	0.173	0.041	0.041	0.041	0.110	0.109	0.105
	3S + 3S + 24C	0.045	0.187	0.188	0.188	0.037	0.039	0.040	0.127	0.128	0.127

	RMSE for MDISC	Results of unidimensional data = criteria	$\rho 1 = 0.00$			$\rho 1 = 0.45$			$\rho 1 = 0.90$		
			$\theta 1 = N(0,1)$ $\theta 2 = N(0,1)$	$\theta 1 = N(-.5,1)$ $\theta 2 = N(0,1)$	$\theta 1 = N(0,1)$ $\theta 2 = N(-1,1)$	$\theta 1 = N(0,1)$ $\theta 2 = N(0,1)$	$\theta 1 = N(-.5,1)$ $\theta 2 = N(0,1)$	$\theta 1 = N(0,1)$ $\theta 2 = N(-1,1)$	$\theta 1 = N(0,1)$ $\theta 2 = N(0,1)$	$\theta 1 = N(-.5,1)$ $\theta 2 = N(0,1)$	$\theta 1 = N(0,1)$ $\theta 2 = N(-1,1)$
Simple items load on the first dimension	24S + 6C	0.038	0.536	0.537	0.535	0.458	0.459	0.458	0.392	0.393	0.390
	18S + 12C	0.040	0.585	0.583	0.583	0.471	0.470	0.468	0.373	0.373	0.372
	12S + 18C	0.043	0.593	0.592	0.590	0.459	0.459	0.458	0.344	0.345	0.347
	6S + 24C	0.045	0.625	0.624	0.625	0.465	0.463	0.461	0.328	0.326	0.329
Simple items load on both dimensions	12S + 12SS + 6C	0.038	0.619	0.619	0.618	0.506	0.506	0.503	0.401	0.401	0.402
	9S + 9S + 12C	0.040	0.620	0.618	0.617	0.492	0.491	0.491	0.378	0.380	0.378
	6S + 6S + 18C	0.043	0.608	0.608	0.609	0.470	0.469	0.469	0.346	0.347	0.350
	3S + 3S + 24C	0.045	0.627	0.628	0.628	0.463	0.466	0.467	0.328	0.328	0.328

	b	Results of unidimensional data = criteria	ρ1 = 0.00			ρ1 = 0.45			ρ1 = 0.90		
			θ1 = N (0,1) θ2 = N (0,1)	θ1 = N (−.5,1) θ2 = N (0,1)	θ1 = N (0,1) θ2 = N (−1,1)	θ1 = N (0,1) θ2 = N (0,1)	θ1 = N (−.5,1) θ2 = N (0,1)	θ1 = N (0,1) θ2 = N (−1,1)	θ1 = N (0,1) θ2 = N (0,1)	θ1 = N (−.5,1) θ2 = N (0,1)	θ1 = N (0,1) θ2 = N (−1,1)
Simple items load on the first dimension	24S + 6C	0.024	0.041	0.503	0.408	0.034	0.479	0.302	0.039	0.455	0.250
	18S + 12C	0.023	0.039	0.496	0.498	0.036	0.455	0.397	0.040	0.418	0.346
	12S + 18C	0.023	0.038	0.483	0.574	0.036	0.421	0.470	0.043	0.375	0.413
	6S + 24C	0.023	0.036	0.442	0.660	0.035	0.367	0.542	0.047	0.325	0.479
Simple items load on both dimensions	12S + 12SS + 6C	0.024	0.061	0.489	1.003	0.043	0.394	0.789	0.040	0.339	0.679
	9S + 9S + 12C	0.023	0.055	0.454	0.900	0.041	0.371	0.743	0.041	0.323	0.646
	6S + 6S + 18C	0.023	0.048	0.426	0.849	0.039	0.353	0.694	0.043	0.310	0.608
	3S + 3S + 24C	0.023	0.037	0.397	0.790	0.038	0.326	0.654	0.047	0.288	0.569

	RMSE for Theta1	Results of unidimensional data = criteria	ρ1 = 0.00			ρ1 = 0.45			ρ1 = 0.90		
			θ1 = N (0,1) θ2 = N (0,1)	θ1 = N (−.5,1) θ2 = N (0,1)	θ1 = N (0,1) θ2 = N (−1,1)	θ1 = N (0,1) θ2 = N (0,1)	θ1 = N (−.5,1) θ2 = N (0,1)	θ1 = N (0,1) θ2 = N (−1,1)	θ1 = N (0,1) θ2 = N (0,1)	θ1 = N (−.5,1) θ2 = N (0,1)	θ1 = N (0,1) θ2 = N (−1,1)
Simple items load on the first dimension	24S + 6C	0.322	0.436	0.670	0.434	0.412	0.656	0.412	0.365	0.622	0.368
	18S + 12C	0.322	0.559	0.756	0.546	0.479	0.698	0.475	0.367	0.623	0.371
	12S + 18C	0.322	0.665	0.835	0.652	0.532	0.735	0.528	0.371	0.625	0.378
	6S + 24C	0.324	0.760	0.911	0.752	0.585	0.771	0.585	0.381	0.632	0.392
Simple items load on both dimensions	12S + 12SS + 6C	0.322	0.812	0.974	0.761	0.631	0.815	0.612	0.413	0.652	0.418
	9S + 9S + 12C	0.322	0.819	0.967	0.796	0.631	0.808	0.621	0.402	0.644	0.410
	6S + 6S + 18C	0.322	0.798	0.948	0.789	0.615	0.797	0.613	0.394	0.640	0.404
	3S + 3S + 24C	0.324	0.810	0.955	0.808	0.619	0.798	0.623	0.390	0.638	0.404

	RMSE for Theta2	Results of unidimensional data = criteria	ρ1 = 0.00			ρ1 = 0.45			ρ1 = 0.90		
			θ1 = N (0,1) θ2 = N (0,1)	θ1 = N (−.5,1) θ2 = N (0,1)	θ1 = N (0,1) θ2 = N (−1,1)	θ1 = N (0,1) θ2 = N (0,1)	θ1 = N (−.5,1) θ2 = N (0,1)	θ1 = N (0,1) θ2 = N (−1,1)	θ1 = N (0,1) θ2 = N (0,1)	θ1 = N (−.5,1) θ2 = N (0,1)	θ1 = N (0,1) θ2 = N (−1,1)
Simple items load on the first dimension	24S + 6C	0.322	1.230	1.225	1.594	0.899	0.895	1.349	0.485	0.491	1.113
	18S + 12C	0.322	1.069	1.068	1.481	0.787	0.785	1.280	0.446	0.450	1.100
	12S + 18C	0.322	0.955	0.953	1.399	0.716	0.719	1.240	0.423	0.426	1.090
	6S + 24C	0.324	0.856	0.855	1.327	0.654	0.654	1.201	0.401	0.405	1.083
Simple items load on both dimensions	12S + 12SS + 6C	0.322	0.828	0.809	1.341	0.642	0.636	1.207	0.414	0.417	1.088
	9S + 9S + 12C	0.322	0.808	0.802	1.302	0.624	0.622	1.193	0.400	0.403	1.084
	6S + 6S + 18C	0.322	0.821	0.816	1.306	0.628	0.627	1.189	0.397	0.399	1.082
	3S + 3S + 24C	0.324	0.803	0.804	1.291	0.616	0.617	1.181	0.390	0.394	1.080

	RMSE for Theta__avg	Results of unidimensional data = criteria	ρ1 = 0.00			ρ1 = 0.45			ρ1 = 0.90		
			θ1 = N (0,1) θ2 = N (0,1)	θ1 = N (−.5,1) θ2 = N (0,1)	θ1 = N (0,1) θ2 = N (−1,1)	θ1 = N (0,1) θ2 = N (0,1)	θ1 = N (−.5,1) θ2 = N (0,1)	θ1 = N (0,1) θ2 = N (−1,1)	θ1 = N (0,1) θ2 = N (0,1)	θ1 = N (−.5,1) θ2 = N (0,1)	θ1 = N (0,1) θ2 = N (−1,1)
Simple items load on the first dimension	24S + 6C = 30	0.322	0.593	0.642	0.783	0.462	0.527	0.685	0.367	0.448	0.622
	18S + 12C = 30	0.322	0.478	0.540	0.703	0.387	0.463	0.638	0.342	0.427	0.611
	12S + 18C = 30	0.322	0.421	0.491	0.664	0.351	0.435	0.618	0.329	0.417	0.604
	6S + 24C = 30	0.324	0.393	0.467	0.644	0.331	0.417	0.606	0.320	0.411	0.603
Simple items load on both dimensions	12S + 12SS+ 6C = 30	0.322	0.416	0.489	0.661	0.361	0.443	0.625	0.348	0.432	0.616
	9S + 9S + 12C = 30	0.322	0.403	0.475	0.647	0.344	0.427	0.616	0.333	0.419	0.609
	6S + 6S + 18C = 30	0.322	0.395	0.470	0.643	0.335	0.421	0.608	0.326	0.415	0.606
	3S + 3S + 24C = 30	0.324	0.390	0.465	0.641	0.328	0.416	0.607	0.320	0.411	0.604

References

Ackerman, T. A. (1989). Unidimensional IRT calibration of compensatory and noncompensatory items. *Applied Psychological Measurement, 13*, 113–127.

Ackerman, T. A. (1992). A didactic explanation of item bias, item impact, and item validity from a multidimensional perspective. *Journal of Educational Measurement, 29*(1), 67–91.

Ansley, T. N., & Forsyth, R. A. (1985). An examination of the characteristics of unidimensional IRT parameter estimates derived from two dimensional data. *Applied Psychological Measurement, 9*(1), 37–48.

Hambleton, R. K., Swaminathan, H., Cook, L. L., Eignor, D. R., & Gifford, J. A. (1978). Developments in latent trait theory: Models, technical issues, and applications. *Review of Educational Research, 48*, 467–510.

Hambleton, R. K., Swaminathan, H., & Rogers, H. J. (1991). *Fundamentals of item response theory*. Newbury Park, CA: Sage.

Harrison, D. A. (1986). Robustness of IRT parameter estimation to violations of the unidimensionality assumption. *Journal of Educational Statistics, 11*(2), 91–115.

Hattie, J. (1985). Methodology review: Assessing unidimensionality of tests and items. *Applied Psychological Measurement, 9*(2), 139–164.

Kahraman, N. (2013). Unidimensional interpretations for multidimensional test items. *Journal of Educational Measurement, 50*(2), 227–246.

Kirisci, L., Hsu, T., & Yu, L. (2001). Robustness of item parameter estimation programs to assumptions of unidimensionality and normality. *Applied Psychological Measurement, 25*, 146–162.

Lord, F. M., & Novick, R. (1968). *Statistical theories of mental test scores*. Reading, MA: Addison-Wesley.

Luecht, R. M., & Miller, T. R. (1992). Unidimensional calibrations and interpretations of composite traits for multidimensional tests. *Applied Psychological Measurement, 16*, 279–293.

McDonald, R. P. (1999). *Test theory: A unified treatment*. Mahwah, NJ: L. Erlbaum Associates.

Raykov, T. (1997). Bias of coefficient alpha for congeneric measures with correlated errors. *Applied Psychological Measurement, 25*, 69–76.

Reckase, M. D., & McKinley, R. L. (1991). The discriminating power of items that measure more than one dimension. *Applied Psychological Measurement, 15*, 361–373.

Reckase, M. D. (1997). A linear logistic multidimensional model for dichotomous item response data. In W. J. van der Linden & R. K. Hambleton (Eds.), *Handbook of modern item response theory* (pp. 271–286). New York: Springer.

Reckase, M. D. (2009). *Multidimensional item response theory (Statistics for social and behavioral sciences)*. New York: Springer.

Reckase, M. D., Ackerman, T. A., & Carlson, J. E. (1988). Building a unidimensional test using multidimensional items. *Journal of Educational Measurement, 25*, 193–203.

Stout, W. (1987). A nonparametric approach for assessing latent trait unidimensionality. *Psychometrika, 52*, 589–617.

Traub, R. E. (1983). A priori considerations in choosing an item response model. In R. K. Hambleton (Ed.), *Applications of item response theory* (pp. 57–70). British Columbia: Educational Research Institute of British Columbia.

Walker, C. M., Azen, R., & Schmitt, T. (2006). Statistical versus substantive dimensionality the effect of distributional differences on dimensionality assessment using DIMTEST. *Educational and Psychological Measurement, 66*(5), 721–738.

Zhang, J. (2005). *Estimating multidimensional item response models with mixed structure*. ETS Research Report, RR-05-04.

Zhang, B. (2008). Application of unidimensional item response models to tests with items sensitive to secondary dimension. *The Journal of Experimental Education, 77*(2), 147–166.

Zhang, J. (2012). Calibration of response data using MIRT models with simple and mixed structures. *Applied Psychological Measurement, 36*, 375–398.

Zinbarg, R. E., Revelle, W., Yovel, I., & Li, W. (2005). Cronbach's α, Revelle's β and McDonald's ω: Their relations with each other and two alternative conceptualizations of reliability. *Psychometrika, 70*(1), 1–11.

Chapter 13
Identifying Feature Sequences from Process Data in Problem-Solving Items with *N*-Grams

Qiwei He and Matthias von Davier

Abstract This article draws on process data from a computer-based large-scale program, the Programme for International Assessment of Adult Competencies (PIAAC), to address how sequences of actions recorded in problem-solving tasks are related to task performance and how feature sequences are identified for different groups. The purpose of this study is twofold: first, to explore and detect action sequence patterns of features that are associated with success or failure on a problem-solving item, and second, to mutually validate the results derived from two feature selection models. Motivated by the methodologies of natural language processing and text mining, we utilized *n*-gram model and two feature selection methods, chi-square statistic (CHI), and weighted log likelihood ratio test (WLLR), in analyzing the process data at a variety of aggregate levels. It was found that action sequence patterns significantly differed by performance groups and were consistent across countries. The two feature selection approaches resulted in a high agreement of feature identification.

Keywords Process data • Computer-based assessment • *N*-gram • Chi-square selection • Weighted log likelihood ratio • Problem-solving item

13.1 Introduction

Complex problem-solving tasks in educational environments are intended to be more engaging for learners and more reflective of real life challenges than traditional test items (Goldhammer et al. 2013). In computer-based assessments (CBAs), one seeks data relating to the process that provide more information than the outcome of the task alone. Therefore, the analyses of process data are necessarily much more involved than those typically performed on traditional tests.

Q. He (✉) • M. von Davier
Research and Development Department, Global Assessment, Educational Testing Service, 660 Rosedale Road, MS-13E, Princeton, NJ 08541, USA
e-mail: qhe@ets.org; mvondavier@ets.org

L.A. van der Ark et al. (eds.), *Quantitative Psychology Research*, Springer Proceedings in Mathematics & Statistics 140, DOI 10.1007/978-3-319-19977-1_13

This study draws on process data from log files from a computer-based large-scale program, the Programme for International Assessment of Adult Competencies (PIAAC; cf. Schleicher 2008), to address how sequences of actions are associated with different ways of cognitive processing and how key actions are identified that lead to success or failure. These results can be useful for test developers, psychometricians, and instructors to help them better understand what distinguishes successful from unsuccessful test takers and may eventually contribute to improved task and assessment design.

13.1.1 Problem-Solving Items in PIAAC

Large-scale survey assessments of skills and knowledge targeting student and adult populations have often been at the forefront of innovations in test design and the use of analytic methodologies (Rutkowski et al. 2014; von Davier et al. 2006; von Davier and Sinharay 2014). PIAAC is no exception. It is the first international household survey of skills predominantly collected using information and communications technology (ICT). The use of computers as the delivery platform enables data collection not just on whether respondents are able to solve the tasks but how they approach the solution and time their efforts. In PIAAC, the items in the domain of problem solving in technology-rich environments (PSTRE) involve more interactive item types and are available only on computer. To give a response in the simulated computer environments that form the PSTRE tasks, participants are required to click buttons or links, select from dropdown menus, drag and drop, copy and paste, and so on.

13.1.2 Action Sequences as Process Data

In CBAs, the dynamic records of actions generated during the item-response process form a distinct sequence that is derived from test-taker input. Following and analyzing these sequences can facilitate the understanding of how individuals plan, evaluate, and select operations to achieve the problem-solving goal.

Sequences are an important type of data that occur frequently in many scientific, medical, security, business, and other applications. They are also often used in natural language processing (NLP) techniques as a proxy for capturing linguistic information (e.g., Su et al. 2000; Lin and Wilbur 2009) as well as in bioinformatics for encoding the genetic makeup of all species and the structure and function of proteins (Dong and Pei 2007; Sukkarieh et al. 2012). The availability of process-log data sequences from educational learning systems such as intelligent tutors and CBAs has stimulated interest in education research (e.g., Graesser et al. 2004; Sonamthiang et al. 2007; Goldhammer et al. 2014) and appears promising. However, research that uses analytic methodologies to explore sequence patterns in the field of educational assessment, with the goal of evaluating the utility of action sequences for explaining test takers' cognitive task performance, is only at a preliminary stage.

13.1.3 Feature Selection for Sequence Patterns

A distinguishing sequence pattern is one that characterizes a family of sequences and distinguishes the family from other sequences (Dong and Pei 2007). Once the set of sequences of process data is determined, there need to be some criteria for selecting the "good" features for potential usage in data mining tasks, for instance, classifying action sequences into correct or incorrect performance groups. A discrimination-based feature selection approach generally identifies preferred features occurring with relatively higher frequency at a desired site or in some selected classes (Dong and Pei 2007).

As Fink (2008) pointed out, the development and increased use of sequential models was closely related to the statistical modeling of texts. Considering the similar structure between action sequences in process data and word sequences in natural language, we were motivated to adapt NLP and text mining into the analysis of process data in the current study. In text categorization, feature selection is a strategy that aims at identifying the key features that contribute more to accurate and efficient classification (Li et al. 2009). A number of feature selection methods have been widely used in NLP and text classification such as document frequency, information gain, mutual information, chi-square test, binormal separation, and weighted log-likelihood ratio (see more in Yang and Pederson 1997; Nigam et al. 2000; Forman 2003; Li et al. 2009). For our interests in testing the statistical independence and likelihood of action sequences in different performance groups, in this study, we chose two feature selection models, chi-square selection algorithm (CHI; Oakes et al. 2001) and weighted log likelihood ratio test (WLLR; Nigam et al. 2000), to analyze the process data at a variety of aggregate levels. We chose these two feature selection methods based on their high efficiency and simplicity. There has been a good amount of literature on the topic (e.g., Forman 2003; Manning and Schütze 1999). The specific features of these two methods will be discussed in the section of methods.

13.1.4 Goals of the Present Study

The purpose of this study is twofold: first, to explore and detect action sequence patterns of features that are associated with success or failure on a PSTRE item, and second, to mutually validate the results derived from two feature selection models. We investigated the utility of behavioral process data for predicting differences in task performance in the PIAAC PSTRE domain. More specifically, we separated the database by two performance groups (correct and incorrect) for a sample item, extracted action sequences, and identified the key sequences that were significantly associated with task completion.

13.2 Method

13.2.1 Sample

For this study, data from the PSTRE domain collected during the 2012 PIAAC main study were used. The PIAAC sample was representative of the population of adults who were age 16–65 and had prior experience with computers.

We chose the United States, the Netherlands, and Japan as exemplary countries from three continents (North America, Europe, and Asia) among the group of participating countries. This selection allowed for a broad range of country performances, as Japan and the Netherlands performed at a high level in PIAAC, while the US was a relatively low-performing country (OECD 2013). This selection also provided countries with high percentages of individuals using computers among their subpopulations, a necessary element to get valid results for the technology-based PSTRE domain. A total of 3926 test takers who completed the PSTRE items in the PIAAC assessment were included in the present study. Of these, 1340 test takers were from the US, 1508 from the Netherlands, and 1078 from Japan. There were 2025 female test takers (51.6 %) and 1901 male test takers (48.4 %). The average age was 39.6 years (SD = 14.0). A plurality (1812) of this sample had an educational level above high school (46.2 %), with 1493 reporting a high school degree (38.0 %), 615 reporting less than high school (15.7 %) and six cases recorded as missing (0.1 %).

To get more accurate population estimates, we took sampling weights into account in the calculations. We standardized the weights to a sum of 5000 in each country[1] to ensure that every country contributed equally (for details on PIAAC sample design and weighting standards, refer to OECD 2010). With this sum normalization, the range of sampling weight is within [0.15, 3.69], [0.39, 2.54], and [0.30, 2.53] for the samples from the US, the Netherlands, and Japan, respectively. In addition, we conducted the same analyses without using sampling weights. Only marginal differences were found between the two conditions with and without sampling weights.

[1]Approximately 5000 people in each country participated in PIAAC, which consists of three constructs: literacy, numeracy, and PSTRE. Only those who had experience in using computers and agreed to use the computer-based tests participated in the PSTRE session. Hence, the realized sample size for PSTRE is, on average, a quarter of the total sample in each country.

13.2.2 Instrumentation

A total of 14 PSTRE items were administered in the PIAAC main study. We focused on the sequence data resulting from the task requirements of one item. This item consists of two environments: a spreadsheet environment that contains a database with the information required to solve the task (and serves as the stimulus), and an email environment to provide the response. The task is to identify the ID number of a specified club member (e.g., "David Smith")[2] and email it to a correspondent. On the spreadsheet (SS) page, four pieces of information for each club member are provided by columns: ID number, name, number of activities this year, and years as a member. There is a checkbox on each line to facilitate flagging the potential correct answer. On the email (E) page, test takers are required to enter the ID number into an email to a correspondent.

An interim score was evaluated based on the email responses only. It meant that an empty or a wrong answer on the email page led to an incorrect result even though the participant might have correctly identified the specified person on the SS page.

The task for this item is situated in a simulated office environment that included tools and functionality similar to those found in Microsoft Excel and email applications, that is, clickable buttons for saving, searching, sorting, sending email, and help; clickable dropdown menus; clickable buttons for switching between the SS and E environments; and so on. The opening page presents the task description on the left side and is always displayed. The working part is on the right side of the screen, which switches upon change in task environment.

13.2.3 Analytic Strategy

To explore the relationship between action sequences and task completion, we divided the sample into two groups: correct and incorrect. It resulted in 2754 individuals (70.1 %) in the correct group, including 882 from the US, 1104 from the Netherlands and 768 from Japan, and a total of 1172 people (29.9 %) in the incorrect group, consisting of 458 test takers from the US, 404 from the Netherlands, and 310 from Japan. The rate of correctness in the US, the Netherlands, and Japan was 65.8 %, 73.2 %, and 71.2 %, respectively.

Motivated by the methodologies and applications in NLP and text mining (e.g., He et al. 2012, 2014), we used the *n*-gram representation model as well as two feature selection models in analyzing the process data in this study. Given concerns that different models may show a preference for different feature selections, it would be wise to double check any features that are selected via different approaches to ensure only valid ones are used in further analysis. In the current study, the data analysis was undertaken in two phases. First, we decomposed the complete sequences into smaller units (*n*-grams) and identified the best features to distinguish

[2]The name of the specified club member differs by language versions.

the correct and incorrect groups. Two feature selection models—CHI and WLLR—were applied to mutually validate the results. Secondly, based on the common features selected via two models, we explored the relationship between sequence patterns and binary classification.

The analysis was conducted across and within countries. The first set of analyses used the extracted actions and action sequences jointly from all three countries selected for this study. The goal of this joint analysis was to examine whether there are features (actions and action sequences) that could distinguish correct and incorrect groups on an aggregate level. However, in order to examine whether the same features would be detected as robust ones for each country as well, we conducted the second set of analyses separately by country.

13.2.4 N-Gram Representation of Sequence Data

N-grams. Analogous to textual data, action sequences collected in computer-based performance tasks can be decomposed into *n*-grams. That is, the unigrams are defined as "bags of actions," where each single action in a sequence collection represents a distinct feature; Moving away from unigrams, which are not informative about transitions between actions, we looked at *n*-grams. Specifically, we considered bigrams and trigrams, which are defined as action vectors that contain either two or three ordered adjacent actions, respectively. For a more efficient coding system, we subsequently combined the actions that always concurrently appear in the same order into one code. For instance, the action "END" is always preceded by "Next_OK", hence, we recoded "Next_OK, END" into one code "FINALENDING". We used the combined code in the subsequent analysis.

Term weight. During the analysis of action sequences we encountered a problem: The actions such as "START" and "FINALENDING" occurred in all the test takers' processing sequences and provided little information in distinguishing the correct and incorrect groups. To solve this problem, a term for a weighting mechanism in text mining—inverse document frequency (IDF; Spärck Jones 1972)—was applied for attenuating the effect of actions or action vectors that occurred too often in the collection to be meaningful.

In this study, we renamed the IDF to speak about inverse sequence frequency (ISF). To scale the weight to each action, we denoted the total number of sequences in the collection by N and defined the ISF of an action i as $\mathrm{ISF}_i = \log\left(N/\mathrm{sf}_i\right) \geq 0$, where N indicates the total number of sequences in the collection, namely, the total number of test takers (3926 in this study) and sf_i is the number of sequences where the action i appears. Thus, the ISF of a rare action is high, whereas the ISF of a frequent action is low. The ISF of an action that occurs in all the sequences namely, used by all the test takers, is zero. Therefore, the low-informative actions such as START or FINALENDING that were used by all test takers were eliminated from further analyses. This can be compared to the removal of frequent words (i.e., stop words) in textual responses such as "an," "a," and "the" (Manning and Schütze 1999).

Another concern about term frequency is about clustering at the individual level. The importance of an action that is taken multiple times by one individual should be different from that when the action is taken once each by multiple individuals. NLP provides a commonly used solution to the problem by dampening the term frequency by a function $f\,(\text{tf}) = 1 + \log(\text{tf})$, $\text{tf} > 0$ because more occurrences of a word indicate higher importance, but not as much relative importance as the undampened count would suggest (Manning and Schütze 1999). We applied rescaling of frequencies in the current study. For example, we used $1 + \log 3$ to slightly dampen the importance of an action with three occurrences in a single respondent sequence than the count of 3 itself. Such a sequence is somewhat more important than a sequence with one occurrence under the rescaling, but not 3 times as important.

Analogous to the weighting scheme in NLP, an action's term frequency tf_{ij} (action i in sequence j) and its ISF was further combined into a single weight as follows:

$$\text{weight}\,(i,j) = \begin{cases} \left[1 + \log\left(\text{tf}_{ij}\right)\right]\log\left(N/\text{sf}_i\right) & \text{if } \text{tf}_{ij} \geq 1 \\ 0 & \text{if } \text{tf}_{ij} = 0 \end{cases}, \tag{13.1}$$

where N is the total number of sequences. The first clause applies to actions occurring in the same sequence, whereas for actions that do not appear ($\text{tf}_{ij} = 0$), we use $\text{weight}\,(i,j) = 0$.

To ensure the reliability of calculation, actions (i.e., unigrams) and action vectors (i.e., bigrams and trigrams) that occurred fewer than five times or had zero ISF weights (i.e., used by all test takers) were deducted from further analyses. As a result, 27 unigrams, 144 bigrams, and 257 trigrams were included in the present study. Table 13.1 presents a total of 27 actions (i.e., unigrams) and their attributes. The interpretation corresponding to each action is presented in the first column. The frequency of sequences (SeqFreq) that contain the action by each row is shown in the third column, following by the raw frequency of actions (ActFreq) in the fourth column. Note that the SeqFreq and ActFreq are not always equal, because an action may occur several times in one sequence, which results in an increment for ActFreq but not SeqFreq. The last four columns of Table 13.1 present the raw and weighted frequency of actions in correct and incorrect groups, respectively.

13.2.5 Chi-Square Selection Model (CHI)

To answer the question regarding which actions or action vectors are the key factors that lead to success or failure in the problem-solving process, we first applied the CHI method to identify robust features. Robust features are generally defined as the "best" features with high information gain in the NLP (Joachims 1998); thus, the use of *robust feature* here is different from the meaning of the term in statistics. The chi-square feature selection model is recommended for use in textual analysis

Table 13.1 Raw and weighted frequency of actions (unigrams) defined in a sample PSTRE item

				Freq in correct		Freq in incorrect	
Interpretation	Action code	SeqFreq	ActFreq	Raw	Wgt	Raw	Wgt
Switch to email page	E	3533	7164	5721	434.02	1443	117.93
Send email	E_S	1676	1814	1384	1102.00	430	324.69
Cancel to continue to the next item	Next_C	564	736	354	591.45	382	651.29
Switch to spreadsheet page	SS	1976	3047	2683	1446.51	364	198.93
Use "Help" on spreadsheet page	SS_H	120	161	116	336.44	45	125.63
Save results on spreadsheet page	SS_Save	169	186	119	350.33	67	201.63
Start searching engine on spreadsheet page	SS_Se	883	952	808	1135.39	144	199.74
Start sorting engine on spreadsheet page	SS_So	445	578	486	905.03	92	168.65
Sort by null in the first choice	SS_So_1_0	11	12	9	58.39	3	11.60
Sort by 1st column (ID number) in the first choice	SS_So_1A	41	43	32	149.11	11	48.52
Sort by 2nd column (Name) in the first choice	SS_So_1B	573	581	518	910.56	63	107.67
Sort by null in the second choice	SS_So_2_0	7	7	5	24.76	2	8.29
Sort by 1st column (ID number) in the second choice	SS_So_2A	56	57	50	191.09	7	24.81
Sort by 2nd column (Name) in the second choice	SS_So_2B	51	52	40	165.67	12	39.25
Sort by 1st column (ID number) in the third choice	SS_So_3A	9	9	7	43.12	2	9.96
Sort by 2nd column (Name) in the third choice	SS_So_3B	20	20	15	68.60	5	23.79
Sort by 4th column (Year as a member) in the third choice	SS_So_3D	6	6	3	15.59	3	14.27

(continued)

Table 13.1 (continued)

Interpretation	Action code	SeqFreq	ActFreq	Freq in correct		Freq in incorrect	
				Raw	Wgt	Raw	Wgt
Cancel sorting	SS_So_C	88	95	69	234.10	26	90.59
Click "OK" after setting sorting conditions	SS_So_OK	596	735	649	1052.88	86	129.43
Type in full name for searching	SS_Type_FN	462	686	569	1022.24	117	208.84
Type in given name for searching	SS_Type_GN	85	154	136	357.31	18	59.76
Type in null for searching	SS_Type_null	25	28	21	113.90	7	36.02
Type in partial given name for searching	SS_Type_PGN	7	12	5	43.38	7	36.39
Type in partial surname for searching	SS_Type_PSN	9	16	12	61.66	4	23.65
Typing with spelling mistakes in searching	SS_Type_SM	115	283	237	585.57	46	100.38
Type in surname for searching	SS_Type_SN	433	644	572	1041.88	72	124.06
Typing with understanding mistakes in searching	SS_Type_UM	25	40	30	104.14	10	35.47

Note. SeqFreq indicates the frequency of sequences that contain the action by each row, i.e., the number of test takers who used the action by each row. ActFreq represents the frequency of actions that occur in the whole collection. Raw and Wgt indicate the raw and weighted frequency of each action that occurs in the correct and incorrect groups, respectively. Actions that occur fewer than five times (ActFreq $<$ 5) or are used by all the test takers (N = 3926) were deducted from the further analysis

due to its high effectiveness in finding robust keywords and for testing the similarity between different text corpora (e.g., Manning and Schütze 1999; He et al. 2012; 2014; for more feature selection models, refer to Forman 2003). Because of the structural similarity between textual and process data, it appears appropriate to apply this approach to detect those actions or action vectors that are highly informative for distinguishing the two performance groups.

To apply the CHI method, the joint frequencies of presence versus absence of each action or action vector crossed by the correctness or incorrectness of the response were arranged into a 2-by-2 contingency table as shown in Table 13.2. The (weighted) number of action occurrences in two groups C_1 (i.e., correct group) and C_2 (i.e., incorrect group) is indicated by n_i and m_i, respectively. The sum of the weighted action occurrences in each group is defined as the group length len(C).

Table 13.2 2-by-2 contingency table for action i in chi-square score calculation

	C_1	C_2
Action i	n_i	m_i
$\neg$ Action i	$\text{len}(C_1) - n_i$	$\text{len}(C_2) - m_i$

Note. C_1 and C_2 represent the two study groups (i.e., correct and incorrect). n_i and m_i indicate the weighted frequency of the action i occurs in C_1 and C_2, respectively. len(C) indicates the sum of the weighted action occurrences in each group

The idea behind this method is to test whether occurrence and nonoccurrence of actions and correctness are independent. Thus, the method compares two groups to determine how far C_1 departs from C_2 in terms of action frequencies.

Under the null hypothesis the two collections are randomly equivalent, so their distribution of actions is proportional to each other. A chi-square value is computed to evaluate the departure from this null hypothesis. For a 2-by-2 contingency table, the chi-square value is computed as

$$\chi^2 = \frac{M(O_{11}O_{22} - O_{12}O_{21})^2}{(O_{11} + O_{12})(O_{11} + O_{21})(O_{12} + O_{22})(O_{21} + O_{22})}, \quad (13.2)$$

where M is the total number of actions in the collection, and O_{ij} represents the weighted counts in each cell in the matrix (see more in Bishop et al. 1975; Agresti 1990). The weighted counts O_{11} and O_{12} are the number of occurrences of an action (vector) in the correct and incorrect group, respectively, while O_{21} and O_{22} are the number of nonoccurrences of this action in the two performance groups.

In this study, we used the chi-square statistic as a measure of association. That is, the statistic divided by the weighted number of actions is a standard estimate of the mean square contingency, which in turn is a squared correlation coefficient. We selected those attributes for which the chi-square was high (according to the 2-by-2 cross-table with the variable of interest, such as correct/incorrect groups). In that way, attributes that were strongly associated with the variable of interest were selected as robust features. Namely, the actions with higher chi-square scores were more discriminative in classification (Manning and Schütze 1999). Therefore, we ranked the chi-square statistic of each action in a descending order. The actions ranked at the top were defined as the robust features. Because we were interested only in ranking the chi-square score for each action (action vector) to find the "best" features, assessing statistical significance of the chi-square was not important in this instance. Further, if the ratio n_i/m_i was larger than the ratio len(C_1)/len(C_2), the action was defined as more typical of group C_1 (as a "positive indicator"); otherwise, it was more typical of group C_2 (as a "negative indicator") (for more details, refer to Oakes et al. 2001).

13.2.6 Weighted Log Likelihood Ratio (WLLR)

In order to compare the results obtained using the chi-square selection using another frequently applied measure, we applied the WLLR in the present study as well. There are two reasons for our choice of WLLR to validate the results from the CHI method: First, WLLR has been proven very efficient in feature selection in text categorization (e.g., Forman 2003; Nigam et al. 2000; Li et al. 2009); second, CHI and WLLR are considered to belong to the same group of measures, which take both category information (i.e., ratio between different classes) and frequency information (i.e., frequency of document and frequency of terms) into account (Li et al. 2009). The WLLR is defined as the product of the probability of each action sequence and the logarithm of the ratio between the conditional probabilities of the sequence in different performance groups. We focused on applying this commonly used feature selection method in this study for comparison with the results derived from the chi-square method rather than questioning its statistical rationale. Analogous to WLLR being applied in feature selection for text categorization (Nigam et al. 2000), the WLLR of each action sequence for the purpose of binary classification (i.e., correct group and incorrect group) can be defined as the following:

$$WLLR\,(a, C_i) = p\,(a|C_i)\log\frac{p\,(a|C_i)}{p\left(a|\overline{C}_i\right)}, \tag{13.3}$$

where $p\,(a|C_i)$ is the conditional probability of action a given in the class C_i and $p\left(a|\overline{C}_i\right)$ is the conditional probability of action a not in the class C_i. In the current analysis, we calculated the WLLR by correct and incorrect groups separately, which resulted in all positive values of ratio scores. The correct and incorrect groups were defined exactly the same as with the chi-square selection method.

13.3 Results

13.3.1 Performance Groups on an Aggregate Level

The first analysis of feature extraction was conducted by performance group via two approaches. Table 13.3 presents the correlation of CHI and WLLR scores for action sequences in different performance groups by n-grams. It was found that the CHI and WLLR scores were moderately correlated in the unigrams and highly correlated in the bigrams and trigrams in both the correct and incorrect groups. The reason might be interpreted as follows. Unigrams are more flexible than bigrams and trigrams. The similar frequency of unigrams in correct and incorrect groups results in a smaller likelihood ratio between the two groups. As shown in formula (13.3), the WLLR is biased toward the action sequences with both high category ratio and high

Table 13.3 Correlation between CHI and WLLR in different performance groups by *n*-grams

	Correct	Incorrect
Unigrams	0.74	0.60
Bigrams	0.87	0.98
Trigrams	0.88	0.94

frequency, which has been proven in earlier studies by Li et al. (2009) and Nigam et al. (2000). In the unigrams, the frequency of action sequences appears to play a more important role than the ratio measurement. Therefore, we can expect that the unigrams that have low frequencies may have a low WLLR score, although the CHI score could be high. Because the frequencies of action sequences that occurred in the correct group are higher on average than the incorrect group, we would expect the correlation between CHI and WLLR also to be higher in the correct group than the incorrect group, as shown in Table 13.3. However, the correlation of CHI and WLLR scores for bigrams and trigrams in the incorrect group was a bit higher than the correct group, which was a different pattern than seen with the unigrams. The reason seems to be the greater possibility of errors when looking at sequential actions (bigram, trigram) instead of just one action (unigram). The results in Table 13.3 also demonstrate that the mini-sequences of bigrams and trigrams are more informative than unigrams to be detected as robust classifiers.

Table 13.4 presents the "best" five features (actions and action sequences) commonly identified by both the CHI and WLLR approaches to distinguish the correct and incorrect groups based on an aggregated sample. The top five features of *n*-grams that typically represent each performance group are listed in descending order according to their chi-square scores. Note that due to space limitations, we only present the top five features, using them as examples to illustrate the results of feature selection. The raw frequency of each action and action sequence in Table 13.4 was within the range from 7 to 3047. We found the rankings of features to be consistent between CHI and WLLR.[3]

Among the unigrams, the actions related to using tools to find clues on the spreadsheet page, such as searching or sorting approaches (e.g., "SS_Type_SN", "SS_So_OK", "SS_So_1B", "SS_Se") were found to be robust features in the correct group. This matches our expectation, as the use of searching or sorting tools plays an important role in simplifying the problem-solving process and facilitates success on this item. Conversely, features that were most salient indicators of the incorrect group involved breakoff actions such as canceling a started sequence (e.g., "Next_C"). These cancel actions suggested that the test takers in the incorrect group were unsure about decisions during the response process and may have decided to cancel what they started as a result. Furthermore, the actions that potentially led to wrong answers (e.g., "SS_So_3D") were also found to be robust indicators for the incorrect group. For instance, the action "SS_So_3D", meaning sorting the fourth

[3]Note that the values of CHI and WLLR in Table 13.4 are on different scales. Thus, one needs to focus on the rankings of the features instead of their values.

Table 13.4 Top five features of action sequences commonly selected via CHI and WLLR to distinguish correct and incorrect group

		Action sequences	CHI	WLLR
Correct	Unigrams	SS	70.72	0.37
		SS_So_OK	64.58	0.11
		SS_Se	22.53	0.11
		SS_So_1B	59.66	0.10
		SS_Type_SN	68.04	0.09
	Bigrams	E, SS	229.99	0.43
		SS, E	191.18	0.38
		SS_So_OK, E	153.90	0.11
		SS_So_1B, SS_So_OK	122.49	0.09
		START, SS_Se	74.03	0.09
	Trigrams	E, SS, E	272.49	0.42
		START, E, SS	226.42	0.20
		SS, E, E_S	211.37	0.17
		SS, E, Next	103.52	0.11
		SS, E, SS	133.85	0.09
Incorrect	Unigrams	Next_C	892.80	0.12
		SS_Save	98.90	0.01
		SS_Type_PGN	33.19	0.00
		SS_So_3D	14.56	0.00
		SS_Type_PSN	3.27	0.00
	Bigrams	START, Next	2416.20	0.53
		Next, Next_C	521.74	0.12
		Next_C, Next	504.22	0.08
		SS_Type_FN, Next	196.80	0.05
		E_S, E_S	492.26	0.05
	Trigrams	START, Next, FINALENDING	2420.26	1.71
		Next, Next_C, Next	478.16	0.08
		START, E, Next	399.01	0.08
		Next_C, Next, FINALENDING	392.59	0.07
		E_S, Next, Next_C	374.83	0.05

column (year as a member) in the third choice in the spreadsheet page, was not helpful in identifying the specified person as required. The use of robust features such as "SS_Save", that is, actions that did not directly relate to the shortest path to success, also suggested that test takers in the incorrect group did not fully understand how to solve the problem. Hence, they frequently aimlessly saved the results on the server.

The extracted features of bigrams and trigrams further supported the initial findings based on unigrams. We noticed that the action sequences identified as typical behaviors in the correct group showed that the test takers had clear subgoals in different environments and well understood how to achieve these goals. For example, the correct group usually chose a tool (searching or sorting) at the very beginning to solve the item (e.g., "START, SS_Se"). On the contrary, the robust n-gram-based incorrect indicators suggested that the first actions taken by test takers in the incorrect groups were more likely to be clicking on "Next" (e.g., "START, Next") or directly switching to the email page (e.g., "START, E, Next"). Further inspection of the robust indicators of incorrect responses showed that some action sequences led to wrong answers due to careless mistakes. For instance, some participants in the incorrect group followed the action sequence "SS_Type_FN, Next", meaning they found the unique result from the search engine that was probably correct in the spreadsheet environment; unfortunately, they then clicked on "Next" and either forgot—or maybe were unaware of the need—to enter this result in the email. The robust incorrect indicators such as "Next, Next_C" and "Next_C, Next" provided additional evidence of the breakoff behavior in the incorrect group, which is consistent with the results obtained based on unigrams.

In addition, we noticed that the process data of action sequences could also be used as indicators of missing data. For instance, the most robust trigram in the incorrect group, "START, Next, FINALENDING", was found 321 times in the dataset, which implied that these 321 participants (which correspond to 8.18 % in the whole sample) simply skipped this item. For better precision, they should be labeled as missing rather than as incorrect responses.

13.3.2 Performance Groups Within Each Country

To investigate whether the features (actions and action sequences) extracted by performance groups on an aggregate level were consistent across countries, we further explored the data by conducting separate analyses within each country. Specifically, we applied the CHI and WLLR methods on each country layer and compared the extracted n-gram features among the three countries. Table 13.5

Table 13.5 Consistency rate of extracted features by performance groups compared between country level and aggregate level

	US	Netherlands	Japan
Correct			
Unigrams	0.8	0.8	0.6
Bigrams	0.6	0.6	0.8
Trigrams	0.8	0.8	0.6
Incorrect			
Unigrams	0.6	0.6	0.4
Bigrams	0.6	0.8	0.8
Trigrams	0.8	0.6	0.6

Note. The calculation is based on the comparison between top five robust features extracted by performance groups within each country and those extracted on an aggregate level as shown in Table 13.4

presents the consistency rate of each performance group. We define consistency rate here as the percentage of overlap among the top five features extracted within each country and on an aggregate level. For instance, the consistency rate is as high as 80 % in the first cell under the column of US, suggesting that four of the top five features extracted from the correct group in the US sample matched the features extracted from the correct group of the aggregate sample. The consistency rate of features in the correct group was within a range of [60 %, 80 %], with an average of 70 %. These results suggested that the extracted features within each country were generally consistent with the features detected from a joint sample. Comparatively, the consistency rate of features in the incorrect group was a bit lower but still acceptable. The range was [40 %, 80 %], with an average of 60 %. The reason for a relatively low consistency rate in the incorrect group was probably the diversity of mistakes that led to wrong actions.

A slightly low consistency rate in the Japanese group, especially in the unigrams (60 % in correct group and 40 % in the incorrect group), aroused our attention. To explore the possible reasons for this issue, we took a further look into the Japanese process data as well as the pilot item in the Japanese version. It was noticed that, in the spreadsheet for the Japanese version, there was a space between individuals' given names and surnames. However, such a space is optional and may or may not appear in daily use in Japanese writings. The optional space caused an increase in repeated searching actions and typing actions with "spelling mistakes" (e.g. "SS_Type_SM") because a number of test takers did not notice the presence of the space in the table. However, this issue didn't seem to have a major impact on the response probabilities or on the overall proficiency level of the Japan group, which is the highest performing PIAAC country.

13.4 Discussion

CBAs provide new sources of evidence to study cognitive abilities and underlying processes by measuring not only the outcome of a task but also behavioral process data that can be interpreted in terms of cognitive processes happening throughout task completion (Goldhammer et al. 2013). This is of interest especially in action-driven items, such as PSTRE items in large-scale assessments.

The goal of this study was to explore associations between action sequences and task completion and to identify the feature action sequences that distinguish between different performance groups. Motivated by NLP and text-mining methodologies, we chose the *n*-gram representation method and the CHI and WLLR feature selection methods to extract action sequence patterns that facilitate differentiation between performance groups and mutually validate the results. It was found that the two feature selection approaches resulted in a high agreement of feature identification. The actions related to using tools such as sorting and searching occurred significantly more often in the group of respondents that produced a correct response, while actions suggesting hesitative behaviors such as repeatedly clicking the cancel button were found more often in the incorrect group. Further, among these robust indicators, we noticed that the correct group had a better understanding of the subgoals of different environments and were more likely to recover from initial errors in the problem-solving process. Conversely, respondents in the incorrect group appeared to have only a relatively vague idea about what was expected in the item and were more likely to use the help function.

Besides the positive results, some limitations also merit discussion. For instance, the present study focused on extracting action sequence patterns by different performance groups without taking background characteristics or timing data into consideration. Background variables such as gender, educational level, working status, and familiarity with computer might be important factors in the problem-solving process and will likely be associated with performance on the PSTRE items as well, which would be interesting to be included in future studies. Also, evidence has shown that timing is highly correlated with the problem-solving process and performance (e.g., Goldhammer et al. 2014). Thus, it might be interesting to develop a model that can take advantage of both timing and process data in an integrative analytic approach.

Future studies will provide more information about the predictive power of feature extraction models. More specifically, action sequences harvested across multiple tasks should be related to proficiency estimates based on scored task responses from the same as well as other proficiency scales that were assessed simultaneously. We would like to recommend selecting features via multiple approaches rather than a unique one because different methods may pick up slightly different distinguishing features (action sequences). It seems advisable to double check the feature selection in order to ensure that robust features are selected and are valid for further analysis of additional datasets. In addition, future studies will benefit from the explorations presented here and will be able to scale up analyses to include more data from a larger variety of countries. For instance, we could compute the Kullback–Leibler divergence (Kullback and Leibler 1951) by averaging the sum of WLLR scores for each action sequence to estimate the likelihood of correctness on an individual level.

In conclusion, with increasing use of CBAs, process data play an increasingly important role in tracking test takers' thinking and action sequences. This pilot study presented what we think is a promising method to analyze process data and extract robust sequence features that are informative for differentiating between performance groups. However, the research regarding process data is still nascent in educational assessments. The benefits that process data can bring and how we can use it are questions waiting to be fully explored. For future studies, we recommend including background characteristics and timing data in the analysis of process data to further explore their interaction effects on performance as well as making a comparative study among different feature selection methods to better identify the key sequences in classification.

References

Agresti, A. (1990). *Categorical data analysis*. New York: Wiley.

Bishop, Y. M. M., Fienberg, S. E., & Holland, P. W. (1975). *Discrete multivariate analysis: Theory and practice*. Cambridge, MA: MIT Press.

Dong, G., & Pei, J. (2007). *Sequence data mining*. New York: Springer.

Fink, G. A. (2008). *Markov models for pattern recognition*. Berlin, Germany: Springer.

Forman, G. (2003). An extensive empirical study of feature selection metrics for text classification. *Journal of Machine Learning Research, 3*, 1289–1305.

Goldhammer, F., Naumann, J., Selter, A., Toth, K., Rolke, H., & Klieme, E. (2014). The time on task effect in reading and problem solving is moderated by task difficulty and skill: Insights from a computer-based large-scale assessment. *Journal of Educational Psychology, 106*(4), 608–626.

Goldhammer, F., Naumann, J., & Keβel, Y. (2013). Assessing individual differences in basic computer skills: Psychometric characteristics of an interactive performance measure. *European Journal of Psychological Assessment, 29*(4), 263–275.

Graesser, A. C., Lu, S., Jackson, G. T., Mitchell, H., Ventura, M., Olney, A., et al. (2004). AutoTutor: A tutor with dialogue in natural language. *Behavioral Research Methods, Instruments, and Computers, 36*, 180–193.

He, Q., Glas, C. A. W., Kosinski, M., Stillwell, D. J., & Veldkamp, B. P. (2014). Predicting self-monitoring skills using textual posts on Facebook. *Computers in Human Behavior, 33*, 69–78.

He, Q., Veldkamp, B. P., & de Vries, T. (2012). Screening for posttraumatic stress disorder using verbal features in self narratives: A text mining approach. *Psychiatry Research, 198*(3), 441–447.

Joachims, T. (1998). Text categorization with support vector machines: Learning with many relevant features. *Machine Learning: ECML-98 Lecture Notes in Computer Science, 1398*, 137–142.

Kullback, S., & Leibler, R. A. (1951). On information and sufficiency. *Annals of Mathematical Statistics, 22*(1), 79–86.

Li, S., Xia, R., Zong, C., & Huang, C. (2009). A framework of feature selection methods for text categorization. In *Proceedings of the 47th Annual Meeting of the ACL and the 4th IJCNLP of the AFNLP* (pp. 692–700).

Lin, J., & Wilbur, W. J. (2009). Modeling actions of PubMed users with n-gram language models. *Information Retrieval, 12*, 487–503.

Manning, C. D., & Schütze, H. (1999). *Foundations of statistical natural language processing*. Cambridge, MA: MIT Press.

Nigam, K., McCallum, A. K., Thurn, S., & Mitchell, T. (2000). Text classification from labeled and unlabeled documents using EM. *Machine Learning, 39*(2-3), 103–134.

Oakes, M., Gaizauskas, R., Fowkes, H., Jonsson, W. A. V., & Beaulieu, M. (2001). A method based on chi-square test for document classification. In *Proceedings of the 24th Annual International ACM SIGIR Conference on Research and Development in Information Retrieval* (pp. 440–441). New York: ACM.

Organisation for Economic Co-operation and Development. (2010). *PIAAC technical standards and guidelines*. Paris, France: Author. http://www.oecd.org/site/piaac/PIAAC-NPM(2010_12)PIAAC_Technical_Standards_and_Guidelines.pdf

Organisation for Economic Co-operation and Development. (2013). *Technical Report of the Survey of Adult Skills (PIAAC)*. Paris, France: Author. http://www.oecd.org/site/piaac/_Technical%20Report_17OCT13.pdf

Rutkowski, L., Gonzalez, E., von Davier, M., & Zhou, Y. (2014). Assessment design for international large-scale assessments. In L. Rutkowski, M. von Davier, & D. Rutkowski (Eds.), *Handbook of international large-scale assessment* (pp. 75–95). Boca Raton, FL: Taylor & Francis.

Schleicher, A. (2008). PIAAC: A new strategy for assessing adult competencies. *International Review of Education, 54*, 627–650.

Sonamthiang, S., Cercone, N., & Naruedomkul, K. (2007). Discovering hierarchical patterns of students' learning behavior in intelligent tutoring systems. In *Proceedings of IEEE International Conference on Granular Computing* (pp. 485–489).

Spärck Jones, K. (1972). A statistical interpretation of term specificity and its application in retrieval. *Journal of Documentation, 28*, 11–21.

Su, Z., Yang, Q., Lu, Y., & Zhang, H. (2000). What next: A prediction system for Web requests using n-gram sequence models. In *Proceedings of the First International Conference on Web Information Systems Engineering* (Vol. 1, pp. 214–221).

Sukkarieh, J. Z., von Davier, M., & Yamamoto, K. (2012). *From biology to education: Scoring and clustering multilingual text sequences and other sequential tasks* (Research Report No. RR-12-25). Princeton, NJ: Educational Testing Service.

von Davier, M., & Sinharay, S. (2014). Analytics in international large-scale assessments: Item response theory and population models. In L. Rutkowski, M. von Davier, & D. Rutkowski (Eds.), *Handbook of international large-scale assessment* (pp. 155–174). Boca Raton, FL: Taylor & Francis.

von Davier, M., Sinharay, S., Oranje, A., & Beaton, A. (2006). Statistical procedures used in the National Assessment of Educational Progress (NAEP): Recent developments and future directions. In C. R. Rao & S. Sinharay (Eds.), *Handbook of statistics (Vol. 26): Psychometrics.* Amsterdam, Netherlands: Elsevier.

Yang, Y., & Pederson, J. O. (1997). A comparative study on feature selection in text categorization. In *Proceedings of the 14th International Conference on Machine Learning* (pp. 412–420).

Chapter 14
Evaluating the Detection of Aberrant Responses in Automated Essay Scoring

Mo Zhang, Jing Chen, and Chunyi Ruan

Abstract As automated essay scoring grows in popularity, the measurement issues associated with it take on greater importance. One such issue is the detection of aberrant responses. In this study, we considered aberrant responses as those that were not suitable for machine scoring because the responses have characteristics that the scoring system cannot process. Since no such system can yet understand language in a way that a human rater does, the detection of aberrant responses is important for all automated essay scoring systems. Successful identification of aberrant responses can happen before and after machine scoring is attempted (i.e., pre-screening and post-hoc screening). Such identification is essential if the technology is to be used as the primary scoring method. In this study, we investigated the functioning of a set of pre-screening advisory flags that have been used in different automated essay scoring systems. In addition, we evaluated whether the size of the human–machine discrepancy could be predicted as a precursor to developing a general post-hoc screening method. These analyses were conducted using one scoring system as a case example. Empirical results suggested that some pre-screening advisories were operating more effectively than others were. With respect to post-hoc screening, relatively little scoring difficulty was found overall, thereby reducing the ability to predict human–machine discrepancy for those responses that passed through pre-screening. Limitations of the study and suggestions for future studies are also provided.

Keywords Aberrant response • Automated essay scoring • Scoring difficulty

14.1 Introduction

Automated scoring is here defined as the machine grading of constructed responses that are not amenable to approaches relying on exact matching (such as correspondence with a list of key words) (Bennett and Zhang 2015). Such responses

M. Zhang (✉) • J. Chen • C. Ruan
Research and Development Division, Educational Testing Service,
Princeton, NJ 08540, USA
e-mail: mzhang@ets.org; jchen003@ets.org; cruan@ets.org

L.A. van der Ark et al. (eds.), *Quantitative Psychology Research*, Springer Proceedings in Mathematics & Statistics 140, DOI 10.1007/978-3-319-19977-1_14

are not amenable to exact matching because the specific form(s) and/or content of the correct answer(s) are not known in advance. Automated scoring has been used in various content domains including mathematics, science, and the English language arts (e.g., for writing and speaking ability). Generally stated, automated scoring involves the extraction and aggregation of features of the constructed responses through both qualitative and quantitative means.

In scoring essay responses, which is the subject of this paper, natural language processing methods are typically used for feature extraction (e.g., grammatical error detection and word association). Following feature extraction, evidence is aggregated, which essentially amounts to assigning weights to the different linguistic features and combining the weighted feature values. In these aggregation models, the weights can be determined by a panel of experts or by regressing the human ratings on the set of features. The model is then used to produce a score similar to what a human rater would have assigned to a given response.

14.1.1 Aberrant Responses in Automated Essay Scoring

Even though the use of automated essay scoring continues to grow in a variety of contexts, including educational assessment, several measurement issues have not been fully addressed, one of which is the detection of aberrant responses. In multiple-choice testing, this concept typically refers to a pattern across responses for an individual that does not meet expectation (e.g., incorrect answers to easy questions and correct answers to more difficult questions). There is a large body of research on the detection of such response patterns via person-fit statistics (e.g., Karabastos 2003; Reise and Due 1991; Rupp 2013). For automated scoring, however, the focus is on the characteristics of a single (but complex) item response rather than on a pattern across responses.

In this study, we considered aberrant responses to be those that are not suitable for machine scoring because the responses have characteristics that the scoring system cannot accurately process but that well-trained human raters can more often effectively handle. Characteristics that may produce an aberrant response include off-topic content, foreign language, unnecessary text repetition, random keystrokes, extensive copying or paraphrasing from source materials, pre-memorized text, unusually creative content (e.g., highly metaphorical), or unexpected organization or format (e.g., a poem).

Several aspects of this definition are worth noting. First, this definition implies that aberrancy is a function of the interaction between the limitations of the scoring system and the behavior of examinees with respect to a type of assessment task. Such limitations may be specific to a scoring system or associated more generally with the state of the art. Second, the definition implies that one common manifestation of aberrancy should be a discrepancy between machine and human scores. Finally, the definition makes no presumptions about the intent underlying examinee behavior. That is, aberrant responses may or may not be intentional attempts to "game" the system. Although it is often difficult to infer the intent, such an inference is not necessary for identification and handling of aberrant responses.

In contrast to the sizeable literature in multiple-choice testing, there is only limited research on aberrant-response detection for automated essay scoring. In one study, Powers et al. (2001) conducted an experiment where the authors attempted to trick a machine scoring system by repeating the same paragraphs multiple times so as to increase text length. In another study, Higgins et al. (2005) developed a method to detect off-topic responses using vocabulary patterns. Finally, several recent papers discussed game-ability in automated scoring (e.g., Bejar et al. 2013; Higgins and Heilman 2014). Most of the above studies were experimental ones that compared scores before and after some manipulation (e.g., by increasing the complexity of the vocabulary, or by adding shell language that did not necessarily connect to the content).

14.1.2 Detection of Aberrant Responses

Why do we want to detect aberrant responses? From a measurement perspective, whether automated scoring is sensitive to, and how it handles, atypical responses affects how we interpret and use the resulting scores. Our confidence in the automated scores will be reduced if the scoring system is not robust against aberrant responses or fails to handle those responses appropriately.

Detection of aberrant responses may happen at two times. The first time is the pre-screening stage, before scoring is attempted. Intentionally or not, examinees may produce responses that are nonsensical or otherwise highly atypical. Such atypical responses may be blank, have random keystrokes, be off-topic, or have unusual linguistic structure. From a modeling perspective, those responses can be considered as outliers and should be excluded from the samples used for calibrating and evaluating automated scoring models. Advisory flags are often used to identify such responses during the pre-screening stage. In some cases, these responses can still be scored automatically without human intervention. Examples include an empty submission, an essay in a language other than the target language, or an essay consisting of a complete copy of the prompt text. In other cases, the aberrant response is routed to a human rater for evaluation, bypassing the automated scoring system.

The second time is the post-hoc screening stage. Because machine scoring may not have the same level of public acceptance for high-stakes uses as does human scoring, most testing programs employ both human and machine scoring methods. Responses that are not suitable for machine scoring (evidenced by, for example, low human–machine agreement) can be identified and routed to additional human graders for evaluation. It is often a policy decision to implement a safeguard so that when the machine score is different from the human rating by more than a predetermined threshold, a second human rating is sought.

Because of the expense and slow turnaround associated with human scoring, many large-volume testing programs (e.g., Common Core State Assessments; ETS 2014a; Partnership for Assessment of Readiness for College and Careers 2010; SMARTER Balanced Assessment Consortium 2010) would prefer to use automated scoring as a primary method. For such use to be viable, the effectiveness of pre-screening and post-hoc methods will need to be convincingly demonstrated. For pre-screening, that demonstration would include confirming that the advisory flags accurately identify atypical responses. For post-hoc screening, it might include devising a method to predict the likelihood that a response would have generated a sizeable human–machine discrepancy had it been scored by a human rater. Specifically, if machine-scoring difficulty can be accurately predicted, then human raters can be brought in only when the automated scores were considered to be potentially problematic. The feasibility of this particular approach, however, has not been widely investigated.

14.1.3 Purpose of This Study

The purpose of this study was to investigate the effectiveness of approaches to detecting aberrant responses, with the ultimate goal of supporting the use of automated scoring as a primary method. Even though various pre-screening advisory flags have been integrated into automated scoring systems (e.g., Intelligent Essay Assessor™, Pearson Education Inc. 2010; IntelliMetric™, Vantage Learning 2012), there has been little published research on the effectiveness of those advisory flags. In this study, we evaluated the effectiveness of such pre-screening flags. In addition, we evaluated whether the size of the human–machine discrepancy could be predicted as a precursor to developing a general post-hoc screening method.

14.1.4 E-rater

The automated scoring system used in this study as a case example was *e-rater*®, which was developed at Educational Testing Service (ETS), and has been incorporated in a number of testing programs (Attali and Burstein 2006). The automated scores produced by e-rater are being used for different purposes ranging from classroom assessment to graduate and professional school admissions (ETS 2014b, c). In most testing programs, e-rater scores are generated through a multiple linear regression. The model is calibrated by regressing human ratings onto such text features as vocabulary complexity, essay organization, accuracy of grammar and mechanics, and writing style (in terms of sentence variety and word use).

There are several pre-screening advisory flags embedded in e-rater. In this study, we analyzed eight advisories that were implemented for the particular essay task we examined. Each of those advisories signals some anomalous aspect in an essay response (see Table 14.1). These anomalous aspects would be expected to occur

Table 14.1 Pre-screening advisory flags in e-rater

ID	Label	Description
#1	Repetition	May contain too many repetitions of words, phrases, sentences, or text sections.
#2	Insufficient development	May not show enough development on topic or concept, or provided insufficient evidence to support the claims.
#3	Off topic	May not be relevant to the assigned topic.
#4	Restatement of prompt text	Appears to be a restatement of the prompt text with few additional concepts.
#5	Too short	May be too short to be reliably automatically scored.
#6	Too long	May be too long to be reliably automatically scored.
#7	Unusual organization	May contain unusual organizational elements which cannot be recognized by the automated scoring system.
#8	Excessive number of problems	May contain unusually large amount of errors in grammar, mechanics, style, and usage which may result in unreliable automated scores.

in most writing assessment programs and, as a consequence, similar pre-screening mechanisms have been included in various other automated scoring systems (Foltz et al. 1999; Page 2003; Vantage Learning 2012).

Some of the testing programs that incorporate e-rater also employ a type of post-hoc screening (in addition to pre-screening using advisories like those above). That post-hoc screening involves evaluating the discrepancy between the automated score and a human rater's score for the same response. In cases where human–machine discrepancy exceeds a tolerable threshold, a second human rating is sought. While the exact discrepancy thresholds being used operationally have not been reported, prior research has evaluated thresholds as low as 0.5 to as high as 1.5 on a 5- or 6-point holistic-scoring scale (e.g., Zhang et al. 2013).

14.2 Research Questions

We pursued two research questions, one concerning the pre-screening stage and the other, post-hoc screening.

Research Question 1. Are the advisory flags at the pre-screening stage effective in detecting the aberrant responses they were designed to identify?

RQ1.1 Is the mean absolute human–machine discrepancy greater for flagged than for non-flagged responses?

RQ1.2 Is human–machine agreement lower for flagged than for non-flagged responses?

Research Question 2. For responses that pass through pre-screening, can the size of the human–machine discrepancy be predicted well enough to support an effective post-screening mechanism?

The motivation for answering these research questions is related to supporting the use of automated scoring as a primary method. An answer to the first question will indicate whether aberrant responses can be successfully filtered at the pre-screening stage so that those responses can be given to human raters for processing. For responses that pass pre-screening, an answer to the second question will suggest whether methods could be developed to predict which essays would have been likely to generate low human–machine discrepancies had they been scored by humans. Such essays could thus bypass human review completely, facilitating the sole use of automated scoring.

14.3 Method

14.3.1 Instrument

An expository essay-writing task was used, which was administered in an assessment for graduate school admission in the U.S. In the task, examinees were asked to share their opinions on a general topic, and provide supporting evidence for their claims. The score scale ranged from integer 1 to 6. Included in this study were 76 different prompts of this task type.

14.3.2 Data Set

Essay responses were collected between April 2013 and March 2014. For research question 1, the total number of responses was approximately 520,000, with 499,537 of those responses not flagged by any advisories. The ones that were flagged accounted for less than 5 % of the total sample. Specifically, there were 2591 responses that were uniquely flagged by advisory #2, 10,243 responses by #4, 52 responses by #5, 360 responses by #6, 7017 responses by #7, and 127 responses by #8. (Responses that received more than one advisory flag were not included; N = 681.) No responses were flagged by advisories #1 or #3, even though those advisories were active. All responses to the essay task were scored by at least one human rater and the automated scoring system, while a subset was further graded by a second randomly-assigned human rater (N = 20,153).

For research question 2, a subset of the total sample consisting of 512,439 essay responses was used to examine the extent to which human–machine discrepancy could be predicted. This data set excluded those flagged responses considered aberrant by the testing program (i.e., #5–8).

14.3.3 Data Analyses

Since advisories are intended to identify responses that the machine would not be expected to accurately score, responses with advisory flags should produce lower human–machine agreement than responses receiving no advisory flag. As a consequence, for research question 1, we compared the means of the absolute differences in human–machine discrepancy between flagged and non-flagged responses separately for each of the six advisories (excluding #1 and #3) using a two-sample independent t-test and Cohen's d. We used the absolute difference because positive and negative differences can cancel out, hiding large differences between scoring methods.

We next compared the machine–human agreements between the flagged and the non-flagged groups. Agreement was measured using the Pearson correlation coefficient, quadratically weighted kappa (QWK), and standardized mean score difference (SMD), with the pooled variance of the machine and human scores as the denominator. The first two statistics reflect human–machine agreement at the individual response level, and the last statistic (SMD) concerns distributional differences.

For research question 2, a two-step approach was taken. In the first step, we evaluated the extent to which the machine had difficulty scoring responses. Scoring difficulty was evaluated in several ways, each of which used the results from cumulative logistic regression of the human ratings on the linguistic features extracted by the machine (Haberman and Sinharay 2010). First, we examined the squared correlation between human scores and the machine scores produced by this regression. A high squared correlation would suggest that the machine had produced scores that emulated human ratings well. Second, we computed the mean squared error (MSE) between machine and human scores. A low MSE would imply a close similarity between machine and human scores. Finally, for each response, we used the probability assigned by the regression to each of the six human-score categories. The standard deviation of those probabilities was computed for each response. A response that was difficult for the machine to score would be expected to have a very small standard deviation, meaning that the probability of assigning a score category was approximately equal across the range. On a six-point scale, a response for which the probabilities were equal for all categories would have a standard deviation of 0, whereas a response with a score-category probability of 1 would have a standard deviation of approximately 0.41. This latter response would have a single score category predicted with certainty, implying no scoring difficulty. To summarize results across the data set, the mean and range of the standard deviations were computed, and the distribution was examined.

To investigate whether the machine had difficulty grading responses at different score levels, we computed both MSE within each score level, and the correlation of the standard deviation of the probabilities with human scores. For purposes of computing MSE, ten score levels were created using the machine scores, running from 1 to 6 in increments of 0.5. The MSE between human and machine scores was computed using both the overall sample and the double human-scored sample. In addition, the MSE between the two human ratings was computed and compared with the machine–human MSE. This comparison was made to identify the extent to which scoring difficulty also existed in human ratings, since such scores are known to have limitations (e.g., scale shrinkage and inconsistency; Zhang 2013a).

In the second step, a linear regression model was calibrated to predict the size of the absolute discrepancy between human scores and the machine scores resulting from the cumulative logistic regression. The predictors were the previously mentioned linguistic features, two advisory flags not used by the testing program for pre-screening (#2: insufficient development and #4: restatement of prompt text), and three additional linguistic features. One of the three additional linguistic features indicated the presence of word repetition (below the level needed to trigger flag #1) and of inappropriate words or phrases (e.g., expletives), both of which could conceivably result in higher machine than human scores. The other two features measured the overlap in vocabulary of the target essay with essays at different score levels. This predictive model was evaluated using the Pearson correlation coefficient between the predicted and observed human–machine discrepancies. A high correlation would suggest that the size of the discrepancy could be predicted and potentially used as part of a post-screening technique.

For all analyses, the indices described above were computed for the overall sample, as well as for the top ten countries/territories based on examinee volume.

14.4 Results

14.4.1 Results for Research Question 1

Table 14.2 shows the results for comparing the mean absolute value of the human–machine discrepancy between flagged and non-flagged response groups. This comparison reflects the extent to which human and machine scores disagree at the level of individual responses.

As the table shows, for three of six advisories, the human–machine discrepancy was noticeably larger for flagged responses than non-flagged responses (i.e., #2: insufficient development, #6: too long, and #8: excessive number of problems). These three advisories showed values of Cohen's d within the range commonly considered to constitute a small effect (i.e., greater than 0.20 and less than 0.50). The largest value was for advisory #8 (excessive number of problems) which had a d equal to 0.44.

Three other advisories showed similar degrees of human–machine discrepancy between the flagged and non-flagged groups. For two of the advisories, the differences were not statistically significant (i.e., #5: too short and #7: unusual organization). Although the remaining advisory #4 (restatement of prompt text) produced statistically significant results, the practical significance of the difference was negligible ($d = 0.08$).

Table 14.2 Comparing absolute human–machine discrepancy between flagged and non-flagged responses

	Flagged group		Non-flagged group			
Flag	N	Mean of $\|\Delta\|$ (SD)	N	Mean of $\|\Delta\|$ (SD)	t value	Cohen's d
#2	2591	0.55 (0.39)	499,573	0.45 (0.35)	14.24*	0.28
#4	10,243	0.48 (0.36)	499,573	0.45 (0.35)	8.20*	0.08
#5	52	0.49 (0.21)	499,573	0.45 (0.35)	0.84	0.12
#6	360	0.52 (0.45)	499,573	0.45 (0.35)	3.93*	0.21
#7	7017	0.44 (0.33)	499,573	0.45 (0.35)	−1.42	−0.02
#8	127	0.60 (0.41)	499,573	0.45 (0.35)	4.94*	0.44

Note. $|\Delta|$ = absolute value of human score minus machine score. * = statistically significant at $p < 0.001$ level. SD = standard deviation. #2 = insufficient development; #4 = restatement of prompt text; #5 = too short; #6 = too long; #7 = unusual organization; #8 = excessive number of problems. No responses were observed for advisory flags #1 (repetition) and #3 (off topic)

Table 14.3 Comparing human–machine agreement between non-flagged and flagged responses

Group	N	SMD (h minus e)	Correlation	QWK
Non-flagged	499,573	0.04	0.81	0.77
Flag #2	2591	0.40	0.86	0.77
Flag #4	10,243	0.16	0.80	0.75
Flag #5	52	1.48	0.41	0.29
Flag #6	360	−0.33	0.53	0.36
Flag #7	7017	−0.10	0.76	0.70
Flag #8	127	0.91	0.59	0.45

Note. Correlation = Pearson correlation coefficient; QWK = quadratically weighted kappa; SMD = standardized mean score difference. #2 = insufficient development; #4 = restatement of prompt text; #5 = too short; #6 = too long; #7 = unusual organization; #8 = excessive number of problems. No responses were observed for advisory flags #1 (repetition) and #3 (off topic)

Table 14.3 presents three additional agreement statistics between human and machine scores for flagged responses and non-flagged responses. Included in the table are the human–machine SMD, Pearson correlation coefficient, and QWK.

For the SMD, all flagged groups produced values greater than the non-flagged group. The largest differences were for advisories #2 (insufficient development), #5 (too short), and #8 (excessive number of problems), each of which identified responses for which the machine gave a notably lower score on average than did the human raters.

With respect to the Pearson correlation coefficient, the values for three advisories (#5: too short, #6: too long, and #8: excessive number of problems) were considerably lower for the flagged groups than for the non-flagged group. That is, the human–machine correlation coefficient was 0.81 for non-flagged responses, while the comparable values were 0.41, 0.53, and 0.59 for the three above groups, respectively. Among the remaining three advisories, one had a higher machine–human agreement (i.e., #2: insufficient development), one had a comparable level of machine–human agreement (i.e., #4: restatement of prompt text), and the last had a lower level but by only a relatively small amount (i.e., #7: unusual organization). Generally similar results were found for the QWK statistic.

14.4.2 Results for Research Question 2

The second research question concerned whether the size of the human–machine discrepancy for a response could be predicted. This question was addressed through a two-step process, with the first step being an evaluation of the extent to which the machine had difficulty in scoring. This step was undertaken because if little difficulty was encountered, human–machine discrepancy would be very rare and hard to predict.

Several indicators of machine-scoring difficulty were examined. The two middle columns in Table 14.4 show (1) the squared correlation between human scores and the machine scores produced by the cumulative logistic regression, and (2) the MSE between human and machine scores. These indices are given for the overall sample and for the top 10 countries/territories based on test-taker volume.

Table 14.4 Indicators of machine scoring difficulty

Test country/Territory	N	R-squared	MSE (SD)	r
Total sample	**512,439**	**0.67**	**0.28 (0.43)**	**−0.53**
United States	325,125	0.64	0.27 (0.41)	−0.55
India	77,870	0.52	0.32 (0.48)	−0.30
China	48,089	0.36	0.34 (0.51)	−0.22
Korea	6252	0.52	0.29 (0.43)	−0.38
Canada	5560	0.62	0.31 (0.46)	−0.56
Taiwan	3270	0.46	0.28 (0.45)	−0.27
Great Britain	3162	0.67	0.34 (0.49)	−0.55
Brazil	2813	0.58	0.22 (0.32)	−0.37
Turkey	2149	0.50	0.28 (0.42)	−0.34
Bangladesh	2096	0.45	0.30 (0.45)	−0.28

Note. R-squared = squared correlation between human scores and the machine scores produced by the cumulative logistic regression. MSE = mean squared error between human and machine scores produced by the cumulative logistic regression. r = Pearson correlation coefficient between the human scores and the standard deviation of the probabilities for the score categories yielded by the cumulative logistic regression

For the total sample, the R-squared of 0.67 suggests a reasonably strong relationship between machine and human scores. However, there are clear differences among countries/territories on this index, suggesting some variation with respect to scoring difficulty. In particular, English-native speaking countries like the U.S., Canada, and Great Britain appeared to have noticeably higher levels of R-squared (0.64, 0.62, and 0.67, respectively) than did such non-English speaking countries/territories as China, Taiwan, and Bangladesh (0.36, 0.46, and 0.45, respectively). In contrast to R-squared, relatively little variation was observed for MSE (which is sensitive to differences in scores for individual responses, as opposed to differences in response ordering). The range across all countries was from 0.22 to 0.34.

Not shown in Table 14.4 is a third scoring-difficulty indicator, the standard deviation of the probabilities assigned to each score level by the cumulative logistic regression. For any given response, this value can range from 0, which reflects the most difficulty in distinguishing among score categories, to approximately 0.41, which reflects no difficulty. The mean standard deviation of the probabilities was 0.25 (SD = 0.03) across all examinees in the sample. Shown in Fig. 14.1 is the distribution of the standard deviations. As the figure indicates, most examinees fall into the upper half of the range of possible values, suggesting a relative lack of scoring difficulty.

We also examined scoring difficulty as a function of score level. Two indices were evaluated. One was the Pearson correlation coefficient between the human

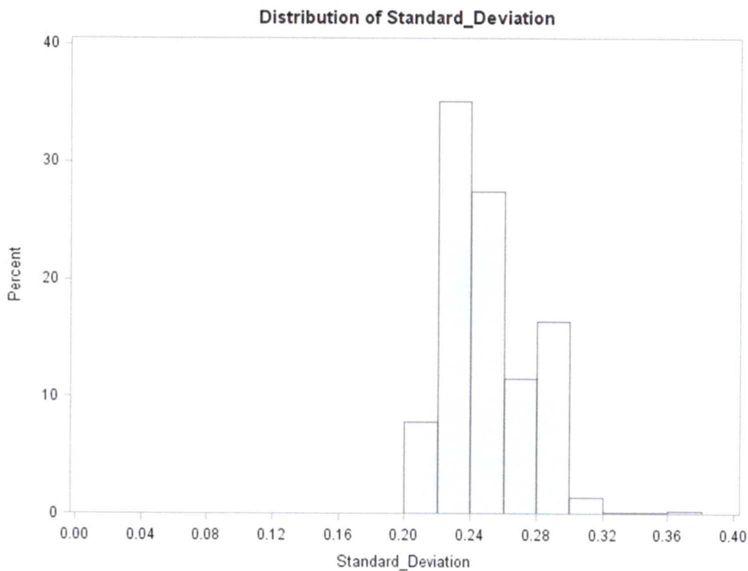

Fig. 14.1 Distribution of the standard deviation of score-level probabilities for the overall sample (N = 512,439)

scores and the standard deviation of the probabilities for the score categories yielded by the cumulative logistic regression. This index is shown in the far-right column of Table 14.4. For the sample as a whole, r = −0.53, indicating a moderate relationship between machine-scoring difficulty and score level, such that the higher the score, the greater the difficulty. This index also has negative values for all top ten countries/territories, though for some countries the relationship was weaker than for others. It is worth noting that the strongest relationships occurred for the English speaking countries/territories, whereas the weaker relationships occurred for non-English speaking countries/territories. This result suggests that scoring difficulty is more evenly distributed across the rubric levels for the non-English speaking countries/territories than for the native English-speaking ones. The former countries/territories had fewer examinees on the higher-end of the scale, where machine scoring would be expected to have the most difficulty due to the greater sophistication of the responses.

The second index used to investigate the association of scoring difficulty with level was conditional MSE (based on the machine scores). As can be seen in Table 14.5, the largest MSEs were for the 4.5-to-5.0 and 5.0-to-5.5 ranges. This result is in line with the negative correlation between the standard deviation of the probabilities and score level reported above. Note that while the MSE for score range 5.5-to-6.0 does not appear to be consistent with this trend, this MSE was not well estimated due to the extremely small sample size.

In Table 14.6 are the MSEs computed by level using the double human-scored sample. Shown are the human–machine MSE and the human–human MSE. The latter MSE gives an estimate of the scoring difficulty present in human rating. Because this MSE can be viewed as a component of the human–machine MSE, a small difference between the two MSEs would suggest that most of the error in the human–machine MSE is attributable to human rating. As the table shows, this difference was always less than half of the human–machine MSE, suggesting that

Table 14.5 Mean squared error by score level for the overall sample

Score level	N	MSE (SD)
[1.0, 1.5)	5373	0.25 (0.33)
[1.5, 2.0)	12,935	0.25 (0.39)
[2.0, 2.5)	38,820	0.28 (0.36)
[2.5, 3.0)	84,006	0.24 (0.39)
[3.0, 3.5)	135,085	0.25 (0.39)
[3.5, 4.0)	121,669	0.29 (0.42)
[4.0, 4.5)	80,190	0.34 (0.51)
[4.5, 5.0)	28,572	0.42 (0.60)
[5.0, 5.5)	5537	0.43 (0.56)
[5.5, 6.0]	252	0.31 (0.67)

Note. MSE = mean squared error between human and machine scores produced by the cumulative logistic regression model. Score levels are based on the machine scores

Table 14.6 Mean squared error by score level for the double human-scored sample

Score level	N	Human–machine MSE (SD)	Human–human MSE (SD)	MSE difference
[1.0, 1.5)	147	0.26 (0.28)	0.16 (0.47)	0.10
[1.5, 2.0)	422	0.22 (0.38)	0.15 (0.59)	0.07
[2.0, 2.5)	1510	0.29 (0.37)	0.21 (0.54)	0.08
[2.5, 3.0)	3140	0.23 (0.40)	0.16 (0.55)	0.07
[3.0, 3.5)	5244	0.25 (0.39)	0.17 (0.52)	0.08
[3.5, 4.0)	4921	0.29 (0.41)	0.18 (0.61)	0.11
[4.0, 4.5)	3311	0.35 (0.52)	0.24 (0.73)	0.11
[4.5, 5.0)	1193	0.44 (0.60)	0.32 (0.92)	0.12
[5.0, 5.5)	255	0.44 (0.58)	0.27 (0.79)	0.17
[5.5, 6.0]	10	0.22 (0.09)	0.40 (0.42)	–*

Note. MSE = mean squared error between the two human ratings, and between human and machine scores produced by the cumulative logistic regression model. Score levels are based on the machine scores. MSE difference = human–machine MSE minus human–human MSE. * = not estimable due to sample size

most of the scoring difficulty can be attributed to unreliability in the human ratings. In addition, the table shows that human raters also encountered greater difficulty at the higher score levels.

In the second step of addressing research question 2, we investigated whether the size of the human–machine discrepancy for a response could be predicted. Table 14.7 provides the correlation coefficient between the predicted and observed absolute human–machine discrepancy. The predictive model was based on the machine scoring features, three additional linguistic features, and two advisory flags. For the overall sample as well as for the individual countries/territories, the prediction accuracy was very limited.

14.5 Discussion

The current study investigated the effectiveness of approaches to detecting aberrant responses in the automated essay scoring context. Aberrant responses were considered to be those that were not suitable for machine scoring because the responses have characteristics that the scoring system cannot process. Successful identification of aberrant responses is essential for using automated scoring as the primary grading method.

Two research questions were posed. One related to the performance of a set of pre-screening advisory flags similar to the ones used in various automated essay scoring systems. The other question concerned the extent of machine scoring diffi-

Table 14.7 Correlation coefficient between the predicted and observed absolute human–machine discrepancy

Test country/Territory	N	r
Total sample	**512,439**	**0.18**
United States	325,125	0.18
India	77,870	0.14
China	48,089	0.19
Korea	6252	0.14
Canada	5560	0.21
Taiwan	3270	0.12
Great Britain	3162	0.24
Brazil	2813	0.06
Turkey	2149	0.15
Bangladesh	2096	0.12

culty and whether the size of the human–machine discrepancy could be predicted as a precursor to developing a general post-hoc screening method.

For the first research question, analyses were concentrated on the performance of a subset of the pre-screening advisory flags used in the automated scoring system, e-rater, as a case example. The results suggested that some advisories were operating considerably more effectively than others. Two advisories (#6: too long and #8: excessive number of problems) produced noticeable differences on all measures evaluated—flagged responses had greater absolute machine–human discrepancies on the individual level, greater SMDs on the distributional level, and lower machine–human agreement than the non-flagged group. A third flag (#5: too short) appeared to be highly sensitive to differences in rank ordering and score distribution, but not to variation in the individual-response level. For this advisory, the human–machine correlation coefficient and QWK were much lower, and the SMD much higher, for the flagged than for the non-flagged groups. In contrast, the mean of the absolute human–machine discrepancies did not distinguish the two groups. For a fourth advisory (#2: insufficient development), the machine–human correlation coefficient and QWK for the flagged group were either slightly higher, or no different from, the non-flagged group. Although this result was contrary to expectation, the magnitude of the differences was small, suggesting a similar rank ordering of machine and human scores in the two groups. But, as expected, the human–machine SMDs and the absolute discrepancies for this advisory were considerably larger for flagged responses than for non-flagged responses. Thus, this flag appeared to be primarily sensitive to level differences.

Two other advisories produced more marginal effects (#4: restatement of prompt text and #7: unusual organization). These advisories were relatively ineffective in distinguishing between flagged and non-flagged groups in terms of absolute human–machine discrepancies. They were also much less effective than other advisories as measured by Pearson correlation coefficient and QWK. Last, although they showed some evidence of distinguishing distributional differences (SMD), the magnitudes were small.

Finally, two advisories (#1: repetition and #3: off topic) were not triggered by any responses and hence the effect of these flags could not be evaluated. It is possible that because the data were collected from a high-stakes testing program, examinees' motivation to game the system through repetition was very low. Similarly, it is possible that all test-takers submitted content-relevant essays; however, it is also possible that this advisory is not sensitive enough towards off-topic responses.

For the second research question, we investigated whether the size of the human–machine discrepancy could be predicted accurately enough to support a post-hoc screening mechanism. As a precursor to that prediction, we evaluated the extent to which the machine had difficulty scoring responses. Results showed relatively little scoring difficulty overall, with the relationship between machine and human scores being reasonably strong. At the same time, there were clear differences among countries/territories with lower difficulty associated with English-native speaking countries and higher levels of difficulty evident in some non-English speaking countries/territories. This result is consistent with the findings of other studies (e.g., Bridgeman et al. 2012; Zhang 2013b), and might be caused by smaller variation in English-language writing proficiency among examinees from those non-native English-speaking countries/territories.[1] Considerably less variation across test countries/territories was found for the MSE, which could reflect the fact that it measures a somewhat different aspect of agreement from R-squared. Additionally, this index is less affected than R-squared by differences in variability from one country/territory to another. Finally, the mean standard deviation of the probabilities also suggested a relative lack of scoring difficulty in the overall sample.

Although scoring difficulty appeared to be relatively small overall, more difficulty was apparent for the upper than for the other levels of the score scale. This phenomenon was evidenced by a moderate negative correlation of the standard deviation of the score-level probabilities with human scores, and by larger MSEs for responses in the upper levels. Interestingly, human raters also showed evidence of greater scoring difficulty at the upper end of the scale, as indicated by MSE. In fact, a sizable portion of the machine–human MSE might be caused by unreliability among human raters, which in turn may reflect ambiguity in the rubric criteria.

Our attempt to predict human–machine discrepancy had limited success. The low level of prediction was not surprising in the context of the scoring difficulty results. For one, machine scores appeared to correlate strongly with human scores overall, leaving relatively little variation in the size of the discrepancies. Second, the small number of examinees who were in the lowest and highest score levels worked further to reduce the variation in discrepancy. Finally, discrepancy did not appear to be constant across score levels making it harder to predict.

[1]The standard deviations of the human scores were 0.86 for the U.S., 0.90 for Canada, and 1.00 for Great Britain; the comparable values were 0.59 for China, 0.66 for Taiwan, and 0.69 for Bangladesh.

Several limitations of this study should be noted. First, for most analyses, only one human score was used. Because human raters (like machines) are fallible, having additional human raters might make for a more reliable and valid criterion against which to evaluate the flags, scoring difficulty, and the discrepancy prediction model. Second, we evaluated advisory flags that covered only six types of aberrant response. There are many other kinds of aberrant response (e.g., responses with many rare or long words) that were not investigated because the system used in this study did not have flags to detect them. Finally, only one test and its automated scoring system were investigated. It is possible that differences in examinee population, test content, test purpose, or automated scoring system would lead to different results.

This study demonstrated how the performance of pre-screening flags for detecting aberrant responses might be analyzed, and the extent to which machine scoring difficulty might be predicted. The approaches used here can be employed by other researchers in evaluating the effectiveness of similar flags, and the extent of scoring difficulty, likely to be found for other systems. That evaluation might inform policy decisions about when it is appropriate to use particular advisory flags, the criteria for determining aberrance, and the subpopulations and scale regions where scoring difficulty might be present. Researchers building automated scoring systems should consider including pre-screening advisory flags similar to the ones found to be effective here.

Future studies should consider the use of qualitative analyses, which might reveal consistent patterns in responses that have large human–machine discrepancy. For post-hoc screening purposes, those patterns can then be used to model scoring difficulty. Inclusion of more linguistic features independent of those used for automated scoring might also improve the accuracy of predicting discrepancy. For pre-screening purposes, timing and process information might be useful (Zhang and Deane in press). As a simple example, if an examinee submits an essay shortly after the test starts (e.g., 30 s), that response is highly likely to be illegitimate. In any case, a stronger portfolio of pre-screening and post-screening techniques will be needed if the sole use of automated scoring is to become viable.

Acknowledgements We would like to thank Shelby Haberman for his substantial help in providing guidance on the design, analyses, and interpretation. We also thank Beata Beigman Klebanov, Nitin Madnani, Don Powers, Andre Rupp, David Williamson, Randy Bennett, and Andries van der Ark for their review and suggestions on the previous versions of this manuscript.

References

Attali, Y., & Burstein, J. (2006). Automated essay scoring with e-rater® v. 2. *The Journal of Technology, Learning and Assessment*, *4*(3).

Bejar, I. I., VanWinkle, W. H., Madnani, N., Lewis, W., & Steier, M. (2013). *Length of textual response as a construct-irrelevant response strategy: The case of shell language* (RR-13-07). Princeton, NJ: Educational Testing Service.

Bennett, R. E., & Zhang, M. (2015). Validity and automated scoring. In F. Drasgow (Ed.), *Technology in testing: Improving educational and psychological measurement*. NCME applications of educational measurement and assessment series. New York, US: Taylors & Francis.
Bridgeman, B., Trapani, C., & Attali, Y. (2012). Comparison of human and machine scoring of essays: Differences by gender, ethnicity, and country. *Applied Measurement in Education, 25*, 27–40.
ETS (2014a). *Coming together to raise achievement new assessments for the Common Core State Standards*. Retrieved from: http://www.k12center.org/rsc/pdf/coming_together_march_2014_rev_1.pdf, on February 25, 2015.
ETS. (2014b). *Criterion®*. Download from http://www.ets.org/criterion
ETS. (2014c). *Understanding your TOEFL iBT® test scores*. Download from http://www.ets.org/toefl/ibt/scores/understand
Foltz, P. W., Laham, D., & Landauer, T. K. (1999). Automated essay scoring: Applications to educational technology. In B. Collis & R. Oliver (Eds.), *Proceedings of World Conference on Educational Multimedia, Hypermedia and Telecommunications* (pp. 939–944). Chesapeake, VA: Association for the Advancement of Computing in Education (AACE).
Haberman, S. J., & Sinharay, S. (2010). The application of the cumulative logistic regression model to automated essay scoring. *Journal of Educational and Behavioral Statistics, 35*, 586–602.
Higgins, D., Burstein, J., & Attali, Y. (2005). Identifying off-topic student essays without topic-specific training data. *Natural Language Engineering, 12*, 145–159.
Higgins, D., & Heilman, M. (2014). Managing what we can measure: Quantifying the susceptibility of automated scoring systems to gaming behavior. *Educational Measurement: Issues and Practice, 33*(4), 36–46.
Karabastos, G. (2003). Comparing the aberrant response detection performance of thirty six person-fit statistics. *Applied Measurement in Education, 16*(4), 277–298.
Page, E. B. (2003). Project Essay Grade: PEG. In M. D. Shermis & J. Burstein (Eds.), *Automated essay scoring: A cross-disciplinary perspective* (pp. 43–54). Mahwah, NJ: Lawrence Erlbaum Associates.
Partnership for Assessment of Readiness for College and Careers. (2010). *The Partnership for Assessment of Readiness for College and Careers (PARCC) application for the Race to the Top comprehensive assessment systems competition*. Retrieved from http://www.parcconline.org/sites/parcc/files/PARCC%20Application%20-%20FINAL.pdf, on February 25, 2015.
Pearson Education Inc. (2010). *Intelligent essay assessor™ (IEA) fact sheet*. Retrieved from http://kt.pearsonassessments.com/download/IEA-FactSheet-20100401.pdf, on October 19, 2014.
Powers, D., Burstein, J., Chodorow, M., Fowles, M., & Kulich, K. (2001). *Stumping e-rater: Challenging the validity of automated essay scoring* (RR-01-03). Princeton, NJ: Educational Testing Service.
Reise, S. P., & Due, A. M. (1991). The influence of test characteristics on the detection of aberrant response patterns. *Applied Psychological Measurement, 15*, 217–226.
Rupp, A. A. (2013). A systematic review of the methodology for person fit research in item response theory: Lessons about generalizability of inferences from the design of simulation studies. *Psychological Test and Assessment Modeling, 55*, 3–38.
SMARTER Balanced Assessment Consortium. (2010). *Race to the Top assessment program application for new grants: Comprehensive assessment systems CFDA Number:* 84.395B. Retrieved from http://www.smarterbalanced.org/wordpress/wp-content/uploads/2011/12/Smarter-Balanced-RttT-Application.pdf, on February 25, 2015.
Vantage Learning. (2012). *IntelliMetric®*. Retrieved from http://www.vantagelearning.com/products/intellimetric, on October 19, 2014.
Zhang, M. (2013a). *Contrasting automated and human scoring of essays* (RDC-21). Princeton, NJ: Educational Testing Service.
Zhang, M. (2013b). *The impact of sampling approach on population invariance in automated scoring of essays* (RR-13-18). Princeton, NJ: Educational Testing Service.

Zhang, M., Breyer, F. J., & Lorenz, F. (2013). *Investigating the suitability of implementing the e-rater scoring engine in a large-scale English language testing program* (RR-13-36). Princeton, NJ: Educational Testing Service.

Zhang, M., & Deane, P. (in press). *Process features in writing: Internal structure and incremental value over product features*. Research Report. Princeton, NJ: Educational Testing Service.

Chapter 15
On Closeness Between Factor Analysis and Principal Component Analysis Under High-Dimensional Conditions

L. Liang, K. Hayashi, and Ke-Hai Yuan

Abstract This article studies the relationship between loadings from factor analysis (FA) and principal component analysis (PCA) when the number of variables p is large. Using the average squared canonical correlation between two matrices as a measure of closeness, results indicate that the average squared canonical correlation between the sample loading matrix from FA and that from PCA approaches 1 as p increases, while the ratio of p/N does not need to approach zero. Thus, the two methods still yield similar results with high-dimensional data. The Fisher-z transformed average canonical correlation between the two loading matrices and the logarithm of p is almost perfectly linearly related.

Keywords Canonical correlation • Factor indeterminacy • Fisher-z transformation • Guttman condition • Large p small N • Ridge factor analysis

15.1 Introduction

Factor analysis (FA) and principal component analysis (PCA) are frequently used multivariate statistical methods for data reduction. In FA (Anderson 2003; Lawley and Maxwell 1971), the p-dimensional mean-centered vector of the observed variables $\boldsymbol{y}$ is linearly related to an m-dimensional vector of latent factors $\boldsymbol{f}$ as $\boldsymbol{y} = \boldsymbol{\Lambda f} + \boldsymbol{\varepsilon}$, where $\boldsymbol{\Lambda}$ is the $p \times m$ matrix of factor loadings (with $p > m$), and $\boldsymbol{\varepsilon}$ is a p-dimensional vector of errors. Typically for the orthogonal factor model,

L. Liang • K. Hayashi (✉)
Department of Psychology, University of Hawaii at Manoa, 2530 Dole Street, Sakamaki C400, Honolulu, HI 96822, USA
e-mail: lianglu@hawaii.edu; hayashik@hawaii.edu

K.-H. Yuan
Department of Psychology, University of Notre Dame, 123A Haggar Hall, Notre Dame, IN 46556, USA
e-mail: kyuan@nd.edu

L.A. van der Ark et al. (eds.), *Quantitative Psychology Research*, Springer Proceedings in Mathematics & Statistics 140, DOI 10.1007/978-3-319-19977-1_15

the three assumptions are imposed: (1) $\boldsymbol{f} \sim N_m(\mathbf{0}, \boldsymbol{I}_m)$; (2) $\boldsymbol{\varepsilon} \sim N_p(\mathbf{0}, \boldsymbol{\Psi})$, where $\boldsymbol{\Psi}$ is a diagonal matrix; (3) $Cov(\boldsymbol{f}, \boldsymbol{\varepsilon}) = \mathbf{0}$. Then, under these three assumptions, the covariance matrix of $\boldsymbol{y}$ is given by $\boldsymbol{\Sigma} = \boldsymbol{\Lambda}\boldsymbol{\Lambda}' + \boldsymbol{\Psi}$.

Let $\boldsymbol{\Lambda}^+$ be the $p \times m$ matrix whose columns are the standardized eigenvectors corresponding to the first m largest eigenvalues of $\boldsymbol{\Sigma}$; $\boldsymbol{\Omega}$ be the $m \times m$ diagonal matrix whose diagonal elements are the first m largest eigenvalues of $\boldsymbol{\Sigma}$; and $\boldsymbol{\Omega}^{1/2}$ be the $m \times m$ diagonal matrix whose diagonal elements are the square root of those in $\boldsymbol{\Omega}$. Then principal components (PCs) (c.f., Anderson 2003) with m elements are obtained as $\boldsymbol{f}^* = \boldsymbol{\Lambda}^{+\prime}\boldsymbol{y}$. Clearly, the PCs are uncorrelated with a covariance matrix $\boldsymbol{\Lambda}^{+\prime}\boldsymbol{\Sigma}\boldsymbol{\Lambda}^+$. When m is properly chosen, there exists $\boldsymbol{\Sigma} \approx \boldsymbol{\Lambda}^+\boldsymbol{\Omega}\boldsymbol{\Lambda}^{+\prime} = \boldsymbol{\Lambda}^*\boldsymbol{\Lambda}^{*\prime}$, where $\boldsymbol{\Lambda}^* = \boldsymbol{\Lambda}^+\boldsymbol{\Omega}^{1/2}$ is the $p \times m$ matrix of PCA loadings.

It has been well known that FA and PCA often yield approximately the same results, especially their loading matrices $\widehat{\boldsymbol{\Lambda}}$ and $\widehat{\boldsymbol{\Lambda}}^*$, respectively. See, e.g., Velicer and Jackson (1990) and the literature cited therein. Conditions under which the two matrices are close to each other are of substantial interest. At the population level, one such condition identified by Guttman (1956) requires that $p \to \infty$ while $m/p \to 0$. For the one-factor model with $\boldsymbol{\Lambda} = \boldsymbol{\lambda}$ and $\boldsymbol{\Lambda}^* = \boldsymbol{\lambda}^*$, under the conditions that $\boldsymbol{\lambda}'\boldsymbol{\lambda} \to \infty$ and there exists an upper bound for unique variances as $p \to \infty$, Bentler and Kano (1990) proved that $\boldsymbol{\lambda}^*$ converges to $\boldsymbol{\lambda}$. Let $\psi_{\max}$ be the largest element of the diagonal matrix $\boldsymbol{\Psi}$ of unique variances, $d_{\min}$ be the smallest eigenvalue of $\boldsymbol{\Lambda}'\boldsymbol{\Lambda}$, and

$$\rho^2(\boldsymbol{\Lambda}, \boldsymbol{\Lambda}^*) = \left(\frac{1}{m}\right) tr\left\{(\boldsymbol{\Lambda}'\boldsymbol{\Lambda})^{-1}(\boldsymbol{\Lambda}'\boldsymbol{\Lambda}^*)(\boldsymbol{\Lambda}^{*\prime}\boldsymbol{\Lambda}^*)^{-1}(\boldsymbol{\Lambda}^{*\prime}\boldsymbol{\Lambda})\right\}$$

be the average squared canonical correlation between $\boldsymbol{\Lambda}$ and $\boldsymbol{\Lambda}^*$. Schneeweiss and Mathes (1995) showed that $\rho^2(\boldsymbol{\Lambda}, \boldsymbol{\Lambda}^*) \to 1$ if $\psi_{\max}/d_{\min} \to 0$. Schneeweiss (1997) further gave a weaker condition: $\delta/d_{\min} \to 0$ where $\delta = \psi_{\max} - \psi_{\min}$ is the difference between the largest and the smallest diagonal element of $\boldsymbol{\Psi}$. Here, note that Guttman's condition is expressed by only p and m, and the role of FA loadings is not mentioned. On the other hand, Schneeweiss-Mathes and Schneeweiss conditions are expressed in terms of the eigenvalue(s) of FA loadings and unique variance(s), and the roles of p and m are not mentioned. Yet, it is known that both are closely related (Hayashi and Bentler 2000; Krijnen 2006).

Recently, with the advancement of computing technology, high-dimensional data with large p arise in many disciplines (see, e.g., Hastie et al. 2009). Consequently, the needs for improving our statistical methodology for analyzing such data are increasing. Large p is also common in the traditional research in social sciences. For example, the Minnesota Multiphasic Personality Inventory-2 (MMPI-2; Butcher et al. 1989) contains 567 items, and the scale has been widely used to assess individual mental health. (Note that MMPI-2 items are binary and we must apply FA for ordered categorical data. In our study, we focus on FA for continuous data.) Also, we often collect data from many questionnaires. As a result, whenever we consider item analysis with multiple questionnaires combined, we have to face the issue of analyzing high-dimensional data. Recently, under high-dimensional setting and when both p and N approach infinity, Bai and Li (2012) studied FA and PCA, and showed that their loading estimates converge to the same asymptotic normal distribution, where an additional assumption of $\sqrt{p}/N \rightarrow 0$ is needed.

Although some authors called data with $p > N$ as high-dimensional (see, e.g., Hastie et al. 2009, Chapter 18; Pourahmadi 2013), we do not require this assumption to accommodate typical social science data. Also, we do not consider covariance matrix that has many zero entries, called sparsity (see, e.g., Buehlmann & van de Geer 2011).

15.2 Purpose of Study

We examine the closeness of the estimates of the two loading matrices from FA and PCA under high-dimensional setting. Thus, the main goal of our work is to investigate whether the closeness measured by the average squared sample canonical correlation $\rho^2\left(\widehat{\boldsymbol{\Lambda}}, \widehat{\boldsymbol{\Lambda}}^*\right)$ approaches 1 under the conditions analytically derived by Guttman (1956), Schneeweiss and Mathes (1995), and Schneeweiss (1997); and also under high-dimensional setting with large p when N is relatively small.

Notice that Schneeweiss and Mathes (1995) and Schneeweiss (1997) only considered the population loading matrices without any sampling errors. In contrast, we considered sampling errors by analyzing the sample correlation matrices with ridge FA (Yuan and Chan 2008) and PCA in a simulation study. Our emphasis is on high-dimensional settings where p is relatively close to N. As we describe in the next section, we consider two scenarios: (1) $\sqrt{p}/N$ decreases while p/N stays constant; (2) p/N increases while $\sqrt{p}/N$ stays constant. The reason for us to choose the ratio $\sqrt{p}/N$ to specify our condition is because $\sqrt{p}/N \rightarrow 0$ is needed for the equivalence of asymptotic distributions of FA and PCA loadings (Bai and Li 2012). To the best of our knowledge, there have not been any studies on systematically examining the relationship between the various closeness conditions and the actual levels of closeness measured by the average squared canonical correlation $\rho^2\left(\widehat{\boldsymbol{\Lambda}}, \widehat{\boldsymbol{\Lambda}}^*\right)$ to date.

We predicted that (1) $\rho^2\left(\widehat{\boldsymbol{\Lambda}}, \widehat{\boldsymbol{\Lambda}}^*\right)$ would approach 1 faster under the condition that $\sqrt{p}/N$ decreases with p/N being a constant than under the condition when p/N increases with $\sqrt{p}/N$ being a constant; (2) $\rho^2\left(\widehat{\boldsymbol{\Lambda}}, \widehat{\boldsymbol{\Lambda}}^*\right)$ would approach 1 faster under equal unique variances than under unequal unique variances.

15.3 Simulation Conditions

The population factor loading matrix in our study is of the following form with three factors ($m = 3$):

$$\mathbf{\Lambda}'_{12} = \begin{pmatrix} \lambda_{11}\ \lambda_{21}\ \lambda_{31}\ \lambda_{41} & 0\ \ 0\ \ 0\ \ 0 & 0 & 0 & 0 & 0 \\ 0\ \ 0\ \ 0\ \ 0 & \lambda_{52}\ \lambda_{62}\ \lambda_{72}\ \lambda_{82} & 0 & 0 & 0 & 0 \\ 0\ \ 0\ \ 0\ \ 0 & 0\ \ 0\ \ 0\ \ 0 & \lambda_{93} & \lambda_{10,3} & \lambda_{11,3} & \lambda_{12,3} \end{pmatrix},$$

where two conditions of population loadings are employed: (1) *equal loadings*: $\lambda_{ij} = 0.8$ for every non-zero factor loading, and (2) *unequal loadings*: $\lambda_{11} = \lambda_{21} = \lambda_{52} = \lambda_{62} = \lambda_{93} = \lambda_{10,3} = 0.8$, $\lambda_{31} = \lambda_{72} = \lambda_{11,3} = 0.75$, $\lambda_{41} = \lambda_{82} = \lambda_{12,3} = 0.7$. The numbers of observed variables are multiples of 12: $p = 12q$, $q = 1, 2, \ldots, 7$; and, when q is more than 1, we stack the structure of $\mathbf{\Lambda}_{12}$ vertically so that $\mathbf{\Lambda} = \mathbf{1}_q \otimes \mathbf{\Lambda}_{12}$, where $\mathbf{1}_q$ is the column vector of q 1's and $\otimes$ is the Kronecker product. The factors are orthogonal so that the population covariance structures are of the form: $\mathbf{\Sigma} = \mathbf{\Lambda}\mathbf{\Lambda}' + \mathbf{\Psi}$, where the diagonal elements of $\mathbf{\Sigma}$ are all 1's. As a result, (1) corresponds to equal unique variances and (2) corresponds to unequal unique variances in the population.

Let $\mathbf{S}$ be the sample covariance matrix, and we perform FA on $\mathbf{S}_a = \mathbf{S} + a\mathbf{I}_p$, and call them ridge FA, where $\mathbf{I}_p$ is a p-dimensional identity matrix and a is a tuning parameter. In the analysis, we let $a = p/N$ as was recommended in Yuan and Chan (2008) and Yuan (2013), which led to more accurate estimates of the factor loadings than performing FA on $\mathbf{S}$. No attempt to identify an optimal tuning parameter is made. Because sparsity is not our focus, we do not apply different regularization methods such as the lasso (Tibshirani 1996). We perform PCA on $\mathbf{S}$, not on $\mathbf{S}_a$.

Regarding conditions of N and p, we examine two different scenarios: (1) *equal* p/N: N increases at the same rate as p; (2) *increased* p/N: p increases faster than N. The increased p/N case corresponds to the scenario in which the ratios $\sqrt{p}/N$ are approximately constant, around .0173. See Table 15.1 and Fig. 15.1 for the two different scenarios for the (N, p) pairs. Regarding the ratios m/p, because m is fixed at 3, m/p decreases as p increases. So, our study also includes part of the Guttman (1956) condition: $m/p \to 0$.

The combinations of two patterns of population covariance matrices and two different series of p/N ratios create four different scenarios in the simulation. For each condition of N, p and $\mathbf{\Sigma}$, we performed 100 replications of samples from the multivariate normal distribution with mean vector $\mathbf{0}$ and covariance matrix $\mathbf{\Sigma}$. For each replication, we computed the $\rho^2\left(\widehat{\mathbf{\Lambda}}, \widehat{\mathbf{\Lambda}}^*\right)$; and, at the end of the 100 replications, the average value of $\rho^2\left(\widehat{\mathbf{\Lambda}}, \widehat{\mathbf{\Lambda}}^*\right)$ across the replications was obtained.

Table 15.1 Combination of (p, N) pairs in the simulation study

Condition with p/N being a constant							
p	12	24	48	96	192		
N	200	400	800	1600	3200		
p/N	0.06	0.06	0.06	0.06	0.06		
$\sqrt{p}/N$	0.0173	0.0122	0.00866	0.00612	0.00433		
Condition with p/N increasing							
p	12	24	48	96	192	384	768
N	200	283	400	566	800	1131	1600
p/N	0.06	0.0848	0.12	0.1696	0.24	0.3395	0.48
$\sqrt{p}/N$	0.0173	0.0173	0.0173	0.0173	0.0173	0.0173	0.0173

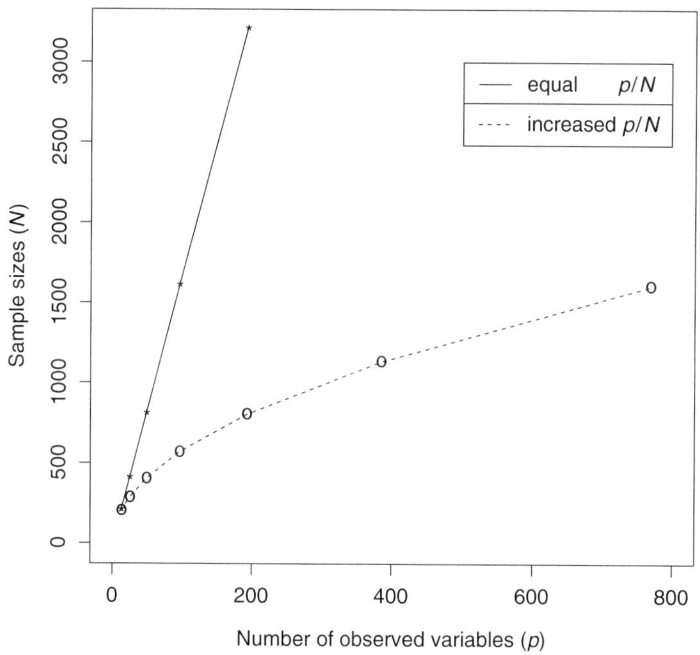

Fig. 15.1 Combination of (N, p) pairs in the simulation study; *Note*: The "equal p/N" corresponds to the scenario in which $\sqrt{p}/N \to 0$, and the "increased p/N" corresponds to the scenario in which $\sqrt{p}/N$ is approximately constant

For FA, we employed the "factanal" function in the R language and modified it to fit our simulation purpose. The "factanal" function employs the "optim" function, a general purpose optimization function. We used the default convergence criterion set by the "optim" function. For PCA, we simply used the "eigen" function to find the eigenvalues and the corresponding standardized eigenvectors.

15.4 Results

(1) In each of the four different combinations of unique variances and *p*/*N* ratios, both $\widehat{\psi}_{\max}/\widehat{d}_{\min}$ and $\widehat{\delta}/\widehat{d}_{\min}$ decrease rather fast with *p* initially, and they tend to stabilize as *p* increases (Figs. 15.2 and 15.3). As *p* increases, both $\widehat{\psi}_{\max}/\widehat{d}_{\min}$ and $\widehat{\delta}/\widehat{d}_{\min}$ converge to zero slightly slower under the condition with unequal unique variances and when *p*/*N* increases.

(2) The average squared canonical correlations $\rho^2\left(\widehat{\mathbf{\Lambda}},\widehat{\mathbf{\Lambda}}^*\right)$ increase rapidly to 1 as *p* increases, especially under the conditions of equal unique variances (Figs. 15.4 and 15.5). The relationship between $\rho^2\left(\widehat{\mathbf{\Lambda}},\widehat{\mathbf{\Lambda}}^*\right)$ and *p* is displayed in Fig. 15.5 after the Fisher-*z* transformation of the average canonical correlation, where $\widehat{z} = (1/2)\log\left\{\left(1+\rho\left(\widehat{\mathbf{\Lambda}},\widehat{\mathbf{\Lambda}}^*\right)\right)/\left(1-\rho\left(\widehat{\mathbf{\Lambda}},\widehat{\mathbf{\Lambda}}^*\right)\right)\right\}$ still keeps increasing as *p* increased from 12 to 768. The differences in the speeds with which $\rho\left(\widehat{\mathbf{\Lambda}},\widehat{\mathbf{\Lambda}}^*\right)$ approaches 1 among the four different scenarios become clearer after the Fisher-*z* transformation (Fig. 15.5). Quite interestingly, the value of the Fisher-*z* transformed average canonical correlation and the logarithm of *p* are almost perfectly linearly related. For the equal unique variance case with the constant *p*/*N* condition, $\widehat{z} = 1.002 + (1.554)log(p)$ with coefficient of determination $r^2 = .9999$; for the equal unique variance case with the increased *p*/*N* condition, $\widehat{z} = 1.699 + (1.280)log(p)$ with $r^2 = .9999$; for the unequal unique variance case with the constant *p*/*N* condition, $\widehat{z} = 1.546+(1.059)log(p)$ with $r^2 = .9997$; and for the unequal unique variance case with the increased *p*/*N* condition, $\widehat{z} = 1.585 + (1.034)log(p)$ with $r^2 = 1.0000$.

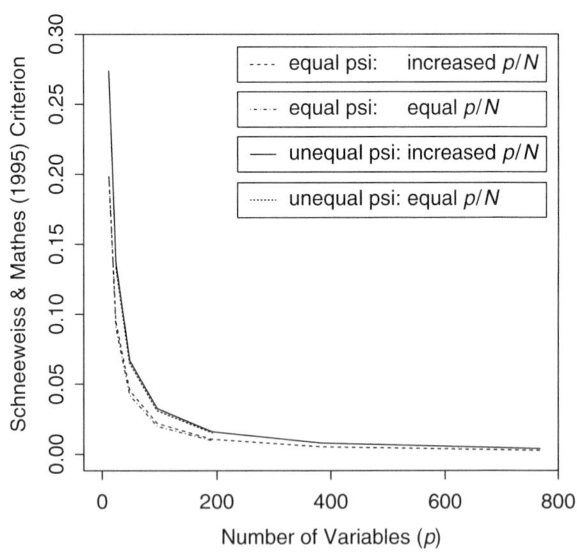

Fig. 15.2 Schneeweiss and Mathes (1995) criterion ($\hat{\psi}_{\max}/\hat{d}_{\min}$) as a function of the number of observed variables (*p*) for four simulation conditions

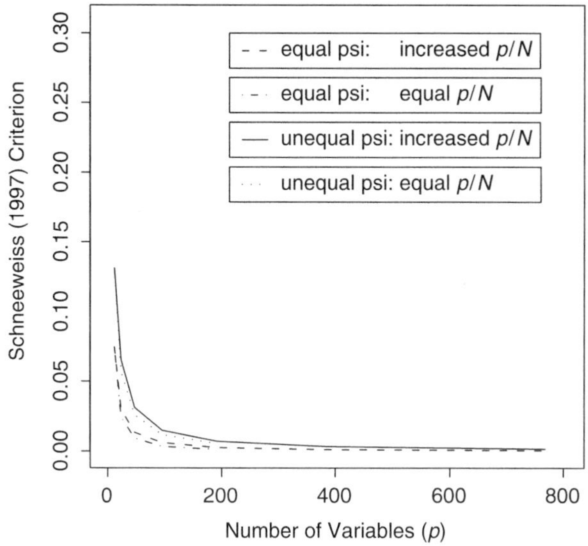

Fig. 15.3 Schneeweiss (1997) criterion ($\hat{\delta}/\hat{d}_{\min}$) as a function of the number of observed variables (p) for four simulation conditions

(3) The average squared canonical correlation $\rho^2\left(\widehat{\mathbf{\Lambda}}, \widehat{\mathbf{\Lambda}}^*\right)$ increases rapidly to 1 as the ratio p/N increases, especially faster under the condition with equal unique variances (Figs. 15.6 and 15.7). Under the increased p/N condition, the value of the Fisher-z transformed average canonical correlation and the logarithm of p/N are also almost perfectly linearly related. For the equal unique variance case, $\widehat{z} = 12.080 + (2.559)log\,(p/N)$ with $r^2 = .9998$, and for the unequal unique variance case, $\widehat{z} = 9.974 + (2.068)log\,(p/N)$ with $r^2 = .9999$.

(4) The average squared canonical correlation $\rho^2\left(\widehat{\mathbf{\Lambda}}, \widehat{\mathbf{\Lambda}}^*\right)$ approaches 1 as $\widehat{\psi}_{\max}/\widehat{d}_{\min}$ approaches 0 (Figs. 15.8 and 15.9), and also as $\widehat{\delta}/\widehat{d}_{\min}$ approaches 0 (Figs. 15.10 and 15.11). The speeds for $\rho^2\left(\widehat{\mathbf{\Lambda}}, \widehat{\mathbf{\Lambda}}^*\right)$ to approach 1 are slightly slower for the conditions with unequal unique variances than those with equal unique variances, as reflected in Figs. 15.8 and 15.10 as well as in Figs. 15.9 and 15.11. However, the speed for $\rho^2\left(\widehat{\mathbf{\Lambda}}, \widehat{\mathbf{\Lambda}}^*\right)$ to approach 1 under the condition with increased p/N was slower than under the condition with constant p/N case, as reflected in Figs. 15.8 and 15.9.

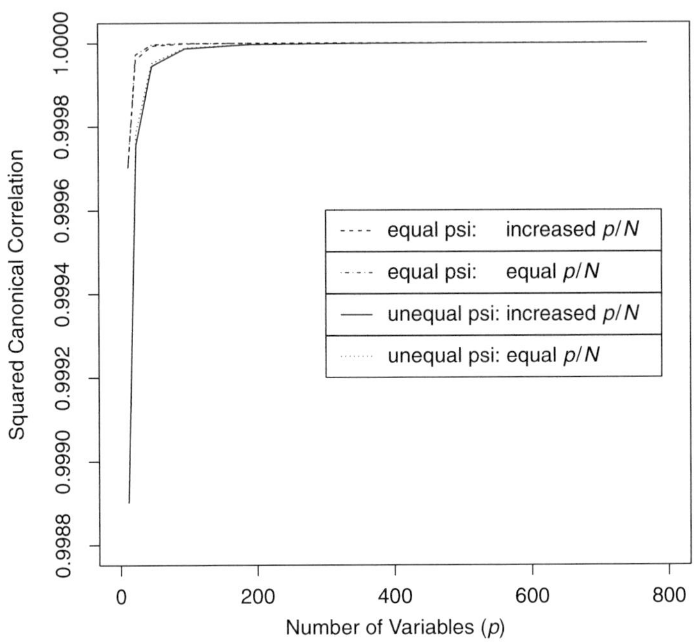

Fig. 15.4 Average squared canonical correlation as a function of the number of observed variables (p) for four simulation conditions

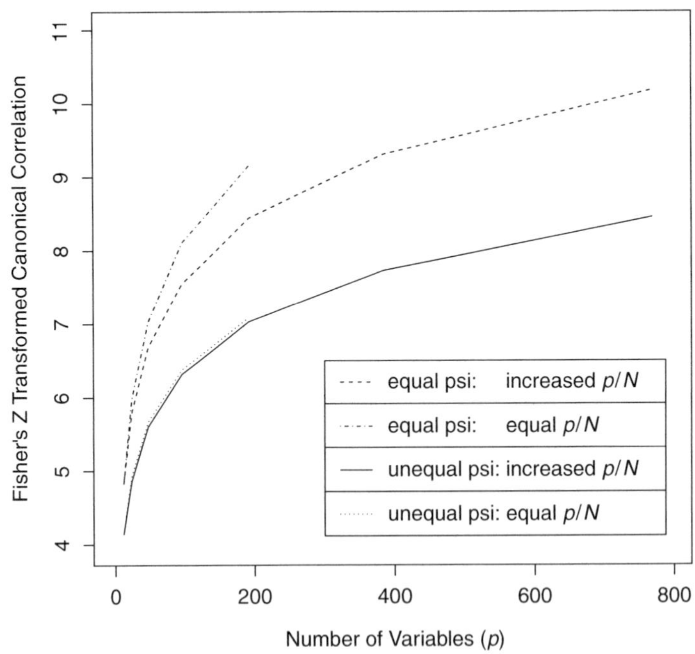

Fig. 15.5 Fisher-z transformed average canonical correlation as a function of the number of observed variables (p) for four simulation conditions

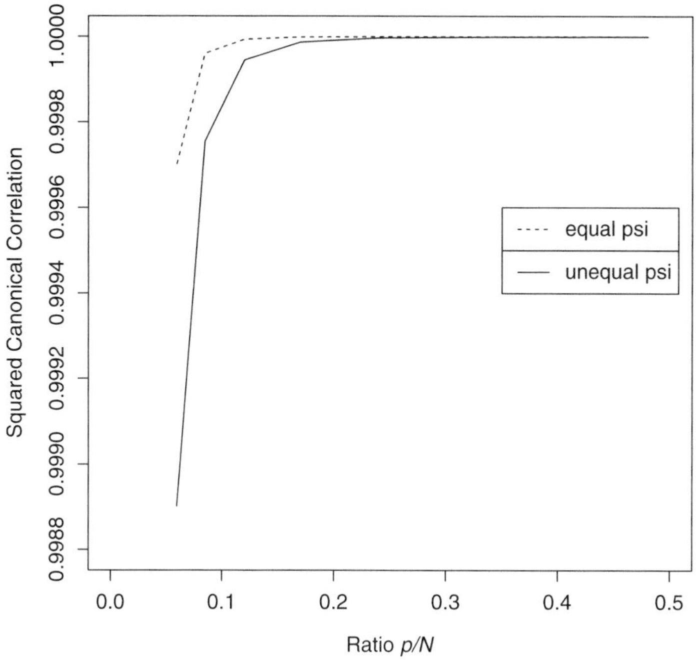

Fig. 15.6 Average squared canonical correlation as a function of the ratio of number of observed variables to sample size (p/N) for the conditions with equal and unequal unique variances

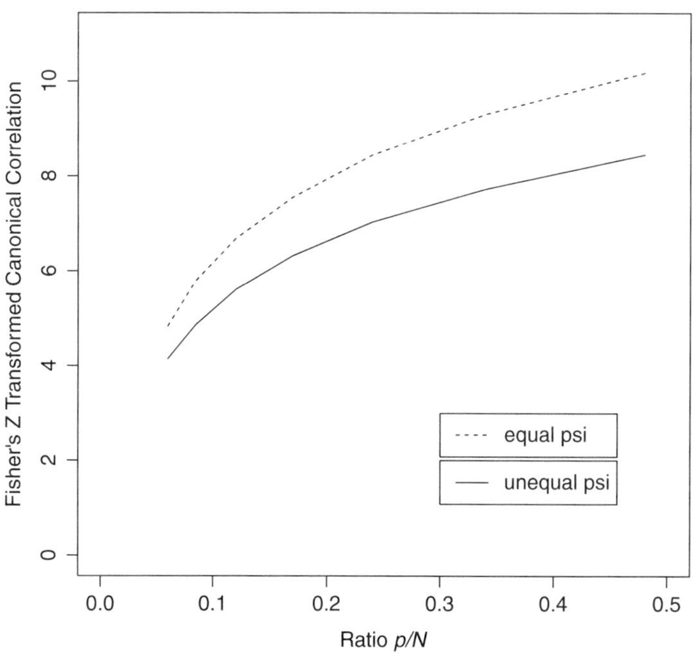

Fig. 15.7 Fisher-z transformed average canonical correlation as a function of the ratio of number of observed variables to sample size (p/N) for the conditions with equal and unequal unique variances

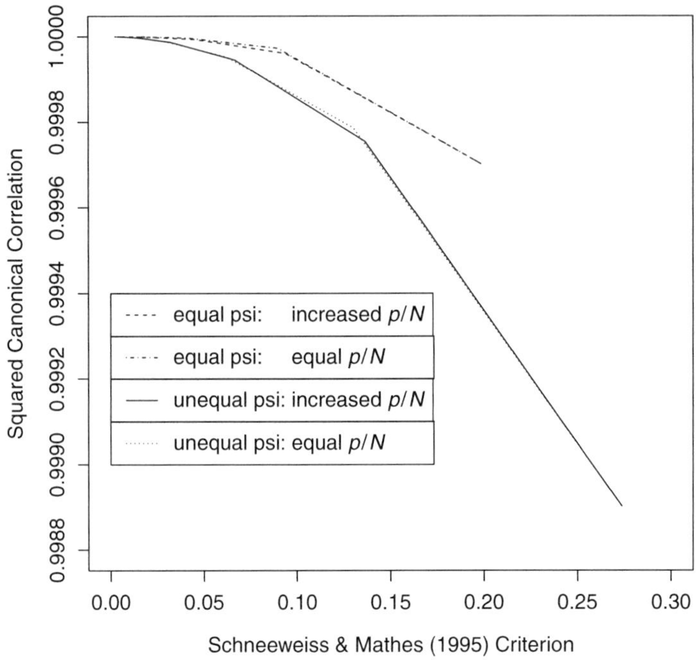

Fig. 15.8 Average squared canonical correlation as a function of Schneeweiss and Mathes (1995) criterion ($\hat{\psi}_{\max}/\hat{d}_{\min}$) for the four simulation conditions

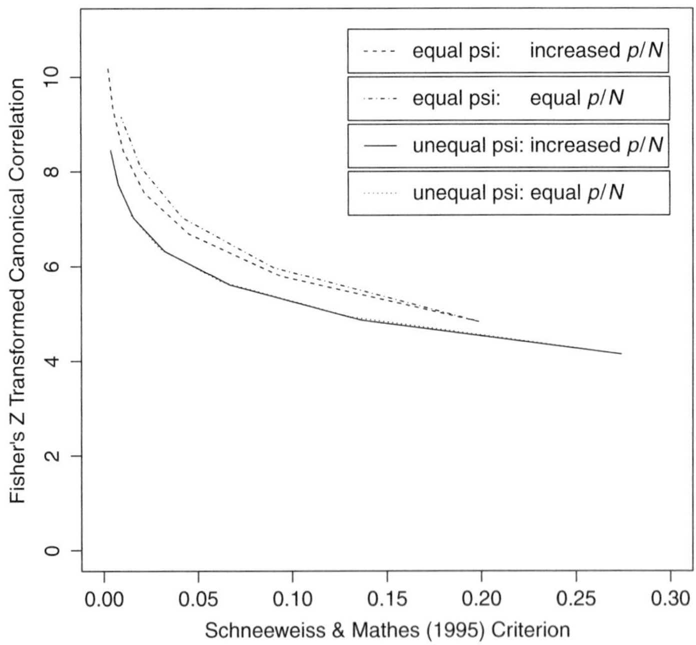

Fig. 15.9 Fisher-z transformed average canonical correlation as a function of Schneeweiss and Mathes (1995) criterion ($\hat{\psi}_{\max}/\hat{d}_{\min}$) for the four simulation conditions

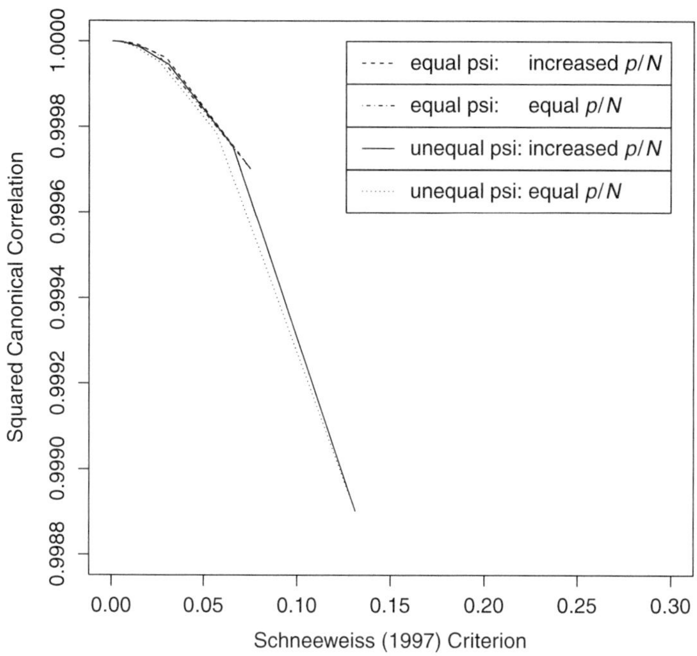

Fig. 15.10 Average squared canonical correlation as a function of Schneeweiss (1997) criterion ($\hat{\delta}/\hat{d}_{\min}$) for the four simulation conditions

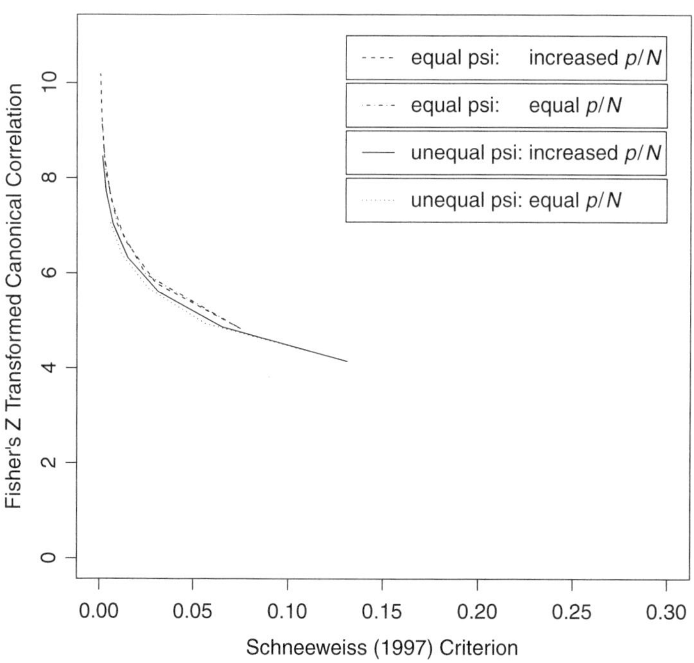

Fig. 15.11 Fisher-z transformed average canonical correlation as a function of Schneeweiss (1997) criterion ($\hat{\delta}/\hat{d}_{\min}$) for the four simulation conditions

15.5 Discussion

Conditions for equivalence between FA and PCA loadings were derived analytically at the population level (Guttman 1956; Schneeweiss and Mathes 1995; Schneeweiss 1997). In contrast, we considered the effect of sampling errors by analyzing the sample correlation matrices with ridge FA and PCA using a simulation, with a focus on high-dimensional situations. More specifically, we investigated whether and how the average squared canonical correlation $\rho^2\left(\widehat{\boldsymbol{\Lambda}}, \widehat{\boldsymbol{\Lambda}}^*\right)$ approaches 1 with large p by including the conditions obtained by Guttman, Schneeweiss and Mathes, and Schneeweiss. Results indicate that the estimates of loadings by FA and PCA are rather close for all the conditions considered. For the condition with increased p/N, we tried to create a situation where p increases faster than N. In our simulation, the results under the condition with increased p/N are still similar to those under the condition with p/N being a constant. Also, the speed for the average squared canonical correlation converging to 1 under the conditions with unequal unique variances was slightly slower than that under the condition with equal unique variances. Our results indicate that the average squared correlation between the sample loading matrix from FA and that from PCA approaches 1 as p increases, while the ratio of p/N (let alone $\sqrt{p}/\mathrm{N}$) does not need to approach zero. Apparently, the results seem to contradict the result theoretically derived by Bai and Li (2012). Further study is needed to explain the discrepancy.

The single most interesting finding by far was that the Fisher-z transformed average canonical correlation and the logarithm of the p are almost perfectly linearly related for every condition examined in the simulation. This implies the functional relationship $\rho\left(\widehat{\boldsymbol{\Lambda}}, \widehat{\boldsymbol{\Lambda}}^*\right) = \left\{1 + 2/\left[e^{2\widehat{\beta}_0} p^{2\widehat{\beta}_1} - 1\right]\right\}^{-1}$ approximately holds, where $\widehat{\beta}_0$ and $\widehat{\beta}_1$ are, respectively, the intercept and slope of the simple regression line of the Fisher-z transformed average canonical correlation on the logarithm of p. Furthermore, under the increased p/N condition, the Fisher-z transformed average canonical correlation and the logarithm of ratio p/N are also almost perfectly linear related. This can be explained from the nature of our simulation design. We chose the two series of pairs (p, N) in such a way that either p/N are a constant or $\sqrt{p}/N$ are a constant. For the latter case, let $\sqrt{p}/N = C$. Then $(1/2)log(p) = log(N) + log(C)$. Thus, using $log(p)$ as a predictor is equivalent to using $log(N)$ as a predictor, and the equation: $log(p/N) = (1/2)log(p) + log(\sqrt{p}/N) = (1/2)log(p) + \log(C)$ explains why both $log(p)$ and $log(p/N)$ had a linear relationship with the Fisher-z transformed average canonical correlation.

Obviously, our simulation design is far from being extensive in a sense that the ratios p/N do not include values greater than 1. More extensive simulation studies might also need to include different covariance structures, with different combinations of p and N, as well as conditions with p/N being greater than 1.

Acknowledgments Ke-Hai Yuan's work was supported by the National Science Foundation under Grant No. SES-1461355. The authors are grateful to comments from Drs. Sy-Miin Chow and Shin-ichi Mayekawa that led to significant improvements of the article.

References

Anderson, T. W. (2003). *An introduction to multivariate statistical analysis* (3rd ed.). New York: Wiley.

Bai, J., & Li, K. (2012). Statistical analysis of factor models of high dimension. *The Annals of Statistics, 40*, 436–465.

Bentler, P. M., & Kano, Y. (1990). On the equivalence of factors and components. *Multivariate Behavioral Research, 25*, 67–74.

Buehlmann, P., & van de Geer, S. (2011). *Statistics for high-dimensional data: Method, theory, and applications*. Heidelberg: Springer.

Butcher, J. N., Dahlstrom, W. G., Graham, J. R., Tellegen, A., & Kaemmer, B. (1989). *The Minnesota Multiphasic Personality Inventory-2 (MMPI-2): Manual for administration and scoring*. Minneapolis, MN: University of Minnesota Press.

Guttman, L. (1956). "Best possible" estimates of communalities. *Psychometrika, 21*, 273–286.

Hastie, T., Tibshirani, R., & Friedman, J. (2009). *The elements of statistical learning* (2nd ed.). New York: Springer.

Hayashi, K., & Bentler, P. M. (2000). On the relations among regular, equal unique variances, and image factor analysis models. *Psychometrika, 65*, 59–72.

Krijnen, W. P. (2006). Convergence of estimates of unique variances in factor analysis, based on the inverse sample covariance matrix. *Psychometrika, 71*, 193–199.

Lawley, D. N., & Maxwell, A. E. (1971). *Factor analysis as a statistical method* (2nd ed.). New York: American Elsevier.

Pourahmadi, M. (2013). *High-dimensional covariance estimation*. New York: Wiley.

Schneeweiss, H. (1997). Factors and principal components in the near spherical case. *Multivariate Behavioral Research, 32*, 375–401.

Schneeweiss, H., & Mathes, H. (1995). Factor analysis and principal components. *Journal of Multivariate Analysis, 55*, 105–124.

Tibshirani, R. (1996). Regression shrinkage and selection via the Lasso. *Journal of the Royal Statistical Society, Series B, 58*, 267–288.

Velicer, W. F., & Jackson, D. N. (1990). Component analysis versus common factor analysis: Some issues in selecting an appropriate procedure. *Multivariate Behavioral Research, 25*, 1–28.

Yuan, K.-H. (2013, July). Ridge structural equation modeling with large p and/or small N. Paper presented at the 78th Annual Meeting of the Psychometric Society (*IMPS2013*), Arnhem, The Netherlands.

Yuan, K.-H., & Chan, W. (2008). Structural equation modeling with near singular covariance matrices. *Computational Statistics and Data Analysis, 52*, 4842–4858.

Chapter 16
The Infinitesimal Jackknife and Analysis of Higher Order Moments

Robert Jennrich and Albert Satorra

Abstract Mean corrected higher order sample moments are asymptotically normally distributed. It is shown that both in the literature and popular software the estimates of their asymptotic covariance matrices are incorrect. An introduction to the infinitesimal jackknife (IJK) is given and it is shown how to use it to correctly estimate the asymptotic covariance matrices of higher order sample moments. Another advantage in using the IJK is the ease with which it may be used when stacking or subsetting estimators. The estimates given are used to test the goodness of fit of a nonlinear factor analysis model. A computationally accelerated form for IJK estimates is given.

16.1 Introduction

Covariance structure analysis is a popular form of analysis in psychometrics and econometrics. It is a form of second order moment structure analysis. We are interested here in moment structure analysis for higher order moments. Unfortunately this is not an immediate generalization of classical covariance structure analysis.

Why higher order moments? Higher order moments permit estimating linear models that are non-identified with just first- and second-order moments. In 1937 Jerzy Neyman conjectured that for a non-normal regressor consistent estimation in the classical errors-in-variables model could be achieved by using third-order moments. Mooijaart (1985) proposes estimation of an exploratory factor analysis model using moments up to order three; Cragg (1997) uses moments up to order four in the estimation of a simple regression with errors in variables.

Higher order moments are also used to estimate interaction and nonlinearities among latent variables. For example, Hausman et al. (1991) estimate a polynomial

---

R. Jennrich (✉)
University of California, Los Angeles, CA, USA
e-mail: rij@stat.ucla.edu

A. Satorra
Universitat Pompeu Fabra, Barcelona, Spain
e-mail: albert.satorra@upf.edu

L.A. van der Ark et al. (eds.), *Quantitative Psychology Research*, Springer Proceedings in Mathematics & Statistics 140, DOI 10.1007/978-3-319-19977-1_16

errors-in-variables model. Mooijaart and Bentler (2010) present a general approach to estimate nonlinear latent variables models based on a moment structure for moments up to order three. Mooijaart and Bentler's approach is implemented in the widely used software EQS (Bentler 2012). More recently, moments involving higher-order moments have also been applied in genetics (Ozaki et al. 2011). In these applications, estimation of the covariance matrix of a vector of sample higher order moments is essential for correct inferences.

We will be primarily interested in the analysis of higher order moments of the form

$$\nu_k = E((x-\mu) \otimes \cdots \otimes (x-\mu))$$

where x is a random vector with mean μ and the kronecker product is of order k. The natural estimate of ν is

$$q_k = \frac{1}{n}\sum_{i=1}^{n}((x_i-\bar{x}) \otimes \cdots \otimes (x_i-\bar{x}))$$

where $x_1, \cdots, x_n$ is a sample from the distribution of x.

We will use the infinitesimal jackknife (IJK) to derive an estimate of the asymptotic covariance matrix for q_k and show that in the literature and in popular software this has been done incorrectly when $k > 2$. Our aim is to produce a computationally simple consistent estimator of the asymptotic covariance matrix of q_k or the asymptotic covariance matrix of a stacked or subsetting vector of q_k's.

The IJK estimates for the asymptotic covariance matrices for q_k can be used to obtain standard errors for parameter estimates in moment structure models involving higher order moments and to test the goodness of fit for these models. We will illustrate this with the classical errors in variable model.

This is an abbreviated version of Jennrich and Satorra (in press) with the focus on the use of the IJK to compute standard errors of higher order moment structures and the element-wise formulae for the IJK estimate of variance, both issues not attended in the main paper. We also provide a Monte Carlo illustration for the errors in variable model, an illustration not included in the *Psychometrika* paper.

16.2 The IJK Estimate of the Variance of Higher Order Moments

The IJK was introduced by Jaeckel (1972) in a Bell Labs technical note. Efron and Tibshirani (1993) and Jennrich (2008) discuss the IJK method.

Let $T(F)$ be a function of an arbitrary distribution F on R^p. The influence function for $T(F)$ at $x \in R^p$ is

$$T'(x,F) = \lim_{\epsilon \to 0} \frac{T((1-\epsilon)F + \epsilon\delta_x) - T(F)}{\epsilon}$$

where δ_x is the distribution that has mass one at x. This measures the change in $T(F)$ resulting from a small change in F at x.

Note the influence function is actually a derivative. More precisely it is the derivative of the function

$$f(\epsilon) = T((1-\epsilon)F + \epsilon\delta_x)$$

at $\epsilon = 0$.

Consider a vector parameter of the form $\theta = T(F)$. Let F_n be the sample distribution function for a sample of size n from the distribution F. Then the plug-in estimator of θ is $\hat{\theta} = T(F_n)$. The IJK estimator for the asymptotic covariance matrix of $\hat{\theta}$ is the sample covariance matrix for the pseudo-values

$$\theta_i^* = T'(x_i, F_n)$$

In symbols

$$\text{acov}^{IJK}(\hat{\theta}) = \text{scov}(\theta_i^*) \tag{16.1}$$

The covariance here is defined dividing by n. This is a very simple way to estimate parameters of the form $\theta = T(F)$ and their asymptotic covariance matrix.

Clearly $\nu_k = T(F)$,

$$T(F) = \int (u - \int x dF(x)) \otimes \cdots \otimes (u - \int x dF(x)) dF(u)$$

where the Kronecker product is of order k. Then q_k is the plug-in estimator of ν_k. Jennrich and Satorra (in press) obtain that the pseudo-values for q_k are

$$q_{ki}^* = \sum_{\ell=1}^{k} T'_\ell(x_i, F_n) + T'_{k+1}(x_i, F_n) \tag{16.2}$$

where for $\ell = 1, \cdots, k$

$$T'_\ell(x_i, F_n) = -\frac{1}{n}\sum_{j=1}^{n}(a_1 \otimes \cdots \otimes a_k)$$

where $a_\ell = -(x_i - \bar{x})$ and all other $a_m = x_j - \bar{x}$, and

$$T'_{k+1}(x_i, F_n) = (x_i - \bar{x}) \otimes \cdots \otimes (x_i - \bar{x}) - q_k$$

the Kronecker product being of order k. In words, the pseudo-values for q_k are minus the mean on j of the distinct permutations of $(x_i - \bar{x}) \otimes (x_j - \bar{x}) \otimes \cdots \otimes (x_j - \bar{x})$ plus $(x_i - \bar{x}) \otimes \cdots \otimes (x_i - \bar{x}) - q_k$ where the products are of order k.

An important case is that for q_3. The pseudo-values for q_3 are

$$\begin{aligned} q_{3i}^* = &-\textstyle\sum_{j=1}^n (x_i - \bar{x}) \otimes (x_j - \bar{x}) \otimes (x_j - \bar{x}) \\ &-\textstyle\sum_{j=1}^n (x_j - \bar{x}) \otimes (x_i - \bar{x}) \otimes (x_j - \bar{x}) \\ &-\textstyle\sum_{j=1}^n (x_j - \bar{x}) \otimes (x_j - \bar{x}) \otimes (x_i - \bar{x}) \\ &+(x_i - \bar{x}) \otimes (x_i - \bar{x}) \otimes (x_i - \bar{x}) - q_3 \end{aligned} \tag{16.3}$$

16.2.1 The Accelerated IJK

Because there is a summation on j for every value of i these formulas can be expensive to evaluate. Fortunately there is an accelerated form. The IJK pseudo-values for q_k can be written in the form

$$q_{ki}^* = -C_k(x_i - \bar{x}) \otimes q_{k-1} + (x_i - \bar{x}) \otimes \cdots \otimes (x_i - \bar{x}) - q_k$$

where C_k is a constant matrix whose value does not depend on data values (for details on C_k, see Jennrich and Satorra Jennrich and Satorra (in press)).

Already for $n = 500$ the basic algorithm is quite expensive and almost prohibitively expensive when $n = 1000$; in contrast, the accelerated algorithm can handle large values of p and n. For example, to compute the pseudo-values of q_3 when $p = 5$ and $n = 1000$ the basic algorithm took 1047 s while the accelerated one needed just 4.91 s.

16.2.2 Functions of Plug-In Estimators

For functions of plug-in estimators, we have the following theorem.

Theorem 1. *If $\hat{\theta}$ is a plug-in estimator of the form*

$$\hat{\theta} = f(T(F_n))$$

then

$$\hat{\theta}_i^* = f'(T(F_n))T'(x_i, F_n)$$

where f' denotes the Jacobian of f.

How might the IJK be used to estimate standard errors for minimum distance estimator (MDE)? If $\hat{\theta}$ is a MDE based on s, then $\hat{\theta} = f(s)$. Thus, if s is a plug-in estimator of the form $s = T(F_n)$, then

$$\theta_i^* = f'(s)s_i^*$$

and

$$\text{acov}^{IJK}(\hat{\theta}) = \text{scov}\,(f'(s)s_i^*)$$

There are well-known formulas for $f'(s)$ when using least squares and normal maximum likelihood deviance functions.

16.2.3 Stacking and Sub-setting

Let $\hat{\theta}_1, \cdots, \hat{\theta}_m$ be plug-in estimators. Then the stack

$$\hat{\theta} = \begin{pmatrix} \hat{\theta}_1 \\ \vdots \\ \hat{\theta}_m \end{pmatrix}$$

is a plug-in estimator and its pseudo-values are simply the stack made up of the pseudo-values for $\hat{\theta}_1, \cdots, \hat{\theta}_m$.

Similarly, let $\hat{\theta}$ be a plug-in estimator and $\hat{\theta}_s$ contain a subset of the components of $\hat{\theta}$. Then $\hat{\theta}_s$ is a plug-in estimator and its pseudo-values are the corresponding subset of the pseudo-values of $\hat{\theta}$.

16.2.4 Component-Wise IJK Estimates of Variance

Let p be the length of x. Then q_3 has p^3 components. Index these by an $\alpha\beta\gamma$ triplet with α, β, and γ each having values from 1 to p and the triplets ordered lexicographically. The pseudo-values of the $\alpha\beta\gamma$ component of q_3 are given by Eq. (16.4), which follows from Eq. (16.3) and some work,

$$\begin{aligned}(q_{3i}^*)_{\alpha\beta\gamma} = {} & (x_i - \bar{x})_\alpha (x_i - \bar{x})_\beta (x_i - \bar{x})_\gamma - (q_3)_{\alpha\beta\gamma} \\ & -(x_i - \bar{x})_\alpha (q_2)_{\beta\gamma} - (x_i - \bar{x})_\beta (q_2)_{\alpha\gamma} - (x_i - \bar{x})_\gamma (q_2)_{\alpha\beta}\end{aligned} \tag{16.4}$$

The extension to other values of k is obvious.

From the subsection above of Stacking and subsetting, the IJK estimate of variance of a moment vector formed by stacking a subset of moments $(q_3)_{\alpha\beta\gamma}$ is the sample covariance matrix of the stacked vector of the corresponding pseudo-values $(q_{3i}^*)_{\alpha\beta\gamma}$.[1]

[1] Note that when computing the sample covariance, the term-$(q_3)_{\alpha\beta\gamma}$ of (16.4) can be suppressed since it does not vary with i.

16.3 Errors in Variables

The Introduction mentioned a number of applications of higher order moments to errors in variables problems. We will use a simple example to show how such problems are related to IJK methods. Let X and Y be two unobserved random variables with

$$Y = \alpha + \beta X$$

Assume X and Y can only be observed with error as

$$x = X + d \quad \text{and} \quad y = Y + e$$

where d and e have mean zero, are independent among themselves and independent also of X and Y.

Let $(x_1, y_1), \ldots, (x_n, y_n)$ be a sample from the joint distribution of (x, y). It is shown by Pal (1980, p. 352) that if the third central moment of X is nonzero, then

$$\hat{\beta} = \frac{\frac{1}{n}\sum_{i=1}^{n}(x_i - \bar{x})(y_i - \bar{y})^2}{\frac{1}{n}\sum_{i=1}^{n}(x_i - \bar{x})^2(y_i - \bar{y})}$$

is a consistent estimator of β. We will show how to use IJK methods to show not only this, but also to show that $\hat{\beta}$ is asymptotically normal and to provide a standard error for $\hat{\beta}$.

Let

$$z_i = \begin{pmatrix} x_i \\ y_i \end{pmatrix}$$

and

$$q_3 = \frac{1}{n}\sum_{i=1}^{n}(z_i - \bar{z}) \otimes (z_i - \bar{z}) \otimes (z_i - \bar{z})$$

The numerator and denominator of the fraction defining $\hat{\beta}$ are the seventh and fourth components of q_3. Note that

$$\hat{\beta} = f(s)$$

where s is the two component vector containing the fourth and seventh components of q_3 and $f(s) = s_1/s_2$. Since s is a sub-vector of q_3, $s = T(F_n)$ and

$$\hat{\beta} = f(T(F_n))$$

This is an asymptotically normal plug-in estimator of $\beta = f(T(F))$. Thus $\hat{\beta}$ is not only consistent, it is also asymptotically normal.

By Theorem 1 the pseudo-values of $\hat{\beta}$ are

$$\beta_i^* = f'(T(F_n))T'(x_i, F_n) = f'(s)s_i^*$$

where s_i^* is the sub-vector of q_{3i}^* containing its fourth and seventh components. These may be used to consistently estimate the asymptotic variance of $\hat{\beta}$ and provide a standard error.

16.4 A Simulation Study

One thousand data sets were generated using $\alpha = 1, \beta = 2$, X distributed as χ_3^2 centered and scaled to have mean zero and variance one, and d and e distributed as $N(0, 1)$.

For each data set, we computed $\hat{\beta}$ and the IJK estimate of the asymptotic variance of $\hat{\beta}$. Let $\text{avar}^{IJK}(\hat{\beta})$ be the IJK estimate of the $\text{avar}(\hat{\beta})$. Then

$$se(\hat{\beta}) = \sqrt{\frac{\text{avar}^{IJK}(\hat{\beta})}{n}}$$

This provides a standard error for $\hat{\beta}$. For large n one expects the statistic

$$z = \frac{\hat{\beta} - \beta}{se(\hat{\beta})}$$

to be approximately standard normal.

Figure 16.1 is a QQ plot of the quantiles of z on the quantiles of the standard normal for samples of size $n = 300$. The line in the figure is a 45 degree line. For testing purposes one would like the plot to approximate this line at least on the range of minus two to plus two. The distribution of $\hat{\beta}$ departs from this line on the left. Its distribution appears to be long-tailed on the left and will reject on the left too often. The empirical rejection rate for a two-sided test with nominal rate of 5 % was 8.8 %.

Figure 16.2 is the QQ plot obtained when $n = 1000$. On the range from minus two to plus two it lies fairly close to the 45 degree line and will probably have a rejection rate approximating 5 %. The empirical rejection rate for a two-sided test with nominal rate of 5 % was 5.7 % which is well within the margin of error of 1.38 % for the simulation. In our experience convergence in distributions is fairly slow when using higher order moments.

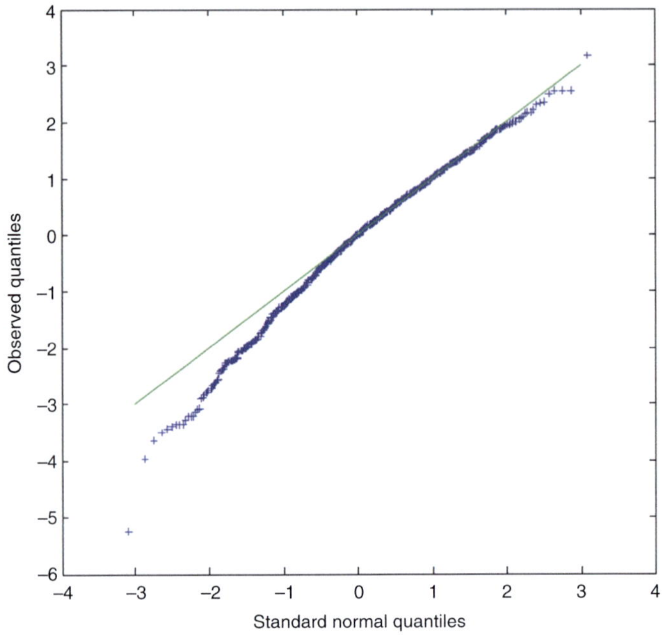

Fig. 16.1 QQ plot when $n = 300$

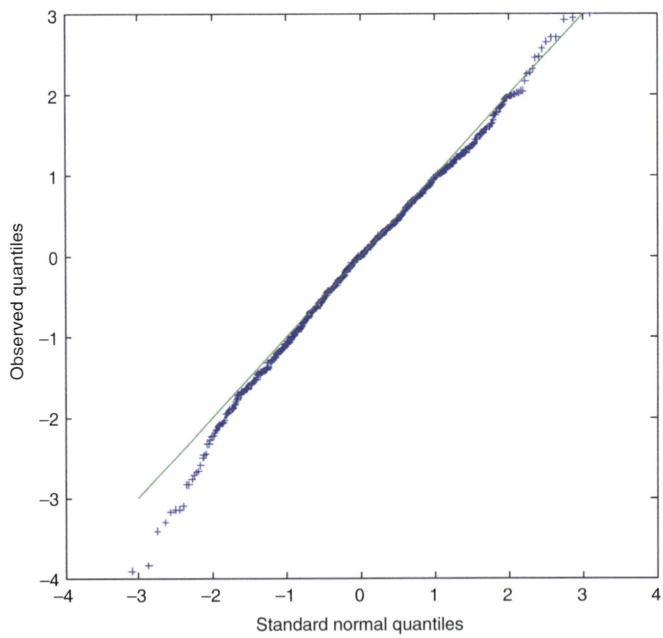

Fig. 16.2 QQ plot when $n = 1000$

References

Bentler, P. M. (2012). *EQS 6 structural equations program manual.* Encino, CA: Multivariate Software.

Cragg, J. G. (1997). Using higher order moments to estimate the simple errors-in-variables model. *The Rand Journal of Economics, 28*, Special Issue in honor of Richard E. Quandt, S71–S91.

Efron, B., & Tibshirani, R. J. (1993). *An introduction to the Bootstrap*. New York: Chapman & Hall.

Hausman, J. A., Newey, W. K., Ichimura, H., & Powell, J. L. (1991). Identification and estimation of polynomial errors-in-variables models. *Journal of Econometrics, 50*, 273–295.

Jaeckel, L. (1972). *The infinitesimal jackknife*. Memorandum #MM 72-1215-11. Murray Hill, NJ: Bell Laboratories.

Jennrich, R. I. (2008). Nonparametric estimation of standard errors in covariance structure analysis. *Psychometrika, 73*, 579–594.

Jennrich, R. I., & Satorra, A. (in press). The infinitesimal jackknife and moment structure analysis using higher order moments. *Psychometrika.*

Mooijaart, A. (1985). Factor analysis of non-normal variables. *Psychometrika, 50*, 323–342.

Mooijaart, A., & Bentler, P. M. (2010). An alternative approach for non-linear latent variable models. *Structural Equation Modeling, 17*, 357–373.

Ozaki, K., Toyoda, H., Iwama, N., Kubo, S., & Ando, J. (2011). Using non-normal SEM to resolve the ACDE model in the classical twin design. *Behavioral Genetics, 41*, 329–339.

Pal, M. (1980). Consistent moment estimators of regression coefficients in the presence of errors in variables. *Journal of Econometrics, 14*, 349–364.

Chapter 17
A General SEM Framework for Integrating Moderation and Mediation: The Constrained Approach

Shu-Ping Chen

Abstract Modeling the combination of latent moderating and mediating effects is a significant issue in the social and behavioral sciences. Chen and Cheng (Structural Equation Modeling: A Multidisciplinary Journal 21: 94–101, 2014) generalized Jöreskog and Yang's (Advanced structural equation modeling: Issues and techniques (pp. 57–88). Mahwah, NJ: Lawrence Erlbaum, 1996) constrained approach to allow for the concurrent modeling of moderation and mediation within the context of SEM. Unfortunately, due to restrictions related to Chen and Cheng's partitioning scheme, their framework cannot completely conceptualize and interpret moderation of indirect effects in a mediated model. In the current study, the Chen and Cheng (abbreviated below as C & C) framework is extended to accommodate situations in which any two pathways that constitute a particular indirect effect in a mediated model can be differentially or collectively moderated by the moderator variable(s). By preserving the inherent advantage of the C & C framework, i.e., the matrix partitioning technique, while at the same time further generalizing its applicability, it is expected that the current framework enhances the potential usefulness of the constrained approach as well as the entire class of the product indicator approaches.

Keywords Moderation • Mediation • The constrained approach

In recent years, the social and behavioral sciences have witnessed a trend toward an increasing number of empirical studies related to mediated moderation (a moderating effect is transmitted through a mediator variable, Baron and Kenny 1986) or moderated mediation (mediation relations are contingent on the level of a moderator, James and Brett 1984). As one example of a study incorporating mediated moderation, Pollack et al. (2012) examined the psychological experience

S.-P. Chen (✉)
Department of Psychology, National Chengchi University, No. 64, Sec. 2, ZhiNan Road, Wenshan District, Taipei City 11605, Taiwan, ROC
e-mail: abby.chen.psy@gmail.com

L.A. van der Ark et al. (eds.), *Quantitative Psychology Research*, Springer Proceedings in Mathematics & Statistics 140, DOI 10.1007/978-3-319-19977-1_17

of entrepreneurs in response to economic stress, finding that the indirect effect of economic stress on entrepreneurial withdrawal intentions through depressed affect is moderated by the level of business-related social ties. Exemplifying the use of moderated mediation, Cole et al. (2008) investigated affective mechanisms linking dysfunctional behavior to performance in work teams. The researchers specified negative team affective tone as a mediator between dysfunctional team behavior and team performance, whereas nonverbal negative expressivity was found to be contingent on the relation of team affective tone on team performance. In general, examples of empirical studies integrating mediation and moderation are quite abundant in the literature of various disciplines, including business and management (e.g., Cole et al. 2008; Pollack et al. 2012), psychology (e.g., Luszczynska et al. 2010), and marketing communications (e.g., Slater et al. 2007), among others. From the above-cited empirical examples, one can surmise that the substantive variables of interest utilized to establish causal connections in the corresponding theoretical models are generally treated as latent variables, each of which is a theoretical definition of a concept and measured by observed indicators.

Complementing the above empirical research examples are studies which propose various analytical procedures aimed at integrating moderation and mediation in the context of moderated regression or path analysis (e.g., Edwards and Lambert 2007; Fairchild and MacKinnon 2009; Preacher et al. 2007). In particular, Hayes (2013) systemically introduced the concepts of mediation analysis and moderation analysis, as well as their combination (i.e., conditional process analysis) and further demonstrated a computational tool (PROCESS macro) for estimation and inference. However, under regression or path analytical frameworks, all variables are assumed to be treated as manifest (non-latent) variables and measured without error. In the presence of measurement error (i.e., unreliability of measures), the regression coefficient of an interactive or moderating effect may produce a biased estimate and reduce the power of statistical tests of significance. One possible reason for this is that the reliability of the nonlinear term is heavily dependent on the reliability of its individual measures (Busemeyer and Jones 1983; Jaccard and Wan 1995). If the problem of measurement error is not corrected, these frameworks may be of limited use in social and behavioral science research such as psychology. Given that structural equation modeling (SEM) is equipped to deal with multivariate models and multiple measures of latent variables while controlling for measurement errors in observed variables (Bollen and Noble 2011), it should be appropriate to introduce SEM as a preferred alternative to regression or path analysis.

Out of multiple recent lines of SEM-based research, a variety of approaches have been developed for the estimation of latent nonlinear effects. Most approaches can be divided into several major categories: product indicator approaches (e.g., Algina and Moulder 2001; Coenders et al. 2008; Jöreskog and Yang 1996; Kelava and Brandt 2009; Kenny and Judd 1984; Marsh et al. 2004, 2006; Wall and Amemiya 2001), maximum likelihood (ML) estimation methods (e.g., Klein and Moosbrugger 2000; Klein and Muthén 2007; Lee and Zhu 2002), and Bayesian estimation methods (e.g., Arminger and Muthén 1998; Lee et al. 2007), among others. A cursory inspection seems to indicate that most of these approaches have been developed primarily to estimate interaction and/or quadratic effects of exogenous latent variables, leaving nonlinear effects of endogenous latent variables unaccounted for. Unfortunately, this means that there is a growing divide between the capability of available nonlinear SEM approaches, on the one hand, and the interests of social science empirical researchers on the other. In particular, current scholars, while continuing to do interaction research involving exogenous latent variables, have increasingly attempted to model endogenous latent variables as moderators in their theoretical models.

While each of the previously mentioned nonlinear SEM approaches could conceivably be developed to incorporate latent nonlinear relations involving endogenous latent variables, the underlying mathematical theories derived by each of these approaches may become overly complex which could lead to some potential problems. For example, within the classes of ML and Bayesian estimation methods, Wall (2009) mentioned that when latent nonlinear models increase in complexity (e.g., larger number of latent variables), the computational algorithms are likely to fail to reach convergence, and even if they do, may become less numerically precise. As another example, within the class of product indicator approaches, the elaborate and tedious nature of the model specification procedure may limit its potential usefulness. Even so, considering the ever-increasing number of complicated latent nonlinear relations (e.g., a combination of mediation and moderation) appearing in empirical applications, it is still imperative that research efforts be made to develop and generalize current nonlinear SEM approaches.

Pursuing this research aim, Chen and Cheng (2014) generalized Jöreskog and Yang's (1996) constrained approach, one of the product indicator methods, to process interaction and/or quadratic effects involving endogenous latent variables. The Chen and Cheng (abbreviated below as C & C) framework thus allows for the concurrent modeling of moderation and mediation within the context of SEM. Unfortunately, however, due to restrictions related to their partitioning scheme, the C & C framework cannot completely conceptualize and interpret moderation of indirect effects in a mediated model. For example, the two moderated mediation models (i.e., the first and second stage moderation model and the total effect moderation model) from Edwards and Lambert (2007) cannot be embedded into the C & C framework.

In the current study, further progress is made on the C & C framework to accommodate situations in which any two pathways that constitute a particular indirect effect in a mediated model (e.g., simple mediator models, parallel multiple mediator models, serial multiple mediator models) can be differentially or collectively moderated by the moderator variable(s). To simplify the model specification procedure without sacrificing generality, the latent variable versions of all the models from Edwards and Lambert (2007) are utilized to demonstrate the proposed partitioning scheme. The present research leverages key attributes of the two above-mentioned studies to create a highly general latent nonlinear framework. First of all, the models considered by Edwards and Lambert are relatively exhaustive and include many forms that integrate moderation and mediation that may be of interest to empirical researchers. Secondly, the proposed approach retains one of the major advantages of the C & C framework: in contrast to specifying constraints in equation form as in Jöreskog and Yang's (1996) constrained approach, we specify constraints in matrix form to simplify the constraint specification procedure and the process of model specification on the part of the researcher.

17.1 Model Partitioning Scheme

In this section, the partitioning scheme of the current nonlinear framework is demonstrated through latent variable versions of the great majority of the models in Edwards and Lambert (2007), with conceptual and statistical diagrams shown in Fig. 17.1. The present partitioning scheme allows latent variables that are themselves nonlinear functions of other latent variables to also influence other endogenous variables in the model in a nonlinear fashion (e.g., in Models D and H from Edwards and Lambert, the term M is influenced by the interaction term XZ, and in turn, interacts with Z to affect Y).

More specifically, with regard to the structural part of the current partitioning scheme (the conceptual diagram shown in Fig. 17.2), latent variables are partitioned into three subvectors (denoted as $\boldsymbol{\eta}_{\mathbf{F}}$, $\boldsymbol{\eta}_{\mathbf{S}}$ and $\boldsymbol{\eta}_{\mathbf{T}}$, where the subscripts, respectively, stand for "First layer," "Second layer," and "Third layer") to support the integration of the two vectors of latent nonlinear variables (denoted as $\boldsymbol{\eta}_{\mathbf{F}^*}$ and $\boldsymbol{\eta}_{\mathbf{S}^*}$). Here, $\boldsymbol{\eta}_{\mathbf{F}^*}$ and $\boldsymbol{\eta}_{\mathbf{S}^*}$ are, respectively, defined as $\mathbf{W}_1\text{vech}(\boldsymbol{\eta}_{\mathbf{F}}\boldsymbol{\eta}_{\mathbf{F}}^{\mathrm{T}})$ and $\mathbf{W}_2\text{vec}(\boldsymbol{\eta}_{\mathbf{S}}\boldsymbol{\eta}_{\mathbf{F}}^{\mathrm{T}})$, where $\mathbf{W}_1$ and $\mathbf{W}_2$ serve as filter matrices (Chen and Cheng 2014) to select a set of latent nonlinear terms that the researcher is interested in. Also note that the vech operator vectorizes a square matrix by stacking the columns from its lower triangle part while the vec operator vectorizes a matrix by stacking its columns (Seber 2007). Examining the interrelations among these partitions, the effects among $\boldsymbol{\eta}_{\mathbf{F}}$, $\boldsymbol{\eta}_{\mathbf{S}}$ and $\boldsymbol{\eta}_{\mathbf{T}}$ are presumed to be unidirectional in the sense that $\boldsymbol{\eta}_{\mathbf{F}}$ can influence $\boldsymbol{\eta}_{\mathbf{S}}$ and/or $\boldsymbol{\eta}_{\mathbf{T}}$, but $\boldsymbol{\eta}_{\mathbf{S}}$ and $\boldsymbol{\eta}_{\mathbf{T}}$ cannot affect $\boldsymbol{\eta}_{\mathbf{F}}$; likewise, $\boldsymbol{\eta}_{\mathbf{S}}$ can influence $\boldsymbol{\eta}_{\mathbf{T}}$, but $\boldsymbol{\eta}_{\mathbf{T}}$ cannot affect $\boldsymbol{\eta}_{\mathbf{S}}$. Meanwhile, with regard to the two vectors of latent nonlinear variables, it is assumed that $\boldsymbol{\eta}_{\mathbf{F}^*}$ can influence $\boldsymbol{\eta}_{\mathbf{S}}$ and/or $\boldsymbol{\eta}_{\mathbf{T}}$ while $\boldsymbol{\eta}_{\mathbf{S}^*}$ can only influence $\boldsymbol{\eta}_{\mathbf{T}}$. On the whole, as revealed in Fig. 17.2, the current partitioning scheme has the capability to incorporate moderation Models B to H from Edwards and Lambert (2007).

With regard to the measurement part of the present partitioning scheme, observed indicators are partitioned into three subvectors utilized as observed indicators of $\boldsymbol{\eta}_{\mathbf{F}}$, $\boldsymbol{\eta}_{\mathbf{S}}$ and $\boldsymbol{\eta}_{\mathbf{T}}$ (denoted as $\mathbf{y}_{\mathbf{F}}$, $\mathbf{y}_{\mathbf{S}}$ and $\mathbf{y}_{\mathbf{T}}$, respectively) which in turn support the integration of product indicators of $\boldsymbol{\eta}_{\mathbf{F}^*}$ and $\boldsymbol{\eta}_{\mathbf{S}^*}$ (denoted as $\mathbf{y}_{\mathbf{F}^*}$ and $\mathbf{y}_{\mathbf{S}^*}$, respectively). Here, $\mathbf{y}_{\mathbf{F}^*}$ and $\mathbf{y}_{\mathbf{S}^*}$ are, respectively, defined as $\mathbf{W}_3\text{vech}(\mathbf{y}_{\mathbf{F}}\mathbf{y}_{\mathbf{F}}^{\mathrm{T}})$ and $\mathbf{W}_4\text{vec}(\mathbf{y}_{\mathbf{S}}\mathbf{y}_{\mathbf{F}}^{\mathrm{T}})$, where $\mathbf{W}_3$ and $\mathbf{W}_4$ serve as filter matrices (Chen and Cheng 2014) to provide the researcher a convenient way of selecting the product indicators associated with $\boldsymbol{\eta}_{\mathbf{F}^*}$ and $\boldsymbol{\eta}_{\mathbf{S}^*}$. In the current partitioning scheme, the effect relating $\mathbf{y}_i$ to $\boldsymbol{\eta}_j$ (for $i = \mathbf{F}, \mathbf{S}, \mathbf{T}$ and $j = \mathbf{F}, \mathbf{S}, \mathbf{T}, \mathbf{F}^*, \mathbf{S}^*$) is assumed to be null for $i \neq j$.

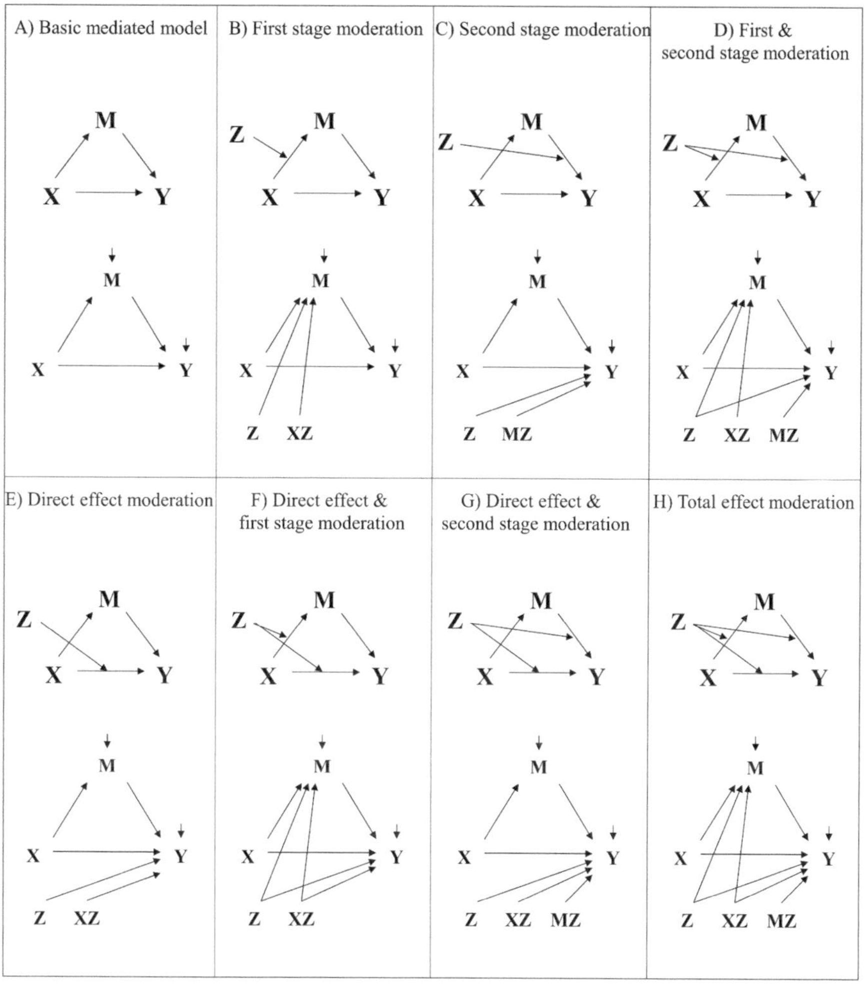

Fig. 17.1 Conceptual and statistical diagrams from Edwards and Lambert

Putting it all together, the current nonlinear framework can be established by integrating the partitioned vectors of latent variables $\boldsymbol{\eta} = \left[\boldsymbol{\eta}_{\mathbf{F}}^{\mathrm{T}} \mid \boldsymbol{\eta}_{\mathbf{S}}^{\mathrm{T}} \mid \boldsymbol{\eta}_{\mathbf{T}}^{\mathrm{T}} \mid \boldsymbol{\eta}_{\mathbf{F}*}^{\mathrm{T}} \mid \boldsymbol{\eta}_{\mathbf{S}*}^{\mathrm{T}}\right]^{\mathrm{T}}$ and observed indicators $\mathbf{y} = \left[\mathbf{y}_{\mathbf{F}}^{\mathrm{T}} \mid \mathbf{y}_{\mathbf{S}}^{\mathrm{T}} \mid \mathbf{y}_{\mathbf{T}}^{\mathrm{T}} \mid \mathbf{y}_{\mathbf{F}*}^{\mathrm{T}} \mid \mathbf{y}_{\mathbf{S}*}^{\mathrm{T}}\right]^{\mathrm{T}}$. The actual construction of this framework and the specification of constraints in matrix form will be illustrated in the next section.

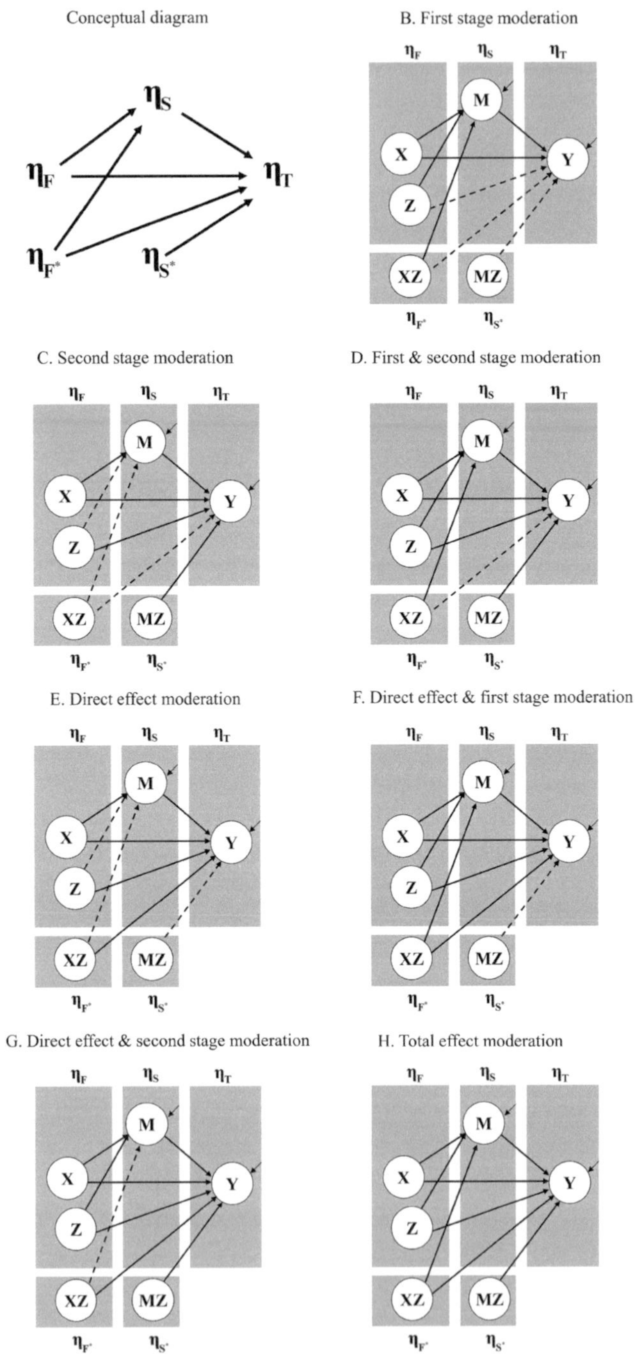

Fig. 17.2 Conceptual diagram and superimposition of the current framework on Models B and H from Edwards and Lambert

17.2 Model Specification

The current partitioned nonlinear framework adopts the notation of Muthén (1984) Case A. The structural and measurement parts, respectively, composed of $(f + s + t + f^* + s^*) \times 1$ and $(p + q + r + p^* + q^*) \times 1$ partitioned vectors of latent variables $\boldsymbol{\eta} = \left[\boldsymbol{\eta}_{\mathbf{F}}^{\mathrm{T}} \mid \boldsymbol{\eta}_{\mathbf{S}}^{\mathrm{T}} \mid \boldsymbol{\eta}_{\mathbf{T}}^{\mathrm{T}} \mid \boldsymbol{\eta}_{\mathbf{F}^*}^{\mathrm{T}} \mid \boldsymbol{\eta}_{\mathbf{S}^*}^{\mathrm{T}}\right]^{\mathrm{T}}$ and observed indicators $\mathbf{y} = \left[\mathbf{y}_{\mathbf{F}}^{\mathrm{T}} \mid \mathbf{y}_{\mathbf{S}}^{\mathrm{T}} \mid \mathbf{y}_{\mathbf{T}}^{\mathrm{T}} \mid \mathbf{y}_{\mathbf{F}^*}^{\mathrm{T}} \mid \mathbf{y}_{\mathbf{S}^*}^{\mathrm{T}}\right]^{\mathrm{T}}$, are shown in Eqs. (17.1) and (17.2).

$$\begin{array}{ccccccc} \boldsymbol{\eta} & = & \boldsymbol{\alpha} & + & \mathbf{B} & \boldsymbol{\eta} & + \ \boldsymbol{\zeta} \end{array}$$
$$\begin{bmatrix} \boldsymbol{\eta}_{\mathrm{F}} \\ \boldsymbol{\eta}_{\mathrm{S}} \\ \boldsymbol{\eta}_{\mathrm{T}} \\ \boldsymbol{\eta}_{\mathrm{F}^*} \\ \boldsymbol{\eta}_{\mathrm{S}^*} \end{bmatrix} = \begin{bmatrix} \boldsymbol{\alpha}_{\mathrm{F}} \\ \boldsymbol{\alpha}_{\mathrm{S}} \\ \boldsymbol{\alpha}_{\mathrm{T}} \\ \mathbf{W}_1\mathbf{L}_f\mathbf{F}_1 \operatorname{vec}\left(\boldsymbol{\alpha}_{\mathrm{F}}\boldsymbol{\alpha}_{\mathrm{F}}^{\mathrm{T}}\right) \\ \mathbf{W}_2\mathbf{S}_1 \operatorname{vec}\left(\boldsymbol{\alpha}_{\mathrm{S}}\boldsymbol{\alpha}_{\mathrm{F}}^{\mathrm{T}}\right) \end{bmatrix} + \begin{bmatrix} \mathbf{B}_{\mathrm{FF}} & \mathbf{0} & \mathbf{0} & \mathbf{0} & \mathbf{0} \\ \mathbf{B}_{\mathrm{SF}} & \mathbf{B}_{\mathrm{SS}} & \mathbf{0} & \mathbf{B}_{\mathrm{SF}^*} & \mathbf{0} \\ \mathbf{B}_{\mathrm{TF}} & \mathbf{B}_{\mathrm{TS}} & \mathbf{B}_{\mathrm{TT}} & \mathbf{B}_{\mathrm{TF}^*} & \mathbf{B}_{\mathrm{TS}^*} \\ \mathbf{0} & \mathbf{0} & \mathbf{0} & \mathbf{0} & \mathbf{0} \\ \mathbf{W}_2\mathbf{S}_1\mathbf{S}_2 & \mathbf{0} & \mathbf{0} & \mathbf{W}_2\mathbf{S}_1\mathbf{S}_3 & \mathbf{0} \end{bmatrix} \begin{bmatrix} \boldsymbol{\eta}_{\mathrm{F}} \\ \boldsymbol{\eta}_{\mathrm{S}} \\ \boldsymbol{\eta}_{\mathrm{T}} \\ \boldsymbol{\eta}_{\mathrm{F}^*} \\ \boldsymbol{\eta}_{\mathrm{S}^*} \end{bmatrix} + \begin{bmatrix} \boldsymbol{\zeta}_{\mathrm{F}} \\ \boldsymbol{\zeta}_{\mathrm{S}} \\ \boldsymbol{\zeta}_{\mathrm{T}} \\ \boldsymbol{\zeta}_{\mathrm{F}^*} \\ \boldsymbol{\zeta}_{\mathrm{S}^*} \end{bmatrix}. \tag{17.1}$$

Here, $\boldsymbol{\alpha}_i$ and $\boldsymbol{\zeta}_i$ are vectors of intercepts and disturbance terms associated with $\boldsymbol{\eta}_i$ (for $i = \mathbf{F}, \mathbf{S}, \mathbf{T}$). $\mathbf{B}_{ij}$ represents the coefficient matrix relating $\boldsymbol{\eta}_i$ to $\boldsymbol{\eta}_j$ (for $i = \mathbf{F}, \mathbf{S}, \mathbf{T}$ and $j = \mathbf{F}, \mathbf{S}, \mathbf{T}, \mathbf{F}^*, \mathbf{S}^*$). More specifically, $\mathbf{B}_{ij}$ (for $i = j$) is specified as a non-null matrix with all diagonal elements restricted to zero; $\mathbf{B}_{ij}$ (for $i \neq j$) is specified as a null or non-null matrix in accordance with the inter-partition relations established for the current partitioning scheme (see Fig. 17.2). The expanded forms of the nonlinear vectors $\boldsymbol{\eta}_{\mathbf{F}^*}$ and $\boldsymbol{\eta}_{\mathbf{S}^*}$ shown in Eq. (17.1) were obtained by plugging the equations $\boldsymbol{\eta}_{\mathbf{F}} = \boldsymbol{\alpha}_{\mathbf{F}} + \mathbf{B}_{\mathbf{FF}}\boldsymbol{\eta}_{\mathbf{F}} + \boldsymbol{\zeta}_{\mathbf{F}}$ and $\boldsymbol{\eta}_{\mathbf{S}} = \boldsymbol{\alpha}_{\mathbf{S}} + \mathbf{B}_{\mathbf{SF}}\boldsymbol{\eta}_{\mathbf{F}} + \mathbf{B}_{\mathbf{SS}}\boldsymbol{\eta}_{\mathbf{S}} + \mathbf{B}_{\mathbf{SF}^*}\boldsymbol{\eta}_{\mathbf{F}^*} + \boldsymbol{\zeta}_{\mathbf{S}}$ from Eq. (17.1) into the equations $\boldsymbol{\eta}_{\mathbf{F}^*} = \mathbf{W}_1 \operatorname{vech}\left(\boldsymbol{\eta}_{\mathbf{F}}\boldsymbol{\eta}_{\mathbf{F}}^{\mathrm{T}}\right)$ and $\boldsymbol{\eta}_{\mathbf{S}^*} = \mathbf{W}_2 \operatorname{vec}\left(\boldsymbol{\eta}_{\mathbf{S}}\boldsymbol{\eta}_{\mathbf{F}}^{\mathrm{T}}\right)$ established in the previous section. Note that the details of these expansions can be found in Appendix A.

$$\begin{array}{ccccccc} \mathbf{y} & = & \boldsymbol{\nu} & + & \boldsymbol{\Lambda} & \boldsymbol{\eta} & + \ \boldsymbol{\varepsilon} \end{array}$$
$$\begin{bmatrix} \mathbf{y}_{\mathrm{F}} \\ \mathbf{y}_{\mathrm{S}} \\ \mathbf{y}_{\mathrm{T}} \\ \mathbf{y}_{\mathrm{F}^*} \\ \mathbf{y}_{\mathrm{S}^*} \end{bmatrix} = \begin{bmatrix} \boldsymbol{\nu}_{\mathrm{F}} \\ \boldsymbol{\nu}_{\mathrm{S}} \\ \boldsymbol{\nu}_{\mathrm{T}} \\ \mathbf{W}_3\mathbf{L}_p \operatorname{vec}\left(\boldsymbol{\nu}_{\mathrm{F}}\boldsymbol{\nu}_{\mathrm{F}}^{\mathrm{T}}\right) \\ \mathbf{W}_4 \operatorname{vec}\left(\boldsymbol{\nu}_{\mathrm{S}}\boldsymbol{\nu}_{\mathrm{F}}^{\mathrm{T}}\right) \end{bmatrix} + \begin{bmatrix} \boldsymbol{\Lambda}_{\mathrm{FF}} & \mathbf{0} & \mathbf{0} & \mathbf{0} & \mathbf{0} \\ \mathbf{0} & \boldsymbol{\Lambda}_{\mathrm{SS}} & \mathbf{0} & \mathbf{0} & \mathbf{0} \\ \mathbf{0} & \mathbf{0} & \boldsymbol{\Lambda}_{\mathrm{TT}} & \mathbf{0} & \mathbf{0} \\ \mathbf{W}_3\mathbf{L}_p\mathbf{E}_1 & \mathbf{0} & \mathbf{0} & \mathbf{W}_3\mathbf{L}_p\mathbf{E}_2\mathbf{D}_f\mathbf{W}_1^{\mathrm{T}} & \mathbf{0} \\ \mathbf{W}_4\mathbf{A}_1 & \mathbf{W}_4\mathbf{A}_2 & \mathbf{0} & \mathbf{0} & \mathbf{W}_4\mathbf{A}_3\mathbf{W}_2^{\mathrm{T}} \end{bmatrix} \begin{bmatrix} \boldsymbol{\eta}_{\mathrm{F}} \\ \boldsymbol{\eta}_{\mathrm{S}} \\ \boldsymbol{\eta}_{\mathrm{T}} \\ \boldsymbol{\eta}_{\mathrm{F}^*} \\ \boldsymbol{\eta}_{\mathrm{S}^*} \end{bmatrix} + \begin{bmatrix} \boldsymbol{\varepsilon}_{\mathrm{F}} \\ \boldsymbol{\varepsilon}_{\mathrm{S}} \\ \boldsymbol{\varepsilon}_{\mathrm{T}} \\ \boldsymbol{\varepsilon}_{\mathrm{F}^*} \\ \boldsymbol{\varepsilon}_{\mathrm{S}^*} \end{bmatrix}. \tag{17.2}$$

Here, $\boldsymbol{\nu}_i$ and $\boldsymbol{\varepsilon}_i$ are vectors of intercepts and measurement errors associated with $\mathbf{y}_i$ (for $i = \mathbf{F}, \mathbf{S}, \mathbf{T}$). Meanwhile, $\boldsymbol{\Lambda}_{ij}$, the factor loading matrix relating $\mathbf{y}_i$ to $\boldsymbol{\eta}_j$ (for $i = \mathbf{F}, \mathbf{S}, \mathbf{T}$ and $j = \mathbf{F}, \mathbf{S}, \mathbf{T}, \mathbf{F}^*, \mathbf{S}^*$), is presumed to be non-null for $i = j$ and null for $i \neq j$. The expanded forms of the nonlinear vectors $\mathbf{y}_{\mathbf{F}^*}$ and $\mathbf{y}_{\mathbf{S}^*}$ shown in Eq. (17.2) were obtained by plugging the equations $\mathbf{y}_{\mathbf{F}} = \boldsymbol{\nu}_{\mathbf{F}} + \boldsymbol{\Lambda}_{\mathbf{FF}}\boldsymbol{\eta}_{\mathbf{F}} + \boldsymbol{\varepsilon}_{\mathbf{F}}$ and $\mathbf{y}_{\mathbf{S}} = \boldsymbol{\nu}_{\mathbf{S}} + \boldsymbol{\Lambda}_{\mathbf{SS}}\boldsymbol{\eta}_{\mathbf{S}} + \boldsymbol{\varepsilon}_{\mathbf{S}}$ from Eq. (17.2) into the equations $\mathbf{y}_{\mathbf{F}^*} = \mathbf{W}_3 \operatorname{vech}\left(\mathbf{y}_{\mathbf{F}}\mathbf{y}_{\mathbf{F}}^{\mathrm{T}}\right)$ and $\mathbf{y}_{\mathbf{S}^*} = \mathbf{W}_4 \operatorname{vec}\left(\mathbf{y}_{\mathbf{S}}\mathbf{y}_{\mathbf{F}}^{\mathrm{T}}\right)$ established in the previous section. Also note that the details of these expansions can be found in Appendix A.

In the current partitioning nonlinear framework, the vectors of disturbance terms and measurement errors from Eqs. (17.1) and (17.2) are assumed to have a multivariate normal distribution as follows:

$$\begin{bmatrix} \boldsymbol{\zeta}_{\mathbf{F}} \\ \boldsymbol{\zeta}_{\mathbf{S}} \\ \boldsymbol{\zeta}_{\mathbf{T}} \\ \boldsymbol{\varepsilon}_{\mathbf{F}} \\ \boldsymbol{\varepsilon}_{\mathbf{S}} \\ \boldsymbol{\varepsilon}_{\mathbf{T}} \end{bmatrix} \sim \mathcal{N}\left(\begin{bmatrix} \mathbf{0} \\ \mathbf{0} \\ \mathbf{0} \\ \mathbf{0} \\ \mathbf{0} \\ \mathbf{0} \end{bmatrix}, \begin{bmatrix} \boldsymbol{\Psi}_{\mathbf{FF}} & & & & & \\ \boldsymbol{\Psi}_{\mathbf{SF}} & \boldsymbol{\Psi}_{\mathbf{SS}} & & & & \\ \boldsymbol{\Psi}_{\mathbf{TF}} & \boldsymbol{\Psi}_{\mathbf{TS}} & \boldsymbol{\Psi}_{\mathbf{TT}} & & & \\ \mathbf{0} & \mathbf{0} & \mathbf{0} & \boldsymbol{\Theta}_{\mathbf{FF}} & & \\ \mathbf{0} & \mathbf{0} & \mathbf{0} & \boldsymbol{\Theta}_{\mathbf{SF}} & \boldsymbol{\Theta}_{\mathbf{SS}} & \\ \mathbf{0} & \mathbf{0} & \mathbf{0} & \boldsymbol{\Theta}_{\mathbf{TF}} & \boldsymbol{\Theta}_{\mathbf{TS}} & \boldsymbol{\Theta}_{\mathbf{TT}} \end{bmatrix}\right). \tag{17.3}$$

Having developed the generalized nonlinear framework as shown in Eqs. (17.1) and (17.2), it is now possible to proceed to examining the specification of constraints in the context of these two equations. The six partitioned matrices ($\boldsymbol{\alpha}$, $\mathbf{B}$, $\boldsymbol{\Psi}$, $\boldsymbol{\nu}$, $\boldsymbol{\Lambda}$ and $\boldsymbol{\Theta}$) along with their respective constraints are described in Eqs. (17.4) through (17.7) and Appendix B. Constraints embedded into $\boldsymbol{\alpha}$, $\boldsymbol{\nu}$, $\boldsymbol{\Psi}$ and $\boldsymbol{\Theta}$ are derived based on the assumption of Expression (17.3) as well as extensions of several properties of the multivariate normal distribution (Magnus and Neudecker 1979; Tracy and Sultan 1993; Ghazal and Neudecker 2000). The details of the derivations of these partitioned matrices are available from the author upon request.

The partitioned vector $\boldsymbol{\alpha}$ is a 5×1 array of the form $\left[\boldsymbol{\alpha}_{\mathbf{F}}^{\mathrm{T}} \mid \boldsymbol{\alpha}_{\mathbf{S}}^{\mathrm{T}} \mid \boldsymbol{\alpha}_{\mathbf{T}}^{\mathrm{T}} \mid \boldsymbol{\alpha}_{\mathbf{F}*}^{\mathrm{T}} \mid \boldsymbol{\alpha}_{\mathbf{S}*}^{\mathrm{T}}\right]^{\mathrm{T}}$. $\boldsymbol{\alpha}_{\mathbf{F}*}$ and $\boldsymbol{\alpha}_{\mathbf{S}*}$, the vectors of intercepts of $\boldsymbol{\eta}_{\mathbf{F}*}$ and $\boldsymbol{\eta}_{\mathbf{S}*}$, encompass the non-null expected values of $\boldsymbol{\zeta}_{\mathbf{F}*}$ and $\boldsymbol{\zeta}_{\mathbf{S}*}$ to meet the assumption inherent to SEM that the expected values of disturbance terms are set to null. The resultant form of $\boldsymbol{\alpha}$ is expressed as

$$\boldsymbol{\alpha} = \begin{bmatrix} \boldsymbol{\alpha}_{\mathbf{F}} \\ \boldsymbol{\alpha}_{\mathbf{S}} \\ \boldsymbol{\alpha}_{\mathbf{T}} \\ \boldsymbol{\alpha}_{\mathbf{F}*} \underline{\underline{\Delta}}\, \mathbf{W}_1 \mathbf{L}_f \mathbf{F}_1 \mathrm{vec}\left(\boldsymbol{\alpha}_{\mathbf{F}} \boldsymbol{\alpha}_{\mathbf{F}}^{\mathrm{T}} + \boldsymbol{\Psi}_{\mathbf{FF}}\right) \\ \boldsymbol{\alpha}_{\mathbf{S}*} \underline{\underline{\Delta}}\, \mathbf{W}_2 \mathbf{S}_1 \left[\mathrm{vec}\left(\boldsymbol{\alpha}_{\mathbf{S}} \boldsymbol{\alpha}_{\mathbf{F}}^{\mathrm{T}}\right) + \mathbf{S}_6 \mathrm{vec}\left(\boldsymbol{\Psi}_{\mathbf{FF}}\right) + \mathrm{vec}\left(\boldsymbol{\Psi}_{\mathbf{SF}}\right)\right] \end{bmatrix} \tag{17.4}$$

(here "$\underline{\underline{\Delta}}$" is the symbol for "defined as").

The general form of the partitioned vector $\boldsymbol{\nu}$ is $\left[\boldsymbol{\nu}_{\mathbf{F}}^{\mathrm{T}} \mid \boldsymbol{\nu}_{\mathbf{S}}^{\mathrm{T}} \mid \boldsymbol{\nu}_{\mathbf{T}}^{\mathrm{T}} \mid \boldsymbol{\nu}_{\mathbf{F}*}^{\mathrm{T}} \mid \boldsymbol{\nu}_{\mathbf{S}*}^{\mathrm{T}}\right]^{\mathrm{T}}$, where $\boldsymbol{\nu}_{\mathbf{F}*}$ and $\boldsymbol{\nu}_{\mathbf{S}*}$ are the vectors of intercepts of $\mathbf{y}_{\mathbf{F}*}$ and $\mathbf{y}_{\mathbf{S}*}$. $\boldsymbol{\nu}_{\mathbf{F}*}$ and $\boldsymbol{\nu}_{\mathbf{S}*}$ subsume the non-null expected values of $\boldsymbol{\varepsilon}_{\mathbf{F}*}$ and $\boldsymbol{\varepsilon}_{\mathbf{S}*}$ to avoid a violation of the assumption inherent to SEM that expected values of measurement errors are set to null. The resultant form of $\boldsymbol{\nu}$ is expressed as

$$\boldsymbol{\nu} = \begin{bmatrix} \boldsymbol{\nu}_{\mathbf{F}} \\ \boldsymbol{\nu}_{\mathbf{S}} \\ \boldsymbol{\nu}_{\mathbf{T}} \\ \boldsymbol{\nu}_{\mathbf{F}^*} \underline{\underline{\Delta}} \mathbf{W}_3\mathbf{L}_p\text{vec}\left(\boldsymbol{\nu}_{\mathbf{F}}\boldsymbol{\nu}_{\mathbf{F}}^{\mathrm{T}} + \boldsymbol{\Theta}_{\mathbf{FF}}\right) \\ \boldsymbol{\nu}_{\mathbf{S}^*} \underline{\underline{\Delta}} \mathbf{W}_4\text{vec}\left(\boldsymbol{\nu}_{\mathbf{S}}\boldsymbol{\nu}_{\mathbf{F}}^{\mathrm{T}} + \boldsymbol{\Theta}_{\mathbf{SF}}\right) \end{bmatrix}. \tag{17.5}$$

The partitioned coefficient matrices $\mathbf{B}$ and $\boldsymbol{\Lambda}$ are taken directly from Eqs. (17.1) and (17.2) to be expressed by Eqs. (17.6) and (17.7), respectively.

$$\mathbf{B} = \begin{bmatrix} \mathbf{B}_{\mathbf{FF}} & \mathbf{0} & \mathbf{0} & \mathbf{0} & \mathbf{0} \\ \mathbf{B}_{\mathbf{SF}} & \mathbf{B}_{\mathbf{SS}} & \mathbf{0} & \mathbf{B}_{\mathbf{SF}^*} & \mathbf{0} \\ \mathbf{B}_{\mathbf{TF}} & \mathbf{B}_{\mathbf{TS}} & \mathbf{B}_{\mathbf{TT}} & \mathbf{B}_{\mathbf{TF}^*} & \mathbf{B}_{\mathbf{TS}^*} \\ \mathbf{0} & \mathbf{0} & \mathbf{0} & \mathbf{0} & \mathbf{0} \\ \mathbf{B}_{\mathbf{S}^*\mathbf{F}} \underline{\underline{\Delta}} \mathbf{W}_2\mathbf{S}_1\mathbf{S}_2 & \mathbf{0} & \mathbf{0} & \mathbf{B}_{\mathbf{S}^*\mathbf{F}^*} \underline{\underline{\Delta}} \mathbf{W}_2\mathbf{S}_1\mathbf{S}_3 & \mathbf{0} \end{bmatrix}. \tag{17.6}$$

$$\boldsymbol{\Lambda} = \begin{bmatrix} \boldsymbol{\Lambda}_{\mathbf{FF}} & \mathbf{0} & \mathbf{0} & \mathbf{0} & \mathbf{0} \\ \mathbf{0} & \boldsymbol{\Lambda}_{\mathbf{SS}} & \mathbf{0} & \mathbf{0} & \mathbf{0} \\ \mathbf{0} & \mathbf{0} & \boldsymbol{\Lambda}_{\mathbf{TT}} & \mathbf{0} & \mathbf{0} \\ \boldsymbol{\Lambda}_{\mathbf{F}^*\mathbf{F}} \underline{\underline{\Delta}} \mathbf{W}_3\mathbf{L}_p\mathbf{E}_1 & \mathbf{0} & \mathbf{0} & \boldsymbol{\Lambda}_{\mathbf{F}^*\mathbf{F}^*} \underline{\underline{\Delta}} \mathbf{W}_3\mathbf{L}_p\mathbf{E}_2\mathbf{D}_f\mathbf{W}_1^{\mathrm{T}} & \mathbf{0} \\ \boldsymbol{\Lambda}_{\mathbf{S}^*\mathbf{F}} \underline{\underline{\Delta}} \mathbf{W}_4\mathbf{A}_1 & \boldsymbol{\Lambda}_{\mathbf{S}^*\mathbf{S}} \underline{\underline{\Delta}} \mathbf{W}_4\mathbf{A}_2 & \mathbf{0} & \mathbf{0} & \boldsymbol{\Lambda}_{\mathbf{S}^*\mathbf{S}^*} \underline{\underline{\Delta}} \mathbf{W}_4\mathbf{A}_3\mathbf{W}_2^{\mathrm{T}} \end{bmatrix}. \tag{17.7}$$

Due to space considerations, details of the partitioning and constraint specification of the disturbance covariance matrix $\boldsymbol{\Psi}$ and the measurement error covariance matrix $\boldsymbol{\Theta}$ are presented in Appendix B.

On the whole, constraints embedded into the six resultant matrices are represented as either the null matrix or a constraint matrix which is a function of one or more of the submatrices associated with η_{F} and η_{S} (i.e., α_{F}, α_{S}, $\mathbf{B}_{\mathbf{FF}}$, $\mathbf{B}_{\mathbf{SF}}$, $\mathbf{B}_{\mathbf{SS}}$, $\boldsymbol{\Psi}_{\mathbf{FF}}$, $\boldsymbol{\Psi}_{\mathbf{SS}}$, $\boldsymbol{\Psi}_{\mathbf{TF}}$ and $\boldsymbol{\Psi}_{\mathbf{TS}}$) and/or submatrices associated with $\mathbf{y}_{\mathbf{F}}$ and $\mathbf{y}_{\mathbf{S}}$ (i.e., $\boldsymbol{\nu}_{\mathbf{F}}$, $\boldsymbol{\nu}_{\mathbf{S}}$, $\boldsymbol{\Lambda}_{\mathbf{FF}}$, $\boldsymbol{\Lambda}_{\mathbf{SS}}$, $\boldsymbol{\Theta}_{\mathbf{FF}}$, $\boldsymbol{\Theta}_{\mathbf{SF}}$, $\boldsymbol{\Theta}_{\mathbf{SS}}$, $\boldsymbol{\Theta}_{\mathbf{TF}}$ and $\boldsymbol{\Theta}_{\mathbf{TS}}$).

In light of the above discussion, it can be seen that the process of constraint specification is neatly incorporated into the nonlinear framework of the present study. It should be noted that the forms of the derived constraint matrices are kept the same regardless of the number and type of latent nonlinear effects and product indicators selected. In the following section, an artificial model is illustrated to demonstrate the usage and validity of the current approach. This model will be implemented in OpenMx, taking advantage of the capability of this SEM package to readily support model construction in matrix form.

17.3 Artificial Interaction Model

The total effect moderation model (Model H) from Edwards and Lambert (2007) was used to validate the extended partitioned scheme detailed earlier. It was assumed that each latent variable was associated with two observed indicators. For a complete graphical depiction of the illustrated model, refer to the path diagram in Fig. 17.3.

In this model, the disturbance terms ($\zeta_1, \ldots, \zeta_4$) and measurement errors ($\varepsilon_1, \ldots, \varepsilon_8$) were assumed to have a multivariate normal distribution with mean zero and have a covariance matrix composed of the elements in $diag(\psi_{11}, \ldots, \psi_{44}, \theta_{11}, \ldots, \theta_{88})$ and the covariance term ψ_{21}. Simulated data were generated by PRELIS 2 with sample size set at 500 observations, while the population parameter values were shown in Table 17.1. The sample mean and covariance matrix for each replication were calculated from noncentered observed variables. Estimates and standard errors of parameters from maximum likelihood (ML) estimation were taken for the first 500 replications in which the estimation procedure converged.

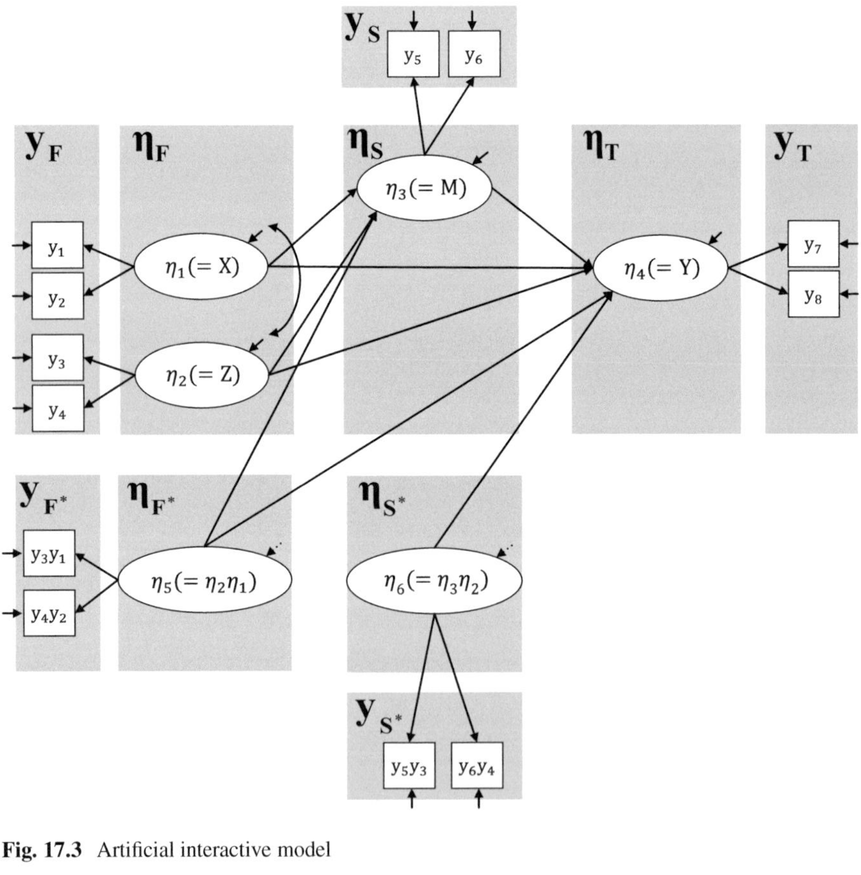

Fig. 17.3 Artificial interactive model

Table 17.1 Total effect moderation model

Parameter (true value)	Bias	*SE*	*SD*	Parameter (true value)	Bias	*SE*	*SD*
$\alpha_1(0.00)$	–	–	–	$\beta_{31}(0.40)$	0.001	0.048	0.070
$\alpha_2(0.00)$	–	–	–	$\beta_{32}(0.40)$	−0.002	0.049	0.064
$\alpha_3(0.00)$	–	–	–	$\beta_{41}(0.40)$	0.002	0.086	0.098
$\alpha_4(0.00)$	–	–	–	$\beta_{42}(0.40)$	−0.007	0.084	0.094
				$\beta_{43}(0.40)$	0.015	0.128	0.143
$\upsilon_1(1.00)$	0.000	0.037	0.064	$\beta_{35}(0.20)$	−0.004	0.041	0.056
$\upsilon_2(1.00)$	0.000	0.030	0.054	$\beta_{45}(0.20)$	0.002	0.096	0.109
$\upsilon_3(1.00)$	0.002	0.031	0.063	$\beta_{46}(0.20)$	0.003	0.084	0.093
$\upsilon_4(1.00)$	0.001	0.025	0.053				
$\upsilon_5(1.00)$	0.001	0.040	0.062	$\psi_{11}(1.00)$	0.002	0.097	0.142
$\upsilon_6(1.00)$	0.001	0.032	0.055	$\psi_{21}(0.30)$	0.000	0.039	0.069
$\upsilon_7(1.00)$	0.004	0.059	0.073	$\psi_{22}(1.00)$	−0.002	0.091	0.132
$\upsilon_8(1.00)$	0.000	0.047	0.056	$\psi_{33}(0.36)$	−0.007	0.060	0.077
				$\psi_{44}(0.36)$	−0.015	0.073	0.076
$\lambda_{11}(1.00)$	–	–	–				
$\lambda_{21}(0.70)$	0.006	0.053	0.072	$\theta_{11}(0.51)$	−0.003	0.074	0.093
$\lambda_{32}(1.00)$	–	–	–	$\theta_{22}(0.51)$	0.000	0.044	0.059
$\lambda_{42}(0.70)$	0.003	0.051	0.069	$\theta_{33}(0.51)$	−0.010	0.076	0.091
$\lambda_{53}(1.00)$	–	–	–	$\theta_{44}(0.51)$	−0.004	0.043	0.052
$\lambda_{63}(0.70)$	0.010	0.047	0.070	$\theta_{55}(0.51)$	−0.001	0.059	0.075
$\lambda_{74}(1.00)$	–	–	–	$\theta_{66}(0.51)$	−0.006	0.037	0.046
$\lambda_{84}(0.70)$	0.002	0.040	0.042	$\theta_{77}(0.51)$	−0.003	0.070	0.071
				$\theta_{88}(0.51)$	0.001	0.044	0.041

Notes. SD = empirical standard error; *SE* = average estimated standard error. *Rate of fully proper solutions* = 95.8 %. To fix scales, α_1 to α_4 are set to zero, and λ_{11}, λ_{32}, λ_{53} and λ_{74} are set to one

Due to space considerations, the OpenMx syntax used in implementing the total effect moderation model example is not provided here, but will be provided by the author upon request.

In order to confirm the validity of the current approach, the bias (calculated as the difference between the mean of the 500 parameter estimates and the population parameter value), the empirical standard deviation (*SD*), and average estimated standard error (*SE*) for each parameter from the simulation study are presented in Table 17.1.

The simulation results indicated that the mean estimates of all parameters were close to the population parameter values and the absolute biases were less than 0.02, confirming the validity of the current approach. The average estimated standard errors (*SE*) tended to be smaller than empirical standard deviations (*SD*), meaning that the estimated standard errors underestimated empirical standard deviation and thus wrongly inflated the level of significance of testing parameters (increasing the Type I error rate). It is important to mention that various simulation studies (cf., Yang-Wallentin and Jöreskog 2001; Moosbrugger et al. 2009; Chen and Cheng 2014) similarly showed that average estimated standard errors of parameters were underestimated when estimating the interaction and/or quadratic effect(s) of latent variables under the constrained approach. Thus, more research is needed to determine whether or not this phenomenon is an inherent feature of the constrained approach.

17.4 Conclusion

The current study established a more general latent nonlinear framework for integrating moderation and mediation. The proposed matrix specification scheme encapsulates many possible forms of moderation models that can accommodate situations in which any two pathways that constitute a particular indirect effect in a mediated model can be differentially or collectively moderated by the moderator variable(s), thereby further broadening the potential usefulness of the class of product indicator approaches, most notably the constrained approach.

Although the proposed framework provides a major step forward in the development of the constrained approach, there are a few caveats to take into consideration. First and foremost, the constraint specification procedure of the proposed framework is based on the assumption that $\boldsymbol{\zeta}_{\mathbf{F}}$, $\boldsymbol{\zeta}_{\mathbf{S}}$, $\boldsymbol{\zeta}_{\mathbf{T}}$, $\boldsymbol{\varepsilon}_{\mathbf{F}}$, $\boldsymbol{\varepsilon}_{\mathbf{S}}$ and $\boldsymbol{\varepsilon}_{\mathbf{T}}$ are multivariate normally distributed. If this assumption is violated, applying the proposed approach might result in unknown bias in the parameter estimates. Secondly, the current framework, focusing on the specification of latent interaction and/or quadratic effects, has no capability to deal with higher-order latent nonlinear effects. Finally, it is important to keep in mind that the current framework estimates latent nonlinear effects through a more generalized version of Jöreskog and Yang's (1996) constrained approach, which is but one of a multitude of approaches (e.g., the unconstrained approach, Marsh et al. 2004, 2006; the latent moderated structural equations approach, Klein and Moosbrugger 2000) that can potentially be used. Further research should be conducted with the aim of possibly developing other approaches that can likewise be used to estimate complex latent nonlinear effects.

Appendix A: Expansions of $\boldsymbol{\eta}_{\mathbf{F}*}$, $\boldsymbol{\eta}_{\mathbf{S}*}$, $\mathbf{y}_{\mathbf{F}*}$, and $\mathbf{y}_{\mathbf{S}*}$

Before $\boldsymbol{\eta}_{\mathbf{F}*}$, $\boldsymbol{\eta}_{\mathbf{S}*}$, $\mathbf{y}_{\mathbf{F}*}$, and $\mathbf{y}_{\mathbf{S}*}$ are discussed in the subsequent paragraph, it is necessary to gain familiarity with the notation of four basic types of matrices. The $n \times n$ identity matrix will be denoted as $\mathbf{I}_n$ and the $mn \times mn$ commutation matrix will be indicated as $\mathbf{K}_{mn}$ for $m \neq n$ and $\mathbf{K}_n$ for $m = n$ (see definition 3.1 of Magnus and Neudecker 1979). The $n(n+1)/2 \times n^2$ elimination matrix and $n^2 \times n(n+1)/2$ duplication matrix will be denoted as $\mathbf{L}_n$ and $\mathbf{D}_n$, respectively (see definitions 3.1a and 3.2a of Magnus and Neudecker 1980).

The expansions of $\boldsymbol{\eta}_{\mathbf{F}^*}$, $\boldsymbol{\eta}_{\mathbf{S}^*}$, $\mathbf{y}_{\mathbf{F}^*}$, and $\mathbf{y}_{\mathbf{S}^*}$ can be obtained with the aid of several theorems and properties of the Kronecker product, vech and vec operators shown in Magnus and Neudecker (1980, 1988). The resulting forms of these expansions are expressed as below.

$$\boldsymbol{\eta}_{\mathbf{F}^*} = \mathbf{W}_1\mathbf{L}_f\mathbf{F}_1\text{vec}\left(\boldsymbol{\alpha}_{\mathbf{F}}\boldsymbol{\alpha}_{\mathbf{F}}^{\mathrm{T}}\right) + \boldsymbol{\zeta}_{\mathbf{F}^*},$$

$$\boldsymbol{\eta}_{\mathbf{S}^*} = \mathbf{W}_2\mathbf{S}_1\text{vec}\left(\boldsymbol{\alpha}_{\mathbf{S}}\boldsymbol{\alpha}_{\mathbf{F}}^{\mathrm{T}}\right) + \mathbf{W}_2\mathbf{S}_1\mathbf{S}_2\boldsymbol{\eta}_{\mathbf{F}} + \mathbf{W}_2\mathbf{S}_1\mathbf{S}_3\boldsymbol{\eta}_{\mathbf{F}}^* + \boldsymbol{\zeta}_{\mathbf{S}^*},$$

$$\mathbf{y}_{\mathbf{F}^*} = \mathbf{W}_3\mathbf{L}_p\text{vec}\left(\boldsymbol{\nu}_{\mathbf{F}}\boldsymbol{\nu}_{\mathbf{F}}^{\mathrm{T}}\right) + \mathbf{W}_3\mathbf{L}_p\mathbf{E}_1\boldsymbol{\eta}_{\mathbf{F}} + \mathbf{W}_3\mathbf{L}_p\mathbf{E}_2\mathbf{D}_f\mathbf{W}_1^{\mathrm{T}}\boldsymbol{\eta}_{\mathbf{F}^*} + \boldsymbol{\varepsilon}_{\mathbf{F}^*},$$

$$\mathbf{y}_{\mathbf{S}^*} = \mathbf{W}_4\text{vec}\left(\boldsymbol{\nu}_{\mathbf{S}}\boldsymbol{\nu}_{\mathbf{F}}^{\mathrm{T}}\right) + \mathbf{W}_4\mathbf{A}_1\boldsymbol{\eta}_{\mathbf{F}} + \mathbf{W}_4\mathbf{A}_2\boldsymbol{\eta}_{\mathbf{S}} + \mathbf{W}_4\mathbf{A}_3\mathbf{W}_2^{\mathrm{T}}\boldsymbol{\eta}_{\mathbf{S}^*} + \boldsymbol{\varepsilon}_{\mathbf{S}^*},$$

where $\boldsymbol{\zeta}_{\mathbf{F}^*} \underset{=}{\Delta} \mathbf{W}_1\mathbf{L}_f\mathbf{F}_1\left(\mathbf{F}_2\boldsymbol{\zeta}_{\mathbf{F}} + \boldsymbol{\zeta}_{\mathbf{F}} \otimes \boldsymbol{\zeta}_{\mathbf{F}}\right)$,

$$\boldsymbol{\zeta}_{\mathbf{S}^*} \underset{=}{\Delta} \mathbf{W}_2\mathbf{S}_1\left[\mathbf{S}_4\boldsymbol{\zeta}_{\mathbf{F}} + \mathbf{S}_5\boldsymbol{\zeta}_{\mathbf{S}} + \mathbf{S}_6\left(\boldsymbol{\zeta}_{\mathbf{F}} \otimes \boldsymbol{\zeta}_{\mathbf{F}}\right) + \mathbf{S}_7\left(\boldsymbol{\zeta}_{\mathbf{F}} \otimes \boldsymbol{\zeta}_{\mathbf{F}} \otimes \boldsymbol{\zeta}_{\mathbf{F}}\right) + \boldsymbol{\zeta}_{\mathbf{F}} \otimes \boldsymbol{\zeta}_{\mathbf{S}}\right],$$

$$\boldsymbol{\varepsilon}_{\mathbf{F}^*} \underset{=}{\Delta} \mathbf{W}_3\mathbf{L}_p\left[\mathbf{E}_3\boldsymbol{\varepsilon}_{\mathbf{F}} + \mathbf{E}_4\left(\boldsymbol{\varepsilon}_{\mathbf{F}} \otimes \boldsymbol{\zeta}_{\mathbf{F}}\right) + \mathbf{E}_5\left(\boldsymbol{\zeta}_{\mathbf{F}} \otimes \boldsymbol{\varepsilon}_{\mathbf{F}}\right) + \boldsymbol{\varepsilon}_{\mathbf{F}} \otimes \boldsymbol{\varepsilon}_{\mathbf{F}}\right],$$

$$\begin{aligned}\boldsymbol{\varepsilon}_{\mathbf{S}^*} \underset{=}{\Delta} \mathbf{W}_4\big[&\mathbf{A}_4\boldsymbol{\varepsilon}_{\mathbf{F}} + \mathbf{A}_5\boldsymbol{\varepsilon}_{\mathbf{S}} + \mathbf{A}_6\left(\boldsymbol{\varepsilon}_{\mathbf{F}} \otimes \boldsymbol{\zeta}_{\mathbf{F}}\right) + \mathbf{A}_7\left(\boldsymbol{\zeta}_{\mathbf{F}} \otimes \boldsymbol{\varepsilon}_{\mathbf{S}}\right) + \mathbf{A}_8\left(\boldsymbol{\varepsilon}_{\mathbf{F}} \otimes \boldsymbol{\zeta}_{\mathbf{S}}\right)\\ &+ \mathbf{A}_9\left(\boldsymbol{\varepsilon}_{\mathbf{F}} \otimes \boldsymbol{\zeta}_{\mathbf{F}} \otimes \boldsymbol{\zeta}_{\mathbf{F}}\right) + \boldsymbol{\varepsilon}_{\mathbf{F}} \otimes \boldsymbol{\varepsilon}_{\mathbf{S}}\big]\end{aligned}$$

(here "$\underset{=}{\Delta}$" is the symbol for "defined as") in which $\mathbf{F}_1 = [(\mathrm{I}_f - \mathbf{B}_{\mathbf{FF}}) \otimes (\mathrm{I}_f - \mathbf{B}_{\mathbf{FF}})]^{-1}$,

$\mathbf{F}_2 = \mathbf{I}_f \otimes \boldsymbol{\alpha}_{\mathbf{F}} + \boldsymbol{\alpha}_{\mathbf{F}} \otimes \mathbf{I}_f$, $\mathbf{S}_1 = [(\mathrm{I}_f - \mathbf{B}_{\mathbf{FF}}) \otimes (\mathbf{I}_s - \mathbf{B}_{\mathbf{SS}})]^{-1}$, $\mathbf{S}_2 = \boldsymbol{\alpha}_{\mathbf{F}} \otimes \mathbf{B}_{\mathbf{SF}}$, $\mathbf{S}_3 = \boldsymbol{\alpha}_{\mathbf{F}} \otimes \mathbf{B}_{\mathbf{SF}^*}$, $\mathbf{S}_4 = \mathbf{I}_f \otimes [\boldsymbol{\alpha}_{\mathbf{S}} + \mathbf{B}_{\mathbf{SF}}(\mathrm{I}_f - \mathbf{B}_{\mathbf{FF}})^{-1}\boldsymbol{\alpha}_{\mathbf{F}} + \mathbf{B}_{\mathbf{SF}^*}\mathbf{W}_1\mathbf{L}_f\mathbf{F}_1(\boldsymbol{\alpha}_{\mathbf{F}} \otimes \boldsymbol{\alpha}_{\mathbf{F}})]$, $\mathbf{S}_5 = \boldsymbol{\alpha}_{\mathbf{F}} \otimes \mathbf{I}_s$, $\mathbf{S}_6 = \mathbf{I}_f \otimes [\mathbf{B}_{\mathbf{SF}}(\mathrm{I}_f - \mathbf{B}_{\mathbf{FF}})^{-1} + \mathbf{B}_{\mathbf{SF}^*}\mathbf{W}_1\mathbf{L}_f\mathbf{F}_1\mathbf{F}_2]$, $\mathbf{S}_7 = \mathbf{I}_f \otimes (\mathbf{B}_{\mathbf{SF}^*}\mathbf{W}_1\mathbf{L}_f\mathbf{F}_1)$, $\mathbf{E}_1 = \boldsymbol{\Lambda}_{\mathbf{FF}} \otimes \boldsymbol{\nu}_{\mathbf{F}} + \boldsymbol{\nu}_{\mathbf{F}} \otimes \boldsymbol{\Lambda}_{\mathbf{FF}}$, $\mathbf{E}_2 = \boldsymbol{\Lambda}_{\mathbf{FF}} \otimes \boldsymbol{\Lambda}_{\mathbf{FF}}$, $\mathbf{E}_3 = \mathbf{I}_p \otimes [\boldsymbol{\nu}_{\mathbf{F}} + \boldsymbol{\Lambda}_{\mathbf{FF}}(\mathrm{I}_f - \mathbf{B}_{\mathbf{FF}})^{-1}\boldsymbol{\alpha}_{\mathbf{F}}] + [\boldsymbol{\nu}_{\mathbf{F}} + \boldsymbol{\Lambda}_{\mathbf{FF}}(\mathrm{I}_f - \mathbf{B}_{\mathbf{FF}})^{-1}\boldsymbol{\alpha}_{\mathbf{F}}] \otimes \mathbf{I}_p$, $\mathbf{E}_4 = \mathbf{I}_p \otimes (\boldsymbol{\Lambda}_{\mathbf{FF}}(\mathrm{I}_f - \mathbf{B}_{\mathbf{FF}})^{-1})$, $\mathbf{E}_5 = (\boldsymbol{\Lambda}_{\mathbf{FF}}(\mathrm{I}_f - \mathbf{B}_{\mathbf{FF}})^{-1}) \otimes \mathbf{I}_p$, $\mathbf{A}_1 = \boldsymbol{\Lambda}_{\mathbf{FF}} \otimes \boldsymbol{\nu}_{\mathbf{S}}$, $\mathbf{A}_2 = \boldsymbol{\nu}_{\mathbf{F}} \otimes \boldsymbol{\Lambda}_{\mathbf{SS}}$, $\mathbf{A}_3 = \boldsymbol{\Lambda}_{\mathbf{FF}} \otimes \boldsymbol{\Lambda}_{\mathbf{SS}}$, $\mathbf{A}_4 = \mathbf{I}_p \otimes [\boldsymbol{\nu}_{\mathbf{S}} + \boldsymbol{\Lambda}_{\mathbf{SS}}(\mathbf{I}_s - \mathbf{B}_{\mathbf{SS}})^{-1}(\boldsymbol{\alpha}_{\mathbf{S}} + \mathbf{B}_{\mathbf{SF}}(\mathrm{I}_f - \mathbf{B}_{\mathbf{FF}})^{-1}\boldsymbol{\alpha}_{\mathbf{F}} + \mathbf{B}_{\mathbf{SF}^*}\mathbf{W}_1\mathbf{L}_f\mathbf{F}_1(\boldsymbol{\alpha}_{\mathbf{F}} \otimes \boldsymbol{\alpha}_{\mathbf{F}}))]$, $\mathbf{A}_5 = [\boldsymbol{\nu}_{\mathbf{F}} + \boldsymbol{\Lambda}_{\mathbf{FF}}(\mathbf{I}_f - \mathbf{B}_{\mathbf{FF}})^{-1}\boldsymbol{\alpha}_{\mathbf{F}}] \otimes \mathbf{I}_q$, $\mathbf{A}_6 = \mathbf{I}_p \otimes [\boldsymbol{\Lambda}_{\mathbf{SS}}(\mathbf{I}_s - \mathbf{B}_{\mathbf{SS}})^{-1}(\mathbf{B}_{\mathbf{SF}}(\mathrm{I}_f - \mathbf{B}_{\mathbf{FF}})^{-1} + \mathbf{B}_{\mathbf{SF}^*}\mathbf{W}_1\mathbf{L}_f\mathbf{F}_1\mathbf{F}_2)]$, $\mathbf{A}_7 = (\boldsymbol{\Lambda}_{\mathbf{FF}}(\mathbf{I}_f - \mathbf{B}_{\mathbf{FF}})^{-1}) \otimes \mathbf{I}_q$, $\mathbf{A}_8 = \mathbf{I}_p \otimes (\boldsymbol{\Lambda}_{\mathbf{SS}}(\mathbf{I}_s - \mathbf{B}_{\mathbf{SS}})^{-1})$ and $\mathbf{A}_9 = \mathbf{I}_p \otimes (\boldsymbol{\Lambda}_{\mathbf{SS}}(\mathbf{I}_s - \mathbf{B}_{\mathbf{SS}})^{-1}\mathbf{B}_{\mathbf{SF}^*}\mathbf{W}_1\mathbf{L}_f\mathbf{F}_1)$.

Here, $\boldsymbol{\zeta}_{\mathbf{F}^*}$ and $\boldsymbol{\zeta}_{\mathbf{S}^*}$ are vectors of disturbance terms of $\boldsymbol{\eta}_{\mathbf{F}^*}$ and $\boldsymbol{\eta}_{\mathbf{S}^*}$, while $\boldsymbol{\varepsilon}_{\mathbf{F}^*}$ and $\boldsymbol{\varepsilon}_{\mathbf{S}^*}$ are vectors of measurement errors of $\mathbf{y}_{\mathbf{F}^*}$ and $\mathbf{y}_{\mathbf{S}^*}$. Meanwhile, $\mathbf{F}_1$, $\mathbf{F}_2$, $\mathbf{S}_1$ to $\mathbf{S}_7$, $\mathbf{E}_1$ to $\mathbf{E}_5$, and $\mathbf{A}_1$ to $\mathbf{A}_9$ are all constant matrices.

Appendix B: Partitioned Matrices $\boldsymbol{\Psi}$ and $\boldsymbol{\Theta}$

The disturbance covariance matrix $\boldsymbol{\Psi}$ is partitioned into a 5×5 array of submatrices as expressed below:

$$\boldsymbol{\Psi} = \begin{bmatrix} \boldsymbol{\Psi}_{\mathbf{FF}} & & & & \\ \boldsymbol{\Psi}_{\mathbf{SF}} & \boldsymbol{\Psi}_{\mathbf{SS}} & & & \\ \boldsymbol{\Psi}_{\mathbf{TF}} & \boldsymbol{\Psi}_{\mathbf{TS}} & \boldsymbol{\Psi}_{\mathbf{TT}} & & \\ \boldsymbol{\Psi}_{\mathbf{F^*F}} & \boldsymbol{\Psi}_{\mathbf{F^*S}} & \boldsymbol{\Psi}_{\mathbf{F^*T}} & \boldsymbol{\Psi}_{\mathbf{F^*F^*}} & \\ \boldsymbol{\Psi}_{\mathbf{S^*F}} & \boldsymbol{\Psi}_{\mathbf{S^*S}} & \boldsymbol{\Psi}_{\mathbf{S^*T}} & \boldsymbol{\Psi}_{\mathbf{S^*F^*}} & \boldsymbol{\Psi}_{\mathbf{S^*S^*}} \end{bmatrix},$$

where $\boldsymbol{\Psi}_{\mathbf{F^*F}} \underline{\underline{\Delta}} \mathbf{W}_1\mathbf{L}_f\mathbf{F}_1\mathbf{F}_2\boldsymbol{\Psi}_{\mathbf{FF}}$, $\boldsymbol{\Psi}_{\mathbf{F^*S}} \underline{\underline{\Delta}} \mathbf{W}_1\mathbf{L}_f\mathbf{F}_1\mathbf{F}_2(\boldsymbol{\Psi}_{\mathbf{SF}})^{\mathrm{T}}$, $\boldsymbol{\Psi}_{\mathbf{F^*T}} \underline{\underline{\Delta}} \mathbf{W}_1\mathbf{L}_f\mathbf{F}_1\mathbf{F}_2(\boldsymbol{\Psi}_{\mathbf{TF}})^{\mathrm{T}}$,

$$\boldsymbol{\Psi}_{\mathbf{F^*F^*}} \underline{\underline{\Delta}} \mathbf{W}_1\mathbf{L}_f\mathbf{F}_1\left[\mathbf{F}_2\boldsymbol{\Psi}_{\mathbf{FF}}\mathbf{F}_2^{\mathrm{T}} + \left(\mathbf{I}_{f^2} + \mathbf{K}_{ff}\right)\left(\boldsymbol{\Psi}_{\mathbf{FF}} \otimes \boldsymbol{\Psi}_{\mathbf{FF}}\right)\right]\mathbf{F}_1^{\mathrm{T}}\mathbf{L}_f^{\mathrm{T}}\mathbf{W}_1^{\mathrm{T}},$$

$$\begin{aligned}\boldsymbol{\Psi}_{\mathbf{S^*F}} \underline{\underline{\Delta}} \mathbf{W}_2\mathbf{S}_1\big[&\mathbf{S}_4\boldsymbol{\Psi}_{\mathbf{FF}} + \mathbf{S}_5\boldsymbol{\Psi}_{\mathbf{SF}} \\ &+ \mathbf{S}_7\Delta_{f^3\times f}\left[\mathbf{K}_{ff^3}\left(\mathrm{vec}\left(\left(\mathbf{I}_{f^2} + \mathbf{K}_{ff}\right)\left(\boldsymbol{\Psi}_{\mathbf{FF}} \otimes \boldsymbol{\Psi}_{\mathbf{FF}}\right)\right)\right.\right. \\ &+ \left.\left.\mathrm{vec}\left(\boldsymbol{\Psi}_{\mathbf{FF}}\right) \otimes \mathrm{vec}\left(\boldsymbol{\Psi}_{\mathbf{FF}}\right)\right)\right]\big],\end{aligned}$$

$$\begin{aligned}\boldsymbol{\Psi}_{\mathbf{S^*S}} \underline{\underline{\Delta}} \mathbf{W}_2\mathbf{S}_1\big[&\mathbf{S}_4(\boldsymbol{\Psi}_{\mathbf{SF}})^{\mathrm{T}} + \mathbf{S}_5\boldsymbol{\Psi}_{\mathbf{SS}} \\ &+ \mathbf{S}_7\Delta_{f^3\times s}\left[\mathbf{K}_{sf^3}\left(\mathrm{vec}\left(\left(\boldsymbol{\Psi}_{\mathbf{FF}} \otimes \boldsymbol{\Psi}_{\mathbf{SF}}\right) + \mathbf{K}_{fs}\left(\boldsymbol{\Psi}_{\mathbf{SF}} \otimes \boldsymbol{\Psi}_{\mathbf{FF}}\right)\right)\right.\right. \\ &+ \left.\left.\mathrm{vec}\left(\boldsymbol{\Psi}_{\mathbf{FF}}\right) \otimes \mathrm{vec}\left(\boldsymbol{\Psi}_{\mathbf{SF}}\right)\right)\right]\big],\end{aligned}$$

$$\begin{aligned}\boldsymbol{\Psi}_{\mathbf{S^*T}} \underline{\underline{\Delta}} \mathbf{W}_2\mathbf{S}_1\big[&\mathbf{S}_4(\boldsymbol{\Psi}_{\mathbf{TF}})^{\mathrm{T}} + \mathbf{S}_5(\boldsymbol{\Psi}_{\mathbf{TS}})^{\mathrm{T}} \\ &+ \mathbf{S}_7\Delta_{f^3\times t}\left[\mathbf{K}_{tf^3}\left(\mathrm{vec}\left(\left(\boldsymbol{\Psi}_{\mathbf{FF}} \otimes \boldsymbol{\Psi}_{\mathbf{TF}}\right) + \mathbf{K}_{ft}\left(\boldsymbol{\Psi}_{\mathbf{TF}} \otimes \boldsymbol{\Psi}_{\mathbf{FF}}\right)\right)\right.\right. \\ &+ \left.\left.\mathrm{vec}\left(\boldsymbol{\Psi}_{\mathbf{FF}}\right) \otimes \mathrm{vec}\left(\boldsymbol{\Psi}_{\mathbf{TF}}\right)\right)\right]\big],\end{aligned}$$

$$\begin{aligned}\boldsymbol{\Psi}_{\mathbf{S^*F^*}} \underline{\underline{\Delta}} \mathbf{W}_2\mathbf{S}_1\big[&\mathbf{S}_4\boldsymbol{\Psi}_{\mathbf{FF}}\mathbf{F}_2^{\mathrm{T}} + \mathbf{S}_5\boldsymbol{\Psi}_{\mathbf{SF}}\mathbf{F}_2^{\mathrm{T}} \\ &+ \mathbf{S}_7\Delta_{f^3\times f}\left[\mathbf{K}_{ff^3}\left(\mathrm{vec}\left(\left(\mathbf{I}_{f^2} + \mathbf{K}_{ff}\right)\left(\boldsymbol{\Psi}_{\mathbf{FF}} \otimes \boldsymbol{\Psi}_{\mathbf{FF}}\right)\right) + \mathrm{vec}\left(\boldsymbol{\Psi}_{\mathbf{FF}}\right) \otimes \mathrm{vec}\left(\boldsymbol{\Psi}_{\mathbf{FF}}\right)\right)\right]\mathbf{F}_2^{\mathrm{T}} \\ &+ \mathbf{S}_6\left(\mathbf{I}_{f^2} + \mathbf{K}_{ff}\right)\left(\boldsymbol{\Psi}_{\mathbf{FF}} \otimes \boldsymbol{\Psi}_{\mathbf{FF}}\right) + \boldsymbol{\Psi}_{\mathbf{FF}} \otimes \boldsymbol{\Psi}_{\mathbf{SF}} + \mathbf{K}_{fs}\left(\boldsymbol{\Psi}_{\mathbf{SF}} \otimes \boldsymbol{\Psi}_{\mathbf{FF}}\right)\big]\mathbf{F}_1^{\mathrm{T}}\mathbf{L}_f^{\mathrm{T}}\mathbf{W}_1^{\mathrm{T}},\end{aligned}$$

$$\begin{aligned}
\boldsymbol{\Psi}_{\mathbf{S^*S^*}} \triangleq\ & \mathbf{W}_2\mathbf{S}_1\big[\mathbf{S}_4\boldsymbol{\Psi}_{\mathbf{FF}}\mathbf{S}_4^{\mathrm{T}} + \mathbf{S}_5\boldsymbol{\Psi}_{\mathbf{SS}}\mathbf{S}_5^{\mathrm{T}} + \mathbf{S}_6\left(\mathbf{I}_{f^2} + \mathbf{K}_{ff}\right)\left(\boldsymbol{\Psi}_{\mathbf{FF}} \otimes \boldsymbol{\Psi}_{\mathbf{FF}}\right)\mathbf{S}_6^{\mathrm{T}} \\
& + \mathbf{S}_7\big[\left(\mathbf{I}_{f^3} + \mathbf{K}_{ff^2} + \mathbf{K}_{f^2f} + \mathbf{I}_f \otimes \mathbf{K}_{ff} + \mathbf{K}_{ff} \otimes \mathbf{I}_f + \left(\mathbf{I}_f \otimes \mathbf{K}_{ff}\right)\mathbf{K}_{ff^2}\right) \\
& \cdot \left(\boldsymbol{\Psi}_{\mathbf{FF}} \otimes \boldsymbol{\Psi}_{\mathbf{FF}} \otimes \boldsymbol{\Psi}_{\mathbf{FF}}\right) + \left(\mathbf{I}_{f^3} + \mathbf{K}_{ff^2} + \mathbf{K}_{f^2f}\right)\left(\left(\mathrm{vec}\left(\boldsymbol{\Psi}_{\mathbf{FF}}\right)\mathrm{vec}(\boldsymbol{\Psi}_{\mathbf{FF}})^{\mathrm{T}}\right) \otimes \boldsymbol{\Psi}_{\mathbf{FF}}\right) \\
& \cdot \left(\mathbf{I}_{f^3} + \mathbf{K}_{ff^2} + \mathbf{K}_{f^2f}\right)\big]\mathbf{S}_7^{\mathrm{T}} + \left(\boldsymbol{\Psi}_{\mathbf{FF}} \otimes \boldsymbol{\Psi}_{\mathbf{SS}}\right) + \mathbf{K}_{fs}\left(\boldsymbol{\Psi}_{\mathbf{SF}} \otimes \left(\boldsymbol{\Psi}_{\mathbf{SF}}\right)^{\mathrm{T}}\right) \\
& + \mathbf{S}_5\boldsymbol{\Psi}_{\mathbf{SF}}\mathbf{S}_4^{\mathrm{T}} + \mathbf{S}_4(\boldsymbol{\Psi}_{\mathbf{SF}})^{\mathrm{T}}\mathbf{S}_5^{\mathrm{T}} \\
& + \mathbf{S}_7\Delta_{f^3\times f}\left[\mathbf{K}_{ff^3}\left(\mathrm{vec}\left(\left(\mathbf{I}_{f^2} + \mathbf{K}_{ff}\right)\left(\boldsymbol{\Psi}_{\mathbf{FF}} \otimes \boldsymbol{\Psi}_{\mathbf{FF}}\right)\right) + \mathrm{vec}\left(\boldsymbol{\Psi}_{\mathbf{FF}}\right) \otimes \mathrm{vec}\left(\boldsymbol{\Psi}_{\mathbf{FF}}\right)\right)\right]\mathbf{S}_4^{\mathrm{T}} \\
& + \mathbf{S}_4\Delta_{f\times f^3}\left[\mathbf{K}_{f^3f}\left(\mathrm{vec}\left(\left(\mathbf{I}_{f^2} + \mathbf{K}_{ff}\right)\left(\boldsymbol{\Psi}_{\mathbf{FF}} \otimes \boldsymbol{\Psi}_{\mathbf{FF}}\right)\right) + \mathrm{vec}\left(\boldsymbol{\Psi}_{\mathbf{FF}}\right) \otimes \mathrm{vec}\left(\boldsymbol{\Psi}_{\mathbf{FF}}\right)\right)\right]\mathbf{S}_7^{\mathrm{T}} \\
& + \mathbf{S}_7\Delta_{f^3\times s}\left[\mathbf{K}_{sf^3}\left(\mathrm{vec}\left(\left(\boldsymbol{\Psi}_{\mathbf{FF}} \otimes \boldsymbol{\Psi}_{\mathbf{SF}}\right) + \mathbf{K}_{fs}\left(\boldsymbol{\Psi}_{\mathbf{SF}} \otimes \boldsymbol{\Psi}_{\mathbf{FF}}\right)\right) + \mathrm{vec}\left(\boldsymbol{\Psi}_{\mathbf{FF}}\right) \otimes \mathrm{vec}\left(\boldsymbol{\Psi}_{\mathbf{SF}}\right)\right)\right]\mathbf{S}_5^{\mathrm{T}} \\
& + \mathbf{S}_5\Delta_{s\times f^3}\left[\mathbf{K}_{f^3s}\left(\mathrm{vec}\left[\left(\left(\boldsymbol{\Psi}_{\mathbf{SF}}\right)^{\mathrm{T}} \otimes \boldsymbol{\Psi}_{\mathbf{FF}}\right) + \mathbf{K}_{ff}\left(\left(\boldsymbol{\Psi}_{\mathbf{SF}}\right)^{\mathrm{T}} \otimes \boldsymbol{\Psi}_{\mathbf{FF}}\right)\right]\right.\right. \\
& \left.\left. + \mathrm{vec}\left(\left(\boldsymbol{\Psi}_{\mathbf{SF}}\right)^{\mathrm{T}}\right) \otimes \mathrm{vec}\left(\boldsymbol{\Psi}_{\mathbf{FF}}\right)\right)\right]\mathbf{S}_7^{\mathrm{T}} \\
& + \left[\left(\boldsymbol{\Psi}_{\mathbf{FF}} \otimes \boldsymbol{\Psi}_{\mathbf{SF}}\right) + \mathbf{K}_{fs}\left(\boldsymbol{\Psi}_{\mathbf{SF}} \otimes \boldsymbol{\Psi}_{\mathbf{FF}}\right)\right]\mathbf{S}_6^{\mathrm{T}} \\
& + \mathbf{S}_6\left[\left(\boldsymbol{\Psi}_{\mathbf{FF}} \otimes \left(\boldsymbol{\Psi}_{\mathbf{SF}}\right)^{\mathrm{T}}\right) + \mathbf{K}_{ff}\left(\boldsymbol{\Psi}_{\mathbf{FF}} \otimes \left(\boldsymbol{\Psi}_{\mathbf{SF}}\right)^{\mathrm{T}}\right)\right]\big]\mathbf{S}_1^{\mathrm{T}}\mathbf{W}_2^{\mathrm{T}}
\end{aligned}$$

(here the symbol "$\Delta_{n\times m}$" is used to transform a $nm \times 1$ vector into an $n \times m$ matrix).

The measurement error covariance matrix $\boldsymbol{\Theta}$ is partitioned into a 5×5 array of submatrices as expressed below:

$$\boldsymbol{\Theta} = \begin{bmatrix} \boldsymbol{\Theta}_{\mathbf{FF}} & & & & \\ \boldsymbol{\Theta}_{\mathbf{SF}} & \boldsymbol{\Theta}_{\mathbf{SS}} & & & \\ \boldsymbol{\Theta}_{\mathbf{TF}} & \boldsymbol{\Theta}_{\mathbf{TS}} & \boldsymbol{\Theta}_{\mathbf{TT}} & & \\ \boldsymbol{\Theta}_{\mathbf{F^*F}} & \boldsymbol{\Theta}_{\mathbf{F^*S}} & \boldsymbol{\Theta}_{\mathbf{F^*T}} & \boldsymbol{\Theta}_{\mathbf{F^*F^*}} & \\ \boldsymbol{\Theta}_{\mathbf{S^*F}} & \boldsymbol{\Theta}_{\mathbf{S^*S}} & \boldsymbol{\Theta}_{\mathbf{S^*T}} & \boldsymbol{\Theta}_{\mathbf{S^*F^*}} & \boldsymbol{\Theta}_{\mathbf{S^*S^*}} \end{bmatrix},$$

where $\boldsymbol{\Theta}_{\mathbf{F^*F}} \triangleq \mathbf{W}_3\mathbf{L}_p\mathbf{E}_3\boldsymbol{\Theta}_{\mathbf{FF}}$, $\boldsymbol{\Theta}_{\mathbf{F^*S}} \triangleq \mathbf{W}_3\mathbf{L}_p\mathbf{E}_3(\boldsymbol{\Theta}_{\mathbf{SF}})^{\mathrm{T}}$, $\boldsymbol{\Theta}_{\mathbf{F^*T}} \triangleq \mathbf{W}_3\mathbf{L}_p\mathbf{E}_3(\boldsymbol{\Theta}_{\mathbf{TF}})^{\mathrm{T}}$,

$$\begin{aligned}
\boldsymbol{\Theta}_{\mathbf{F^*F^*}} \triangleq\ & \mathbf{W}_3\mathbf{L}_p\big[\mathbf{E}_3\boldsymbol{\Theta}_{\mathbf{FF}}\mathbf{E}_3^{\mathrm{T}} + \mathbf{E}_4\left(\boldsymbol{\Theta}_{\mathbf{FF}} \otimes \boldsymbol{\Psi}_{\mathbf{FF}}\right)\mathbf{E}_4^{\mathrm{T}} + \mathbf{E}_5\left(\boldsymbol{\Psi}_{\mathbf{FF}} \otimes \boldsymbol{\Theta}_{\mathbf{FF}}\right)\mathbf{E}_5^{\mathrm{T}} \\
& + \left(\mathbf{I}_{p^2} + \mathbf{K}_{pp}\right)\left(\boldsymbol{\Theta}_{\mathbf{FF}} \otimes \boldsymbol{\Theta}_{\mathbf{FF}}\right) + \mathbf{E}_5\mathbf{K}_{fp}\left(\boldsymbol{\Theta}_{\mathbf{FF}} \otimes \boldsymbol{\Psi}_{\mathbf{FF}}\right)\mathbf{E}_4^{\mathrm{T}} \\
& + \mathbf{E}_4\mathbf{K}_{pf}\left(\boldsymbol{\Psi}_{\mathbf{FF}} \otimes \boldsymbol{\Theta}_{\mathbf{FF}}\right)\mathbf{E}_5^{\mathrm{T}}\big]\mathbf{L}_p^{\mathrm{T}}\mathbf{W}_3^{\mathrm{T}},
\end{aligned}$$

$$\boldsymbol{\Theta}_{\mathbf{S^*F}} \triangleq \mathbf{W}_4\left[\mathbf{A}_4\boldsymbol{\Theta}_{\mathbf{FF}} + \mathbf{A}_5\boldsymbol{\Theta}_{\mathbf{SF}} + \mathbf{A}_9\Delta_{(pf^2)\times p}\left[\mathbf{K}_{p(pf^2)}\mathrm{vec}\left(\mathbf{K}_{fp}\left(\boldsymbol{\Theta}_{\mathbf{FF}} \otimes \boldsymbol{\Psi}_{\mathbf{FF}}\right)\right)\right]\right],$$

$$\boldsymbol{\Theta}_{\mathbf{S}^*\mathbf{S}} \triangleq \mathbf{W}_4\left[\mathbf{A}_4(\boldsymbol{\Theta}_{\mathbf{SF}})^{\mathrm{T}} + \mathbf{A}_5\boldsymbol{\Theta}_{\mathbf{SS}} + \mathbf{A}_9\Delta_{(pf^2)\times q}\left[\mathbf{K}_{q(pf^2)}\mathrm{vec}\left(\mathbf{K}_{fq}\left(\boldsymbol{\Theta}_{\mathbf{SF}}\otimes\boldsymbol{\Psi}_{\mathbf{FF}}\right)\right)\right]\right],$$

$$\boldsymbol{\Theta}_{\mathbf{S}^*\mathbf{T}} \triangleq \mathbf{W}_4\left[\mathbf{A}_4(\boldsymbol{\Theta}_{\mathbf{TF}})^{\mathrm{T}} + \mathbf{A}_5(\boldsymbol{\Theta}_{\mathbf{TS}})^{\mathrm{T}} + \mathbf{A}_9\Delta_{(pf^2)\times r}\left[\mathbf{K}_{r(pf^2)}\mathrm{vec}\left(\mathbf{K}_{fr}\left(\boldsymbol{\Theta}_{\mathbf{TF}}\otimes\boldsymbol{\Psi}_{\mathbf{FF}}\right)\right)\right]\right],$$

$$\begin{aligned}\boldsymbol{\Theta}_{\mathbf{S}^*\mathbf{F}^*} \triangleq\ & \mathbf{W}_4\big[\mathbf{A}_4\boldsymbol{\Theta}_{\mathbf{FF}}\mathbf{E}_3^{\mathrm{T}} + \mathbf{A}_5\boldsymbol{\Theta}_{\mathbf{SF}}\mathbf{E}_3^{\mathrm{T}}\\
&+ \mathbf{A}_9\Delta_{(pf^2)\times p}\left[\mathbf{K}_{p(pf^2)}\mathrm{vec}\left(\mathbf{K}_{fp}\left(\boldsymbol{\Theta}_{\mathbf{FF}}\otimes\boldsymbol{\Psi}_{\mathbf{FF}}\right)\right)\right]\mathbf{E}_3^{\mathrm{T}}\\
&+ \mathbf{A}_6\left(\boldsymbol{\Theta}_{\mathbf{FF}}\otimes\boldsymbol{\Psi}_{\mathbf{FF}}\right)\mathbf{E}_4^{\mathrm{T}} + \mathbf{A}_7\mathbf{K}_{fq}\left(\boldsymbol{\Theta}_{\mathbf{SF}}\otimes\boldsymbol{\Psi}_{\mathbf{FF}}\right)\mathbf{E}_4^{\mathrm{T}} + \mathbf{A}_8\left(\boldsymbol{\Theta}_{\mathbf{FF}}\otimes\boldsymbol{\Psi}_{\mathbf{SF}}\right)\mathbf{E}_4^{\mathrm{T}}\\
&+ \mathbf{A}_6\mathbf{K}_{pf}\left(\boldsymbol{\Psi}_{\mathbf{FF}}\otimes\boldsymbol{\Theta}_{\mathbf{FF}}\right)\mathbf{E}_5^{\mathrm{T}} + \mathbf{A}_7\left(\boldsymbol{\Psi}_{\mathbf{FF}}\otimes\boldsymbol{\Theta}_{\mathbf{SF}}\right)\mathbf{E}_5^{\mathrm{T}} + \mathbf{A}_8\mathbf{K}_{ps}\left(\boldsymbol{\Psi}_{\mathbf{SF}}\otimes\boldsymbol{\Theta}_{\mathbf{FF}}\right)\mathbf{E}_5^{\mathrm{T}}\\
&+ \left(\boldsymbol{\Theta}_{\mathbf{FF}}\otimes\boldsymbol{\Theta}_{\mathbf{SF}}\right) + \mathbf{K}_{pq}\left(\boldsymbol{\Theta}_{\mathbf{SF}}\otimes\boldsymbol{\Theta}_{\mathbf{FF}}\right)\big]\mathbf{L}_p^{\mathrm{T}}\mathbf{W}_3^{\mathrm{T}},\end{aligned}$$

$$\begin{aligned}\boldsymbol{\Theta}_{\mathbf{S}^*\mathbf{S}^*} =\ & \mathbf{W}_4\big[\mathbf{A}_4\boldsymbol{\Theta}_{\mathbf{FF}}\mathbf{A}_4^{\mathrm{T}} + \mathbf{A}_5\boldsymbol{\Theta}_{\mathbf{SS}}\mathbf{A}_5^{\mathrm{T}} + \mathbf{A}_6\left(\boldsymbol{\Theta}_{\mathbf{FF}}\otimes\boldsymbol{\Psi}_{\mathbf{FF}}\right)\mathbf{A}_6^{\mathrm{T}}\\
&+ \mathbf{A}_7\left(\boldsymbol{\Psi}_{\mathbf{FF}}\otimes\boldsymbol{\Theta}_{\mathbf{SS}}\right)\mathbf{A}_7^{\mathrm{T}} + \mathbf{A}_8\left(\boldsymbol{\Theta}_{\mathbf{FF}}\otimes\boldsymbol{\Psi}_{\mathbf{SS}}\right)\mathbf{A}_8^{\mathrm{T}}\\
&+ \mathbf{A}_9\big[\left(\mathbf{I}_{pf^2} + \mathbf{I}_p\otimes\mathbf{K}_{ff}\right)\left(\boldsymbol{\Theta}_{\mathbf{FF}}\otimes\boldsymbol{\Psi}_{\mathbf{FF}}\otimes\boldsymbol{\Psi}_{\mathbf{FF}}\right)\\
&+ \mathbf{K}_{p(f^2)}\left(\left(\mathrm{vec}\left(\boldsymbol{\Psi}_{\mathbf{FF}}\right)\mathrm{vec}(\boldsymbol{\Psi}_{\mathbf{FF}})^{\mathrm{T}}\right)\otimes\boldsymbol{\Theta}_{\mathbf{FF}}\right)\mathbf{K}_{(f^2)p}\big]\mathbf{A}_9^{\mathrm{T}}\\
&+ \left(\boldsymbol{\Theta}_{\mathbf{FF}}\otimes\boldsymbol{\Theta}_{\mathbf{SS}}\right) + \mathbf{K}_{pq}\left(\boldsymbol{\Theta}_{\mathbf{SF}}\otimes(\boldsymbol{\Theta}_{\mathbf{SF}})^{\mathrm{T}}\right)\\
&+ \mathbf{A}_5\boldsymbol{\Theta}_{\mathbf{SF}}\mathbf{A}_4^{\mathrm{T}} + \mathbf{A}_9\Delta_{(pf^2)\times p}\left[\mathbf{K}_{p(pf^2)}\mathrm{vec}\left(\mathbf{K}_{fp}\left(\boldsymbol{\Theta}_{\mathbf{FF}}\otimes\boldsymbol{\Psi}_{\mathbf{FF}}\right)\right)\right]\mathbf{A}_4^{\mathrm{T}}\\
&+ \mathbf{A}_4(\boldsymbol{\Theta}_{\mathbf{SF}})^{\mathrm{T}}\mathbf{A}_5^{\mathrm{T}} + \mathbf{A}_9\Delta_{(pf^2)\times q}\left[\mathbf{K}_{q(pf^2)}\mathrm{vec}\left(\mathbf{K}_{fq}\left(\boldsymbol{\Theta}_{\mathbf{SF}}\otimes\boldsymbol{\Psi}_{\mathbf{FF}}\right)\right)\right]\mathbf{A}_5^{\mathrm{T}}\\
&+ \mathbf{A}_7\mathbf{K}_{fq}\left(\boldsymbol{\Theta}_{\mathbf{SF}}\otimes\boldsymbol{\Psi}_{\mathbf{FF}}\right)\mathbf{A}_6^{\mathrm{T}} + \mathbf{A}_8\left(\boldsymbol{\Theta}_{\mathbf{FF}}\otimes\boldsymbol{\Psi}_{\mathbf{SF}}\right)\mathbf{A}_6^{\mathrm{T}}\\
&+ \mathbf{A}_6\mathbf{K}_{pf}\left(\boldsymbol{\Psi}_{\mathbf{FF}}\otimes(\boldsymbol{\Theta}_{\mathbf{SF}})^{\mathrm{T}}\right)\mathbf{A}_7^{\mathrm{T}} + \mathbf{A}_8\mathbf{K}_{ps}\left(\boldsymbol{\Psi}_{\mathbf{SF}}\otimes(\boldsymbol{\Theta}_{\mathbf{SF}})^{\mathrm{T}}\right)\mathbf{A}_7^{\mathrm{T}}\\
&+ \mathbf{A}_6\left(\boldsymbol{\Theta}_{\mathbf{FF}}\otimes(\boldsymbol{\Psi}_{\mathbf{SF}})^{\mathrm{T}}\right)\mathbf{A}_8^{\mathrm{T}} + \mathbf{A}_7\mathbf{K}_{fq}\left(\boldsymbol{\Theta}_{\mathbf{SF}}\otimes(\boldsymbol{\Psi}_{\mathbf{SF}})^{\mathrm{T}}\right)\mathbf{A}_8^{\mathrm{T}}\\
&+ \mathbf{A}_4\Delta_{p\times(pf^2)}\left[\mathbf{K}_{(pf^2)p}\left(\mathrm{vec}\left(\boldsymbol{\Theta}_{\mathbf{FF}}\right)\otimes\mathrm{vec}\left(\boldsymbol{\Psi}_{\mathbf{FF}}\right)\right)\right]\mathbf{A}_9^{\mathrm{T}}\\
&+ \mathbf{A}_5\Delta_{q\times(pf^2)}\left[\mathbf{K}_{(pf^2)q}\left(\mathrm{vec}\left((\boldsymbol{\Theta}_{\mathbf{SF}})^{\mathrm{T}}\right)\otimes\mathrm{vec}\left(\boldsymbol{\Psi}_{\mathbf{FF}}\right)\right)\right]\mathbf{A}_9^{\mathrm{T}}\big]\mathbf{W}_4^{\mathrm{T}}.\end{aligned}$$

References

Algina, J., & Moulder, B. C. (2001). A note on estimating the Jöreskog-Yang model for latent variable interaction using LISREL 8.3. *Structural Equation Modeling: A Multidisciplinary Journal, 8*, 40–52. doi:10.1207/S15328007SEM0801_3.

Arminger, G., & Muthén, B. O. (1998). A Bayesian approach to nonlinear latent variable models using the Gibbs sampler and the Metropolis-Hastings algorithm. *Psychometrika, 63*, 271–300. doi:10.1007/BF02294856.

Baron, R. M., & Kenny, D. A. (1986). The moderator–mediator variable distinction in social psychological research: Conceptual, strategic, and statistical considerations. *Journal of Personality and Social Psychology, 51*, 1173–1182. doi:10.1037/0022-3514.51.6.1173.

Bollen, K. A., & Noble, M. D. (2011). Structural equation models and the quantification of behavior. *Proceedings of the National Academy of Sciences, 108*, 15639–15646. doi:10.1073/pnas.1010661108.

Busemeyer, J. R., & Jones, L. E. (1983). Analysis of multiplicative combination rules when the causal variables are measured with error. *Psychological Bulletin, 93*, 549–562. doi:10.1037/0033-2909.93.3.549.

Chen, S.-P., & Cheng, C.-P. (2014). Model specification for latent interactive and quadratic effects in matrix form. *Structural Equation Modeling: A Multidisciplinary Journal, 21*, 94–101. doi:10.1080/10705511.2014.859509.

Coenders, G., Batista-Foguet, J. M., & Saris, W. E. (2008). Simple, efficient and distribution-free approach to interaction effects in complex structural equation models. *Quality & Quantity, 42*, 369–396. doi:10.1007/s11135-006-9050-6.

Cole, M. S., Walter, F., & Bruch, H. (2008). Affective mechanisms linking dysfunctional behavior to performance in work teams: A moderated mediation study. *Journal of Applied Psychology, 93*, 945–958. doi:10.1037/0021-9010.93.5.945.

Edwards, J. R., & Lambert, L. S. (2007). Methods for integrating moderation and mediation: A general analytical framework using moderated path analysis. *Psychological Methods, 12*, 1–22. doi:10.1037/1082-989X.12.1.1.

Fairchild, A. J., & MacKinnon, D. P. (2009). A general model for testing mediation and moderation effects. *Prevention Science, 10*, 87–99. doi:10.1007/s11121-008-0109-6.

Ghazal, G. A., & Neudecker, H. (2000). On second-order and fourth-order moments of jointly distributed random matrices: A survey. *Linear Algebra and its Applications, 321*, 61–93. doi:10.1016/S0024-3795(00)00181-6.

Hayes, A. F. (2013). *Introduction to mediation, moderation, and conditional process analysis*. New York, NY: Guilford Press.

Jaccard, J., & Wan, C. K. (1995). Measurement error in the analysis of interaction effects between continuous predictors using multiple regression: Multiple indicator and structural equation approaches. *Psychological Bulletin, 117*, 348–357. doi:10.1037/0033-2909.117.2.348.

James, L. R., & Brett, J. M. (1984). Mediators, moderators, and tests for mediation. *Journal of Applied Psychology, 69*, 307–321. doi:10.1037/0021-9010.69.2.307.

Jöreskog, K. G., & Yang, F. (1996). Nonlinear structural equation models: The Kenny-Judd model with interaction effects. In G. A. Marcoulides & R. E. Schumacker (Eds.), *Advanced structural equation modeling: Issues and techniques* (pp. 57–88). Mahwah, NJ: Lawrence Erlbaum.

Kelava, A., & Brandt, H. (2009). Estimation of nonlinear latent structural equation models using the extended unconstrained approach. *Review of Psychology, 16*(2), 123–131.

Kenny, D. A., & Judd, C. M. (1984). Estimating the nonlinear and interactive effects of latent variables. *Psychological Bulletin, 96*, 201–210. doi:10.1037/0033-2909.96.1.201.

Klein, A. G., & Muthén, B. O. (2007). Quasi-maximum likelihood estimation of structural equation models with multiple interaction and quadratic effects. *Multivariate Behavioral Research, 42*, 647–673. doi:10.1080/00273170701710205.

Klein, A., & Moosbrugger, H. (2000). Maximum likelihood estimation of latent interaction effects with the LMS method. *Psychometrika, 65*, 457–474. doi:10.1007/BF02296338.

Lee, S.-Y., Song, X.-Y., & Tang, N.-S. (2007). Bayesian methods for analyzing structural equation models with covariates, interaction, and quadratic latent variables. *Structural Equation Modeling: A Multidisciplinary Journal, 14*, 404–434. doi:10.1080/10705510701301511.

Lee, S.-Y., & Zhu, H.-T. (2002). Maximum likelihood estimation of nonlinear structural equation models. *Psychometrika, 67*, 189–210. doi:10.1007/BF02294842.

Luszczynska, A., Cao, D. S., Mallach, N., Pietron, K., Mazurkiewicz, M., & Schwarzer, R. (2010). Intentions, planning, and self-efficacy predict physical activity in Chinese and polish adolescents: Two moderated mediation analyses. *International Journal of Clinical and Health Psychology, 10*(2), 265–278.

Magnus, J. R., & Neudecker, H. (1979). The commutation matrix: Some properties and applications. *The Annals of Statistics, 7*, 237–466. doi:10.1214/aos/1176344621.

Magnus, J. R., & Neudecker, H. (1980). The elimination matrix: Some lemmas and applications. *SIAM Journal on Algebraic Discrete Methods, 1*, 422–449. doi:10.1137/0601049.

Magnus, J. R., & Neudecker, H. (1988). *Matrix differential calculus with applications in statistics and econometrics*. New York, NY: John Wiley & Sons.

Marsh, H. W., Wen, Z., & Hau, K.-T. (2004). Structural equation models of latent interactions: Evaluation of alternative estimation strategies and indicator construction. *Psychological Methods, 9*, 275–300. doi:10.1037/1082-989X.9.3.275.

Marsh, H. W., Wen, Z., & Hau, K.-T. (2006). Structural equation models of latent interaction and quadratic effects. In G. R. Hancock & R. O. Mueller (Eds.), *Structural equation modeling: A second course* (pp. 225–265). Greenwich, CT: Information Age Publishing.

Moosbrugger, H., Schermelleh-Engel, K., Kelava, A., & Klein, A. G. (2009). Testing multiple nonlinear effects in structural equation modeling: A comparison of alternative estimation approaches. In T. Teo & M. S. Khine (Eds.), *Structural equation modelling in educational research: Concepts and applications* (pp. 103–136). Rotterdam, NL: Sense Publishers.

Muthén, B. (1984). A general structural equation model with dichotomous, ordered categorical, and continuous latent variable indicators. *Psychometrika, 49*, 115–132. doi:10.1007/BF02294210.

Pollack, J. M., Vanepps, E. M., & Hayes, A. F. (2012). The moderating role of social ties on entrepreneurs' depressed affect and withdrawal intentions in response to economic stress. *Journal of Organizational Behavior, 33*, 789–810. doi:10.1002/job.1794.

Preacher, K. J., Rucker, D. D., & Hayes, A. F. (2007). Addressing moderated mediation hypotheses: Theory, methods, and prescriptions. *Multivariate Behavioral Research, 42*, 185–227. doi:10.1080/00273170701341316.

Seber, G. A. F. (2007). *A matrix handbook for statisticians*. New York, NY: John Wiley & Sons.

Slater, M. D., Hayes, A. F., & Ford, V. L. (2007). Examining the moderating and mediating roles of news exposure and attention on adolescent judgments of alcohol-related risks. *Communication Research, 34*, 355–381. doi:10.1177/0093650207302783.

Tracy, D. S., & Sultan, S. A. (1993). Higher order moments of multivariate normal distribution using matrix derivatives. *Stochastic Analysis and Applications, 11*, 337–348. doi:10.1080/07362999308809320.

Wall, M. M. (2009). Maximum likelihood and Bayesian estimation for nonlinear structural equation models. In R. E. Millsap & A. Maydeu-Olivares (Eds.), *The SAGE handbook of quantitative methods in psychology* (pp. 540–567). London, England: Sage.

Wall, M. M., & Amemiya, Y. (2001). Generalized appended product indicator procedure for nonlinear structural equation analysis. *Journal of Educational and Behavioral Statistics, 26*, 1–29. doi:10.3102/10769986026001001.

Yang-Wallentin, F., & Jöreskog, K. G. (2001). Robust standard errors and chi-squares for interaction models. In G. A. Marcoulides & R. E. Schumacker (Eds.), *New developments and techniques in structural equation modeling* (pp. 159–171). Mahwah, NJ: Erlbaum.

Chapter 18
Mastery Classification of Diagnostic Classification Models

Yuehmei Chien, Ning Yan, and Chingwei D. Shin

Abstract The purpose of diagnostic classification models (DCMs) is to determine mastery or non-mastery of a set of attributes or skills. There are two statistics directly obtained from DCMs that can be used for mastery classification—the posterior marginal probabilities for attributes and the posterior probability for attribute profile.

When using the posterior marginal probabilities for mastery classification, a threshold of a probability is required to determine the mastery or non-mastery status for each attribute. It is not uncommon that a 0.5 threshold is adopted in real assessment for binary classification. However, 0.5 might not be the best choice in some cases. Therefore, a simulation-based threshold approach is proposed to evaluate several possible thresholds and even determine the optimal threshold. In addition to non-mastery and mastery, another category called the indifference region, for those probabilities around 0.5, seems justifiable. However, use of the indifference region category should be used with caution because there may not be any response vector falling in the indifference region based on the item parameters of the test.

Another statistic used for mastery classification is the posterior probability for attribute profile, which is more straightforward than the posterior marginal probability. However, it also has an issue—multiple-maximum—when a test is not well designed. The practitioners and the stakeholders of testing programs should be aware of the existence of the two potential issues when the DCMs are used for the mastery classification purpose.

Y. Chien (✉) • C.D. Shin
Pearson, 2510 N Dodge Street, Iowa City, IA 52245, USA
e-mail: yuehmei.chien@pearson.com; david.shin@pearson.com

N. Yan
59-3-406 Southwest Residential Village, Tianjin, China
e-mail: ning.now@gmail.com

L.A. van der Ark et al. (eds.), *Quantitative Psychology Research*, Springer Proceedings in Mathematics & Statistics 140, DOI 10.1007/978-3-319-19977-1_18

18.1 Introduction

The diagnostic classification models (DCM) are latent variable models for cognitive diagnosis, which assumes the latent classes (i.e., mastery or non-mastery of particular skills/attributes/knowledge components) can be represented by binary latent variables. Recently, DCM has drawn much attention of the practitioners because of its promising use in aligning teaching, learning, and assessment. DCMs aim to determine mastery or non-mastery of a set of attributes or skills, or to provide timely diagnostic feedback by knowing students' weaknesses and strengths to guide teaching and learning. In particular, the use of DCM in formative assessments in classroom has been increasing quickly.

The use of DCM is twofold regarding what can be obtained from the model and provided to individual students: the strength and weakness profiles based on estimated attribute mastery probabilities for each attribute, and the classification of mastery or non-mastery based on estimated profile probabilities. For example, a set of estimated attribute mastery probabilities for three skills—0.92, 0.41, and 0.22—indicates the student is strong on Skill 1, but may require some additional learning or practice on the other two skills, especially for Skill 3.

For the mastery classification, there are two statistics obtained from DCM that can be used to determine the mastery or non-mastery status for each attribute. The first statistic is *the posterior probability for attribute profile*. Using DCM, the posterior probabilities for all possible attribute profiles are obtainable and the attribute profile can be the profile with the maximum posterior probability. This estimation method is the maximum likelihood estimation (MLE) or maximum a posteriori (MAP) if a prior applied multiplies the likelihood function. For ease of reference, the method to obtain the mastery classification is referred to as the MLE profile estimation.

Another way to obtain the mastery classification is based on different statistics obtained from DCM, that is *the posterior marginal probabilities for attributes*. To obtain the classification results, a threshold or a cut-off of a probability must be predefined and then used to determine the mastery or non-mastery status. It is not uncommon that a 0.5 threshold is adopted in real assessment. Using 0.5 as a threshold, the previous example has classification [1, 0, 0], where 1 indicates mastery and 0 indicates non-mastery. Similarly, for ease of reference, this method to obtain the mastery classification is referred to as the threshold approach.

In this paper, the focus is on estimation of mastery classification. For classification using the posterior marginal probabilities for attributes, two issues were addressed. First, for binary classification, a simulation-based approach is suggested to evaluate the different thresholds. Second, for the indifference region, in addition to binary classification, evidence demonstrates that examining the values of posterior marginal probabilities for different response patterns or total scores is rational and necessary because there may not have any probability falling in the indifference region. For classification using the posterior probability for attribute profile, the issue of the multiple maximums on the likelihood in the MLE profile estimation is addressed. Prior to mentioning those focused aspects, DCMs are briefly introduced. Some discussions are also provided at the end of this paper.

18.2 Models

In the literature, there are many cognitive diagnostic models including the rule space model (Tatsuoka 1983), the Bayesian inference network (Mislevy et al. 1999), and the fusion model (Hartz 2002; Hartz et al. 2002), the deterministic inputs, noisy "and" gate (DINA) model (Doignon and Falmagne 1999; Haertel 1989; Junker and Sijtsma 2001), the Deterministic Input, Noisy "Or" Gate (DINO) model (Templin and Henson 2006), the generalized deterministic inputs, noisy "and" gate (G-DINA) model (de la Torre 2011), the log-linear CDM (Henson et al. 2009), and the general diagnostic model (GDM; von Davier 2005). (See more detailed information for various DCMs from Rupp et al. 2010.)

Among those models, DINA and DINO are popular models for educational assessment and for psychological tests, respectively, due to their simplicity. DINA is a noncompensatory model, which assumes the deficiency on one attribute cannot be compensated by the mastery of other attributes. DINA models the probability of a correct response as a function of a slipping parameter for the mastery latent class and as guessing for the non-mastery latent class. On the contrary, the DINO model is a compensatory model, which assumes the deficiency in one attribute can be compensated by the mastery of other attributes.

18.3 The Threshold Approach

To obtain the mastery classification from DCM, the most used approach is the threshold approach (e.g., Hartz 2002; Jang 2005). In practice, the classification of mastery or non-mastery of each attribute is determined by applying cut-offs on the posterior marginal probabilities for attributes. When a binary classification is desired, a convention/intuitive threshold 0.5 is commonly used as the threshold to obtain the mastery ($>= 0.5$) and non-mastery states (<0.5) for each attributes (e.g., DeCarlo 2011). A threshold of 0.5 is statistically sound and a possible optimal threshold in many cases when the classification is binary. However, depending on the Q-matrix structure and the item quality (i.e., the discrimination power), 0.5 might not be the best choice in some cases. Therefore, using a simulation to examine the distribution of the posterior marginal probabilities for attributes and then evaluating several possible thresholds is important for the binary classification.

The simulation-based approach first applies a set of cut-offs, for example, from 0.5 to 0.6 by 0.01. Then the best cut-off for each attribute that results in the largest attribute classification accuracy for each attribute can be obtained. It is possible that different attributes have different cut-offs.

Table 18.1 The classification accuracy using 0.5 vs. the optimal set of cut-offs

	Cut-off = 0.5 for all attributes	Cut-offs = 0.5, 0.51, 0.56, 0.59, 0.6, 0.6
Profile	41.4 %	43.7 %
Attributes	79.4 %, 81.3 %, 84.8 %, 86.4 %, 83.5 %, 85 %	79.4 %, 81.4 %, 85.5 %, 87.1 %, 84.8 %, 87.6 %

Table 18.1 is an example showing the difference of using the convention threshold and using the best cut-offs obtained from the simulation, which is 0.5, 0.51, 0.56, 0.59, 0.6, and 0.6, respectively. The overall profile classification accuracy increased from 41.4 to 43.7 % and the attribute mastery classification accuracy also slightly increased for the attributes 2 to 6.

Note that the largest classification accuracy obtained in the simulation, given a specific cut-off for an attribute, is not population invariant, which means the optimal cut-off obtained might be varied for different populations that are composed of different proportions of student in each of the profiles. Therefore, it is important that the population of simulees can be drawn from an empirical population that represents the real population closely.

A common alternative method to classify students, instead of using binary classification with large uncertainty around the cut-off, is to allow an indifference region aside from the mastery and non-mastery. An indifference region found in the literature is defined between 0.4 and 0.6 (e.g., Hartz 2002; Jang 2005). However, we suggest that the indifference region is defined carefully. Figure 18.1 shows a histogram of the posterior marginal probabilities for an attribute for 2700 students under different test lengths, where n in figure indicates the test length. The original data set contains 8 items measuring one attribute (as shown as $n = 8$ in the figure). The slip parameters are between 0.06 and 0.12 and the guessing parameters are between 0.20 and 0.25 for those 8 items. Because the test length is 8, the possible total scores are 0, 1, 2, 3, 4, 5, 6, 7, or 8. Three hundred students' responses are generated for each of the nine different total scores. To evaluate with shorter test lengths, the posterior marginal probabilities are re-estimated with only the first n items, where $n = 3$ to 7. In total, six different test lengths were evaluated and the results were represented in Fig. 18.1.

For test length = 8, only 21 students fall into the indifference region as defined between 0.4 and 0.6. Note that, in the data set of test length = 8, there are 300 students with a total score 4 and another 300 students with a total score 5, which are the tests with larger measurement error if classification decisions are made. Also, note only test lengths 5 or 8 have some students falling in the indifference region, while other four test lengths have none. Defining an indifference region on the posterior marginal probabilities of attributes and using it to classify students might not obtain the desired results. To further examine the posterior marginal probability for the total scores of 4 and 5, a scatter plot is created, as shown in Fig. 18.2; the total score = 4 all have very low probability values that are obviously classified

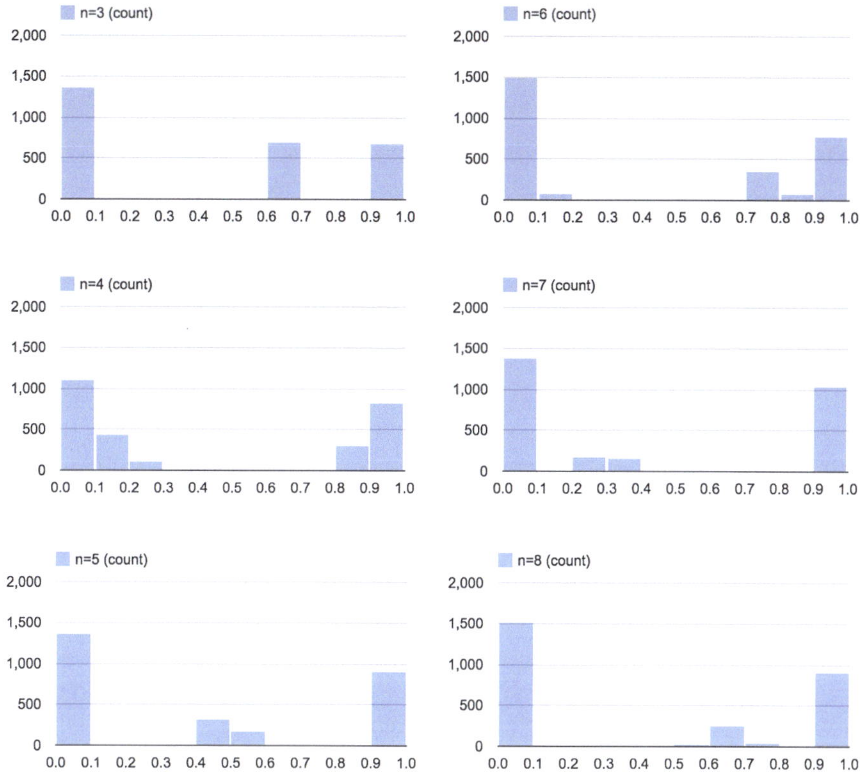

Fig. 18.1 A histogram of the posterior marginal probabilities for an attribute for 2700 students under different test lengths

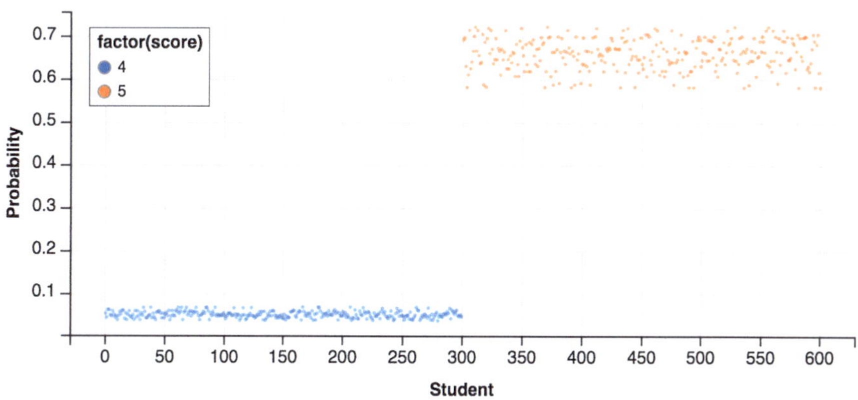

Fig. 18.2 A scatter plot of the posterior marginal probability for the total scores of 4 and 5

as non-mastery, while the total score = 5 have probability values around 0.57 to 0.73 that may be classified as indifference region. This example shows setting up an indifference region might not be straightforward and examining the posterior marginal probability given different responses patterns and different total scores are critical. Indeed, more research is necessary in this area.

18.4 Multiple Maxima (Ties in Posterior Probability)

18.4.1 The Paradox in the Fraction Subtraction Data

The well-known fraction-subtraction (FS) data set was collected by Dr. Kikumi Tatsuoka in 1984. Curtis Tatsuoka released the data in 2002 and made it publicly available at http://onlinelibrary.wiley.com/journal/10.1111/(ISSN)1467-9876/homepage/fractionsdata.txt. The FS data set contains responses to twenty fraction subtraction test items from 536 middle school students. This test measures eight fine-grained attributes in the domain of fraction subtraction, which includes—(1) convert a whole number to a fraction; (2) separate a whole number from a fraction; (3) simplify before subtracting; (4) find a common denominator; (5) borrow from whole number part; (6) column borrow to subtract the second numerator from the first; (7) subtract numerators; (8) and reduce answers to simplest form. The Q-matrix, which specifies which attributes are measured by each item, is listed in Table 18.2. With eight attributes, the maximum number of latent classes is two hundreds and fifty six, without considering whether some combinations are unlikely such as mastery of "borrow from whole number part" without mastery of "subtract numerators".

Figure 18.3 shows the likelihood of those 256 latent classes for a student with a total score of 4. It clearly shows there are four latent classes with exactly the same posterior probability. Figure 18.4 demonstrates a more extreme example with a total score of zero, where there are sixty-four latent classes having exactly the same posterior probability. The first latent class and the last latent class among those sixty four are "00000000" and "10111101", respectively. As mentioned previously, DINA is a conjunctive model that requires all skills measured are mastered to be able to answer an item correctly besides guessing. Therefore, for an incorrect response, depending on the number of attributes measured, DINA may not be able to statistically provide useful information about the state of mastery or non-mastery. In the FS data, items 6, 8, and 9 are simple items, which only measure one attribute, Attribute 7, Attribute 7, and Attribute 2, respectively. The rest of items are complex items measuring more than one attribute. For the all-zero responses in the FS data set, only items 6, 8, and 9 can provide information about the high chance of being non-mastery for attributes 2 and 7; therefore, the mastery status is non-mastery for attributes 2 and 7 while half-half chance for the rest of six attributes.

Table 18.2 The Q-matrix of the FS data

Item\ Attribute	1	2	3	4	5	6	7	8
1	0	0	0	1	0	1	1	0
2	0	0	0	1	0	0	1	0
3	0	0	0	1	0	0	1	0
4	0	1	1	0	1	0	1	0
5	0	1	0	1	0	0	1	1
6	0	0	0	0	0	0	1	0
7	1	1	0	0	0	0	1	0
8	0	0	0	0	0	0	1	0
9	0	1	0	0	0	0	0	0
10	0	1	0	0	1	0	1	1
11	0	1	0	0	1	0	1	0
12	0	0	0	0	0	0	1	1
13	0	1	0	1	1	0	1	0
14	0	1	0	0	0	0	1	0
15	1	0	0	0	0	0	1	0
16	0	1	0	0	0	0	1	0
17	0	1	0	0	1	0	1	0
18	0	1	0	0	1	1	1	0
19	1	1	1	0	1	0	1	0
20	0	1	1	0	1	0	1	0

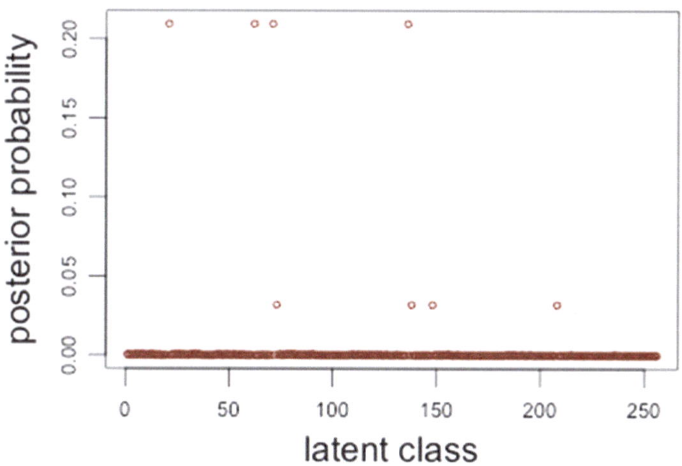

Fig. 18.3 A response vector with a total score of four

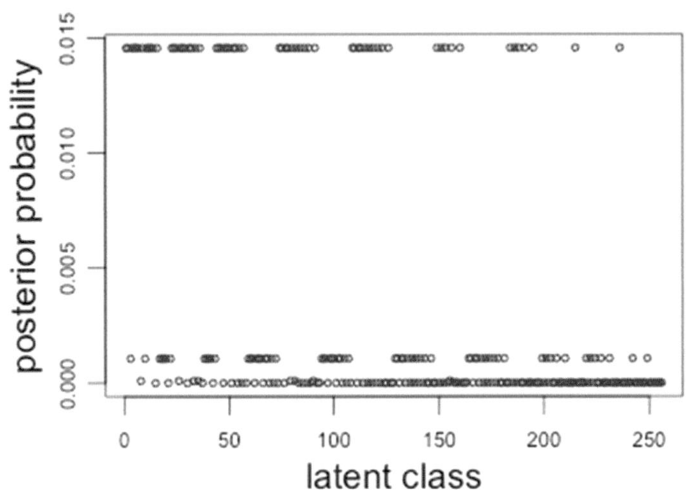

Fig. 18.4 A response vector with a total score of zero

18.4.2 Q-score (The Ideal Response)

In item response theory, the possible local maximum on likelihood of a continuum latent ability scale is a well-known issue of using the MLE. That means the estimated parameter is not universally best but only in some cases. In other words, the solution found on likelihood is not a real solution. Similarly in DCM, there is a profile estimation issue called multiple-maximum caused by using MLE. That is, given the observed responses on a test, there may be multiple latent classes with exactly the same highest probability. This multiple maxima issue has not been explicitly described in the literature, but is mentioned as a parameter-identification problem (e.g., Zhang 2014). Because of the existence of multiple maximum, the profile estimate using DCMs is not always identifiable for some diagnostic tests when the *Q*-matrix or the test is not well designed.

Depending on the structure of the Q-matrix, two different mastery profiles over a set of latent classes could be equivalent; these two mastery profiles generate exactly the same probability distribution of item response patterns, so that they cannot be distinguished on the basis of item response data. To identify this equivalence relationship from the Q-matrix, a simple method is proposed. First, a Q-score is defined as the most likely observed score on the item for a respondent with the given latent class; i.e., Q-score, is the true score for the items given the latent classes. Then, by examining whether there are any two latent classes with the same Q-score, the possible existence of a multiple-maximum can be known.

Table 18.3 A Q-matrix of three attributes for four items

Item\Attribute	1	2	3
1	1	1	0
2	1	0	1
3	0	1	1
4	1	1	1

Table 18.4 A Q-score using the condensation rule of the DINA model

	1	2	3	4
000	0	0	0	0
100	0	0	0	0
010	0	0	0	0
001	0	0	0	0
110	1	0	0	0
101	0	1	0	0
011	0	0	1	0
111	1	1	1	1

Table 18.5 A Q-score using the condensation rule of the DINO model

	1	2	3	4
000	0	0	0	0
100	1	1	0	1
010	1	0	1	1
001	0	1	1	1
110	1	1	1	1
101	1	1	1	1
011	1	1	1	1
111	1	1	1	1

The following is a simple example with four items and three attributes (see Table 18.3) to demonstrate the use of the Q-score for finding the possible existence of the multiple-maxima in the mastery profile estimates. Table 18.4 lists the Q-score under the conjunctive assumption of the DINA model. The first four latent classes, or the mastery profiles, all generate exactly the same Q-scores. In other words, a respondent who has an observed total score of zero is equally likely to belong to any of the first four latent classes.

The Q-score rule can be applied to any DCM that has one Q-matrix with a clearly defined condensation rule to specify the relationship between the correct response of each item and the attributes measured by the item. Table 18.5 lists the Q-score of the same four-item test, but using the condensation rule of the DINO model. The last four latent classes, or the mastery profiles, all generate exactly the same Q-scores under the condensation rule of the DINO model. Therefore, a respondent who has answered the four items correctly is equally likely to belong to any of the last four latent classes.

18.5 Discussion and Future Research

It is statistically sound that the attribute is classified into "mastery" if $p > 0.5$, and "non-mastery" otherwise, where p is the posterior marginal probability of mastery for the attribute. However, because of the complexity of the model used and the structure of Q-matrix, it is suggested that the different threshold values should be used to examine the possible effect on classification. If a sample of population can be obtained and represents the population well, a simulation approach can be used to find a set of optimal thresholds for attributes. To emphasize the importance of this issue, Fig. 18.5 shows the posterior marginal probabilities for those eight attributes, where many posterior marginal probabilities are surround 0.5, and the convention threshold .5 definitely is not a good choice. One might argue that the FS data is not perfect; and yes, the test design regarding whether a complex Q-matrix was employed by the FS test is flawed and therefore, it seriously suffered from uncertainty of the classification and from the multiple-maximum. Therefore, it is even more important to examine the distribution of the posterior marginal probability before a cut-off (for non-mastery and mastery) or two cut-offs (for non-mastery, indifference, and mastery) are applied for classification.

Another importance of this paper is to explicitly call the practitioners' attention to the multiple-maximum issue. The multiple latent classes might cause a misleading mastery classification for either using the posterior probability for attribute profile or using the posterior marginal probability for attributes. As shown by DeCarlo (2011), the attribute probability for a zero score could be as high as 0.985 for a zero score of the FS data using the DINA model. To avoid this multiple-maximum, simple structure items (solely measuring one attribute) should be added to the test (as suggested by DeCarlo 2011) to make a complete Q-matrix (Chiu et al. 2009) during test construction.

However, DCMs might be used to fit existing items by tagging them with associated attributes (e.g., von Davier 2005). Thus, adding simple structure items into the existing test become cumbersome. Furthermore, with the emergence of cognitive diagnostic computerized adaptive testing (CD-CAT; e.g., Cheng 2009), the interim profile estimates must be calculated based on the items administered so far, and the effect of the multiple-maximum on the CD-CAT is worthy of further research.

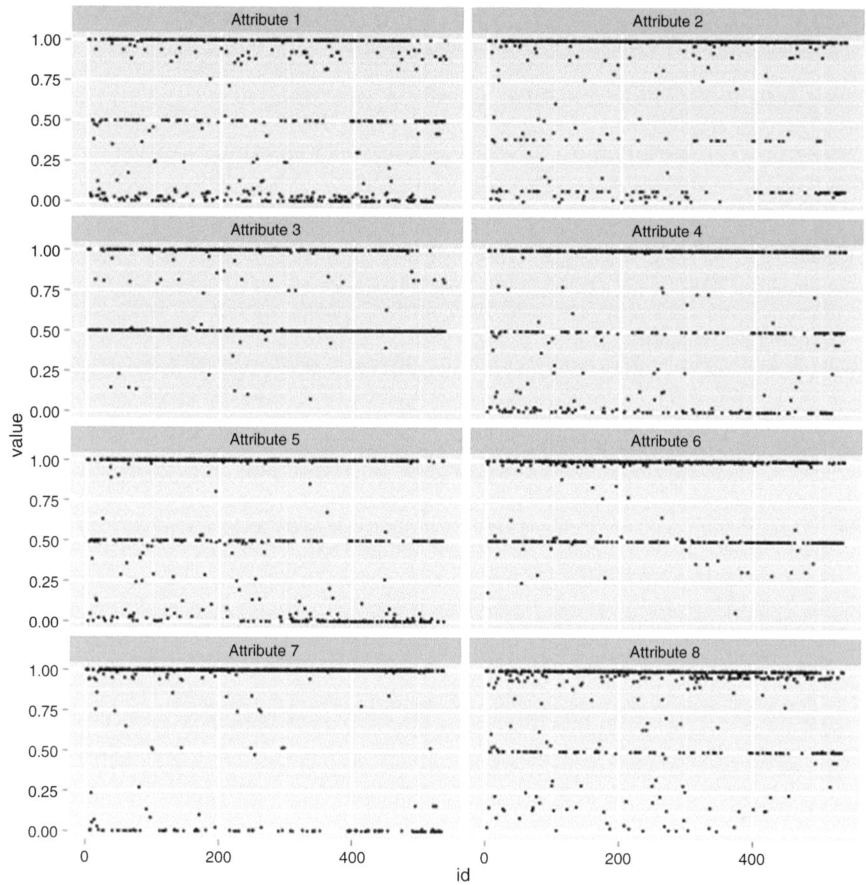

Fig. 18.5 The posterior marginal probabilities for those eight attributes of the FS data

References

Cheng, Y. (2009). When cognitive diagnosis meets computerized adaptive testing: CDCAT. *Psychometrika, 74*, 619–632.

Chiu, C.-Y., Douglas, J., & Li, X. (2009). Cluster analysis for cognitive diagnosis: Theory and applications. *Psychometrika, 74*, 633–665.

de la Torre, J. (2011). The generalized DINA model framework. *Psychometrika, 76*, 179–199.

DeCarlo, L. T. (2011). On the analysis of fraction subtraction data: The DINA model, classification, latent class sizes, and the Q-matrix. *Applied Psychological Measurement, 35*, 8–26.

Doignon, J. P., & Falmagne, J. C. (1999). *Knowledge spaces*. New York, NY: Springer.

Haertel, E. H. (1989). Using restricted latent class models to map the skill structure of achievement items. *Journal of Educational Measurement, 26*, 333–352.

Hartz, S. M. (2002). *A Bayesian framework for the unified model for assessing cognitive abilities: Blending theory with practicality*. Unpublished doctoral dissertation, University of Illinois at Urbana-Champaign, Champaign, IL.

Hartz, S., Roussos, L., & Stout, W. (2002). *Skills diagnosis: Theory and practice* [User manual for Arpeggio software]. Princeton, NJ: Educational Testing Service.

Henson, R., Templin, J., & Willse, J. (2009). Defining a family of cognitive diagnosis models using log-linear models with latent variables. *Psychometrika, 74*, 191–210.

Jang, E. (2005). *A validity narrative: Effects of reading skills diagnosis on teaching and learning in the context of NG TOEFL*. Doctoral dissertation, University of Illinois at Urbana-Champaign.

Junker, B. W., & Sijtsma, K. (2001). Cognitive assessment models with few assumptions, and connections with nonparametric item response theory. *Applied Psychological Measurement, 25*, 258–272.

Mislevy, R. J., Almond, R. G., Yan, D., & Steinberg, L. S. (1999). Bayes nets in educational assessment: Where do the numbers come from? In K. B. Laskey & H. Prade (Eds.), *Proceedings of the fifteenth conference on uncertainty in artificial intelligence* (pp. 437–446). San Mateo, CA: Morgan Kaufmann.

Rupp, A. A., Templin, J., & Henson, R. A. (2010). *Diagnostic measurement: Theory, methods, and practice*. New York, NY: Guilford.

Tatsuoka, K. K. (1983). Rule space: An approach for dealing with misconceptions based on item response theory. *Journal of Educational Measurement, 20*, 345–354.

Templin, J. L., & Henson, R. (2006). Measurement of psychological disorders using cognitive diagnosis models. *Psychological Methods, 11*, 287–305.

von Davier, M. (2005). *A general diagnostic model applied to language testing data*, ETS Research Report RR-05-16. Princeton, NJ: Educational Testing Service. Retrieved from http://www.ets.org/Media/Research/pdf/RR-05-16.pdf

Zhang, S. S. (2014). *Statistical inference and experimental design for Q-matrix based cognitive diagnosis models*. Doctoral dissertation, Columbia University.

Chapter 19
Exploring Joint Maximum Likelihood Estimation for Cognitive Diagnosis Models

Chia-Yi Chiu, Hans-Friedrich Köhn, Yi Zheng, and Robert Henson

Abstract Current methods for fitting cognitive diagnosis models (CDMs) to educational data typically rely on expectation maximization (EM) or Markov chain Monte Carlo (MCMC) for estimating the item parameters and examinees' proficiency class memberships. However, for advanced, more complex CDMs like the reduced reparameterized unified model (Reduced RUM) and the (saturated) loglinear cognitive diagnosis model (LCDM), EM and Markov chain Monte Carlo (MCMC) have the reputation of often consuming excessive CPU times. Joint maximum likelihood estimation (JMLE) is proposed as an alternative to EM and MCMC. The maximization of the joint likelihood is typically accomplished in a few iterations, thereby drastically reducing the CPU times usually needed for fitting advanced CDMs like the Reduced RUM or the (saturated) LCDM. As another attractive feature, the JMLE algorithm presented here resolves the traditional issue of JMLE estimators—their lack of statistical consistency—by using an external, statistically consistent estimator to obtain initial estimates of examinees' class memberships as starting values. It can be proven that under this condition the JMLE item parameter estimators are also statistically consistent. The computational performance of the proposed JMLE algorithm is evaluated in two comprehensive simulation studies.

Keywords Cognitive diagnosis • Joint maximum likelihood estimation • Non-parametric classification • Consistency

---

C.-Y. Chiu (✉)
Rutgers, The State University of New Jersey, New Brunswick, NJ, USA
e-mail: chia-yi.chiu@gse.rutgers.edu

H.-F. Köhn
University of Illinois at Urbana-Champaign, Champaign, IL, USA
e-mail: hkoehn@cyrus.psych.illinois.edu

Y. Zheng
Arizona State University, Tempe, AZ, USA
e-mail: Yi.Isabel.Zheng@asu.edu

R. Henson
University of North Carolina, Greensboro, NC, USA
e-mail: rahenson@uncg.edu

L.A. van der Ark et al. (eds.), *Quantitative Psychology Research*, Springer Proceedings in Mathematics & Statistics 140, DOI 10.1007/978-3-319-19977-1_19

19.1 Introduction

Cognitive diagnosis in educational assessment (DiBello et al. 2007; Haberman and von Davier 2007; Leighton and Gierl 2007; Rupp et al. 2010) perceives an examinee's ability in a domain as a composite of binary (latent) cognitive skills called attributes, each of which an examinee may or may not have mastered. Distinct patterns of attributes define classes of intellectual proficiency. Modeling educational testing data within a cognitive diagnosis perspective seeks to (a) assign examinees to proficiency classes (i.e., estimate their individual attribute patterns from the observed item responses); (b) estimate the item parameters (that allow to assess the probability of a correct response). Current methods for estimating examinees' proficiency class memberships and the item parameters either use the expectation maximization (EM) algorithm or MCMC techniques. However, when attempting to model educational test performance with more advanced and complex CDMs like the reduced reparameterized unified model (Reduced RUM; Hartz 2002; Hartz and Roussos 2008) and the (saturated) loglinear cognitive diagnosis model (LCDM; Henson et al. 2009; Rupp et al. 2010; Templin and Bradshaw 2014), EM and MCMC often consume excessive amounts of CPU time, which limits their usefulness in research and practice.

Hence, in this article, an alternative estimation method for CDMs is proposed that uses joint maximum likelihood estimation (JMLE) of the item parameters and examinees' attribute patterns. The maximization of the joint likelihood is typically accomplished in a few iterations, thereby drastically reducing the CPU times needed for fitting advanced CDMs like the Reduced RUM or the (saturated) LCDM. As another highly attractive feature, the proposed JMLE algorithm resolves the traditional issue of JMLE parameter estimators: their lack of statistical consistency (Baker and Kim 2004; Neyman and Scott 1948). (For this reason, JMLE has been mostly avoided in psychometrics despite the mathematical convenience of simple likelihood functions.) The JMLE algorithm presented here uses an external, statistically consistent estimator to obtain initial estimates of examinees' proficiency class memberships as starting values. Chiu et al. (2013) proved that under this condition the JMLE item parameter estimators are also statistically consistent.

The subsequent section briefly reviews key features of CDMs and the nonparametric classification (NPC) method that is used to obtain statistically consistent estimators of examinees' attribute patterns. The rationale and layout of the JMLE algorithm are described in the third section. Section four reports the results of several simulation studies that compare the performance of the JMLE method with that of the EM algorithm and MCMC under finite data conditions. The paper concludes with a discussion of the findings and directions for future research.

19.2 Definitions and Technical Concepts

19.2.1 Cognitive Diagnosis Models

CDMs model the functional relation between attribute mastery and the probability of a correct item response. CDMs differ in how mastery and nonmastery of the attributes are believed to affect an examinee's performance on a test item (e.g., compensatory models versus non-compensatory models; conjunctive models versus disjunctive models; for a detailed discussion, see Henson et al. 2009).

Suppose that K latent binary attributes constitute a certain ability domain; there are then 2^K distinct attribute patterns composed of these K attributes representing $2^K = M$ distinct classes of intellectual proficiency. (Note that an attribute pattern of a proficiency class can consist of all zeroes, because it is possible for an examinee not to have mastered any attributes at all.) Let the K-dimensional vector, $\boldsymbol{\alpha}_m = (\alpha_{m1}, \alpha_{m2}, \ldots, \alpha_{mK})'$, denote the binary attribute pattern of proficiency class $\mathscr{C}_m$, $m = 1, 2, \ldots, M$, where the *kth* entry indicates whether the respective attribute has been mastered. Y_{ij} is the observed response of examinee i, $i = 1, 2, \ldots, N$, to binary item j, $j = 1, 2, \ldots, J$. The attribute pattern of examinee $i \in \mathscr{C}_m$, $\boldsymbol{\alpha}_{i \in \mathscr{C}_m}$, is written as $\boldsymbol{\alpha}_i = (\alpha_{i1}, \alpha_{i2}, \ldots, \alpha_{iK})'$.

Consider a test of J items for assessing ability in the domain. Each individual item j is associated with a K-dimensional binary vector $\mathbf{q}_j$ called the item-attribute pattern, where $q_{jk} = 1$, $k = 1, 2, \ldots, K$, if a correct answer requires mastery of the *kth* attribute, and 0 otherwise. Note that item-attribute patterns consisting entirely of zeroes are inadmissible, because they correspond to items that require no skills at all. Hence, given K attributes, there are at most $2^K - 1$ distinct item-attribute patterns. The J item-attribute patterns of a test constitute its Q-matrix, $\mathbf{Q} = \{q_{jk}\}_{(J \times K)}$, (Tatsuoka 1985) that summarizes the constraints specifying the associations between items and attributes.

19.2.2 The NPC Method

The NPC method developed by Chiu and Douglas (2013) is used here to obtain initial estimates of examinees' attribute patterns $\boldsymbol{\alpha}$ (i.e., their proficiency class memberships) that are needed as starting input to the JMLE algorithm. The NPC method assigns examinees to proficiency classes by comparing their observed item response patterns with each of the ideal response patterns of the $M = 2^K$ possible proficiency classes. The ideal response is a function of the q-vector of item j, $\mathbf{q}_j$, and the attribute pattern $\boldsymbol{\alpha}_m$ of proficiency class $\mathscr{C}_m$. The ideal response to item j, ξ_{mj}, is the score that would be realized by the examinees in proficiency class $\mathscr{C}_m$ (having attribute pattern $\boldsymbol{\alpha}_m$) if no "slipping" (failing to answer item j correctly despite having the skills required to do so) or "guessing" occurred (answering item j correctly despite lacking the skills required to do so). Let $\boldsymbol{\xi}_m = \left(\xi_{m1}, \xi_{m2}, \ldots, \xi_{mJ}\right)'$

denote the J-dimensional vector of ideal item responses of proficiency class $\mathscr{C}_m$. The NPC estimator $\tilde{\boldsymbol{\alpha}}$ of an examinee's attribute pattern is defined as the attribute pattern associated with that $\boldsymbol{\xi}_m$ minimizing the distance between all $2^K = M$ ideal item response patterns, $\boldsymbol{\xi}_1, \boldsymbol{\xi}_2, \ldots, \boldsymbol{\xi}_M$, and an examinee's observed item response pattern $\mathbf{y}$: $\tilde{\boldsymbol{\alpha}} = \arg\min_m \big(d\big(\mathbf{y}, \boldsymbol{\xi}_m\big)\big)$. (Recall the one-to-one correspondence between $\boldsymbol{\xi}_m$ and $\boldsymbol{\alpha}_m$.) Said differently, the estimator $\tilde{\boldsymbol{\alpha}}$ identifies the attribute pattern underlying that ideal item response pattern, which among all possible $\boldsymbol{\xi}_m$ is closest—or most similar—to the observed item response pattern $\mathbf{y}$. (For brevity, the examinee index i is dropped if the context permits.) For binary data, a natural and frequently used distance measure is the Hamming distance, which simply counts the number of disagreements between two vectors. Here, a weighted version of the Hamming distance is used to accommodate for differential item variability. Let $\bar{p}_j$ be the proportion of examinees responding correctly to item j. Then the weighted Hamming distance is

$$d_{wH}(\mathbf{y}, \boldsymbol{\xi}) = \sum_{j=1}^{J} \frac{1}{\bar{p}_j(1-\bar{p}_j)} \mid y_j - \xi_j \mid$$

Simulation studies by Chiu and Douglas (2013) demonstrated the computational speed and efficiency of the NPC method; it attained classification-correct rates almost as high as those obtainable from parametric maximum likelihood estimation (MLE) methods. But perhaps most important, Wang and Douglas (2015) proved that the NPC estimator of $\boldsymbol{\alpha}$ is statistically consistent if the data conform to the Deterministic Input Noisy Output "AND" gate (DINA) model (Junker and Sijtsma 2001; Macready and Dayton 1977), the Deterministic Input Noisy Output "OR" gate (DINO) model (Templin and Henson 2006), the Reduced RUM, or the Noisy Input Deterministic Output "And" gate (NIDA) model (Junker and Sijtsma 2001; Maris 1999).

19.3 The JMLE Algorithm

Let $\mathbf{Y} = (\mathbf{y}_1, \mathbf{y}_2, \ldots, \mathbf{y}_N)'$ denote the $N \times J$ matrix of observed item responses, where $\mathbf{y}_i = (y_{i1}, y_{i2}, \ldots, y_{iJ})'$ is the observed item response pattern, or vector, for examinee i. (Note that $\mathbf{Y}$ can also be written as a collection of J N-dimensional response vectors of items $1, 2, \ldots, J$, $\mathbf{y}_1, \mathbf{y}_2, \ldots, \mathbf{y}_J$.) For the observed item responses, conditional independence is assumed (given attribute pattern $\boldsymbol{\alpha}$). JMLE seeks to estimate examinees' attribute patterns and the item parameters by maximizing the joint likelihood $L(\boldsymbol{\alpha}, \boldsymbol{\Theta}; \mathbf{Y})$

$$L(\boldsymbol{\alpha}, \boldsymbol{\Theta}; \mathbf{Y}) = \prod_{i=1}^{N} L_i(\boldsymbol{\alpha}_i, \boldsymbol{\Theta}; \mathbf{y}_i) = \prod_{i=1}^{N} \prod_{j=1}^{J} f(y_{ij} | \boldsymbol{\alpha}_i, \boldsymbol{\theta}_j) \tag{19.1}$$

where $\boldsymbol{\Theta} = (\boldsymbol{\theta}_1, \boldsymbol{\theta}_2, \ldots, \boldsymbol{\theta}_J)$ denotes the matrix of item parameters. For the JLME algorithm proposed here, Birnbaum's paradigm (Birnbaum 1968), a two-stage procedure for JMLE (Baker and Kim 2004; Embretson and Reise 2000), was adopted: examinees' attribute patterns and the item parameters are treated as two sets where one is assumed to consist of known parameters whereas those in the second set are to be estimated. The algorithm is initialized with the estimates of examinees' attribute patterns as input, which are obtained by the consistent estimator of the NPC method. The joint likelihood in Eq. (19.1) then reduces to a function of only the item parameters. The estimator of $\boldsymbol{\theta}_j$ is derived by maximizing the logarithm of the item likelihood, $L_j(\boldsymbol{\theta}_j; \mathbf{y}_j, \boldsymbol{\alpha})$

$$\log L_j(\boldsymbol{\theta}_j; \mathbf{y}_j, \boldsymbol{\alpha}) = \sum_{i=1}^{N} \log \left(f(y_{ij} | \boldsymbol{\theta}_j, \boldsymbol{\alpha}_i) \right)$$

(The entire set of item parameters is estimated by maximizing $\log L(\boldsymbol{\Theta}; \mathbf{Y}, \boldsymbol{\alpha})$.) The item parameter estimates obtained from this first stage are then used in the second stage for (re-)estimating the examinees' attribute patterns by maximizing $L(\boldsymbol{\alpha}; \mathbf{Y}, \boldsymbol{\Theta})$, and so on. The steps of the JLME algorithm can be summarized as follows:

(1) Estimate examinees' attribute patterns $\tilde{\boldsymbol{\alpha}}$ using the NPC method; the matrix of estimated attribute patterns is denoted by $\tilde{\boldsymbol{\alpha}}^{(0)}$.
(2) Set the initial values of examinees' attribute patterns to $\tilde{\boldsymbol{\alpha}}^{(0)}$ and obtain the item parameter estimates $\tilde{\boldsymbol{\Theta}}^{(1)}$.
(3) Use $\tilde{\boldsymbol{\Theta}}^{(1)}$ as input and update the examinees' attribute patterns to $\tilde{\boldsymbol{\alpha}}^{(1)}$ by maximizing the (reduced) log-likelihood $\log L\big(\boldsymbol{\alpha}; \mathbf{Y}, \tilde{\boldsymbol{\Theta}}^{(1)}\big)$.
(4) Use $\tilde{\boldsymbol{\alpha}}^{(1)}$ as input for the examinees' attribute patterns and update $\tilde{\boldsymbol{\Theta}}^{(1)}$ to $\tilde{\boldsymbol{\Theta}}^{(2)}$ by maximizing the (reduced) log-likelihood $\log L\big(\boldsymbol{\Theta}; \mathbf{Y}, \tilde{\boldsymbol{\alpha}}^{(1)}\big)$.

Steps 3 and 4 are iterated until the estimates converge.

19.4 Simulation Studies

Two simulation studies were conducted to evaluate the computational performance of the JMLE algorithm on artificial data sets under varying experimental conditions. The item parameter estimates and the classification of examinees obtained from JMLE were compared to those obtained from EM-based MLE and MCMC. In addition, all data sets were also fitted by a procedure called conditional maximum likelihood estimation (CMLE). CMLE uses the examinees' (known) true attribute patterns as input when estimating the item parameters, and the (known) true item parameters as input when estimating examinees' attribute patterns. Thus,

CMLE provided a most conservative benchmark for the results obtained from JMLE, EM, and MCMC.

19.4.1 Study I

The purpose of Study I was to assess the accuracy of the JMLE estimates (i.e., item parameters and examinees' attribute patterns) on a large scale with a substantial number of replicated data sets. However, as mentioned earlier, estimation methods using the EM algorithm or MCMC techniques typically cause a computational bottleneck when employed with advanced, complex CDMs so that numerical experiments with a large number of replicated data sets are computationally infeasible—unless the test data sets conform to the DINA model or the DINO model. Because for these two CDMs closed form solutions for the maximum of the marginal likelihood guarantee fast and computationally efficient implementations of the EM algorithm (e.g., in the `R` package `CDM`; Robitzsch et al. 2014). Thus, it was decided to use artificial data sets generated from the DINA model so that a large number of replicated data sets could be used. The item response function (IRF) of the DINA model is

$$P(Y_{ij} = 1 \mid \boldsymbol{\alpha}_i, s_j, g_j) = (1 - s_j)^{\eta_{ij}} g_j^{(1-\eta_{ij})} \tag{19.2}$$

where the conjunction parameter η_{ij} corresponds to the ideal response

$$\eta_{ij} = \prod_{k=1}^{K} \alpha_{ik}^{q_{jk}}$$

The item parameters $s_j = P(Y_{ij} = 0 \mid \eta_{ij} = 1)$ and $g_j = P(Y_{ij} = 1 \mid \eta_{ij} = 0)$ represent the probabilities of "slipping" and "guessing," respectively.
The JMLE estimators of s_j and g_j, denoted as $\tilde{s}_j$ and $\tilde{g}_j$, are obtained by applying the following closed forms:

$$\tilde{s}_j = \frac{\sum_{i=1}^{N} \tilde{\eta}_{ij}(1 - Y_{ij})}{\sum_{i=1}^{N} \tilde{\eta}_{ij}} \tag{19.3}$$

and

$$\tilde{g}_j = \frac{\sum_{i=1}^{N}(1 - \tilde{\eta}_{ij})Y_{ij}}{\sum_{i=1}^{N}(1 - \tilde{\eta}_{ij})}, \tag{19.4}$$

where $\tilde{\eta}_{ij}$ is the ideal response computed by using $\tilde{\boldsymbol{\alpha}}$, the estimator of $\boldsymbol{\alpha}$ obtained by using the NPC method. It should be noted that the statistical consistency of these estimators has been proven by Chiu et al. (2013).

19.4.1.1 Design

The experimental design included five variables: (a) the number of examinees, $N = 100, 500, 1000$; (b) the number of attributes, $K = 3, 5$; (c) the number of items, $J = 30, 60$; (d) the distribution from which examinees' attribute patterns were sampled: discrete uniform or multivariate normal (for details, consult Chiu et al. 2009, p. 649); and (e) the distribution of the slipping and guessing item parameters, s_j and g_j: continuous uniform $\mathcal{U}(0, 0.1)$, continuous uniform $\mathcal{U}(0, 0.3)$, and continuous uniform $\mathcal{U}(0, 0.5)$.

For $K = 3$ attributes, $2^3 - 1 = 7$ distinct binary item attribute patterns were generated (recall that $\mathbf{q} = (000)$ is not admissible as item attribute pattern). The template Q-matrix for $J = 30$ items was generated by replicating these 7-item attribute patterns four times; the last two items used $\mathbf{q}_{29} = \mathbf{q}_{30} = (111)$. For $K = 5$ attributes, $2^5 - 2 = 30$ distinct binary item-attribute patterns were generated (in omitting the first and the last pattern consisting of all zeroes and all ones, respectively). For $J = 60$ items, the 30-item Q-matrices were simply doubled.

Examinees' manifest item responses were sampled from a Bernoulli distribution, with $P(Y_{ij} = 1)$ determined by the IRF of the DINA model (see Eq. (19.2)). Study I in total consisted of $2 \times 2 \times 3 \times 3 = 36$ cells; for each cell, 100 replicated data sets were generated. For each replicated data set, examinees' attribute patterns and responses were re-sampled, whereas the Q-matrix and the item parameters were held constant.

19.4.1.2 Results

The data were analyzed using the NCP, JMLE, and CMLE implementations available in the (newly released) R package NPCD (Zheng and Chiu 2014) and the EM algorithm for the DINA model in the R package CDM (Robitzsch et al. 2014). The JMLE algorithm terminated upon reaching the convergence criteria. For the estimates of examinee's attribute patterns, the convergence criterion was defined as

$$\frac{1}{N}\sum_{i=1}^{N} I[\tilde{\boldsymbol{\alpha}}_i^{(t)} = \tilde{\boldsymbol{\alpha}}_i^{(t-1)}] \geq 0.99$$

($t-1$ and t refer to consecutive iterations; $I[\cdot]$ denotes the indicator function). For the slipping and guessing parameter estimates, the convergence criterion was defined (in generic θ-notation) as

$$\max_{j=1}^{J}(|\tilde{\theta}_j^{(t)} - \tilde{\theta}_j^{(t-1)}|) \leq 0.001$$

For each replicated data set, the accuracy of the classification of examinees was evaluated by (a) the pattern-wise agreement rate (PAR) defined as the proportion of correctly estimated attribute patterns

$$PAR = \frac{1}{N}\sum_{i=1}^{N} I[\tilde{\boldsymbol{\alpha}}_i = \boldsymbol{\alpha}_i]$$

and (b) the attribute-wise agreement rate (AAR), which is the proportion of correctly estimated attributes defined as

$$AAR = \frac{1}{N \times K}\sum_{i=1}^{N}\sum_{k=1}^{K} I[\tilde{\alpha}_{ik} = \alpha_{ik}]$$

The accuracy of the item parameter estimates, $\tilde{s}_j$ and $\tilde{g}_j$, was assessed by their root mean squared error (RMSE) defined as

$$RMSE(\tilde{s}) = \sqrt{\frac{1}{J}\sum_{j=1}^{J}(\tilde{\theta}_j - \theta_j)^2}$$

In the subsequent tables, the averages of these indices computed for each cell across its 100 replications are reported. The results obtained for the two distributions underlying the examinees' attribute patterns were very similar; hence, only the results for the multivariate normal distribution are presented.

Estimation of Examinees Attribute Patterns The number of examinees had a negligible effect on AAR and PAR of $\boldsymbol{\alpha}$; thus, only the results for $N = 500$ are reported in Table 19.1, as they were obtained by the JMLE method, the EM algorithm, and the CMLE method. For completeness, the AAR and the PAR values realized by the NPC method are also reported. For all four methods, the AAR and PAR scores were close and indicated excellent recovery of examinees' attribute patterns—most of the AAR scores were greater than 0.9. The largest absolute difference between JMLE and the best-performing method was 6.2 % for PAR in experimental condition $K = 5$; $J = 30$; $s_j, g_j \sim \mathcal{U}(0, 0.5)$ Not too surprising, the PAR scores were generally lower than the AAR scores. In summary, the AAR and PAR scores increased when the number of items increased, the number of attributes decreased, or the level of error perturbation decreased.

Table 19.1 Study I: DINA data—AAR and PAR of $\boldsymbol{\alpha}$, $N = 500$

			$J = 30$			$J = 60$		
	K		0.1	0.3	0.5	0.1	0.3	0.5
AAR	3	JMLE	0.999	0.982	0.897	1.000	0.997	0.975
		EM	0.999	0.984	0.907	1.000	0.997	0.977
		NPC	0.998	0.971	0.880	1.000	0.994	0.950
		CMLE	1.000	0.985	0.908	1.000	0.997	0.977
	5	JMLE	0.969	0.904	0.813	0.995	0.967	0.879
		EM	0.978	0.922	0.833	0.996	0.972	0.891
		NPC	0.973	0.903	0.806	0.993	0.957	0.873
		CMLE	0.980	0.931	0.847	0.996	0.971	0.892
PAR	3	JMLE	0.998	0.951	0.751	1.000	0.991	0.930
		EM	0.998	0.955	0.771	1.000	0.991	0.935
		NPC	0.995	0.921	0.708	1.000	0.982	0.863
		CMLE	0.999	0.957	0.775	1.000	0.992	0.936
	5	JMLE	0.887	0.706	0.498	0.976	0.866	0.637
		EM	0.913	0.742	0.541	0.980	0.883	0.663
		NPC	0.891	0.690	0.480	0.967	0.830	0.603
		CMLE	0.921	0.758	0.560	0.981	0.880	0.667

Item Parameter Estimation Table 19.2 presents the RMSE of the estimates of the slipping and guessing parameters obtained by using the JMLE method, the EM algorithm, and the CMLE method. Overall, the RMSE values of the three estimation methods were very close and reasonably small (recall that small RMSE values imply high estimation accuracy). In summary, the RMSE decreased when the number of examinees increased, the number of attributes decreased, or the level of error perturbation decreased.

19.4.2 Study II

The purpose of Study II was to demonstrate the applicability of the JMLE method to an advanced and more complex CDM. The Reduced RUM was chosen because it has been frequently studied in simulations and applications to real world data sets (e.g., Feng et al. 2014; Henson and Douglas 2005; Henson et al. 2008, 2007; Henson and Templin 2007; Kim 2011; Liu et al. 2009; Templin et al. 2008). Researchers have appreciated the flexibility of the Reduced RUM in modeling the probability of correct item responses for different attribute profile patterns. The IRF of the Reduced RUM is

$$P(Y_{ij} = 1 \mid \boldsymbol{\alpha}_i) = \pi_j^* \prod_{k=1}^{K} r_{jk}^{*\; q_{jk}(1-\alpha_{ik})}$$

Table 19.2 Study I: DINA data—RMSE of item parameter estimates from the JMLE, EM, CMLE methods

				$J = 30$			$J = 60$		
	K	N		0.1	0.3	0.5	0.1	0.3	0.5
s	3	100	JMLE	0.042	0.070	0.088	0.042	0.071	0.079
			EM	0.041	0.068	0.085	0.042	0.071	0.079
			CMLE	0.041	0.066	0.081	0.042	0.071	0.079
		500	JMLE	0.016	0.030	0.044	0.020	0.031	0.035
			EM	0.016	0.029	0.035	0.020	0.031	0.035
			CMLE	0.016	0.029	0.034	0.020	0.030	0.035
		1000	JMLE	0.014	0.022	0.029	0.013	0.020	0.026
			EM	0.014	0.021	0.026	0.013	0.020	0.026
			CMLE	0.014	0.021	0.025	0.013	0.020	0.026
	5	100	JMLE	0.061	0.100	0.122	0.052	0.088	0.112
			EM	0.059	0.091	0.107	0.052	0.086	0.107
			CMLE	0.058	0.085	0.093	0.052	0.085	0.104
		500	JMLE	0.024	0.049	0.065	0.021	0.041	0.052
			EM	0.021	0.039	0.046	0.021	0.038	0.047
			CMLE	0.021	0.038	0.042	0.021	0.038	0.046
		1000	JMLE	0.021	0.025	0.051	0.017	0.030	0.033
			EM	0.017	0.022	0.030	0.017	0.027	0.030
			CMLE	0.017	0.021	0.026	0.017	0.027	0.029
g	3	100	JMLE	0.030	0.056	0.065	0.031	0.041	0.058
			EM	0.029	0.054	0.062	0.031	0.041	0.058
			CMLE	0.029	0.051	0.053	0.031	0.041	0.056
		500	JMLE	0.013	0.024	0.041	0.012	0.022	0.027
			EM	0.013	0.022	0.030	0.012	0.022	0.026
			CMLE	0.013	0.021	0.025	0.012	0.022	0.025
		1000	JMLE	0.009	0.016	0.032	0.009	0.016	0.018
			EM	0.009	0.016	0.021	0.009	0.016	0.018
			CMLE	0.009	0.015	0.018	0.009	0.016	0.017
	5	100	JMLE	0.036	0.070	0.097	0.027	0.051	0.062
			EM	0.036	0.069	0.085	0.026	0.047	0.058
			CMLE	0.024	0.042	0.052	0.025	0.043	0.050
		500	JMLE	0.030	0.053	0.063	0.014	0.027	0.039
			EM	0.016	0.027	0.045	0.012	0.021	0.031
			CMLE	0.012	0.017	0.022	0.012	0.019	0.024
		1000	JMLE	0.024	0.035	0.078	0.011	0.021	0.022
			EM	0.011	0.016	0.023	0.009	0.015	0.017
			CMLE	0.009	0.013	0.016	0.009	0.014	0.016

where π_j^* is the probability of answering item j correctly if an examinee masters all the required attributes for item j; the parameter $0 < r_{jk}^* < 1$ denotes a penalty term for lacking the kth attribute required for item j.

The estimators of π_j^* and r_{jk}^* under the proposed JMLE framework are obtained by solving for π_j^* and r_{jk}^* in the following normal equations for all k:

$$\sum_{i=1}^{N} \frac{Y_{ij} - \pi_j^* \prod_{k=1}^{K} r_{jk}^{*(1-\tilde{\alpha}_{ik})q_{jk}}}{1 - \pi_j^* \prod_{k=1}^{K} r_{jk}^{*(1-\tilde{\alpha}_{ik})q_{jk}}} = 0 \tag{19.5}$$

and

$$\sum_{i=1}^{N} \frac{(1-\tilde{\alpha}_{ik})q_{jk}(Y_{ij} - \pi_j^* \prod_{k=1}^{K} r_{jk}^{*(1-\tilde{\alpha}_{ik})q_{jk}})}{1 - \pi_j^* \prod_{k=1}^{K} r_{jk}^{*(1-\tilde{\alpha}_{ik})q_{jk}}} = 0. \tag{19.6}$$

Note that there are no closed forms for Eqs. (19.5) and (19.6). Therefore, like MMLE with the EM algorithm, some optimization package may be needed to solve the equations.

As mentioned earlier, extant estimation methods for the Reduced RUM consume prohibitive amounts of CPU time, which makes the Reduced RUM a prime candidate for exploring the potential computational benefits of JMLE. The performance of JMLE was contrasted with that of the presumably most commonly used estimation method for the Reduced RUM: MCMC (using the implementation in `OpenBUGS`; Lunn et al. 2009). Like in Study I, the results of CMLE served as a benchmark.

19.4.2.1 Design

The design of Study II had to accommodate the CPU time requirements of MCMC. So, only the condition with $K = 3$ attributes and $J = 30$ items (and the corresponding Q-matrix from Study I) were used (which might be representative for many real-world test settings). The item parameters were fixed at $\pi^* = 0.90$ and $r_1^* = r_2^* = r_3^* = 0.60$ for all j. In total, 25 data sets were generated, each with $N = 3000$ examinees, whose attribute patterns were derived from the multivariate normal distribution.

19.4.2.2 Results

For all three estimation methods, the accuracy of the estimates of examinees' attribute patterns (i.e., AAR and PAR), the item parameter estimates and their RMSE, and the CPU times are reported.

Table 19.3 shows the average item parameter estimates obtained from JMLE, MCMC, and CMLE. JMLE and MCMC produced estimates reasonably close to the true item parameters. (As expected, the CMLE item parameter estimates were even closer to the true parameters.)

Table 19.4 reports the RMSE of the item parameter estimates, the AAR and PAR scores for examinees' estimated attribute patterns (i.e., the accuracy of their classification), and the CPU times used by the three estimation methods. The RMSE in Table 19.4 confirm that JMLE and MCMC attained comparable levels of accuracy in estimating the item parameters. The AAR and PAR scores show that JMLE and MCMC also performed comparably in classifying examinees. However, on average, MCMC required roughly 125 times the amount of CPU time that JMLE used.

19.5 Discussion

In this article, JMLE was presented as an alternative MLE method for fitting CDMs to educational testing data—that is, for estimating the item parameters and examinees' proficiency class memberships. JMLE has been barely used in Psychometrics because JMLE-parameter estimates typically lack statistical consistency. The JMLE method proposed here, however, was proven to provide statistically consistent estimators if the estimator used to obtain estimates of examinees' proficiency class memberships for initializing the JMLE algorithm is itself consistent (Chiu et al. 2013). (These authors presented a theorem on the consistency of JMLE item parameter estimators. The proof relied on two lemmas. Consider the slipping parameters as an example. Lemma 1 claims that the sampling distribution of the estimator $\hat{s}_j$—obtained when using examinees' true attribute profiles $\boldsymbol{\alpha}$ as input to JMLE—converges to a normal distribution. When the consistent estimator $\tilde{\boldsymbol{\alpha}}$ of examinees' attribute profiles is used as input to JMLE, then, as Lemma 2 states, the corresponding item parameter estimator $\tilde{s}_j$ converges in probability to $\hat{s}_j$ for all items j. Building on Lemmas 1 and 2, the claim of the Consistency Theorem that $\tilde{s}_j$ converges to s_j in probability is proven. A stronger version of consistency, usually referred to as *uniform consistency*, is formulated in the second Consistency Theorem, the proof of which also depends on Lemmas 1 and 2.) Two simulation studies were conducted to evaluate the computational performance of the proposed JMLE method. Study I consisted of a large-scale evaluation of JMLE. The results demonstrated that the estimates of the item parameters and examinees' attribute patterns obtained from JMLE were almost as accurate as those obtained from EM-based MLE. In Study II, the performance of JMLE was compared to that of MCMC, which is often the method of choice for fitting advanced, more complex CDMs, for example, the Reduced RUM. The findings of Study II showed that the JMLE and MCMC estimates of item parameters and examinees' attribute patterns have comparable accuracy. However, JMLE is about 125 times faster than MCMC.

These results suggest that JMLE might indeed offer a viable computational alternative to MCMC for fitting the Reduced RUM. The Reduced RUM can also

Table 19.3 Study II: Reduced RUM—item parameter estimates obtained from JMLE, MCMC, and CMLE

	JMLE				MCMC				CMLE			
Item	$\hat{\pi}^*$	$\hat{r}_1^*$	$\hat{r}_2^*$	$\hat{r}_3^*$	$\hat{\pi}^*$	$\hat{r}_1^*$	$\hat{r}_2^*$	$\hat{r}_3^*$	$\hat{\pi}^*$	$\hat{r}_1^*$	$\hat{r}_2^*$	$\hat{r}_3^*$
1	0.904	0.563	–	–	0.886	0.556	–	–	0.899	0.601	–	–
2	0.902	–	0.560	–	0.852	–	0.604	–	0.899	–	0.600	–
3	0.906	–	–	0.559	0.903	–	–	0.630	0.902	–	–	0.599
4	0.908	0.566	0.560	–	0.890	0.565	0.556	–	0.901	0.597	0.596	–
5	0.907	0.575	–	0.568	0.895	0.621	–	0.587	0.900	0.603	–	0.604
6	0.905	–	0.566	0.569	0.895	–	0.612	0.590	0.900	–	0.604	0.599
7	0.912	0.574	0.557	0.575	0.895	0.586	0.576	0.594	0.900	0.600	0.597	0.603
8	0.906	0.560	–	–	0.883	0.582	–	–	0.902	0.598	–	–
9	0.903	–	0.562	–	0.881	–	0.588	–	0.899	–	0.603	–
10	0.903	–	–	0.564	0.903	–	–	0.625	0.899	–	–	0.604
11	0.908	0.570	0.566	–	0.890	0.573	0.565	–	0.900	0.606	0.599	–
12	0.904	0.573	–	0.558	0.890	0.615	–	0.585	0.896	0.601	–	0.598
13	0.911	–	0.563	0.567	0.898	–	0.615	0.588	0.902	–	0.602	0.603
14	0.909	0.571	0.582	0.566	0.891	0.589	0.599	0.582	0.899	0.601	0.609	0.597
15	0.907	0.561	–	–	0.885	0.579	–	–	0.902	0.601	–	–
16	0.902	–	0.562	–	0.883	–	0.585	–	0.900	–	0.601	–
17	0.898	–	–	0.570	0.900	–	–	0.628	0.897	–	–	0.604
18	0.906	0.572	0.569	–	0.890	0.571	0.565	–	0.899	0.603	0.604	–
19	0.906	0.564	–	0.562	0.892	0.613	–	0.582	0.898	0.593	–	0.600
20	0.911	–	0.570	0.558	0.899	–	0.611	0.585	0.902	–	0.608	0.593
21	0.906	0.574	0.564	0.573	0.887	0.590	0.579	0.592	0.896	0.600	0.592	0.605
22	0.905	0.559	–	–	0.882	0.580	–	–	0.900	0.598	–	–
23	0.902	–	0.562	–	0.882	–	0.585	–	0.899	–	0.602	–
24	0.905	–	–	0.563	0.905	–	–	0.626	0.902	–	–	0.602
25	0.908	0.561	0.567	–	0.891	0.561	0.567	–	0.899	0.597	0.601	–
26	0.908	0.567	–	0.564	0.894	0.616	–	0.584	0.901	0.602	–	0.595
27	0.907	–	0.554	0.574	0.895	–	0.602	0.594	0.900	–	0.596	0.602
28	0.913	0.576	0.562	0.576	0.895	0.594	0.585	0.587	0.903	0.598	0.603	0.599
29	0.912	0.570	0.568	0.580	0.894	0.589	0.584	0.593	0.901	0.600	0.602	0.606
30	0.912	0.584	0.576	0.560	0.893	0.606	0.593	0.579	0.900	0.614	0.605	0.594

Table 19.4 Study II: Reduced RUM—RMSE, AAR and PAR, and CPU times (in seconds) for JMLE, MCMC, and CMLE

	RMSE				
Method	$\hat{\pi}^*$	$\hat{r}_1^*$	AAR	PAR	CPU time
JMLE	0.013	0.046	0.903	0.753	89.451
MCMC	0.019	0.038	0.904	0.754	11,172.640
CMLE	0.009	0.022	0.911	0.773	52.195

be fitted with the EM algorithm, but with CPU times similar to those of MCMC. However, as a presumably even bigger limitation, the EM algorithm can presently only be used with models that do not involve more than $K = 2$ attributes.

In conclusion, future research should focus on the extension of JMLE as a computational device for fitting a larger array of advanced CDMs—and most important, general CDMs like the GDM (von Davier 2005, 2008), the (saturated) LCDM or the G-DINA model (de la Torre 2011). However, this would first require to prove that the NPC method does also provide a consistent estimator of examinees' attribute pattern $\boldsymbol{\alpha}$ in case of general CDMs.

References

Baker, F. B., & Kim, S.-H. (2004). *Item response theory: Parameter estimation techniques* (2nd ed.). New York: Marcel Dekker.

Birnbaum, A. (1968). Some latent trait models and their use in inferring an examinee's ability. In F. M. Load & M. R. Novick (Eds.), *Statistical theories of mental test scores* (pp. 397–479). Reading, MA: Addison-Wesley.

Chiu, C.-Y., & Douglas, J. A. (2013). A nonparametric approach to cognitive diagnosis by proximity to ideal response profiles. *Journal of Classification, 30*, 225–250.

Chiu, C.-Y., Douglas, J. A., & Li, X. (2009). Cluster analysis for cognitive diagnosis: Theory and applications. *Psychometrika, 74*, 633–665.

Chiu, C.-Y., Zheng, Y., & Henson, R. (2013) Joint maximum likelihood estimation for cognitive diagnostic models in conjunction with proximity to ideal response patterns. *Psychometrika* (Manuscript under revision).

de la Torre, J. (2011). The generalized DINA model framework. *Psychometrika, 76*, 179–199.

DiBello, L. V., Roussos, L. A., & Stout, W. F. (2007). Review of cognitively diagnostic assessment and a summary of psychometric models. In C. R. Rao & S. Sinharay (Eds.), *Handbook of statistics: Psychometrics* (Vol. 26, pp. 979–1030). Amsterdam: Elsevier.

Embretson, S. E., & Reise, S. P. (2000). *Item response theory for psychologists*. Mahwah, NJ: Erlbaum.

Feng, Y., Habing, B. T., & Huebner, A. (2014). Parameter estimation of the reduced RUM using the EM algorithm. *Applied Psychological Measurement, 38*, 137–150.

Haberman, S. J., & von Davier, M. (2007). Some notes on models for cognitively based skill diagnosis. In C. R. Rao & S. Sinharay (Eds.), *Handbook of statistics: Psychometrics* (Vol. 26, pp. 1031–1038). Amsterdam: Elsevier.

Hartz, S. M. (2002). *A Bayesian framework for the unified model for assessing cognitive abilities: Blending theory with practicality*. (Doctoral dissertation) Available from ProQuest Dissertations and Theses database (UMI No. 3044108).

Hartz, S. M., & Roussos, L. A. (2008, October). *The fusion model for skill diagnosis: Blending theory with practicality* (Research report No. RR-08-71). Princeton, NJ: Educational Testing Service.

Henson, R., & Douglas, J. (2005). Test construction for cognitive diagnosis. *Applied Psychological Measurement, 29*, 262–277.

Henson, R., Roussos, L. A., Douglas, J., & He, X. (2008). Cognitive diagnostic attribute-level discrimination indices. *Applied Psychological Measurement, 32*, 275–288.

Henson, R., Templin, J. L., & Douglas, J. (2007). Using efficient model based sum-scores for conducting skills diagnoses. *Journal of Educational Measurement, 44*, 361–376.

Henson, R. A., & Templin, J. (2007, April). *Large-scale language assessment using cognitive diagnosis models*. Paper presented at the Annual Meeting of the National Council on Measurement in Education, Chicago, IL.

Henson, R. A., Templin, J. L., & Willse, J. T. (2009). Defining a family of cognitive diagnosis models using log-linear models with latent variables. *Psychometrika, 74*, 191–210.

Junker, B. W., & Sijtsma, K. (2001). Cognitive assessment models with few assumptions, and connections with nonparametric item response theory. *Applied Psychological Measurement, 25*, 258–272.

Kim, Y.-H. (2011). Diagnosing EAP writing ability using the reduced reparameterized unified model. *Language Testing, 28*, 509–541.

Leighton, J., & Gierl, M. (2007) *Cognitive diagnostic assessment for education: Theory and applications*. Cambridge, UK: Cambridge University Press.

Liu, Y., Douglas, J. A., & Henson, R. A. (2009). Testing person fit in cognitive diagnosis. *Applied Psychological Measurement, 33*, 579–598.

Lunn, D., Spiegelhalter, D., Thomas, A., & Best, N. (2009). The BUGS project: Evolution, critique, and future directions. *Statistics in Medicine, 28*, 3049–3067.

Macready, G. B., & Dayton, C. M. (1977). The use of probabilistic models in the assessment of mastery. *Journal of Educational Statistics, 33*, 379–416.

Maris, E. (1999). Estimating multiple classification latent class models. *Psychometrika, 64*, 187–212.

Neyman, J., & Scott, E. L. (1948). Consistent estimates based on partially consistent observations. *Econometrica, 16*, 1–32.

Robitzsch, A., Kiefer, T., George, A. C., & Uenlue, A. (2014). *CDM: Cognitive diagnosis modeling. R package version 3.1-14*. Retrieved from the Comprehensive R Archive Network [CRAN] website http://CRAN.R-project.org/package=CDM

Rupp, A. A., & Templin, J. L., & Henson, R. A. (2010). *Diagnostic measurement: Theory, methods, and applications*. New York: Guilford.

Tatsuoka, K. K. (1985). A probabilistic model for diagnosing misconception in the pattern classification approach. *Journal of Educational Statistics, 12*, 55–73.

Templin, J., & Bradshaw, L. (2014). Hierarchical diagnostic classification models: A family of models for estimating and testing attribute hierarchies. *Psychometrika, 79*, 317–339.

Templin, J. L., & Henson, R. A. (2006). Measurement of psychological disorders using cognitive diagnosis models. *Psychological Methods, 11*, 287–305.

Templin, J. L., Henson, R. A., Templin, S. E., & Roussos, L. A. (2008). Robustness of hierarchical modeling of skill association in cognitive diagnosis models. *Applied Psychological Measurement, 32*, 559–574.

von Davier, M. (2005, September). *A general diagnostic model applied to language testing data* (Research report No. RR-05-16). Princeton, NJ: Educational Testing Service.

von Davier, M. (2008). A general diagnostic model applied to language testing data. *British Journal of Mathematical and Statistical Psychology, 61*, 287–301.

Wang, S., & Douglas, J. (2015). Consistency of nonparametric classification in cognitive diagnosis. *Psychometrika, 80*, 85–100.

Zheng, Y., & Chiu, C.-Y. (2014). *NPCD: Nonparametric methods for cognitive diagnosis. R package version 1.0-5*. Retrieved from the Comprehensive R Archive Network [CRAN] website http://CRAN.R-project.org/package=NPCD

Chapter 20
Neural Networks for Propensity Score Estimation: Simulation Results and Recommendations

Bryan Keller, Jee-Seon Kim, and Peter M. Steiner

Abstract Neural networks have been noted as promising for propensity score estimation because they algorithmically handle nonlinear relationships and interactions. We examine the performance neural networks as compared with main-effects logistic regression for propensity score estimation via simulation study. When the main-effects logistic propensity score model is correctly specified, the two approaches yield almost identical mean square error. When the logistic propensity score model is misspecified due to the addition of quadratic terms and interactions to the data-generating propensity score model, neural networks perform better in terms of bias and mean square error. We link the performance results to balance on observed covariates and demonstrate that our results underscore the importance of checking balance on higher-order covariate terms.

Keywords Propensity score analysis • Neural networks • Logistic regression • Data mining • Covariate balance

20.1 Introduction

The goal of propensity score analysis is to correct for bias due to confounding in a non-randomized experiment. The *propensity score* is defined as the probability of assignment to the treatment group—we assume a dichotomous treatment variable—given the observed covariates (Rosenbaum and Rubin 1983). The application of propensity score analysis involves (1) estimating the propensity score for each participant and (2) conditioning on the estimated propensity scores to estimate an average treatment effect.

B. Keller (✉)
Teachers College, Columbia University, New York, NY, USA
e-mail: keller4@tc.columbia.edu

J.-S. Kim • P.M. Steiner
University of Wisconsin-Madison, Madison, WI, USA
e-mail: jeeseonkim@wisc.edu; psteiner@wisc.edu

L.A. van der Ark et al. (eds.), *Quantitative Psychology Research*, Springer Proceedings in Mathematics & Statistics 140, DOI 10.1007/978-3-319-19977-1_20

In practice, propensity scores are most often estimated by logistic regression. However, data-mining techniques that algorithmically handle nonlinear relationships have been noted as promising for propensity score estimation because they are able to adapt to complex response surfaces in their naive implementations (Westreich et al. 2010).

To our best knowledge the performance of neural networks for propensity score estimation has been examined via simulation in only one study (Setoguchi et al. 2008). The results of that study suggested that neural networks are a viable alternative to main-effects logistic regression for propensity score estimation, though the authors caution that more work is needed over a broader range of scenarios.

We respond to the need for empirical evaluation by contributing a simulation study which examines the performance of neural networks as compared with main-effects logistic regression for propensity score estimation. Although we describe the simulation study in detail below, two aspects deserve particular attention. First, we use a *weight decay* smoothing parameter to inhibit over-fitting with neural networks. Second, we generate data from a pair of models: the propensity score data-generation model and the outcome data-generation model. The unique aspect here is that we consider the effect of nonlinear terms in the outcome data-generation model. In fact, we hypothesize that it is precisely when there are confounding higher-order terms in *both* the propensity score data-generation model and the outcome data-generation model that neural networks will have the potential to most drastically outperform main-effects logistic regression in terms of bias and mean square error.

The remainder of the paper is organized as follows: in the remainder of this section we describe propensity score analysis and assumptions required to estimate the average treatment effect for a population. In the next section we describe logistic regression and neural networks for propensity score estimation. We then discuss the method used to condition on the propensity score: optimal full matching. We then describe the design and results of the simulation study and conclude with some recommendations.

20.1.1 The Average Treatment Effect

The *potential outcomes* notation is based on the Neyman–Rubin framework for causal inference (Holland 1986). Let $Z_i = 1$ if the ith unit was assigned to the treatment group and $Z_i = 0$ otherwise. Let Y_i^j be a response variable such that each experimental unit has two potential outcomes, Y_i^1 and Y_i^0, depending on assignment Z_i.

Two causal quantities which are most commonly of interest are the overall population average treatment effect τ and the population average treatment effect for the treated τ_T (Imbens 2004; Schafer and Kang 2008; Steiner and Cook 2013):

$$\tau = E(Y_i^1 - Y_i^0) = E(Y_i^1) - E(Y_i^0) \tag{20.1}$$

and

$$\tau_T = E(Y_i^1 - Y_i^0|Z_i = 1) = E(Y_i^1|Z_i = 1) - E(Y_i^0|Z_i = 1). \tag{20.2}$$

We focus on the average treatment effect on the treated, τ_T, in the simulation study because it provides an estimate of the effect of treatment on those who received it, which is often more interesting than the overall treatment effect (Morgan and Winship 2007).

20.1.2 Assumptions for Identifying and Estimating the Average Treatment Effect

The propensity score (PS) is defined as the conditional probability of assignment to the treatment group given the observed covariates $X = (X_1, \ldots, X_p)'$ (Rosenbaum and Rubin 1983). That is,

$$\text{PS}(X) = P(Z = 1|X). \tag{20.3}$$

Propensity scores may be conditioned upon in an application such as matching, stratification, or weighting in order to restore covariate balance across groups to what would have been expected from a randomized experiment. In order for the propensity score to be effective in eliminating bias some assumptions are necessary. First, the treatment assignment must be *strongly ignorable* (Rosenbaum and Rubin 1983; Rubin 1978). Strong ignorability specifies (a) that the potential outcomes are independent of the treatment assignment given the observed covariates and (b) that each experimental unit in the population has a true propensity score that lies strictly between zero and one. That is,

$$Y^1, Y^0 \perp\!\!\!\perp Z|X \tag{20.4}$$

and

$$0 < P(Z = 1|X) < 1. \tag{20.5}$$

In practice, strong ignorability is satisfied when all of the confounding covariates (i.e., those that are associated with both treatment assignment and the outcome) are observed, there is overlap between the propensity score distributions of the treatment and control groups, and the covariates are measured reliably (Steiner et al. 2011). When there is a lack of overlap, τ_T is only identified for the subpopulation of overlapping units.

Second, it is assumed that there is only one version of the treatment and that the value of each potential outcome is independent of the particular assignment pattern in Z. These two assumptions are referred to collectively as the stable unit treatment value assumption (SUTVA; Rubin 1978, 1980).

Finally, since true propensity scores are not known in observational study settings, they must be estimated. Assuming strong ignorability and SUTVA hold, an additional analytic assumption required for consistent estimation is that the propensity score estimates are adequate for bias removal. Although the necessary and sufficient conditions for estimation of adequate propensity scores depend on the method used to condition on them (Waernbaum 2010), one way to ensure adequate propensity score estimates is to correctly specify the relationship between selection Z and covariates X in a parametric model.

In practice, however, the model is never exactly correct. Thus, the focus of the propensity score estimation literature is on the proposal and evaluation of methods that attempt to approximately satisfy this analytic assumption.

20.1.3 Covariate Balance

If strong ignorability and SUTVA are satisfied, the propensity score is a *balancing score* for X (Rosenbaum and Rubin 1983); that is,

$$X \perp\!\!\!\perp Z|\mathrm{PS}(X). \tag{20.6}$$

As a result, the extent to which covariate distributions are balanced across treatment groups may be used as a diagnostic tool for checking the adequacy of the propensity score estimates.

Balance measures based on means are easy to calculate and have been shown to outperform other methods in simulation studies (Ali et al. 2014; Belitser et al. 2011), thus, we measure covariate balance with standardized mean differences. The standardized mean difference for covariate X is

$$d = \frac{\bar{X}_T - \bar{X}_C}{\hat{\sigma}_T} \tag{20.7}$$

where $\bar{X}_T$ and $\bar{X}_C$ are the means of treated and control units, respectively, and $\hat{\sigma}_T$ is the estimated standard deviation for X for treated units. We divide by the standard deviation of the treated cases instead of the pooled standard deviation across groups because the value of $\hat{\sigma}_T$ is not affected by propensity score weighting when estimating τ_T (McCaffrey et al. 2004).

To summarize balance over multiple covariates, both measures can be extended by taking averages. For covariates $X_1, X_2, \ldots, X_p$, the average standardized absolute mean difference (ASAMD) is

$$\mathrm{ASAMD} = \frac{1}{p}\sum_{i=1}^{p} |d_i|. \tag{20.8}$$

20.2 Propensity Score Estimation

Logistic regression is the most frequently used method for estimating propensity scores. For dichotomous outcome Z and covariates $X_1, X_2, \ldots, X_p$, each vectors of length N, the multiple logistic regression model is

$$log\left[\frac{P(Z=1|X_1,X_2,\ldots,X_p)}{1-P(Z=1|X_1,X_2,\ldots,X_p)}\right] = \beta_0 + \beta_1 X_1 + \beta_2 X_2 + \cdots + \beta_p X_p. \quad (20.9)$$

We refer to the model in Eq. (20.9) as the *main-effects logistic regression* because the model contains one first-order term for each covariate.

The single-layer feed-forward neural network consists of an input layer of p observed covariates and a constant term, an output layer containing a single unit for dichotomous classification, and one hidden layer of M unobserved variables and a constant term (see Fig. 20.1).

The hidden units ($\mathbf{H} = H_1, \ldots, H_M$ in Fig. 20.1) are created by forming weighted linear combinations of the input variables and then applying the logistic function $f(t) = 1/(1 + e^{-t})$.

The dichotomous exposure variable Z is then used as the outcome in a logistic regression on the hidden units in the final step. The weights of the network are similar to regression coefficients in a traditional regression analysis in that larger weights indicate sharper changes in the slope of the response surface predicted by the model.

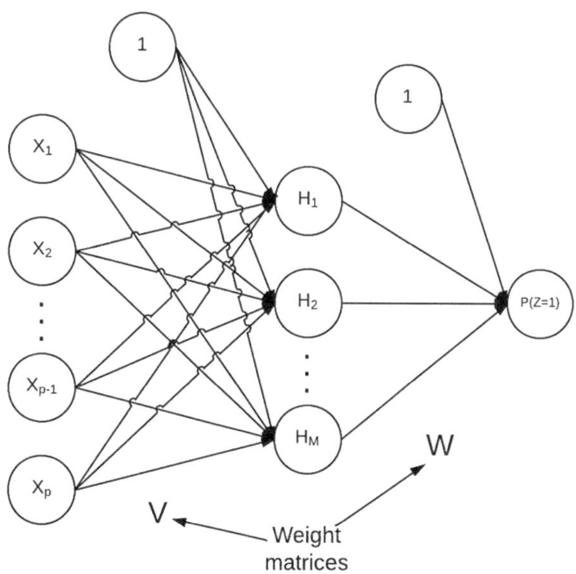

Fig. 20.1 Neural network with p inputs, M hidden nodes, and 1 classification output. The 1s represent intercepts

The model may be expressed as follows:

$$P(Z = 1|\mathbf{X}) = f(f(\mathbf{X}\mathbf{V}^T)\mathbf{W}^T), \tag{20.10}$$

where $\mathbf{X}_{N\times(p+1)}$ is the matrix of predictors, augmented to include a column of ones, and $\mathbf{V}_{M\times(p+1)}$ and $\mathbf{W}_{1\times(M+1)}$ are weight matrices containing the coefficients for the network. The hidden layer $\mathbf{H} = f(\mathbf{X}\mathbf{V}^T)$ is also augmented to include a column of 1s before being multiplied by $\mathbf{W}^T$. These augmentations are analogous to including the constant term for the intercept in the design matrix of a multiple regression and are represented by encircled 1s in Fig. 20.1.

The size of the hidden layer (M) determines how many parameters the model will have and, thus, how flexible the network will be in modeling the relationship between the predictors and the output. Increased flexibility, however, comes at the cost of an increased risk of overfitting random noise in the data. *Weight decay* is a technique which imposes penalties on large weights in the network, as in ridge regression for linear models, thereby smoothing boundaries and preventing over-adaptation to the particularities of the data (Hastie et al. 2009; Ripley 1996).

20.3 Propensity Score Application

The goal of the propensity score application step is to condition the outcome on the estimated propensity score, thereby restoring balance to the observed covariates and allowing for unbiased estimation of the average treatment effect. Matching techniques aim to accomplish this goal by identifying groups of individuals from the treatment and control groups that are as alike as possible according to the logit of the estimated propensity score. This may be done in a one-to-one, one-to-many, or many-to-many fashion; *full matching* refers to the latter case.

The goal of *optimal* full matching is to define S mutually exclusive strata each containing at least one treated and one control unit such that the configuration minimizes a global measure of distance (Rosenbaum 2002). Because optimal matching minimizes an overall measure of distance, it avoids the problem of different results based on matching order which occurs with other matching algorithms such as nearest neighbor matching.

After groups have been formed by optimal full matching, τ_T may be estimated by taking the difference of weighted averages across treatment and comparison groups. For τ_T, weights are calculated as follows:

$$\lambda_i = Z_i + (1 - Z_i)\frac{N_C n_T}{N_T n_C}, \tag{20.11}$$

where N is the overall sample size, N_T and N_C are the number of treated and comparison units, respectively, and n_T and n_C are the number of treated and comparison units in the subclass to which unit i belongs, respectively.

Let T be the set of indexes assigned to the treated condition and let C be the set of indexes assigned to the comparison condition. Then the estimator for τ_T is

$$\hat{\tau}_T = \frac{\sum_{i \in T} \lambda_i Y_i}{\sum_{i \in T} \lambda_i} - \frac{\sum_{i \in C} \lambda_i Y_i}{\sum_{i \in C} \lambda_i}. \tag{20.12}$$

20.4 Simulation Study

The purpose of the simulation is to examine the effect of propensity score estimation method on bias and mean square error of the treatment effect estimates and on balance on observed covariates.

20.4.1 Data Generation and Simulation Design

Twelve covariates were independently generated from a standard normal distribution. A correlation structure was induced via Cholesky decomposition so that $\rho_{ij} = 0.3$ for all $i \neq j$, where ρ is the Pearson product-moment correlation coefficient. The main-effects propensity score model is

$$\text{PS}_1 = (1 + \exp\{-(\beta_0 + \beta_1 X_1 + \beta_2 X_2 + \cdots + \beta_{12} X_{12}\})^{-1}. \tag{20.13}$$

The complex propensity score model,

$$\begin{aligned} \text{PS}_2 = (1 + \exp\{-(&\beta_0 + \beta_1 X_1 + \beta_2 X_2 + \cdots + \beta_{12} X_{12} + \\ &\beta_{13} X_1 X_{12} + \beta_{14} X_2 X_{11} + \beta_{15} X_2 X_{10} + \beta_{16} X_4 X_{12} + \beta_{17} X_1 X_8 + \\ &\beta_{18} X_2^2 + \beta_{19} X_5^2 + \beta_{20} X_8^2 + \beta_{21} X_{11}^2)\})^{-1}, \end{aligned} \tag{20.14}$$

includes five two-way interaction terms and four quadratic terms in addition to the main-effects in PS_1. The regression coefficients for the propensity score models were specified as follows:

$\beta_0, \cdots, \beta_6 =$	−1.00	−0.49,	−0.18,	−0.40,	−0.26,	−0.16,	0.51,
$\beta_7, \cdots, \beta_{12} =$		−0.84,	0.08,	−0.31,	0.73,	−0.04,	−0.34,
$\beta_{13}, \cdots, \beta_{17} =$			−0.42,	−0.26,	0.16,	−0.36,	0.31,
$\beta_{18}, \cdots, \beta_{21} =$				−0.50,	0.46,	0.30,	0.36.

The regression models used to generate the continuous outcome are shown in Eqs. (20.15) and (20.16). The main-effects outcome model is

$$\text{Y}_1 = \alpha_0 + \alpha_1 X_1 + \alpha_2 X_2 + \cdots + \alpha_{12} X_{12} + \gamma Z. \tag{20.15}$$

The complex outcome model is

$$\begin{aligned}Y_2 =& \alpha_0 + \alpha_1 X_1 + \alpha_2 X_2 + \cdots + \alpha_{12} X_{12} + \\ & \alpha_{13} X_1 X_{12} + \alpha_{14} X_1 X_{11} + \alpha_{15} X_2 X_{11} + \alpha_{16} X_3 X_{12} + \alpha_{17} X_4 X_{12} + \\ & \alpha_{18} X_2^2 + \alpha_{19} X_3^2 + \alpha_{20} X_5^2 + \alpha_{21} X_{11}^2 + \alpha_{22} X_{12}^2 + \gamma Z. \end{aligned} \quad (20.16)$$

For each case i, the dichotomous selection variable Z_i was generated by comparing the propensity score to a random uniform draw from [0,1]. If the uniform draw was less than or equal to the propensity score for case i, Z_i was assigned to be 1; otherwise, Z_i was assigned to be 0. In both models, the selection variable was multiplied by the constant treatment effect $\gamma = -0.40$. The regression coefficients for the outcome models were specified as follows.

$$\begin{array}{rrrrrrrr} \alpha_0, \cdots, \alpha_6 = 1.00, & 0.24, & 0.38, & -0.50, & 0.40, & -0.60, & -0.30, \\ \alpha_7, \cdots, \alpha_{12} = & 0.06, & -0.66, & 0.58, & 0.34, & -0.58, & -0.40, \\ \alpha_{13}, \cdots, \alpha_{17} = & & -0.21, & -0.14, & -0.49, & 0.11, & 0.22, \\ \alpha_{18}, \cdots, \alpha_{22} = & & -0.30, & 0.41, & 0.31, & 0.26, & -0.20. \end{array}$$

The two PS models were crossed with the two outcome models to create four data-generation conditions. One thousand data sets were simulated and analyzed for each of the four conditions based on a sample size of 2000. Table 20.1 displays the standardized initial biases and the probability of treatment assignment for each of the four scenarios. The standardized initial bias was calculated as the unadjusted mean difference (treatment minus control) minus the true treatment effect of −0.4 divided by the standard deviation of the treatment group. The probability of assignment to the treatment group is simply the proportion of simulated participants in the population assigned to the treatment group.

Table 20.1 Population standardized initial bias and probability of assignment to treatment for each of four data generation scenarios

Scenario	Standardized initial bias	$P(Z = 1)$
$PS_1 \times Y_1$	0.257	0.332
$PS_1 \times Y_2$	0.214	0.332
$PS_2 \times Y_1$	0.231	0.418
$PS_2 \times Y_2$	0.462	0.418

Note: PS_1 and PS_2 represent the linear and nonlinear PS data-generating models, respectively; Y_1 and Y_2 represent the linear and nonlinear outcome data-generating models, respectively.

20.4.2 Analysis

Logistic regression was run with main effects only for $X_1, \cdots, X_{12}$, as in Eq. (20.9); neural networks were fit with eight hidden nodes and the weight decay tuning parameter set at $\lambda = 0.10$ for the scenarios with linear propensity score model and $\lambda = 0.13$ for the nonlinear propensity score models. For the last two data-generation scenarios (both with PS_2) we also estimated propensity scores with the correctly specified model, displayed in Eq. (20.14), in order to have a baseline for comparison with the other methods.

In practice, with a single data set, an analyst would select optimal tuning parameter values for a data mining method by searching over a grid of many possible choices and settling on the combination which produced the best cross-validated prediction or the best balance. In order to avoid the prohibitive computational cost of running a cross-validated grid search at each iteration, we ran such a grid search on five data sets generated from the linear PS and five data sets generated from the nonlinear PS and used the results to select sensible values. Our approach for selecting the value of weight decay (λ) for the neural networks was motivated by the usual design-based recommendations for propensity score model fitting: we selected the value of λ that was associated with the best covariate balance (though ten-fold cross validation based on prediction yielded similar results).

To assess covariate balance we used a weighted composite of the ASAMD on first-order terms and the ASAMD on second-order terms. These were weighted equally in order to assign the same conceptual importance to the class of first-order terms as the class of second-order terms in determining the resultant balance. For each dataset, as the value of λ increased, the balance improved for a period and then began to decrease. For the linear propensity score model optimal balance was attained at about $\lambda = 0.10$; for the nonlinear propensity score model, optimal balance was attained at about $\lambda = 0.13$. Thus these values were used throughout all 1000 simulation replications.

For each replication and for each propensity score estimation method, cases in the treatment or control group with no counterpart in the opposite group within 0.1 pooled standard deviations of the propensity score logit were considered non-overlapping and discarded from the analysis. After discarding cases, propensity scores were re-estimated on the remaining cases and those values were used going forward. For PS_1, both methods resulted in about 4 % of cases being discarded due to lack of overlap. For PS_2, 1 and 7 % of cases were discarded for main-effects logistic regression and neural networks, respectively.

20.4.3 Results

For the first and second scenarios, the main-effects logistic regression model (see Eq. (20.13); abbreviated MELR in Table 20.2) was the correctly specified model.

Table 20.2 Performance metrics averaged over 1000 replications; optimal full matching was used to estimate the average treatment effect on the treated

Metric	Method	Scenario			
		$PS_1 \times Y_1$	$PS_1 \times Y_2$	$PS_2 \times Y_1$	$PS_2 \times Y_2$
Bias and MSE					
|Bias (%)|	MELR	0.07	0.03	25.14	173.80
	NN	3.58	3.08	12.73	13.90
	LR-20.14	NA	NA	0.85	1.94
Bias	MELR	0.000	0.000	0.101	0.695
	NN	−0.014	−0.012	−0.051	0.056
	LR-20.14	NA	NA	0.003	0.008
SE	MELR	0.002	0.004	0.002	0.003
	NN	0.002	0.004	0.003	0.004
	LR-20.14	NA	NA	0.003	0.004
MSE	MELR	0.006	0.018	0.014	0.495
	NN	0.006	0.016	0.012	0.020
	LR-20.14	NA	NA	0.012	0.018
Covariate balance					
ASAMD on 1st-order terms	MELR	0.042	0.042	0.047	0.048
	NN	0.044	0.044	0.074	0.073
	LR-20.14	NA	NA	0.053	0.055
ASAMD on 2nd-order terms	MELR	0.067	0.067	0.118	0.118
	NN	0.059	0.060	0.069	0.069
	LR-20.14	NA	NA	0.071	0.071

Note: PS_1 and PS_2 represent the simple and complex propensity score data-generating models, respectively; Y_1 and Y_2 represent the simple and complex outcome data-generating models, respectively; MELR: main-effects logistic regression as in Eq. (20.13); NN: neural networks; LR-20.14: logistic regression as in Eq. (20.14); ASAMD: average standardized absolute mean difference across the covariates (see Eq. (20.8)); SE: simulation standard error; and MSE: simulation mean square error

Note that biases associated with MELR were both within two simulation standard errors of zero, indicating they are not significantly different from zero. For the third and fourth scenarios, the data-generating model (see Eq. (20.14); abbreviated LR-20.14 in Table 20.2) was also used to estimate propensity scores. The estimates based on LR-20.14 for the last two scenarios were also within two simulation standard errors from zero. Thus, when the propensity score model was correctly specified, estimates based on optimal full matching were not significantly biased.

Estimates based on neural networks were associated with lower mean square error than main-effects logistic regression for all four scenarios, including the first two scenarios, for which the main-effects logistic model was correctly specified. This finding is not altogether surprising because the feed-forward neural network can be thought of as a generalization of logistic regression. In particular, by setting the coefficients in the matrix $\mathbf{V}$ and vector $\mathbf{v}_0$ all equal to zero, the feed-forward neural network described above is identical to main-effects logistic regression.

When the data-generating propensity score model was complex, estimates based on neural networks were far less biased than those based on main-effects logistic regression. In the last scenario, in which the propensity score and outcome data-generation models both contained second-order terms, estimates based on main-effects logistic regression were biased by 174 % of the magnitude of the treatment effect, while neural networks yielded about 14 % residual bias. Across all four scenarios, propensity scores based on neural networks resulted in less than 14 % bias.

Regarding covariate balance on first-order terms, the balance attained by the main-effects logistic regression was better than that attained by neural networks across the board. On second-order terms, however, the opposite held true, with greater disparities evident when the data-generating propensity score model was complex.

20.4.4 Discussion

The results of the simulation study suggest that if the relationship between covariates and selection involves only first-order terms, it does not make much difference in terms of bias or mean square error whether main-effects logistic regression or neural networks is used to estimate propensity scores. For the first two scenarios, both methods were less than 4 % biased, with nearly identical mean square error.

If the true selection model involves more than just linear terms, misspecification of the logistic propensity score estimation model by way of omitting higher-order terms creates the potential for bias, the magnitude of which depends on the relationship between the covariates and the outcome. If nonlinear terms omitted from the propensity score estimation model are also related to the outcome, as was the case in scenario 4 (note the common terms in Eqs. (20.14) and (20.16)), the bias may be very large because the omitted terms act as confounding variables that have not been accounted for.

Importantly, we found that balance checks on first-order terms did not help in diagnosing this problem. The last column of Table 20.2 reveals that model selection based exclusively on first-order balance would have favored the main-effects logistic model over both neural networks and the correctly specified logistic model.

While these results clearly highlight the importance of checking balance on higher-order terms, they also raise questions. First, in practice, what is the highest-degree covariate transformation on which balance should be assessed? Second, how should balance measures on higher-order terms be weighted when comparing propensity score estimation models or techniques? For example, for an analysis with 10 covariates there are 10, 55, and 220 possible first, second, and third-order terms, respectively whereas, for an analysis with 20 covariates there are 20, 210, and 1540 possible first, second, and third-order terms, respectively. Further research aimed at addressing these questions would be useful.

20.5 Conclusion

Propensity scores are most often estimated by logistic regression in practice because it is familiar, available in most statistical software packages, and easy to implement. The most challenging aspect associated with its use is the need for iterative respecification of the model based on balance checking, which, with many covariates, is tedious at best and untenable, due either to exhaustion of degrees of freedom or exhaustion of the analyst, at worst.

Neural networks are promising for propensity score estimation because they algorithmically deal with nonlinearities in the selection surface, making iterative respecification unnecessary. We found, through simulation, that propensity scores estimated by neural networks resulted in better balance on second-order terms than those estimated by main-effects logistic regression. In practice, the analyst will not know which higher-order terms (if any) are actually predictive of selection. The most useful algorithmic approach for propensity score estimation is one which automatically detects such terms and accounts for them in the propensity score estimates, which is what neural networks did here.

There are some potential challenges with the implementation of neural networks as well. First, while the selection of optimal tuning parameter values related to weight decay and the number of hidden units can be carried out automatically using packages designed to do cross-validation (we used package `caret` Kuhn 2014 in R Core Team 2014), the process is computationally expensive, ranging anywhere from several seconds to several hours of computational time, depending on the size of the problem and the speed of the computer. Second, if the neural network results in poor covariate balance even after selecting optimal tuning parameters, there is no guidance as to how an analyst should alter the model to improve the balance. For this second point, however, neural networks are flexible enough such that, if tuning parameters are carefully selected, this should be a relatively rare occurrence which might suggest a problem with the suitability of the data for propensity score analysis, rather than a problem with the neural network specification. Finally, even with the use of the weight decay smoothing parameter it is possible that with many noisy covariates neural networks may still overfit the data.

Although neural networks performed favorably relative to main-effects logistic regression, further research is needed to determine if neural networks continue to perform well in cases with many weak predictors, when coupled with other approaches for conditioning on the estimated propensity scores, and compared with other data-mining methods.

Finally, while we compared neural networks to main-effects logistic regression because it is the approach most often used in practice, the undiscerning use of the main-effects logistic model for propensity score estimation is not recommended. In practice, an analyst using a logistic regression framework for modeling selection would experiment with various formulations of the model in an iterative process aimed at maximizing covariate balance. While this approach is difficult to mimic in a simulation study, the performance of neural networks could be compared with a custom logistic model created by an experienced analyst in a case study setting.

Acknowledgements This research was supported in part by the Institute of Education Sciences, U.S. Department of Education, through Grant R305D120005. The opinions expressed are those of the authors and do not represent views of the Institute or the U.S. Department of Education.

References

Ali, M. S., Groenwold, R. H. H., Pestman, W. R., Belitser, S. V., Roes, K. C. B., Hoes, A. W., et al. (2014). Propensity score balance measures in pharmacoepidemiology: A simulation study. *Pharmacoepidemiology and Drug Safety, 23*, 802–811.

Belitser, S. V., Martens, E. P., Pestman, W. R., Groenwold, R. H. H., de Boer, A., & Klungel, O. H. (2011). Measuring balance and model selection in propensity score methods. *Pharmacoepidemiology and Drug Safety, 29*, 1115–1129.

Hastie, T., Tibshirani, R., & Friedman, J. (2009). *The elements of statistical learning* (2nd ed.). New York, NY: Springer.

Holland, P. W. (1986). Statistics and causal inference. *Journal of the American Statistical Association, 81*, 945–970.

Imbens, G. W. (2004). Nonparametric estimation of average treatment effects under exogeneity: A review. *The Review of Economics and Statistics, 86*, 4–29.

Kuhn, M. (2014). Caret: Classification and regression training. R package version 6.0-35. http://CRAN.R-project.org/package=caret.

McCaffrey, D. F., Ridgeway, G., & Morral, A. R. (2004). Propensity score estimation with boosted regression for evaluating causal effects in observational studies. *Psychological Methods, 9*, 403–425.

Morgan, S. L., & Winship, C. (2007). *Counterfactuals and causal inference: Methods and principles for social research*. New York, NY: Cambridge University Press.

R Core Team. (2014). *R: A language and environment for statistical computing*. Vienna, Austria: R Foundation for Statistical Computing. http://www.R-project.org/.

Ripley, B. D. (1996). *Pattern recognition and neural networks*. New York, NY: Cambridge University Press.

Rosenbaum, P. R. (2002). *Observational studies* (2nd ed.). New York, NY: Springer.

Rosenbaum, P. R., Rubin, D. B. (1983). The central role of the propensity score in observational studies for causal effects. *Biometrika, 70*, 41–55.

Rubin, D. B. (1978) Bayesian inference for causal effects: The role of randomization. *Annals of Statistics, 6*, 34–58.

Rubin, D. B. (1980). Randomization analysis of experimental data: The Fisher randomization test comment. *Journal of the American Statistical Association, 75*, 591–593.

Schafer, J., & Kang, J. (2008). Average causal effects from nonrandomized studies: A practical guide and simulated example. *Psychological Methods, 13*, 279–313.

Setoguchi, S., Schneeweiss, S., Brookhart, M. A., Glynn, R. J., & Cook, E. F. (2008). Evaluating uses of data mining techniques in propensity score estimation: A simulation study. *Pharmacoepidemiology and Drug Safety, 17*, 546–555.

Steiner, P. M., & Cook, T. D. (2013). Matching and propensity scores. In T. Little (Ed.), *Oxford handbook of quantitative methods*. Oxford: Oxford University Press.

Steiner, P. M., Cook, T. D., & Shadish, W. R. (2011). On the importance of reliable covariate measurement in selection bias adjustments using propensity scores. *Journal of Educational and Behavioral Statistics, 36*, 213–236.

Waernbaum, I. (2010). Propensity score model specification for estimation of average treatment effects. *Journal of Statistical Planning and Inference, 140*, 1948–1956.

Westreich, D., Lessler, J., & Funk, M. J. (2010). Propensity score estimation: Neural networks, support vector machines, decision trees (CART), and meta-classifiers as alternatives to logistic regression. *Journal of Clinical Epidemiology, 63*, 826–833.

Chapter 21
Multilevel Propensity Score Methods for Estimating Causal Effects: A Latent Class Modeling Strategy

Jee-Seon Kim and Peter M. Steiner

Abstract Despite their appeal, randomized experiments cannot always be conducted, for example, due to ethical or practical reasons. In order to remove selection bias and draw causal inferences from observational data, propensity score matching techniques have gained increased popularity during the past three decades. Although propensity score methods have been studied extensively for single-level data, the additional assumptions and necessary modifications for applications with multilevel data are understudied. This is troublesome considering the abundance of nested structures and multilevel data in the social sciences. This study summarizes issues and challenges for causal inference with observational multilevel data in comparison with single-level data, and discusses strategies for multilevel matching methods. We investigate within- and across-cluster matching strategies and emphasize the importance of examining both overlap within clusters and potential heterogeneity in the data before pooling cases across clusters. We introduce a multilevel latent class logit model approach that encompasses the strengths of within- and across-matching techniques. Simulation results support the effectiveness of our method in estimating treatment effects with multilevel data even when selection processes vary across clusters and a lack of overlap exists within clusters.

Keywords Propensity score matching • Multilevel models • Hierarchical linear models • Latent class analysis • Finite mixture models • Causal inference

21.1 Introduction

Causal inference has been an important topic in many disciplines, and randomized experiments (a.k.a. randomized controlled trials) have been used widely for estimating causal effects of treatments or interventions. However, in social science research

---

J.-S. Kim (✉) • P.M. Steiner
University of Wisconsin-Madison, 1025 West Johnson Street, Madison, WI 53706, USA
e-mail: jeeseonkim@wisc.edu; psteiner@wisc.edu

L.A. van der Ark et al. (eds.), *Quantitative Psychology Research*, Springer Proceedings in Mathematics & Statistics 140, DOI 10.1007/978-3-319-19977-1_21

randomization is not always feasible due to practical or ethical reasons. For example, the effect of retaining students in a grade level is difficult to evaluate due to selection bias in natural settings, yet it would be unethical to randomly assign students to retention and promotion groups for the purpose of estimating the effect of retention.

The multilevel or clustered structure of data adds an additional layer of complexity. Importantly, the selection mechanism (e.g., retention policy) may vary considerably across schools. The observations within clusters are usually not independent from each other, and thus the dependency within clusters, variability across clusters, and potentially different treatment effects for different clusters should also be accounted for in data analysis.

When randomized experiments are not attainable, quasi-experiments like regression discontinuity designs, interrupted time series designs, instrumental variables, or non-equivalent control group designs are frequently used as alternative methods (Shadish et al. 2002). In particular, the popularity of propensity score (PS) techniques for matching non-equivalent groups (e.g., PS matching, inverse-propensity weighting, or PS stratification) has increased during the last two decades (see Thoemmes and Kim 2011). While a large body of literature exists with regard to standard PS designs and techniques, corresponding strategies for matching non-equivalent control groups in the context of multilevel data are still underdeveloped.

In comparison with single-level data, the main challenges with multilevel data are that (1) units within clusters are typically not independent, (2) interventions or treatments may be implemented at different levels (e.g., student, classroom, school, or district), and (3) selection processes may simultaneously take place at different levels, differ from cluster to cluster, and/or introduce biases of different directions at different levels. For these reasons, standard matching techniques that ignore the clustering or multisite structure are, in general, not directly applicable. If the multilevel structure is ignored or not correctly reflected in matching treatment and comparison units, we will very likely obtain biased impact estimates of the treatment effect.

Although some methodological publications on PS designs with multilevel data exist (Arpino and Mealli 2011; Hong and Raudenbush 2006; Kelcey 2009; Kim and Seltzer 2007; Steiner et al. 2013; Stuart 2007; Thoemmes and West 2011), many aspects of the methods are not well enough studied in the context of clustered or nested data structures. While most of these studies focus on different methods for estimating the PS (e.g., fixed vs. random effects models), there is less research on different matching strategies within and across clusters, for example the question whether the clusters are comparable enough to be pooled together for an across-cluster matching.

This chapter adds to the limited literature and investigates fundamental issues and challenges in evaluating treatment effects from multilevel observational studies with treatment selection among level-one units. We propose a matching strategy that first identifies with respect to the selection process homogeneous classes of clusters and then matches units across clusters but within the homogeneous classes. Such a matching strategy has the advantage that the overlap of treated and untreated units within classes (but across clusters) is better than the overlap within each single cluster and that it reduces the risk of a grossly misspecified joint PS model. Moreover, creating homogeneous classes with respect to the selection process allows for a direct investigation of heterogeneous treatment effects across classes. In a simulation study we compare the proposed matching strategy to within- and across-cluster matching. The simulation indicates that matching across clusters within homogeneous classes results in better overlap between treatment and control units and in less biased estimates.

21.2 Matching Strategies for Observational Multilevel Data

21.2.1 Within-Cluster and Across-Cluster Matching

For multilevel observational data with selection at the highest level (e.g., district-level selection where districts are the highest level in the data), the issue of matching treated and untreated groups is relatively straightforward compared to selection at a lower level, because the highest-level units are independent (Stuart 2007). In this case, well-developed PS techniques for single-level data can be applied with some modifications. Two common practices are to match highest-level units only (with aggregated lower-level variables) or to match sequentially from the highest level to lower levels.

By contrast, multilevel observational data with selection at level-one entails more complexity as the treated and untreated units are not independent. Two main strategies for matching level-one units exist (Arpino and Mealli 2011; Kim and Seltzer 2007; Steiner et al. 2013; Stuart 2007; Thoemmes and West 2011): (1) within-cluster matching where matches are only formed within clusters and (2) across-cluster matching where treatment and control units are matched across clusters. Both strategies have their advantages and disadvantages. Within-cluster matching does not need any cluster-level covariates and, thus, the identification and estimation of causal effects relies on weaker ignorability assumptions than across-cluster matching which also requires the correct modeling of cluster-level covariates. However, within-cluster matching frequently lacks satisfactory overlap between treatment and control units. For example, consider retaining (vs. promoting) a student as the treatment of interest. Since retention is a very extreme selection process, it is rather hard to find a comparable promoted student for each retained student within each school. However, across schools the overlap between retained and promoted students is typically better than within clusters (due to larger sample size and heterogeneity of selection across clusters). Thus, in choosing between within- and across-cluster matching one faces a bias tradeoff between the lack of overlap within clusters and the correct specification of the PS model across clusters. In the next section, we propose an alternative method to within- and across-cluster matching.

21.2.2 Across-Cluster Matching Within Homogeneous Groups of Clusters

We suggest a PS matching strategy that encompasses the advantages of within- and across-cluster matching and avoids their disadvantages. The idea is to first identify groups of clusters that are homogeneous with respect to the selection model, and then to estimate the PS and treatment effect within each of the homogeneous groups. The clusters' group memberships might be known or unknown. Group membership is known if one has a good knowledge about the selection process in each cluster (e.g., when school administrators assign students according to different but known rules across schools). We refer to the known groups as "manifest classes." If the homogeneous groups are unknown, we refer to them as "latent classes," and the method for classifying units into homogeneous groups follows standard practice using finite mixture models or latent class analysis (Clogg 1995; McLachlan and Peel 2000).

The strategy of matching units across clusters within homogeneous classes has three main advantages. First, for homogeneous classes of clusters it is easier to get the PS model specification approximately right (the need for and the correct modeling of level-two covariates should be less important). Second, overlap within classes should be better than within single clusters. Third, because a different selection process across classes likely results in heterogeneous treatment effects, one can directly investigate treatment effect heterogeneity.

21.3 Estimation of Propensity Scores and Treatment Effects

21.3.1 Within-Cluster and Across-Cluster Matching

Depending on the matching strategy, the estimation procedures for the unknown PS and the treatment effect are slightly different. For within-cluster matching, the PS is estimated for each cluster separately (thus, the cluster-specific PS models only require the correct modeling of level-one covariates, level-two covariates are not needed). The cluster-specific PSs are then used to estimate a PS-adjusted treatment effect for each cluster separately. The PS-adjustment can be implemented as PS matching, PS stratification, or as inverse-propensity weighting (Rosenbaum and Rubin 1983; Schafer and Kang 2008; Steiner and Cook 2013). An average treatment effect for the entire population can be obtained by pooling the cluster-specific estimates. The cluster-specific and overall treatment effects can be consistently estimated if the observed level-one covariates are able to remove the selection bias in each cluster (i.e., the strong ignorability assumption is met; Rosenbaum and Rubin 1983) and if the PS model is correctly specified for each cluster.

For the across-cluster matching strategy, a joint PS model is estimated for all clusters together. The PS model typically involves level-one and level-two covariates and cross-level interactions, but also random or fixed effects for the clusters (Kelcey 2009; Kim and Seltzer 2007; Thoemmes and Kim 2011). In comparison with the cluster-specific models of the within-cluster matching strategy, the correct specification of the joint PS model is more challenging because heterogeneities across clusters need to be considered. Once the PS is estimated, the average treatment effect is estimated via one of the PS-adjustments mentioned above. In order to obtain an appropriate standard error for the treatment effect, the clustered data structure needs to be taken into account (e.g., via random or fixed effects for the clusters). Selection bias is successfully removed only if the confounding variables at both levels (one and two) are reliably measured and the joint PS model is correctly specified.

21.3.2 *Across-Cluster Matching Within Homogeneous Groups of Clusters*

If the clusters' class memberships are unknown, they first need to be estimated from the observed data. Our proposed strategy can be considered as an application of multilevel latent class logit modeling to the selection process and can be presented as

$$logit(\pi_{ijs}) = \alpha_{js} + \beta_{js}X_{ijs} + \gamma_{js}W_{js} + \delta_{js}X_{ijs}W_{js}, \tag{21.1}$$

where π_{ijs} is the propensity of receiving a treatment or intervention for a level-one unit i ($i = 1, \ldots, n_j$) in cluster j ($j = 1, \ldots, M_s$) in latent class s ($s = 1, \ldots, K$), X_{ijs} is a level-one covariate, W_{js} is a level-two covariate, and $X_{ijs}W_{js}$ is the cross-level interaction, respectively. Regression coefficients α_{js}, β_{js}, γ_{js}, and δ_{js} may vary across clusters and latent classes. For simplicity, the equation only consists of two levels and one covariate at each level, but it can be generalized to three or more levels and multiple covariates at each level. The observed treatment status $Z_{ijs} \in 0, 1$ ($0 =$ untreated; $1 =$ treated) is modeled as a Bernoulli distributed random variable with probability $\pi_{ijs} : Z_{ijs} \sim$ Bernoulli (π_{ijs}). Standard latent class models and finite mixture models have been modified to multilevel models, and these multilevel latent class models can be estimated by latent class analysis software such as Latent GOLD, or alternatively various R packages for finite mixture models. We used the R package FlexMix (Grün and Leisch 2008) in this chapter.

When the selection process and the class membership are determined by multiple variables (X, W) as in Eq. (21.1), latent class regression can effectively classify units into several latent classes, such that the coefficients are similar within latent classes but different between latent classes. Note that this latent class approach is different from random coefficient models with random intercepts and random slopes. In random coefficient models, regression coefficients are assumed to be unobserved continuous variables (often assumed to be normally distributed) and the variance–covariance matrix of these coefficients is estimated. In latent class regression, coefficients are parameters that are allowed to be different across classes. Therefore, outcomes of latent class regression include multiple sets of coefficient estimates without any assumptions about relationships or distributions among the estimated values.

The procedure to implement multilevel latent class logit modeling in regard to a selection process is similar to standard latent class analysis when adding a cluster identification variable and defining the logit link function in the model specification. One can fit models with varying numbers of classes and compare model fit using heuristic model comparison criteria such as AIC, BIC, and their variations. If a one-class model fits better than multiple-class models, it is likely that the selection process was comparable across the clusters. If a two-class model substantially improves the model fit, this suggests that at least two distinctive selection processes were used for the treatment assignment. Three and more classes can be considered next. It is important to note that formal statistical tests (e.g., likelihood ratio test) cannot be used to determine the number of classes, as models with different numbers of latent classes ($K \geq 2$) are not nested even though the other model specification is identical.

Once the latent classes are determined or if the classes are known (manifest classes), units can be pooled across clusters but within classes. A separate PS model is then estimated for each manifest or latent class. As with the across-cluster matching strategy, both level-one and level-two covariates as well as cross-level interactions should be modeled. Variations across clusters are modeled by random or fixed effects. However, in contrast to across-cluster matching, the class-specific PS models should be less sensitive to model misspecification because the classes represent homogeneous groups with respect to the cluster's selection models (i.e., the strong ignorability assumption is more likely met for homogeneous groups of clusters than for the entire population of clusters). Matching cases from different clusters within classes is more justifiable than matching across all clusters of the entire data set, as selection processes should be similar among clusters and thus the direction and degree of selection bias would likely be similar within latent classes. Once the class-specific PSs are estimated, the treatment effect is estimated for each class as described for the across-cluster matching strategy. An overall treatment effect can be estimated by pooling the class-specific effects.

In the next section, we conducted a simulation study examining the effectiveness of our multilevel latent class logit model approach for identifying different selection processes and removing selection bias. We compare our approach to within-cluster matching, across-cluster matching, and also across-cluster matching within known classes where it is possible to know which units used which selection processes.

21.4 Simulation

21.4.1 Data Generating Models

We use a model with two level-one (X_1, X_2) and two level-two (W_1, W_2) covariates in the simulation. In order to create three different groups ("classes") of clusters we used different coefficient matrices for the data-generating selection models and outcome models. While the heterogeneity in the outcome models is moderate (i.e., coefficients have the same sign across classes), the classes differ considerably in their selection processes (i.e., coefficients have opposite signs). For the first class, selection is positively determined by the two level-one covariates but negatively determined by the two level-two covariates. In the second class, the two level-one covariates have a negative effect on selection while the two level-two covariates have a positive effect on selection. Thus, the two selection processes are of opposite directions. Finally, the third class is characterized by a selection process that is only very weakly determined by the level-one covariates (here, treatment assignment almost resembles a random assignment procedure). For each of the three classes, Fig. 21.1 shows for a single simulated data set the relation between the first level-one covariate X_1 and the logit of the PS (for each class, the second level-one covariate X_2 has about the same relation to the PS logit as X_1).

According to the data-generating selection model, overlap within clusters, classes, and the entire data differs. Figure 21.2 shows for each of the three classes the distribution of the level-one covariate X_1 by treatment status. The plots clearly indicate that the selection mechanisms are quite different. Table 21.1 shows the average percentage of overlapping cases with respect to the logit of the PS. Overall, the within-cluster overlap between treatment and control cases amounts to 84 % (i.e., 16 % of the cases lack overlap), but across clusters the overlap is 97 %.

Figure 21.3 shows that the outcome models also vary considerably across classes (though the slopes of the level-one covariates are all positive). We also allowed for different treatment effects across classes: 5, 15, and 10 for Classes 1, 2, and 3, respectively. Note that it is realistic for multilevel structures to have very different selection processes but similar data-generating outcome models. While the rationales of teachers, parents, students, and peers for selecting into a treatment might strongly differ from school to school (or district to district), the data-generating outcome model is usually more robust across schools and districts.

In simulating repeated draws from the population of clusters and units, we sampled 30, 18, and 12 clusters from each of the three classes, respectively. A cluster consisted on average of 300 level-one units (sampled from a normal distribution with mean 300 and SD 50). In each iteration of our simulation, we first estimated different PS models, then the mixture selection models in order to determine the latent group membership (assuming it is not known), and, finally, we estimated the treatment effect using different PS techniques.

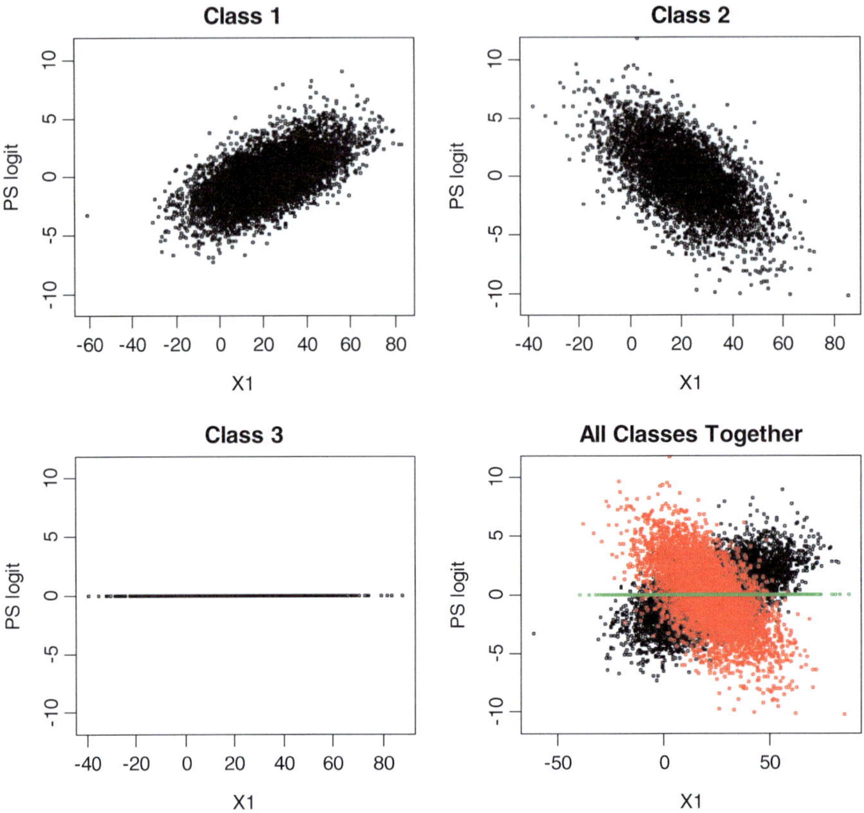

Fig. 21.1 Class-specific selection models with respect to the level-one covariate X_1

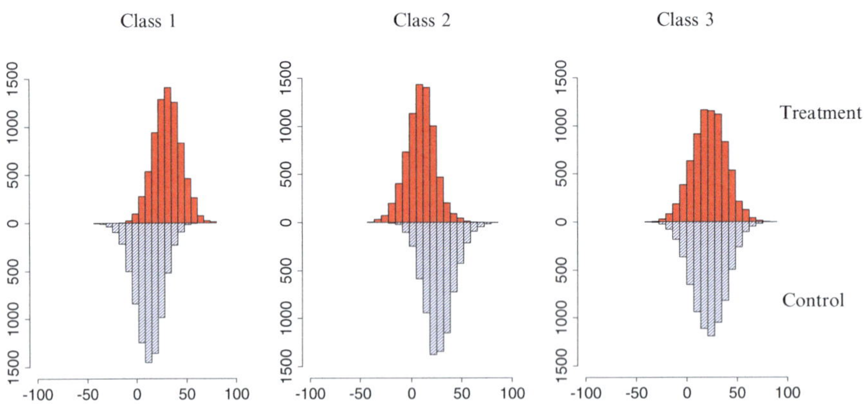

Fig. 21.2 Distribution of level-one covariate X_1 by treatment status and by class

Table 21.1 Overlap within clusters and classes (in percent of the total number of units)

	Class 1	Class 2	Class 3	Overall
Overlap within clusters	85.6	72.9	98.6	84.4
Overlap within classes	97.3	91.3	99.9	97.0

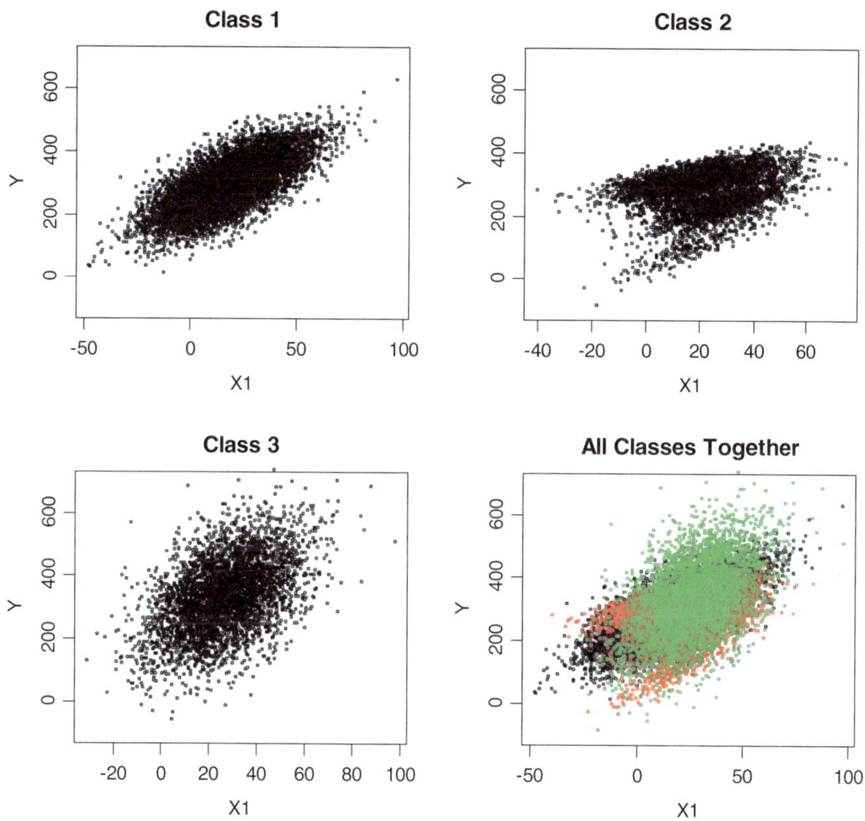

Fig. 21.3 Class-specific outcome models with respect to the level-one covariate X_1

21.4.2 *PS Estimation and Matching via Inverse-Propensity Weighting*

In estimating the unknown PS we used different models, some of them including cluster fixed effects. The models are estimated in different ways: (i) within each cluster separately (for within-cluster matching), (ii) across clusters but within the three known classes (for across-cluster matching within manifest classes), (iii) across clusters but within the three estimated latent classes (for across-cluster matching within latent classes, where class membership is estimated using a multilevel latent class logit model), and (iv) across all clusters without using any grouping information (for a complete across-cluster matching). While the PS models for (i) only include the two level-one covariates as predictors, the models for (ii)–(iv) include in addition cluster-fixed effects (thus the inclusion of level-two covariates was not necessary). Given the heterogeneity of the selection models, it is clear that the PS model for (iv) does not adequately model the different selection procedures across the three classes. We used the estimated PS to derive inverse-propensity weights for the average treatment effect (ATE). We only focus on inverse-propensity weighting because our simulations, as well as other studies, revealed that the choice of a specific PS method does not make a significant difference.

21.4.3 *Estimation of Treatment Effects*

Since we implemented the "matching" as inverse-propensity weighting, we ran a weighted multilevel model with the treatment indicator as sole predictor. Depending on the matching strategy, we either estimated the treatment effect (i) within clusters (in this case it is a simple regression model), (ii) within the three manifest classes, (iii) within the three latent classes, or (iv) across all clusters simultaneously. Thus, analyses (i)–(iii) produced either cluster- or class-specific estimates. In order to obtain overall ATE estimates we computed the weighted average across clusters or classes, respectively (with weights based on level-one units).

21.4.4 *Simulation Results*

The results of our simulation study are shown in Tables 21.2 and 21.3. Table 21.2 shows the estimated class sizes and the percent of misclassified units when we derived the class membership from the estimated mixture model (with respect to the selection process). The estimated class sizes were close to the true class sizes; 0.5, 0.3, and 0.2. Despite the quite different selection processes across classes, overall

Table 21.2 Estimated class sizes (in percent) and misclassification rates

	Class 1	Class 2	Class 3	Overall
Estimated class size[a]	48.5	29.8	21.7	100.0
Misclassification percentage	8.2	8.1	7.2	8.0

[a]Data were generated by sampling 30, 18, and 12 clusters from the three classes. True class sizes vary slightly over replications as level-one units were sampled from a normal distribution with mean 300 and SD 50.x

Table 21.3 Treatment effect estimates by classes and overall

	Class 1	Class 2	Class 3	Overall
True treatment effects	5	15	10	9
Prima facie effect (unadjusted effect)	73.799	−28.893	9.875	30.171
Across-cluster PS	67.363	−32.150	−0.132	22.004
Within-cluster PS	8.333	9.555	10.065	9.051
Within-class PS (manifest classes)	2.578	16.537	10.010	8.263
Within-class PS (latent classes)[a]	4.160	15.645	10.278	8.997

[a]For the estimated classes, the true effects within the latent classes slightly differ from the ones given above

only 8 % of the units were misclassified. Table 21.3 shows the estimated ATEs we obtained from the different matching strategies. The *prima facie effects*; that is, the unadjusted mean differences between treatment and control units, amount to 74, −29, and 10 points for Classes 1, 2, and 3, respectively (in effect sizes: 1.1, 0.3, and 0.1 SD). Given that the corresponding true effects are 5, 15, and 10 points, the selection biases within the first two groups are rather large. According to the data-generating selection model, we have a positive selection bias in the first group but a negative selection bias in the second group. There is essentially no selection bias in group 3 because selection was extremely weak and close to random assignment. Overall, across the three classes, selection bias is still considerably large because the prima facie effect of 30 is much greater than the true effect of 9 points.

If one estimates the ATE based on a PS that has been estimated across all clusters, selection bias is removed but only a small part of it. The across-cluster estimate of 22 points is not even close to the true effect of 9 points. Though the across-cluster PS model includes the level-one covariates and cluster-fixed effects, it fails to provide a reasonable estimate of ATE because the PS model did not allow for the varying slopes across classes. Within-cluster matching overcomes this misspecification issue, but fails to provide accurate estimates for each of the three classes because of the lack of overlap within clusters. However, the overall estimate (averaged across all clusters) is 9.05 and thus very close to the true effect. But this is only a coincidence due to the simulation setup. In general, the overall estimate obtained from within-cluster matching will be biased as well (given a lack of overlap within clusters).

A better performance is achieved by across-cluster matching within known or estimated classes. If the class membership is known, then the class-specific and the overall estimates are rather close to the true treatment effects. However, with the estimated class membership, the estimates are even less biased. The overall effect averaged across the three classes (8.997) is essentially identical to the true effect of 9 points. Thus, with the implementation of the latent class approach, we achieve a less biased result than with the known class variable where the overall estimate amounts to 8.263 points. This is not surprising because, in estimating the class membership from the observed data, clusters that are outlying with respect to their actual class get classified into a class that better represents the outlying clusters' selection process.

21.5 Conclusions

This chapter considers challenges and strategies for estimating treatment effects with observational data, particularly focusing on propensity score matching methods. Although cases can be "borrowed" or "pooled" across clusters in multilevel data, pooling across all clusters simultaneously may be harmful when the data are heterogeneous and, thus, difficult to model correctly. This study showed that imposing common selection and outcome models to heterogeneous data would result in misspecified models and may yield a severely biased average treatment effect (ATE). Instead of pooling cases automatically by fitting a multilevel model to the entire data, we propose to examine first if a common selection process is reasonable for the data.

For example, schools may provide extra mathematics sessions to their students for different reasons, such as enhancing the growth of high achieving students or preventing the failure of low performing students. In this case, the selection process may be positively related to student performance for some schools, while negatively related for others. Selection processes may also be related to other characteristics of students, parents, teachers, and school administrators. If it is possible to know which units used which selection processes, we argue that one should classify units into multiple groups (i.e., manifest classes) according to the selection processes, and conduct PS analysis for each manifest class separately. If the estimated treated effects are very similar despite distinctive selection processes, the result suggests that the different selection mechanisms did not influence the direction or degree of the treatment effects, and ATE appears meaningful. However, it is more likely that treatment effects are different corresponding to distinctive selection processes, and in that case one estimate of ATE would be an oversimplification at best and distortion at worst.

In sum, our matching strategies for estimating treatment effects with observational multilevel data consist of three main elements: (1) check overlap for each of the clusters. If overlap is satisfactory and sample size is sufficient for all clusters, within-cluster matching would be recommended and within-cluster effects can be pooled for ATE. In most cases, however, not all within-cluster effects can be estimated reliably even in large-scale data due to a small portion of clusters without sufficient overlap. In the simulation, 84 % of clusters have overlap but within-cluster matching was far short of removing selection bias. Therefore, across-cluster matching is often necessary in multilevel data. Before pooling the entire data, (2) we suggest to seek if it is possible to know which units used which selection processes and, if so, form manifest classes according to the selection processes. If this information cannot be collected, (3) we recommend the proposed multilevel latent class logit model as the selection model to examine if different selection processes were used in the data. Once units are classified into a small number of either manifest or latent classes, one can estimate propensity scores and treatment effects by pooling cases across clusters but within classes. This chapter demonstrated that identifying homogeneous latent classes can help in avoiding severe model misspecifications and likely reduce selection bias more successfully.

The aim of this chapter is to provide guidelines and suggestions for researchers in choosing an appropriate and effective matching strategy for their multilevel data. Particularly if selection models are heterogeneous across clusters, estimating the treatment effects within homogenous classes allows one to obtain less biased ATE estimates within classes as well as for the entire data. Such a matching strategy also has the advantage that it enables the investigation of heterogeneous treatment effects in the data. In this study we demonstrated how to form homogenous latent classes according to the selection process. Alternatively one could also construct homogeneous classes with respect to other sources of heterogeneity such as the outcome model, or the selection and outcome model together.

Acknowledgements This research was in part supported by the Institute of Education Sciences, U.S. Department of Education, through Grant R305D120005. The opinions expressed are those of the authors and do not represent views of the Institute or the U.S. Department of Education.

References

Arpino, B., & Mealli, F. (2011). The specification of the propensity score in multilevel studies. *Computational Statistics and Data Analysis, 55*, 1770–1780.

Clogg, C. C. (1995). Latent class models. In G. Arminger, C. C. Clogg, & M. E. Sobel (Eds.), *Handbook of statistical modeling for the social and behavioral sciences* (Ch. 6, pp. 311–359). New York: Plenum.

Grün, B., & Leisch, F. (2008). FlexMix version 2: Finite mixtures with concomitant variables and varying and constant parameters. *Journal of Statistical Software, 28*, 1–35.

Hong, G., & Raudenbush, S. W. (2006). Evaluating kindergarten retention policy: A case study of causal inference for multi-level observational data. *Journal of the American Statistical Association, 101*, 901–910.

Kelcey, B. M. (2009). Improving and assessing propensity score based causal inferences in multilevel and nonlinear settings. Dissertation at The University of Michigan. http://deepblue.lib.umich.edu/bitstream/2027.42/63716/1/bkelcey_1.pdf.

Kim, J., & Seltzer, M. (2007). Causal inference in multilevel settings in which selection process vary across schools. Working Paper 708, Center for the Study of Evaluation (CSE), UCLA: Los Angeles.

McLachlan, G. J., & Peel, D. (2000). *Finite mixture models*. New York: Wiley.

Rosenbaum, P. R., & Rubin, D. B. (1983). The central role of the propensity score in observational studies for causal effects. *Biometrika, 70*, 41–55.

Schafer, J. L., & Kang, J. (2008). Average causal effects from non-randomized studies: A practical guide and simulated example. *Psychological Methods, 13*(4), 279–313.

Shadish, W. R., Cook, T. D., & Campbell, D. T. (2002). *Experimental and quasiexperimental designs for generalized causal inference*. Boston, MA: Houghton-Mifflin.

Steiner, P. M., & Cook, D. L. (2013). Matching and propensity scores. In T. D. Little (Ed.), *The Oxford handbook of quantitative methods, volume 1, foundations*. New York, NY: Oxford University Press.

Steiner, P. M., Kim, J.-S., & Thoemmes, F. (2013). Matching strategies for observational multilevel data. In *JSM proceedings* (pp. 5020–5032). Alexandria, VA: American Statistical Association.

Stuart, E. (2007). Estimating causal effects using school-level datasets. *Educational Researcher, 36*, 187–198.

Thoemmes, F., & Kim, E. S. (2011). A systematic review of propensity score methods in the social sciences. *Multivariate Behavioral Research, 46*, 90–118.

Thoemmes, F., & West, S. G. (2011). The use of propensity scores for nonrandomized designs with clustered data. *Multivariate Behavioral Research, 46*, 514–543.

Chapter 22
The Sensitivity Analysis of Two-Level Hierarchical Linear Models to Outliers

Jue Wang, Zhenqiu Lu, and Allan S. Cohen

Abstract The hierarchical linear model (HLM) has become popular in behavioral research, and has been widely used in various educational studies in recent years. Violations of model assumptions can have significant impact on the model estimates. The purpose of this study is to conduct a sensitivity analysis of two-level HLM by exploring the influence of outliers on parameter estimates of HLM under normality assumptions. A simulation study is performed to examine the bias of parameter estimates with different numbers and magnitudes of outliers given different sample sizes. Results indicated that the bias of parameter estimates increased with the magnitudes and number of outliers. The estimates have bias with a few outliers. A robust method Huber sandwich estimator corrected the standard errors efficiently when there was a large proportion of outliers.

Keywords Hierarchical linear models • Outliers • Robust method

22.1 Introduction

The hierarchical linear model (HLM) has become popular in behavioral research, and has been widely used in various educational studies in recent years. Compared to general linear models (GLM), HLM is favored by a number of researchers (e.g., Field 2009). Morris (1995) claimed that "hierarchical models are extremely promising tools for data analysis" (p. 85). For GLM, the distributional assumption requires independent and identically distributed error terms (Frank 1998). However, data in educational research studies are usually hierarchical. For example, students as subjects are actually nested within their classes, and classes are nested within schools. Data from those students are not independent from each other. With multilevel models, aggregation bias (Cronbach and Webb 1975; Robinson 1950) can be attenuated. The problem of misestimated precision can be taken care of with multilevel models as well (e.g., Aitkin et al. 1981). Besides, the ordinary

J. Wang (✉) • Z. Lu • A.S. Cohen
University of Georgia, Athens, GA, USA
e-mail: cherish@uga.edu; zlu@uga.edu; acohen@uga.edu

L.A. van der Ark et al. (eds.), *Quantitative Psychology Research*, Springer Proceedings in Mathematics & Statistics 140, DOI 10.1007/978-3-319-19977-1_22

linear "squared (OLS)" estimation fails to include covariance components in the standard error estimates when applied to the nested data (Bijleveld et al. 1998). HLM can estimate variance components with unbalanced or nested data and divide the variability across different levels. Field (2009) summarized three crucial benefits of HLM that "cast aside the assumption of homogeneity of regression slopes," "say 'bye-bye' to the assumption of independence," and "laugh in the face of missing data" (p. 729).

As the increase in popularity of HLM, it is important to investigate whether model estimation can be easily influenced by extreme observations. For traditional HLM, residual terms at all levels of HLM are assumed to be normally distributed. But based on previous studies, statistical models with an assumption of normality can be highly sensitive to outlying cases (Hogg 1979; Mosteller and Tukey 1977), so nonnormality is one factor that affects the standard errors for the fixed-effects estimates and in turn affect the test statistics in HLM. Outliers for two-level HLM may due to outlying level-1 units given the regression equation for a particular level-2 unit, or represent an atypical regression coefficient of a level-2 unit. Rachman-Moore and Wolfe (1984) indicated that even one outlier at level-1 can affect the estimates of the level-2 unit aggregates and other level-1 unit contributions, impacting the estimation of fixed effects. Studies have been conducted indicating that point estimates and intervals for fixed effects may be sensitive to outliers at all levels (Seltzer 1993; Seltzer et al. 2002). Seltzer and Choi (2003) indicated that results were not excessively influenced by one or two extreme outlying values at level 1 by reanalyzing real data with level-1 outliers. There was little change in the fixed effects. This finding was distinct from the previous results. The leading sensitivity analyses for HLM adopted real data analyses and then compared results across different assumptions or employed robust methods to fit the real data. Actually, different estimation methods, computational algorithms, assumptions, sample sizes, and severity of outliers may impact the results of parameter estimation. One purpose of this study is to conduct a well-performed simulation study, which explores the bias of parameter estimates in various conditions from the true parameters. Practical instructions can be provided for educational researchers in using HLM when outliers exist. Applying a robust method to correct the standard errors is a practical recommendation. An asymptotically consistent robust method called the "Huber sandwich estimator" is popular for correcting standard errors. Freedman (2006) indicated that the "Huber sandwich estimator" can be useful when the model is misspecified. He also noted that when the model is nearly correct, there is no evident benefit from the robustification of the Huber sandwich estimator for correcting the usual standard errors. Additionally, the cost of increasing robustness is more computational complexity. If the Huber sandwich estimator does not perform better than the Full maximum likelihood estimation (FMLE) method, the value of the robust method is compromised in dealing with outliers for HLM. Another purpose of this study is to compare the performance of the Huber Sandwich estimator with FMLE.

In summary, we have two purposes of this study. First, we explore the bias of the parameter estimates of HLM with different magnitudes of outliers; and second, we investigate the correction of the standard errors for fixed-effects estimates in the presence of outliers.

22.2 Theoretical Background

22.2.1 *Hierarchical Linear Model*

Raudenbush and Bryk (2002) introduced a general HLM model. It is a generalization of traditional linear models. HLM not only incorporates the hierarchical structure of the data, but also partitions the covariance components and tests the cross-level effects. At each level, HLM shares the linearity, normality, and homoscedasticity assumptions of OLS regression. Apart from that, HLM can adjust for the non-independence of error terms. The independence among all the observations required by OLS is not required for HLM. In turn, HLM assumes residuals at different levels need to be uncorrelated and the observations at the highest level should be independent of each other. HLM also can accommodate the missing data and an unbalanced design.

The general form of two-level HLM with random intercepts and random slopes is as follows:

$$\begin{aligned} \text{Level-1} \quad Y_{ij} &= \beta_{0j} + \beta_{1j}X_{ij} + r_{ij} \\ \text{Level-2} \quad \beta_{0j} &= \gamma_{00} + u_{0j} \\ \beta_{1j} &= \gamma_{10} + u_{1j} \end{aligned} \tag{22.1}$$

or in a combined form:

$$Y_{ij} = (\gamma_{00} + \gamma_{10}X_{ij}) + (u_{0j} + u_{1j}X_{ij} + r_{ij}) \tag{22.2}$$

where i and j represent the level-1 and level-2 units, respectively. The parameters β_{0j} and β_{1j} are the random intercept and the random slope of the regression equation at level-2 unit j, correspondingly. r_{ij} represents the error term at level-1 γ_{00} and γ_{10} represent the fixed-effects estimates of the random intercept β_{0j} and the random slope β_{1j}, correspondingly. The random effects of the regression coefficients are u_{0j} and u_{1j}. The mean structure part of this HLM model is $(\gamma_{00} + \gamma_{10}X_{ij})$. And the residual part is $(u_{0j} + u_{1j}X_{ij} + r_{ij})$. Let $\mathbf{u}$ be the vector of random effects u_{0j} and u_{1j}, and $\boldsymbol{\epsilon}$ be the vector of residual variances. Based on normality assumption, we have

$$\mathbb{E}\begin{bmatrix} \mathbf{u} \\ \boldsymbol{\epsilon} \end{bmatrix} = \begin{bmatrix} \mathbf{0} \\ \mathbf{0} \end{bmatrix}, \text{ and}$$

$$\mathbb{V}ar\begin{bmatrix}\mathbf{u}\\ \epsilon\end{bmatrix}=\begin{bmatrix}\mathbf{G} & \mathbf{0}\\ \mathbf{0} & \mathbf{R}\end{bmatrix},$$

where $\mathbf{G}=\begin{bmatrix}\tau_{00} & \tau_{01}\\ \tau_{01} & \tau_{11}\end{bmatrix}$ and $\mathbf{R}=\sigma^2\mathbf{I}_n$.

22.2.2 Maximum Likelihood Estimation

Maximum likelihood estimation (MLE) produces parameter estimates of a statistical model that maximize the likelihood function. The MLE produces consistent and efficient estimates. It is also scale free and scale invariant. Scale free indicates that the value of the fit function is the same for the correlation matrix, covariance matrix, or any other changes of the scale. Scale invariant implies that the parameter estimates are not affected by the transformation of variables. FMLE provides both regression coefficients, including the fixed-effects estimates (intercepts and slopes), and the random-effects estimates (variance components) for HLM; the restricted maximum likelihood estimation (RMLE) is mainly used to estimate the covariance components. The FMLE method is employed in the estimation procedure of this study.

For two-level HLM, we assume the data $\mathbf{y}$ follow $N(\mathbf{X}\boldsymbol{\beta},\mathbf{V})$. The likelihood function regarding $\boldsymbol{\beta}$ and $\mathbf{V}$ of FMLE is as below (Searle et al. 1992):

$$L(\boldsymbol{\beta},\mathbf{V};\mathbf{y})=\frac{1}{(2\pi)^{\frac{N}{2}}|\mathbf{V}|^{\frac{1}{2}}}\mathrm{e}^{-\frac{1}{2}(\mathbf{y}-\mathbf{X}\boldsymbol{\beta})'\mathbf{V}^{-1}(\mathbf{y}-\mathbf{X}\boldsymbol{\beta})} \tag{22.3}$$

Then the log-likelihood function is as follows:

$$\log L(\boldsymbol{\beta},\mathbf{V};\mathbf{y})=-\frac{N}{2}(\log 2\pi)-\frac{1}{2}\log|\mathbf{V}|-\frac{1}{2}(\mathbf{r}'\mathbf{V}^{-1}\mathbf{r}) \tag{22.4}$$

where $\mathbf{r}=\mathbf{y}-\mathbf{X}\boldsymbol{\beta}$. SAS Proc Mixed procedure (SAS Institute Inc. 2013) employs a ridge-stabilized Newton–Raphson algorithm to maximize the log-likelihood function, or minimize $-2\log L(\boldsymbol{\beta},\mathbf{V};\mathbf{y})$, to look for the linear approximation of the function roots through an iterative process (Ypma 1995). The estimators for fixed-effects $\boldsymbol{\beta}$ and random-effects $\mathbf{u}$ (Littell et al. 2006) are

$$\hat{\boldsymbol{\beta}}=\left(\sum_{j=1}^{m}\mathbf{X}_j'\mathbf{V}_j^{-1}\mathbf{X}_j\right)^{-1}\left(\sum_{j=1}^{m}\mathbf{X}_j'\mathbf{V}_j^{-1}\mathbf{y}_j\right) \tag{22.5}$$

$$\hat{\mathbf{u}}=\sum_{j=1}^{m}\hat{\mathbf{G}}\mathbf{Z}'\hat{\mathbf{V}}_j^{-1}(\mathbf{y}_j-\mathbf{X}_j\hat{\boldsymbol{\beta}}) \tag{22.6}$$

where m represents the number of units at level 2; $\mathbf{X}_j$ and $\mathbf{V}_j$ are the design matrix and the covariance matrix for level-2 unit j, respectively; $\mathbf{Z}$ denotes as a design matrix for random-effects estimates. The variance of $\hat{\boldsymbol{\beta}}$ is estimated by

$$var(\hat{\boldsymbol{\beta}}) = \left(\mathbf{X}'\hat{\mathbf{V}}^{-1}\mathbf{X}\right)^{-1}. \tag{22.7}$$

22.2.3 Outliers and Huber Sandwich Estimator

One concern about FMLE is the assumption of multivariate normality. Grubbs (1969) stated that an outlier is one that seems to deviate markedly from other data of the sample. It may be merely an extreme indication of the random variability inherent in the data or it may also be the result of a gross deviation from the experimental process or data processing. Barnett and Lewis (1994) defined outliers to be observations that are inconsistent with the rest of the data. Researchers would not like to simply delete outliers. However, the presence of outliers has serious effects on the modeling, monitoring, and diagnosis (Zou et al. 2014). Before applying the model to fit the data, it is necessary to do a sensitivity analysis of the model to the outliers. Using robust methods to estimate standard errors is one way. Huber (1967) and White (1982) introduced a robust covariance matrix estimator referred to as the Huber sandwich estimator, which is commonly used in generalized estimating equations (GEE, Diggle et al. 1994; Huber 1967; Liang and Zeger 1986; White 1980). The Huber sandwich estimator does not change parameter estimates. It provides robust standard errors of fixed-effects estimates which in turn corrects the test of significance (King and Roberts 2012). Huber sandwich estimator is an implemented robust method for correcting standard errors in the SAS software. Different from the FMLE covariance matrix estimator, the Huber sandwich estimator is based on the quasi-likelihood GEE and computes the covariance matrix for the fixed-effects estimates as below (Liang and Zeger 1986):

$$(\mathbf{X}'\hat{\mathbf{V}}^{-1}\mathbf{X})^{-1}\left(\sum_{j=1}^{m}\mathbf{X}_j'\hat{\mathbf{V}}_j^{-1}\hat{\epsilon}_j\hat{\epsilon}_j'\mathbf{X}_j\hat{\mathbf{V}}_j^{-1}\right)(\mathbf{X}'\hat{\mathbf{V}}^{-1}\mathbf{X})^{-1} \tag{22.8}$$

where j refers to the level-2 unit and m is the number of units at level 2, $\hat{\epsilon}_j = \mathbf{y}_j - \mathbf{X}_j\hat{\boldsymbol{\beta}}$, is the estimated residual part of the model, $\mathbf{X}_j$ and $\hat{\mathbf{V}}_j$ are the design matrix and the covariance matrix for unit j, respectively. The generalized inverse in the equation is appropriate as the matrix is singular. The consistent covariance estimation is obtained in the presence of heteroskedasticity (White 1980). The left and right part of the equation are the FMLE covariance matrix estimator. When data are normally distributed, the middle part will be canceled out and the Huber sandwich estimator would yield the same result as the FMLE.

22.3 A Simulation Study

22.3.1 *Design*

A simulation study was performed to investigate the sensitivity of HLM to outliers. Data sets with three different sample sizes were simulated based on the random-coefficients regression model. In order to maintain the same ratio of the number of level-1 units to the number of level-2 units, the three sample sizes were set as 200 (20 level-1 units by 10 level-2 units), 1250 (50 level-1 units by 25 level-2 units), and 5000 (100 level-1 units by 50 level-2 units).

Step 1, normally distributed data were generated based on the random-coefficients regression model, $Y_{ij} = (\gamma_{00} + \gamma_{10}X_{ij}) + (u_{0j} + u_{ij}X_{ij} + r_{ij})$. The true values of parameters were set as follows: $\gamma_{00} = 5$, $\gamma_{10} = 1$, $\tau_{00} = 1$, $\tau_{11} = 4$, $\tau_{01} = 1$, and $\sigma^2 = 4$. The correlation between τ_{00} and τ_{11} was .50.

Step 2, two types of outliers (3 SD and 5 SD) were defined based on the sample standard deviations. The mathematical equation for creating outliers was $\bar{Y}_{outlier} = \bar{Y} + n\hat{\sigma}$ where $n = 3$ or 5. The sample mean $\bar{Y}$ and the sample standard deviation $\hat{\sigma}$ were estimated by using the simulated datasets without outliers. The 3 SD outliers are three standard deviations from the sample mean. Similarly, the 5 SD outliers are five standard deviations from the sample mean. All the outliers were created in the positive direction, in order to avoid the trade-off effects of outliers and better investigate the influence of violating normality assumption. Several specific numbers of outliers with 3 SD and 5 SD were created for the dependent variable and substituted for the real data. For the datasets with a sample size of 200, 1, 2, 5, 8, 10, and 20 outliers were created. The percentage of the outliers in the datasets of sample size 200 were .50, 1.00, 2.50, 4.00, 5.00, and 10.00 %. For the data sets with a sample size of 1250, 2, 5, 10, 25, 50, 75, and 125 outliers have been created. The corresponding percentages were .16, .40, .80, 2.00, 4.00, 6.00, and 10.00 %. For the data sets with a sample size of 5000, 2, 5, 10, 20, 30, 40, 50, 100, 150, 250, and 500 outliers were created. The percentages of outliers were then .04, .10, .20, .40, .60, .80, 1.00, 2.00, 3.00, 5.00, and 10.00 %.

Step 3, the FMLE method with the Newton–Raphson algorithm was adopted to estimate parameters with the correctly specified model.

Step 4, the fixed-effects and random-effects estimates were compared with the true values of the parameters. The indices for the comparisons are absolute bias and relative bias. The bias of a statistic $\hat{\theta}$ is defined as $\mathbb{B}(\hat{\theta}) = \mathbb{E}(\hat{\theta}) - \hat{\theta}$, which is the distance of the expectation of the estimate and the estimate itself. The absolute bias is the absolute value of the difference between estimates and the values of true parameters. The relative bias represents the ratio of the absolute bias to the values of true parameters, which is the percentage of the relative difference between the mean estimate and the single estimate. Both the absolute bias and relative bias indicate the sensitivity of the model with a specific estimation method to the outliers. The Q-Q plots of the scaled residuals for the dependent variable were used to display the distribution of residuals. When data are correlated, the vector of residuals instead of each separate residual can be scaled, accounting for the covariances among the observations. The Cholesky residuals were used. As described in the SAS/STAT(R) 9.22 User's Guide, if $\mathbb{V}ar(Y) = C'C$, then $C'^{-1}Y$ is a vector of uncorrelated variables with unit variance which has uniform dispersion. Those residuals are expressed as $\hat{\varepsilon}_c = C'^{-1}(Y - X\hat{\beta})$.

Step 5, the robust method Huber sandwich estimator for correcting the standard errors and test statistics on the fixed-effects estimates was examined. The estimated covariance matrix of fixed-effects estimates by the Huber sandwich estimator was compared with those obtained by the FMLE method. For each condition, 100 replications were conducted to carry out the simulation study.

22.3.2 Results

In order to recover the parameters, the random-coefficients regression model was employed to fit the simulated data without outliers. The absolute bias and the relative bias of the estimates were acceptable with all absolute bias less than .20 and relative bias ranging from .01 to 8.06 % (Table 22.1). The Pearson correlation between true values and the estimates was strongly positive, $r = .999$, $p < .01$, indicating the parameters were successfully recovered. The Q-Q plot and histogram for the scaled residuals of the dependent variable indicated that the simulated data were normally distributed (Fig. 22.1a). The Q-Q plots of the scaled residuals for the dependent variable showed how the outliers affect the normal distribution of the data (Fig. 22.1b). In the presence of a few outliers, the distributions of the scaled residuals appeared normal. With larger numbers of outliers, however, the scaled residuals had more variability around the line. In the presence of extreme outliers, the scaled residual did not appear to be normally distributed. For the three sample sizes, the patterns look similar, so we took the sample size of 200 as an illustration Results are shown in the Table 22.2.

The intercept estimate γ_{00} appeared to be affected by outliers. The absolute bias of the estimates increased as the number of outliers increased (Fig. 22.2a). The relative bias of γ_{00} ranged from .53 to 35.63 %. The independent sample t-test for the differences of absolute/relative bias on γ_{00} between different types of outliers was not significant, $t(46) = -1.40, p = .17$.

The slope estimate of γ_{10} was much less susceptible to outliers, compared with the estimate of γ_{00} (Fig. 22.2a). The range of relative bias of γ_{10} was 1.53–12.55 %. The independent sample t-test indicated that there was no significant difference in the absolute bias of the γ_{10} estimation between 3 SD and 5 SD outliers, $t(77.46) = -1.23, p = .22$.

The outliers had the most influential effects on the estimation of σ^2. With an increase in the numbers of outliers, the absolute bias increased rapidly (Fig. 22.2a).

Table 22.1 Summary of parameter recovery

Sample sizes	Parameters	True values	Estimates	Standard errors	Absolute bias	Relative bias (%)
200	γ_{00}	5.00	5.00	.32	.00	.01
200	γ_{10}	1.00	1.01	.61	.01	1.11
200	σ^2	4.00	3.96	.42	.04	1.06
200	τ_{00}	1.00	.93	.51	.07	6.63
200	τ_{01}	1.00	.97	.73	.03	3.36
200	τ_{11}	4.00	3.80	1.80	.20	4.89
1250	γ_{00}	5.00	5.00	.20	.00	.08
1250	γ_{10}	1.00	1.00	.40	.00	.28
1250	σ^2	4.00	4.04	.16	.04	.88
1250	τ_{00}	1.00	.98	.30	.02	2.22
1250	τ_{01}	1.00	.92	.45	.08	8.06
1250	τ_{11}	4.00	3.90	1.13	.10	2.38
5000	γ_{00}	5.00	5.00	.14	.00	.04
5000	γ_{10}	1.00	.97	.28	.03	3.30
5000	σ^2	4.00	3.99	.08	.01	.18
5000	τ_{00}	1.00	1.00	.21	.00	.08
5000	τ_{01}	1.00	.96	.32	.04	3.89
5000	τ_{11}	4.00	3.86	.78	.14	3.40
Mean					.04	2.33
SD					.05	2.40

Note: γ_{00} and γ_{10} represent the fixed-effects estimates of the random intercept and the slope. σ^2 is the error term at level 1. τ_{00} is the variance of the random intercept and τ_{11} is the variance of the random slope. τ_{01} represents the covariance of the random intercept and slope

The range of relative bias was 16.97–733.97 %, 10–20 times wider than other estimates. In the presence of 10.00 % outliers in the data, the largest absolute and relative bias were observed.

The variance component of the intercept, τ_{00}, was affected in a similar way to γ_{00} (Fig. 22.2a). The range of relative bias was 10.47–97.99 %. There was a significant difference in the absolute bias for estimates of τ_{00} across the three sample sizes, $F(2, 45) = 11.92, p < .001$.

The relative bias of variance component of the slope τ_{11} was large with only .50 % outliers and then increased slightly up to 5.00 %; however, the 10.00 % outliers completely distort the estimates of τ_{11} (Fig. 22.2a). The absolute bias with 5 SD outliers were not significantly different from those with 3 SD outliers based on the independent sample t-test, $t(10) = .43, p = .68$.

The covariance of the intercept and slope was τ_{01}. The distribution of absolute bias did not display a clear pattern (Fig. 22.2a). The absolute bias appeared to be similar across numbers and types of outliers. The range of relative bias was 1.92–26.14 %. The independent sample t-test for the differences of absolute bias on the τ_{01} was not significantly different between 3 SD and 5 SD outliers, $t(46) = .57$,

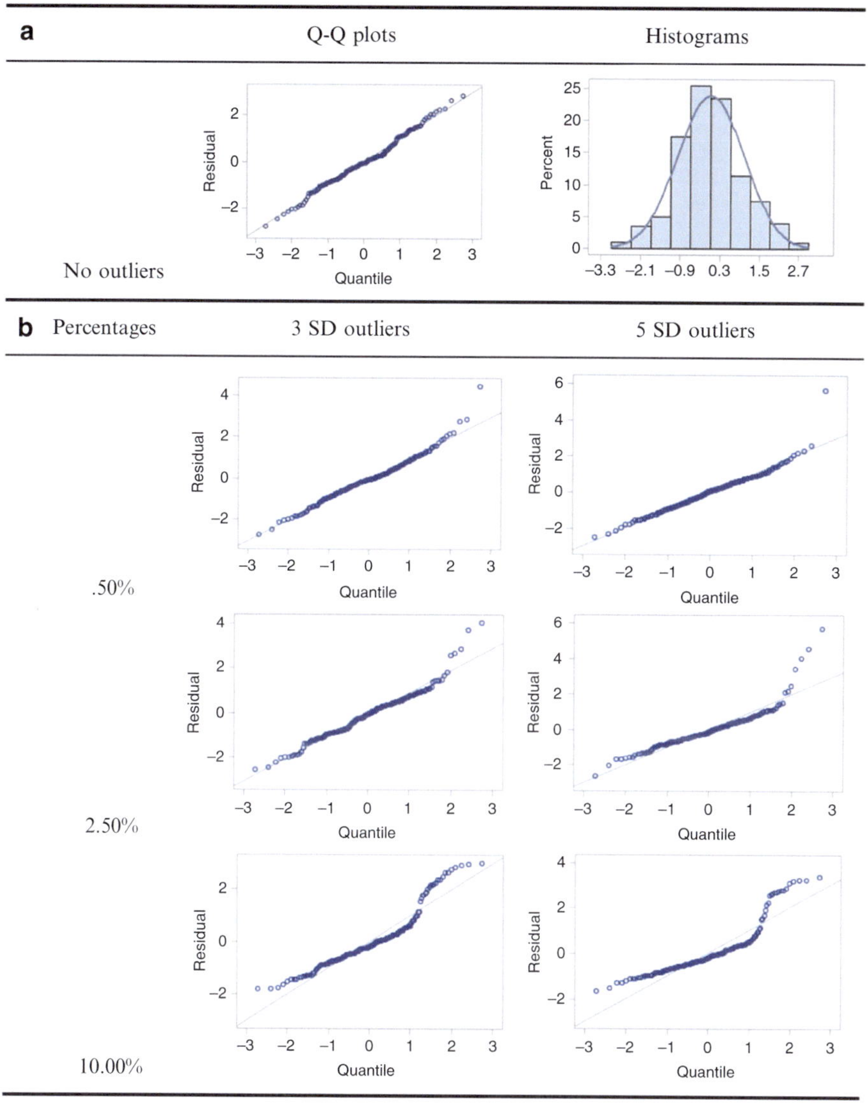

Fig. 22.1 (**a**) Plots for data without outliers and (**b**) QQ plots for data with outliers

$p = .57$. In addition, the one-way ANOVA for testing the differences of absolute bias across sample sizes was significant, $F(2, 45) = 7.77, p < .001$.

Comparing the FMLE and the Huber-sandwich estimator for estimating standard errors of fixed-effects estimates, there was no significant difference between the FMLE standard errors and Huber standard errors. The standard errors of FMLE and of Huber-sandwich estimator were close to each other with less than 4.00 % outliers (Fig. 22.2b). With more than 4.00 % outliers, the Huber-sandwich estimator

Table 22.2 Fixed-effects and random-effects estimates with 3 SD outliers and sample size 200

Parameters	Percents (%)	True values	Estimates	Standard errors	Absolute bias	Relative bias (%)
γ_{00}	.50	5.00	5.03	.32	.03	.53
	2.50	5.00	5.24	.32	.24	4.79
	10.00	5.00	6.09	.32	1.09	21.87
γ_{10}	.50	1.00	.93	.60	.07	7.19
	2.50	1.00	.97	.60	.03	3.12
	10.00	1.00	.93	.58	.07	7.12
σ^2	.50	4.00	4.68	.49	.68	16.97
	2.50	4.00	6.83	.72	2.83	70.79
	10.00	4.00	14.92	1.56	10.92	272.89
τ_{00}	.50	1.00	.85	.50	.15	14.95
	2.50	1.00	.70	.49	.30	29.61
	10.00	1.00	.30	.58	.70	70.05
τ_{11}	.50	4.00	3.57	1.72	.43	10.81
	2.50	4.00	3.42	1.71	.58	14.41
	10.00	4.00	2.80	1.70	1.20	30.07
τ_{01}	.50	1.00	.78	.68	.22	21.98
	2.50	1.00	.80	.69	.20	20.49
	10.00	1.00	.77	.66	.23	22.70

Note: Notations are the same as above. Only part of the results are listed in the table

provided smaller standard errors than the FMLE. With 10.00 % outliers, the difference between standard errors of γ_{00} with 5 SD outliers was larger than those with 3 SD outliers. A similar situation happened for γ_{10} as well, but the mean differences between the two estimation methods were not significant given a sample size of 200, $t(46) = .34, p = .74$. The mean difference between the two estimation methods was not significant as well, $t(86) = -.001, p = .999$, which indicated that the Huber-sandwich estimator tended to provide robust standard errors only when the outliers were extreme.

22.4 Discussion

Outliers had influences on the estimates of the random-coefficients regression model under the FMLE. The estimate of σ^2 was influenced the most. The effects on the γ_{00} were increased with more outliers. The bias of γ_{00} with 5 SD outliers was clearly larger than those with 3 SD outliers. The estimate of τ_{00} was affected in a similar way to the estimate of γ_{00}. Relatively speaking, the estimate of γ_{10} was less influenced by outliers. Moreover, the estimate γ_{10} had no specific influence pattern related to outliers. The estimate τ_{11} had more random variations. With 10.00 % 5 SD

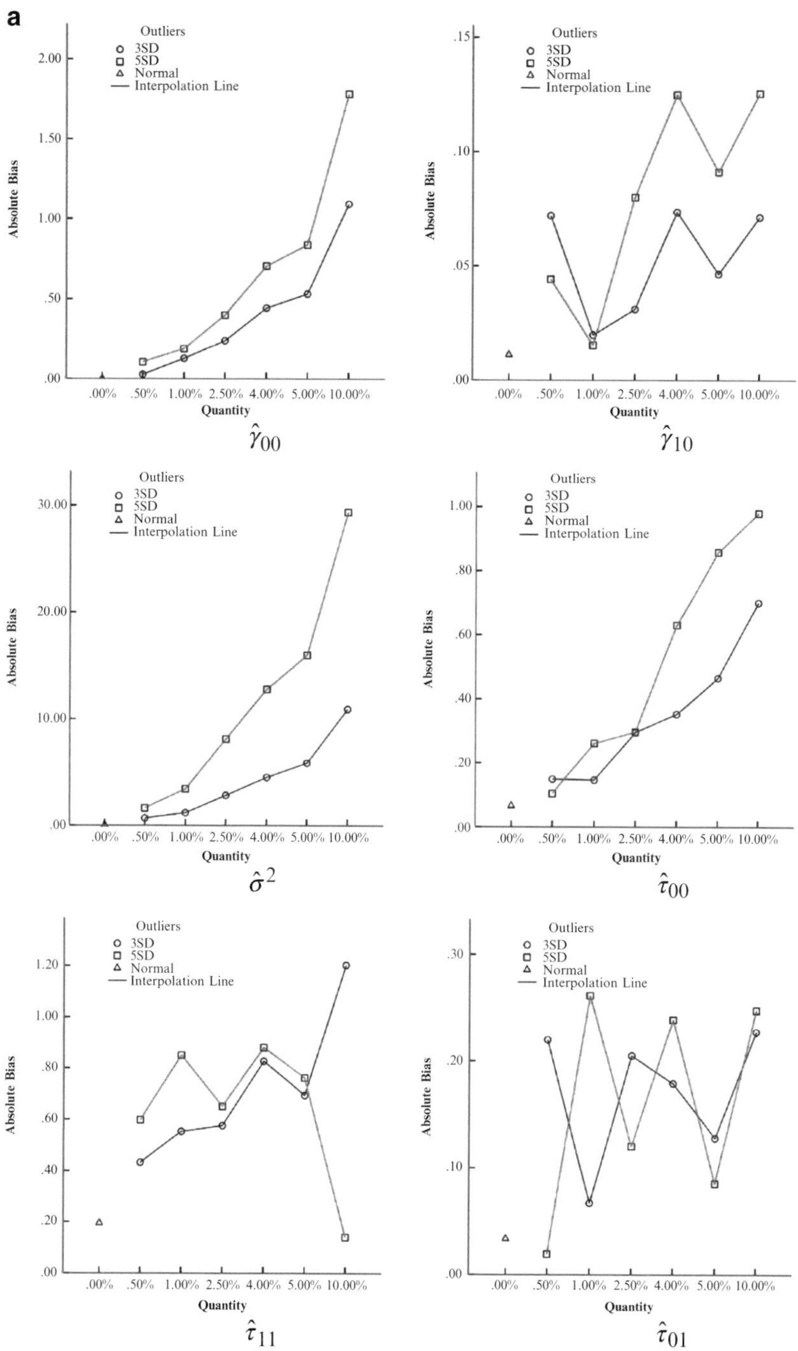

Fig. 22.2 (**a**) Absolute bias of estimates and (**b**) comparison between FMLE and Huber estimator

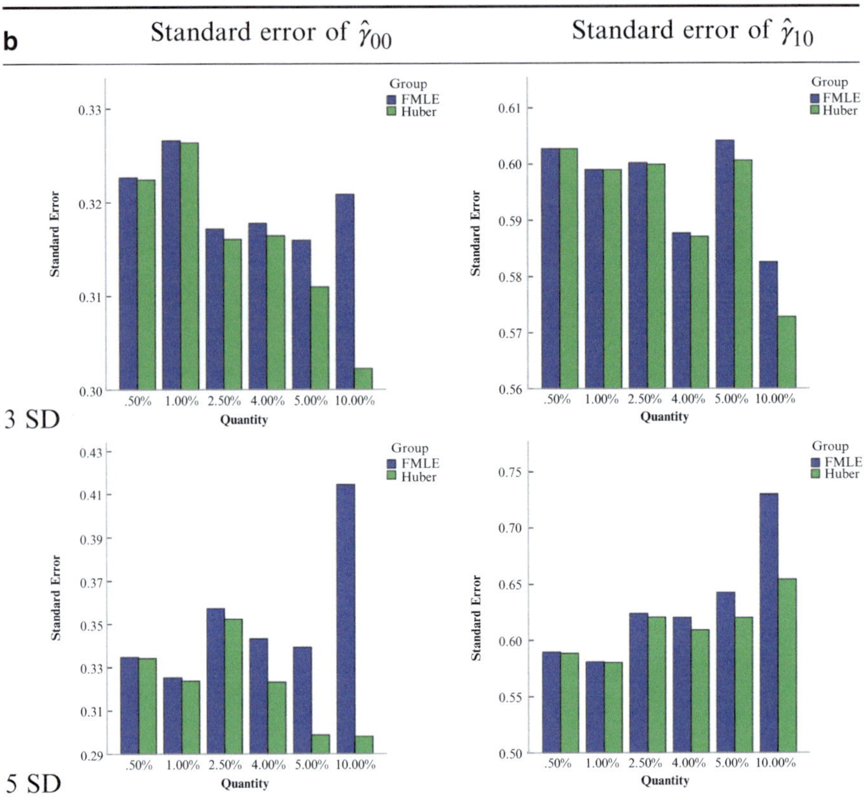

Fig. 22.2 (continued)

outliers and a sample size of 200, τ_{11} had the lowest absolute and relative bias, however, the estimation was not convincing. The standard errors were very large, indicating that the estimate of τ_{11} has been distorted. The estimate of τ_{00} increased with large proportions of 5 SD outliers. The estimate of τ_{01} with a sample size of 200 was not stable in the presence of outliers. 10.00 % outliers in a sample size of 200 was a large proportion, which can perhaps no longer be viewed as outliers. With 10.00 % 3 SD outliers in a sample size of 200, 1 out of 100 replications of the model estimation procedures in the SAS software did not converge after 10^6 iterations. With 5.00 and 10.00 % 5 SD outliers given a sample size of 200, there were 5 out of 100 replications of the model estimation procedures that did not converge after 10^6 iterations. Therefore, the stability of parameter estimation in HLM will be compromised with a large proportion of outliers.

No standard acceptable criterion can be established for the absolute bias and relative bias. Based on the tables, the researchers can look up the absolute and relative bias according to the corresponding types and numbers of outliers given a specific sample size. A larger sample size is typically better for estimation. Except for the bias of the estimates γ_{00} and σ^2, the bias of the estimates γ_{10}, τ_{00}, τ_{11}, and τ_{01} have been significantly different across sample sizes. However, since the outliers were created in the positive direction, the bias was exaggerated.

The Huber sandwich estimator corrected the standard errors efficiently only when there was a large proportion of outliers. The Huber-sandwich estimator was more efficient in correcting the standard errors with 5 SD outliers than with 3 SD outliers. Therefore, the Huber-sandwich estimator did not work efficiently across conditions in this study.

Future research will investigate the correction for standard errors and the parameter estimates with other robust methods. A *t*-distribution assumption will be employed in the parameter estimation, compared with a normal distribution assumption as well.

22.5 Conclusion

The simulation study investigated the bias of estimates of the parameters to evaluate the sensitivity of two-level HLM to outliers. The 2 types of outliers (3SD and 5SD) with various magnitudes of different sample sizes have been examined. By having different types and magnitudes of outliers, the model assumption of normality has been violated to various extents. Violations of model assumptions had significant impact on the model. The bias of parameter estimates for σ^2, γ_{00}, and τ_{00} increased with a larger number of outliers. For other estimates, the bias had different extents of random variation across various conditions. The 5 SD outliers had significantly more severe influence than 3 SD outliers on the estimate of σ^2. But for the other estimates, there was no significant difference of bias between 3 SD outliers and 5 SD outliers. With a limited number of outliers, the estimates had very small bias. The robust method Huber sandwich estimator corrected the standard errors efficiently only with a large proportion of outliers. Therefore, the robust methods are not always correcting the bias resulting from outliers efficiently.

The researchers should be cautious in selecting among various robust methods. Different from Huber sandwich estimator, applying a *t*-distribution in model estimation is another robust method. By using a *t*-distribution, the model is not restricted with the normality assumption. With different degrees of freedom in *t*-distributions, it may be able to deal with various magnitudes of outliers. The outliers do not need to be restricted into one direction, either. In the future studies, we will explore the possibilities of applying a *t*-distribution in correcting bias in HLM.

References

Aitkin, M., Anderson, D., & Hinde, J. (1981). Statistical modeling of data on teaching styles. *Journal of the Royal Statistical Society, Series A, 144*(4), 419–461.

Barnett, V., & Lewis, T. (1994). *Outliers in statistical data* (Vol. 3). New York: Wiley.

Bijleveld, C. C. J. H., van der Kamp, L. J. T., Mooijaart, A., van der Kloot, W. A., van der Leeden, R., & van der Burg, E. (1998). *Longitudinal data analysis: Designs, models and methods.* Thousand Oaks, CA: Sage.

Cronbach, L. J., & Webb, N. (1975). Between and within-class effects in a reported aptitude-by-treatment interaction: Reanalysis of a study by G. L. Anderson. *Journal of Educational Psychology, 6*, 717–724.

Diggle, P., Liang, K.-Y., & Zeger, S. (1994). *Analysis of longitudinal data.* Oxford: Clarendon.

Field, A. P. (2009). *Discovering statistics using spss (and sex and drugs and rock 'n' roll)* (3rd ed.). Los Angeles/London: Sage.

Frank, K. A. (1998). Quantitative methods for studying social context in multilevels and through interpersonal relations. *Review of Research in Education, 23*, 171–216.

Freedman, D. A. (2006). On the so-called 'Huber sandwich estimator' and 'robust standard errors'. *The American Statistician, 60*(4), 299. doi:10.2307/27643806.

Grubbs, F. E. (1969). Procedures for detecting outlying observations in samples. *Technometrics, 11*(1). 1–21.

Hogg, R. (1979). Statistical robustness: One view of its use in applications today. *American Statistician, 33*, 108–115.

Huber, P. J. (1967). *The behavior of maximum likelihood estimates under nonstandard conditions.* Paper presented at the Proceedings of the Fifth Berkeley Symposium on Mathematical Statistics and Probability.

King, G., & Roberts, M. (2012). How robust standard errors expose methodological problems they do not fix. *Annual Meeting of the Society for Political Methodology*, Duke University.

Liang, K.-Y., & Zeger, S. L. (1986). Longitudinal data analysis using generalized linear models. *Biometrika, 73*(1), 13–22.

Littell, R. C., Milliken, G. A., Stroup, W. W., Wolfinger, R. D., & Schabenberger, O. (2006) *'SAS®' System for Mixed Models* (2nd ed.). Cary, NC: SAS Institute Inc.

Morris, C. N. (1995). Hierarchical models for educational data: An overview. *Journal of Educational and Behavioral Statistics, 20*(2), 190–200.

Mosteller, F., & Tukey, J. W. (1977). Data analysis and regression: a second course in statistics. *Addison-Wesley Series in Behavioral Science: Quantitative Methods.*

Rachman-Moore, D., & Wolfe, R. G. (1984). Robust analysis of a nonlinear model for multilevel educational survey data. *Journal of Educational Statistics, 9*(4), 277–293.

Raudenbush, S. W., & Bryk, A. S. (2002). *Hierarchical linear models applications and data analysis methods* (2nd ed.). Thousand Oaks, CA: Sage.

Robinson, W. S. (1950). Ecological correlations and the behavior of individuals. *American Sociological Review, 15*, 351–357.

SAS Institute Inc. (2013). *SAS/STAT®13.1 user's guide.* Cary, NC: SAS Institute Inc.

Searle, S. R., Casella, G., & McCulloch, C. E. (1992). *Variance components.* New York: Wiley.

Seltzer, M. (1993). Sensitivity analysis for fixed effects in the hierarchical model: A Gibbs sampling approach. *Journal of Educational Statistics, 18*(3), 207–235.

Seltzer, M., & Choi, K. (2003). Sensitivity analysis for hierarchical models: Downweighting and identifying extreme cases using the t distribution. *Multilevel modeling: Methodological advances, issues, and applications*, 25–52.

Seltzer, M., Novak, J., Choi, K., & Lim, N. (2002). Sensitivity analysis for hierarchical models employing "t" level-1 assumptions. *Journal of Educational and Behavioral Statistics, 27*(2), 181–222.

White, H. (1980). A heteroskedasticity-consistent covariance matrix estimator and a direct test for heteroskedasticity. *Econometrica: Journal of the Econometric Society, 48*, 817–838.

White, H. (1982). Maximum likelihood estimation of misspecified models. *Econometrica, 50*, 1–25.

Ypma, T. J. (1995). Historical development of the Newton-Raphson method. *SIAM Review, 37*(4), 531–551.

Zou, C., Tseng, S.-T., & Wang, Z. (2014). Outlier detection in general profiles using penalized regression method. *IIE Transactions, 46*(2), 106–117.

Chapter 23
Doubly Robust Estimation of Treatment Effects from Observational Multilevel Data

Courtney E. Hall, Peter M. Steiner, and Jee-Seon Kim

Abstract When randomized experiments cannot be conducted, propensity score (PS) matching and regression techniques are frequently used for estimating causal treatment effects from observational data. These methods remove bias caused by baseline differences in the treatment and control groups. Instead of using a PS technique or an outcome regression singly, one might use a doubly robust estimator that combines a PS technique (matching, stratification, or inverse propensity weighting) with an outcome regression in an attempt to address bias more effectively. Theoretically, if the PS or outcome model is correctly specified, a doubly robust estimator will produce an unbiased estimate of the average treatment effect (ATE). Doubly robust estimators are not yet well studied for multilevel data where selection into treatment takes place among level-one units within clusters. Using four simulated multilevel populations, we compare doubly robust estimators to standard PS and regression estimators and investigate their relative performance with respect to bias reduction.

Keywords Propensity score • Observational study • Doubly robust estimator • Multilevel modeling

When educational researchers are unable to conduct randomized controlled trials (RCTs) because of practical or ethical limitations, they must frequently rely on observational data to draw causal conclusions. Researchers commonly face two challenges when working with observational data in education: Selection bias (also called confounding bias) due to differential selection into the treatment and control conditions and the hierarchically nested structure of the data. Thus, the identification and estimation of causal treatment effects requires researchers to remove selection bias by conditioning on observed covariates and to take the clustered data structure

---

IMPS 2014 Proceedings

C.E. Hall (✉) • P.M. Steiner • J.-S. Kim
University of Wisconsin-Madison, 1025 West Johnson Street, Madison, WI 53703, USA
e-mail: cehall@wisc.edu; Psteiner@wisc.edu; Jeeseonkim@wisc.edu

L.A. van der Ark et al. (eds.), *Quantitative Psychology Research*, Springer Proceedings in Mathematics & Statistics 140, DOI 10.1007/978-3-319-19977-1_23

into account. In comparison to single level data, causal inference with multilevel data is typically more complex because selection might occur at different levels and vary considerably across clusters. In addition, the nested data structure requires standard errors that account for the dependence of observations within clusters.

If one succeeds in reliably measuring all confounding covariates or at least a set of covariates that blocks the confounding paths such that the *strong ignorability assumption* holds (Rosenbaum and Rubin 1983), the causal treatment effect is identified and can be consistently or even unbiasedly estimated from observational data. Two of the most popular classes of estimators for the average treatment effect (ATE) are propensity score (PS) estimators and outcome regression estimators (i.e., an effect estimator implemented as standard regression with a set of observed covariates as controls). The rationale of the two estimator classes is quite different: PS analysis attempts to remove baseline differences in observed covariates between the treatment and control groups by first modeling the selection mechanism and then by matching, stratifying, or weighting cases on the basis of the estimated PS. Outcome regression analysis directly models the outcome and, thus, removes selection bias by partialling out the effects of the baseline covariates included in the outcome model. Parametric regression estimators typically rely on stronger functional form assumptions than non- or semi-parametric PS estimators. However, if one misspecifies the PS model or the outcome regression model misspecification bias will result even if the strong ignorability assumption holds.

Instead of using either a PS technique or an outcome regression singly, one might combine them together in the hope to minimize the misspecification bias left by either of the methods. Such doubly robust estimators that combine a PS estimator with an outcome regression estimator are appealing to practitioners because they address the selection bias via modeling the selection process and the outcome mechanism simultaneously. If one or both of the mechanisms are correctly specified, then the doubly robust estimator consistently estimates ATE (Bang and Robins 2005). Since it is rarely possible to have full knowledge of the selection or outcome mechanism, doubly robust estimators provide researchers a second chance to remove all the selection bias.

So far, doubly robust estimators have been primarily investigated for single level data, where selection takes place on a single level only (e.g., Bang and Robins 2005; Kang and Schafer 2007). Identification and estimation of ATEs are more difficult when selection can take place at multiple levels and differs across sites or clusters (level-2 units) as it is typical for observational data in education and psychology. This study investigates a doubly robust estimator for estimating the ATE from multilevel data and compares its performance to PS estimators and outcome regression estimators. We use a simulation study to examine how well the three types of estimators remove bias in samples taken from four different multilevel populations.

23.1 Identification of Causal Estimands and Estimators

23.1.1 Potential Outcomes Framework and Identification

In order to motivate the identification of causal treatment effects we use the potential outcomes framework of the Rubin Causal Model (Rubin 1974). Suppose that there exists a population of J clusters $j = 1, \ldots, J$, each with N_j units such that the total number of level-1 units is given by $\sum_{j=1}^{J} N_j = N$. Within each cluster, level-1 units select or get assigned into a treatment condition ($Z = 1$) or a control condition ($Z = 0$). We assume that selection into treatment is driven by level-1 and level-2 covariates **X** and **W**, respectively. Each level-1 unit i in cluster j has two potential outcomes, Y_{ij}^0 and Y_{ij}^1, where Y_{ij}^0 is the outcome of unit ij if it were assigned to the control group and Y_{ij}^1 is the outcome of unit ij if it were assigned to the treatment group. Thus, the observed outcomes are given by $Y_{ij} = Y_{ij}^1 Z_{ij} + Y_{ij}^0 (1 - Z_{ij})$. Though it is never possible to observe both potential outcomes simultaneously, we can define the individual and average treatment effect (abbreviated ITE and ATE, respectively) as $\text{ITE} = Y_{ij}^1 - Y_{ij}^0$ and $\text{ATE} = \text{E}[\text{ITE}] = \text{E}[Y_{ij}^1 - Y_{ij}^0] = \text{E}[Y_{ij}^1] - \text{E}[Y_{ij}^0]$. When treatment assignment is randomized, as in a perfectly implemented RCT with no attrition, the ATE is identified as the difference in the treatment and control group's expectation, $\text{ATE} = \text{E}[Y_{ij}|Z_{ij} = 1] - \text{E}[Y_{ij}|Z_{ij} = 0]$, since the potential outcomes are independent of Z and, thus, $\text{E}[Y_{ij}|Z_{ij} = 1] = \text{E}[Y_{ij}^1|Z_{ij} = 1] = \text{E}[Y_{ij}^1]$ and $\text{E}[Y_{ij}|Z_{ij} = 0] = \text{E}[Y_{ij}^0|Z_{ij} = 0] = \text{E}[Y_{ij}^0]$.

When treatment assignment is not randomized, as in observational studies, there are likely variables that confound the relationship between the treatment Z and the outcome Y. That is, the conditional expectations of the treatment and control groups can no longer be assumed to be equal to the unconditional expectations of the potential outcome as in the RCT case (Holland 1986; Rubin 1974). The bias that results because of differential selection into the treatment and control group is called selection or confounding bias.

To identify causal effects from observational data, it is necessary to condition on all confounding variables (or at least a set of covariates that block the confounding paths), which need to be observed and reliably measured. If one is willing to rely on linear functional form assumptions, ATE can then be estimated via an outcome regression analysis—a fixed or random effects model for hierarchically structured data. Another way to adjust for confounding bias is to construct a composite score from covariates $\mathbf{V} = (\mathbf{X}, \mathbf{W})$ and the observed treatment status Z, called a balancing score, $b_{\mathbf{V},Z}(\mathbf{v})$, such that $(Y^0, Y^1) \perp\!\!\!\perp Z | b_{\mathbf{V},Z}(\mathbf{v})$ (Hong and Raudenbush 2005; Rosenbaum and Rubin 1983; Steiner et al. 2015). Rosenbaum and Rubin (1983) showed that the balancing score $b_{\mathbf{V},Z}(\mathbf{v})$ is sufficient for the identification of the treatment effect, given strong ignorability holds. One such balancing score is the propensity score, which is defined as the probability of being selected into treatment conditional on $\mathbf{V} = (\mathbf{X}, \mathbf{W})$: $e_{\mathbf{V},Z}(\mathbf{v}) = \text{P}(Z = 1 | \mathbf{V} = \mathbf{v})$. Since the PS is typically not known, it needs to be estimated from observed baseline covariates using logistic regression or other PS estimation technique such as random forests or neural networks (Keller et al. 2013). The estimated PS is then used to estimate ATE via PS matching, PS stratification, or inverse-propensity weighting.

23.1.2 *Doubly Robust Estimators*

Not only parametric but also nonparametric estimation techniques require researchers to make some assumptions about the selection and outcome mechanisms, for instance functional form assumptions when estimating the logit of the PS or the outcome regression model. If the assumptions are not met, biased effect estimates due to model misspecification will result. Doubly robust estimators give researchers at least two chances to remove all the selection bias: by correctly specifying either the PS model or the outcome regression model. ATE is consistently estimated only if either the PS balances the baseline covariates between the treatment and control group or the outcome model is correctly specified (Bang and Robins 2005). If both the selection and the outcome model are incorrectly specified, bias very likely remains—bias might even increase as compared to using a PS or regression adjustment alone (Kang and Schafer 2007).

Previous research has focused mainly on doubly robust methods for single level data. Research on PS analyses in multilevel contexts is in general limited (Hong 2010; Kelcey 2011; Kim and Seltzer 2007; Li et al. 2012; Steiner et al. 2013) and the literature on doubly robust estimators for multilevel data is even more sparse.

There are few studies comparing doubly robust estimators with PS-only and regression-only approaches. Those that do exist are limited to single level data as well as to relatively simple data generating models (DGMs) (Waernbaum 2012; Kang and Schafer 2007; Kreif et al. 2011). In this study, we will use more complex and realistic DGMs to emulate multilevel situations that could be observed in practice. The research question we investigate in this study is: How well do doubly robust estimators remove selection bias in multilevel observational data when the PS or outcome model is incorrectly specified, that is, the multilevel nature of the data is not taken into account, not all confounding covariates are included, or the functional form is not correctly specified?

23.2 Simulation Design and Methods

In order to assess the effectiveness of doubly robust estimators in removing selection bias from multilevel data, we conduct a simulation which compares doubly robust estimators with standard PS and regression estimators under a variety of conditions. Specifically, we vary (1) the underlying data structure (i.e., the data generating selection and outcome models) and (2) the functional form of PS and regression

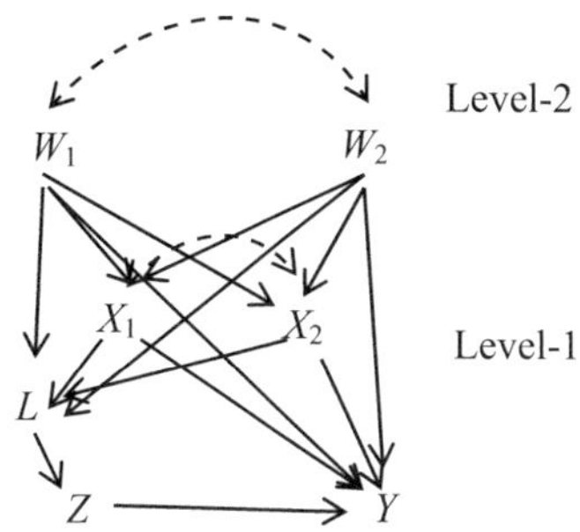

Fig. 23.1 Graph of data generating model (DGM). *Notes*: W_1 and W_2 are the level-2 covariates, and X_1 and X_2 are the level-1 covariates. L is the logit of the PS, Z is the treatment assignment, and Y is the outcome

estimators. The simulation uses four different DGMs in order to cover a range of plausible scenarios. Since all covariates are assumed to be observed and reliably measured, strong ignorability is met for all four simulated data sets. Thus, biases in estimators can only be due to incorrectly specified PS or outcome models. Since the primary advantage of doubly robust estimators is that they continue to remove bias even when either the PS or outcome model is misspecified (but the other model is correctly specified), the simulation varies the degree of model misspecification, that is, the models vary with respect to the inclusion of level-2 covariates, interaction terms, random effects, and fixed effects.

23.2.1 Data Generation

All data sets were generated with different multilevel selection and outcome models (with random intercepts and slopes). The graph of the DGMs is shown in Fig. 23.1. The selection into treatment Z is determined by the latent PS logit (L) which we generated as a linear function of level-1 and level-2 covariates $\mathbf{X} = (X_1, X_2)$ and $\mathbf{W} = (W_1, W_2)$, respectively. Also the outcome Y is obtained as a linear combination of level-1 and level-2 covariates, plus a treatment effect (Z) and a normally distributed error term. Thus, the identification of ATE requires conditioning on $\mathbf{X}$ and $\mathbf{W}$ since these covariates confound the relation between Z and Y. Note that the level-2 covariates $\mathbf{W}$ affect Y and L (and thus Z) also via cross-level interaction effect, that is, the effect of the level-1 covariates on L and Y depends on the values of level-2 covariates. In order to investigate the performance of different ATE estimators, we generated four different populations each consisting of 5000 clusters with 250–350 level-1 units.

The four populations were generated by crossing two selection models with two outcome models. The variations in the models were achieved by varying the effects of the level-2 covariates on the level-1 coefficients while we tried to hold the intraclass correlations (ICCs between 0.3 and 0.4) and initial selection biases constant across populations and clusters. For a sample of clusters, Fig. 23.2 illustrates for each of the two outcome mechanisms the relation between Y and X_1

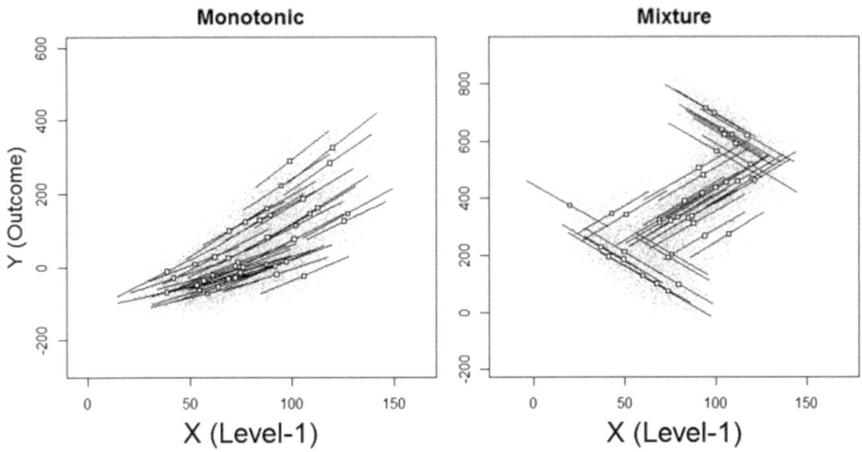

Fig. 23.2 Data generating outcome model (for level-1 covariate X_1)

where the lines represent the cluster-specific regression lines. The points on the regression lines indicate the cluster averages $(\overline{X}_{1j}, \overline{Y}_j)$. Since the cluster-specific relations between Y and X_2 are the same they are not displayed.

The first data generating outcome model in Fig. 23.2 is called "monotonic" because all the slopes are positive and monotonically increasing as the cluster means $\overline{X}_{1j}$ increase. Also note that the cluster means $\overline{Y}_j$ and the within-cluster ranges of Y increase as the cluster means $\overline{X}_{1j}$ increase. The second DGM in Fig. 23.2 represents a "mixture" model with three classes. Within each of three classes, clusters have approximately the same slopes (with some random variation) but slopes differ across classes: they are negative for the first (left) and third (right) class and positive for the middle class. Clusters were assigned to the first class (negative slopes) if both W_1 and W_2 fell below the 40th percentile of the distribution of $\mathbf{W}$ and assigned to the third class if both level-2 scores were above the 60th percentile. Otherwise, clusters were assigned to the middle class with positive slopes.

The corresponding data generating selection models are shown in Fig. 23.3. They are analogous to the outcome DGMs, except that each cluster has been mean-centered such that each cluster has a comparable distribution of the propensity score logit which implies that each cluster will have approximately the same proportion of treated cases.

23.2.2 PS and ATE Estimation

For each of the four populations, we drew 1000 samples and then estimated the treatment effects for each of them. The samples were selected via cluster random sampling by randomly selecting 40 clusters from each population and then selecting

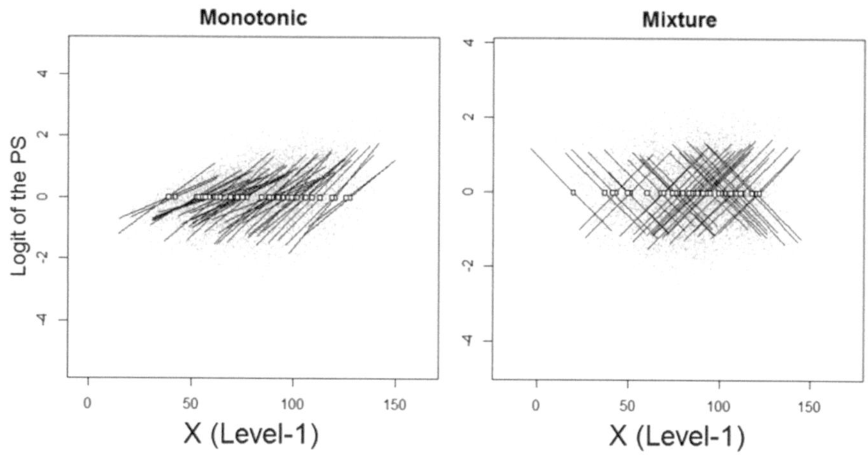

Fig. 23.3 Data generating selection model (for level-1 covariate X_1)

40 % of the units within each cluster, for an average of 120 units per cluster. We estimated ATE using three estimators: a PS stratification estimator, a linear regression estimator, and a doubly robust estimator that combines PS stratification with an additional covariate adjustment. The estimators' performance was then assessed in terms of the remaining bias.

For each of the three estimators, we used different model specifications in order to simulate different degrees of model misspecification. For the PS stratification estimator, we estimated the PS logit, L, in seven different ways using logistic regression. The estimated models particularly differ in how the multilevel structure is taken into account:

S_0) Single Level—No Level-2 Covariates:

$$L_{ij} = \lambda_0 + \lambda_1 X_{1ij} + \lambda_2 X_{2ij}$$

S_1) Single Level—Main Effects Only:

$$L_{ij} = \lambda_0 + \lambda_1 X_{1ij} + \lambda_2 X_{2ij} + \lambda_3 W_{1j} + \lambda_4 W_{2j}$$

S_2) Single Level—Cross-Level Interactions:

$$L_{ij} = \lambda_0 + \lambda_1 X_{1ij} + \lambda_2 X_{2ij} + \lambda_3 W_{1j} + \lambda_4 W_{2j} + \lambda_5 X_{1ij} W_{1j} \\ + \lambda_6 X_{1ij} W_{2j} + \lambda_7 X_{2ij} W_{1j} + \lambda_8 X_{2ij} W_{2j}$$

F_1) Fixed Effects (with cluster dummies S_1 to S_{39}):

$$L_{ij} = \lambda_0 + \lambda_1 X_{1ij} + \lambda_2 X_{2ij} + \xi_1 S_1 + \cdots + \xi_{39} S_{39}$$

F_2) Fixed Effects with Interactions between Cluster Dummies and Level-1 Covariates:

$$L_{ij} = \lambda_0 + \lambda_1 X_{1ij} + \lambda_2 X_{2ij} + \xi_1 S_1 + \cdots + \xi_{39} S_{39} + \\ + X_{1ij}\left(\xi_{40} S_1 + \cdots + \xi_{78} S_{39}\right) + X_{2ij}\left(\xi_{79} S_1 + \cdots + \xi_{117} S_{39}\right)$$

R_1) Random Intercepts:

$$L_{ij} = \lambda_{0j} + \lambda_1 X_{1ij} + \lambda_2 X_{2ij}$$
$$\lambda_{0j} = \delta_{00} + \upsilon_{0j}$$

R_2) Random Intercepts and Slopes with Cross-Level Interactions:

$$L_{ij} = \lambda_{0j} + \lambda_{1j} X_{1ij} + \lambda_{2j} X_{2ij}$$
$$\lambda_{0j} = \delta_{00} + \delta_{01} W_{1j} + \delta_{02} W_{2j} + \upsilon_{0j}$$
$$\lambda_{1j} = \delta_{10} + \delta_{11} W_{1j} + \delta_{12} W_{2j} + \upsilon_{1j}$$
$$\lambda_{2j} = \delta_{20} + \delta_{21} W_{1j} + \delta_{22} W_{2j} + \upsilon_{2j}$$

Note that PS model R_2 with random intercepts and slopes with cross-level interactions is the correctly specified model. PS stratification, implemented as marginal mean weighting, was then used to estimate the treatment effect. We first divided the treated and control cases into five strata based on the quintiles of the PS-logit distribution. If a stratum contained only treated or control cases, the corresponding stratum was deleted from the analysis because we wanted to avoid bias due to violations of the common support assumption. We then estimated ATE with a weighted multilevel regression analysis with random intercepts and the treatment status as sole predictor, $Y_{ij} = \alpha_j + \tau_{PS} Z_{ij} + \varepsilon_{ij}$. The regression weights were obtained as marginal mean weights derived from the proportion of treated and control cases within each stratum (for further details, see Hong 2010). Thus, the PS estimator for ATE is given by $\widehat{\tau}_{PS}$. This specific form of the PS stratification estimator implies that the PS adjustment is implemented across clusters rather than within each cluster separately (Steiner et al. 2013). Since a within-cluster PS adjustment is frequently not possible due to a lack of overlap or small sample sizes we decided to only investigate across-cluster PS stratification.

We also used seven model specifications for the outcome regression estimator. The seven outcome models are equivalent to the PS estimation models S_0 to R_2, except for the dependent variable L which is replaced by Y and an additional error term in all single level and level-1 equations. In order to accurately estimate the ATE, rather than a variance-of-treatment weighted ATE (Angrist and Pischke 2009), we used a marginal structural modeling approach (Robins et al. 2000; Schafer and Kang 2008) and estimated each model separately for the treated cases and the control cases (thus, there is no treatment indicator Z in the models). From the two estimated models we then obtained the predicted treatment and control outcomes ($\hat{Y}^1_{ij}$ and $\hat{Y}^0_{ij}$) for all cases in the sample and used them to estimate the ATE as the average difference in predicted treatment and control outcomes, $\widehat{\tau}_R = \frac{1}{N}\sum_j \sum_i \left(\widehat{Y}^1_{ij} - \widehat{Y}^0_{ij}\right)$. As an example consider model S_0 which is estimated for both the treatment and control group:

$$Y^0_{ij} = \beta_{00} + \beta_{01}X_{1ij} + \beta_{02}X_{2ij} + \varepsilon_{0ij} \quad \text{for } \{i : Z_i = 0\} \text{ and}$$

$$Y^1_{ij} = \beta_{10} + \beta_{11}X_{1ij} + \beta_{12}X_{2ij} + \varepsilon_{1ij} \quad \text{for } \{i : Z_i = 1\}.$$

The predicted outcomes $\hat{Y}^1_{ij}$ and $\hat{Y}^0_{ij}$ are then used to obtain the regression estimate $\widehat{\tau}_R$.

For the doubly robust estimation we combine the PS stratification estimator (i.e., marginal mean weighting) with the outcome regression. That is, the outcome regression models are run as weighted regressions with the marginal mean weights discussed above. As before, weighted regression models were estimated separately for the treatment and control cases. The predicted treatment and control outcomes from the weighted analyses ($\hat{Y}^1_{wij}, \hat{Y}^0_{wij}$) were then used for the doubly robust ATE estimator, $\widehat{\tau}_{DR} = \frac{1}{N}\sum_j \sum_i \left(\widehat{Y}^1_{wij} - \widehat{Y}^0_{wij}\right)$. In order to limit the number of doubly robust estimates we combined the seven outcome regression models with the marginal mean weights from only two different PS models, the single-level PS model without any level-2 covariates (S_0) and the most flexible fixed effects PS model (F_2). Thus, we obtain 14 doubly robust estimates for each population.

23.3 Simulation Results

Across the 1000 replications for each population, we evaluate the performance of the different estimators with respect to the percent bias remaining. Not surprisingly, the results from this study demonstrate that doubly robust estimators work similarly in multilevel contexts as in single level contexts. That is, if either the selection or the outcome mechanism is correctly specified, the doubly robust ATE estimate will be approximately unbiased. And if both models are misspecified bias might actually increase.

23.3.1 PS Stratification and Outcome Regression Estimates

For all four populations, Table 23.1 contains the remaining bias for the PS-only estimates. They are also displayed in the four subplots of Fig. 23.4. The four subplots show the bias remaining for the PS stratification estimator for each of the four populations, which differ by their selection (rows) and outcome mechanisms (columns). The models used to estimate the PS are labeled along the bottom of

Table 23.1 Percent bias remaining in PS stratification estimators (PS only) for each of the four populations

Selection DGM–Outcome DGM		Populations			
		Monotonic–Monotonic	Monotonic–Mixture	Mixture–Monotonic	Mixture–Mixture
PS model	S_0: Single level and X only	7.2 % (0.12)	−126.6 % (53.18)	−38.6 % (9.9)	57.8 % (0.18)
	S_1: Single level and **X**, **W** main effects	20.3 % (0.09)	7.8 % (7.41)	−7.8 % (9.8)	92.4 % (0.09)
	S_2: Single level, **X**, **W** and **XW** interactions	13.0 % (0.09)	6.1 % (10.24)	−4.1 % (7.11)	88.6 % (0.10)
	F_1: Fixed effects via cluster dummies, **X** main effects	15.1 % (0.09)	−6.6 % (8.19)	−51.6 % (19.44)	68.3 % (0.14)
	F_2: Fixed effects via cluster dummies and interactions with **X**	11.8 % (0.08)	18.4 % (4.12)	−15.0 % (0.84)	−10.4 % (0.10)
	R_1: Random intercepts	16.0 % (0.09)	8.2 % (13.93)	−6.2 % (8.72)	90.8 % (0.10)
	R_2: Random slopes	12.3 % (0.09)	5.5 % (16.48)	1.2 % (9.16)	9.3 % (0.13)

Notes: Simulation standard deviations are shown in parentheses. Models S_0 to R_2 represent the PS models as outlined in section on PS and ATE estimation

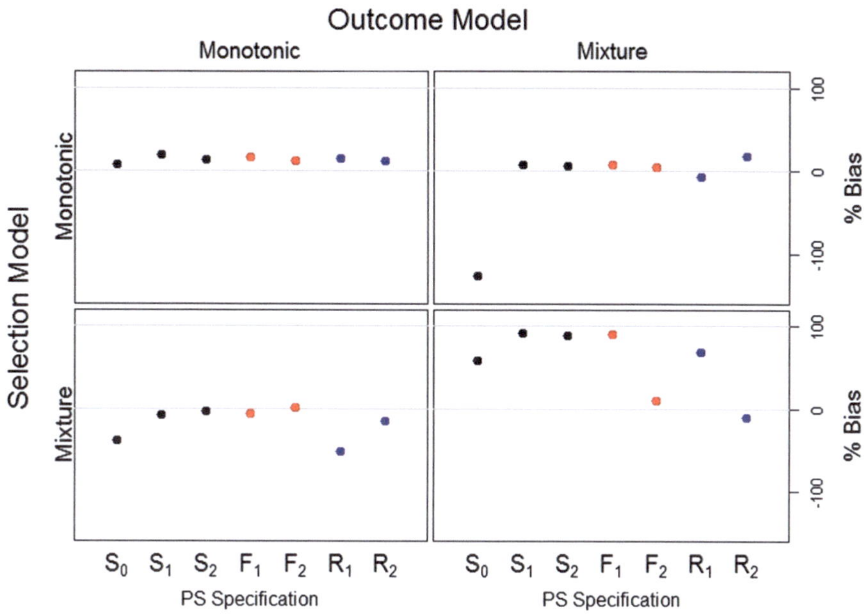

Fig. 23.4 Percent bias remaining in PS stratification estimators (PS only) for each of the four populations

the plots (see the model equations above). For example, the top left subplot shows the results for the population generated with a monotonic selection mechanism and a monotonic outcome mechanism. For this population, between 7 and 20 % of the bias remains regardless of which PS specification is used to estimate the ATE (given that we used only five strata, one can expect that 10 % of the bias is remaining due to the roughness of the strata; Rosenbaum and Rubin 1983). The effect of misspecifying of the PS model is small because the selection DGM is rather simple—all cluster-specific slopes are positive and only depend monotonically on level-2 covariates. Thus, though the misspecifications result in biased estimates of the PSs, the misspecifications have almost no effect on the determination of the PS strata. This is so because the misspecifications of the PS model only resulted in a monotonic transformation of the true PS which does not affect the creation of PS strata (Waernbaum 2012). However, this does not hold for PS model S_0 which failed to include the confounding level-2 covariates. Nonetheless, we get almost unbiased results because the outcome DGM is monotonic and, thus, of low complexity as well. Turning to the top right subplot where the outcome DGM is a mixture model, we can see that PS stratification with PSs from model S_0 now results in severely biased estimates (−126.6 %) while all other PS models do very well in removing selection bias. Again, as long as all confounding covariates are included in the PS model, the ATE estimates are rather robust to monotonic misspecifications of the PS model (i.e., the rank order of the PSs estimated from the misspecified model is the same as the rank order from the correctly specified model).

The second row of plots in Fig. 23.4 shows the results for the populations with a mixture DGM for the selection process. If the outcome DGM is of monotonic type (bottom left subplot), ATE estimates are again rather insensitive to PS model misspecifications. Though some of the misspecifications result in a non-monotonic transformation of the correctly estimated PS model we still get approximately unbiased estimates (expect for S_0 and R_1 which neither include covariates **W** nor random slopes) because the misspecifications are harmless with regard to the monotonic outcome DGM. Thus, the simplicity of the monotonic outcome DGM guarantees some robustness with respect to the misspecification of the outcome model. However, if the DGMs of both the selection and outcome mechanism are more complex (i.e., mixtures), then the correct specification of the PS model matters. In the bottom right subplot of Fig. 23.4, only the fixed effects model F_2 and the random slopes model R_2 are able to produce nearly unbiased effect estimates (these are the only two models that correctly reflect the complexity of the selection process).

Looking at all four subplots together, it is apparent that the amount of remaining bias depends not only on the specification of the PS model, but also on the population's data generating mechanism. In general, there is less remaining bias when the PS model has a functional form that correctly incorporates the multilevel structure of the data (i.e., models R_2 and F_2). The correct specification of the PS is crucial for obtaining unbiased treatment effect estimates if the population has selection and outcome DGMs that strongly vary across clusters (Mixture–Mixture population).

Figure 23.5 and Table 23.2 show the estimated treatment effects for the outcome regression estimator (i.e., when regression adjustments are used). The model labels along the bottom of the plots now indicate the regression models used. Since our selection and outcome DGMs were linear, the regression-based results are essentially the same as for the PS-stratification estimator and, thus, will not be discussed in detail here. However, note that the results might significantly differ for highly nonlinear DGMs.

23.3.2 Doubly Robust Estimates

Figures 23.6 and 23.7 (and the corresponding data in Tables 23.3 and 23.4) show the results for the doubly robust estimators. The outcome regression models used to estimate the ATE are labeled along the bottom of the plots. Model E indicates the empty outcome model that includes no predictors except for the treatment indicator but uses the marginal mean weights derived from the PS strata—thus, model E represents the PS stratification estimator. The outcome regression models are the same for the two figures and tables, but the PS estimator differs (i.e., the marginal mean weights). Figure 23.6 and Table 23.3 show the remaining bias when the most complex fixed effects PS specification (F_2) is used, while Fig. 23.7 and Table 23.4 show the doubly robust results when the misspecified single level PS model S_0 is

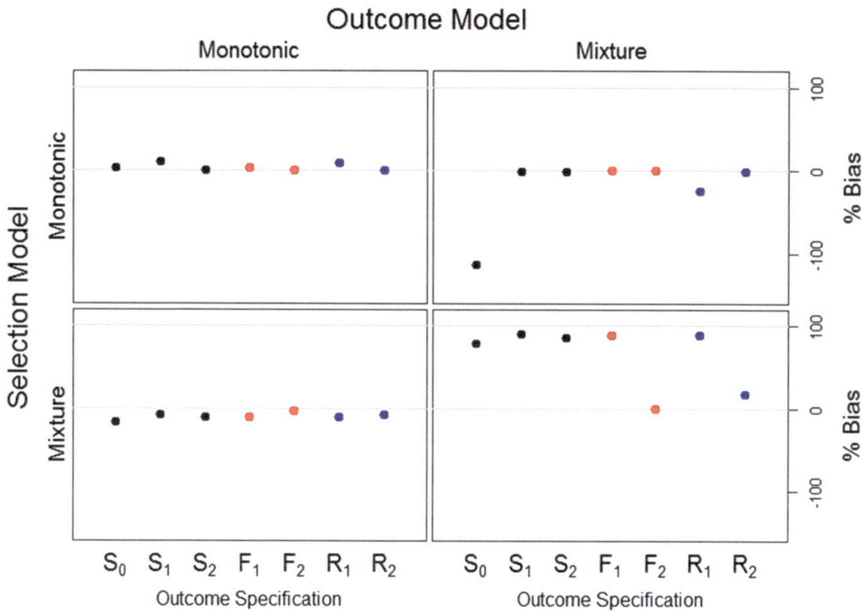

Fig. 23.5 Percent bias remaining in outcome regression estimators (regression only) for each of the four populations

used. The fixed effects PS model F_2 allows each cluster to have its own slope and intercept, thus, it is flexible enough to correctly specify the selection DGM (we could have also used the random intercept and slopes PS model R_2 which results in very similar estimates). In Fig. 23.6, all four populations show little remaining bias for even the grossly misspecified outcome regression model (such as S_0 and S_1) because the PS model is correctly specified. This result is in accordance with the theory on doubly robust estimators: When the PS model is correctly specified, the outcome mechanism (the covariate adjustment) can be misspecified and we still get unbiased results.

Figure 23.7 illustrates what happens when the PS model is misspecified. The PS model in this case is the single level model S_0. Now, in all of the populations, except for the Monotonic–Monotonic one, only the outcome models that allow each cluster to have a separate slope and intercept (F_2 and R_2) are essentially unbiased. However, for the monotonic outcome DGM combined with the mixture selection DGM (bottom left plot), also the misspecified regression models remove most of the bias (as it was already the case for the regression only results). However, when both the PS and the outcome model do not properly take the cluster structure into account, remaining bias is often greater than when only one misspecified model is used. For example, in the Monotonic–Mixture population (top right plot), the remaining bias of −135.7 % when the PS and regression adjustment are both single level models (S_0) is greater than the −114.2 % bias remaining when only the regression model

Table 23.2 Percent bias remaining in outcome regression estimators (regression only) for each of the four populations

		Populations			
Selection DGM–Outcome DGM		Monotonic–Monotonic	Monotonic–Mixture	Mixture–Monotonic	Mixture–Mixture
Regression model	S_0	4.2 % (0.13)	−114.2 % (55.03)	−16.2 % (11.32)	79.0 % (0.13)
	S_1	11.1 % (0.1)	−0.4 % (9.48)	−8.4 % (11.6)	90.2 % (0.1)
	S_2	1.0 % (0.1)	−0.2 % (11.01)	−11.4 % (7.41)	86.1 % (0.11)
	F_1	9.8 % (0.09)	−23.8 % (20.53)	−11.1 % (7.63)	88.3 % (0.11)
	F_2	0.8 % (0.09)	−0.2 % (15.82)	−8.2 % (6.39)	16.6 % (0.12)
	R_1	3.7 % (0.09)	−0.2 % (14.45)	−11.0 % (3.98)	88.8 % (0.11)
	R_2	1.0 % (0.1)	0.2 % (17.95)	−3.3 % (8.86)	−0.6 % (0.13)

Notes: Simulation standard deviations are shown in parentheses. Models S_0 to R_2 are regression only models as outlined in section on PS and ATE estimation

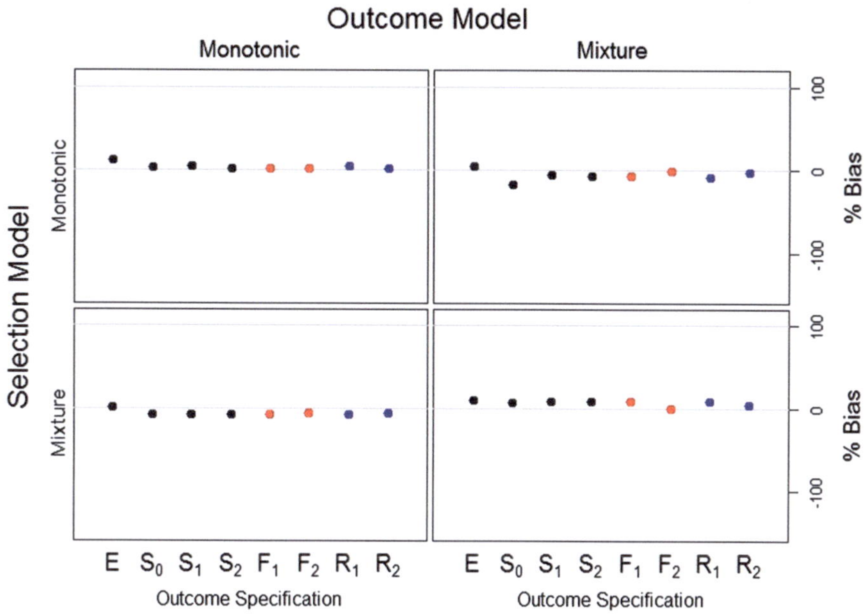

Fig. 23.6 Percent bias remaining for doubly robust estimators using PS model F_2 (fixed effects) for each of the four populations

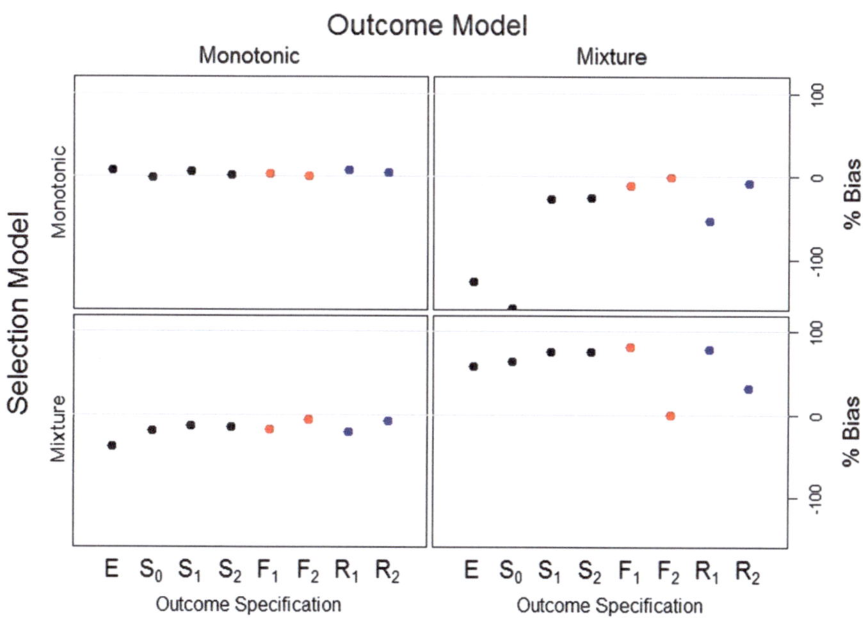

Fig. 23.7 Percent bias remaining for doubly robust estimators using PS model S_0 (level-1 main effects only)

Table 23.3 Percent bias remaining for doubly robust estimators using PS model F_2 (fixed effects with cluster interactions) for each of the four populations

		Populations			
Selection DGM–Outcome DGM		Monotonic–Monotonic	Monotonic–Mixture	Mixture–Monotonic	Mixture–Mixture
Regression model	S_0	3.8 % (0.09)	−13.9 % (20.19)	−5.7 % (9.06)	7.2 % (0.13)
	S_1	4.5 % (0.09)	−3.9 % (15.39)	−2.3 % (9.27)	8.2 % (0.13)
	S_2	1.4 % (0.1)	−5.3 % (16.55)	−4.2 % (7.97)	7.8 % (0.13)
	F_1	4.4 % (0.09)	−5.6 % (15.99)	−3.3 % (4.41)	8.2 % (0.13)
	F_2	1.3 % (0.1)	−1.4 % (14.99)	−4.4 % (8.8)	1.2 % (0.14)
	R_1	2.7 % (0.1)	−5.1 % (15.6)	−4.1 % (6.16)	8.3 % (0.13)
	R_2	1.3 % (0.1)	−0.3 % (13.66)	−3.2 % (8.27)	−0.4 % (0.14)

Notes: Simulation standard deviations are shown in parentheses. Models S_0 to R_2 are regression only models as outlined in section on PS and ATE estimation

Table 23.4 Percent bias remaining for doubly robust estimators using PS model S_0 (level-1 main effects only)

		Populations			
Selection DGM–Outcome DGM		Monotonic–Monotonic	Monotonic–Mixture	Mixture–Monotonic	Mixture–Mixture
Regression model	S_0	−1.3 % (0.12)	−135.7 % (61.68)	−12.1 % (7.18)	63.9 % (0.16)
	S_1	6.5 % (0.11)	−25.0 % (14.62)	−5.2 % (7.26)	75.8 % (0.13)
	S_2	1.4 % (0.1)	−17.5 % (14.98)	−9.3 % (6.35)	74.9 % (0.13)
	F_1	8.2 % (0.09)	−30.3 % (22.00)	−9.9 % (5.99)	81.6 % (0.13)
	F_2	1.1 % (0.09)	−1.4 % (15.49)	−8.5 % (6.31)	15.4 % (0.13)
	R_1	3.3 % (0.09)	−6.1 % (15.38)	−10.1 % (3.89)	83.1 % (0.12)
	R_2	1.0 % (0.1)	−0.1 % (17.68)	−3.4 % (8.4)	−0.7 % (0.13)

Notes: Simulation standard deviations are shown in parentheses. Models S_0 to R_2 are regression only models as outlined in section on PS and ATE estimation

S_0 is used or the $-126.6\,\%$ bias remaining when the PS model S_0 is used alone (the latter is shown in the plot as Model E). For the Mixture–Mixture population (bottom right plot of Fig. 23.7), the additional regression adjustments generally result in an increasing bias in comparison with the PS stratification used singly (model E in the plot). Only when the regression models correctly capture the variations of the outcome model across clusters (i.e., R_2 and F_2) the doubly robust estimator performs better than the PS stratification estimator.

23.4 Discussion

The populations examined in this study demonstrate how doubly robust estimators work for two selection and two outcome mechanisms. Despite the fact that only four populations were examined, the mechanisms highlighted here represent two contrasting relationships that could occur in practice. The Mixture–Mixture population in particular represents an extreme cluster structure where some clusters have positive relationships and some have negative relationships, which cannot be modeled correctly without including cluster-level characteristics either in the selection or outcome model—as the results demonstrate. Unless the selection or outcome models are complex enough to allow each cluster to have its own intercept and slope, via fixed or random effects, the ATE estimates can be extremely biased for all three types of estimators discussed here (PS only, regression, and doubly robust). At the other extreme, for the Monotonic–Monotonic population the within-cluster relationships between the dependent and independent variables are all of the same direction, thus, even strongly misspecified PS or outcome models succeed in removing almost all of the selection bias. The comparison of PS and outcome regression estimators revealed that, according to theory, doubly robust estimators succeed in removing all the selection bias as long as one of the models is correctly specified (or at least sufficiently flexible to capture the variations across clusters).

Although our results are in accordance with theory, the results of our simulations do not necessarily generalize to different settings. First, we only looked at four populations generated from two selection and outcome DGMs. Though we attempted to create populations that could match data in practice, one cannot derive strong conclusion about the performance of doubly robust estimators in general. However, we tested several other populations with alternate data generating processes, and the results shown here continue to hold. Second, we only investigated PS stratification. Results might slightly differ for PS matching or inverse-probability weighting. Third, the analysis scenarios assumed that strong ignorability is met. With the exception of model S_0, all estimation models included all covariates that were used to generate the data, which may overstate the effectiveness of the estimators in practice. Finally, the treatment effects we generated were assumed to be homogenous and there was strong overlap between treated and control cases in the populations. With heterogeneous treatment effects and weak overlap the performance of estimators might change.

Future research could address some of these limitations. Future studies could expand upon the populations used for this study by generating data using different coefficient matrices that create new relationships between the level-1 and level-2 variables. More realistic populations could be generated that introduce heterogeneous treatment effects, more covariates, and/or additional hierarchies (such as level-3 covariates). The analysis could be expanded to explore other PS methods, different doubly robust estimators, and scenarios where strong ignorability is not met.

Acknowledgements The research reported here was supported by the Institute of Education Sciences, U.S. Department of Education, through Grant R305D120005. The opinions expressed are those of the authors and do not represent views of the Institute or the U.S. Department of Education.

References

Angrist, J., & Pischke, J. (2009). *Mostly harmless econometrics: An empiricist's companion*. Princeton, NJ: Princeton University Press.

Bang, H., & Robins, J. (2005). Doubly robust estimation in missing data and causal inference models. *Biometrics, 64*(4), 962–973. Retrieved from http://www.jstor.org/stable/3695907.

Holland, P. (1986). Statistics and causal inference. *Journal of the American Statistical Association, 81*, 945–970.

Hong, G. (2010). Marginal mean weighting through stratification: Adjustment for selection bias in multilevel data. *Journal of Educational and Behavioral Statistics, 35*(5), 433–531.

Hong, G., & Raudenbush, S. W. (2005). Effects of kindergarten retention policy on children's cognitive growth in reading and mathematics. *Educational Evaluation and Policy Analysis, 27*(3), 205–224.

Kang, J. D. Y., & Schafer, J. L. (2007). Demystifying double robustness: A comparison of alternative strategies for estimating a population mean from incomplete data. *Statistical Science, 22*(4), 523–539. Retrieved from http://arxiv.org/pdf/0804.2958.pdf.

Kelcey, B. (2011). Assessing the effects of teachers' reading knowledge on students' achievement using multilevel propensity score stratification. *Educational Evaluation and Policy Analysis, 33*(4), 458–482.

Keller, B., Kim, J.-S., & Steiner, P. (2013). Data mining alternatives to logistic regression for propensity score estimation: Neural networks and support vector machines. *Multivariate Behavioral Research, 48*(1), 165.

Kim, J., & Seltzer, M. (2007). *Causal inference in multilevel settings in which selection process vary across schools*. Working Paper 708, Center for the Study of Evaluation (CSE), UCLA, Los Angeles.

Kreif, N., Grieve, R., Radice, R., & Sekhon, J. (2011). Regression-adjusted matching and double-robust methods for estimating average treatment effects in health economic evaluation. *Health Services and Outcomes Research Methodology, 13*, (2–4), 174–202.

Li, F., Zaslavsky, A., & Landrum, M. (2012). Propensity score weighting with multilevel data. *Statistics in Medicine, 32*, 3373–3387.

Robins, J., Hernan, M., & Brumback, B. (2000). Marginal structural models and causal inference in epidemiology. *Epidemiology, 11*(5), 550–560.

Rosenbaum, P., & Rubin, D. (1983). The central role of the propensity score in observational studies for causal effects. *Biometrika, 70*(1), 41–55.

Rubin, D. (1974). Estimating causal effects of treatments in randomized and nonrandomized studies. *Journal of Educational Psychology, 66*, 688–701.
Schafer, J., & Kang, J. (2008). Average causal effects from nonrandomized studies: A practical guide and simulated example. *Psychological Methods, 13*(4), 279–313.
Steiner, P., Kim, Y., Hall, C., & Su, D. (2015). Graphical models for quasi-experimental designs. *Sociological Methods & Research,* 0049124115582272
Steiner, P., Kim, J.-S., & Thoemmes, F. (2013). Matching strategies for observational multilevel data. In *JSM Proceedings* (pp. 5020–5032). Alexandria, VA: American Statistical Association.
Waernbaum, I. (2012). Model misspecification and robustness in causal inference: Comparing matching with doubly robust estimation. *Statistics in Medicine, 31*(15), 1572–1581.

Chapter 24
Mediation Analysis with Missing Data Through Multiple Imputation and Bootstrap

Zhiyong Zhang, Lijuan Wang, and Xin Tong

Abstract A method using multiple imputation and bootstrap for dealing with missing data in mediation analysis is introduced and implemented in both SAS and R. Through simulation studies, it is shown that the method performs well for both MCAR and MAR data without and with auxiliary variables. It is also shown that the method can work for MNAR data if auxiliary variables related to missingness are included. The application of the method is demonstrated through the analysis of a subset of data from the National Longitudinal Survey of Youth. Mediation analysis with missing data can be conducted using the provided SAS macros and R package bmem.

Keywords Mediation analysis • Missing data • Multiple imputation • Bootstrap

24.1 Introduction

Mediation models and mediation analysis are widely used in behavioral and social sciences as well as in health and medical research. Mediation models are very useful for theory development and testing as well as for identification of intervention points in applied work. Although mediation models were first developed in psychology (e.g., MacCorquodale and Meehl 1948; Woodworth 1928), they have been recognized and used in many disciplines where the mediation effect is also known as the indirect effect (Sociology, Alwin and Hauser 1975) and the surrogate or intermediate endpoint effect (Epidemiology, Freedman and Schatzkin 1992).

Figure 24.1 depicts the path diagram of a simple mediation model. In this figure, X, M, and Y represent the independent or input variable, the mediation variable (mediator), and the dependent or outcome variable, respectively. The e_M and e_Y are

Z. Zhang (✉) • L. Wang
University of Notre Dame, Notre Dame, IN 46556, USA
e-mail: zzhang4@nd.edu; lwang4@nd.edu

X. Tong
University of Virginia, Charlottesville, VA 22904, USA
e-mail: xtong@virginia.edu

L.A. van der Ark et al. (eds.), *Quantitative Psychology Research*, Springer Proceedings in Mathematics & Statistics 140, DOI 10.1007/978-3-319-19977-1_24

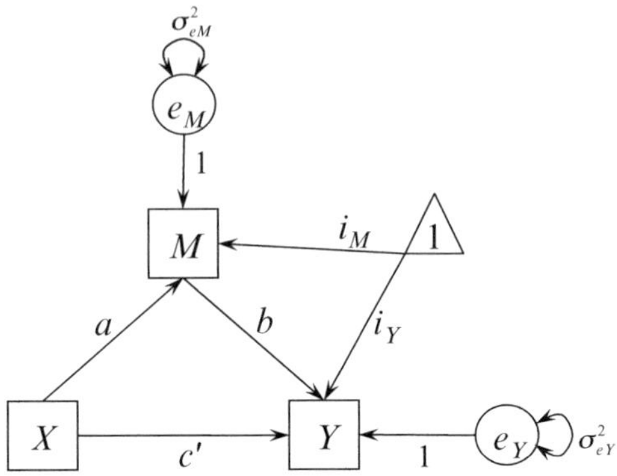

Fig. 24.1 Path diagram demonstration of a mediation model

residuals or disturbances with variances σ^2_{eM} and σ^2_{eY}. The coefficient c' is called the direct effect, and the mediation effect or indirect effect is measured by the product term $ab = a \times b$ as an indirect path from X to Y through M. The other parameters in this model include the intercepts i_M and i_Y.

Statistical approaches to estimating and testing mediation effects with complete data have been discussed extensively in the psychological literature (e.g., Baron and Kenny 1986; Bollen and Stine 1990; MacKinnon et al. 2007, 2002; Shrout and Bolger 2002). One way to test mediation effects is to test $H_0 : ab = 0$. If a large sample is available, the normal approximation method can be used, which constructs the standard error of $\widehat{ab}$ through the delta method so that $s.e.(\widehat{ab}) = \sqrt{\hat{b}^2\widehat{\sigma_a^2} + 2\hat{a}\hat{b}\hat{\sigma}_{ab} + \hat{a}^2\widehat{\sigma_b^2}}$ with the parameter estimates $\hat{a}$ and $\hat{b}$, their estimated variances $\widehat{\sigma_a^2}$ and $\widehat{\sigma_b^2}$, and covariance $\hat{\sigma}_{ab}$ (e.g., Sobel 1982, 1986). Many researchers suggested that the distribution of a mediation effect may not be normal especially when the sample size is small although with large sample sizes the distribution may still approach normality (Bollen and Stine 1990; MacKinnon et al. 2002). Thus, bootstrap methods have been recommended to obtain the empirical distribution and confidence interval of a mediation effect (MacKinnon et al. 2004; Mallinckrodt et al. 2006; Preacher and Hayes 2008; Shrout and Bolger 2002; Zhang and Wang 2008).

Missing data is continuously a challenge even for a well-designed study. Although there are approaches to dealing with missing data for path analysis in general (for a recent review, see Graham 2009), there are few studies focusing on the treatment of missing data in mediation analysis. Mediation analysis is different from typical path analysis because the focus is on the product of multiple path coefficients. A common practice is to analyze complete data through listwise deletion or pairwise deletion (e.g., Chen et al. 2005; Preacher and Hayes 2004). Recently, Zhang and Wang (2013b) discussed how to deal with missing data in mediation analysis through multiple imputation and full information maximum likelihood. However, the number of imputations needed to get reliable results remains unclear.

In this study, we discuss how to deal with missing data for mediation analysis through multiple imputation (MI) and bootstrap. We will first present some technical aspects of multiple imputation for mediation analysis with missing data. Then, we will present two simulation studies to evaluate the performance of MI for mediation analysis with missing data. In particular, we investigate the number of imputations needed for mediation analysis. Next, an empirical example will be used to demonstrate the application of the method. Finally, we discuss the limitations of the study and future directions. Instructions on how to use SAS and R to conduct mediation analysis through multiple imputation and bootstrap are provided online as supplemental materials.

24.2 Method

24.2.1 Complete Data Mediation Analysis

We focus our discussion on the simple mediation model to better illustrate the method although the approach works for the general mediation model. In its mathematical form, the mediation model displayed in Fig. 24.1 can be expressed using two equations,

$$
\begin{aligned}
M &= i_M + aX + e_M \\
Y &= i_Y + bM + c'X + e_Y, \qquad (24.1)
\end{aligned}
$$

which can be viewed as a collection of two linear regression models. To obtain the parameter estimates in the model, the maximum likelihood estimation method for structural equation modeling (SEM) can be used. Specifically for the simple mediation model, the mediation effect estimate is $\widehat{ab} = \hat{a}\hat{b}$ with

$$
\begin{aligned}
\hat{a} &= s_{XM}/s_X^2 \\
\hat{b} &= (s_{MY}s_X^2 - s_{XM}s_{XY})/(s_X^2 s_M^2 - s_{XM}^2) \qquad (24.2)
\end{aligned}
$$

where $s_X^2, s_M^2, s_Y^2, s_{XM}, s_{MY}, s_{XY}$ are sample variances and covariances of X, M, Y, respectively.

24.2.2 Missingness Mechanisms

Little and Rubin (1987, 2002) have distinguished three types of missing data—missing completely at random (MCAR), missing at random (MAR), and missing not at random (MNAR). Let $D = (X, M, Y)$ denote all data that can be potentially observed in a mediation model. D_{obs} and D_{miss} denote data that are actually observed and data that are not observed, respectively. Let R denote an indicator matrix of zeros and ones with the same dimension as D. If a datum in D is missing, the corresponding element in R is equal to 1. Otherwise, it is equal to 0. Finally, let A denote the auxiliary variables that are related to the missingness of D but not a component of the mediation model.

If the missing mechanism is MCAR, then we have

$$\Pr(R|D_{obs}, D_{miss}, \boldsymbol{\theta}) = \Pr(R|\boldsymbol{\theta}),$$

where the vector $\boldsymbol{\theta}$ represents all model parameters in the mediation model. This suggests that missing data D_{miss} are a simple random sample of D and not related to the data observed or auxiliary variables A. If the missing mechanism is MAR, then

$$\Pr(R|D_{obs}, D_{miss}, \boldsymbol{\theta}) = \Pr(R|D_{obs}, \boldsymbol{\theta}),$$

which indicates that the probability that a datum is missing is related to the observed data D_{obs} but not to the missing data D_{miss}.

Finally, if the probability that a datum is missing is related to the missing data D_{miss} or auxiliary variables A but A are not considered in the data analysis, the missing mechanism is MNAR. In particular, we want to emphasize the MNAR mechanism with auxiliary variables where

$$\Pr(R|D_{obs}, D_{miss}, \boldsymbol{\theta}) = \Pr(R|D_{obs}, A, \boldsymbol{\theta}).$$

Note that although the missingness is MNAR if only D is modeled, the overall missingness becomes to MAR if D and A are jointly modeled. Therefore, one way to deal with MNAR is to identify and include the auxiliary variables that are related to missingness.

24.2.3 *Multiple Imputation for Mediation Analysis with Missing Data*

Most techniques dealing with missing data, including multiple imputation, in general require missing data to be either MCAR or MAR (see also, e.g., Little and Rubin 2002; Schafer 1997). For MNAR, the missing mechanism has to be known to correctly recover model parameters (e.g., Lu et al. 2011; Zhang and Wang 2012). Practically, researchers have suggested including auxiliary variables to facilitate MNAR missing data analysis (Graham 2003; Savalei and Bentler 2009). After including appropriate auxiliary variables, we may be able to assume that data from both model variables and auxiliary variables are MAR.

Assume that a set of $p(p \geq 0)$ auxiliary variables $A_1, A_2, \ldots, A_p$ are available. These auxiliary variables may or may not be related to missingness of the mediation model variables. By augmenting the auxiliary variables with the mediation model variables, we have $D = (X, M, Y, A_1, \ldots, A_p)$, e.g., for the simple mediation model. To proceed, we assume that the missing mechanism is MAR after including the auxiliary variables.

Multiple imputation (Little and Rubin 2002; Rubin 1976; Schafer 1997) is a procedure to fill each missing value with a set of plausible values. The multiple imputed data sets are then analyzed using standard procedures for complete data and the results from these analyses are combined for obtaining point estimates of model parameters and their standard errors. For mediation analysis with missing data, the following steps can be implemented for obtaining point estimates of mediation model parameters:

1. Assuming that $D = (X, M, Y, A_1, \ldots, A_p)$ are from a multivariate normal distribution, generate K sets of values for each missing value. Combine the generated values with the observed data to produce K sets of complete data (Schafer 1997).
2. For each of the K sets of complete data, apply the formula in Eq. (24.2) or use the SEM method to obtain a point mediation effect estimate $\widehat{ab}_k = \hat{a}_k\hat{b}_k$ ($j = 1, \ldots, K$).
3. The point estimate for the mediation effect through multiple imputation is the average of the K complete data mediation effect estimates:

$$\widehat{ab} = \hat{a}\hat{b} = \frac{1}{K}\sum_{k=1}^{K} \hat{a}_k\hat{b}_k.$$

Parameter estimates for other model parameters can be obtained in the same way.

24.2.4 *Testing Mediation Effects Through the Bootstrap Method*

The procedure described above is implemented to obtain point estimates of mediation effects. The bootstrap method has been used to test the significance of the mediation effects (e.g., Bollen and Stine 1990). This method has no distribution assumption on the indirect effect. Instead, it approximates the distribution of the indirect effect using its bootstrap empirical distribution. The bootstrap method can be applied along with multiple imputation to obtain standard errors of mediation effect estimates and confidence intervals for mediation analysis with missing data. Specifically, the following procedure can be used.

1. Using the *original data set* (sample size = N) as a population, draw a bootstrap sample of N persons randomly with replacement from the original data set. This bootstrap sample generally would contain missing data.

2. With the bootstrap sample, implement the K multiple imputation procedure described in the above section to obtain point estimates of model parameters and a point estimate of the mediation effect.
3. Repeat Steps 1 and 2 for a total of B times. B is called the number of bootstrap samples.
4. Empirical distributions of model parameters and the mediation effect are then obtained using the B sets of bootstrap point estimates. Thus, confidence intervals of model parameters and the mediation effect can be constructed.

The procedure described above can be considered as a procedure of K multiple imputations nested within B bootstrap samples. Using the B bootstrap sample point estimates, one can obtain bootstrap standard errors and confidence intervals of model parameters and mediation effects conveniently. Let $\boldsymbol{\theta}$ denote a vector of model parameters and the mediation effects. With data from each bootstrap, we can obtain $\hat{\boldsymbol{\theta}}^b$, $b = 1, \ldots, B$. The standard error estimate of the pth parameter $\hat{\theta}_p$ can be calculated as

$$\widehat{s.e.(\hat{\theta}_p)} = \sqrt{\sum_{b=1}^{B}(\hat{\theta}_p^b - \bar{\hat{\theta}}_p^b)^2/(B-1)}$$

with $\bar{\hat{\theta}}_p^b = \sum_{b=1}^{B} \hat{\theta}_p^b / B$.

Many methods for constructing confidence intervals from $\hat{\boldsymbol{\theta}}^b$ have been proposed such as the percentile interval, the bias-corrected (BC) interval, and the bias-corrected and accelerated (BCa) interval (Efron 1987; MacKinnon et al. 2004). In the present study, we focus on the BC interval because MacKinnon et al. (2004) showed that, in general, the BC confidence intervals have performed better in terms of Type I error and statistical power among many different confidence intervals. The $1-2\alpha$ BC interval for the pth element of $\boldsymbol{\theta}$ can be constructed using the percentiles $\hat{\theta}_p^b(\tilde{\alpha}_l)$ and $\hat{\theta}_p^b(\tilde{\alpha}_u)$ of $\hat{\theta}_p^b$ with $\tilde{\alpha}_l = \Phi(2z_0 + z^{(\alpha)})$ and $\tilde{\alpha}_u = \Phi(2z_0 + z^{(1-\alpha)})$ where Φ is the standard cumulative normal distribution function and $z^{(\alpha)}$ is the α percentile of the standard normal distribution and

$$z_0 = \Phi^{-1}\left[\frac{\text{number of times that } \hat{\theta}_p^b < \hat{\theta}_p}{B}\right].$$

24.3 Simulation Studies

In this section, we conduct two simulation studies to evaluate the performance of the proposed method for mediation analysis with missing data. We first evaluate its performance under different missing data mechanisms including MCAR, MAR, and MNAR without and with auxiliary variables. Then, we investigate how many imputations are needed for different proportions of missing data.

24.3.1 Simulation Study 1: Estimate of Mediation Effects Under MCAR, MAR, and MNAR Data

24.3.1.1 Simulation Design

For mediation analysis with complete data, simulation studies have been conducted to investigate a variety of features of mediation models (e.g., MacKinnon et al. 2002, 2004). For the current study, we follow the parameter setup from the previous literature and set the population parameter values to be $a = b = .39$, $c' = 0$, $i_M = i_Y = 0$, and $\sigma^2_{eM} = \sigma^2_{eY} = \sigma^2_{eX} = 1$. Furthermore, we fix the sample size at $N = 100$ and consider three proportions of missingness with missing data percentages at 10, 20, and 40 %, respectively. To facilitate the comparisons among different missing mechanisms, missing data are only allowed in M and Y although our software programs also allow missingness in X. Two auxiliary variables (A_1 and A_2) are also generated where the correlation between A_1 and M and the correlation between A_2 and Y are both 0.5.

Missing data are generated in the following way. First, 1000 sets of complete data are generated. Second, for MCAR, each data value has the same probability of missing for M and Y. Third, for the MAR data, the probability of missingness in Y and M depends only on X. Specifically, if X is smaller than a given percentile, M is missing and if X is larger than a given percentile, Y is missing. Finally, to generate MNAR data, we assume that missingness of M depends on A_1 and missingness of Y depends on A_2. If A_1 is smaller than a given percentile, M is missing, and if A_2 is smaller than a percentile, Y is missing. Clearly, if auxiliary variables A_1 and A_2 are included in an analysis, the missing mechanism becomes MAR. However, if the auxiliary are not considered, the missing mechanism is MNAR.

The generated data are analyzed using the R package bmem. To estimate the mediation effects, the sample covariance matrix of the imputed data is first estimated. Then, the mediation model is fitted to the estimated covariance matrix to obtain the model parameters through the SEM maximum likelihood estimation method (Bollen 1989). Finally, the mediation effects are calculated as the product of the corresponding direct effects.

24.3.1.2 Results

The parameter estimate bias, coverage probability, and power for MCAR, MAR, and MNAR data with 10, 20, and 40 % missing data were obtained without and with auxiliary variables and are summarized in Table 24.1. Based on the results, we can conclude the following. First, the bias of the parameter estimates under the

Table 24.1 Bias, coverage probability, and power under MCAR

	Without auxiliary variables			With auxiliary variables		
	Bias	Coverage	Power	Bias	Coverage	Power
MCAR						
10 %	0.219	0.967	0.900	0.263	0.967	0.920
20 %	−1.222	0.966	0.808	−0.593	0.963	0.845
40 %	−0.716	0.946	0.531	0.112	0.950	0.615
MAR						
10 %	−0.119	0.957	0.870	−0.403	0.961	0.893
20 %	−0.546	0.962	0.767	−1.940	0.958	0.791
40 %	−2.932	0.960	0.511	−1.747	0.955	0.599
MNAR						
10 %	−32.633	0.831	0.800	−0.513	0.951	0.925
20 %	−49.117	0.673	0.570	−2.583	0.941	0.815
40 %	−66.815	0.559	0.305	−2.951	0.951	0.642

Note: We have also investigated other conditions where the sample size, population parameters, and correlation between auxiliary variables and model variables are different. We observed the same patterns in the results.

studied MCAR conditions was small enough to be ignored. Second, the coverage probability was close to the nominal level 0.95. Third, the inclusion of auxiliary variables in MCAR did not seem to influence the accuracy of parameter estimates and coverage probability. The use of auxiliary variables, however, boosted the power of detecting the mediation effect especially when the missing proportion was large (e.g., 40 %). The findings from MAR data are similar to those from MCAR data and thus are not repeated here. However, the power of detecting mediation effects from MAR data were smaller than that from MCAR data given the same proportion of missing data.

The results for MNAR data clearly showed that when auxiliary variables were not included, parameter estimates were highly underestimated especially when the missing data proportion was large, e.g., about 67 % bias with 40 % missing data for the mediation effect. Correspondingly, coverage probability was highly underestimated, too. For example, with 40 % of missing data, the coverage probability was only about 56 %. However, with the inclusion of auxiliary variables, the parameter estimate bias dramatically decreased to less than 3 % and the coverage probabilities were close to 95 %. Thus, multiple imputation can be used to analyze MNAR data and recover true parameter values by including auxiliary variables that can explain missingness of the variables in the mediation model. This is because the inclusion of the auxiliary variables converts the missingness mechanism to MAR. However, this does not mean that the inclusion of auxiliary variables can always address the non-ignorable problems and more discussion on this can be found in Zhang and Wang (2013b)

24.3.2 Simulation Study 2: Impact of the Number of Imputations

One difficulty in applying multiple imputation is to decide on how many imputations are sufficient. For example, Rubin (1987) has suggested that five imputations are sufficient in the case of 50 % missing data for estimating the simple mean. But Graham et al. (2007) recommend that many more imputations than what Rubin recommended should be used. Although one may always choose to use a very large number of imputations for mediation analysis with missing data, this may not be practically possible because of the amount of computational time involved.

In this simulation study, we investigate the impact of the number of imputations on point estimates and standard error estimates of mediation effects with different proportions of missing data. The same model in the first simulation study is used. The data are generated in the following way. First, two groups of 100 sets of complete data with two auxiliary variables are generated so that the correlation between the auxiliary variables and the mediation model variables is ρ =0.1 for the first group and $\rho = 0.4$ for the second group, respectively. Second, 10 and 40 % of missing data are generated, respectively, for each group of the 100 sets of complete data, where the missingness is related to the auxiliary variables as in the first simulation study. Therefore, in total, we have 4 groups of 100 sets of missing data.

For each data set, we obtain the results from the data analysis including auxiliary variables with the number of imputations ranging from 10 to 100 at intervals of 10. Note that the overall missingness is MAR. After that, we calculate the average mediation effect and standard error estimates from the 100 sets of data. For better comparison, we calculate the relative deviance of mediation effect estimates and their standard error estimates from those estimates with 100 imputations. The relative deviance from the simulation is plotted in Fig. 24.2. Since the results were based on 100 replications of simulation, the absolute difference was small as a result. Therefore, we rescaled the relative deviance by 1000 times to focus on the relative change of the deviance corresponding to the number of imputations. We have found that the analysis of individual data sets showed the similar pattern but with much larger deviance.

Comparing the results with 10 % missing data in Fig. 24.2a, c and the results with 40 % missing data in Fig. 24.2b, d, it is clear that there are more fluctuations in both mediation effect estimates and their standard errors with more missing data regardless of $\rho = 0.1$ or 0.5. Therefore, a greater number of imputations is needed with more missing data. More specifically, with 10 % missing data, the parameter estimates, especially the standard estimates, seem to become stable with more than 40 or 50 imputations. With 40 % missing data, however, the relative deviance of point estimates and standard error estimates does not appear stabilized until with more than 80 imputations. In our simulation study, the choice of 100 imputations appears to be adequate based on this simulation. The conclusion on the specific number of imputations here only applies to the simple mediation model. For more complex mediation analysis, more imputations might be needed.

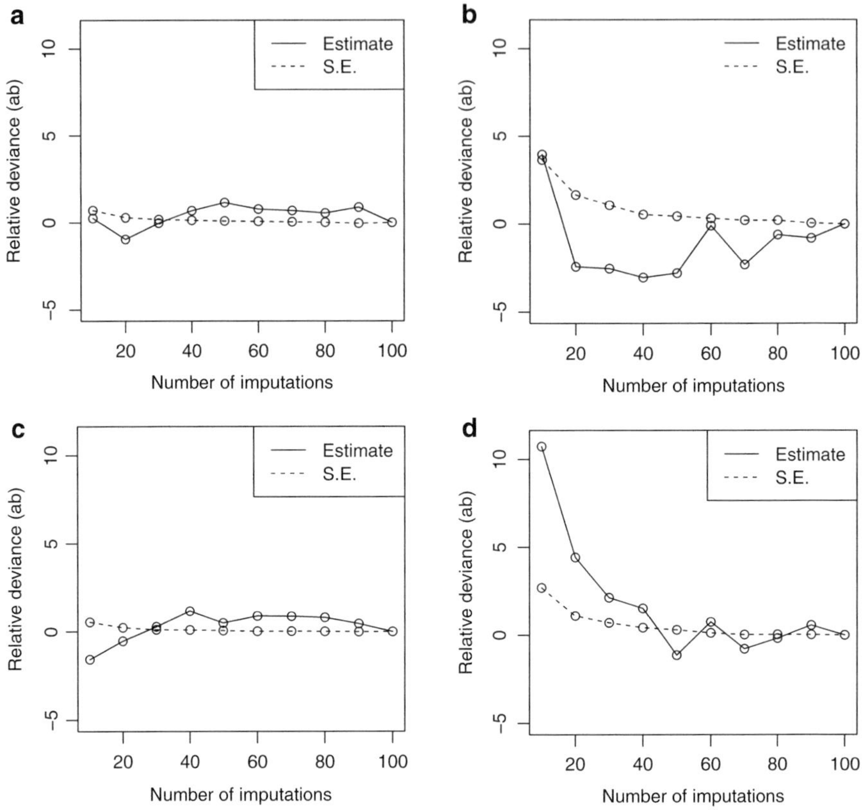

Fig. 24.2 The impact of different numbers of imputations on the accuracy of point estimates and bootstrap standard error estimates. (**a**) $\rho = 0.1$, 10 % missing data, (**b**) $\rho = 0.1$, 40 % missing data, (**c**) $\rho = 0.5$, 10 % missing data, (**d**) $\rho = 0.5$, 40 % missing data

24.4 An Empirical Example

In this section, we apply the proposed method to a real study to illustrate its application. Research has found that parental education levels can influence adolescent mathematical achievement directly and indirectly. For example, Davis-Kean (2005) showed that parental education levels are related to child academic achievement through parental beliefs and behaviors. To test a similar hypothesis, we investigate whether home environment is a mediator in the relation between mother's education and child mathematical achievement.

Data used in this example are from the National Longitudinal Survey of Youth, the 1979 cohort (NLSY79, Center for Human Resource Research 2006). Data were collected in 1986 from $N = 475$ families on mother's education level (ME), home environment (HE), child mathematical achievement (Math), child behavior problem index (BPI), and child reading recognition and reading comprehension achievement.

Table 24.2 Missing data patterns of the empirical data set

Pattern	ME	HE	Math	Sample size
1	O	O	O	417
2	O	X	O	36
3	O	O	X	14
4	O	X	X	8
Total				475

Note: *O* observed, *X* missing, *ME* mother's education level, *HE* home environments, *Math* mathematical achievement

Table 24.3 Mediation effect of home environment on the relationship between mother's education and child mathematical achievement

	Without auxiliary variable				With auxiliary variable			
Parameter	Estimate	S.E.	95 % BC		Estimate	S.E.	95 % BC	
a	0.035	0.049	0.018	0.162	0.036	0.049	0.018	0.163
b	0.475	0.126	0.252	0.754	0.458	0.125	0.221	0.711
c'	0.134	0.191	0.071	0.611	0.134	0.188	0.072	0.609
ab	0.017	0.021	0.005	0.071	0.016	0.021	0.005	0.067
i_Y	7.953	2.047	3.530	9.825	8.045	2.025	3.778	10.006
i_M	5.330	0.556	3.949	5.641	5.327	0.558	3.945	5.646
σ^2_{eY}	4.532	0.269	4.093	5.211	4.520	0.268	4.075	5.141
σ^2_{eM}	1.660	0.061	1.545	1.789	1.660	0.061	1.542	1.790

Note: The results are based on 1000 bootstrap samples and 100 imputations
S.E. bootstrap standard error, *BC* bias-corrected confidence interval

For the mediation analysis, mother's education is the independent variable, home environment is the mediator, and child mathematical achievement is the outcome variable. The missing data patterns and the sample size of each pattern are presented in Table 24.2. In this data set, 417 families have complete data and 58 families have missing data on at least one of the two model variables: home environment and child mathematical achievement. In this study, BPI and child reading recognition and reading comprehension achievement are used as auxiliary variables because they have been found to be related to mathematical achievement in the literature (e.g., Grimm 2008; Wu et al. 2014). In addition, it is reasonable to believe that it is more difficult to collect data from children with behavior problems and children with reading problems can have a harder time to complete tests on mathematics, which, therefore, could lead to more missing data.

In Table 24.3, the results from the empirical data analysis using the proposed method without and with the auxiliary variables are presented. The results reveal that the inclusion of the auxiliary variables only slightly changed the parameter estimates, standard errors, and the BC confidence intervals. This indicates that the auxiliary variables may not be related to the missingness in the mediation model variables. The results also show that home environment partially mediates the relationship between mother's education and child mathematical achievement because both the indirect effect ab and the direct effect c' are significant.

24.5 Software

We have developed both SAS macros and an R package bmem (Zhang and Wang 2013a) for mediation analysis with missing data through multiple imputation and bootstrap. Instructions on how to use the SAS macros and the R package can be found on our website at http://psychstat.org/imps2014. The SAS macros are designed for the simple mediation model and have computational advantages that make them run faster than bmem. The R package bmem, however, can handle more complex mediation analysis with multiple mediators and latent variables. Both programs can utilize auxiliary variables to potentially handle MNAR data.

24.6 Discussion

In this study, we discussed how to conduct mediation analysis with missing data through multiple imputation and bootstrap. Through simulation studies, we demonstrated that the proposed method performed well for both MCAR and MAR without and with auxiliary variables. It is also shown that multiple imputation worked equally well for MNAR if auxiliary variables related to missingness were included, because the overall missingness becomes essentially MAR. The analysis the NLSY79 data revealed that home environment partially mediated the relationship between mother's education and child mathematical achievement.

24.6.1 Strength of the Proposed Method

The multiple imputation and bootstrap method for mediation analysis with missing data has several advantages. First, the idea of imputation and bootstrap is easy to understand. Second, multiple imputation has been widely implemented in both free and commercial software and thus can be extended to mediation analysis relatively easily. Third, it is natural and easy to include auxiliary variables in multiple imputation. Fourth, unlike the full information maximum likelihood method, multiple imputation does not assume a specific model when imputing data.

24.6.2 Assumptions and Limitations

There are several assumptions and limitations of the current study. First, the current SAS program is based on a simple mediation model. In the future, the program should be expanded to allow more complex mediation analysis. Second, in applying multiple imputation, we have assumed that all variables are multivariate normally distributed. However, it is possible that one or more variables are not normally distributed. Third, the current mediation model only focuses on the cross-sectional data analysis. Some researchers have suggested that the time variable should be considered in mediation analysis (e.g., Cole and Maxwell 2003; MacKinnon 2008; Wang et al. 2009). Fourth, in dealing with MNAR data, we assume that useful auxiliary variables that can explain missingness in the mediation model variables are available. Therefore, the true missingness mechanism is actually MAR. However, sometimes the auxiliary variables may not be available. Other methods for dealing with MNAR data can be investigated in the future.

In summary, a method using multiple imputation and bootstrap for mediation analysis with missing data is introduced. Simulation results show that the method works well in dealing with missing data for mediation analysis under different missing mechanisms. Both SAS macros and an R package are provided to conduct mediation analysis with missing data, which is expected to promote the use of advanced techniques in dealing with missing data for mediation analysis in the future.

References

Alwin, D. F., & Hauser, R. M. (1975). The decomposition of effects in path analysis. *American Sociological Review, 40*, 37–47.

Baron, R. M., & Kenny, D. A. (1986). The moderator-mediator variable distinction in social psychological research: Conceptual, strategic, and statistical considerations. *Journal of Personality and Social Psychology, 51*, 1173–1182.

Bollen, K. A. (1989). *Structural equations with latent variables*. New York: Wiley.

Bollen, K. A., & Stine, R. A. (1990). Direct and indirect effects: Classical and bootstrap estimates of variability. *Sociological Methodology, 20*, 115–140.

Center for Human Resource Research. (2006). *NLSY79 CHILD & YOUNG ADULT DATA USERS GUIDE: A Guide to the 1986–2004 Child Data*. Columbus, OH: The Ohio State University

Chen, Z. X., Aryee, S., & Lee, C. (2005). Test of a mediation model of perceived organizational support. *Journal of Vocational Behavior, 66*(3), 457–470.

Cole, D. A., & Maxwell, S. E. (2003). Testing mediational models with longitudinal data: Questions and tips in the use of structural equation modeling. *Journal of Abnormal Psychology, 112*, 558–577.

Davis-Kean, P. E. (2005). The influence of parent education and family income on child achievement: The indirect role of parental expectations and the home environment. *Journal of Family Psychology, 19*, 294–304.

Efron, B. (1987). Better bootstrap confidence intervals. *Journal of the American Statistical Association, 82*(397), 171–185.

Freedman, L. S., & Schatzkin, A. (1992). Sample size for studying intermediate endpoints within intervention trails or observational studies. *American Journal of Epidemiology, 136*, 1148–1159.

Graham, J. W. (2003). Adding missing-data-relevant variables to fiml-based structural equation models. *Structural Equation Modeling, 10*, 80–100.

Graham, J. W. (2009). Missing data analysis: Making it work in the real world. *Annual Review of Psychology, 60*, 549–576.

Graham, J. W., Olchowski, A. E., & Gilreath, T. D. (2007). How many imputations are really needed? Some practical clarifications of multiple imputation theory. *Prevention Science, 8*, 206–213.

Grimm, K. J. (2008). Longitudinal associations between reading and mathematics. *Developmental Neuropsychology, 33*, 410–426.

Little, R. J. A., & Rubin, D. B. (1987). *Statistical analysis with missing data*. New York, NY: Wiley.

Little, R. J. A., & Rubin, D. B. (2002). *Statistical analysis with missing data* (2nd ed.). New York, NY: Wiley-Interscience.

Lu, Z., Zhang, Z., & Lubke, G. (2011). Bayesian inference for growth mixture models with non-ignorable missing data. *Mulitvariate Behavioral Research, 46*, 567–597.

MacCorquodale, K., & Meehl, P. E. (1948). On a distinction between hypothetical constructs and intervening variables. *Psychological Review, 55*(2), 95–107.

MacKinnon, D. P. (2008). *Introduction to statistical mediation analysis*. New York, NY: Taylor & Francis.

MacKinnon, D. P., Fairchild, A. J., & Fritz, M. S. (2007). Mediation analysis. *Annual Review of Psychology, 58*, 593–614.

MacKinnon, D. P., Lockwood, C. M., Hoffman, J. M., West, S. G., & Sheets, V. (2002). A comparison of methods to test mediation and other intervening variable effects. *Psychological Methods, 7*, 83–104.

MacKinnon, D. P., Lockwood, C. M., & Williams, J. (2004). Confidence limits for the indirect effect: Distribution of the product and resampling methods. *Multivariate Behavioral Research, 39*(1), 99–128.

Mallinckrodt, B., Abraham, T. W., Wei, M., & Russell, D. W. (2006). Advance in testing statistical significance of mediation effects. *Journal of Counseling Psychology, 53*(3), 372–378.

Preacher, K. J., & Hayes, A. F. (2004). Spss and sas procedures for estimating indirect effects in simple mediation models. *Behavior Research Methods, Instruments, & Computers, 36*, 717–731.

Preacher, K. J., & Hayes, A. F. (2008). Asymptotic and resampling strategies for assessing and comparing indirect effects in multiple mediator models. *Behavioral Research Methods, 40*, 879–891.

Rubin, D. B. (1976). Inference and missing data. *Biometrika, 63*(3), 581–592.

Rubin, D. B. (1987). *Multiple imputation for nonresponse in surveys*. New York: Wiley.

Savalei, V., & Bentler, P. M. (2009). A two-stage approach to missing data: Theory and application to auxiliary variables. *Structural Equation Modeling, 16*, 477–497.

Schafer, J. L. (1997). *Analysis of incomplete multivariate data*. London: Chapman & Hall/CRC.

Shrout, P. E., & Bolger, N. (2002). Mediation in experimental and nonexperimental studies: New procedures and recommendations. *Psychological Methods, 7*, 422–445.

Sobel, M. E. (1982). Asymptotic confidence intervals for indirect effects in structural equation models. In S. Leinhardt (Ed.), *Sociological methodology* (pp. 290–312). San Francisco: Jossey-Bass.

Sobel, M. E. (1986). Some new results on indirect effects and their standard errors in covariance structure models. In N. Tuma (Ed.), *Sociological methodology* (pp. 159–186). Washington, DC: American Sociological Association.

Wang, L., Zhang, Z., & Estabrook, R. (2009). Longitudinal mediation analysis of training intervention effects. In S. M. Chow, E. Ferrer, & F. Hsieh (Eds.), *Statistical methods for modeling human dynamics: An interdisciplinary dialogue* (pp. 349–380). New Jersey: Lawrence Erlbaum Associates.

Woodworth, R. S. (1928). Dynamic psychology. In C. Murchison (Ed.), *Psychologies of 1925* (pp. 111–126). Worcester, MA: Clark Universal Academy Press, Inc.

Wu, S. S., Willcutt, E., Escovar, E., & Menon, V. (2014). Mathematics achievement, anxiety and their relation to internalizing and externalizing behaviors. *Journal of Learning Disorders, 47*(6), 503–514.

Zhang, Z., & Wang, L. (2008). Methods for evaluating mediation effects: Rationale and comparison. In K. Shigemasu, A. Okada, T. Imaizumi, & T. Hoshino (Eds.), *New trends in psychometrics* (pp. 595–604). Tokyo: Universal Academy Press, Inc.

Zhang, Z., & Wang, L. (2012). A note on the robustness of a full Bayesian method for non-ignorable missing data analysis. *Brazilian Journal of Probability and Statistics, 26*(3), 244–264.

Zhang, Z., & Wang, L. (2013a). *bmem: Mediation analysis with missing data using bootstrap. R package version 1.5.* https://cran.r-project.org/web/packages/bmem/index.html.

Zhang, Z., & Wang, L. (2013b). Methods for mediation analysis with missing data. *Psychometrika, 78*, 154–184.

Chapter 25
Issues in Aggregating Time Series: Illustration Through an AR(1) Model

Zhenqiu (Laura) Lu and Zhiyong Zhang

Abstract Intra-individual variation is time dependent variation within a single participant's time series. When data are collected from more than one subject, methods developed for single subject intra-individual relationship may not fully work and laws governing inter-individual relationship may not apply to intra-individual relationship. There are relative few methods in dealing with the analysis of pooling multiple time series. This article ·aims to investigate empirically the comparability of methods for pooling time series data and to address related issues through an AR(1) model. In this article, multiple time series are formulated, pooling estimation methods are derived and compared, simulation studies results are summarized, and related practical issues are addressed.

Keywords Time series analysis • First-order autoregressive model • Pooling multiple subjects • Longitudinal analysis • Maximum likelihood estimation

25.1 Introduction

The variation analysis in psychological, social, and behavioral researches has many ramifications. Among them two main branches are inter-individual variation and intra-individual variation. Inter-individual variation is the variation between individuals, and also widely known as the analysis of cross-sectional data in many researches. Intra-individual variation is the time dependent variation within a single participant's time series. It is also known as the analysis of time series data or P-technique in Cattell (1952) data-box (Cattell 1952). In this type of study, usually one subject is measured and the variables of interests are collected from each of a large number of occasions. Data collected in this way do not have

Z. (Laura) Lu (✉)
University of Georgia, Athens, GA 30602, USA
e-mail: zlu@uga.edu

Z. Zhang
University of Notre Dame, Notre Dame, IN 46556, USA
e-mail: zhangzhiyong@nd.edu

L.A. van der Ark et al. (eds.), *Quantitative Psychology Research*, Springer Proceedings in Mathematics & Statistics 140, DOI 10.1007/978-3-319-19977-1_25

inter-individual differences since there is only one subject involved, but they can reflect changes across occasions. Intra-individual analysis has become popular advanced by Nesselroade, Molenaar, and colleagues. Many methods are available for single time series analysis (e.g., Cattell et al. 1947; Molenaar 1985; Nesselroade and Molenaar 2003).

In this article, attention will be drawn to multiple subjects intra-individual variation analysis. In many researches intra-individual relationship data are collected from more than one subject. When multiple subjects are involved, methods developed for single subject intra-individual relationship may not fully work. Also, laws governing inter-individual relationship may not apply to intra-individual relationship (e.g., Molenaar 2004; Nesselroade and Ram 2004). So far there are relative few methods in literature dealing with the analysis of pooling multiple time series (e.g., Cattell and Scheier 1961; Daly et al. 1974; Molenaar et al. 2003; Nesselroade and Molenaar 1999). This article aims to investigate empirically the comparability of methods for pooling time series and to address related issues by illustrating through an AR(1) model. We focus on five estimation methods for multiple time series: pooling conditional likelihood estimation, pooling exact likelihood estimation, connecting data conditional likelihood, connecting data exact likelihood, and multivariate analysis.

This article is organized as follows. In the next section some introductory remarks about time series are given. First single series and multiple series focusing on the AR(1) model are described and formulated. And then different estimation methods for multiple time series are introduced and derived. Then follows a section of simulation studies in which the performance of four estimating methods is investigated under various conditions. Simulation results are provided after the description of simulation design and implementation. The closing part of this article summarizes the simulation results, compares different estimation methods of aggregating time series, and provides practical implication.

25.2 Models

In this section, time series models and the corresponding estimation methods will be introduced. We first focus on single time series analysis, and then extend to multiple time series analysis.

25.2.1 Single Time Series AR(1) Model and Estimation

The simplest and the most popular single time series model to describe intra-individual relationship is the first-order autoregressive model, also known as AR(1). It can be expressed as follows:

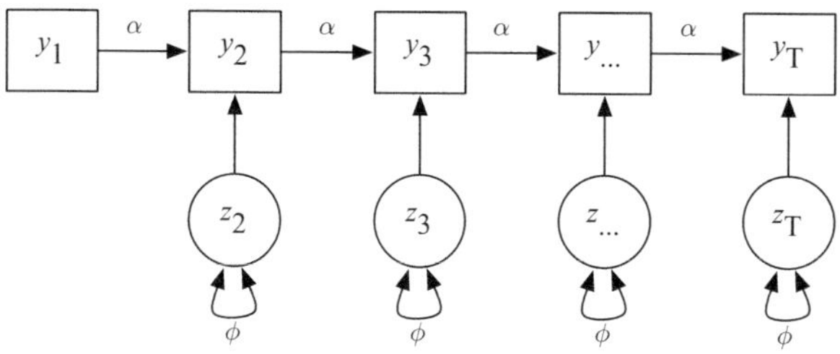

Fig. 25.1 The AR(1) model

$$\begin{aligned} & y_1 : \text{the initial value} \\ & y_t = \mu + \alpha\, y_{t-1} + z_t \quad (t > 1) \\ & z_t \sim i.i.d.\ N(0, \phi) \end{aligned} \tag{25.1}$$

where y_t is the observed value at time point t, α is the model autoregressive coefficient at lag 1, μ is an unknown parameter related to the mean of y, and z is a random shock or a white noise, which is assumed to follow a normal distribution with a mean of 0 and a variance of ϕ. The joint density function of y_t $(t = 1, \ldots, T)$ given the AR(1) model in Eq. (25.2) is

$$p(y_1, y_2, \ldots, y_T) = p(y_1) \prod_{t=2}^{T} p(y_t | y_{t-1}).$$

The path diagram of the AR(1) model is shown in Fig. 25.1.

There are two maximum likelihood estimation (MLE) methods for AR(1), conditional MLE and exact MLE. The former treats the initial value y_1 as deterministic and focuses only on the conditional distribution in Eq. (25.2). By maximizing the conditional likelihood function without y_1, this estimation method makes analysis relatively easy. Parameters are obtained by maximizing the conditional likelihood function as follows:

$$L_c(\alpha, \mu, \phi | \mathbf{y}) = \prod_{t=2}^{T} p(y_t | y_{t-1}, \alpha, \mu, \phi) = \prod_{t=2}^{T} \frac{1}{\sqrt{2\pi\phi}} \exp\left[-\frac{(y_t - \mu - \alpha\, y_{t-1})^2}{2\phi} \right].$$

Instead of treating y_1 as deterministic, the latter (exact MLE) estimation treats y_1 as random. It maximizes the exact likelihood function which includes the distribution of y_1. When exact MLE is adopted, a stationarity procedure is required. By assuming $|\alpha| < 1$, the covariance of y_t in AR(1) is shown stationary, and we have

$$\begin{aligned} & y_1 \sim N\left(\frac{\mu}{1-\alpha}, \frac{\phi}{1-\alpha^2}\right), \\ & y_t | y_{t-1} \sim N(\mu + \alpha\, y_{t-1}, \phi), (t > 1). \end{aligned}$$

With this assumption, the exact likelihood function of $\mathbf{y}$ is

$$L_e(\alpha, \mu, \phi|\mathbf{y}) = p(y_1|\alpha, \mu, \phi)L_c(\alpha, \mu, \phi|\mathbf{y})$$

$$= \frac{1}{\sqrt{2\pi(\frac{\phi}{1-\alpha^2})}} \exp\left[-\frac{(y_1 - \frac{\mu}{1-\alpha})^2}{2\,(\frac{\phi}{1-\alpha^2})}\right]\left\{\prod_{t=2}^{T} \frac{1}{\sqrt{2\pi\phi}} \exp\left[-\frac{(y_t - \mu - \alpha\, y_{t-1})^2}{2\phi}\right]\right\}.$$

25.2.2 *Multiple Time Series and Estimation*

The AR(1) model introduced above is for single time series analysis. In reality, however, multiple time series are prevalent. There are many sources of multiple time series. For example, multiple-subject time series, in which data are collected from multiple similar subjects; multivariate time series, in which multiple dependent variables are collected from the same subjects; and multiple session time series, in which data are collected at different sessions from the same subjects.

Suppose there are N individuals (or sessions or other forms of series). Without loss of generality, we assume each individual has T observations collected from different time points, so totally there are NT observations. The model for individual i at time point t is expressed as follows:

$$y_{it} = \mu + \alpha\, y_{i(t-1)} + z_{it}, \quad (i = 1, \ldots, N;\ t = 2, \ldots, T)$$

where $z_{it} \sim \ i.i.d.\ N(0, \phi)$.

25.2.2.1 Pooling Likelihoods

There are various methods to estimate parameters μ, α, and ϕ in multiple time series analysis. They can be estimated by pooling likelihood functions across all individuals. Based on different forms of likelihood function, there are pooled conditional likelihood MLE and pooled exact likelihood MLE.

In the following analysis, we assume the N individuals are from one population and have the same parameters μ, α, and ϕ. But these assumptions can be relax. Pooled likelihood methods allow μ, α, and ϕ to vary and estimate.

The pooled conditional likelihood of a stationary AR(1) for N individuals is

$$L_c(\alpha, \mu, \phi|\mathbf{y}) = \prod_{i=1}^{N}\prod_{t=2}^{T} p(y_{it}|y_{i(t-1)}, \alpha, \mu, \phi)$$

$$= \prod_{i=1}^{N}\prod_{t=2}^{T} \frac{1}{\sqrt{2\pi\phi}} \exp\left[-\frac{(y_{it} - \mu - \alpha\, y_{i(t-1)})^2}{2\phi}\right]. \quad (25.2)$$

To obtain the MLE of μ, α, and ϕ, we make the first derivative with respect to each parameter equal to 0 and make their corresponding second derivatives negative at $\hat{\boldsymbol{\theta}} = (\hat{\mu}, \hat{\alpha}, \hat{\phi})$. We have

$$\hat{\mu} = \frac{(\sum_{i=1}^{N}\sum_{t=2}^{T} y_{i(t-1)}^2)(\sum_{i=1}^{N}\sum_{t=2}^{T} y_{it}) - (\sum_{i=1}^{N}\sum_{t=2}^{T} y_{i(t-1)})(\sum_{i=1}^{N}\sum_{t=2}^{T} y_{i(t-1)}y_{it})}{N(T-1)\sum_{i=1}^{N}\sum_{t=2}^{T} y_{i(t-1)}^2 - (\sum_{i=1}^{N}\sum_{t=2}^{T} y_{i(t-1)})^2},$$

$$\hat{\alpha} = \frac{N(T-1)(\sum_{i=1}^{N}\sum_{t=2}^{T} y_{i(t-1)}y_{it}) - (\sum_{i=1}^{N}\sum_{t=2}^{T} y_{i(t-1)})(\sum_{i=1}^{N}\sum_{t=2}^{T} y_{it})}{N(T-1)\sum_{i=1}^{N}\sum_{t=2}^{T} y_{i(t-1)}^2 - (\sum_{i=1}^{N}\sum_{t=2}^{T} y_{i(t-1)})^2},$$

$$\hat{\phi} = \frac{1}{N(T-1)}\sum_{i=1}^{N}\sum_{t=2}^{T}(y_{it} - \hat{\mu} - \hat{\alpha}\, y_{i(t-1)})^2. \tag{25.3}$$

Assumptions of the pooling conditional likelihood functions include the same parameters, μ, α, and ϕ, across all individuals.

Parameters can also be estimated by maximizing the pooled exact likelihood function including the distribution of initial values.

$$L_e(\alpha, \mu, \phi|\mathbf{y}) = \prod_{i=1}^{N}\left[p(y_{i1}|\alpha, \mu, \phi)\prod_{t=2}^{T} p(y_{it}|y_{i(t-1)}, \alpha, \mu, \phi)\right]$$

Unfortunately, there is no analytic solution for $\hat{\boldsymbol{\theta}} = (\hat{\mu}, \hat{\alpha}, \hat{\phi})$ in terms of $\{y_{it}\}$, $(1 \leq i \leq N, 1 \leq t \leq T)$. Instead, we have to adopt iterative algorithms to obtain numerical solutions. Assumptions of the pooling exact likelihood functions include the same parameters, μ, α, and ϕ, across all individuals, and a stationary time series $\alpha < 1$. This method is recommended when participants are almost identical, or multiple sessions.

25.2.2.2 Connecting Data

In practice, people also analyze data by connecting all series from multiple subjects as from a single subject. Figure 25.2 shows the series connected by individuals. This method assumes connecting points do not matter, so that y_{iT} and $y_{(i+1)1}$ can be

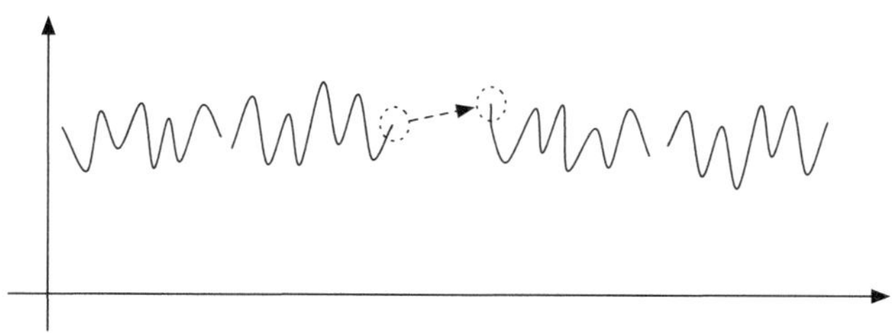

Fig. 25.2 Connecting data from multiple subjects

connected. Also, it assumes all series share the same μ, α, and ϕ. The assumption of equal μ can be relax, though. It can be centered through centering means.

Based on different likelihood functions, there are conditional MLE and exact MLE for connected data. Let j ($j = 1, 2, \ldots, NT$) be the new subscript for the connected series. For conditional MLE, the conditional likelihood function of the connected data is

$$L(\alpha, \mu, \phi|\mathbf{y}) = \prod_{j=2}^{NT} p(y_j|\alpha, \mu, \phi) = \prod_{j=2}^{NT} \frac{1}{\sqrt{2\pi\phi}} \exp\left[-\frac{(y_j - \mu - \alpha\, y_{j-1})^2}{2\phi}\right].$$

By making the first derivatives with respect to all parameters equal to 0, we have analytical solutions for conditional MLE

$$\hat{\mu} = \frac{(\sum_{j=2}^{NT} y_{j-1}^2)(\sum_{t=2}^{NT} y_j) - (\sum_{j=2}^{NT} y_{j-1})(\sum_{j=2}^{NT} y_{j-1} y_j)}{(NT-1)\sum_{j=2}^{NT} y_{j-1}^2 - (\sum_{j=2}^{NT} y_{j-1})^2},$$

$$\hat{\alpha} = \frac{(NT-1)(\sum_{j=2}^{NT} y_{j-1} y_j) - (\sum_{j=2}^{NT} y_{j-1})(\sum_{j=2}^{NT} y_j)}{(NT-1)\sum_{j=2}^{NT} y_{j-1}^2 - (\sum_{j=2}^{NT} y_{j-1})^2},$$

$$\hat{\phi} = \frac{1}{NT-1} \sum_{j=2}^{NT} (y_j - \hat{\mu} - \hat{\alpha}\, y_{j-1})^2.$$

For exact MLE, it requires a stationary AR(1) model. The exact likelihood functions of the connected data is

$$L(\alpha, \mu, \phi|\mathbf{y}) = p(y_1|\alpha, \mu, \phi) \prod_{j=2}^{NT} p(y_j|\alpha, \mu, \phi)$$

$$= \frac{1}{\sqrt{2\pi(\frac{\phi}{1-\alpha^2})}} \exp\left[-\frac{(y_1 - \frac{\mu}{1-\alpha})^2}{2\,(\frac{\phi}{1-\alpha^2})}\right] \left\{\prod_{j=2}^{NT} \frac{1}{\sqrt{2\pi\phi}} \exp\left[-\frac{(y_j - \mu - \alpha\, y_{j-1})^2}{2\phi}\right]\right\}.$$

Again, there is no analytical solutions for $\hat{\boldsymbol{\theta}} = (\hat{\mu}, \hat{\alpha}, \hat{\phi})$.

25.2.2.3 Multivariate Time Series Analysis

Multivariate analysis is another alternative approach to multiple time series analysis. It views each time series as an N-dimensional multivariate variable. It also allows subject dependence. This method is relatively difficult to use comparing the other two methods. It requires data be measured at the same time points, so all individuals have the same time series length.

Let $\mathbf{Y}_t$, $\mathbf{Y}_{t-1}$, and $\mathbf{z}_t$ be three N-dimensional column vectors, $\mathbf{Y}_t' = (y_{1t}, y_{2t}, \ldots, y_{Nt})$, $\mathbf{Y}_{t-1}' = (y_{1(t-1)}, y_{2(t-1)}, \ldots, y_{N(t-1)})$, and $\mathbf{z}_t' = (z_{1t}, z_{2t}, \ldots, z_{Nt})$, and $\boldsymbol{\beta}$ be a (2×1) vector including parameters μ and α. At time point t, the multiple time series can be expressed as $\mathbf{Y}_t = (\mathbf{1}, \mathbf{Y}_{t-1})\boldsymbol{\beta} + \mathbf{z}_t$, which is

$$\begin{pmatrix} y_{1t} \\ y_{2t} \\ \vdots \\ y_{Nt} \end{pmatrix} = \begin{pmatrix} 1 & y_{1(t-1)} \\ 1 & y_{2(t-1)} \\ \vdots & \vdots \\ 1 & y_{N(t-1)} \end{pmatrix} \begin{pmatrix} \mu \\ \alpha \end{pmatrix} + \begin{pmatrix} z_{1t} \\ z_{2t} \\ \vdots \\ z_{Nt} \end{pmatrix}.$$

If we combine all time points t from 2 to T, then we have the least-squares (LS) estimate of $\boldsymbol{\beta}$,

$$\hat{\boldsymbol{\beta}} = \begin{bmatrix} \hat{\mu} \\ \hat{\alpha} \end{bmatrix} = \begin{bmatrix} N(T-1) & \sum_{t=2}^{T} \sum_{i=1}^{N} y_{i(t-1)} \\ \sum_{t=2}^{T} \sum_{i=1}^{N} y_{i(t-1)} & \sum_{t=2}^{T} \sum_{i=1}^{N} y_{i(t-1)}^2 \end{bmatrix}^{-1} \begin{bmatrix} \sum_{t=2}^{T} \sum_{i=1}^{N} y_{it} \\ \sum_{t=2}^{T} \sum_{i=1}^{N} y_{i(t-1)} y_{it} \end{bmatrix}.$$

Note that with normal distribution, maximizing (25.2) with respect to μ and α is equivalent to minimizing

$$\sum_{i=1}^{N} \sum_{t=2}^{T} (y_{it} - \mu - \alpha\, y_{i(t-1)})^2$$

with respect to μ and α, so the LS solution for $\boldsymbol{\theta} = (\mu, \alpha, \phi)$ is exactly the same as the pooled conditional likelihood MLE solution as shown in (25.3).

25.3 Simulation Study

To investigate the performance of different pooling methods on estimating multiple times series, we conducted a simulation study.

25.3.1 Design and Implementation

First, multiple time series under various conditions were generated. We used the AR(1) model. The true parameter values were $\mu = 0$, $\alpha = 0.5$, and $\phi = 0.25$. As one main difference among various methods on parameter estimation is the influence of the initial value y_1, we generated data under three conditions: (a) with a fixed y_1 at 0, (b) with a random y_1 drew from $N(0, \phi)$, and (c) with a random y_1 drew from $N(\frac{\mu}{1-\alpha}, \frac{\phi}{1-\alpha^2})$. Other conditions included the lengths of series or the number of time points, $T = (5, 10, 15, 20, 30)$, and the number of subjects,

$N = (10, 20, 30, 40, 50)$. Totally, there are $3 \times 5 \times 5 = 75$ different types of data sets generated. For each data set, 1000 replications were generated.

Second, model parameters (μ, α, and ϕ) were estimated by using different multiple time series estimation methods. As the multivariate LS estimation method yields the same results as the pooled likelihood conditional MLE when data are normally distributed, we adopted four estimation methods in this study: pooled likelihood conditional MLE, pooled likelihood exact MLE, pooled data conditional MLE, and pooled data exact MLE. As there is no analytical solutions for exact MLE, iterative algorithms were employed to obtain numerical solutions.

Finally, results were summarized across all simulation replications. For each parameter, *Est.* is the average estimate across 1000 replications; the absolute bias (*Bias.abs*) was calculated as the absolute value of the difference between an estimated value and its true value; the relative bias (*Bias.rel*) of an estimate was the ratio of its absolute bias to its true value; the empirical s.e. (*SE.emp*) was calculated based on the estimates across 1000 replications; the average s.e. (*SE.avg*) was the average standard error across 1000 replications; the mean square error (*MSE*) of each parameter estimate was calculated as $MSE = Bias_abs^2 + SE_emp^2$; and the *Cover* is its coverage rate.

In the simulation study, we used R language to generate data, estimate parameters, and summarize results. No R package was involved.

25.3.2 Results

Totally, there were $3 \times 5 \times 5 = 75$ simulation result summary tables. Due to the limited space, we only showed part of the results here. Tables 25.1, 25.2, 25.3, 25.4, 25.5 and 25.6 summarized the estimates from four estimation methods, pooling likelihood (P.L.) conditional MLE, pooling likelihood (P.L.) exact MLE, connecting data (C.D.) conditional MLE, and connecting data (C.D.) exact MLE.

The *SE.emp* and *SE.avg* in all tables were quite close to each other, which indicates that those estimates methods work well. Based on the 75 simulation result tables, we have the following findings:

1. In general, the *Bias.abs*, *Bias.rel*, *SE.emp*, *SE.avg*, and *MSE* values for large T or large N (e.g., see Tables 25.2, 25.4 and 25.6) were smaller than those for small T or small N (e.g., see Tables 25.1, 25.3 and 25.5). The coverage rates for large T or large N were more close to 0.95 than those for small T or small N. Both indicated that for these four estimation methods, although the data sets had different initial values, (a) the longer the time series, the more accurate the estimate, and (b) the more individuals participated, the more accurate the estimate.
2. By comparing bias statistics (such as *Bias.abs* and *Bias.rel*) and coverage rates (*Cover*) across all tables, in most cases the pooled likelihood methods outperformed the connecting data methods. For the situation of large T and small N, connecting data methods also estimated well.

3. The pooled likelihood conditional MLE performed best, especially on the recovery of the autoregressive coefficient α (see Tables 25.1, 25.2, 25.3, 25.4, 25.5 and 25.6), except when initial value $y_1 \sim N(\frac{\mu}{1-\alpha}, \frac{\phi}{1-\alpha^2})$ both the pooled likelihood conditional MLE and the pooled likelihood exact MLE performed well (e.g., see Tables 25.5 and 25.6).
4. For large T and small N, conditional MLE performed similarly as the exact MLE;
5. For small T and large N, exact MLE is more efficient but may have large bias depending on the state of y_1 and stationarity of time series.
6. The parameter coverages for data with random initial values were more close to 0.95 than the rates for fixed initial value $y_1 = 0$. Among two types of random initial values, the one drew from the stationary distribution $y_1 \sim N(\frac{\mu}{1-\alpha}, \frac{\phi}{1-\alpha^2})$ performed better than the other distribution.
7. For the data with fixed initial values $y_1 = 0$, the parameter coverage rates were low, especially for ϕ (see Table 25.1).

Table 25.1 Parameter estimate summary based on the simulation study of fixed $y_1 = 0, N = 10$ individuals, $T = 5$ observations, and 1000 replications

		True[a]	Est.[b]	Bias.abs[c]	Bias.rel[d]	SE.emp[e]	SE.avg[f]	MSE[g]	Cover[h]
P.L.[i]									
Exact[j]	μ	0	−0.0027	0.0027	0.0027	0.0640	0.0574	0.0041	0.9440
	α	0.5	0.3567	0.1433	0.2867	0.1399	0.1318	0.0401	0.8250
	ϕ	0.25	0.1942	0.0558	0.2234	0.0466	0.0392	0.0053	0.5990
Cond.[k]	μ	0	−0.0039	0.0039	0.0039	0.0884	0.0782	0.0078	0.9200
	α	0.5	0.4534	0.0466	0.0932	0.1794	0.1693	0.0344	0.9330
	ϕ	0.25	0.2372	0.0128	0.0510	0.0572	0.0531	0.0034	0.8750
C.D.[l]									
Exact	μ	0	−0.0032	0.0032	0.0032	0.0708	0.0641	0.0050	0.9370
	α	0.5	0.3245	0.1755	0.3509	0.1325	0.1325	0.0484	0.7630
	ϕ	0.25	0.2039	0.0461	0.1845	0.0501	0.0408	0.0046	0.6480
Cond.	μ	0	−0.0033	0.0033	0.0033	0.0729	0.0660	0.0053	0.9350
	α	0.5	0.3310	0.1690	0.3381	0.1353	0.1355	0.0469	0.7790
	ϕ	0.25	0.2078	0.0422	0.1686	0.0511	0.0420	0.0044	0.6830

[a]The true value of the corresponding parameter
[b]The average of the estimate of the corresponding parameter across 1000 replications
[c]The absolute bias of the estimate
[d]The relative bias of the estimate
[e]The empirical s.e. across 1000 replications
[f]The average of the s.e. obtained from the model
[g]The mean square error of the estimate, $MSE = Bias.abs^2 + SE.emp^2$
[h]The coverage probability of the estimate
[i]The method of pooling likelihood functions
[j]Parameters are estimated by maximizing the exact likelihood function of the original data
[k]Parameters are estimated by maximizing the conditional likelihood function of the original data
[l]The method of connecting data

Table 25.2 Parameter estimate summary based on the simulation study of fixed $y_1 = 0$, $N = 50$ individuals, $T = 30$ observations, and 1000 replications

		True	Est.	Bias.abs	Bias.rel	SE.emp	SE.avg	MSE	Cover
P.L.									
Exact	μ	0	0.0002	0.0002	0.0002	0.0126	0.0123	0.0002	0.9450
	α	0.5	0.4810	0.0190	0.0380	0.0225	0.0223	0.0009	0.8680
	ϕ	0.25	0.2413	0.0087	0.0348	0.0087	0.0088	0.0002	0.8280
Cond.	μ	0	0.0002	0.0002	0.0002	0.0134	0.0131	0.0002	0.9450
	α	0.5	0.4974	0.0026	0.0052	0.0233	0.0233	0.0005	0.9590
	ϕ	0.25	0.2495	0.0005	0.0019	0.0090	0.0093	0.0001	0.9560
C.D.									
Exact	μ	0	0.0002	0.0002	0.0002	0.0131	0.0128	0.0002	0.9410
	α	0.5	0.4802	0.0198	0.0397	0.0227	0.0226	0.0009	0.8580
	ϕ	0.25	0.2438	0.0062	0.0248	0.0088	0.0089	0.0001	0.8720
Cond.	μ	0	0.0002	0.0002	0.0002	0.0131	0.0128	0.0002	0.9410
	α	0.5	0.4805	0.0195	0.0391	0.0227	0.0227	0.0009	0.8600
	ϕ	0.25	0.2440	0.0060	0.0241	0.0088	0.0089	0.0001	0.8780

Note: With the same notations as in Table 25.1

Table 25.3 Parameter estimate summary based on the simulation study of fixed $y_1 \sim N(0, \phi)$, $N = 10$ individuals, $T = 5$ observations, and 1000 replications

		True	Est.	Bias.abs	Bias.rel	SE.emp	SE.avg	MSE	Cover
P.L.									
Exact	μ	0	−0.0007	0.0007	0.0007	0.0657	0.0604	0.0043	0.9470
	α	0.5	0.4387	0.0613	0.1225	0.1345	0.1318	0.0218	0.9370
	ϕ	0.25	0.2301	0.0199	0.0795	0.0481	0.0466	0.0027	0.8550
Cond.	μ	0	−0.0008	0.0008	0.0008	0.0874	0.0786	0.0076	0.9230
	α	0.5	0.4638	0.0362	0.0724	0.1491	0.1443	0.0235	0.9310
	ϕ	0.25	0.2382	0.0118	0.0473	0.0550	0.0533	0.0032	0.8890
C.D.									
Exact	μ	0	−0.0009	0.0009	0.0009	0.0753	0.0713	0.0057	0.9450
	α	0.5	0.3613	0.1387	0.2775	0.1322	0.1312	0.0367	0.8450
	ϕ	0.25	0.2512	0.0012	0.0048	0.0535	0.0503	0.0029	0.9140
Cond.	μ	0	−0.0004	0.0004	0.0004	0.0772	0.0729	0.0060	0.9370
	α	0.5	0.3621	0.1379	0.2757	0.1331	0.1319	0.0367	0.8470
	ϕ	0.25	0.2517	0.0017	0.0069	0.0537	0.0509	0.0029	0.9170

Note: With the same notations as in Table 25.1

Table 25.4 Parameter estimate summary based on the simulation study of fixed $y_1 \sim N(0, \phi)$, $N = 50$ individuals, $T = 30$ observations, and 1000 replications

		True	Est.	Bias.abs	Bias.rel	SE.emp	SE.avg	MSE	Cover
P.L.									
Exact	μ	0	0.0007	0.0007	0.0007	0.0125	0.0125	0.0002	0.9490
	α	0.5	0.4949	0.0051	0.0103	0.0236	0.0225	0.0006	0.9320
	ϕ	0.25	0.2474	0.0026	0.0103	0.0092	0.0090	0.0001	0.9280
Cond.	μ	0	0.0009	0.0009	0.0009	0.0132	0.0131	0.0002	0.9480
	α	0.5	0.4989	0.0011	0.0022	0.0241	0.0229	0.0006	0.9340
	ϕ	0.25	0.2494	0.0006	0.0022	0.0094	0.0093	0.0001	0.9390
C.D.									
Exact	μ	0	0.0007	0.0007	0.0007	0.0130	0.0130	0.0002	0.9490
	α	0.5	0.4822	0.0178	0.0356	0.0238	0.0226	0.0009	0.8650
	ϕ	0.25	0.2521	0.0021	0.0084	0.0094	0.0092	0.0001	0.9300
Cond.	μ	0	0.0007	0.0007	0.0007	0.0131	0.0130	0.0002	0.9480
	α	0.5	0.4823	0.0177	0.0355	0.0238	0.0226	0.0009	0.8680
	ϕ	0.25	0.2521	0.0021	0.0086	0.0094	0.0092	0.0001	0.9280

Note: With the same notations as in Table 25.1

Table 25.5 Parameter estimate summary based on the simulation study of fixed $y_1 \sim N(\frac{\mu}{1-\alpha}, \frac{\phi}{1-\alpha^2})$, $N = 10$ individuals, $T = 5$ observations, and 1000 replications

		True	Est.	Bias.abs	Bias.rel	SE.emp	SE.avg	MSE	Cover
P.L.									
Exact	μ	0	−0.0006	0.0006	0.0006	0.0692	0.0616	0.0048	0.9400
	α	0.5	0.4561	0.0439	0.0879	0.1384	0.1325	0.0211	0.9380
	ϕ	0.25	0.2417	0.0083	0.0333	0.0501	0.0490	0.0026	0.9010
Cond.	μ	0	−0.0011	0.0011	0.0011	0.0896	0.0789	0.0080	0.9120
	α	0.5	0.4603	0.0397	0.0794	0.1505	0.1392	0.0242	0.9250
	ϕ	0.25	0.2382	0.0118	0.0470	0.0551	0.0533	0.0032	0.8920
C.D.									
Exact	μ	0	−0.0004	0.0004	0.0004	0.0800	0.0736	0.0064	0.9310
	α	0.5	0.3666	0.1334	0.2669	0.1324	0.1311	0.0353	0.8500
	ϕ	0.25	0.2670	0.0170	0.0680	0.0586	0.0534	0.0037	0.9230
Cond.	μ	0	−0.0011	0.0011	0.0011	0.0820	0.0752	0.0067	0.9290
	α	0.5	0.3662	0.1338	0.2675	0.1327	0.1315	0.0355	0.8490
	ϕ	0.25	0.2668	0.0168	0.0672	0.0593	0.0539	0.0038	0.9190

Note: With the same notations as in Table 25.1

Table 25.6 Parameter estimate summary based on the simulation study of fixed $y_1 \sim N(\frac{\mu}{1-\alpha}, \frac{\phi}{1-\alpha^2})$, $N = 50$ individuals, $T = 30$ observations, and 1000 replications

		True	Est.	Bias.abs	Bias.rel	SE.emp	SE.avg	MSE	Cover
P.L.									
Exact	μ	0	−0.0002	0.0002	0.0002	0.0127	0.0125	0.0002	0.9540
	α	0.5	0.4998	0.0002	0.0003	0.0220	0.0225	0.0005	0.9470
	ϕ	0.25	0.2495	0.0005	0.0021	0.0091	0.0091	0.0001	0.9570
Cond.	μ	0	−0.0001	0.0001	0.0001	0.0134	0.0131	0.0002	0.9540
	α	0.5	0.4997	0.0003	0.0007	0.0222	0.0227	0.0005	0.9440
	ϕ	0.25	0.2494	0.0006	0.0024	0.0093	0.0093	0.0001	0.9530
C.D.									
Exact	μ	0	−0.0002	0.0002	0.0002	0.0132	0.0130	0.0002	0.9560
	α	0.5	0.4833	0.0167	0.0334	0.0222	0.0226	0.0008	0.8900
	ϕ	0.25	0.2549	0.0049	0.0195	0.0095	0.0093	0.0001	0.9260
Cond.	μ	0	−0.0002	0.0002	0.0002	0.0133	0.0131	0.0002	0.9560
	α	0.5	0.4833	0.0167	0.0334	0.0221	0.0226	0.0008	0.8900
	ϕ	0.25	0.2549	0.0049	0.0195	0.0095	0.0093	0.0001	0.9260

Note: With the same notations as in Table 25.1

25.4 Comparisons and Practical Implications

In this section, we compare different estimation methods for pooling multiple time series. Table 25.7 shows the summary.

Regarding the number of participants and length of time series, we plotted the information curve as in Fig. 25.3.

Based on the study, practical implications include (1) focusing on process oriented, intra-individual variability and change analysis, (2) collecting as many data with controlled quality as possible from each individual, (3) selecting multiple individuals from a homogeneous group, and (4) testing poolability of parameters μ, α, and ϕ.

References

Cattell, R. B. (1952). The three basic factor-analytic research designs—Their interrelations and derivatives. *Psychological Bulletin, 49*, 499–520.

Cattell, R. B., Cattell, A. K. S., & Rhymer, R. M. (1947). P-technique demonstrated in determining psychophysical source traits in a normal individual. *Psychometrika, 12*, 267–288.

Cattell, R. B., & Scheier, I. H. (1961). *The meaning and measurement of neuroticism and anxiety*. New York: Ronald.

Daly, D. L., Bath, K. E., & Nesselroade, J. R. (1974). On the confounding of inter—And intraindividual variability in examining change patterns. *Journal of Clinical Psychology, 30*, 33–36.

Table 25.7 A comparison of multiple time series estimation methods

Pooling method	Comparison
Connecting data	Easy to use
	Allow μ to vary through centering
	Can be used for large T and small N situation
Pooling likelihood	Easy to use
	Allow μ, α, ϕ to vary and estimate
	For large T and small N, Conditional MLE $\approx$ Exact MLE
	For small T and large N, Exact MLE is more efficient but may have large bias depending on the state of y_1 and stationarity of time series
Multivariate method	Relatively difficult to use
	The same time series length
	Data measured at the same time
	Allow subject dependence

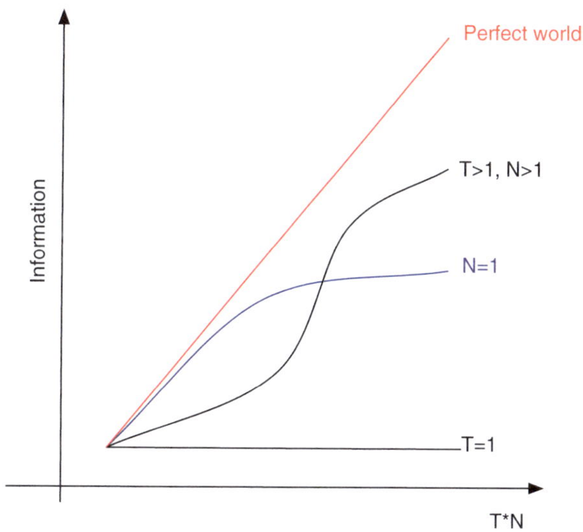

Fig. 25.3 The information curve for multiple time series analysis

Molenaar, P. (1985). A dynamic factor model for the analysis of multivariate time series. *Psychometrika, 50*, 181–202.

Molenaar, P. C. M. (2004). A manifesto on psychology as idiographic science: Bringing the person back into scientific psychology—this time forever. *Measurement: Interdisciplinary Research and Perspectives, 2*, 201–218.

Molenaar, P. C. M., Huizenga, H. M., & Nesselroade, J. R. (2003). The relationship between the structure of interindividual and intraindividual variability: A theoretical and empirical vindication of developmental systems theory. In U. M. Staudinger & U. Lindenberger (Eds.), *Understanding human development: Dialogues with lifespan psychology* (pp. 339–360). Norwell: Kluwer Academic Publishers.

Nesselroade, J. R., & Molenaar, P. (2003). Quantitative models for developmental processes. In J. Valsiner & K. Connolly (Eds.), *Handbook of developmental psychology* (pp. 622–639). London: Sage.

Nesselroade, J. R., & Molenaar, P. C. M. (1999). Pooling lagged covariance structures based on short, multivariate time-series for dynamic factor analysis. In R. H. Hoyle (Ed.), *Statistical strategies for small sample research* (pp. 224–250). Newbury Park, CA: Sage.

Nesselroade, J. R., & Ram, N. (2004). Studying intraindividual variability: What we have learned that will help us understand lives in context. *Research in Human Development, 1*, 9–29.

Chapter 26
Path Diagrams: Layout Algorithms, Styles, and Views

Yiu-Fai Yung

Abstract Path diagrams are valuable visualization tools in practical structural equation modeling (SEM). They provide intuitively appealing representations of modeling ideas and results. As a part of the computational process of modeling, path diagrams can be viewed as input device or as output results. This paper discusses the latter role of path diagrams. The modeling scenario of interest is to produce path diagrams given the syntactic input of structural models. The process-flow, grouped-flow, and GRIP layout algorithms for producing path diagrams are described and discussed. Emphases are on building intuitions about these layout algorithms and hence the appropriate use of these algorithms for producing path diagrams for different types of models. Steps that automate the selection among these layout algorithms for a given model are proposed. Finally, adjustments that are needed for producing path diagrams with different styles and views are discussed. Path diagram examples are used throughout the paper to illustrate the layout algorithms, the proposed automatic selection steps, and different styles and views.

Keywords Path diagram • Structural equation model • Layout algorithms • Statistical graphics

26.1 Introduction

In structural equation modeling (SEM), researchers often use path diagrams to present their modeling ideas and analysis results. The most appealing feature of path diagrams is the visualization of the functional or causal relationships among variables in models. Variables are represented by various shapes and the directed or correlated relationships are represented by arrows. After model estimation, path or effect estimates are displayed in path diagrams to aid interpretations. Fit summary statistics are sometimes included in path diagrams to show how well the model fits the data.

Y.-F. Yung (✉)
Multivariate Modeling R & D, SAS Institute Inc., SAS Campus Drive, Cary, NC 27513, USA
e-mail: Yiu-Fai.Yung@sas.com

L.A. van der Ark et al. (eds.), *Quantitative Psychology Research*, Springer Proceedings in Mathematics & Statistics 140, DOI 10.1007/978-3-319-19977-1_26

Because of the intuitive nature of path diagrams for representing multivariate relationships, many commercial software implement path diagram interface for users to specify structural equation models. In such an interface, users specify models by "drawing" variables and paths in a virtual drawing panel. After model is estimated, statistical results such as estimates and standard errors are put into the path diagram. For example, computer packages such as AMOS (Arbuckle 2010), EQS (Bentler 2006), and SAS-SEM (SAS Institute Inc. 2013) all have this kind of path diagram interface for inputting models.

Instead of using the path diagram as an input device, this paper considers the automatic production of path diagrams from syntactic model input (that is, computer code). There are several important scenarios that warrant the study of the automatic path diagram output. In the first scenario, an adept structural equation modeler does not consider drawing path diagrams to be more intuitive than specifying the model by computer code. To such a user, the path diagram interface is actually not as efficient as the syntactical input. Nonetheless, he or she might still want to present the results in the form of a path diagram once the model is estimated. In the second scenario, a modeler has quite a lot of variables in the model. It would be very tedious for the modeler to manually draw an aesthetically pleasing path diagram in the input interface. By automating the production of path diagrams from syntactic input, the modeler can avoid the tedious drawing. Moreover, the layout algorithms for drawing path diagrams might be able to create path diagrams that are reasonably good-looking. In the third scenario, the modeler needs to create several path diagrams with different views or styles (representation schemes) from a single model input. For example, he or she might want to create a path diagram that contains only latent factors for presentation purposes, while producing a full path diagram for his or her own reference. Automatic path diagram production facilitates such a flexible rendering of path diagrams with different views and styles.

In the field of SEM, research on creating path diagram output has been scarce (but see Boker et al. 2002; Epskamp et al. 2012). However, in the field of computer graphics, graph drawing is a well-established topic (see, e.g., Battista et al. 1999). The methods that draw graphs by computational steps are called layout algorithms. This paper introduces some of these layout algorithms, describes their characteristics, and discusses how they are applied to create path diagrams. Because different algorithms result in different path diagrams, this paper proposes steps that select among these algorithms automatically given the model specification by computer code. This paper also identifies and resolves some issues that are related to the production of path diagrams with different styles or views.

26.2 Layout Algorithms: Some Intuitions

This section provides some high-level descriptions of the layout algorithms for producing graphs and shows how these algorithms can be adapted to path diagrams. We start with a simple description of a graph. There are two main elements in a graph: Nodes (or points) and links (or edges). Nodes are connection points or end points that represent objects or process. They are usually drawn as two-dimensional shapes such as rectangular, oval, and so on. Links are connections between nodes. Undirected links are simply lines that connect nodes, while directed links are drawn as lines with arrow-heads that show the direction of connections.

Depending on the application domain, graphs have different terminologies. In a social network diagram, the nodes are individuals and the links show the connections between individuals. In a computer network diagram, the nodes are device components and the links show the data transmission process. In a process flow diagram, the nodes are major equipment and the links show the flow of the work processes. All these diagrams are essentially graphs. To extend the graph-theoretic concepts to path diagrams for structural equation models, the nodes are variables and the links show the functional or causal relationships between variables.

A layout algorithm for a graph is a computational procedure that determines the placement of nodes in a two-dimensional space (or sometimes three-dimensional space—but this is out of the current scope). There have been many layout algorithms developed for graphs (Battista et al. 1999). To provide intuitions in a simplified setting, this section considers only three layout algorithms that have been implemented in the CALIS procedure (SAS Institute Inc. 2014). Other layout algorithms are discussed in the final section.

The GRIP Layout Algorithm: The GRIP (Graph dRawing with Intelligent Placement) layout algorithm (Gajer et al. 2004; Gajer and Kobourov 2002) starts with a small set of initial nodes. It places these nodes in the two-dimensional space either directly or by projecting them from higher dimensional space. Sets of nodes are then added successively and the placement of nodes are refined with the additions of new nodes. After all nodes are added, links are added to complete the final graph (Gajer and Kobourov 2002). To illustrate the GRIP layout algorithm, consider the well-known data example from Wheaton et al. (1977). The following pseudo code represents the functional relationships in the model:

```
Alien67   →   Anomie67    Powerless67
Alien71   →   Anomie71    Powerless71
SES       →   Education   SEI
SES       →   Alien67     Alien71
Alien67   →   Alien71
```

Variables Anomie67, Powerless67, Anomie71, Powerless71, Education, and SEI are observed variables in the model, while SES, Alien67, and Alien71 are latent factors. Notice that error variables are not explicitly defined in the specification. At this point, there is no need to introduce the role of error variables in the model (but this will be addressed later in this paper). The GRIP algorithm produces the path diagram in Fig. 26.1.

Unlike many types of graphs in which nodes are represented by the same shape, the path diagram convention is to use rectangles for observed variables and ovals for latent factors. This adaptation is shown in Fig. 26.1. Some other characteristics of the path diagram produced by the GRIP algorithm are noted:

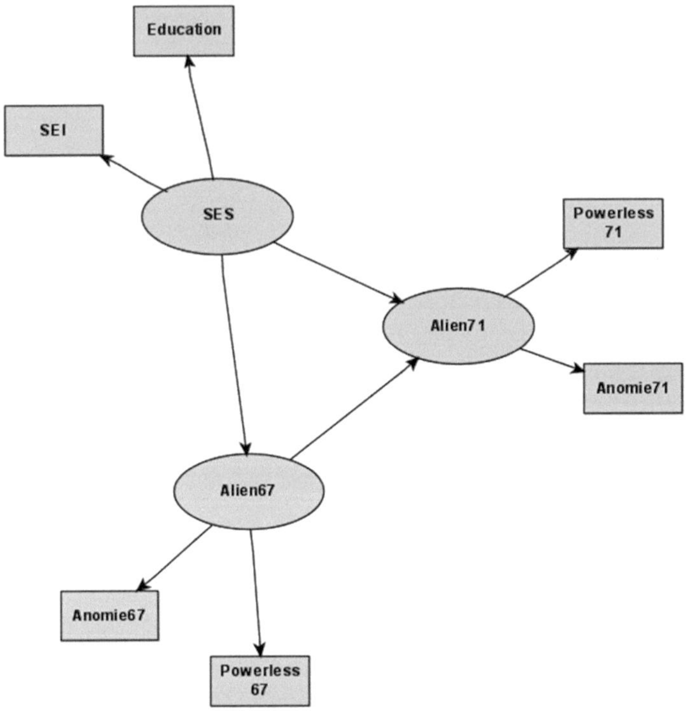

Fig. 26.1 Path diagram by using the GRIP layout algorithm

- The GRIP layout algorithm does not take the path directions (links) into considerations when placing variables (nodes). In the path diagram, variables are more or less evenly dispersed and a sequential ordering of the variables is not visually emphasized (for example, by putting the variables of a causal sequence in a straight line).
- To make the linkage between a factor and its associated observed indicators more apparent in the path diagram, the original GRIP algorithm has been modified so that the paths between a latent factor and its associated observed indicators are shorter than those between factors.

Although the GRIP algorithm works well in general, it does not depict the "causal" order of the variables vividly. For example, consider the following pseudo code that represents a confirmatory factor model with one factor:

```
Factor →    X1 X2 X3 X4 X5 X6
```

The GRIP algorithm produces the path diagram in Fig. 26.2. Although this is still a well-balanced and eye-pleasing path diagram, it does not depict explicitly that the factor and the observed variables are at different levels of ordering.

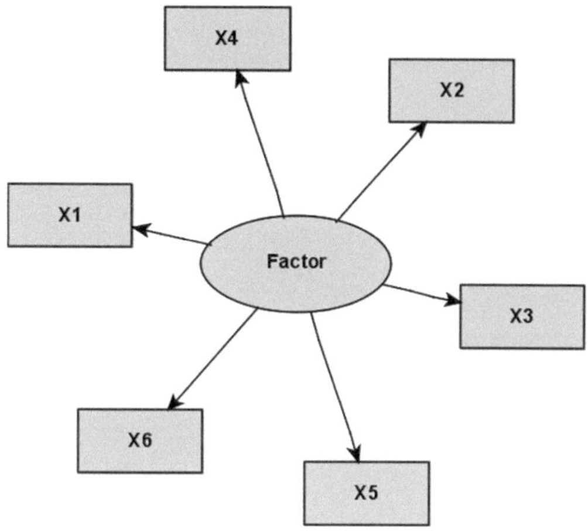

Fig. 26.2 A confirmatory factor model by using the GRIP layout algorithm

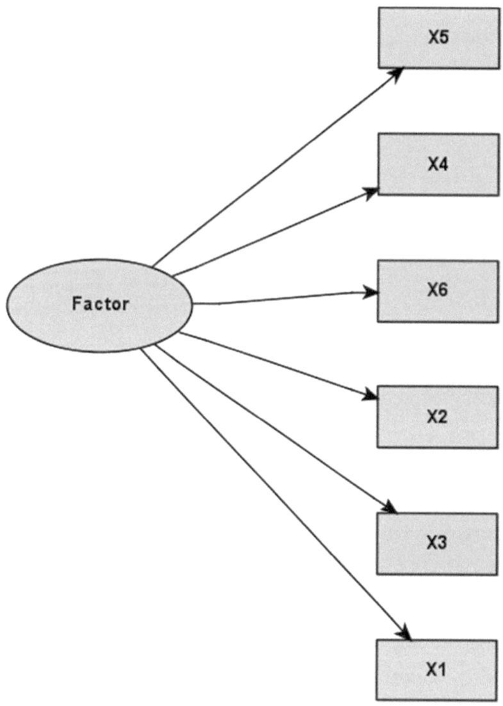

Fig. 26.3 A confirmatory factor model by using the process-flow layout algorithm

The Process-Flow Layout Algorithm: In contrast, the process-flow layout algorithm arranges variables in the path diagram according to their causal or functional order in the model. Indeed, the basic idea of process-flow idea is very similar to that of Boker et al. (2002). Figure 26.3 shows the path diagram for the preceding confirmatory factor model by using the process-flow algorithm.

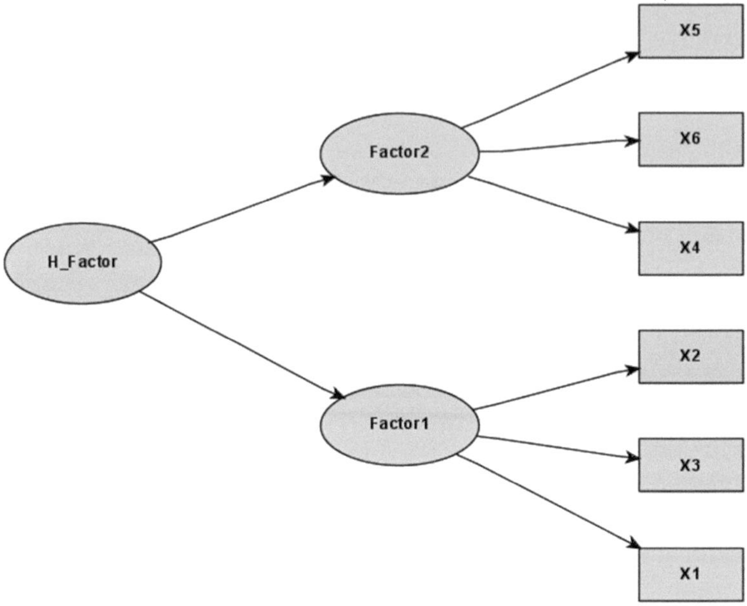

Fig. 26.4 A second-order factor model by using the process-flow layout algorithm

Another situation that the process-flow layout algorithm is deemed desirable is for producing the path diagram for the higher-order factor model, as exemplified by the following pseudo code:

```
Factor1    →   X1 X2 X3
Factor2    →   X4 X5 X6
G_Factor   →   Factor1 Factor2
```

Figure 26.4 shows that the process-flow algorithm is able to display the causal/functional order of variables in a hierarchical manner. However, the process-flow algorithm might fail to produce a visually pleasing picture when the higher-order factor model has observed indicators in the higher-order factors. For example, Fig. 26.5 shows the path diagram that is produced for the following pseudo code:

```
Factor1    →   X1 X2
Factor2    →   X3 X4
G_Factor   →   X5 X6
G_Factor   →   Factor1 Factor2
```

It is disconcerting to see that observed variables X5 and X6 are at the same level as the latent factors Factor1 and Factor2. Some characteristics of the process-flow algorithm are noted:

- To determine the placement of the variables, the process-flow layout algorithm analyzes the causal or functional ordering of the variables in the model.

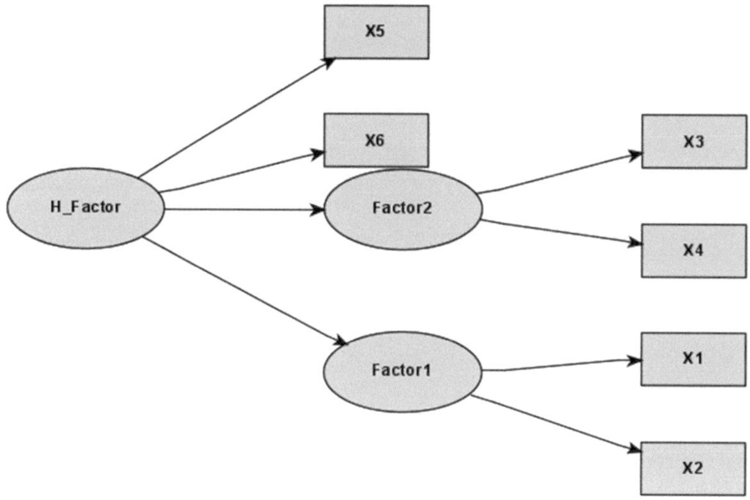

Fig. 26.5 An illustration of the problem of mixed variable types by using the process-flow algorithm

- The path diagram produced by the process-flow algorithm might not be as balanced as that produced by the GRIP algorithm.
- The process-flow algorithm might not produce good-looking path diagrams when there are mixed types of variables at some level of the ordering.

The Grouped-Flow Layout Algorithm: Instead of utilizing the ordering of all variables in the layout process, one can focus on the ordering of a particular set of variables in the model. In the preceding example, it might be more desirable to focus on the ordering of the latent factors alone when laying out the variables. This amounts to applying the process-flow layout algorithm to the three factor-indicators clusters in the model; hence, the name *grouped*-flow layout algorithm. By using the grouped-flow algorithm, Fig. 26.6 shows the path diagram produced for the preceding model. Now the path diagram clearly shows the hierarchical-ordering in the factor clusters.

Some remarks on the grouped-flow layout algorithm are now in order:

- The grouped-flow algorithm is essentially the same as the process-flow algorithm being applied to the latent factors alone. However, once the ordering of the latent factors are determined, space must be reserved for displaying the entire factor clusters rather than for displaying the individual factors.
- The grouped-flow algorithm is unique to the path diagrams in SEM because visually distinctive shapes are used to represent different types of variables in models. Otherwise, when all the nodes/variables are of the same type (such as in other types of graphs), the process-flow algorithm is all one needs to layout nodes/variables in graphs/path diagrams that emphasize the ordering of nodes/variables (for example, regression models with observed variables only).

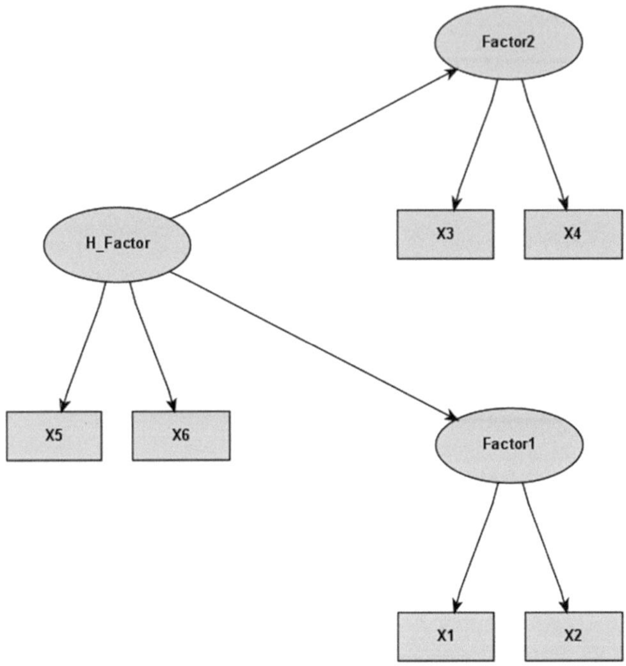

Fig. 26.6 An illustration of the grouped-flow algorithm

26.3 Automatic Determination of the Layout Algorithm

The intuition built from the preceding section suggests that while the GRIP layout algorithm is appropriate for producing path diagrams in general situations, models that exhibit some kind of "strong" causal/functional ordering properties in variables are better organized using the process-flow or grouped-flow algorithm to show the ordering properties in path diagrams. Based on this observation, the following steps are suggested to automatically determine among the three layout algorithms for a given model:

1. Assign a level value to each variable (observed variable or latent factor, excluding error variable) in the model, starting from the exogenous variables that do not receive any effects from any other variables (that is, they do not have paths pointing to them). Assign 1 as the level value to these exogenous variables.
2. Assign $j + 1$ as the level value to the variables that are directly pointed to by the level-j variables. Repeat the assignment process. If the assignment of the $j + 1$ level value is applied to a variable that has been assigned previously, stop the assignment and go to Step 4. Otherwise, continue until all variables are assigned. Go to Step 3.

3. All variables should now have unique level values. Check the set of variables at each level. If there is at least one set of variables that contains both observed variables and latent factors, go to Step 4. Otherwise, quit the steps and use the process-flow algorithm.
4. Consider only the set of latent factors in the model. Assign each latent factor a level value by restarting the same process as described in Steps 1 and 2 (but only with latent factors). If the assignment of the $j + 1$ level value is applied to a latent factor that has been assigned previously, quit the steps and use the GRIP algorithm.
5. All latent factors should now have unique level values. Use the grouped-flow algorithm.

Some remarks on these steps should be noted:

- The determination of the layout algorithm does not consider the error variables or the bi-directional links (that is, double-headed paths that represent covariance) in the model.
- The process-flow algorithm requires a unique ordering of all variables, while the grouped-flow algorithm requires a unique ordering of the latent factors.
- In order to use the process-flow algorithm, Step 3 checks to ensure that variables at the same level are of the same type. This avoids the oddity of aligning observed variables and latent factors vertically (or horizontally) in the path diagram (see Fig. 26.5).
- These steps do not aim at finding the "best" algorithm for a given model. The definition of "best" is somewhat subjective and is also dependent on the particular purpose in the mind of the modeler. For example, a process-flow algorithm might still be good enough for producing a path diagram even if there is no unique ordering of variables in the model. Rather, these steps do guarantee that it can detect models that have the idealized ordering patterns for which the process-flow and grouped-flow algorithms are specifically designed.

How do these steps work for the mentioned examples? Will they produce "good" path diagrams that are consistent with the intuition built in the preceding section? To illustrate the selection of the process-flow algorithm, consider again the one-factor model that is specified by the following pseudo code:

```
Factor →    X1 X2 X3 X4 X5 X6
```

The proposed steps will be able to assign a unique level to each variable in the model, as illustrated in Fig. 26.7, where the process-flow algorithm is used to draw the path diagram. The resultant path diagram would be exactly the same as the one shown in Fig. 26.3.

To illustrate the selection of the grouped-flow algorithm, consider again the path diagram in Fig. 26.5. The corresponding model is specified by the following pseudo code:

```
Factor1   →   X1 X2
Factor2   →   X3 X4
G_Factor  →   X5 X6
G_Factor  →   Factor1 Factor2
```

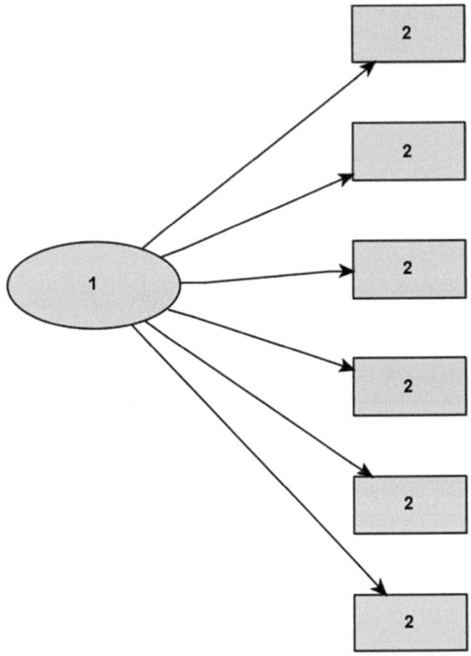

Fig. 26.7 Level assignments of a confirmatory factor model

As discussed previously, the process-flow algorithm that produces the diagram in Fig. 26.5 is less-than-desirable because there are mixed variable types at the second level. By using the proposed steps for assigning the level values to variables, Fig. 26.8 shows that variables at level 2 are not all of the same type. Step 3 detects such mixed variable types and so the process-flow layout algorithm is not chosen. However, when the set of variables is limited to the latent factors in Step 4, the latent factors do have unique level values. Hence, the grouped-flow algorithm is used and the resultant path diagram would be exactly the same as the one shown in Fig. 26.6.

To illustrate the selection of the GRIP algorithm, consider again the path diagram in Fig. 26.1 that represents the model with the following pseudo code:

```
Alien67   →   Anomie67    Powerless67
Alien71   →   Anomie71    Powerless71
SES       →   Education   SEI
SES       →   Alien67     Alien71
Alien67   →   Alien71
```

Figure 26.9 shows the level values of the variables. Because latent factor Alien71 can be assigned to either level 2 or 3 (that is, SES→Alien71, or SES→Alien67→Alien71), neither the process-flow nor the grouped-flow is selected. Hence, the GRIP algorithm is used and the resultant path diagram is exactly the same as the one shown in Fig. 26.1.

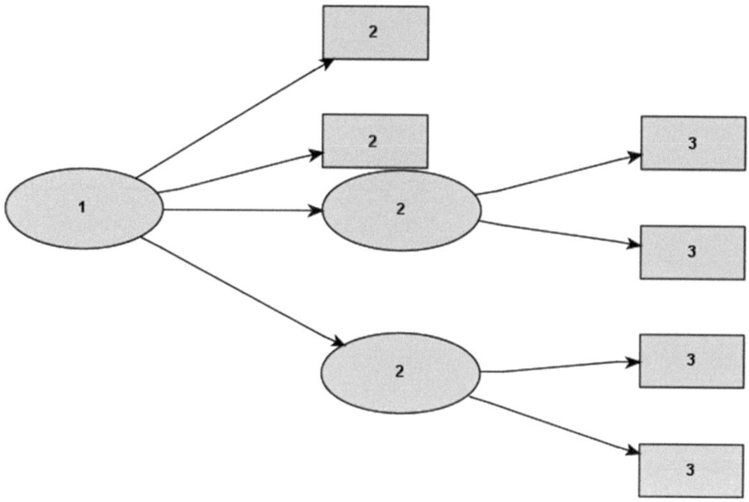

Fig. 26.8 Illustration of a model that has mixed variable types at level 2

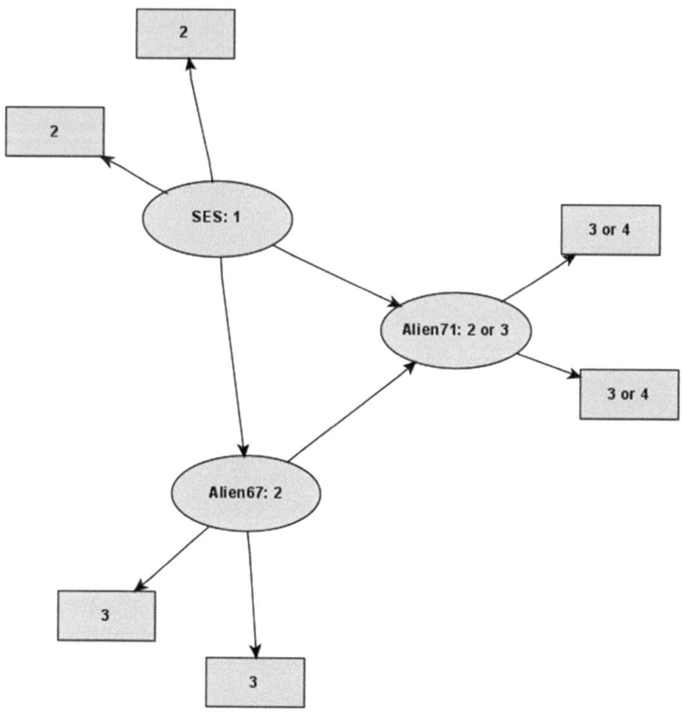

Fig. 26.9 Illustration of model that does not have unique level assignments

26.4 Styles and Views of Path Diagrams: Some Proposed Solutions

So far the discussion of layout algorithms ignores the representation of the error variables in models and in path diagrams. There are good reasons for that. First, error variables, as they are defined, are not systematic part of the model. Omitting the error variables from path diagrams usually would not compromise the main interpretations of the model. In fact, in the so-called RAM model, which is one of the major formulations of structural equation models, error variables in path diagrams are never explicitly represented (McArdle and McDonald 1984). Second, showing the error variables tends to add to the complexity of the graphics. It might make the resultant path diagrams more complicated than necessary. Third, even if showing error variables in path diagrams is desirable in some situations, the proposed steps that select the layout algorithm would still need to exclude the error variables in the decision process. Because all error variables are exogenous by definition, they would all be assigned to level 1 in the level assignment steps. This leads to one of the following two consequences. First, perfect process-flow or grouped-flow patterns could not be detected by the aforementioned steps. The otherwise important casual/functional chain of effects in the non-error variables would not be shown clearly in the path diagram. Second, even if the process-flow algorithm is selected for producing the path diagram, the error variables effects (that is, paths from error variables) might complicate the path diagram quite a bit.

This brings out the issue about the styles (or representation schemes) of path diagrams. For example, in the EQS program (Bentler 2006), error variables are explicitly specified in models. Naturally, EQS users would expect to have error variables shown in path diagrams. Should one still use the proposed steps in the preceding section? Would it still work fine? The answer is positive. All the proposed steps described in the preceding section can still be used to determine the layout algorithm. The only thing needs to be adjusted is to reserve space for all endogenous variables so that their corresponding error variables could be "tagged" to them after the layout of the non-error variables. For example, error variables that have been "hidden" in the path diagram in Fig. 26.1 (or Fig. 26.9) can be shown with error variables by essentially using the same layout algorithm. Figure 26.10 shows the resultant EQS-style path diagram that displays error variables explicitly. As an example of path diagram results, estimates for path effects and variances are also displayed. As can be seen, the placement of the non-error variables are essentially the same for the current path diagram and the one in Fig. 26.1.

Similarly, to draw the RAM-style path diagram, the proposed steps for determining the layout algorithm is applied in the same way. However, unlike the EQS-style, no space for error variables needs to be reserved for the RAM-style path diagram. Figure 26.11 shows the RAM-style path diagram that is comparable to the EQS-style path diagram in Fig. 26.10. Per RAM-style, the error variance estimates are now attached as double-headed arrows to the endogenous variables in Fig. 26.11, whereas they are attached to the error variables directly in the EQS-style path diagram in Fig. 26.10.

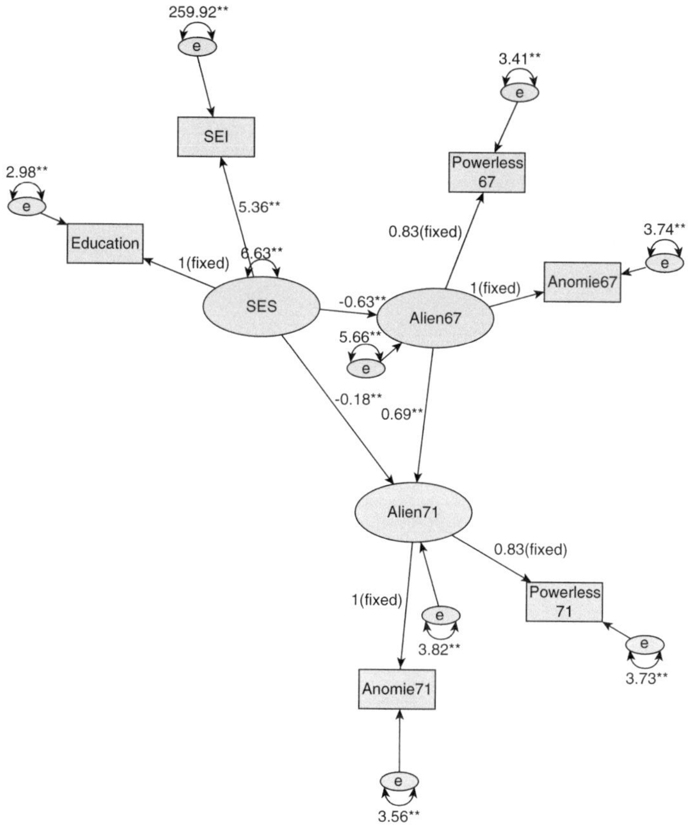

Fig. 26.10 An illustration of an EQS-style path diagram

In addition to styles, SEM modelers often distinguish between the structural component and the measurement component in the model. In fact, this distinction is one of the main features in the original formulation of the LISREL model (Jöreskog and Sörbom 1996). Roughly speaking, the structural component contains only the latent factors and their functional relationships. The measurement component contains the relationships between the latent factors and their observed indicators. Because of the theoretical importance of the structural components, very often researchers would like to focus on the structural components in their path diagrams.

Two ways for producing path diagrams that focus on the structural component are proposed here. The first one is pretty straightforward. By considering only the set of latent variables and their relationships, all the techniques and steps proposed earlier in this paper are applied. Figure 26.12 shows the path diagram of the structural component of the model, of which the full path diagram is shown in Fig. 26.11. The second way is to de-emphasize the observed variables by minimizing their sizes and by omitting their labels and corresponding estimates. Again, all the layout

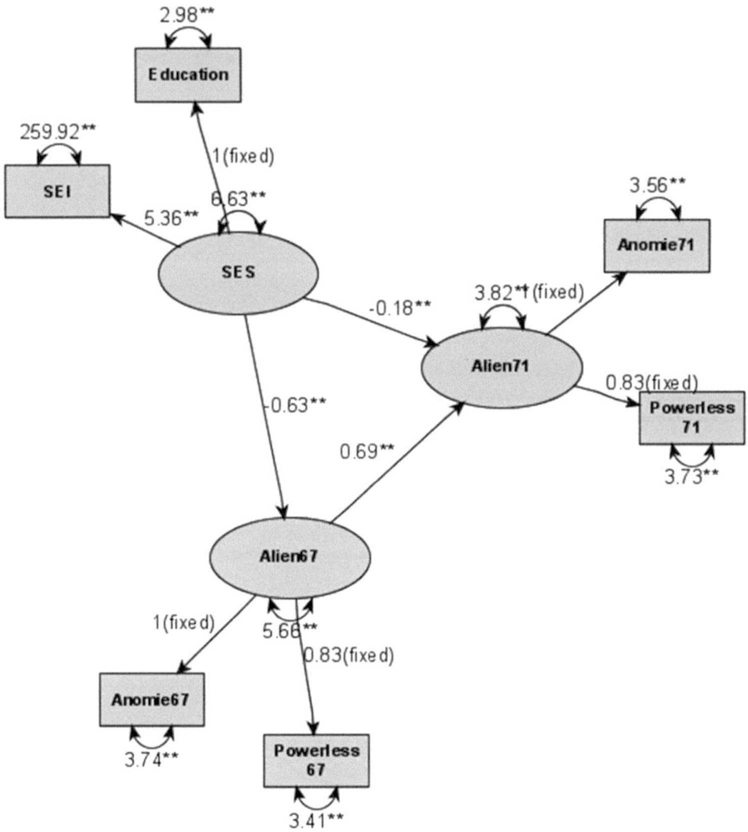

Fig. 26.11 An illustration of a RAM-style path diagram

algorithms and steps discussed previously are applied to draw this path diagram—only now less drawing space is needed for the observed variables. Figure 26.13 shows the resultant path diagram that is based on de-emphasizing the measurement component.

26.5 Concluding Comments

This paper describes the GRIP, process-flow, and grouped-flow algorithms for laying out variables in path diagrams. Steps that determine among these three algorithms for a given structural equation model are proposed and discussed. This paper also discusses the adjustments needed to produce path diagrams with different styles or views from a single model input. The techniques described in this paper has

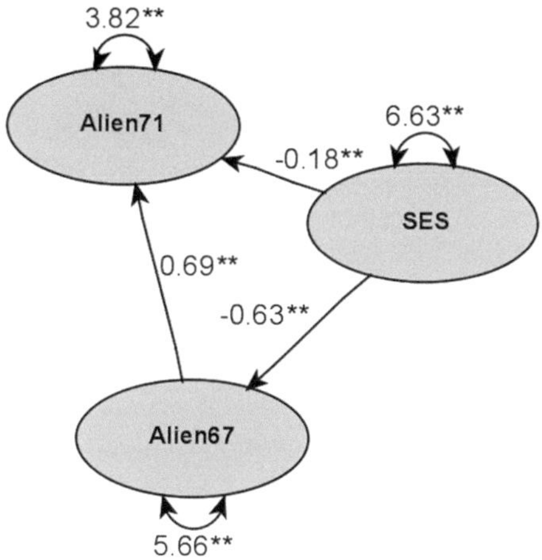

Fig. 26.12 An illustration of showing the structural component alone

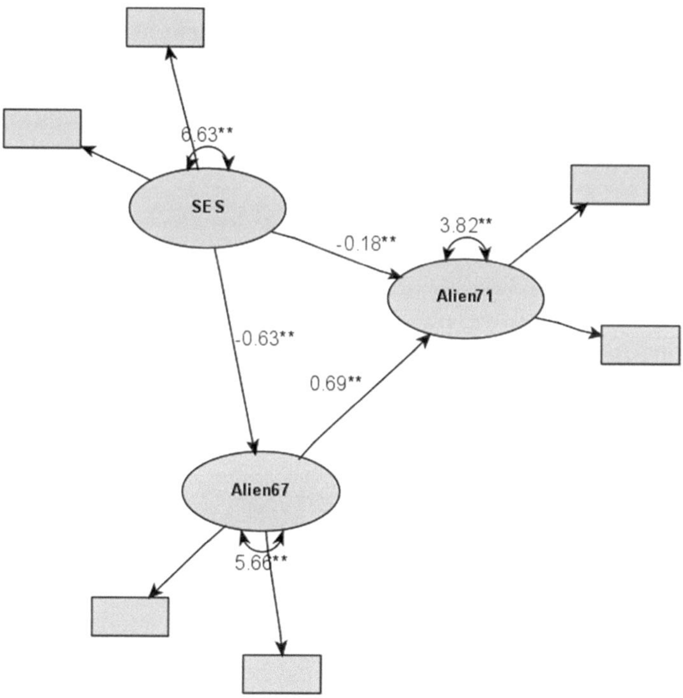

Fig. 26.13 An illustration of emphasizing the structural component

been implemented in a recent edition of the CALIS and FACTOR procedures (SAS Institute Inc. 2014). For details about the control of layout algorithms, styles, and views, see the documentations of the procedures (SAS Institute Inc. 2014) or Yung (2014).

Due to the simplistic setting for showing the basic graphical ideas, our discussion of layout algorithms for path diagrams has been limited. Several other software can also produce path diagrams from syntactic model input. For example, the PD command of LISREL (Jöreskog and Sörbom 1996) offers such a functionality. However, the layout algorithm that LISREL uses is unclear to the author. Epskamp (2014) describes it as a "tree" layout. It appears that some aspects of this "tree" layout is similar to the grouped-flow algorithm described. That is, the arrangement of nodes is mostly dependent on the ordering of the latent factors. But the "tree" layout is unique in its placement of the measurement components. Unlike the grouped-flow algorithm that always places the measured variables under the latent factors, the "tree" layout tends to spread out the measured variables. LISREL does not seem to have additional control on the styles or views of path diagrams.

In contrast, the R package semPlot (Epskamp 2014) considers different layouts and styles in its semPaths() call. For example, it has three variations of the "tree" layout ("tree," "tree2," and "tree3") and three variations of "circular" layout ("circle," "circle2," and "circle3"). It considers different styles such as "LISREL" and "mx." The many options offered in semPaths() appear to be able to create different views too. Although semPaths() and the author's own implement in the CALIS procedure are totally independent software, it is clear that both consider various layout algorithms, styles, and views as important elements in path diagram creation. Hopefully, this paper has covered the basic ideas of these important elements.

A final comment is that path diagrams created by any layout algorithms will not be "perfect"—it might never match exactly what is in the mind of the modeler. For example, labels for estimates might collide or variables are not put at the most desirable locations. Therefore, post-editing of path diagrams in some graphic editors might be indispensable. But the promise of the layout algorithms is that they would make the whole progress more efficient by producing reasonably good-looking path diagrams automatically.

References

Arbuckle, J. L. (2010). *IBM SPSS Amos 19 user's guide*. Chicago: IBM.

Battista, G. D., Eader, P., Tamassia, R., & Tollis, I. G. (1999). *Graph drawing: Algorithms for the visualization of graphs*. New Jersey: Prentice Hall.

Bentler, P. M. (2006). *EQS 6 structural equations program manual*. Encino, CA: Multivariate Software, Inc.

Boker, S. M., McArdle, J. J., & Neale, M. (2002). An algorithm for the hierarchical organization of path diagrams and calculation of components of expected covariance. *Structural Equation Modeling, 9*, 174–194.

Epskamp, S. (2014). semPlot: Unified visualizations of structural equation models. *Psychoco 2014*, Tuebingen, Germany. http://www.sachaepskamp.com/files/semPlot.pdf

Epskamp, S., Cramer, A. O. J., Waldorp, L. J., Schmittmann, V. D., & Borsboom, D. (2012). qgraph: Network visualizations of relationships in psychometric data. *Journal of Statistical Software, 48*(4), 1–18.

Gajer, P., Goodrich, M. T., & Kobourov, S. G. (2004). A multi-dimensional approach to force-directed layouts of large graphs. *Computational Geometry: Theory and Applications, 29*(1), 3–18.

Gajer, P., & Kobourov, S. G. (2002). GRIP: Graph drawing with intelligent placement. *Journal of Graph Algorithms and Applications, 6*(3), 203–224.

Jöreskog, K. G., & Sörbom, D. (1996). *LISREL 8 user's reference guide*. Mooresville, IN: Scientific Software.

McArdle, J. J., & McDonald, R. P. (1984). Some algebraic properties of the Reticular Action Model. *British Journal of Mathematical and Statistical Psychology, 37*, 234–251.

SAS Institute Inc. (2013). *SAS structural equation modeling 2 for JMP*. NC: Author.

SAS Institute Inc. (2014). *SAS/STAT 13.2 user's guide*. NC: Author.

Wheaton, B., Muthén, B. O., Alwin, D. F., & Summers, G. F. (1977). Assessing reliability and stability in panel models. In D. R. Heise (Ed.), *Sociological methodology*. San Francisco: Jossey-Bass.

Yung, Y. F. (2014). *Creating path diagrams that impress: A new graphical capability of the CALIS procedure*. http://support.sas.com/rnd/app/stat/papers/2014/yungpd2014.pdf

MIX
Papier aus verantwortungsvollen Quellen
Paper from responsible sources
FSC® C105338
www.fsc.org

If you have any concerns about our products,
you can contact us on
ProductSafety@springernature.com

In case Publisher is established outside the EU,
the EU authorized representative is:
Springer Nature Customer Service Center GmbH
Europaplatz 3, 69115 Heidelberg, Germany

Printed by Libri Plureos GmbH
in Hamburg, Germany